1,000 Lowfat Recipes

1,000 Lowfat Recipes

Terry Blonder Golson

Macmillan·USA

MACMILLAN
A Simon & Schuster Macmillan Company
1633 Broadway
New York, NY 10019-6785

Macmillan Publishing books may be purchased for business or sales promotional use.
For information please write: Special Markets Department, Macmillan Publishing USA,
1633 Broadway, New York, NY 10019.

Copyright ©1997 by Terry Blonder Golson
Illustrations copyright © by Sally Mara Sturman

Library of Congress Cataloging-in-Publication Data

Golson, Terry Blonder.
1,000 lowfat recipes cookbook / Terry Blonder Golson.
   p. cm.
   Includes index (p.).
   ISBN 0-02-860354-0
   1. Cookery. 2. Lowfat diet—Recipes. I. Title.
TX714.G6487 1998   97-28738
641.5'638—dc21   CIP

Book design by Amy Trombat

Manufactured in the United States of America
10 9 8 7 6

Contents

Acknowledgments ix

Introduction 1
What to Eat, Why, and How, 2
Following the Recipes, 6
Glossary, 8
Menu Planning, 9
Stocking the Healthy Kitchen, 11
Kitchen Design and Organization, 16
Essential Kitchen Equipment, 17

Small Bites and Finger Foods 20

Chips and Nuts, 22
Dips and Spreads, 25
Finger Foods, 33
Crostini and Bruschetta, 42
Mini-Frittatas, 45
Skewered Hors D'oeuvres, 47
Won Tons, 49

Salads 52

Dressings, 55
Green Salads, 61
Cucumber Salads, 68
Tomato Salads, 70
Assorted Vegetable Salads, 73
Slaws, 78
Potato Salads, 82
Pasta Salads, 86
Rice and Grain Salads, 92
Bean Salads, 98
Poultry and Fish Salads, 103

Soups 108

Broths, 110
Chilled Soups, 113
Pureed Soups, 119
Vegetable and Grain Soups 126
Bean Soups, 133
Fish Soups, 142
Chicken Soups, 144

Entrées: Poultry and Meat 152

Breaded Chicken, 155
Grilled and Broiled Chicken, 159
Kebabs, 162
Baked Chicken, 166
Roasted Chicken, 176
Casseroles, 181
Stovetop Cooking, 188
Wok Cooking, 201
Turkey Cutlets, 207
Cooking with Lean Ground Beef, 211

Entrées: Fish and Shellfish 219

Baked Fish, 222
Whole Trout, 233
Grilled and Broiled Fish, 234
Poached Fish, 241
Stovetop Cooking, 244
Shrimp and Shellfish, 250
Risottos, 260
Mussels, 262

Entrées: Vegetarian 264

Stuffed Vegetables, 266
From the Oven, 269
Lasagnas, 277
Ravioli, 282
Stovetop Cooking, 285
Stir-Fries and Dumplings, 296
Stews and Chilis, 298
Risottos, 304

Vegetables, 308

Apples, 311
Asparagus, 313
Beets, 317
Broccoli, 319
Brussels Sprouts, 323
Carrots, 325
Cauliflower, 328
Corn, 330
Green Beans, 333
Greens, 337
Mushrooms, 342
Peas, 345
Potatoes, 347
Root Vegetables, 359
Winter Squash, 360
Summer Squash, 364
Tomatoes, 368
Vegetable Medleys, 370

Pastas, Grains, and Beans 375

Pasta, 375
Couscous, 384
Rice, 386
Other Grains, 396
Beans, 399
Polenta, 407
Stuffing and Bread, 409

Casual Meals 416

Stuffed Potatoes, 418
Burritos, 420
Quesadillas, 423
Sandwiches, 425
Sandwich Fillings, 429
Burgers, 432
Pizza, 436

Breakfasts 446

Bread Spreads, 448
Cereal, 449
Pancakes, 452
Waffles, 456
French Toast, 458
Frittatas, 462
Fruits and Vegetables, 466

Yeast Breads, Quick Breads, and Muffins 471

Muffins, 473
Scones, 482
Corn Bread, 486
Quick Breads, 488
Yeast Breads, 493
Focaccia, 502

Desserts 508

Fruit Desserts, 508
Pies, 521
Cakes, 530
Glazes, 544
Cookies, 571
Brownies and Bars, 556
Cobblers, 561
Puddings, 564
Frozen Desserts, 571
Syrups, Sauces, and Other Toppings, 576

Sauces, Salsas, Pantry Staples, and Beverages 581

Tomato Sauces, 583
Barbeque Sauces, 587
Pestos, 589
Salsas, 592
Chutneys, 594
Fish Sauces, 598
Other Sauces, 600
Dipping Sauces, 602
Homemade Pantry Staples, 603
Beverages, 609

Index 612

Acknowledgments

Many people have helped me during the course of the three years that it took to write this book. Without Carla Glasser, my agent, I would not be published. Justin Schwartz was the editor who started this project and Jennifer Griffin saw it to completion. Along the way there have been many professionals working on the manuscript, from copy editors to designers. I thank them all.

Some of these recipes first appeared in my two previous cookbooks (now out of print). Thank you to the people at Camden House for publishing me, and especially to Sandy Taylor, my editor there, who taught me a lot about what it takes to write a good book.

The nutritional analyses were done by registered dietician Tammi Hancock, who did much more than just run the numbers through her computer. Not only do the analyses reflect her knowledge of cooking, but the recipes themselves are better due to her careful reading and insistence on accuracy and consistency.

Often food writing is a lonely profession, first in the kitchen and then in front of the computer. Not so this book. When I enlisted the help of some home cooks to recipe test, I had no idea that I would receive far more than their enthusiastic (and honest) feedback on the hundreds of recipes that they prepared. Molly Gayley Gnichtel, Susan Hollingworth, Regina Knight, Beverly Koenigsberg, Bettina Messana, Elizabeth Parson, Carolyn Shohet, and Ingrid Wheeler encouraged and inspired me. They have become friends beyond the confines of the creation of this book and my life has been enriched by them. Thanks also to friends Lois Wurts and Emily Anhalt who tested several recipes and to Ann Owen who contributed her Belizean Stew recipe.

Iz Cohen has been generous with his phenomenal knowledge of baking. I am fortunate to benefit from his decades of experience. However, his humor and friendship mean more to me than all of his advice on glazes and yeasts. Thanks, Iz.

Food writing is home-based work and my family had no choice but to be involved. Thankfully, they embraced the project and stayed positive throughout—despite the dinners that were all rice pilafs, or the memorable meal of winter squash in which every dish was orange! My husband, Steve, has been supportive and generous in many small and large ways. He often takes time out of his workday so that I can finish mine. He keeps my computer running and the copier filled with paper. He also keeps my days filled with love and companionship. My stepson Jordan is ever helpful in the kitchen and his enthusiasm never wanes. He brought a teenager's palate to the mix. The Beef and Noodles recipe is for him. For the bulk of the recipe testing I kept Daniel, the toddler, out of the kitchen and harm's way. However, we frequently cook together (especially when the tasks are easy, like stirring a batter), and his very presence fills the kitchen, and house, with joy. I was pregnant with Jacob while finishing the writing, and his kicking reminded me that there is more to life than a publisher's deadline. He arrived in time to keep me company while finishing the last edits on the book, and, in fact, is cooing and cuddling in my arms as I write this.

This book was nurtured and written with the love and friendship of family and friends. I hope that the end result reflects all that they have given me.

Introduction

There is no longer any doubt that we are what we eat. Foods promote health and cause disease; they affect our looks, moods, and energy levels. But in the quest for better health through diet, we have lost sight of the fact that food is more than an alphabet soup of nutrients. We eat not only to sate our hunger, but also for pleasure and companionship, to celebrate and to console. I've worked as a chef at a very strict health spa, where no fat at all was used, and I've cooked in a French restaurant where a $1/4$ stick of butter in a vegetable dish was considered "moderate." So I have experienced the extremes of eating solely for health and eating decadently in spite of health. It was clear to me that neither way was the approach that normal, busy people could follow on a daily basis.

And eating well, day in and day out, is the goal. Diets don't work. They are temporary and the results never last. I wanted a healthy way to eat in which good food was an enjoyable and integral part of daily life. Over the last ten years I have cooked for myself and my family and taught cooking classes, always with this goal in mind. My students are home cooks, and they too want an approach where food is good for their bodies but doesn't control their lives, in which meals fulfill their desires for delicious foods but don't require a professional's skill in the kitchen. This book is for my students and for others who want to make healthy home cooking part of their lives.

I believe that eating well begins in the home kitchen. Too often we eat in a rush, away from home. Fast foods are high in calories and fat but low in nutrients. Although it is possible to find healthy meals in restaurants or lowfat prepared foods in markets, home-cooked meals are healthier, tastier, and more economical. In almost all cases, the foods you make at home will be fresher and more wholesome than anything found at a market. You know exactly what is in your meal when it is home-cooked and you can adjust the seasonings or ingredients exactly to your liking. There is also an intangible benefit to cooking at home: the aroma of a pot simmering on the stove or a cake in the oven increases the pleasure of the meal, makes a home more inviting, and draws family and guests together. Single people cooking for themselves eat in a less rushed fashion when a home-cooked meal, rather than a carton of take-out, is set on the table.

Often people who want to cook healthy foods don't know how to start. The big picture gets lost among the hype over "magic" foods, miracle diets, and the seemingly continual changes in nutritional advice. However, despite this barrage of (mis)information, there is a growing consensus about what constitutes a healthy diet, and it is much more reasonable and logical than many people imagine. This healthy way of eating is plant-based and lowfat, the protein is lean, and the calories are reduced. Although this might appear far different from the average high-fat, high-calorie menu that centers around meat, it has many similarities. Most of the foods are the same, only the proportions change. Vegetables move to the center of the plate, standard ingredients are replaced with more healthful versions, and cooking techniques are used to lighten recipes.

This book is filled with recipes to help you cook good food at home. My recipes have no value if they are not used. The highest compliment I've received on my previous two books was when a reader told me that a neighbor borrowed the books and wouldn't give them back—because she was cooking from them. I've heard this many times. My recipes are designed so that even the busiest parent or the most inexperienced cook can prepare healthful meals throughout the week. It is how I cook for myself and my family. As much as I like to cook, I save my recreational cooking for special occasions. For everyday meals, I want quick, uncomplicated recipes that are easy to follow. Although I have access to specialty food shops, it is a rare day when I have time to stop at more than one store, so I prefer recipes with ingredients that can be found at the supermarket. I like interesting flavors but don't have the desire to recreate exotic cuisine at home—I'd rather have the authentic version when dining out. I like recipes that are easy to clean up (unlike the commercial kitchens where I've worked, there are no hired dishwashers in my home!). When creating the recipes, it wasn't enough that the dish was easy to prepare and fit within sound nutritional parameters; it also had to be the sort of thing that I wanted to make more than once. All of the recipes in this book have passed this test.

It also wasn't enough that I could cook the recipes. I wanted to make sure that anyone could, so after I was satisfied with a recipe, I sent it to one of eight testers. These testers made my recipes in their own homes and fed them to their families and friends. They let me know if the recipe worked in their ovens, in their pans, and with their ingredients. I benefited from their varied backgrounds. Only one of my testers had professional cooking experience. One tester's household consisted of three children in their late teens and early twenties and a husband with a history of heart disease; another tester was the mother of toddlers; a third was single. One woman had begun cooking only three years before, in her early forties; another had been a cookbook collector and recreational cook for a decade. The input from these testers assures that the recipes will work in any home kitchen, prepared by any cook.

Along with the recipes, I've written sections on what constitutes a healthy diet and given information to help you achieve that on a daily basis. Throughout the book I've shared information and tricks of the trade that I learned as a professional chef that will help you handle ingredients with confidence and work in your kitchen efficiently. This knowledge takes the hassle out of cooking and turns it into a pleasurable experience. But the core of this book is the recipes. One thousand recipes makes it obvious that this isn't a restrictive diet, but a broad approach to good eating with lots of options to fit everyone's lifestyle and tastes.

What to Eat, Why, and How

Our bodies are incredibly intricate organisms, and what they need for fuel and maintenance is equally complex. Scientists are only beginning to understand how food affects the body. The roles of the "phytochemicals" (molecules in plants), how different types of fibers interact with the digestive system, or how the various types of oils affect the blood are a few of the topics currently being investigated. But there is no doubt that food affects our health. It is estimated that 35 percent of all cancer deaths are related to diet, especially high-fat, low-fiber diets. Diabetes, a debilitating disease and the fourth-largest cause of death in the United States, has three risk factors: obesity, inactivity, and old age. Two of those are preventable. The reassuring news is that although nutritionists and others will be arguing over the details for years to come, there is a consensus about how to eat for health, and that this broad picture of good eating is delicious and within the reach of every home cook.

Eat your vegetables. All of the research points to the importance of vegetables and fruits in the diet, for their phytochemicals, nutrients, fiber, and other, still undefined components. The evidence confirms that eating a plant-based diet, with fresh vegetables and whole carbohydrates (such as brown rice and whole wheat) providing the bulk, is one of the best things people can do for themselves. Among other benefits, vegetables help reduce the risk of cancers, diabetes, heart disease, and blindness, and relieve constipation and diverticulosis. This is not something that you can take a pill for. Research indicates that these foods are most beneficial when eaten in their whole forms. When cooking at home, it is easy to consume more than the recommended five servings of vegetables and fruits in a day. Drink juice instead of soda, and have fresh fruit salad and cut vegetables in the refrigerator. Select recipes that are filled with vegetables and eat vegetarian meals several times a week. When meat is on the table, serve vegetable side dishes and a grain so that the meat is there for interest, but the vegetables are there for bulk.

Eat more fiber. The National Cancer Institute recommends that Americans double the amount of fiber in their daily diets from about 11 grams to between 20 and 30 grams. This advice is based on many studies, one of which showed that men who ate 29 grams of fiber a day cut their risk of heart attack by over 40 percent compared to men who consumed about 13 grams. As with the studies on vegetables, positive results are more consistently achieved when foods are eaten in their whole form, rather than continuing on a typical diet that is augmented by fiber from a jar.

If you are eating more vegetables, beans, and whole grains you are well on your way to eating enough fiber. All of recipes in this book have been analyzed for fiber. Labels on store-bought foods also list fiber. In fact, a good clue to how healthful a store-bought food is for you is to look at the fiber content on the nutritional label.

Eat less fat. Fat is a large part of most people's diets. Average Americans consume about 40 percent of their calories from fat. Although some fat is necessary for good health, such a high proportion of fat in the diet carries with it major problems. Fat is high in calories and so contributes to obesity, which in turn increases the risk factors for many diseases. Fat is linked to colon, prostate, and skin cancers; heart attack; and stroke. Because of this, lowfat diets are seen as a healthy alternative.

Avoid saturated and hydrogenated (trans) fats. There are several types of fats, and those with the worst reputations (and deservedly so) are saturated fats and those formed when manufacturers take liquid fats (polyunsaturates) and make them solid by a process called hydrogenation. These fats increase the blood levels of LDL cholesterol (the "bad cholesterol" that increases heart disease and stroke risk).

Saturated fats are found mostly in high-fat dairy products, chicken skin, and red meats. Trans fats are found in fried foods, margarine, and many processed foods. The label might say "100% vegetable oil," but if it lists hydrogenated oil in the ingredients, beware. This is not healthy fat.

When you watch out for saturated fat, you are also keeping an eye on dietary cholesterol. This is because cholesterol is found only in animal products, most notably in high-fat dairy and fatty meats. Cholesterol is not found in foods derived from vegetables; even avocados and olives are cholesterol-free. Although the levels of cholesterol in your blood are an indicator of heart disease risk, there is not a clear link between how much cholesterol you eat and your blood levels. Saturated fats raise blood cholesterol levels more than eating cholesterol does. Still, limiting cholesterol is prudent. It was easy to keep all of my recipes well within heathful bounds because I use few high-fat animal products. I do cook with eggs: they are a wonderful source of protein and iron, and although they contain cholesterol, they are low in overall fat.

It is not difficult for the home cook to greatly reduce the amount of saturated fat in the diet. The solution ties in with eating a plant-based diet. Eat more vegetables than meat, and when you do cook with meat, use lean cuts. Use lowfat dairy products and find alternatives to butter and cream-filled recipes. Avoid hydrogenated fats by limiting the amount of fried foods, margarine, and commercially baked goods and snacks that you consume. Find healthier alternatives or make them yourself.

Do not avoid all fats. A prudent goal is to get about 20 percent of one's daily calories from fat. Within these bounds, the average person can have up to 50 grams of fat. For a cook, this lowfat—not nonfat—diet is good news because fat can do a tremendous amount for a recipe, from improving texture and color to contributing flavor. If most of your food is home-cooked, you can make excellent use of those 50 grams of fat. I use oils such as Asian sesame oil and canola, but I especially rely on olive oil because studies suggest that olive oil is heart-healthy and

improves HDL cholesterol levels in the blood. At times, when saturated fat is essential for a recipe, such as in a dessert, I use real butter, but in the smallest amounts necessary.

Nuts are good food. There are some foods that are high in fat that shouldn't be avoided or eliminated from the diet. Nuts have been shown to lower blood cholesterol levels, protect against some cancers, and are excellent sources of vitamins (2 ounces provide about 40 percent of the RDA for vitamin B and 50 percent of vitamin E) as well as minerals like magnesium. They are packed with protein, and so are important for vegetarians. Their only downside is that they are high in calories, so they should be eaten in moderation if weight gain is a concern. Nuts are a boon for the lowfat cook because of their rich flavors and textures.

Watch your salt intake. Although there is controversy over how important it is to limit salt in your diet, the general recommendation of getting no more than 2,400 milligrams a day of sodium (a little more than a teaspoon of table salt) is probably good advice. For some people, cutting salt definitely reduces the risk and severity of high blood pressure. Others won't reap such clear benefits. Unfortunately, there is no test to perform to tell which group you fall into.

Between 65 to 85 percent of the salt consumed in the United States comes from processed foods. By eating fresh-cooked foods from the home kitchen, you'll see immediate reductions in your salt intake. Yet salt is essential in many recipes and without it foods are often unpalatable. It is not necessary to go to extremes and do without salt. Use enough salt for flavor, but not so much as to be a health risk.

Protein needs are easily met. On average, adults need about 50 grams of protein a day, a teenager 44 to 60 grams, and a 7- to 10-year-old about 28 grams. In this country, protein is abundant. For people who consume dairy and small amounts of lean meats, protein requirements are met without even trying. For example, a ¼-pound serving of turkey cutlets provides about 28 grams of protein. Vegetarian foods can also be good sources of protein. A serving of my Bean Enchiladas (page 273) provides 23 grams.

Eat quantities in moderation. How much we eat is as important as what we eat. Eating more calories than the body requires causes a person to become fat. As a nation, we have been putting on weight at an alarming rate. Across all age groups, people have gained eight to ten pounds in the last decade. Obesity in children under age 12 has increased 54 percent since 1974. Twenty-five percent of children are overweight, as are almost half of all adults. Obesity is a risk factor for many diseases and has been linked to heart disease, cancer, and diabetes. Obese children reach puberty earlier, which in turn causes these children to grow into adults at high risk for breast cancer and reduced longevity. Losing weight can cause dramatic improvements in health. In one study, when just ten pounds were lost and kept off for two years, the chance of getting diabetes decreased 30 percent. Shedding eight to ten pounds and doing light exercise can cut blood pressure in half.

Calories are naturally reduced when eating home-cooked, lowfat meals centered around vegetables and carbohydrates. Because the foods are high in fiber, they are filling for fewer calories. They are nutrient-rich, promote health, and are very satisfying. On the other hand, commercial lowfat foods are not the answer. Lowfat does not mean low-calorie, but most people simply eat more of a "lowfat" food and thus still consume too many calories. Also, packaged lowfat foods are rarely healthy. Besides often being high in calories, they lack nutrients

and fiber. Eating nonfat bologna sandwiches and lowfat cake does not reduce weight or improve health. However, reduced-fat products, when used as ingredients, are very helpful within the context of healthful home cooking.

Get fit. You don't have to enter an iron-man competition to reap the benefits of exercise. Moderate exercise, such as three 30-minute walks a week, can improve health (even such light exercise can reduce the risk of heart disease in postmenopausal women by half). There are many reasons to get fit. Exercise reduces the risk of cancer, reverses and prevents heart disease, boosts the immune system, improves memory, relieves anxiety, and leads to a longer and more productive life.

This is not a spa cookbook, and so the servings are not minuscule. However, they shouldn't be judged against oversized restaurant and fast-food portions. (Some Italian restaurants, for instance, offer a plate of spaghetti and meatballs that could easily serve three people.) When determining servings per recipe, I assumed that the recipe was part of a larger meal. For example, soups are ladled out as first courses, not the main event. Also, serving size varies depending on a recipe's texture, bulk, and flavor. For example, a portion of a sweet chilled fruit soup is smaller than a bowl of chicken noodle.

Since each family's appetites are different, I was careful to specify "servings" and not declare how many it serves. Households with teenagers or those with physically demanding jobs understand how appetites can vary. View each serving as a moderate portion. If some in your family always have seconds, take that into account. If you serve a limited menu (for example, pizza and salad, but no bread or soup) adjust the number of servings you need accordingly.

Most of these recipes make four to six servings, so smaller households may end up with leftovers. Many freeze well or are equally good the next day. If you have a large family, you might need to double recipes. This is often quite easy to do, but use common sense. Allow more time for preparation and cooking. Not all recipes can be cooked in a larger pan. Lowfat foods heat differently since the fat is not there to conduct heat to the core. Because of this, liquid recipes like soups can be doubled in a larger pot, but most casseroles should be cooked in the suggested pan size; just use two pans. Not all seasonings should be multiplied, so taste as you cook.

The recipes have been analyzed for seven items: calories, protein, fat, saturated fat, carbohydrates, fiber, and sodium. Since few of the recipes include ingredients that contribute cholesterol, I have left that number out. Besides, saturated fat content is of more importance in heart health than dietary cholesterol. A registered dietician put all of the recipes through a computer program. Her database has nutritional data on thousands of ingredients and products, and she used her knowledge of nutrition and food preparation to adjust the results for cooking methods. Still, these numbers are not exact (for that, each food would have to be analyzed in a lab several times), and so she rounded them off to the nearest whole number.

I rarely look at nutritional analyses of my home-cooked recipes. Because I start with healthful ingredients, I trust that the end results are equally healthful. Seeing the nutritionist's numbers just confirms this trust. However, for those on restricted diets or for diabetics, the information might be necessary for the formulation of a weekly meal plan. On the other hand, for most people, it is important to look at the big picture, not a single nutrient. Rather than counting grams, ask yourself if you are eating enough vegetables, fiber, and lean protein, and

whether the menu is low in fat and reasonable in calories. All of these recipes fit these criteria. As my grandmother Nana Rose used to say, "With the best ingredients, how can it be bad?"

Following the Recipes

Completing a recipe can require following a great many steps, tools, and ingredients. If the cook isn't organized, a recipe can get out of hand and the cooking experience becomes annoying instead of gratifying. Even if you look forward to spending hours in the kitchen, it is unlikely that you enjoy tedious tasks (like peeling garlic), dirty dishes, or the frustration of not being able to finish a recipe because you are missing an ingredient. Taking time to get organized can make the cooking process itself quite easy and enjoyable.

Choose recipes and menus that fit your schedule and kitchen. Of utmost importance is having a recipe that is straightforward. I've tried to write mine as clearly as possible. The ingredients are listed in the order that they are needed. The method is divided into steps. Each recipe stands on its own, but if you desire more information, turn to the "about" notes or use the index to look for further help.

When following a recipe, first read it all the way through. Not only will this give you a good idea of what the finished recipe will be like, but it will alert you to whether you have all of the necessary equipment. Next, read through the ingredients listing again and pull out all of the ingredients. If you are missing something, you will realize it before the crucial moment that it has to be added. In most cases, all ingredients should be prepared and measured out before the cooking begins.

When reading the ingredient list, realize that I assume that all vegetables are washed and trimmed or peeled before chopping; that bell peppers have their cores, seeds, and membranes removed; and that cloves of garlic are peeled. Also, all eggs should be large. I've been very specific about quantities and often give both weight and size. However, recognize that many foods do not come in uniform sizes and that items like heads of broccoli can vary a great deal. For example, even if two heads weigh the same, one might be mostly stem, the other mostly florets. Use your judgment.

I've been very specific in terminology, and have followed government guidelines for lowfat and other products. For example, I specify "reduced-sodium" chicken broth, because the brand I use is "reduced" not "low-salt." If a recipe calls for "reduced-fat" cheese, that is what it was written for, not "lowfat." Often, I've tested the recipe several times, using various ingredients. This book contains the results of that work. Rarely will a recipe be as good if you substitute a lower-fat ingredient. This is notable with cheesecake. You can make a cheesecake with nonfat cream cheese, but it won't be worth eating. On the other hand, if you use a mix of reduced-fat and lowfat ingredients, you will have a superb dessert.

Read through the recipe's directions. If several ingredients are to be added all at once, measure them into a bowl first, then add them to the recipe as directed. This allows you to do preparation ahead of time, leaving the actual cooking until later. It is also helpful when following recipes that say "add the remaining ingredients and cook for 3 minutes." By the time you've added those ingredients one by one into the pan, the 3 minutes will be long gone and the first ingredients will be overcooked. But

if added all at once, there is less rush and the timing will be accurate.

Think ahead with the equipment as well. If you are going to transfer foods from one pan to another, have them all out (and coated with cooking spray if necessary). Make sure that the equipment you have is the right size. (Mixing batter in a too-small bowl is a lesson in frustration, and messy besides.) Water takes up to 20 minutes to come to a boil, so start that right away. Ovens need to preheat for at least that much time to be evenly hot. (I put these tasks at the beginning of the recipes so that they get started in time.)

If making several recipes at one time, think through which ingredients and equipment can be used for both. If both require boiling water, perhaps you can use the same pot for the two tasks. If you need 1 cup of chopped onions for one recipe and 1/2 cup for another, chop them all at the same time. If you are using a mixing bowl for a vinaigrette and also need a bowl for a marinade, perhaps you can use the same bowl with just a rinsing between tasks. All of these small efficiencies add to to a tremendous saving in time and effort.

Clean up as you go along. Put dirty dishes in a sink of water so that dish washing is easy later. Wipe off the cutting surface as you work. Have the garbage can next to your work surface so that you don't have to walk back and forth. Put ingredients that you no longer need back where they belong. Since there are few sights more depressing than a messy kitchen after dinner, I do as much clean-up as possible beforehand. Taking a few moments to tidy up as you are waiting for something to simmer can save a lot of time later.

Finally, don't lose sight of the fact that cooking engages all of your senses and can be a very pleasurable activity. Take a moment to smell the aromas, enjoy the sight of a beautiful vegetable, and get your hands messy feeling the food. One of the best parts of being the cook is that you are supposed to taste as you go along. Enjoy it!

Measuring

There are two different types of measuring cups. Those for dry ingredients come nested, each size a separate measurer. These can be leveled off with the flat edge of a knife for accuracy. Liquid measuring cups have the sizes written on the glass so that the cook can check the reading at eye level. Most of the recipes don't demand perfect measuring, but keeping all the ingredients in the right proportions is always a good idea. Some recipes, like those for baked goods, do require exact amounts. It speeds preparation when the largest measure is used; for example, I specify $1/4$ cup, rather than 4 tablespoons. Still, it helps to know the breakdowns, as explained in the following chart.

Measurement Equivalents

3 teaspoons = 1 tablespoon

2 tablespoons = 1 fluid ounce

4 tablespoons = $1/4$ cup = 2 fluid ounces

$5 1/3$ tablespoons = $1/3$ cup

8 tablespoons = $1/2$ cup

$1/2$ cup = 4 fluid ounces

16 tablespoons = 1 cup

2 cups = 1 pint = 16 fluid ounces

4 cups = 1 quart = 32 fluid ounces

8 cups = 2 quarts = $1/2$ gallon

4 quarts = 1 gallon

Glossary

To help you follow the recipes, here are descriptions of frequently used cooking terms.

Bake: An oven is considered a "dry" heat source. The heat surrounds the baking dish on all sides. Unless otherwise specified, always bake the recipe in the center of the oven.

Blanch: Immersing a food in boiling water for about 2 minutes, then cooling it quickly in a bowl of cold water is blanching. This technique is used to peel some fruits and vegetables, such as peaches and tomatoes. It also is perfect for removing the raw flavor of an ingredient yet leaving the crunch, for example, with snow peas or carrots. The cold water is necessary to stop the cooking, otherwise retained heat would further cook the ingredients.

Blend: Often a recipe says "blend until smooth" or "combine ingredients until well blended." This means that there are are no lumps or streaks in the mixture. Sometimes blending is easily accomplished with a whisk or even a spoon. If an electric blender is necessary, this is specified in the recipe. Take care using electric blenders, as you might end up liquefying instead of blending.

Boil: If a recipe requests a boil, this is a full, vigorous boil, where the bubbles that rise and burst on the surface are numerous and large. It often takes a few moments between the time a liquid comes to a simmer to when it finally reaches a boil. Wait for the boil if that is what a recipe specifies.

Broil: Broiled food is cooked under a heating element. The heat source is above the food and doesn't surround it as when the food is baked. Broilers cook at very high temperatures, and restaurant broilers reach well over the home kitchen's 500°F. Some stoves have a separate broiler, others are in the oven. Some require preheating.

Chop: When foods are cut into evenly sized pieces, they are chopped. "Coarsely chopped" is when the appearance isn't important and the food is chopped into irregularly sized pieces. "Chopped" usually means pieces about $2/3$ to $1/2$ inch in size.

Dice: Foods are cut into small cubes, about $1/4$ inch in size.

Dredge: A piece of food is dipped in a dry coating until thoroughly coated, then the excess is shaken off. For example, fish fillets might be dredged in a flour mixture before cooking.

Dust: To dust means to give a very light coating of a dry ingredient, such as a final, decorative sprinkle of sugar on a cake.

Mince: A mince is a very fine chop, with pieces smaller than grains of rice.

Sauté: Foods cooked in a thin, hot layer of oil or other fat are sautéed. The pan is always heated first, the oil added, and then the ingredients are stirred in. There should be a sizzle when the ingredients hit the oil. Once the cooking begins, the heat can be lowered.

Simmer: The cooking liquid is brought to a gentle boil, in which the bubbles that rise to the surface and break are not large and vigorous, like a boil, but smaller and less energetic.

Steam: Foods are cooked in a perforated basket over boiling water.

Menu Planning

In reality, the average home cook has a repertoire of fewer than a dozen recipes that he or she repeats week in and week out. This is not necessarily bad. Familiar recipes are easy to shop for, easy to cook, and are known to please the family. Rarely does the cook have to write down a menu or shopping list, since it has become rote. But if you want change, whether for variety or for health, writing up a menu becomes necessary.

To start, write down a list of the meals that you already prepare frequently. No one will be happy if this is replaced overnight with an entirely different menu. Determine which recipes can stay as is. Begin your new menu with these old favorites. Look for other recipes that can be adapted to a healthier diet. More nutritious versions of some popular recipes can be found in this book, such as spaghetti with meatballs or burgers. Next, decide which recipes should be replaced with entirely new recipes. Do this gradually. Adding one new recipe every

two weeks is plenty. Review the menu to see if it includes enough fruits, vegetables, and whole grains and beans. If not, a simple way to improve a meal is to add a salad, a vegetable side dish, or a whole grain.

Be realistic about how much time you have to cook. You don't have to put out a complicated gourmet meal every night. I always like to prepare a slightly simpler meal than I think I have time for, so that I don't feel harried and so that I have time for the unexpected. Also, pick recipes that can be prepared ahead but cooked or reheated at the last minute. Plan your menu so that all foods don't have to come to the table piping hot. This will alleviate a lot of time pressure just before the meal.

Don't plan on preparing too many new recipes each week. Design your menu to include leftovers or a mixture of convenience foods and homemade. For example, buy a cooked rotisserie chicken and quality whole-grain bread, and put your efforts into the side dishes of salad and carbohydrate. Make enough for leftovers so that the next night the only new recipe to cook is the main dish.

Think through the menu so that you can make the most use of fresh ingredients, have less waste, and save time. For example, if buying fresh spinach, plan on a fresh spinach salad one day and a cooked spinach dish another. Wash and pick through it all the first night, so that there is almost no prep the second day. If roasting a chicken on a Friday, make a chicken casserole using leftovers on Sunday. If serving a side dish of plain cooked rice, have fried rice the next evening.

Although most meals are centered around a main dish, that is not a rule written in stone. Especially in the summertime, a selection of salads and a soup can be a superb meal. Many health experts suggest eating at least two or three vegetarian meals a week. A vegetarian meal does not have to include a main dish, but can be a plate of several hearty side dishes.

When designing a menu I think not only about flavor combinations but also about presentation. What the dinner looks like affects how appetizing it is. Especially when introducing new foods, appearances are important. I always think back to what happened at a spa where I worked. I had recently left my job there when I got a desperate call asking me to come back. It turned out that my replacement was color blind and had served an entirely green meal. Although all-green meals are unusual, I've seen plenty of beige meals, for example, composed of a chicken breast, baked potato, and cauliflower. Small changes like serving a sweet potato and broccoli would make that meal far more appealing without any additional work.

Here are some suggestions for both weekday meals and fancy feasts, guaranteed to be beautiful and delicious, but with a thousand recipes in this book, this list is obviously incomplete.

Menu for a Busy Day

Tortellini Soup
Turkey Cutlets with Gremolata Sauce
Baby-Cut Carrots in a Honey-Mustard Glaze
Caesar-Style Salad
Cinnamon Raisin Bread Pudding

No-Fuss Dinner

Salad Bar Pesto Soup
Chicken Baked in Mustard
Buttered Egg Noodles
Tossed Salad with Dressing
Baked Apples

Chinese Banquet

Velvet Corn Soup
Ginger Greens Dumplings
Shrimp Fried Rice
Kung Pao Chicken
Snow Peas and Water Chestnuts
Cooked White Rice
Five-Spice Orange Slices

Pizza Party

Any 2 Pizza Recipes
American Garlic Bread
Tossed Salad with Dressing
Mousselike Cheesecake with Cherry Topping

Vegetarian Dinner

Black Bean Chili
Brown Rice
Molasses Cornbread
Mixed Greens and Mango Salad
Butterscotch Chip Brownies

Summer Luncheon

Corn Gazpacho
Raspberry Chicken and Greens Salad
Garlic Toasts
Honey of a Lemonade
Orange Biscotti
Pineapple Sherbet

On The Grill

Maple-Mustard Glazed Chicken
Grilled Zucchini
Grilled Portobello Mushrooms
Roasted Corn on the Cob
Honey Vanilla Frozen Ice Cream
Chocolate Syrup

Meat and Potatoes

Turkey Meatloaf
Mushroom Gravy
Mashed Potatoes with Roasted Garlic
Carrots and Peas
Tossed Salad with Dressing
Yellow Layer Cake with Seven-Minute Frosting

Kid's Menu for the Entire Family

Honey-Mustard Chicken Nuggets or Fish Sticks
Buttered Peas
Sweet Potato Spears
Applesauce
Cupcakes with Honey Fudge Frosting

Southwestern Fiesta

Tortilla Soup with Crab
Chicken or Vegetable Fajitas
Chili and Lime Corn
Southwestern Black Beans
Orange and Pineapple Salsa
Flan

Brunch for a Crowd

Blueberry Lemon Muffins
Breakfast Polenta
Granola with Nonfat Yogurt and 1% Lowfat Milk
Sausage and Cheese Egg Casserole
Strawberry and Melon Compote
Pear Spice Coffee Cake

A Special Family Gathering

Salad with Orange and Fennel
Herb Roasted Chicken
Apple and Nut Stuffing
Pearl Onions, Mushrooms, and Peas
Harvard Beets
Carrot Cake with Cream Cheese Frosting

Stocking the Healthy Kitchen

Most kitchens contain all that is necessary to start cooking healthy recipes. If you have spices, flour, canned beans, pasta, and rice in your cabinets and vegetables in your refrigerator, you are off to a good start. Listing every spice and grain and other detail that I use in this book does not make sense—with a thousand recipes, there is a little bit of everything here. Instead, look through this book and pick out five recipes you would like to try and make a shopping list from that. Gradually build up your pantry as you build your repertoire.

Most of the ingredients in my recipes are familiar, but some products might need an introduction and others need more explanation to get the most out of them. Here they are, in alphabetical order.

Asian sesame oil: Asian sesame oil goes by many names, including toasted sesame oil and dark sesame oil. It is used more as a flavor enhancer than a cooking oil because it smokes at low temperatures. A small amount packs a lot of distinctive flavor. Sesame oil that is light in color and mild in taste is not toasted oil and cannot be used interchangeably with Asian sesame oil.

Bacon: Because of its high fat and saturated fat content, bacon is not frequently consumed in a healthful diet. However, it can be used as a seasoning. Because I use it rarely and in small amounts, I buy the best that I can find. For example, a maple-cured bacon made in Vermont has a sweet, smoky taste and is not too salty. Since I use only a slice or two at a time, I keep the bacon in the freezer and remove only what I need.

Buttermilk: Buttermilk's name derives from the fact that in the past, when milk was churned into butter, what was left over was the "buttermilk." It is still lowfat, sometimes even nonfat. I've used 1% fat buttermilk in this book. Buttermilk, like yogurt, is cultured. It gets thicker with time. Shake the container before using it. Do not substitute powdered buttermilk; the results will not be as good. I use buttermilk a lot in baking. It softens the texture, adds body without fat, and helps quick breads rise. The slight tang contrasts nicely with the sugar in the batter.

Calamata olives: Calamata and other brine-cured olives have a salty and intense flavor that is totally different from the black olives sold in cans. They rarely come pitted, so this messy task must be done at home. To remove the pits, press down on an olive until the skin cracks (this can be done with the flat side of a chef's knife), then roll the olive until the pit is released. Pull out and discard. The resulting pitted olive will not look pretty, but it will taste great.

Capers: Capers are the buds from a shrub grown in the Mediterreanean. They are pickled in a salty brine. "Drained capers" are specified to prevent the salty liquid from overpowering a recipe. Capers come in several sizes. Some are the size of olives, and eaten whole as hors d'oeurves. Others are the size of peas. The most common, however—and the most useful for cooking—are the smallest capers. Once opened, if the jar is kept in the refrigerator and there is enough brine in the bottle to cover the capers, they will last for many months.

Dutch-processed cocoa: Dutch-processed cocoa goes through a procedure that raises its pH, darkens the color, and removes the harsh edges from the flavor. "Dutched" cocoa tastes milder but more chocolatey. For those who have grown up with Hershey's and still enjoy their chocolate bars, regular cocoa can be substituted. (Hershey's, by the way, also makes Dutch-processed cocoa.) I've found a tremendous difference in flavor between cocoa powder brands. It is worth buying several, making hot chocolate (the ultimate test), and deciding which you prefer.

Chili powder and **pure ground chilies:** These are different spices, though they can be used interchangeably. Chili powder is a blend of several spices; along with ground chili peppers there may be salt, coriander, oregano, and other seasonings. Pure ground chilies are dried, roasted chilies ground to a fine powder. I like the purity of flavor that pure ground chilies lend to a dish. It is often hotter and spicier than the chili powder blend found in supermarkets.

Garlic: In the form of fresh, peeled cloves, garlic is an essential element in countless recipes, but peeling it is one of the most annoying tasks in the kitchen. The papery peel sticks to your skin and the smell clings to your hands. You can avoid peeling garlic altogether and purchase peeled cloves at the market. The peeled cloves, without oil or preservatives, will stay fresh and firm if kept in a container in the refrigerator. Or use the same idea but peel the garlic bulb yourself. What you want to avoid is having to peel the garlic, clove by clove, each time you need some for a recipe, which is tedious and time-consuming. It is much better to do it once and get the task over with.

When buying garlic, look for very firm, dry, papery-skinned bulbs without blackish spots. To peel, rub off the loose skin, then put the bulb on a board and come down on it with a closed fist. The cloves will separate (smashed with too much force, though, they'll fly across the counter). Using the flat side of a large knife, hit each clove hard enough to split the skin but not flatten the clove. Do all of the cloves. Next, cut off the hard brown ends, then peel off the paper. Or you can purchase a nifty gadget that is a plastic tube that looks like a cannelloni shell. Put a few cloves of garlic in the tube, press, and roll, and the skins slip right off. Stored in a glass jar in the refrigerator, cloves stay fresh for at least one month.

Don't buy the minced garlic packed in oil, both because of the fat content and because of the slightly rancid flavor that this product has.

Ginger: Fresh ginger is one of my top ten favorite flavors. Dried powdered ginger is also wonderful, but not the same. Fresh ginger looks awkward to use yet is actually a user-friendly ingredient. Ginger is a root, with knobs or branches. It is displayed in the market in large pieces, but you do not have to buy the entire piece. Break off a knob the size you require; it will easily snap off at the joints. The outside of the ginger should be dry and beige, with no soft or wrinkled areas. The inside should be light yellow, fragrant, and as firm and moist as a potato.

Do not wrap the ginger or store it in the refrigerator because it will soften and mold. Instead, keep the ginger in a cool, dry, dark place. The exposed ends will quickly dry up and seal in the moisture from the root's interior. It will remain fresh for at least a week and often much longer.

Ginger is hard and fribrous, which makes it difficult to mince finely. So instead of using a knife, use a small hand-held grater, the same

tool used for Parmesan cheese. Peel it first, then grate. The tough fibers end up on the top of the grater, the usable ginger and its juices finely grated below. Grate only what is needed and put the rest of the knob, still unwrapped, back in storage until needed again. (Stored too long ginger will shrink and harden until no longer edible. But don't let it go to waste; use it in a hot bathtub for a relaxing, fragrant soak.)

Hoisin sauce: Hoisin sauce is a dark paste of fermented soybeans sweetened with sugar and flavored with chili, sesame oil, and other seasonings. Used in marinades and dipping sauces, it adds a complex sweet-and-salty flavor to foods. Hoisin sauce is available in the specialty foods section of your supermarket (look near the soy sauce) and in most Asian markets. Once opened, it lasts indefinitely in the refrigerator.

Kosher salt: Kosher salt differs on many counts from regular table salt. The crystals are larger and thus stick to food with more tenacity. It is purer than table salt because it doesn't contain the additives that keep regular salt pourable. Not only does this give it a cleaner taste, but I've found that table salt absorbs flavors, especially bitter ones, and with time, old salt will taste terrible. I've ruined a recipe cooking with old salt that had been stored near a stovetop for two years.

Kosher salt comes in a large box. Keep some in a small glass jar on the counter where you use it and refill as necessary. I do use regular salt for baking (it dissolves better in batters).

Lemon juice and **lime juice:** Bottled lemon and lime juices do not have fresh-squeezed flavor, so I never use them. But I still don't have to squeeze a lemon each time I need juice. Since both lemon and lime juices freeze well, I make my own frozen juice. Whenever I am using a fresh lemon or lime, I squeeze out all of the juice, not just what the recipe at the moment requires. Any extra is frozen in an ice cube tray. Once the juice is solid, the cubes are popped out and stored in a freezer bag. That way, when I need only a tablespoon or two of citrus juice, I always have some fresh-squeezed available. If I'm in a hurry, I defrost it in the microwave. Frozen pure lemon juice can also be purchased in the market. It is stocked next to the frozen juices. This product is pasteurized, so once thawed it will stay fresh for up to four weeks in the refrigerator.

Maple syrup: Maple syrup is made by boiling the sap of maple trees. Heating and reducing this liquid turns it into a thick, dark syrup with a complicated, rich taste. Imitation maple syrup was one of the first artificial flavors invented, but it still isn't half as good as the real thing. Grade A maple syrup is the lightest in color and mildest in flavor. I prefer grade B, which has a more pronounced maple flavor. Once opened, maple syrup needs to be kept refrigerated, but will stay fresh for many months.

Mirin: Mirin is a sweetened Asian cooking wine. If unavailable, use sweet sherry.

Oyster sauce: Oyster sauce is a thick Chinese liquid made from oyster extract, salt, and spices. Contrary to its name, it does not taste strongly of oysters, but does lend a distinctive, deep flavor to Asian recipes. Once opened, it will keep indefinitely in the refrigerator.

Parsley: Parsley is an herb that loses its flavor when dried, so it should always be used fresh. But fresh parsley often goes to waste. All too often a recipe calls for only 1 tablespoon of

parsley, so a sprig is pulled off and the remainder of the greens are put back in the fridge, where they quickly sag and are eventually thrown out. This doesn't have to happen.

The day that the parsley is brought home from the market, the entire bunch should be washed very well in cool water, tough stems torn off, then the leaves dried in a salad spinner. (The leaves must be very dry.) Stored in a loosely closed plastic bag in the produce drawer of the refrigerator, parsley will stay crisp for one week.

If the bag of prepped parsley is still too much for your weekly needs, it can be frozen, either as is or after mincing. Frozen parsley remains bright green and fresh for months. Once defrosted, it will wilt, so it is best for cooked foods, not salads.

Two types of parsley are available in the market, the tightly curled parsley and the Italian flat-leaf parsley. Both are good for cooking, although the flat-leaf has a milder flavor.

Peanut butter: Peanut butter for cooking needs to be unsalted and unsweetened. Most jarred brands are whipped smooth with extra oils and are sweetened and salted. This is great for sandwiches, but can ruin a sauce for pasta. The best peanut butter for cooking is freshly ground, and is nothing but peanuts. It is often coarse, and the oil might separate and need to be stirred back in, but the flavor is pure peanuts. Some national brands make low-sodium, low-sugar peanut butter; use these only if the fresh-ground is unavailable.

Quinoa: Quinoa is a South American grain sold in natural food stores. It must be rinsed thoroughly under cool running water before cooking (use a fine mesh sieve because the grains are tiny) because its outer covering foams and tastes soapy. It also tastes best when toasted before boiling. Vegetarians like it because of its high protein content, chefs like it because of its unique squashlike flavor, and home cooks like it because it cooks in under 20 minutes.

Rice vinegar: Rice vinegar is as familiar to Asian cooks as apple cider vinegar is to New England cooks. It has a strong and distinctive flavor. Although white wine vinegar can be substituted, the results will be different than if made with rice vinegar. Natural food stores sell brown rice vinegar, which can be used when rice vinegar is called for, although the color is darker and the flavor a bit more intense.

Scallions: Scallions are long, narrow green shoots with small white bulbs at the end. Sometimes they are called green onions. Except for the roots and the wilted tops, all of the scallion can be used. The white and light green sections contain the most flavor; the green tops contribute color. They can be eaten raw or cooked.

Shredded cheese: Shredded cheese is used in many recipes. The cook has a choice to buy already shredded cheese in a pouch, or to shred her or his own. I almost always opt to shred a block of cheese in the processor. Because freshly grated cheese is not as dried out, nor does it have anticaking powders in it, I get more volume for the weight. Shredding cheese in the processor takes only a minute. Store unused cheese in a container in the refrigerator. Use it up quickly, though, because it molds more quickly than block cheese.

Soba noodles: Soba noodles are Asian noodles made from buckwheat. Some are 100 percent buckwheat, but I prefer those with some wheat to lighten up the flavor and texture. They have a rich, earthy taste and are a nice change from white pasta. Soba noodles are available at most natural food stores and many gourmet shops.

Soy sauce: Soy sauce is a combination of soybeans, wheat, water, and salt that has been aged. It not only adds flavor but also heightens the flavors of the foods to which it is added. Soy sauces vary according to brand. La Choy soy sauce, and other inexpensive soys are not aged and are made from a soybean slurry that is quickly processed in a chemical bath, which is then sweetened and flavored with caramel and sugar. My recipes are not designed for these products. Kikkoman is a traditionally made soy sauce, available in most supermarkets and appropriate for these recipes. Tamari is a relative of soy sauce—close, but not the same. It is saltier, stronger, and does not contain wheat. It should not be substituted for soy sauce. Soy sauce is high in sodium, but I prefer not to use the low-sodium as I can detect a flavor difference. However, if you are on a salt-restricted diet, do use a reduced-sodium soy sauce.

Tahini: Tahini is ground sesame seeds, sometimes called sesame paste. It is available toasted, but all of my recipes use the untoasted variety. It varies in thickness. During storage, the oil from the seeds separates out, rises to the surface, and can be difficult to stir back in because the paste can be quite stiff and solid. One way around this is to store the unopened jar upside down. When opened, the oil will be on the bottom. If it is still impossible to stir, put it all in a blender or food processor and puree.

Udon noodles: Udon noodles are Japanese wheat noodles that are thick, flat, and have a distinct, slightly salty flavor. They are excellent whether eaten hot or cold and add an authentic touch to some Asian recipes. If unavailable, substitute linguine.

Vegetables: It is true that eating well means eating lots of vegetables. Not everyone likes to cut and chop, but that doesn't mean you have to go without fresh ingredients. If a recipe calls for diced carrots, buy carrot sticks and cut across the bundle to form little cubes. Sometimes onions are available chopped, in bags. Chopped onions are also in the freezer section, though they exude a lot of liquid when sautéed, so are best for soups or stews. Coleslaw mix can be used whenever chopped cabbage is called for. Winter squash comes peeled, mushrooms sliced, and melons cut and cubed. Although you pay a premium for these packaged vegetables, everything purchased is edible (unlike, for example, whole carrots, where you are also paying for the peel and the ends), so it is not as prohibitive as might be thought.

Also make use of the supermarket salad bar, where you can get sliced celery, peppers, and other ingredients already trimmed and in the exact amount for a specific recipe. You might need to cut the vegetables into the required sizes, but most of the work is already done. Although it is true that some of the nutritional value of a vegetable deteriorates when surfaces are cut and exposed to air, not all of the nutrients lose their potency, and it is far better to have fresh vegetables from the salad bar than none at all.

Though the textures of frozen vegetables and fruits are rarely a match for fresh, their flavor can be excellent. Some vegetables, like peas, corn, and spinach, are often better from the freezer than the produce department. Others to keep in the freezer are berries, rhubarb, and sugarsnap peas.

Kitchen Design and Organization

The kitchen is the heart of the home, a gathering place for the family, a place to read the mail, have a snack, do homework, talk over a cup of tea. The smells and promises of cooking draw people into the room. Unfortunately, all too often the design, organization, or appearance of the kitchen discourages the cook. It is worthwhile to take a look around, evaluate the space, and see what can be improved. A welcoming, user-friendly kitchen can make all the difference between whether the family eats take-out or homemade, or eats meals together or on the run.

Some changes take very little time and resources. Others are costly. Full-scale renovations should be done with the help of a kitchen designer, but there are several ways to improve the kitchen almost immediately.

First, look at the overall environment. Do you enjoy being in the kitchen? Perhaps a coat of paint or colorful prints on the walls will make a difference. Is it too dark? Too bright, with shadows? Good lighting can relieve eye strain and make a room more cheerful.

Evaluate the area where you do most of the food preparation. It should be large enough to fit a good-size cutting board as well as the ingredients needed for a recipe. The work space surface should not be cluttered with decorative items, food stuffs, or jars of wooden spoons. When the space is kept open, it is easier to keep track of the ingredients for a recipe, easier to cook, and easier to clean up. Hopefully this work space is next to the stovetop, the sink, and the refrigerator so that there is little wasted motion between these areas. If the kitchen is not so efficiently designed, the cook can save time by being as organized as possible. For example, wash all vegetables at the sink at one time, then carry them in a bowl to the cutting board instead of carrying them one by one from fridge to sink to work area.

Next, look at how your equipment and ingredients are stored and arranged. Only a few pots, pans, and utensils are used on a daily basis. Keep these within easy reach. My favorite pots hang from a pot rack and my smaller tools are on the counter in a brass tub. Measurers and knives are within easy reach. If possible, make a place on the counter for the electric tools, like the food processor. If a tool is in a hard-to-access cabinet, you'll be unlikely to use it.

I believe it is the small, frustrating moments that drive people away from cooking. For example, extricating a pot lid from a drawer jammed with lids—many of which don't even match pots anymore—can be an exasperating experience. Don't make it hard to find your tools. Keep items such as the pots, lids, and baking dishes most frequently used in an easily accessible place. If it takes several minutes to find and untangle the piece of equipment you need, you'll see cooking as an annoying activity instead of a pleasure.

Another small frustration is the hunt for the right herb or spice. Get a spice rack and keep the jars in alphabetical order. It may take time to set up, but you will be amply repaid when you can find exactly what you want the moment you need it. But don't keep the spices on the counter exposed to sunlight and heat, both of which cause them to deteriorate rapidly. A dark cabinet is best.

All of this discussion about organization and efficiency is not intended to turn cooking into serious work. Rather, it is meant to improve the process, leaving more time for the pleasurable aspects.

Essential Kitchen Equipment

Although almost everyone's cabinets are filled with pots, baking pans, and utensils, the reality is that very few of the items are needed for daily cooking. Although my kitchen is filled with an assortment of items that I pull out now and then, there are only a few I use day in and day out. There are also a few that, though not essential, make life much easier. Here is my short list of what a basic kitchen should contain.

Knives: Buy the best knives you can afford; they will last a lifetime. The handle should feel balanced and comfortable in your hand. Only three knives are essential: a 6- or 8-inch chef's knife, a paring knife, and a serrated bread knife. Keep them sharp by using a knife sharpener before each use. I use one that is preset at the correct angles so all I have to do is pull the knife through the slots. Keep knives stored in a knife rack. Never put them loose in a drawer. Not only is it extremely dangerous, but the knife tips and edges might be harmed. A swivel vegetable peeler is also essential. Replace it every few years.

Cutting Boards: Have at least two boards, one for meat, the other for all else. I use a plastic board for meat because it can go in the dishwasher, but I prefer to chop vegetables on a wooden board. It should be large enough so that the vegetables don't roll off and onto the counter as they are being cut. Use one side for garlic, onions, and other savory vegetables; use the other side for fruit and for vegetables that shouldn't taste like garlic. It is useful to have a small board for small tasks.

Small Utensils: Wooden spoons, wooden and rubber spatulas, flat spatulas, whisks, ladles, and slotted spoons all have important jobs to do in the kitchen. Have at least two sets of measuring spoons and cups and a glass 2-cup measuring cup within reach. A child's plastic ruler is surprisingly useful. Also have a small hand-held grater and a larger box grater (a box grater is a tall rectangle that stands on its own and has different-size holes on each of its four sides).

Thermometers: Keep a thermometer in the refrigerator (where the temperature should be between 38 and 40°F), one in the freezer (which should be around 0°F), and one in the oven. For checking the temperature of food, an instant-read thermometer is more useful than a meat thermometer since it can be used for everything from bread to sauces to chicken.

Countertop Electric Appliances: Food processors and blenders both blend and puree, though, depending on the recipe, one usually does a better job than the other. If you have to choose one, get the processor. A mini-processsor is a handy tool and can mince garlic or chop nuts better than the larger version. An electric mixer is necessary for some recipes. A hand-held mixer can usually do the job, though a stand mixer is a wonderful tool, and is an appliance that cooks grow to love.

Pots and Pans: High-quality pots are worth the investment because they will last a lifetime. Thin, poorly made pots scorch foods, warp, and become useless in a few years. Purchase pots that conduct heat well and have thick bottoms and comfortable handles. Not all pots have to be nonstick, although it is best if sauté pans and small pots are. Recent innovations in nonstick surfaces are far superior to previous versions—the best ones now do not peel, are hard to scratch, and last a long time.

These are the essential pots: a medium-size sauté pan (about 8 inches), a larger skillet (about 12 inches), a large wok (13 inches), a 2½-quart saucepan, a 4-quart pot, and a larger pot for soups and broths. A Dutch oven is a pot that can go from the stovetop into the oven and is very useful. Have at least one, about 4 quarts in size. Depending on the quantities that you usually cook, is also helpful to have either a smaller or larger Dutch oven as well.

Baking Pans and Baking Sheets: Cookie sheets and rimmed sheets are useful for more than dessert baking, since both chicken and fish can be cooked on them. Baking pans in several sizes—including 9×13 and an 8- or 9-inch square—are useful as is a large roasting pan. Have at least two wire cooling racks.

Casseroles: I do not like to bake in clear glass casseroles, but if you do, always lower the oven temperature by 25°F or the recipe will dry out. I prefer ceramic or porcelain casseroles. My recipes have been tested in the Corning Ware French White dishes (although my recipes have also been made in my recipe testers' homes in other casseroles, too). The two most useful sizes are 2½-quart and 3- to 4-quart.

Other Equipment: Have at least one set of mixing bowls but preferably more, a wooden rolling pin, a salad spinner, a colander, and a wire-mesh sieve. Keep heat-proof oven mitts within reach near the stove. Lots of cloth kitchen towels come in very handy.

Miscellaneous: A reamer (a wooden tool used to juice citrus), a funnel, and a vegetable scrub brush are all frequently used in my kitchen. My favorite gadget is a device that that peels, cores, and slices apples all in a crank of a handle. I couldn't survive apple-picking season without it. The one item, though, that draws the most comment is my big ball of rubber bands. Our mail is delivered held together with a rubber band, and every day I add another band to my ball. I use rubber bands to keep the brown sugar bag so tightly closed that the sugar never goes hard, to reseal bags of frozen vegetables, and to keep plastic wrapped airtight around cheese. Rubber bands are one of the most useful items in my kitchen and the ball keeps them tidy and in one place.

Small Bites and Finger Foods

Chips and Nuts
22

Spiced Nuts

Sweet Curried Spiced Nuts

Snack Mix

Baked Tortilla Chips

Chili-Spiced Tortilla Chips

Fat-Free Crispy Pita Chips

Garlic Oil Pita Chips

Dips and Spreads
35

Spinach Dip

Curry Orange Dip

Sun-Dried Tomato Dip

Roasted Red Pepper Dip

Vegetable Platter for Dips

Guacamole

Guacamole Caliente

Baba Ganouj

Baba Ganouj with Mint
and Cumin

Eggplant Caviar

Hummus with Tahini

Garlic and Lime Chickpea Dip

Chickpea and
Pine Nut Spread

Black Bean Dip

Layered Black Bean Dip

Herb and Garlic Yogurt
Cheese Spread

Chutney Cream Cheese Spread

Smoked Fish Spread

Smoked Fish Spread
with Horseradish

Finger Foods
34

Jicama Spears

Asparagus Wrapped with
Smoked Salmon

Smoked Salmon Canapés

Cream Cheese and Caviar
Canapés

Deviled Eggs

Stuffed Eggs with
Smoked Salmon

Curried Stuffed Eggs

Chutney Pinwheels

Chili-Cheese Pinwheels

Herbed Roast Beef Pinwheels

Whole Wheat Tostadas

Tostadas with Salsa and
Goat Cheese

Jalapeño-Cheese Mini-Muffins

Potato Cups Filled with
Sour Cream and Caviar

Polenta Squares with Pepper
Relish and Goat Cheese

Polenta, Cheese, and
Vegetable Tart

Bacon-Stuffed Mushroom Caps

Stuffed Mushroom Caps

Crostini and Bruschetta
42

Tomato and Basil Crostini or Bruschetta

Tomato and Feta Crostini or Bruschetta

Greens and Raisins Crostini or Bruschetta

Tomato Olivada Crostini or Bruschetta

Roasted Red Pepper Crostini or Bruschetta

Mini-Frittatas
45

Ricotta-Mushroom Mini-Frittatas

Broccoli-Pepper Mini-Frittatas

Crabmeat Mini-Frittatas

Skewered Hors D'oeuvres
47

Tortellini Skewers

Latin Turkey Skewers

Red-Cooked Turkey Skewers

Steamed Marinated Shrimp

Horseradish Cocktail Sauce

Barbecued Shrimp

Won Tons
49

Vegetable Won Tons

Scallop Won Tons

Spinach and Mushroom Won Tons

Finger foods, from dips and chips to savory little mouthfuls, are often all that is needed for many gatherings. Whether you call these foods hors d'oeuvres, appetizers, or small bites, their role is the same: to provide interesting nibbles for your guests as they meet and converse. However, little appetizers are often the fattiest part of a meal. Cheese platters are obviously sources of fat, but those tiny filled pastry shells, turnovers, and quiches are also extremely high in fat. The alternative selection offered here keeps food festive *and* healthy.

Chips and Nuts

When planning which recipes to serve, keep in mind how casual the party is—some recipes are more elegant than others. Also consider how messy the food is to eat. If your guests are wearing silk they won't appreciate sticky barbequed finger foods. If there are few places to sit, don't serve foods that need to be eaten with a knife or fork. Always have plenty of napkins and obvious places, such as trays, to leave the soiled paper and dirty dishes.

For larger parties, I like to have both foods for passing and others at stationary sites. Having some foods circulating in the room keeps the guests from crowding around one table. Also, hot hors d'oeuvres (such as stuffed mushroom caps) are best when eaten immediately, which will happen if they are taken from person to person at the party.

It can be difficult to decide how much to make. I've discovered that if you are having a party at a meal time and your guests arrive hungry, you'll need twice as much because they'll make a meal out of the finger food—even if they know that they'll sit down to a full dinner in an hour. For many parties, a selection of three or four passed appetizers (three pieces per person) and two appetizers at stationary sites (such as a dip and crackers and a vegetable platter) is ideal.

Spiced Nuts

Makes: 12 servings (1 ounce each)

Although nuts are high in fat, they can have a place in a healthy diet. For more, see page 7.

3 cups whole shelled nuts
1 teaspoon chili powder
1/4 teaspoon kosher salt
1/8 teaspoon cayenne pepper
1/4 teaspoon ground ginger
1/2 teaspoon ground cinnamon
1/3 cup sugar
1 egg white
1 tablespoon orange liqueur

1) Preheat the oven to 325°F. Coat a large rimmed baking sheet with nonstick spray.

2) Toss the nuts with the dry ingredients. Lightly whisk the egg white with the orange liqueur, and stir into the spiced nuts until all is moist.

3) Spread the nuts on the baking sheet in one layer. Bake for 15 minutes. Using a spatula, turn the nuts over. Continue to bake for about 15 minutes longer until the surface of the nuts is dried out. After they have cooled, store in a tightly lidded container.

Per Serving: Calories 189; Protein 4g; Fat 16g (Saturated 1g); Carbohydrates 11g; Fiber 1g; Sodium 49mg

Sweet Curried Spiced Nuts

Makes: 12 servings (1 ounce each)

Although curried, these are more sweet than hot.

1/2 cup sugar
1 tablespoon orange juice
1/2 teaspoon ground cinnamon
1/4 teaspoon ground cloves
1/4 teaspoon ground ginger
2 teaspoons curry powder
1 egg white
3 cups whole shelled nuts

1) Preheat the oven to 325°F. Coat a large rimmed baking sheet with nonstick spray.

2) In a medium bowl, blend together all the ingredients except the nuts. Toss the nuts into this mixture and stir until they are well coated.

3) Spread the nuts on the baking sheet in one layer. Bake for 15 minutes. Using a spatula, break the clumps of nuts apart and turn over. Bake for another 8 minutes. The nuts at the edges of the baking sheet might brown more quickly. Keep an eye on them and stir as needed.

4) Remove the nuts from the baking sheet. After they have cooled, store in a tightly lidded container.

Per Serving: Calories 196; Protein 4g; Fat 16g (Saturated 1g); Carbohydrates 13g; Fiber 1g; Sodium 7mg

Snack Mix

Makes: 14 servings (1/2 cup each)

This healthy version of an old favorite is a welcome sight at casual gatherings.

2 cups corn cereal squares
2 cups whole wheat cereal squares
1/2 cup unsalted, dry roasted peanuts
2 cups small pretzel twists
2 tablespoons melted butter
1 teaspoon honey
1 1/2 teaspoons vegetable oil
1/2 teaspoon ground cinnamon
1 teaspoon vanilla extract
1 cup raisins

1) Preheat the oven to 350°F. Coat a baking sheet with butter-flavored nonstick spray.

2) Put the cereal, peanuts, and pretzels in a bowl. Combine the butter and honey and, if necessary, warm the mixture until the honey is thin and pourable. Stir in the oil, cinnamon, and vanilla. Pour over the cereal mixture and toss to coat.

3) Spread the snack mix on the baking sheet. Lightly coat with the nonstick spray. Bake for 6 minutes, stir, and continue to bake for another 8 to 10 minutes until golden. Let cool. Stir in the raisins.

Per Serving: Calories 150; Protein 3g; Fat 5g (Saturated 2g); Carbohydrates 25g; Fiber 2g; Sodium 207mg

Baked Tortilla Chips

Makes: 48 chips

Serve these immediately, hot and crispy from the oven.

8 corn tortillas

1) Preheat the oven to 400°F.

2) Cut each tortilla into 6 wedges. To save time, stack several, then cut.

3) Place tortillas wedges in a single layer on a baking sheet and bake for 8 to 12 minutes, until crispy.

Per Chip: Calories 6; Protein 0g; Fat 0g (Saturated 0g); Carbohydrates 1g; Fiber 0g; Sodium 5mg

Chili-Spiced Tortilla Chips

Makes: 48 chips

A light coating of olive oil spray can be used in place of brushing the tortillas with oil.

8 corn tortillas
2 teaspoons vegetable oil
1/4 teaspoon ground cumin
1/2 teaspoon chili powder

1) Preheat the oven to 400°F.

2) Cut each tortilla into 6 wedges. To save time, stack several, then cut.

3) Pour the oil into a very small bowl. Using a pastry brush, moisten one side of each wedge with a little oil. (I keep a pastry brush just for oils and savory foods, and another for desserts.) Dust with the spices (you might not need to use all).

4) Place in a single layer on a baking sheet and bake for 10 to 12 minutes, until crispy. Serve immediately.

Per Chip: Calories 8; Protein 0g; Fat 0g (Saturated 0g); Carbohydrates 1g; Fiber 0g; Sodium 5mg

Fat-Free Crispy Pita Chips

Makes: 32 chips

These are absolutely wonderful right out of the oven, but can be made several hours in advance.

Four 7-inch pita breads

1) Preheat the oven to 375°F.

2) Peel each bread apart into 2 rounds apiece. Cut each round into 8 wedges. To save time, stack, then cut.

3) Place in a single layer on a baking sheet and bake for 7 to 10 minutes, until crispy.

Per Chip: Calories 21; Protein 1g; Fat 0g (Saturated 0g); Carbohydrates 4g; Fiber 0g; Sodium 40mg

Garlic Oil Pita Chips

Makes: 32 chips

Other flavored oils, such as chili or rosemary, would also be excellent.

Four 7-inch pita breads
1 1/2 tablespoons garlic oil (recipe page 607)

1) Preheat the oven to 375°F.

2) Peel each bread apart into 2 rounds apiece. Cut each round into 8 wedges. To save time, stack first, then cut.

3) Pour the olive oil into a very small bowl. Using a pastry brush, moisten the inside (rough side) of each wedge with a little garlic oil. (I keep a pastry brush just for oils and savory foods, and another for desserts.)

4) Place in a single layer on a baking sheet and bake for 7 to 10 minutes, until crispy and lightly browned around the edges.

Per Chip: Calories 26; Protein 1g; Fat 1g (Saturated 0g); Carbohydrates 4g; Fiber 0g; Sodium 40mg

Dips and Spreads

The easiest foods to serve at a party are dips and spreads, but nothing signals the end of a party more than an empty bowl of dip. To keep it looking fresh, I use a dish that is smaller than the quantity I've prepared, then fill it to the top several times during the party so that it always looks fresh and abundant.

Dips lose nothing except the fat when made with lowfat dairy products; the texture and flavor are as good as the full-fat versions. Equally wonderful are dips made with beans or spiced and mashed vegetables (like eggplant). Some of the best-tasting crackers on the market are lowfat. No longer should anyone arrive at a party with the worry that they will have to look but not eat.

Spinach Dip

Makes: 13 servings (3 tablespoons each)

This dip can be prepared a day ahead.

2 cloves garlic
4 scallions, cut into 2-inch lengths
One 10-ounce package frozen spinach, cooked
    according to package directions
1 tablespoon lemon juice
$1/8$ teaspoon ground nutmeg
$1/4$ teaspoon ground coriander
1 teaspoon kosher salt
$1/4$ teaspoon freshly ground pepper
$1/4$ teaspoon Tabasco sauce (optional)
1 cup lowfat sour cream
$1/2$ cup nonfat yogurt

1) Mince the garlic and scallions in a food processor.

2) Squeeze the excess moisture out of the spinach. Pulse the spinach in with the garlic and scallions. Add the next 6 ingredients and puree. Pulse in the sour cream and yogurt until smooth.

Per Serving: Calories 34; Protein 2g; Fat 1g (Saturated 1g); Carbohydrates 5g; Fiber 1g; Sodium 190mg

Curry Orange Dip

Makes: 20 servings (3 tablespoons each)

This dip tastes best when chilled before serving.

1 pound 1% lowfat cottage cheese
$1/4$ cup nonfat yogurt
$1/4$ teaspoon lemon juice
2 tablespoons frozen orange juice concentrate
1 teaspoon curry powder
$1/4$ teaspoon ground cardamom
$1/16$ teaspoon cayenne pepper

Puree all the ingredients in a food processor fitted with a metal blade until the texture is smooth and creamy.

Per Serving: Calories 21; Protein 3g; Fat 0g (Saturated 0g); Carbohydrates 2g; Fiber 0g; Sodium 95mg

Sun-Dried Tomato Dip

Makes: 13 servings (3 tablespoons each)

Sun-dried tomatoes bring a lot of intense flavor to this dip. Serve with a platter of cut vegetables.

20 sun-dried tomato halves (not packed in oil)
$1/2$ cup fresh parsley
1 clove garlic
$1/2$ teaspoon kosher salt
$1/2$ teaspoon freshly ground pepper
1 teaspoon lemon juice
1 pound lowfat or nonfat sour cream

1) To soften the tomatoes, place them in a microwavable bowl. Cover with 1 inch of water. Cover loosely with plastic wrap and microwave on high for about 4 minutes. Let rest for 10 minutes. Alternatively, put the tomatoes in a pot of boiling water and cook for 2 minutes, then let rest.

2) Chop the parsley and garlic in a food processor. Drain the tomatoes, reserving the liquid. Drop the tomatoes in the bowl and finely chop. Add the salt, pepper, and lemon juice. Then, with the machine running, pour in enough of the tomato soaking water to get a coarse puree (about 1/4 cup). You might need to scrape down the sides of the bowl once or twice. Discard the rest of the soaking water.

3) Remove the puree from the processor to a bowl and stir in the sour cream until the tomato mixture is distributed smoothly throughout.

Per Serving: Calories 52; Protein 2g; Fat 2g (Saturated 2g); Carbohydrates 7g; Fiber 1g; Sodium 110mg

Roasted Red Pepper Dip

Makes: 16 servings (about 3 tablespoons each)

The Roasted Red Pepper Topping can be made several days in advance, but the sour cream should be stirred in within a few hours of the party.

1 recipe Roasted Red Pepper Topping for
　　Bruschetta (page 45)
1 pound lowfat sour cream

Stir the sour cream into the red pepper mixture.

Per Serving: Calories 35; Protein 1g; Fat 2g (Saturated 1g); Carbohydrates 4g; Fiber 0g; Sodium 158mg

Vegetable Platter for Dips

Makes: 20 servings

Use this recipe as a jumping off point. What is important is that the vegetables are fresh and brightly colored. Although carrots are the most popular dip vegetable, other vegetables can be offered. After a quick steaming, both asparagus and green beans are lovely on a platter, as are raw mushrooms and jicama.

1 head broccoli
1 head cauliflower
2 red or green bell peppers
1 pint cherry tomatoes
2 pounds baby-cut carrots

1) Cut the broccoli and cauliflower into florets that can be eaten in 2 bites. Slice the peppers into strips, taking care to remove all seeds and whitish membranes. Wash and stem the tomatoes.

2) Although they can be served raw, many hard vegetables—such as carrots, broccoli, and cauliflower—benefit from steaming. They must be steamed long enough to taste cooked, yet not so soft that they lose their crunch. Once cooked to the desired tenderness, immerse them in a bowl of cold or iced water to stop the cooking and retain their bright color. Then drain them. Vegetables can be prepared up to a day ahead of time and refrigerated individually in sealable plastic bags.

3) Arrange half the vegetables on a serving platter and replenish with the other half as necessary. If all the vegetables are put out at once, by the middle of your party the platter will look sparse and ragged.

Per Serving: Calories 26; Protein 1g; Fat 0g (Saturated 0g); Carbohydrates 6g; Fiber 2g; Sodium 21mg

Guacamole

Makes: 13 servings (3 tablespoons each)

Hard, unripe avocados lack the flavor of ripe ones. They are poor choices for dips because, even even if pureed in a food processor, they will lack the smooth, rich texture of ripe avocados.

1 large ripe avocado
4 plum tomatoes, seeded
1/2 cup minced red onions
1 tablespoon lemon juice
2 teaspoons fresh lime juice
1/2 teaspoon kosher salt
1/8 teaspoon Tabasco sauce

1) Quarter the avocado, discard the pit, and peel away the skin. Mash the pulp; a potato masher works well for this. Chop the tomatoes. This is easily done with a few pulses in the food processor.

2) Mix together all the ingredients. If not serving immediately, cover with plastic wrap so that the plastic touches the guacamole. The absence of air will prevent browning.

Per Serving: Calories 32; Protein 1g; Fat 2g (Saturated 0g); Carbohydrates 3g; Fiber 1g; Sodium 78mg

Guacamole Caliente

Makes: 16 servings (3 tablespoons each)

The fat in the avocados mellows the hot spices.

2 large ripe avocados
4 plum tomatoes, seeded
1 clove garlic, minced
2 jalapeño peppers, seeded and minced (wear rubber gloves)
1/4 cup minced red onions
1 tablespoon lemon juice
1 tablespoon fresh lime juice
1/2 teaspoon kosher salt
1/4 teaspoon Tabasco sauce
2 tablespoons chopped fresh cilantro

1) Quarter the avocado, discard the pit, and peel away the skin. Mash the pulp. Chop the tomatoes. This is easily done with a few pulses in the food processor. The garlic and jalapeños can be minced in a small spice grinder or mini-processor.

2) Mix together all ingredients. If not serving immediately, cover with plastic wrap so that the plastic touches the guacamole. The absence of air will prevent browning.

Per Serving: Calories 48; Protein 1g; Fat 4g (Saturated 1g); Carbohydrates 4g; Fiber 1g; Sodium 65mg

Baba Ganouj

Makes: 13 servings (3 tablespoons each)

Baba Ganouj is also excellent as a pita pocket sandwich filling.

Two 1-pound eggplants
2 cloves garlic
1/4 cup fresh parsley
1/4 cup tahini
1/4 cup lemon juice
1 teaspoon kosher salt
1/4 teaspoon freshly ground pepper

1) Broil the eggplants, turning frequently until slightly charred and soft, about 15 minutes. (They can also be grilled, or baked at 375°F for 1 hour, but I find broiling the easiest and quickest method.) Remove from the oven and let rest until cool enough to handle. Slice in half lengthwise and scrape the flesh into a colander. Drain out the bitter liquid by setting the colander in the sink or in a bowl for about 15 minutes.

2) Drop the garlic into a food processor and mince, then add the parsley and chop. Scrape down the sides of the bowl and add the remaining ingredients and the eggplant pulp. Process until coarsely chopped.

3) Taste and add more lemon juice if desired.

Per Serving: Calories 49; Protein 1g; Fat 3g (Saturated 0g); Carbohydrates 6g; Fiber 2g; Sodium 150mg

Baba Ganouj with Mint and Cumin

Makes: 13 servings (3 tablespoons each)

The mint and cumin contribute aroma and flavor to this version of the popular Middle Eastern dip.

1 recipe Baba Ganouj (opposite)
1/2 teaspoon kosher salt
2 tablespoons chopped fresh mint leaves
1 teaspoon ground cumin
1/4 teaspoon Tabasco sauce

1) Follow the directions for Baba Ganouj.

2) Add the additional salt and the mint, cumin, and Tabasco in step 2 after the parsley is pulsed in.

Per Serving: Calories 50; Protein 2g; Fat 3g (Saturated 0g); Carbohydrates 6g; Fiber 2g; Sodium 226mg

Eggplant Caviar

Makes: 16 servings (3 tablespoons each)

An old tale tells how this eggplant dip was passed off as real caviar in a royal court, hence its name. Although I don't see a direct resemblance, the combination of sharp, sweet, and salty is wonderful.

Two 1-pound eggplants
1 tablespoon olive oil
2 cups chopped onions
4 cloves garlic, chopped
3 tablespoons tomato paste
1 teaspoon sugar
1 1/2 tablespoons balsamic vinegar
1 teaspoon kosher salt
1/4 teaspoon freshly ground pepper

1) Broil the eggplants, turning frequently until slightly charred and soft, about 15 to 25 minutes. (They can also be grilled, or baked at 375°F for 1 hour, but I find broiling the easiest and quickest method.) Remove from the oven and let rest until cool enough to handle. Slice in half lengthwise and scrape the flesh into a colander. Drain out the bitter liquid by setting the colander in the sink or in a bowl for about 15 minutes.

2) Meanwhile, heat the oil in a heavy-bottomed saucepan. Cook the onions and garlic in the pot until softened and golden, about 10 minutes. Keep the pot covered between stirrings.

3) Add the tomato paste, sugar, vinegar, salt, pepper, and eggplant pulp. Cook until the sharp vinegar aroma disappears, about 3 minutes.

4) Put the mixture into a food processor and pulse until coarsely chopped.

Per Serving: Calories 36; Protein 1g; Fat 1g (Saturated 0g); Carbohydrates 7g; Fiber 2g; Sodium 130mg

Hummus with Tahini

Makes: 10 servings (3 tablespoons each)

This classic version of hummus is very easy to make and will last a week in the refrigerator.

2 cloves garlic
2 cups cooked chickpeas, drained and rinsed
1/3 cup tahini
3 tablespoons lemon juice
1/3 cup water
1/2 teaspoon kosher salt
1/8 teaspoon cayenne pepper

Mince the garlic in a food processor fitted with a metal blade. Add the remaining ingredients and puree until smooth, using additional liquid if needed.

Per Serving: Calories 104; Protein 4g; Fat 5g (Saturated 1g); Carbohydrates 11g; Fiber 2g; Sodium 99mg

Garlic and Lime Chickpea Dip

Makes: 9 servings (3 tablespoons each)

Lime juice gives this dip a fresh and unexpected flavor.

4 cloves garlic
2 cups cooked chickpeas, rinsed and drained
2 tablespoons olive oil
2 tablespoons water
2 tablespoons fresh lime juice
1 1/2 teaspoons kosher salt
1 teaspoon paprika
1/4 teaspoon Tabasco sauce
2 tablespoons chopped fresh parsley

Mince the garlic in a food processor. Add the remaining ingredients except for the parsley. Process until smooth. Pulse in the parsley.

Per Serving: Calories 90; Protein 3g; Fat 4g (Saturated 1g); Carbohydrates 11g; Fiber 2g; Sodium 324mg

Chickpea and Pine Nut Spread

Makes: 9 servings (3 tablespoons each)

Pine nuts have a subtle though unmistakeable flavor. Some of the nuts used in this spread are left coarsely chopped so that their flavor comes through.

2 cups cooked chickpeas, drained and rinsed
2 cloves garlic
5 tablespoons pine nuts
3 tablespoons lemon juice
1 teaspoon kosher salt
1/8 teaspoon Tabasco sauce
2 tablespoons water
2 tablespoons chopped fresh parsley

1) Drop the chickpeas and garlic into a running food processor. Process until minced. Scrape down the sides of the bowl.

2) Add 4 tablespoons of the nuts along with the lemon juice, salt, Tabasco, and water. Process until a smooth paste forms.

3) Pulse in the parsley and the remaining tablespoon of pine nuts until mixed, but not smooth (about 4 pulses).

Per Serving: Calories 84; Protein 4g; Fat 3g (Saturated 0g); Carbohydrates 11g; Fiber 2g; Sodium 217mg

Black Bean Dip

Makes: 12 servings (3 tablespoons each)

Cilantro is an herb that can be difficult to find. If unavailable, use a store-bought salsa that lists cilantro as an ingredient (often available in the dairy case).

2 cups cooked black beans, drained and rinsed
1 cup red salsa (homemade or store-bought)
2 tablespoons chopped fresh cilantro (optional)
1/4 cup lowfat sour cream
1/4 cup nonfat yogurt
2 teaspoons Worcestershire sauce
1/2 teaspoon Tabasco sauce (optional)

Mash the beans, either with a food processor or by hand, until the beans are mostly smooth. Pulse or stir in the remaining ingredients.

Per Serving: Calories 54; Protein 3g; Fat 0g (Saturated 0g); Carbohydrates 9g; Fiber 3g; Sodium 232mg

Layered Black Bean Dip

Makes: 16 servings (about $1/4$ cup each)

Large triangles of tortilla chips are best for scooping this up.

2 cups cooked black beans, drained and rinsed
1 tablespoon fresh lime juice
1 teaspoon ground cumin
1 teaspoon kosher salt
$1/4$ teaspoon Tabasco sauce
1 cup lowfat or nonfat sour cream
1 roasted pepper (jarred or recipe page 603), chopped
1 tomato, cored and chopped
2 scallions, sliced
2 tablespoons chopped fresh parsley or cilantro

1) Mash the beans with the lime juice, cumin, salt, and Tabasco. If the beans appear dry, add a little extra lime juice. Spread into a serving dish so that the beans are about $1/2$ inch thick.

2) Spread the sour cream on top of the beans.

3) Combine the chopped pepper and tomato and distribute on top of the sour cream. Then top with the scallions and parsley or cilantro.

Per Serving: Calories 50; Protein 3g; Fat 1g (Saturated 1g); Carbohydrates 8g; Fiber 2g; Sodium 137mg

Herb and Garlic Yogurt Cheese Spread

Makes: 10 servings
(about $1 1/2$ tablespoons each)

Not only is this good as a dip, but it is also delicious as an alternative to mayonnaise on turkey sandwiches. Fines herbes is a medley of classic aromatic garden herbs. If you don't have any, combine parsley, tarragon, and chives, or use other herbs of your choice.

8 ounces nonfat yogurt
4 ounces reduced-fat cream cheese, softened
1 clove garlic, finely minced
1 teaspoon fines herbes
1 teaspoon minced fresh herbs, such as dill (if unavailable add 1 teaspoon more dried fines herbes)
$1/2$ teaspoon lemon juice
$1/4$ teaspoon kosher salt
$1/8$ teaspoon freshly ground pepper

1) Put the yogurt in a coffee filter or a piece of cheesecloth, set in a colander in a bowl, and place in the refrigerator to allow the whey to drain out. After 6 hours you will have a creamy nonfat spread. Drain for several more hours if a denser, firmer cheese is desired.

2) Using an electric mixer on low speed, combine the thickened yogurt with the remaining ingredients. Beat until smooth.

Per Serving: Calories 42; Protein 3g; Fat 2g (Saturated 2g); Carbohydrates 2g; Fiber 0g; Sodium 114mg

Chutney Cream Cheese Spread

Makes: 10 servings
(about 1 1/2 tablespoons each)

A good chutney will make this simple spread incredibly elegant. I search for interesting chutneys at farmstands to use for this recipe. Both a ginger-apple chutney and a jar of cherry-plum were memorable.

One 8-ounce package reduced-fat cream cheese
1/2 to 2/3 cup store-bought or homemade chutney
(pages 594–596)

Spread the cream cheese 1/2 inch thick on a serving dish. Cover with the chutney. Serve with fat-free crackers.

Per Serving: Calories 76; Protein 3g; Fat 5g (Saturated 3g); Carbohydrates 6g; Fiber 0g; Sodium 98mg

Smoked Fish Spread

Makes: 12 servings (about 2 tablespoons each)

The flavor of smoked fish varies according to type of fish and the handling by the smokehouse. This has been successfully tested with both a strong-tasting bluefish and a milder trout.

1/2 pound smoked fish, skin and bones removed
2 tablespoons lowfat sour cream
1 tablespoon lowfat mayonnaise
1 tablespoon nonfat cream cheese
2 teaspoons minced fresh chives or scallions
1 teaspoon minced fresh parsley
1 tablespoon minced red onions
2 teaspoons lemon juice
1/4 teaspoon kosher salt
1/4 teaspoon freshly ground pepper

1) Flake the fish with a fork before adding it to the mixture.

2) Beat the sour cream, mayonnaise, and cream cheese until smooth. Stir in the remaining ingredients.

Per Serving: Calories 27; Protein 5g; Fat 0g (Saturated 0g); Carbohydrates 1g; Fiber 0g; Sodium 254mg

Smoked Fish Spread with Horseradish

Makes: 10 servings (2 tablespoons each)

Serve this dip with plain crackers, such as melba toasts.

3 scallions, cut into 3-inch pieces
1/4 cup lowfat sour cream
1/4 cup nonfat or lowfat ricotta cheese
1 tablespoon store-bought bottled horseradish
1 teaspoon Dijon mustard
1 teaspoon soy sauce
2 teaspoons lemon juice
1/2 pound smoked fish, skin and bones removed
1/4 teaspoon kosher salt
1/4 teaspoon freshly ground pepper

1) Mince the scallions in a food processor. Remove from the bowl and set aside.

2) Puree the next 6 ingredients (sour cream through lemon juice) until smooth. Pulse in the fish, salt, and pepper until well mixed but not smooth. Stir in the scallions.

Per Serving: Calories 39; Protein 6g; Fat 1g (Saturated 0g); Carbohydrates 2g; Fiber 0g; Sodium 346mg

Finger Foods

Jicama Spears

Makes: 12 servings

Jicama is a crunchy, sweet root vegetable very popular in Central and South America. Purchase jicama that is firm and a uniform light brown color.

1 1/2 pounds jicama (about 1 large)
1 lemon
1 lime
1/4 teaspoon kosher salt
1 teaspoon chili powder or pure ground chili

1) Quarter the jicama and peel with a paring knife. Slice into spears.

2) Arrange on a serving plate. Juice the lemon and lime over the jicama, taking care to discard any citrus seeds. Dust with the salt and chili. Serve chilled.

Per Serving: Calories 22; Protein 0g; Fat 0g (Saturated 0g); Carbohydrates 5g; Fiber 2g; Sodium 44mg

Asparagus Wrapped with Smoked Salmon

Makes: about 24 spears

These are elegant and delicious, and worth the expense of the salmon.

1 pound asparagus, medium width
    (about 24 spears)
1/3 pound smoked salmon, thinly sliced
1 tablespoon Honey-Mustard Sauce (page 601)

1) Trim and steam the asparagus according to the directions on page 314. Once cooked, the asparagus should be pliable but still a bit crisp. If you haven't already done so, trim the jagged ends with a knife.

2) Cut the salmon into strips about 1 inch wide. Lightly brush one side of a strip of salmon with the sauce, then wrap the salmon around the stalk, starting near the tip and spiraling down. If the asparagus are pencil-thin, wrap 2 in a bundle. Place on a serving platter.

Per Spear: Calories 14; Protein 2g; Fat 0g (Saturated 0g); Carbohydrates 1g; Fiber 0g; Sodium 52mg

Smoked Salmon Canapés

Makes: 24 canapés

There are several choices for the type of bread to use. Those long square loaves of cocktail pumpernickel bread are convenient and tasty. Triangles of thinly sliced homemade Whole Wheat Bread (page 497) or slices of narrow French bread loaves would also be good.

1 seedless cucumber (also called imported
    European)
2/3 cup reduced-fat cream cheese
1 tablespoon store-bought bottled horseradish
24 slices thinly sliced bread, about 1 1/2 inches
    square
4 ounces thinly sliced smoked salmon
1/2 small bunch fresh dill, washed and dried

1) Thinly slice the cucumber into rounds. Or peel long strips of cucumber and cut into decorative shapes with vegetable or cookie cutters.

2) Mix the cream cheese and horseradish until smooth using a whisk or an electric mixer.

3) Spread a thin layer of the cream cheese mixture on each piece of bread. Top with a slice of cucumber, then a piece of salmon and a sprig of dill. Arrange on a platter and pass to your guests.

Per Canapé: Calories 50; Protein 3g; Fat 2g (Saturated 1g); Carbohydrates 5g; Fiber 1g; Sodium 125mg

Cream Cheese and Caviar Canapés

Makes: 45 canapés

The appearance of this red, white, and green canapé is very festive.

1 recipe Smoked Salmon Cream Cheese Spread (page 448)
1/2 pound loaf cocktail bread, each slice cut in half diagonally
1 cucumber, peeled, halved lengthwise, and sliced
2/3 cup reduced-fat cream cheese
1 1/2 ounces red caviar

1) Spread a thin layer of the cheese spread on each piece of bread. Place cucumber slice on top (without the cheese, the cucumber slips off).

2) Top each cucumber slice with about a 1/2-teaspoon dollop of cream cheese, then top with a small amount of caviar (about 1/16 teaspoon). Serve immediately.

Per Canapé: Calories 39; Protein 2g; Fat 2g (Saturated 1g); Carbohydrates 3g; Fiber 0g; Sodium 89mg

Deviled Eggs

Makes: 12 deviled eggs

If you don't have a deviled egg serving platter, cut very thin slices off of the bottoms so that the eggs stay put.

6 hard-boiled eggs
2 tablespoons reduced-fat cream cheese
2 tablespoons lowfat sour cream
2 tablespoons reduced-fat mayonnaise
1/4 teaspoon kosher salt
1/8 teaspoon freshly ground pepper
1/4 teaspoon ground turmeric
1 tablespoon sweet pickle relish
1 teaspoon Dijon mustard
1 teaspoon Worcestershire sauce
Paprika for garnish

1) Peel the eggs (see page 607). Cut them in half lengthwise and remove the yolks. Put one yolk in a food processor fitted with a steel blade and discard the rest.

2) Add all remaining ingredients except the paprika to the processor bowl. Pulse until the mixture is well blended but not pureed (over-processing will make the filling runny). Scrape down the sides twice during processing.

3) To fill the eggs, use a teaspoon or a pastry bag fitted with a large decorative tip. Garnish with paprika.

Per Deviled Egg: Calories 59; Protein 4g; Fat 4g (Saturated 1g); Carbohydrates 1g; Fiber 0g; Sodium 128mg

Stuffed Eggs with Smoked Salmon

Makes: 12 deviled eggs

The salmon lends an appealing rosy color to these eggs.

6 hard-boiled eggs
2 tablespoons reduced-fat cream cheese
1/4 cup nonfat sour cream
1 ounce smoked salmon
1 teaspoon lemon juice
1 tablespoon fresh dill
1 teaspoon capers, drained

1) Peel the eggs (see page 607). Cut them in half lengthwise and remove the yolks. Put 2 yolks in a food processor fitted with a steel blade and discard the rest.

2) Add the cream cheese, sour cream, salmon, and lemon juice to the processor bowl. Pulse until the mixture is well blended but not pureed (overprocessing will make the filling runny). Scrape down the sides twice during processing.

3) To fill the eggs, use a teaspoon or a pastry bag fitted with a large decorative tip. Garnish each egg half with a small sprig of dill and 3 capers.

Per Deviled Egg: Calories 53; Protein 4g; Fat 3g (Saturated 1g); Carbohydrates 1g; Fiber 0g; Sodium 73mg

Curried Stuffed Eggs

Makes: 12 deviled eggs

Major Grey's, a classic, mango-based chutney, is available in most supermarkets.

6 hard-boiled eggs
1/2 cup reduced-fat cream cheese, softened
2 tablespoons reduced-fat mayonnaise
1 teaspoon fresh lime juice
2 tablespoons Major Grey's chutney
1/8 teaspoon Tabasco sauce
1/2 teaspoon curry powder
1/4 teaspoon kosher salt
1 tablespoon minced scallions or fresh chives
   for garnish

1) Peel the eggs (see page 607). Cut them in half lengthwise and remove the yolks.

2) Beat the cream cheese until smooth. Put 1 egg yolk in the bowl and mash it with the cream cheese. Discard the rest of the yolks. Add the remaining ingredients except the scallions or chives to the bowl. Mash until smooth.

3) To fill the eggs, use a teaspoon or a pastry bag fitted with a large decorative tip. Garnish each egg half with a touch of scallions.

Per Deviled Egg: Calories 79; Protein 4g; Fat 6g (Saturated 3g); Carbohydrates 2g; Fiber 0g; Sodium 143mg

Chutney Pinwheels

Makes: 32 pinwheels

The tighter these are rolled up, the better they hold together and the prettier they look on the serving platter.

4 ounces reduced-fat cream cheese
1/2 teaspoon curry powder
3 tablespoons chutney
4 large flour tortillas
1/3 cup thin slices red onions
1 cup tomatoes, seeded and chopped

1) Blend the cream cheese, curry powder, and chutney. A small wire whisk is useful for this task.

2) Thinly spread the cheese mixture onto the tortillas. Top with the red onions and tomatoes.

3) Roll up the filled tortillas. Wrap snugly in plastic wrap and refrigerate for 2 to 6 hours. When ready to serve, slice into thick rounds. Display with the whirls showing.

Per Pinwheel: Calories 36; Protein 1g; Fat 1g (Saturated 1g); Carbohydrates 5g; Fiber 0g; Sodium 53mg

Chili-Cheese Pinwheels

Makes: 32 pinwheels

Serve these pinwheels at a casual party along with foods such as salsa, chips, guacamole, and chili.

4 ounces lowfat cream cheese
4 large flour tortillas
1 cup finely shredded lowfat cheddar cheese
2 tablespoons chopped scallions
One 8-ounce can whole green chilies (or jalapeños if desired)
1/2 cup cooked black beans, drained and rinsed well

1) Thinly spread the cream cheese on the tortillas. Top with the cheddar and scallions. Halve the chilies. Scrape out the seeds and membranes, dry on a towel, then slice. Place chili strips on the tortillas. Distribute the beans on top.

2) Roll up as tightly as you can, wrap snugly in plastic wrap, and refrigerate for 2 to 6 hours. When ready to serve, slice into thick rounds and display with the whirls showing.

Per Pinwheel: Calories 44; Protein 2g; Fat 2g (Saturated 1g); Carbohydrates 5g; Fiber 1g; Sodium 106mg

Herbed Roast Beef Pinwheels

Makes: 32 pinwheels

You can use a commercial lowfat Boursin-style cheese, or make you own with the recipe for Herb and Garlic Yogurt Cheese Spread on page 32.

4 ounces lowfat Boursin-style cheese
4 large flour tortillas
1/4 pound deli roast beef, thinly sliced
4 Bibb lettuce leaves, center rib removed
1/4 cup minced scallions or chives
1 cup sliced roasted red bell peppers

1) Thinly spread the cheese on the tortillas. Top with the beef, lettuce, and scallions. Blot the peppers dry on a paper towel and distribute across the tortillas.

2) Roll the tortillas up as tightly as you can, wrap snugly in plastic wrap, and refrigerate for 2 to 6 hours. When ready to serve, slice into thick rounds and display with the whirls showing.

Per pinwheel: Calories 38; Protein 2g; Fat 1g (Saturated 1g); Carbohydrates 4g; Fiber 0g; Sodium 86mg

Whole Wheat Tostadas

Makes: 4 servings

Tostadas can be cut into triangles and passed at a party, or cut into quarters and served as a first course.

Four 6- to 7-inch whole wheat flour tortillas
1 cup salsa (variety of your choice)
3/4 cup cooked black beans, drained and rinsed
1/2 cup shredded reduced-fat cheddar cheese

1) Preheat the oven to 400°F. Coat 2 baking sheets with nonstick spray.

2) Place the tortillas on the baking sheets. If the salsa is watery, drain off excess liquid. Spread the salsa on the tortillas. Top with the beans, followed by the cheese.

3) Bake for 10 minutes. Rotate the baking sheets and switch racks halfway through baking.

Per Serving: Calories 163; Protein 9g; Fat 2g (Saturated 1g); Carbohydrates 32g; Fiber 7g; Sodium 877mg

Tostadas with Salsa and Goat Cheese

Makes: 4 servings

The red, black, and white colors of the salsa, beans, and cheese makes these dramatically attractive.

Four 6- to 7-inch flour tortillas
1 cup salsa (variety of your choice)
1/2 cup cooked black beans, drained and rinsed
1/4 cup crumbled goat cheese (about 2 1/2 ounces)

1) Preheat the oven to 400°F. Coat 2 baking sheets with nonstick spray.

2) Place the tortillas on the sheets. Spread the salsa on the tortillas. Top with the beans, followed by the cheese.

3) Bake for 10 minutes. Rotate the baking sheets and switch racks halfway through baking.

4) Cut each tostada into quarters.

Per Serving: Calories 186; Protein 9g; Fat 6g (Saturated 4g); Carbohydrates 30g; Fiber 6g; Sodium 903mg

Jalapeño-Cheese Mini-Muffins

Makes: 36 muffins

The jalapeños make these appetizers spicy bursts of flavor in your mouth. Substitute canned mild chili peppers if you prefer a more subtle experience.

2 tablespoons sugar
1 1/2 cups unbleached, all-purpose white flour
1 cup cornmeal
1 teaspoon baking soda
2 teaspoons baking powder
1/2 teaspoon salt
1 1/4 cups buttermilk
3 tablespoons vegetable oil
1/2 cup shredded reduced-fat jack or cheddar cheese
1/4 cup chopped canned jalapeños

1) Preheat the oven to 375°F. Coat mini-muffin pans with nonstick spray.

2) Sift together the sugar, flour, cornmeal, baking soda, baking powder, and salt. Add the bits of cornmeal left in the sifter in with the dry ingredients. Stir in the buttermilk and oil until the batter is moist but lumpy. Stir in the cheese and jalapeños.

3) Fill the muffin cups. Bake 15 to 20 minutes until firm and beginning to turn light brown around the edges. These are best if served warm from the oven.

Per Muffin: Calories 52; Protein 1g; Fat 2g (Saturated 0g); Carbohydrates 8g; Fiber 0g; Sodium 122mg

Potato Cups Filled with Sour Cream and Caviar

Makes: 24 pieces

The potatoes can be baked, scooped out, and refrigerated for up to a day. Before filling, warm them in the microwave or oven.

24 very small new potatoes (about 1 1/2 pounds)
2 teaspoons olive oil
1/4 teaspoon freshly ground pepper
1/2 cup lowfat sour cream
2 teaspoons caviar

1) Preheat the oven to 425°F.

2) Scrub the potatoes clean and toss them with the oil until shiny. Place in a single layer in a rimmed baking sheet and bake for about 30 minutes, until tender. Set aside until they are cool enough to handle.

3) Slice a thin piece off the bottom of each potato so that they will sit upright without rolling. Using a melon baller, scoop out the center of each potato, leaving enough flesh attached to the skin to help the potato keep its shape. At this point the potato cups can be refrigerated for up to one day.

4) The potato cups should be warm, but not hot enough to melt the sour cream; if necessary, warm the potatoes in the microwave or oven. Dust the insides with pepper. Fill with sour cream and top with caviar.

Per Cup: Calories 33; Protein 1g; Fat 1g (Saturated 0g); Carbohydrates 6g; Fiber 0g; Sodium 13mg

Polenta Squares with Pepper Relish and Goat Cheese

Makes: 32 pieces

These are very pretty and would be just right as the opening note of a formal dinner party. The polenta can be made one day in advance.

1 recipe Polenta (page 407)
1 red bell pepper
1 green bell pepper
1 yellow bell pepper (if not available, use red)
1 small yellow onion
2 cloves garlic, skin on
1 teaspoon balsamic vinegar
1/2 teaspoon kosher salt
1/4 teaspoon freshly ground pepper
1 tablespoon olive oil
6 ounces goat cheese

1) Prepare the polenta and pour it into a small loaf pan. Chill until firm.

2) Meanwhile, halve the peppers and remove the seeds and ribs. Cut the onion in half but leave the skin on. Line a baking sheet with foil and place peppers and onion cut sides down on it. Add the garlic. Preheat the broiler and place the rack 6 to 8 inches from the heat source. Broil the vegetables until they blister and blacken, about 8 to 10 minutes. Let cool. Peel off and discard the charred skins.

3) Coarsely chop the vegetables by hand or in a food processor. Stir in the vinegar, salt, and pepper. This relish can be made up to one day in advance. Bring to room temperature or warm lightly in the microwave before using.

4) Coat a baking sheet with nonstick spray. Preheat the broiler. Remove the polenta from the pan. Cut into 1/4-inch-thick slices, then halve the slices diagonally into triangles or quarter them into squares. Place the polenta on the baking sheet and brush with olive oil. Broil for 5 to 7 minutes, until crispy, then turn over and broil another 5 minutes. Place on a serving platter. Top with a small teaspoonful of relish and a little goat cheese and serve.

Per Piece: Calories 42; Protein 2g; Fat 2g (Saturated 1g); Carbohydrates 4g; Fiber 0g; Sodium 89mg

Polenta, Cheese, and Vegetable Tart

Makes: 8 servings

Like a quiche, this can be sliced into squares and served as an appetizer, or it can be cut into wedges and served as a first course.

2 1/3 cups water
2/3 cup cornmeal
1/2 teaspoon kosher salt
1 egg white
1/2 cup reduced-fat cream cheese
2 ounces goat cheese
1/2 teaspoon dried thyme
1/4 teaspoon kosher salt
1/8 teaspoon freshly ground pepper
2 small zucchini, thinly sliced into rounds
2 cloves garlic, minced
1 teaspoon olive oil
4 plum tomatoes, cored and sliced into rounds
1 tablespoon grated Parmesan cheese

1) Warm the water in a pot. Stir in the cornmeal and salt. Bring to a gentle simmer. Stir frequently until the polenta thickens and begins to pull away from the sides of the pot, about 15 to 20 minutes. Coat a 9-inch round tart pan with a removable bottom with nonstick spray, or use a springform pan. Pour the cooked polenta into the pan, spreading it evenly on the bottom. Let it rest until the polenta sets, or refrigerate for up to one day.

2) Preheat the oven to 425°F. Using a food processor or mixer, combine the egg white, cream cheese, goat cheese, thyme, salt, and pepper until smooth. Spread the cheese mixture onto the polenta base.

3) Sauté the zucchini and garlic in the olive oil until wilted. Arrange the zucchini and tomato slices decoratively in concentric, overlapping circles over the cheese mixture. Dust with the Parmesan cheese.

4) Bake for 15 to 20 minutes.

Per Serving: Calories 126, Protein 6g; Fat 7g (Saturated 4g); Carbohydrates 11g; Fiber 2g; Sodium 316mg

Bacon-Stuffed Mushroom Caps

Makes: 20 mushrooms

Select unblemished mushroom caps. They can, however, be slightly opened, which provides more room for the filling.

20 medium to large mushrooms, cleaned
2 teaspoons olive oil
1/4 cup minced onions
3 tablespoons dry sherry
3 slices bacon, cooked and chopped
1/2 cup soft breadcrumbs
1/4 cup lowfat ricotta cheese
1/2 teaspoon kosher salt
1/4 teaspoon freshly ground pepper
1/2 teaspoon dried marjoram

1) Preheat the oven to 400°F.

2) Remove the mushroom stems and finely chop the stems to get 1 cup (easily done in a food processor). Discard the rest. If necessary, cut a thin slice off the cap of each mushroom so that it sits flat when turned upside down. Put the caps stem sides down on a nonstick or coated baking sheet.

3) Heat the oil in a large nonstick sauté pan. Stir in the onions and cook until lightly golden. Add the chopped mushroom stems and sherry. Cook over high heat until the stems soften and the alcohol partly cooks down. Scrape the sauté into a bowl and stir in the remaining ingredients.

4) Bake the caps for 5 minutes, until they begin to soften. Remove from the oven. Using a teaspoon, stuff each mushroom with the filling, mounding slightly. Set the caps, filling sides up, back on the baking sheet. Bake for 6 to 10 minutes, until lightly golden. Serve immediately.

Per Mushroom: Calories 23; Protein 1g; Fat 1g (Saturated 0g); Carbohydrates 2g; Fiber 0g; Sodium 73mg

Stuffed Mushroom Caps

Makes: 24 mushrooms

The combination of walnuts, currants, and cheese is wonderful. These are best served hot.

24 medium to large mushrooms, cleaned
2 teaspoons olive oil
5 tablespoons chopped walnuts
1/4 cup dry sherry
1/4 cup currants
1/4 cup Italian seasoned breadcrumbs
1 cup reduced-fat ricotta cheese
1/2 teaspoon kosher salt
3 scallions, minced

1) Preheat the oven to 400°F.

2) Remove the stems from the mushrooms. Coarsely chop the stems to get 1 cup. Discard the rest. If necessary, cut a thin slice off the cap of each mushroom so that it sits flat when turned upside down. Put the caps stem sides down on a nonstick or coated baking sheet.

3) In a large nonstick sauté pan, heat the oil. Stir in the nuts and cook briefly until lightly toasted. Stir in the chopped mushroom stems and sherry. Cook over high heat until the stems soften. Scrape the sauté into a bowl and stir in the remaining ingredients.

4) Bake the caps for 5 minutes, until they begin to soften. Remove from the oven. Using a teaspoon, stuff each mushroom with the filling, mounding slightly. Set the caps, filling sides up, back on the baking sheet. Bake for 10 to 14 minutes, until lightly golden. Serve immediately.

Per Mushroom: Calories 35; Protein 2g; Fat 2g (Saturated 0g); Carbohydrates 3g; Fiber 0g; Sodium 68mg

Crostini and Bruschetta

Crostini and bruschetta, two types of toasted bread appetizers, originated in Italy. In the United States the differences between them are blurred and at times the terms are used interchangeably.

Usually crostini are small, thin toasts topped with a diverse selection of delectable mixtures. They are ideal as appetizers, although a selection can make a lovely lunch. A true bruschetta also starts with toasted or grilled bread, which is then rubbed with raw garlic cloves and brushed with olive oil. Bruschetta are usually larger than crostini but similarly topped, and they make wonderful open-faced sandwiches.

Both crostini and bruschetta are finger foods at their best, although a knife and fork might be necessary for the larger ones. Good bread is essential. It should have a crusty exterior and a soft middle. Don't use loaves that are too big around, or the middles will drop out when the toasts are topped.

Once made, these appetizers should be eaten immediately. However, many of the toppings can be put together up to a day or two ahead of time, so that last-minute preparation is minimal.

The following recipes, which appear elsewhere in the book, make great bruschetta and crostini toppings:

Marinated Tomato Salad (page 71)
Oven-Baked Ratatouille (page 271)
Roasted Garlic and Greens (page 339)
White Bean Stew (page 404)
Roasted Tomato Sauce (page 585)

Tomato and Basil Crostini or Bruschetta

Makes: 20 crostini or 12 bruschetta

Letting the ingredients come to room temperature and having them rest for an hour greatly enhances the flavor of these crostini.

10 plum tomatoes, seeded and chopped
1/4 cup chopped fresh basil leaves
1 clove garlic, minced
1/4 cup finely chopped red onions (optional)
1 teaspoon dried oregano
1 teaspoon balsamic vinegar
1 teaspoon olive oil
1/2 teaspoon kosher salt
1/2 teaspoon freshly ground pepper
1 long loaf crusty bread

1) Chop all ingredients except the bread by hand or in a food processor. Toss together and let rest at room temperature for 1 hour.

2) Slice the bread. If long and thin, cut 20 slices for crostini. If wider, cut 12 slices for bruschetta. Grill or toast.

3) Place spoonfuls of the topping on the toasts.

Per Crostini: Calories 71; Protein 2g; Fat 1g (Saturated 0g); Carbohydrates 13g; Fiber 1g; Sodium 183mg

Tomato and Feta Crostini or Bruschetta

Makes: 10 crostini or 5 bruschetta

Serve these right after topping so that the bread stays crisp.

One 14 1/2-ounce can diced tomatoes
1 teaspoon olive oil
2 shallots, minced
1 teaspoon balsamic vinegar
1 teaspoon red wine vinegar
1/4 cup crumbled feta cheese
1/2 long loaf crusty bread

1) Drain the tomatoes in a colander until all excess liquid drips out.

2) Heat the oil in a small nonstick pan. Cook the shallots until golden. Stir in the tomatoes and vinegars. Warm through. Stir in the feta.

3) Slice the bread. If long and thin, cut 10 slices for crostini. If wider, cut 6 slices for bruschetta. Grill or toast.

4) Place spoonfuls of the topping on the toasts.

Per Crostini: Calories 82; Protein 3g; Fat 2g (Saturated 1g); Carbohydrates 13g; Fiber 1g; Sodium 210mg

Greens and Raisins Crostini or Bruschetta

Makes: 15 crostini or 10 bruschetta

For this crostini, the slices of bread are a bit thicker, so a long loaf yields 15 crostini slices.

1 long loaf crusty bread
1/2 pound Swiss chard, spinach, or escarole leaves
1 1/2 teaspoons olive oil
4 cloves garlic, minced
1/4 cup golden raisins
1/4 teaspoon kosher salt
1/4 teaspoon freshly ground pepper
1 1/2 teaspoons balsamic vinegar
1/2 cup shredded reduced-fat mozzarella

1) Slice the bread. If long and thin, cut 15 slices for crostini. If wider, cut 10 slices for bruschetta. Grill or toast.

2) Wash the greens well, discard the tough stems, and coarsely chop the leaves.

3) In a large skillet or wok, heat the oil. Stir in the greens, garlic, and raisins. Cook until the greens wilt. If the skillet is too small to fit them all in with room to maneuver, do this in two batches.

4) Stir in the salt, pepper, and vinegar. Cook over high heat until most of the liquid boils off.

5) Preheat the broiler. Place the greens mixture on top of each slice of grilled or toasted bread and set on a baking sheet. Top the toasts with the cheese and put under the broiler until the cheese begins to melt.

Per Crostini: Calories 86; Protein 3g; Fat 2g (Saturated 1g); Carbohydrates 15g; Fiber 1g; Sodium 212mg

Tomato Olivada Crostini or Bruschetta

Makes: 20 crostini or 12 bruschetta

The tomatoes must be seasonal and ripe for this recipe to be successful.

2 cloves garlic, peeled
2 ripe tomatoes, peeled and seeded (about 1 pound)
2 pepperoncini
1 tablespoon drained capers
2 tablespoons fresh parsley (packed in measurer)
1/2 cup pitted Calamata or other brine-cured olives
1 long loaf crusty bread

1) Pulse the garlic in a food processor until it is finely chopped. Add the remaining ingredients except the bread and puree. Leave grainy but not chunky.

2) Slice the bread. If long and thin, cut 20 slices for crostini. If wider, cut 12 slices for bruschetta. Grill or toast.

3) Top the bread with the olivada and serve.

Per Crostini: Calories 73; Protein 2g; Fat 2g (Saturated 0g); Carbohydrates 12g; Fiber 1g; Sodium 216mg

Roasted Red Pepper Crostini or Bruschetta

Makes: 10 crostini or 6 bruschetta

The garlic oil is is optional and is not necessary if the topping is going to be used immediately, but if making this ahead of time, it will add a sheen and hold in flavors.

2 roasted red bell peppers (recipe page 603),
    seeds and veins removed
3 tablespoons fresh parsley leaves
2 tablespoons fresh basil leaves (about 10)
1 1/2 teaspoons drained capers
1 tablespoon lemon juice
1 teaspoon kosher salt
1/4 teaspoon freshly ground pepper
1 tablespoon Garlic Oil (optional; page 607)
1/2 long loaf crusty bread

1) Pat the peppers dry with a paper towel.

2) Chop all the ingredients except the bread. If using a food processor, take care to pulse coarsely and not puree.

3) Slice the bread. If long and thin, cut 10 slices for crostini. If wider, cut 6 slices for bruschetta. Grill or toast.

4) Top with the red pepper mixture and serve immediately.

Per Crostini: Calories 67; Protein 2g; Fat 1g (Saturated 0g); Carbohydrates 13g; Fiber 1g; Sodium 341mg

Mini-Frittatas

Mini-frittatas are little puffs of eggs baked in the oven. They can be made up to a day ahead and reheated briefly in the microwave or oven. You can also freeze them and put them directly in a warm oven when needed. They are a lowfat alternative to hors d'oeuvre quiches.

Ricotta-Mushroom Mini-Frittatas

Makes: 16 mini-frittatas

The red bell pepper brings color and a touch of sweetness to these frittatas.

1/2 cup reduced-fat ricotta cheese
2 tablespoons grated Parmesan cheese
1/2 cup chopped mushrooms
1/2 cup diced roasted red bell peppers
1 egg
2 egg whites
1/2 teaspoon dried basil
1/4 teaspoon kosher salt
1/8 teaspoon freshly ground pepper

1) Preheat the oven to 375°F. Spray 16 mini-muffin or tartlet cups with butter-flavored non-stick spray.

2) Mix together all the ingredients. Fill the muffin cups. Bake for 20 minutes, until puffy and lightly browned.

Per Frittata: Calories 20; Protein 2g; Fat 1g (Saturated 0g); Carbohydrates 1g; Fiber 0g; Sodium 62mg

Broccoli-Pepper Mini-Frittatas

Makes: 16 mini-frittatas

Marjoram, like basil, is a sweet herb and though milder, it has a unique flavor. It is just unexpected enough to bring extra interest to these frittatas.

$1/4$ cup crumbled feta cheese
1 tablespoon grated Parmesan cheese
$1/2$ cup finely chopped broccoli florets
$1/2$ cup diced roasted red bell peppers, patted dry
1 tablespoon minced shallots
1 egg
2 egg whites
$1/2$ teaspoon dried marjoram
$1/8$ teaspoon freshly ground pepper

1) Preheat the oven to 375°F. Spray 16 mini-muffin or tartlet cups with butter-flavored non-stick spray.

2) Mix together all the ingredients. Fill the muffin cups. Bake for 20 minutes, until puffy and lightly browned.

Per Frittata: Calories 16; Protein 1g; Fat 1g (Saturated 0g); Carbohydrates 1g; Fiber 0g; Sodium 38mg

Crabmeat Mini-Frittatas

Makes: 12 mini-frittatas

For color and a spicy bite, garnish each of these with a dab of red salsa.

One 6-ounce can fancy white crabmeat
    (slightly less than 1 cup)
1 tablespoon minced fresh parsley
1 tablespoon minced fresh chives
1 tablespoon minced shallots
1 egg
2 egg whites
1 teaspoon Worcestershire sauce
$1/8$ teaspoon freshly ground pepper
$1/8$ teaspoon kosher salt

1) Preheat the oven to 375°F. Spray 12 mini-muffin or tartlet cups with butter-flavored non-stick spray.

2) If necessary, pick over the crabmeat to remove bits of shell and cartilage, then chop the meat. Mix together all the ingredients. Fill the muffin cups. Bake for 12 to 15 minutes, until puffy and lightly browned.

Per Frittata: Calories 20; Protein 3g; Fat 1g (Saturated 0g); Carbohydrates 0g; Fiber 0g; Sodium 73mg

Skewered Hors d'oeuvres

Small skewers of delectable foods are familiar party fare. Having portions on a tidy, hand-held stick are perfect for cocktail parties. To avoid burning the wooden skewers, they must be soaked in water before cooking. Also, each skewer must contain only a bite or two of food, otherwise it will be difficult to eat and no longer a small morsel.

If feeding a large crowd, threading so many skewers may be too time-consuming. If so, serve the morsels from a bowl, with large, sturdy toothpicks on the side.

Tortellini Skewers

Makes: 16 servings
(about 5 tortellini per serving)

As an alternative to the cherry tomatoes, you can use strips of red roasted pepper or circles of grilled zucchini.

One 15- to 16-ounce package frozen cheese
    tortellini
1/2 cup pesto (see pages 589–91 for a selection)
2 pints cherry tomatoes

1) Cook the tortellini according to the package directions, taking care not to overcook it. Drain and immediately toss with the pesto.

2) For each skewer, thread a tortellini, a tomato, and another tortellini.

Per Serving: Calories 107; Protein 5g; Fat 4g (Saturated 1g);
Carbohydrates 15g; Fiber 1g; Sodium 64mg

Latin Turkey Skewers

Makes: 16 servings

These are interesting and flavorful morsels; the brown sugar and cinnamon balance the strong, hot spices of cumin and chili powder and the lime and pineapple juices contribute a Latin flavor. All in all, these are a good start to a lively party.

2 pounds skinless, boneless turkey breast
1 teaspoon ground cumin
1 tablespoon ground chili powder
1 tablespoon ground coriander
1/8 teaspoon cayenne pepper
1/2 teaspoon freshly ground pepper
1 teaspoon ground cinnamon
1 tablespoon light brown sugar
1/4 teaspoon kosher salt
2 teaspoons fresh lime juice
3 tablespoons unsweetened pineapple juice
One 15-ounce can pineapple chunks

1) Cut the turkey into cubes about 3/4 to 1 inch square. Combine the spices and lime and pineapple juices in a sealable plastic bag. Add the turkey and toss until the meat is evenly coated. Place in the refrigerator for between 2 and 8 hours.

2) Preheat the oven to 375°F. Coat 2 baking sheets with nonstick spray. Thread the turkey and pineapple chunks on skewers. Place the skewers on the baking sheets in 1 layer, not touching each other. Bake for 8 to 10 minutes, turning once, until the turkey is cooked through.

Per Serving: Calories 76; Protein 14g; Fat 1g (Saturated 0g);
Carbohydrates 3g; Fiber 0g; Sodium 34mg

Red-Cooked Turkey Skewers

Makes: 16 servings

Red cooking is a Chinese technique that permeates the meat with the rich flavors. Normally slow-cooked in special clay pots, this recipe lets you create the taste with a long marination.

2 pounds skinless, boneless turkey breast
2 tablespoons light brown sugar
1 tablespoon hoisin sauce
1 tablespoon soy sauce
2 tablespoons dry sherry
1 teaspoon Asian sesame oil
1 tablespoon grated fresh ginger
3 cloves garlic, minced

1) Cut the turkey into cubes about 3/4 to 1 inch square. Combine the remaining ingredients in a sealable plastic bag. Add the turkey and toss until the meat is evenly coated. Place in the refrigerator for between 2 and 8 hours. You can refrigerate the turkey in a bowl, but it will have to be stirred several times to ensure that all marinates evenly.

2) Preheat the oven to 375°F. Coat 2 baking sheets with nonstick spray. Thread the turkey on skewers. Place the skewers on the baking sheets in 1 layer, not touching each other. Bake for 8 to 12 minutes, turning once, until the turkey is cooked through.

Per Serving: Calories 66; Protein 14g; Fat 1g (Saturated 0g); Carbohydrates 1g; Fiber 0g; Sodium 43mg

Steamed Marinated Shrimp

Makes: 16 servings

Steamed shrimp are a classic hors d'oeuvre and welcome at festivities. They can be offered hot or chilled with any number of dipping sauces. Horseradish Cocktail Sauce (recipe follows) is a traditional option, or pick one from the selection of dipping sauces on page 602.

2 pounds medium to large raw shrimp
1 tablespoon lemon juice
2 tablespoons dry sherry
1/8 teaspoon Tabasco sauce
2 cloves garlic, crushed
4 slices fresh ginger
1/2 teaspoon kosher salt

1) Peel the shrimp, leaving the shell on the tails intact (this makes a natural handle for later dining). Most shrimp will already have the backs of the shells slit and the dark vein removed to make shelling easy. If your shrimp aren't so prepped, you will have to do this task.

2) Combine the remaining ingredients in a bowl and toss in the shrimp. Cover refrigerate for 30 minutes to 2 hours.

3) Remove the shrimp from the marinade and steam in a basket set over boiling water for 3 to 4 minutes. Overcooking makes shrimp rubbery, so they must be removed from the steamer as soon as they turn pink.

Per Serving: Calories 35; Protein 7g; Fat 0g (Saturated 0g); Carbohydrates 0g; Fiber 0g; Sodium 92mg

Horseradish Cocktail Sauce

Makes: 12 servings (1 tablespoon each)

This sauce—a neccessity for plain steamed shrimp—is so easy to make and much better than the store-bought kind.

1/2 cup ketchup
3 tablespoons store-bought bottled horseradish
1/4 to 1/2 teaspoon Tabasco sauce
2 tablespoons lemon juice
1 teaspoon Worcestershire sauce

Blend together all ingredients.

Per Serving: Calories 13; Protein 0g; Fat 0g (Saturated 0g); Carbohydrates 3g; Fiber 0g; Sodium 130mg

Barbequed Shrimp

Makes: 8 servings

Serve on skewers or in a bowl with toothpicks on the side, with extra barbeque sauce in a bowl for dipping.

2 pounds medium to large raw shrimp, peeled
1 cup barbeque sauce of choice

1) Toss the shrimp and sauce together in a bowl. Cover and refrigerate for 2 to 8 hours.

2) Prepare a grill or broiler. If using skewers, thread 2 shrimp per stick. Oil the cooking surface. Take the shrimp out of the marinade, shake off the excess sauce, and cook 6 inches away from the heat source, or over a moderate grill, for 2 minutes. Turn and cook until pink through, about 2 to 3 minutes more, depending on the heat of the grill.

Per Serving: Calories 94; Protein 18g; Fat 1g (Saturated 0g); Carbohydrates 2g; Fiber 0g; Sodium 313mg

Won Tons

Won ton wrappers are available in most produce sections of supermarkets or in Asian food stores. Since won ton wrappers dry out quickly and crack, keeping them moist is essential, so it's best to set up your work area before starting to assemble the won tons. Clean a smooth flat surface (countertop or marble slab, not wood); spray a sheet pan with nonstick spray, then dust lightly with flour. Pour some water into a small bowl and get out a pastry brush. Dampen 2 cloth kitchen towels. Open the package of won ton skins and keep it covered with 1 towel. Use the other towel to cover the finished won tons.

If, despite your best efforts, the won ton skins crack, it might be that the won tons were already dried out to begin with. I've had this frustrating experience. You might find that the won tons on the bottom of the package are usable. Won tons with cracks in the dough can be pan-fried, but will fall apart if simmered or steamed.

Won tons can be frozen. Put the sheet pan in the freezer. Once the won tons are frozen solid, store them in a sealable freezer bag. Don't leave uncovered in the freezer for more than a few hours because self-defrosting freezers dehydrate food. Frozen won tons should not be defrosted, but should go from the freezer directly into a steamer basket lined with lettuce leaves (to prevent them from sticking).

Vegetable Won Tons

Makes: 50 won tons

All the ingredients can be finely minced in a food processor. There is some leeway with the proportions, so if you are grating one carrot and it yields 2/3 cup, go ahead and use all of it.

1 clove garlic
1 teaspoon minced fresh ginger
One 8-ounce can water chestnuts, drained and finely chopped
3 scallions, minced
1/2 cup finely chopped bok choy or Chinese cabbage
1/2 cup finely grated carrots
1/2 cup chopped mung bean sprouts
1/2 cup finely chopped mushrooms
1 tablespoon soy sauce
2 teaspoons Asian sesame oil
1 teaspoon cornstarch
About 50 won ton wrappers

1) Mix together all the ingredients except the won ton wrappers so that a chunky paste forms.

2) Place a won ton square on the work surface so that it faces you in a diamond shape. Paint the bottom edges of the won ton with water. Put a teaspoon of filling in the center. Fold in half to form a triangle and press the seams closed. Pick up the won ton and bring the left and right triangle points together and press tightly to seal. Set the filled won ton on the baking sheet, cover with the other damp towel, and go on to the next wrapper. Once you get a feel for this, the task goes quicker if you lay out 6 won ton skins at a time and work as if on an assembly line. But you must work quickly to keep them from drying out.

3) There are three ways to cook won tons: steaming, boiling, and pan-frying. Steam them for 3 to 5 minutes in a steamer basket lined with lettuce leaves (to prevent them from sticking). To boil, simmer them for the same amount of time in a pot of water or chicken broth. For crispy won tons, pan-fry them in a small amount of oil in a nonstick pan, and cook them on all sides until brown. Serve hot with dipping sauces (a selection appears on page 602).

Per Won Ton: Calories 28; Protein 1g; Fat 0g (Saturated 0g); Carbohydrates 5g; Fiber 0g; Sodium 27mg

Scallop Won Tons

Makes: 50 won tons

Making won tons can seem fussy, but one batch feeds a number of people and keeps them happy. Also, because they can be frozen, one stint of effort in the kitchen reaps benefits more than once.

2 cloves garlic
One 8-ounce can water chestnuts, drained
3 scallions, cut into 2-inch lengths
$2/3$ cup loosely packed shiitake mushrooms (fresh or reconstituted from dried), stems discarded
1 tablespoon soy sauce
1 teaspoon Asian sesame oil
1 teaspoon minced fresh ginger
1 teaspoon cornstarch
2 egg whites
$1/2$ pound scallops
About 50 won ton wrappers

1) Mince the garlic in a food processor. Drop in the water chestnuts, scallions, and mushrooms and pulse until finely chopped. Add the soy sauce, sesame oil, ginger, cornstarch, egg whites, and scallops. Process until a paste forms.

2) Follow steps 2 and 3 of the Vegetable Won Ton recipe.

Per Won Ton: Calories 32; Protein 2g; Fat 0g (Saturated 0g); Carbohydrates 6g; Fiber 0g; Sodium 36mg

Spinach and Mushroom Won Tons

Makes: 60 won tons

White mushrooms cannot be substituted. The intense flavor of dark mushrooms such as shiitakes is essential for this recipe.

$1/3$ to $1/2$ cup bean thread noodles
One 10-ounce package frozen chopped spinach, thawed and water squeezed out
1 scallion, minced
$1/4$ cup chopped shiitake or portobello mushrooms
$1/4$ cup mung bean sprouts
1 tablespoon soy sauce
1 teaspoon Asian sesame oil
1 teaspoon dry sherry
$1/4$ teaspoon kosher salt
1 teaspoon cornstarch
About 60 won ton wrappers

1) Soak the noodles in water until soft, about 10 minutes. Bean thread noodles are impossible to break or cut before soaking, which is why an approximate amount is given. They'll probably come packaged in small bundles. One "nest" of noodles is about the right quantity. Once softened, drain and chop into $1/2$-inch pieces.

2) Combine the noodles, spinach, scallion, mushrooms, and bean sprouts. Stir in the soy sauce, sesame oil, sherry, salt, and cornstarch and mix thoroughly.

3) Follow steps 2 and 3 of the Vegetable Won Ton recipe.

Per Won Ton: Calories 29; Protein 1g; Fat 0g (Saturated 0g); Carbohydrates 6g; Fiber 0g; Sodium 34mg

Salads

Dressings
55

Balsamic Vinaigrette

Red Wine Vinaigrette

Tomato Vinaigrette

Mustard Vinaigrette

Honey–Poppy Seed Vinaigrette

Orange-Sesame Vinaigrette

Chinese Vinaigrette

Chili-Orange Vinaigrette

Greek Oregano Vinaigrette

Tomato-Tarragon Dressing

French Dressing

Creamy Herb Dressing

Mild Yogurt Curry Dressing

Two-Mustard Dressing

Caesar-Style Dressing

Green Salads
61

Apple, Walnut, and
Greens Salad

Mixed Greens and
Mango Salad

Green, Spiced Nuts, and Warm
Goat Cheese Salad

Strawberry-Spinach Salad

Strawberry-Spinach Salad
with Almonds

Salad with Orange and Fennel

Oriental Orange and
Spinach Salad

Greek Salad

Caesar-Style Salad

Caesar Salad with Apple
Dressing and Currants

Raspberry Chicken and
Greens Salad

Greens, Grapefruit, and
Smoked Turkey Salad

Mixed Vegetable Salad

Cucumber Salads
68

Cucumber and Chives Salad

Marinated Cucumber Salad

Chinese Cucumber Salad

Cucumber Yogurt Salad
with Dill

Greek Cucumber Yogurt Salad

Cucumber Raita

Tomato Salads
70

Summer Herb Tomato Salad

Basil and Tomato Salad

Greek Tomato Salad

Marinated Tomato Salad

Red and Purple Salad

Corn and Tomato Salad

Cherry Tomato and
Watercress Salad

Assorted Vegetable Salads
73

Soy-Dressed Asparagus

Mustard, Dill, and Green Bean Salad

Snap Peas in Mint Vinaigrette

Southwestern Corn Salad

Marinated Carrot Sticks

Pickled Beets

Minty Beet Salad

Beet and Orange Salad

Waldorf Salad

Slaws
78

Classic Picnic Slaw

Coleslaw with Horseradish Dressing

Apple and Carrot Coleslaw

Apple and Celery Slaw with Honey Dressing

Carrot and Walnut Salad

Carrot and Mint Salad

Sesame Carrot Slaw

North African Carrot Salad

Zucchini Slaw

Potato Salads
82

Picnic Potato Salad

Picnic Potato Salad with Herbs and Mustard

Picnic Potato Salad with Relish and Eggs

Pesto Potato Salad

Dilly Potato Salad

Pommery Potato Salad

Garlicky Garden Potato Salad

Sweet Potato and Chutney Salad

Pasta Salads
86

Macaroni and Vegetable Salad

Springtime Pasta Salad

Pesto Pasta Salad

Tortellini with Pesto and Sun-Dried Tomato Salad

Tuna and Shells Salad

Tropical Chicken and Pasta Salad

Japanese Noodle Salad

Sesame Soba Salad

Chinese Broccoli and Pasta Salad

Chinese Chicken and Noodle Salad

Asian Beef and Noodle Salad

Rice and Grain Salads
92

Herbed Rice Salad

Indonesian Rice Salad

Wild Rice, Corn, and Broccoli Salad

Wild Rice, Smoked Turkey, and Grape Salad

Curried Chicken, Fruit, and Rice Salad

Spanish Rice Salad

Toasted Quinoa Salad

Bulgur Wheat Salad

Bulgur and Feta Salad

Sunburst Salad

Wheat Berry and Barley Salad

Pita Salad

Bean Salads
98

Many-Bean Salad

All-Season Black Bean Salad

Black Bean and Corn Salad

Black Bean and Yellow Rice Salad

Chickpea, Broccoli, and Pasta Salad

Chickpea and Roasted Red Pepper Salad

Red Lentil Salad

White Bean and Tuna Salad

Poultry and Fish Salads
103

Poached Chicken for Salads

Chicken and Artichoke Heart Salad

Curried Chicken Salad

Turkey Salad

Turkey, Walnut, and Grape Salad

Tuna Salad with Capers and Artichoke Hearts

Blissful Tuna Salad

Snow Pea and Shrimp Salad

Ocean and Grape Salad

Salmon Salad

Dressings

Most traditional, full-fat salad dressings are a balance of oil and vinegar. Oil mellows the bite of the vinegar while leaving its essential sharpness intact. If the oil is eliminated and water or a similar liquid is used, the vinegar's flavor is diluted and the dressing tastes insipid. Oil would be missed in other ways as well. It blends the other flavors together, making the dressing taste whole. Additionally, it helps the dressing cling to the salad. Without it the dressing pools in the bottom of the bowl and the salad is tasteless.

That said, a dressing does not have to be two-thirds oil (as a classic vinaigrette is) to taste good. Commercial makers of dressings use gums and emulsifiers to fulfill the roles of oil. I use a number of tricks, all more accessible to the home cook. First, I take great care to balance sweet and sour flavors, which is critical without the mellowing effect of fat. In lieu of large quantities of oil, I use vegetable juices, dairy products, and a judicious amount of oil. Many of my dressings call for the more flavorful extra-virgin olive oil, so that a little contributes a lot of flavor.

Salad dressings are astonishingly easy to make. A whisk and a bowl is all you need. Store them in glass jars in the refrigerator. I reuse store-bought salad dressing bottles because they are designed for the job. Bring the dressing to room temperature before using so that the olive oil liquefies and clears. Mix by shaking the jar, then pour. Many vinaigrettes will remain fresh for several months in the refrigerator.

Balsamic Vinaigrette

Makes: 8 servings (1 tablespoon each)

The best balsamic vinegars can be sipped like fine cognac (although they never are; they are incredibly expensive and rare and the lucky owner shakes a few drops over a recipe before dining). On the other end of the spectrum are cheap balsamic vinegars, which are little more than colored and flavored red wine vinegar. For cooking and salad making, a moderately priced balsamic vinegar that has been aged at least five years will provide the mellow depth of flavor unique to this special vinegar. If the label doesn't state the balsamic's age, pass on it.

1/4 cup extra-virgin olive oil
3 tablespoons balsamic vinegar
1 tablespoon lemon juice
1/8 teaspoon kosher salt
1/8 teaspoon freshly ground pepper

Whisk together all the ingredients.

Per Serving: Calories 65; Protein 0g; Fat 7g (Saturated 1g); Carbohydrates 1g; Fiber 0g; Sodium 31mg

Red Wine Vinaigrette

Makes: 8 servings (1 tablespoon each)

1 tablespoon lemon juice
1 tablespoon red wine vinegar
1 tablespoon red wine
2 tablespoons extra-virgin olive oil
1 teaspoon water
1/4 teaspoon kosher salt
1/8 teaspoon freshly ground pepper
1/2 teaspoon dry mustard
1/2 teaspoon Dijon mustard
1 teaspoon dried basil
1 small clove garlic, finely minced
1 tablespoon finely minced onions

Whisk together all the ingredients.

Per Serving: Calories 35; Protein 0g; Fat 3g (Saturated 0g);
Carbohydrates 1g; Fiber 0g; Sodium 68mg

Tomato Vinaigrette

Makes: 48 servings (1 tablespoon each)

1 cup red wine vinegar
1/4 cup extra-virgin olive oil
1/4 cup frozen apple juice concentrate, thawed
1 1/2 cups tomato juice
1 small clove garlic, minced
1 teaspoon onion powder
1 tablespoon Dijon mustard
1 teaspoon dried oregano
1/2 teaspoon dried tarragon
1/16 teaspoon cayenne pepper

Whisk together all the ingredients.

Per Serving: Calories 16; Protein 0g; Fat 1g (Saturated 0g);
Carbohydrates 2g; Fiber 0g; Sodium 36mg

Mustard Vinaigrette

Makes: 8 servings (1 tablespoon each)

Simple and classic, this dressing is also good on steamed carrots.

1/4 cup extra-virgin olive oil
1/4 cup red wine vinegar
1 teaspoon Dijon mustard
1/4 teaspoon soy sauce
1 teaspoon lemon juice
1/4 teaspoon freshly ground pepper

Whisk together all the ingredients.

Per Serving: Calories 63; Protein 0g; Fat 7g (Saturated 1g);
Carbohydrates 1g; Fiber 0g; Sodium 27mg

Honey–Poppy Seed Vinaigrette

Makes: 16 servings (1 tablespoon each)

This sweet and sour blend is so popular in my house that if I run out, our teenager will pull out the recipe and make it himself.

1/4 cup balsamic vinegar
1/4 cup red wine vinegar
2 tablespoons honey
1 teaspoon Dijon mustard
1/8 teaspoon kosher salt
1/4 cup extra-virgin olive oil
1 tablespoon poppy seeds

Whisk together all the ingredients.

Per Serving: Calories 46; Protein 0g; Fat 4g (Saturated 0g);
Carbohydrates 4g; Fiber 0g; Sodium 24mg

Orange-Sesame Vinaigrette

Makes: 8 servings (1 tablespoon each)

For an Asian-themed meal, toss this dressing with salad or chilled, steamed vegetables.

1/4 cup orange juice
1/4 cup white wine vinegar or rice vinegar
1 1/2 tablespoons soy sauce
1/4 teaspoon dry mustard
1 tablespoon peanut oil
1 1/2 teaspoons Asian sesame oil
1 teaspoon sugar
1 teaspoon toasted sesame seeds

Whisk together all the ingredients.

Per Serving: Calories 36; Protein 0g; Fat 3g (Saturated 0g); Carbohydrates 2g; Fiber 0g; Sodium 193mg

Chinese Vinaigrette

Makes: 8 servings (1 tablespoon each)

Try this dressing tossed with chopped cucumbers and tomatoes for a summer salad.

1/4 cup soy sauce
2 tablespoons white wine or rice vinegar
2 tablespoons sugar
1 large slice fresh ginger
1 teaspoon sherry
1 teaspoon water
1 tablespoon Asian sesame oil

Whisk together all the ingredients. Store in a glass jar for several hours or longer to let the dressing absorb the ginger flavor. Discard the ginger slice before using.

Per Serving: Calories 34; Protein 0g; Fat 2g (Saturated 0g); Carbohydrates 4g; Fiber 0g; Sodium 514mg

Chili-Orange Vinaigrette

Makes: 16 servings (1 tablespoon each)

For a meal with an assertive, spicy main course (like fajitas), a mild salad will pale by comparison, but a salad dressed with this vinaigrette will complement the menu and hold its own.

1/3 cup orange juice
1/4 cup apple cider vinegar
1/4 cup olive or peanut oil
1 teaspoon chili powder
1/4 teaspoon kosher salt
1/16 teaspoon Tabasco sauce, or more to taste
1 clove garlic, minced

Whisk together all the ingredients.

Per Serving: Calories 33; Protein 0g; Fat 3g (Saturated 0g); Carbohydrates 1g; Fiber 0g; Sodium 32mg

Greek Oregano Vinaigrette

Makes: 6 servings (1 tablespoon each)

Use this both tossed in salads and splashed in pita pocket sandwiches.

3 tablespoons extra-virgin olive oil
3 tablespoons red wine vinegar
1 tablespoon water
1 teaspoon dried oregano, or 1 tablespoon chopped fresh
1/2 teaspoon kosher salt
1/4 teaspoon freshly ground pepper
1 clove garlic, minced (optional)

Whisk together all the ingredients.

Per Serving: Calories 63; Protein 0g; Fat 7g (Saturated 1g); Carbohydrates 1g; Fiber 0g; Sodium 160mg

Tomato-Tarragon Dressing

Makes: 26 servings (1 tablespoon each)

The distinctive aroma and flavor of tarragon brings a light, French style to this vinaigrette. Serve a salad dressed with this along with a classic meal of roast chicken and potatoes.

2 whole canned tomatoes, with $3/4$ cup juice from the can
$1/2$ cup red wine vinegar
1 tablespoon Dijon mustard
$1/8$ teaspoon freshly ground pepper
$1/2$ teaspoon kosher salt
$1 1/2$ tablespoons honey
1 tablespoon dried tarragon
$1/2$ cup extra-virgin olive oil

This recipe can be made in the food processor. Start by pureeing the tomatoes and juice. Then pulse in all the remaining ingredients except the oil. Add the oil in a slow, steady stream as the machine is running. Alternatively, the tomatoes can be pureed in a blender, then whisked by hand into the remaining ingredients. In either case, make sure the honey is warm enough to be pourable, so that it doesn't remain a lump at the bottom of the bowl.

Per Serving: Calories 45; Protein 0g; Fat 4g (Saturated 1g); Carbohydrates 2g; Fiber 0g; Sodium 63mg

French Dressing

Makes: 20 servings (1 tablespoon each)

Growing up, I loved a similar thick ketchup and mayonnaise–based dressing. Try it with crispy iceberg lettuce and ripe tomatoes, or spread it on a turkey sandwich.

1 cup ketchup
$1/2$ cup reduced-fat mayonnaise
3 tablespoons honey
3 tablespoons apple cider vinegar
1 tablespoon olive oil
2 tablespoons water
1 tablespoon lemon juice
$1/2$ teaspoon dry mustard
$1/2$ teaspoon kosher salt

Using a blender, mix together all the ingredients until smooth.

Per Serving: Calories 49; Protein 0g; Fat 3g (Saturated 0g); Carbohydrates 7g; Fiber 0g; Sodium 239mg

Creamy Herb Dressing

Makes: 10 servings (1 tablespoon each)

If you have garlic oil (page 607) in your pantry, you can use it instead of olive oil and omit the minced garlic. This will not only reduce the prep work, but the dressing won't smell so strongly of garlic the second day. Fines herbes is a medley of classic aromatic garden herbs. If you don't have any, combine parsley, tarragon, and chives, or use other herbs of your choice.

$1/2$ cup buttermilk
1 tablespoon apple cider vinegar
1 clove garlic, minced
1 tablespoon Dijon mustard
2 teaspoons honey
1 tablespoon olive oil
$1/4$ teaspoon kosher salt
$1/8$ teaspoon celery seed
$1/8$ teaspoon freshly ground pepper
$1/8$ teaspoon Tabasco sauce
1 teaspoon dried fines herbes

Whisk together all the ingredients. Store the dressing in a glass jar in the refrigerator, where it will remain fresh for up to 4 days.

Per Serving: Calories 24; Protein 1g; Fat 2g (Saturated 0g); Carbohydrates 2g; Fiber 0g; Sodium 99mg

Mild Yogurt Curry Dressing

Makes: 10 servings (2 tablespoons each)

Yogurts vary in tartness. Adjust the lemon juice to taste.

$3/4$ cup plain nonfat yogurt
$1/4$ cup 1% lowfat milk
1 tablespoon lemon juice
3 tablespoons orange juice
$1/2$ teaspoon ground cumin
$1/2$ teaspoon curry powder
$1/4$ teaspoon kosher salt
$1/4$ teaspoon freshly ground pepper

Whisk together all the ingredients. Store the dressing in a glass jar in the refrigerator, where it will remain fresh for up to 3 days.

Per Serving: Calories 16; Protein 1g; Fat 0g (Saturated 0g); Carbohydrates 2g; Fiber 0g; Sodium 65mg

Two-Mustard Dressing

Makes: 36 servings (1 tablespoon each)

Although incredibly simple, this recipe is wonderful. I've taught it in many cooking classes and I've heard that it has become a staple in many homes. For variations, substitute specialty mustards for the coarse.

2 cups buttermilk
2 tablespoons Dijon mustard
3 tablespoons coarse mustard
1 tablespoon frozen apple juice concentrate, thawed

Whisk together all the ingredients. Store the dressing in a glass jar in the refrigerator, where it will remain fresh for up to 4 days.

Per Serving: Calories 9; Protein 1g; Fat 0g (Saturated 0g); Carbohydrates 1g; Fiber 0g; Sodium 65mg

Caesar-Style Dressing

Makes: 10 servings (1 tablespoon each)

Regular Caesar dressing is high in fat, especially saturated fat. This dressing cuts the fat without sacrificing any of the flavor.

1 clove garlic, minced
$1/3$ cup plain nonfat yogurt
$1/4$ cup lowfat mayonnaise
1 teaspoon Dijon mustard
1 teaspoon anchovy paste
1 tablespoon red wine vinegar
$1/2$ teaspoon Worcestershire sauce
2 tablespoons grated Parmesan cheese
$1/4$ teaspoon freshly ground pepper

Using a food processor or whisk, blend together all the ingredients. Chill before using and serve within 1 day of preparation.

Per Serving: Calories 26; Protein 1g; Fat 1g (Saturated 0g); Carbohydrates 3g; Fiber 0g; Sodium 185mg

Green Salads

I like the taste and crunchiness of iceberg lettuce, and it keeps better than most other lettuces, so it is often useful. But its crispy, mild-flavored leaves are best suited to simple side salads; many recipes require more. Leaf lettuces, from evergreen-dark romaine to buttery Bibb lettuce, add color, texture, flavor, and more nutrients to the salad bowl than does iceberg. Although these lettuces aren't as firm as iceberg, they should be crisp, with a fresh sheen and few blemishes.

Care and Handling of Salad Greens

As soon as you bring the greens home, trim off any broken, mushy, or discolored leaves before storing the lettuce in the vegetable bin of your refrigerator. Once you are ready to use it, wash and prep the entire head, even if you are only going to eat half of it that evening. Not only does it save time to do all the prep work at one time, but washed lettuce is more likely to be eaten later than a wilting half a head of lettuce that requires time and effort to be edible. Lettuce that has been cleaned and dried in a salad spinner stays fresh—stored loosely in an open plastic bag in the refrigerator—for four days, which makes the initial prep work worthwhile.

To wash the lettuce, fill up a sink with cool water, snap the leaves off the core, submerge them in the water, and swirl. If dirty, let the lettuce soak for a few minutes. Very gritty lettuce might require a second wash. Next, dry the lettuce leaves (either whole or torn into pieces) in a salad spinner to rid them of clinging water. This is important because water on the leaves prevents the dressing from sticking, and lettuce stored wet deteriorates rapidly.

If you are going to eat the salad right away you can cut the leaves with a large, sharp knife. However, leaves that are torn by hand stay fresher longer. Handle it gently. Do not crush the leaves as you tear them. I like lettuce small enough so that the diner can eat it without cutting it first (cutting lettuce in one's salad bowl can be awkward and trying to fit a large piece of lettuce into one's mouth can be messy and embarrassing).

These days, there are many alternatives for those who find prepping lettuce too time-consuming. Bags of lettuce that has already been torn can be found in most produce sections. It is more costly, but if buying these means there will be salad on your table, it is a convenience worth paying for. Purchase these as carefully as you would a head of lettuce. Check the sell-by date. Sort through, wash, and spin-dry before eating. One head of romaine or leaf lettuce equals about 12 to 14 cups of prepared or bagged lettuce.

Apple, Walnut, and Greens Salad

Makes: 6 servings

I love the combination of apples and walnuts. The nuts are toasted first to get the most flavor out of them. Also, the salad is topped, not tossed, with them. I've found that if tossed, most of the nuts end up at the bottom of the salad bowl.

2 large firm red apples, cored and diced
2 teaspoons lemon juice
1 rib celery, sliced
1 head leaf or romaine lettuce, washed, dried, and torn into pieces
4 teaspoons apple cider vinegar
2 tablespoons maple syrup
4 teaspoons extra-virgin olive oil
1 1/2 teaspoons Dijon mustard
1/2 teaspoons kosher salt
1/4 teaspoon freshly ground pepper
1/2 cup raisins
1/2 cup walnut or pecan pieces, toasted

1) To prevent browning, toss the diced apples with the lemon juice, then toss the apples with the celery and lettuce.

2) Whisk together the vinegar, maple syrup, oil, mustard, salt, and pepper. Toss with the salad. Top with the raisins and nuts.

Per Serving: Calories 212; Protein 4g; Fat 10g (Saturated 1g); Carbohydrates 32g; Fiber 4g; Sodium 207mg

Mixed Greens and Mango Salad

Makes: 7 servings

The sweetness of the mango is balanced by the curry in the dressing.

10 cups mixed salad greens, washed, dried, and torn into pieces
1 cup thinly sliced red onions
1 mango, peeled, pitted, and diced into 1/2-inch cubes
1 recipe Mild Yogurt Curry Dressing (page 59)

1) Toss together the salad greens and onions and all but 1/2 cup of the mango in a salad bowl. Pour in the dressing and toss again.

2) Top with the reserved 1/2 cup mango.

Per Serving: Calories 64; Protein 4g; Fat 1g (Saturated 0g); Carbohydrates 13g; Fiber 3g; Sodium 115mg

Greens, Spiced Nuts, and Warm Goat Cheese Salad

Makes: 4 servings

This salad is higher in fat than other recipes, but much of it comes from nuts and the portions are large enough for a main course lunch.

6 cups mixed salad greens, washed, dried, and torn into pieces
1/3 cup thinly sliced red onions
3 tablespoons Honey–Poppy Seed Vinaigrette (page 56), or other dressing of choice
1 cup Spiced Nuts or Sweet Curried Spiced Nuts (page 22 or 23)
3 ounces log-shaped goat cheese, cut into 8 rounds
1 to 2 tablespoons dry breadcrumbs

1) Toss together the salad greens, onions, and dressing. Place on individual serving plates. Distribute the nuts on top.

2) Preheat the broiler. Dip the rounds of cheese in the breadcrumbs so that they are lightly coated. Place on a baking sheet and cook for 3 minutes, until warmed and softened. Place 2 rounds on each salad. Serve immediately.

Per Serving: Calories 326; Protein 10g; Fat 25g (Saturated 6g); Carbohydrates 19g; Fiber 3g; Sodium 212mg

Strawberry-Spinach Salad

Makes: 6 servings

Salads similar to this are in the repertoire of many catering companies because the components are easy to prepare and can be readied ahead of time, and the end result is elegant and delicious.

10 cups fresh spinach, loosely packed
1 1/2 cups strawberries
1 cup sliced mushrooms (1/4 pound)
1/3 cup thinly sliced red onions
1/3 cup Honey-Poppy Seed Vinaigrette (page 56)

1) Wash the spinach well, then dry it in a salad spinner. Trim off the thick stems. Tear the largest leaves into smaller pieces, making sure the leaves are manageable with a fork. The spinach can be prepared several hours ahead of time if it is dried well and then kept in the refrigerator.

2) Remove the hulls and then slice the strawberries. Don't do this more than 1 hour before serving or the strawberries will get mushy.

3) Toss 1 cup of the berries with the spinach, mushroom, and onions. Reserve the remaining berries for garnish.

4) Just prior to serving, toss the salad with the dressing and arrange the reserved strawberries on top.

Per Serving: Calories 80; Protein 4g; Fat 4g (Saturated 1g); Carbohydrates 11g; Fiber 4g; Sodium 96mg

Strawberry-Spinach Salad with Almonds

Makes: 6 servings

Cool toasted nuts before adding them to a salad or they will wilt the greens.

1 recipe Strawberry-Spinach Salad (opposite)
1/2 cup sliced almonds, lightly toasted

Prepare Strawberry-Spinach Salad, adding the almonds along with the reserved strawberries in step 4.

Per Serving: Calories 132; Protein 5g; Fat 8g (Saturated 1g); Carbohydrates 12g; Fiber 4g; Sodium 97mg

Salad with Orange and Fennel

Makes: 7 servings

Fennel has a cooling, mild licorice flavor and is crisp and refreshing when served raw in a salad.

4 navel oranges
1 head fennel
6 cups romaine lettuce leaves, washed, dried, and torn into pieces
1/2 cup pitted brine-cured olives
1 cup thinly sliced red onions
1 1/2 tablespoons extra-virgin olive oil
1 tablespoon red wine vinegar
1 teaspoon lemon juice
1 teaspoon orange juice
1/4 teaspoon kosher salt
1/4 teaspoon freshly ground pepper

1) Using a sharp knife, cut the peel and white pith away from the oranges, then slice the oranges and place in a large salad bowl.

2) Cut the stalks off of the fennel and slice off the very bottom. Quarter the head and cut out and discard the core, as if cutting up a cabbage. Thinly slice the fennel and add it to the bowl.

3) Place the lettuce, olives, and red onions in the bowl and toss the salad.

4) Whisk together the remaining ingredients, pour over the salad, and toss once more.

Per Serving: Calories 113; Protein 2g; Fat 5g (Saturated 1g); Carbohydrates 16g; Fiber 4g; Sodium 223mg

Oriental Orange and Spinach Salad

Makes: 6 servings

Spinach is a stongly flavored green and is best complemented by an equally assertive dressing. The slight bitterness of dark green salads is also balanced by the addition of fruit. This salad has both an interesting dressing and the sweetness of citrus, making a wonderful combination.

8 cups fresh spinach (about 1/2 pound)
1/2 cup fresh mung bean sprouts, washed
2 scallions, sliced
1 1/2 cups sliced mushrooms (about 6 ounces)
1/4 cup Orange-Sesame Vinaigrette (page 57)
1 seedless orange

1) Wash the spinach well, discarding tough stems and wilted leaves. Break into large pieces and dry in a salad spinner. Place in a salad bowl.

2) Toss together the sprouts, scallions, and mushrooms. Place on top of the spinach.

3) Whisk the dressing just prior to pouring it on the salad. Toss it into the salad. The spinach will wilt slightly from the dressing.

4) Cut the peel and white pith away from the orange. With a sharp paring knife, remove the segments from the membranes. Arrange the orange segments on top of the salad.

Per Serving: Calories 54; Protein 2g; Fat 2g (Saturated 0g); Carbohydrates 8g; Fiber 2g; Sodium 161mg

Greek Salad

Makes: 6 servings

Canned pitted black olives don't have the salty intensity of flavor that the brine-cured olives do, which is why I specify the latter.

1 head romaine lettuce, washed, dried, and torn into pieces
4 tablespoons Greek Oregano Vinaigrette (page 57)
1 cucumber, peeled, halved lengthwise, and sliced
1/2 cup thinly sliced red onions
1 green bell pepper, chopped or julienned
8 brine-cured olives, pitted and halved
2 tomatoes, cored and cut into 8 wedges each
2 ounces feta cheese (2×1-inch piece)
Two 8-inch pita pockets, cut into 8 wedges each

1) Place the lettuce in a large salad bowl. Toss with 2 tablespoons of the dressing.

2) Toss together the cucumber, onions, and pepper. Distribute on top of the lettuce.

3) Arrange the olives and tomatoes on top of the vegetables. Crumble the feta cheese on top. Drizzle the remaining 2 tablespoons of dressing over the salad. Serve with the pita bread.

Per Serving: Calories 192; Protein 7g; Fat 9g (Saturated 2g); Carbohydrates 23g; Fiber 3g; Sodium 448mg

Caesar-Style Salad

Makes: 7 servings

My family loves this salad. Leftovers (when there are any) go on sliced turkey sandwiches.

1 head romaine lettuce, washed, dried, and torn into pieces
1 cup cherry tomatoes, halved
1 recipe Caesar-Style Dressing (page 60)
2 cups fat-free croutons
2 tablespoons grated Parmesan cheese

Place the lettuce and tomatoes in a large salad bowl. Toss with the dressing. Transfer to a serving bowl. Top with the croutons and dust with the cheese.

Per Serving: Calories 84; Protein 5g; Fat 2g (Saturated 1g); Carbohydrates 11g; Fiber 2g; Sodium 354mg

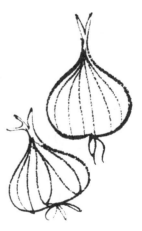

Caesar Salad with Apple Dressing and Currants

Makes: 10 servings

Leave out the watercress if it is difficult to find. In its place you might want to add a sharp-flavored green, like radicchio or escarole.

1 head romaine lettuce, washed, dried, and torn into pieces
1 head leaf lettuce, washed, dried, and torn into pieces
1 bunch watercress, stems removed (optional)
1 cup currants
1 clove garlic
3 medium Granny Smith apples, cored, peeled, and quartered
2 tablespoons apple cider vinegar
2 tablespoons lemon juice
1/4 cup reduced-fat mayonnaise
1/4 cup plain nonfat yogurt
2 tablespoons Dijon mustard
1/2 teaspoon kosher salt
1/4 teaspoon freshly ground pepper
1/4 cup grated Parmesan cheese, divided
2 tablespoons extra-virgin olive oil
2 cups fat-free croutons

1) Prepare the lettuces and watercress. Toss with the currants and chill.

2) Mince the garlic in a food processor, then add the apples, vinegar, and lemon juice. Puree. Pulse in the mayonnaise, yogurt, mustard, salt, pepper, and half the Parmesan cheese. Process until smooth. With the machine running, pour in the olive oil.

3) Toss the dressing with the salad. Top with the remaining Parmesan and the croutons.

Per Serving: Calories 126; Protein 4g; Fat 6g (Saturated 1g); Carbohydrates 15g; Fiber 3g; Sodium 311mg

Raspberry Chicken and Greens Salad

Makes: 4 servings

This main course salad is beautiful, delicious, and ideal for a summer dinner when the grill is the favored place to cook, the raspberries and greens are from local gardens, and the cantaloupe is sweet and ripe.

1/2 cup raspberry preserves, preferably seedless
2 tablespoons balsamic vinegar
2 tablespoons raspberry vinegar
1 teaspoon Dijon mustard
1 pound skinless, boneless chicken breast
8 cups mixed greens or spinach, washed, dried, and torn into pieces
1/2 cantaloupe, peeled, seeded, and sliced into thin half-moons
1 cup fresh raspberries
2 tablespoons water
2 teaspoons olive oil

1) Preheat the grill or broiler. Line a baking sheet with foil or oil the grill. Whisk together the preserves, vinegars, and mustard. Set aside 1/2 cup.

2) Brush the chicken generously with the marinade. Place on the baking sheet or grill. Cook for 5 minutes. Turn over. Brush with the marinade and cook until the chicken is cooked through, about 4 to 6 minutes more. (Be prepared for smoke! Glazes with sugars tend to burn where they touch the pan. I have to turn off my smoke detector with this recipe.)

3) When the chicken is cool enough to handle, slice.

4) Place the greens in a serving bowl or on individual plates. Arrange the cantaloupe and chicken in overlapping layers on the lettuces. Decorate with the raspberries.

5) Whisk the water and oil into the reserved $1/2$ cup of marinade. Drizzle some over the salad and serve the rest on the side.

Per Serving: Calories 387; Protein 29g; Fat 4g (Saturated 1g); Carbohydrates 40g; Fiber 4g; Sodium 157mg

Greens, Grapefruit, and Smoked Turkey Salad

Makes: 5 servings

If buying turkey at the deli, ask for it in one piece, $1/2$ inch thick, and cut it into cubes at home.

1 large ruby red grapefruit
3 tablespoons honey
2 tablespoons olive oil
2 teaspoons Dijon mustard
$1/8$ teaspoon Tabasco sauce
$1/4$ teaspoon kosher salt
1 head leaf or romaine lettuce, washed, dried, and torn into pieces
$1/2$ cup sliced red onions
$1/2$ pound smoked or roasted turkey breast, cut into $1/2$-inch dice

1) Cut the peel and white pith away from the grapefruit. With a sharp knife, cut the segments away from the membranes. Squeeze the pulp to get $1/4$ cup of grapefruit juice, and place it in a small bowl.

2) Whisk together the grapefruit juice, honey, oil, mustard, Tabasco, and salt.

3) Gently toss together the lettuce, onions, turkey, and grapefruit segments. Toss again with the dressing.

Per Serving: Calories 180; Protein 13g; Fat 7g (Saturated 1g); Carbohydrates 20g; Fiber 3g; Sodium 805mg

Mixed Vegetable Salad

Makes: 8 servings

This recipe shows that you don't need a leaf of lettuce to make a tossed salad. What follows is only a guide. Use what is in season and what you like. The idea is to have a selection of vegetables abundantly and attractively displayed on a plate, sort of like a salad bar on a platter.

2 cups shredded carrots
2 cups frozen peas, thawed under hot running water
1 cucumber, peeled and sliced
$1 1/2$ cups cooked baby or sliced beets
1 cup green beans, trimmed and steamed
1 cup nonfat or lowfat salad dressing of choice

Arrange the vegetables on a platter with an eye for color, shape, and texture. For large buffet parties, have extra vegetables prepared and on hand in containers in the refrigerator. Use these to replenish the platter as necessary. Put the salad dressing (or a selection of dressings) in a cruet on the side.

Per Serving: Calories 96; Protein 3g; Fat 0g (Saturated 0g); Carbohydrates 20g; Fiber 4g; Sodium 397mg

Cucumber Salads

Seeding Cucumbers

Many of my recipes with cucumbers call for seeding. To do this, cut the cucumber in half lengthwise, then scoop out the seeds with a teaspoon. If left in, the seeds and their membranes exude liquid that can dilute the dressing. Also, salads look more elegant without the seeds. But if the salad is going to be consumed immediately, or if the cucumbers are small and firm, seeding isn't always necessary.

Cucumber and Chives Salad

Makes: 5 servings

Chives have an onionlike flavor without the latter's sharpness or crunch, which makes them naturally suited to use in salads.

1/2 cup plain nonfat yogurt
1 teaspoon minced fresh chives
1/4 teaspoon kosher salt
1/4 teaspoon freshly ground pepper
1 tablespoon lemon juice
1 tablespoon white wine vinegar
2 cucumbers, peeled, seeded, and sliced

Combine all the ingredients and allow to rest for about 1 hour before serving.

Per Serving: Calories 31; Protein 2g; Fat 0g (Saturated 0g); Carbohydrates 6g; Fiber 1g; Sodium 117mg

Marinated Cucumber Salad

Makes: 6 servings

If fresh dill is unavailable, dried dill will do (1 teaspoon), but allow the salad to marinate for a day before serving.

1/2 cup thinly sliced red onions
1 tablespoon fresh dill, minced
2 tablespoons lemon juice
1/2 cup water
2 tablespoons frozen apple juice concentrate, thawed
3 cucumbers, seeded and sliced

1) Whisk together the onions, dill, lemon juice, water, and apple juice.

2) Add the cucumbers and stir until well blended. Chill for several hours before serving.

Per Serving: Calories 36; Protein 1g; Fat 0g (Saturated 0g); Carbohydrates 8g; Fiber 1g; Sodium 6mg

Chinese Cucumber Salad

Makes: 5 servings

This salad improves with a few hours rest and is still excellent the second day.

1 teaspoon Asian sesame oil
1 tablespoon honey
1 tablespoon soy sauce
1 tablespoon rice vinegar
2 cucumbers, peeled, seeded, and thinly sliced

1) Whisk together the oil, honey, soy, and vinegar.

2) Toss the cucumbers in the dressing, coating them well. Refrigerate the salad before serving.

Per Serving: Calories 38; Protein 1g; Fat 1g (Saturated 0g); Carbohydrates 7g; Fiber 1g; Sodium 208mg

Cucumber Yogurt Salad with Dill

Makes: 5 servings

This is a refreshing alternative to side potato salads.

$1/3$ cup plain nonfat yogurt
1 tablespoon lemon juice
$1/4$ teaspoon celery seed
1 teaspoon fresh dill, minced, or $1/2$ teaspoon dry
$1/4$ teaspoon kosher salt
$1/8$ teaspoon freshly ground pepper
2 cucumbers, peeled, seeded, and sliced thick
$1/2$ cup chopped red onions

1.Whisk together the first 6 ingredients.

2) Stir in the cucumbers and onions and chill before serving.

Per Serving: Calories 32; Protein 2g; Fat 0g (Saturated 0g); Carbohydrates 6g; Fiber 1g; Sodium 112mg

Greek Cucumber Yogurt Salad

Makes: 6 servings

The fresh garlic will get stronger and more aromatic as time goes on, so any leftovers are suitable only for true garlic aficionados.

2 cucumbers, peeled and seeded
1 cup plain lowfat or nonfat yogurt
1 teaspoon lemon juice
1 clove garlic, minced
1 tablespoon chopped fresh parsley
1 teaspoon dried oregano
$1/4$ teaspoon kosher salt
$1/8$ teaspoon freshly ground pepper

1) Chop the cucumbers, by first slicing each half into three long strips. Then, holding them all in a loglike pile, slice across the cucumbers in rhythmic strokes. With little effort this will give you tidily chopped pieces of just the right size.

2) Stir the yogurt and seasonings together, then stir in the cucumbers. Serve immediately.

Per Serving: Calories 41; Protein 3g; Fat 1g (Saturated 0g); Carbohydrates 6g; Fiber 1g; Sodium 11mg

Cucumber Raita

Makes: 4 servings

This cooling salad is served as an accompaniment to spicy Middle Eastern or Indian foods.

$1/2$ cup plain lowfat or nonfat yogurt
2 teaspoons lemon juice
1 teaspoon minced fresh mint
$1/4$ teaspoon ground cumin
1 cucumber, peeled, seeded, and diced

Whisk together the yogurt, lemon juice, mint, and cumin in a bowl. Stir in the cucumber and mix well.

Per Serving: Calories 31; Protein 2g; Fat 1g (Saturated 0g); Carbohydrates 5g; Fiber 1g; Sodium 23mg

Tomato Salads

Tomato salads are summer recipes. If the tomatoes are ripe and luscious, these salads will be extraordinary. But if the tomatoes are hard and pink, the salads won't be worth eating. Tomato sizes vary, and one person's large tomato is another person's medium, which is why I specify both quantity and weight.

Unlike cucumber salads, which are often best served chilled, tomato salads are best when offered at room temperature. In fact, tomatoes should not be refrigerated because cold storage causes their flavor to disappear. Leftovers should be refrigerated, but always bring them back to room temperature to restore some of the lost flavor.

Summer Herb Tomato Salad

Makes: 7 servings

Mint and oregano are a good combination with feta cheese. If using goat cheese, other, milder herbs would be fine, such as marjoram and chervil.

4 large ripe tomatoes, cored and diced (about 2 pounds)
1 small cucumber, peeled and diced
1 tablespoon chopped fresh mint
1/4 cup chopped fresh parsley
1 teaspoon chopped fresh oregano
2 ounces feta or goat cheese, crumbled, about 1/2 cup (optional)
2 tablespoons lemon juice
1 1/2 teaspoons extra-virgin olive oil
1/2 teaspoon kosher salt
1/4 teaspoon freshly ground pepper
1 clove garlic, minced (optional)

1) Toss together the tomatoes, cucumber, herbs, and cheese.

2) Whisk together the lemon juice, oil, salt, pepper, and garlic. Pour over the salad and toss. Let sit for a half hour, then serve.

Per Serving: Calories 43; Protein 1g; Fat 1g (Saturated 0g); Carbohydrates 8g; Fiber 2g; Sodium 151mg

Basil and Tomato Salad

Makes: 4 servings

Make this salad only when ripe, flavorful tomatoes are available.

2 to 3 large ripe tomatoes, cored and thickly sliced (about 1 1/4 pounds)
6 large fresh basil leaves, thinly sliced
1 1/2 teaspoons balsamic vinegar
1 1/2 teaspoons extra-virgin olive oil
1/8 teaspoon kosher salt
1/8 teaspoon freshly ground pepper
2 ounces goat cheese or fresh mozzarella, sliced (optional)

1) Arrange the tomatoes in an overlapping layer on a plate.

2) Distribute the basil across the tomatoes. Sprinkle with the vinegar and oil. Dust with the salt and pepper. Garnish with cheese, if desired.

Per Serving: Calories 47; Protein 1g; Fat 2g (Saturated 0g); Carbohydrates 7g; Fiber 1g; Sodium 73mg

Greek Tomato Salad

Makes: 8 servings

Unlike most tomato salads, leftovers from this one can be refrigerated and served the next day. For fullest flavor, however, bring it to room temperature before eating.

4 large ripe tomatoes, cored and cubed
    (about 2 pounds)
1 cucumber, peeled and cubed
1 large green bell pepper, cut into $1/2$-inch squares
$1/2$ cup red onions, thinly sliced into 1-inch pieces
2 tablespoons red wine vinegar
1 tablespoon extra-virgin olive oil
1 teaspoon kosher salt
1 teaspoon dried oregano
4 brine-cured olives, pitted and chopped
2 ounces feta cheese, crumbled, about $1/2$ cup
    (optional)

1) Toss together the tomatoes, cucumber, bell pepper, and onions.

2) Whisk together the vinegar, oil, salt, and oregano. Pour over the salad. Toss in the olives. Garnish with feta cheese if desired.

Per Serving: Calories 58; Protein 1g; Fat 3g (Saturated 0g); Carbohydrates 9g; Fiber 2g; Sodium 288mg

Marinated Tomato Salad

Makes: 5 servings

This can be served as a side salad, or, if the tomatoes are diced, it can be used as a relish on grilled chicken or burgers.

4 medium tomatoes (about $1^1/2$ pounds)
2 cloves garlic, peeled and crushed
$1/2$ red onion, thinly sliced and cut into thirds ($1/2$ cup)
2 tablespoons minced fresh parsley
1 tablespoon extra-virgin olive oil
2 tablespoons lemon juice
1 teaspoon balsamic vinegar
$1/2$ teaspoon yellow mustard seeds, slightly crushed
$1/4$ teaspoon ground coriander
$1/4$ teaspoon kosher salt
$1/4$ teaspoon freshly ground pepper

1) Core the tomatoes, then seed them by cutting them in half at their equators and gently pushing the seeds and watery juice out with your fingers. Slice the tomatoes.

2) Put a toothpick through the garlic cloves so they will be easier to find and remove later.

3) Combine the tomatoes, garlic, onions, and parsley.

4) Whisk together the remaining ingredients. Pour the dressing over the tomatoes. Stir gently. Let the salad rest 1 hour before serving. Remove and discard the garlic just prior to serving.

Per Serving: Calories 54; Protein 1g; Fat 3g (Saturated 0g); Carbohydrates 7g; Fiber 1g; Sodium 106mg

Red and Purple Salad

Makes: 8 servings

If shallots are unavailable, use minced red onion.

1 shallot, minced (about 1 tablespoon)
1 tablespoon minced fresh parsley
1 1/2 tablespoons minced fresh basil
1/2 cup thinly sliced red onions
4 medium tomatoes, cut into wedges
    (about 1 1/2 pounds)
1 clove garlic, peeled and crushed
1/2 cup red wine vinegar
2 tablespoons extra-virgin olive oil
1/2 teaspoon kosher salt

1) Toss together the shallots, parsley, basil, onions, tomatoes, and garlic.

2) Whisk together the vinegar, oil, and salt. Pour over the salad and toss.

3) Let rest for at least 4 hours before serving. Remove the garlic before serving.

Per Serving: Calories 58; Protein 1g; Fat 4g (Saturated 0g); Carbohydrates 7g; Fiber 1g; Sodium 128mg

Corn and Tomato Salad

Makes: 7 servings

This salad is a good way to use leftover corn on the cob, but it can also be made with lightly cooked frozen corn.

3 cups corn kernels, cooked (from 4 ears of corn)
2 cups diced fresh ripe tomatoes, or 1 pint cherry
    tomatoes, quartered
1 cucumber, peeled and diced
1/2 cup chopped scallions
1 tablespoon fresh chopped basil, or
    1 teaspoon dried
1 1/2 teaspoons red wine vinegar
2 tablespoons extra-virgin olive oil
1 teaspoon kosher salt, or more to taste
1/4 teaspoon freshly ground pepper, or more
    to taste

1) Toss together the corn, tomatoes, cucumber, scallions, and basil.

2) In another bowl, whisk together the vinegar, oil, salt, and pepper. Pour over the salad. Adjust the salt and pepper if desired.

Per Serving: Calories 110; Protein 3g; Fat 5g (Saturated 1g); Carbohydrates 17g; Fiber 3g; Sodium 291mg

Cherry Tomato and Watercress Salad

Makes: 7 servings

Serve this salad within an hour of making it, or the watercress will wilt.

1 bunch watercress, washed and spun dry (about 4 cups)
4 cups cherry tomatoes, halved
1/2 cup diced red onions
2 tablespoons white wine vinegar
1 tablespoon extra-virgin olive oil
1 teaspoon sugar
1/2 teaspoon kosher salt
1/4 teaspoon freshly ground pepper

1) Cut through the pile of watercress to make pieces no longer than a torn lettuce leaf for salad (but do not chop into small bits). Toss together the watercress, tomatoes, and onions.

2) Whisk together the remaining ingredients. Pour over the salad and toss.

Per Serving: Calories 55; Protein 2g; Fat 2g (Saturated 0g); Carbohydrates 8g; Fiber 2g; Sodium 157mg

Assorted Vegetable Salads

Soy-Dressed Asparagus

Makes: 4 servings

Serve this along with an Asian noodle salad for a luncheon, or as a side vegetable on a hot summer night.

1 slice ginger (about the size of a quarter)
1 1/2 teaspoons rice vinegar or white wine vinegar
1/4 teaspoon honey
1 teaspoon Asian sesame oil
1 1/2 teaspoons soy sauce
4 drops Tabasco sauce
1 pound asparagus, tough ends snapped off

1) In a medium bowl, whisk together all but the asparagus.

2) Steam the asparagus until it is cooked but still has "snap," sometimes referred to as crisp-tender. Cut the asparagus in thirds or leave whole. While the asparagus is still hot, toss it with the dressing.

3) Discard the ginger before serving. Serve at room temperature.

Per Serving: Calories 32; Protein 2g; Fat 1g (Saturated 0g); Carbohydrates 4g; Fiber 2g; Sodium 131mg

Mustard, Dill, and Green Bean Salad

Makes: 8 servings

Unlike in other salads, the color of the green beans won't fade here, even after several days, which makes Mustard, Dill, and Green Bean Salad ideal for preparing ahead or for picnics.

2 pounds green beans, trimmed, and halved
    if large
1/4 cup thinly sliced red onions
2 tablespoons minced fresh dill
1 tablespoon balsamic vinegar
1 tablespoon red wine vinegar
1 teaspoon sugar
2 tablespoons extra-virgin olive oil
1 1/2 tablespoons Dijon mustard
1/4 teaspoon kosher salt
1/4 teaspoon freshly ground pepper

1) Bring a large pot of salted water to a boil (about 2 teaspoons salt per quart). Drop in the green beans, bring back to a boil, and cook about 2 minutes until crisp-tender. Drain and immerse the beans in a bowl of cold water to stop the cooking process.

2) Toss the beans with the onions and dill.

3) Whisk together the remaining ingredients and toss with the salad. Bring to room temperature before serving.

Per Serving: Calories 75; Protein 2g; Fat 4g (Saturated 0g); Carbohydrates 10g; Fiber 4g; Sodium 139mg

Snap Peas in Mint Vinaigrette

Makes: 6 servings

The vegetables and dressing can be prepared up to a day ahead of time, but shouldn't be tossed together until the last moment or the peas will discolor.

1 pound snap peas (4 to 5 cups)
1/2 red bell pepper, julienned into 1 1/2-inch strips
1/4 cup thinly sliced red onions, cut into
    1/2-inch pieces
1 tablespoon lemon juice
1 tablespoon red wine vinegar
1 tablespoon minced fresh mint
2 teaspoons coarse mustard
1 tablespoon extra-virgin olive oil
1 tablespoon honey

1) Snap the tip off each snap pea and peel off the string (unless it is a stringless hybrid). Leave the peas whole or cut them in half on the diagonal.

2) Bring a pot of water to a boil. Drop in the peas and cook them for about 1 minute, until they turn bright green. Remove from water and immediately immerse them in cold water.

3) Mix together the peas, bell pepper, and onions.

4) Whisk together the remaining ingredients. Pour the dressing over the vegetables and toss until the peas glisten with an even coating of dressing.

Per Serving: Calories 71; Protein 2g; Fat 3g (Saturated 0g); Carbohydrates 10g; Fiber 2g; Sodium 46mg

Southwestern Corn Salad

Makes: 6 servings

The quality of the ingredients for this salad is not linked to the seasons, so this is good all year long.

3 1/2 to 4 cups corn kernels, cooked, fresh from
    4 ears of corn, or from frozen
1 bell pepper, chopped
4 scallions, sliced
4 cherry tomatoes, halved
2 teaspoons olive oil
3 tablespoons fresh lime juice
3 tablespoons minced fresh parsley or cilantro
1/8 teaspoon cayenne pepper
1/4 teaspoon kosher salt

1) Toss together the corn, bell pepper, scallions, and tomatoes in a bowl.

2) Whisk together the remaining ingredients, pour over the vegetables, and stir.

Per Serving: Calories 101; Protein 3g; Fat 3g (Saturated 0g); Carbohydrates 20g; Fiber 3g; Sodium 97mg

Marinated Carrot Sticks

Makes: 8 servings

Carrot sticks can be used as hors d'oeuvres, in a salad, as finger food, or on an antipasto platter. They will remain fresh for 2 weeks in the refrigerator.

1 pound carrots, peeled and cut into sticks
    3 inches long
1 teaspoon yellow mustard seeds
1 teaspoon dill seeds
1/2 cup apple cider vinegar
1 1/2 tablespoons honey
1 cup water
1 teaspoon kosher salt
1 teaspoon dry mustard

1) Drop the carrots into a pot of boiling water and cook for 2 minutes. Immediately drain and cool under running water in order to stop the cooking process. Pack into a heatproof jar.

2) Heat a saucepan over a moderate flame. Put in the mustard seeds and dill seeds. Toast them over this dry heat until the mustard seeds pop. Do not let them turn dark brown.

3) Pour the vinegar, honey, and water into the saucepan. Be careful not to burn yourself; the liquid will splatter as it hits the hot surface.

4) Add the salt and dry mustard. Boil for 2 minutes. Pour the liquid over the carrots. Chill.

Per Serving: Calories 27; Protein 1g; Fat 0g (Saturated 0g); Carbohydrates 6g; Fiber 1g; Sodium 95mg

Pickled Beets

Makes: 8 servings

Pickled beets can be served on their own, or tossed in with salads.

1 cup apple cider vinegar
2 tablespoons honey
1 cup water
3 peppercorns
1 bay leaf
2 whole cloves
1 cup sliced onions
5 cups beets, cooked, peeled, and sliced

1) Bring the vinegar, honey, and water to a boil in a small saucepan. Add the peppercorns, bay leaf, and cloves. Simmer for 10 minutes.

2) Place the onions and beets in the bottom of a heatproof jar or bowl. Pour the hot liquid over the vegetables and cover.

3) Keep in the refrigerator to marinate for at least 1 day before serving.

Per Serving: Calories 47; Protein 2g; Fat 0g (Saturated 0g); Carbohydrates 11g; Fiber 3g; Sodium 67mg

Minty Beet Salad

Makes: 6 servings

The mint brightens all the flavors. This would complement a grilled chicken supper or would be a welcome additon to a family reunion picnic.

1 1/2 pounds fresh beets, cooked and sliced, or 3 cups canned sliced beets
2 tablespoons fresh mint, chopped or cut into fine strips
1/4 cup thinly sliced red onions, cut into 1-inch pieces
1 tablespoon balsamic vinegar
1 tablespoon white wine vinegar
1 tablespoon honey
1 tablespoon extra-virgin olive oil

1) Toss the beets with the mint and onions.

2) Whisk together the remaining ingredients. Pour the dressing over the beets and toss until the beets are evenly coated. Serve at room temperature.

Per Serving: Calories 86; Protein 2g; Fat 2g (Saturated 0g); Carbohydrates 15g; Fiber 3g; Sodium 90mg

Beet and Orange Salad

Makes: 4 servings

Beet salads can often be stored for several days without loss of flavor or texture. This one can be kept in a glass container in the refrigerator for up to a week.

2 oranges
1 pound fresh beets, cooked and sliced, or 2 cups
    canned sliced beets
1/3 cup thinly sliced red onions, cut into
    1-inch pieces
2 tablespoons orange juice
1 tablespoon honey
2 tablespoons apple cider vinegar
1/4 teaspoon kosher salt
1/8 teaspoon freshly ground pepper

1) Cut the oranges in half. Cut out the segments as you would a grapefruit. Combine these with the beets and onions.

2) Squeeze the orange halves to extract the 2 tablespoons of juice needed for the recipe. Strain out the seeds and put the juice in a bowl. Whisk the juice with the honey, vinegar, salt, and pepper.

3) Pour the dressing over the beet mixture. Stir to combine.

Per Serving: Calories 102; Protein 3g; Fat 0g (Saturated 0g); Carbohydrates 25g; Fiber 5g; Sodium 209mg

Waldorf Salad

Makes: 8 servings

The use of raisins reduces the amount of nuts used, and therefore keeps the fat content low.

1 tablespoon lemon juice
3 large firm apples, such as Granny Smith
2 ribs celery, chopped
1/2 cup golden raisins
1/2 cup walnut pieces, toasted
1 tablespoon lowfat or nonfat sour cream
2 tablespoons reduced-fat mayonnaise
1 teaspoon honey

1) Place the lemon juice in a large bowl. Core the apples and cut into wedges, then cut the wedges into 4 pieces each. Toss immediately in the lemon juice to prevent browning. Stir in the celery, raisins, and walnuts.

2) In a small bowl, whisk together the sour cream, mayonnaise, and honey. Pour over the salad and toss to combine.

Per Serving: Calories 146; Protein 2g; Fat 6g (Saturated 1g); Carbohydrates 23g; Fiber 2g; Sodium 41mg

Slaws

In my mind, slaws are shredded vegetable salads made of crunchy vegetables. Often, though not always, cabbage is the main ingredient. They are quite easy to make; usually the shredding takes only a few moments in the food processor and the dressing can be blended using a whisk. If buying a large head of cabbage is too much, purchase slaw mix in the produce department. Another convenience food is broccoli slaw made from broccoli stalks and carrots. It makes a wonderful side salad. As a general rule, one head of cabbage weighs over two pounds. Take off the loose, dark green leaves and cut out the core, and it weighs about 1 1/2 pounds, and will yield 8 cups when shredded.

I like slaws dressed with light and invigorating flavors that taste less heavy and are lower in fat and calories than commercial slaws (some slaws from the deli weigh in at 14 grams of fat per serving). The mayonnaise I use is reduced-fat, and I often cut it with vinegars, yogurt, or citrus juices. Some slaws have no mayonnaise at all. Most stay fresh for several days and travel well; it is no wonder that slaw is an essential picnic food.

Classic Picnic Slaw

Makes: 10 servings

This is a lighter version of the traditional mayonnaise-based salad. I often add interest to it by using an herb- or garlic-infused vinegar.

8 cups shredded green cabbage
2 carrots, peeled and grated
1/2 medium red onion, shredded or chopped fine
1/2 cup lowfat sour cream
1/2 cup reduced-fat mayonnaise
3 tablespoons white wine vinegar
1 tablespoon sugar
1/2 teaspoon celery seed
1/4 teaspoon freshly ground pepper
1/2 teaspoon kosher salt

1) Mix together the cabbage, carrots, and onion in a large bowl.

2) Whisk together the remaining ingredients. Stir into the vegetables. Chill before serving.

Per Serving: Calories 86; Protein 2g; Fat 5g (Saturated 1g); Carbohydrates 10g; Fiber 2g; Sodium 218mg

Coleslaw with Horseradish Dressing

Makes: 8 servings

This coleslaw forgoes the mayonnaise for a light, bright-tasting vinegar-based dressing. It remains fresh for several days in the refrigerator.

2 tablespoons lemon juice
2 teaspoons white wine vinegar
1 tablespoon olive oil
1/4 teaspoon store-bought white horseradish
1/4 teaspoon freshly ground pepper, or to taste
3 1/2 cups shredded green cabbage
1 carrot, shredded
1/3 cup thinly sliced red onions

1) Whisk together the lemon juice, vinegar, oil, horseradish, and pepper in a large bowl.

2) Toss in the vegetables, stir, and chill.

Per Serving: Calories 30; Protein 1g; Fat 2g (Saturated 0g); Carbohydrates 3g; Fiber 1g; Sodium 9mg

Apple and Carrot Coleslaw

Makes: 8 servings

This version of a carrot slaw doesn't have raisins. Instead, it has apples and a light curry dressing.

2 tablespoons lemon juice
2 tablespoons apple cider vinegar
1 tablespoon vegetable oil
1 tablespoon honey
1 tablespoon Dijon mustard
1 teaspoon mild curry powder
1/4 teaspoon kosher salt
1/8 teaspoon freshly ground pepper
2 firm apples, cored
4 cups shredded green cabbage
2 medium carrots
1/2 medium red onion

1) Whisk together the lemon juice, vinegar, oil, honey, mustard, curry, salt, and pepper.

2) Grate the apples and vegetables with a large-holed grater (easily accomplished with a food processor). Don't peel the apples unless they have been heavily waxed.

3) Toss the apples and vegetables with the dressing. You can make this several hours ahead of time.

Per Serving: Calories 63; Protein 1g; Fat 2g (Saturated 0g); Carbohydrates 12g; Fiber 2g; Sodium 118mg

Apple and Celery Slaw with Honey Dressing

Makes: 10 servings

Celery gives this slaw a nice crunch.

3 large firm red apples, cored and diced
3 tablespoons lemon juice
2 cups diced celery (about 4 ribs)
1/2 cup raisins
2 cups shredded green cabbage
3 tablespoons honey
1/4 cup plain nonfat yogurt
1 tablespoon reduced-fat mayonnaise
1 teaspoon celery seed
1/4 teaspoon freshly ground pepper

1) Toss the diced apples with the lemon juice to prevent browning. Mix in the celery, raisins, and cabbage.

2) Whisk together the remaining ingredients. Stir into the salad. Served chilled.

Per Serving: Calories 99; Protein 1g; Fat 1g (Saturated 0g); Carbohydrates 24g; Fiber 2g; Sodium 41mg

Carrot and Walnut Salad

Makes: 4 servings

The Tabasco gives this salad a bite and keeps the carrots from tasting too sweet.

1 tablespoon extra-virgin olive oil
1/2 cup orange juice
2 tablespoons lemon juice
2 teaspoons sugar
1/2 teaspoon kosher salt
1/8 teaspoon Tabasco
3 cups shredded carrots (about 1 pound)
2 tablespoons chopped walnuts, lightly toasted

1) Whisk together the oil, juices, sugar, salt, and Tabasco.

2) Place the carrots and walnuts in a bowl and stir in the dressing.

Per Serving: Calories 113; Protein 2g; Fat 6g (Saturated 1g); Carbohydrates 15g; Fiber 2g; Sodium 271mg

Carrot and Mint Salad

Makes: 4 servings

Serve this salad warm as soon as it is dressed, or chill and serve up to a day later.

1 1/2 tablespoons minced red onions
1 tablespoon apple cider vinegar
3 tablespoons water, divided
1 1/2 tablespoons minced fresh mint
1/4 teaspoon kosher salt
1 teaspoon lemon juice
4 carrots, grated on largest hole
1 teaspoon olive oil

1) Combine the onions, vinegar, 1 tablespoon of the water, mint, salt, and lemon juice, blending well.

2) Sauté the carrots in the oil and remaining water until they just start to soften. Toss the dressing in with the hot carrots.

Per Serving: Calories 44; Protein 1g; Fat 1g (Saturated 0g); Carbohydrates 8g; Fiber 2g; Sodium 147mg

Sesame Carrot Slaw

Makes: 6 servings

This can be made up to a day ahead of time, but if doing so, wait and toss the sesame seeds on just prior to serving.

3 cups shredded carrots (about 1 pound)
1 cup shredded red or green cabbage
2 tablespoons lemon juice
2 teaspoons sugar
1 tablespoon vegetable oil or Garlic Oil
    (page 607)
1/2 teaspoon kosher salt
1/4 teaspoon freshly ground pepper
2 tablespoons sesame seeds, lightly toasted

1) Stir together the carrots and cabbage.

2) Whisk together the remaining ingredients and pour over the vegetables. Toss with the sesame seeds and serve.

Per Serving: Calories 72; Protein 2g; Fat 4g (Saturated 0g); Carbohydrates 8g; Fiber 2g; Sodium 183mg

North African Carrot Salad

Makes: 8 servings

Cumin and cinnamon give this salad a lot of flavor without making it spicy-hot.

1 pound carrots, peeled and shredded
    (about 3 cups)
1 1/2 tablespoons lemon juice
1 1/2 teaspoons apple cider vinegar
1 tablespoon extra-virgin olive oil
1 1/2 teaspoons honey
1 1/2 teaspoons paprika
1/2 teaspoon ground cumin
1/2 teaspoon ground cinnamon
1 teaspoon kosher salt
1/8 teaspoon freshly ground pepper
2 tablespoons minced fresh parsley

1) Steam or microwave the carrots until just tender. If microwaving, first add a few tablespoons of water to keep them moist. Drain in a colander.

2) While the carrots are cooking, whisk together the remaining ingredients except for the parsley. If the honey is too thick, warm it for 20 seconds in the microwave to make it pourable.

3) While the carrots are still warm, toss them with the dressing. Let cool to room temperature and stir in the parsley.

Per Serving: Calories 47; Protein 1g; Fat 2g (Saturated 0g); Carbohydrates 8g; Fiber 2g; Sodium 261mg

Zucchini Slaw

Makes: 10 servings

Carrots are added to the zucchini for their crunchy texture and bright color. Serve within a day of preparation because, with time, the zucchini will wilt out water.

3 cups shredded green cabbage
2 cups shredded zucchini
    (about 1 medium zucchini)
2 cups shredded carrots
3 tablespoons white wine or rice vinegar
1 tablespoon lemon juice
2 tablespoons light brown sugar
1 tablespoon vegetable oil
1 teaspoon soy sauce
1/4 teaspoon dry mustard
1/2 teaspoon kosher salt

1) Toss together the cabbage, zucchini, and carrots.

2) In another bowl, whisk together the remaining ingredients. Pour over the vegetables and toss.

Per Serving: Calories 45; Protein 1g; Fat 2g (Saturated 0g); Carbohydrates 7g; Fiber 1g; Sodium 144mg

Potato Salads

Waxy potatoes, such as red bliss, are made for potato salads. They hold their shape and texture even when boiled. Peel the potatoes if their skins are blemished or are green. (Exposure to sunlight causes this discoloration, and any green tinge, on skin or in the flesh should also be cut away since it is bitter.) But if the potatoes are thin-skinned and fresh, scrub them well and leave the skins on. Tiny round potatoes are especially nice for potato salads. They can go in whole, which not only looks pretty but is less work for the cook.

Potatoes can be cut, then steamed for potato salad, or whole potatoes can be boiled before cutting. When a recipe says to cook until "fork tender" it means that a fork can be inserted easily into the center of the potato. There shouldn't be any crunch, but don't cook them so long that the outsides of the potatoes turn mushy. Once the potatoes are cooked through, drain, then immerse them in a bowl of cool water to stop the cooking process, then drain again. Also, unless specified, the dressing should not be tossed with hot potatoes because it will curdle.

Picnic Potato Salad

Makes: 12 servings

This classic salad is easy to make and remains fresh for several days in the refrigerator.

3 pounds red- or white-skinned waxy potatoes, cut into 1-inch pieces
1 teaspoon celery seed
2 tablespoons lemon juice
2/3 cup reduced-fat mayonnaise
1/2 teaspoon kosher salt
1/4 teaspoon freshly ground pepper
6 scallions, sliced
2 ribs celery, chopped
Paprika for garnish (optional)

1) Steam the potatoes until fork tender. Drain in a colander and let cool.

2) Whisk together the celery seed, lemon juice, mayonnaise, salt, and pepper. Stir into the potatoes. Toss in the scallions and celery. Garnish with paprika, if desired.

Per Serving: Calories 138; Protein 3g; Fat 5g (Saturated 1g); Carbohydrates 22g; Fiber 2g; Sodium 196mg

Picnic Potato Salad with Herbs and Mustard

Makes: 12 servings

Jazz up the basic salad with fresh herbs and an interesting mustard. Coarse mustard and dill are just suggestions—be creative.

1 recipe Picnic Potato Salad (above)
1 tablespoon coarse mustard
1 tablespoon chopped fresh dill
1/2 cup chopped fresh parsley

Follow the directions for Picnic Potato salad except in Step 2, whisk in the mustard with the mayonnaise and toss in the herbs with the scallions and celery.

Per Serving: Calories 146 Protein 3g; Fat 5g (Saturated 1g); Carbohydrates 22g; Fiber 2g; Sodium 227mg

Picnic Potato Salad with Relish and Eggs

Makes: 12 servings

Vegetarians will like this as a main course salad. I like the texture and flavor that eggs bring to the recipe.

1 recipe Picnic Potato Salad (opposite)
1 1/2 tablespoons Dijon mustard
1/2 teaspoon Worcestershire sauce
1/4 teaspoon Tabasco sauce
3 hard-boiled eggs, 2 yolks discarded
3 tablespoons pickle relish

Follow the directions for Picnic Potato salad except in Step 2, whisk in the mustard, Worcestershire sauce, and Tabasco with the mayonnaise. Chop the eggs and toss in with the scallions and celery.

Per Serving: Calories 155; Protein 4g; Fat 5g (Saturated 1g); Carbohydrates 24g; Fiber 2g; Sodium 288mg

Pesto Potato Salad

Makes: 10 servings

This is an easy recipe to make, yet it looks as if it was purchased at a gourmet take-out shop.

2 pounds waxy potatoes, such as red bliss, cubed or thickly sliced
1/4 cup Basil Pesto (page 589 or store-bought)
2 tablespoons reduced-fat mayonnaise
2 tablespoons water
1/2 teaspoon kosher salt
1/4 teaspoon freshly ground pepper
8 cherry tomatoes, halved
1/2 cup sliced red onions

1) Steam or boil the potato cubes until fork tender, about 12 minutes. Immerse in cool water to stop further cooking. Drain.

2) Whisk together the pesto, mayonnaise, water, salt, and pepper. Combine with the potatoes until they are nicely coated with dressing. Toss in the tomatoes and onions.

Per Serving: Calories 106; Protein 3g; Fat 3g (Saturated 1g); Carbohydrates 18g; Fiber 2g; Sodium 138mg

Dilly Potato Salad

Makes: 8 servings

One way to achieve a full-flavored potato salad is to pour a vinaigrette over the potatoes while they are still hot. This allows the potatoes to soak up the flavors of the dressing.

6 medium potatoes, cut into cubes (1 1/2 pounds)
1/2 cup thinly sliced red onions, cut in 1/2-inch pieces
2 ribs celery, chopped
1 large dill pickle, chopped
1 tablespoon chopped fresh parsley
1 tablespoon minced fresh dill
1/4 cup apple cider vinegar
2 tablespoons vegetable oil
1/4 teaspoon dry mustard
1/2 teaspoon sugar
1/8 teaspoon paprika
1/2 teaspoon kosher salt
1/4 teaspoon freshly ground pepper

1) Cook the potatoes until fork tender.

2) Meanwhile, combine the onions, celery, pickle, parsley, and dill in a large bowl.

3) Whisk together the remaining ingredients.

4) When the potatoes are cooked, drain them and place them in the bowl with the other vegetables. Pour the dressing over all and toss well. Serve this salad immediately while still hot, or later at room temperature.

Per Serving: Calories 106; Protein 2g; Fat 4g (Saturated 0g); Carbohydrates 17g; Fiber 2g; Sodium 239mg

Pommery Potato Salad

Makes: 8 servings

Instead of mayonnaise, this salad uses a combination of cottage cheese and yogurt, which blends well with the coarse mustard and spices.

5 cups baby red potatoes, cut into cubes
  (about 2 pounds)
1 green bell pepper, chopped
1 red bell pepper, chopped
2 ribs celery, chopped
6 scallions, sliced
2 tablespoons minced fresh parsley
2 cloves garlic
1 cup 1% lowfat cottage cheese
1/2 cup plain nonfat yogurt
1 teaspoon sugar
3 tablespoons coarse mustard, such as Pommery
1 1/2 teaspoons soy sauce
1/8 teaspoon paprika
1/8 teaspoon freshly ground pepper
1/2 teaspoon celery seed
2 teaspoons minced fresh dill, or 1/2 teaspoon dry

1) Steam the potatoes until fork tender, then let cool to room temperature

2) Toss the potatoes with the peppers, celery, scallions, and parsley.

3) Mince the garlic in a food processor and then add the remaining ingredients to the work bowl. Puree until thick and smooth. Pour the dressing over the vegetables and toss.

Per Serving: Calories 138; Protein 7g; Fat 1g (Saturated 0g); Carbohydrates 26g; Fiber 3g; Sodium 344mg

Garlicky Garden Potato Salad

Makes: 6 servings

The garlic aroma will increase with time. By the next day it will be quite assertive.

1 or 2 cloves garlic
1 tablespoon extra-virgin olive oil
3 tablespoons apple cider vinegar
1 teaspoon kosher salt
1/2 teaspoon freshly ground pepper
1/4 teaspoon celery seed
1 pound small red potatoes, cut into cubes
  (about 8 to 10 potatoes)
1 cup vegetable of choice (such as green beans,
  cucumber, or broccoli)
1/2 cup chopped red bell pepper
1/3 cup chopped red onions
1 tablespoon chopped fresh parsley
1/2 cup peas, lightly steamed

1) Puree the garlic with the oil, vinegar, salt, and pepper until the garlic is smoothly incorporated into the liquid. Stir in the celery seed.

2) Cook the potatoes until fork-tender, then immediately pour the dressing over the potatoes.

3) Cut the chosen vegetable into bite-size pieces. You may want to steam it lightly to reduce crunch.

4) Once the potatoes are cool, toss in the vegetable, bell pepper, onions, parsley, and peas. Let the salad rest for a couple of hours before serving to allow the flavors to permeate the potatoes.

Per Serving: Calories 104; Protein 3g; Fat 2g (Saturated 0g); Carbohydrates 19g; Fiber 3g; Sodium 327mg

Sweet Potato and Chutney Salad

Makes: 8 servings

Potato salads shouldn't be limited to white potatoes. This one includes sweet potatoes. Not only is the color gorgeous, but the flavors of lime, curry, and chutney make this interesting and delicious.

1 pound sweet potatoes (about 2 large)
1 pound waxy white potatoes
4 scallions, sliced
3 tablespoons chopped fresh parsley
1/3 cup chutney, large pieces chopped if necessary
2 tablespoons lemon juice
1 tablespoon fresh lime juice
1 1/2 tablespoons curry powder
1/2 to 1 teaspoon kosher salt
2 tablespoons reduced-fat mayonnaise

1) Peel the potatoes and cut into cubes. Steam until tender. Immerse in a bowl of cold water to chill. Drain. Toss with the scallions and parsley.

2) Whisk together the remaining ingredients. Pour over the potatoes and toss gently until all is evenly coated with the dressing. Serve at room temperature.

Per Serving: Calories 118; Protein 2g; Fat 2g (Saturated 0g); Carbohydrates 25g; Fiber 3g; Sodium 183mg

Pasta Salads

Cooking Pasta for Salads

Cook pasta thoroughly for pasta salads. Although "al dente" (with a chewy texture) is right for hot pasta entrees, pasta that is to be eaten cold needs to be cooked through (until soft but not mushy) because pasta firms up as it cools off. Once cooked, drain the pasta and immerse in a bowl of cool water. Swirl it around until cooled and drain again. This stops the cooking and rinses off the starch, preventing stickiness.

Macaroni and Vegetable Salad

Makes: 8 servings

Macaroni salad pairs well with burgers from the grill for a summer supper, or with sandwiches at lunch. It will stay fresh for several days in the refrigerator.

2 cups uncooked elbow macaroni (about 8 ounces)
1/2 cup chopped red onions
1 green bell pepper, diced
2 cups small broccoli florets, lightly steamed
1 rib celery, diced
1 carrot, peeled and diced
1 cucumber, peeled, seeded, and diced
1/2 cup lowfat mayonnaise
1/4 cup 1% lowfat milk
2 tablespoons red wine vinegar
1/2 teaspoon kosher salt
1/4 teaspoon freshly ground pepper
1/2 teaspoon dried basil

1) Cook the macaroni in a large pot of boiling water until tender. Drain, immerse in a bowl of cold water, drain again, and toss with the onions, bell pepper, broccoli, celery, carrot, and cucumber.

2) Whisk together the remaining ingredients. Pour over the salad, then toss to coat.

Per Serving: Calories 146; Protein 5g; Fat 2g (Saturated 0g); Carbohydrates 29g; Fiber 2g; Sodium 277mg

Springtime Pasta Salad

Makes: 4 servings

For a special occasion, add 1 cup smoked salmon or trout.

1 1/2 cups uncooked pasta, preferably a short, stubby type
10 asparagus spears, cut into 1-inch pieces
2/3 cup peas
1/2 cup thinly sliced red onions, cut into 1-inch pieces
1/2 red bell pepper, julienned into 1-inch strips
2 tablespoons red wine vinegar
1/2 tablespoon balsamic vinegar
2 tablespoons Garlic Oil (page 607)
1 teaspoon Dijon mustard
1/2 teaspoon kosher salt
1/4 teaspoon freshly ground pepper
1 teaspoon dried basil
1/2 teaspoon dried marjoram
2 tablespoons minced fresh parsley

1) Cook the pasta, drain, immerse in cold water, and drain again.

2) Steam the asparagus until it turns a brighter shade of green and is tender but not soft. Cook the peas in the same manner, but not at the same time as the asparagus, since they take less time to cook. Once steamed, immerse the vegetables in cold water to prevent them from overcooking. Drain.

3) Toss together the asparagus, peas, pasta, onions, and bell pepper.

4) Whisk together the remaining ingredients. Pour the dressing over the pasta and vegetables and toss to coat.

Per Serving: Calories 250; Protein 8g; Fat 8g (Saturated 1g); Carbohydrates 38g; Fiber 4g; Sodium 279mg

Pesto Pasta Salad

Makes: 4 servings

Having pesto on hand makes preparing a pasta salad an easy task—just toss and serve.

1 red bell pepper, julienned
1 1/2 cups broccoli florets, lightly steamed
3 cups cooked pasta, preferably a fat and stubby shape, such as wheels or rotini
3 tablespoons Basil Pesto (page 589 or store-bought)
1/2 teaspoon kosher salt
1/4 teaspoon freshly ground pepper

Toss together the bell pepper, broccoli, and pasta. Mix in the pesto, salt, and pepper until evenly coated.

Per Serving: Calories 193; Protein 7g; Fat 4g (Saturated 1g); Carbohydrates 32g; Fiber 2g; Sodium 269mg

Tortellini with Pesto and Sun-Dried Tomato Salad

Makes: 5 servings

Test the tortellini for doneness before draining. I've found that the manufacturers vary in what they consider to be fully cooked and their suggestions are not always accurate.

One 10- to 16-ounce package frozen cheese tortellini

2 teaspoons extra-virgin olive oil

1/4 cup sun-dried tomatoes (not packed in oil)

2 tablespoons Basil Pesto (page 589 or store-bought)

1 teaspoon balsamic vinegar

1/2 teaspoon kosher salt (optional)

2 cups small broccoli florets, steamed until crisp-tender

8 cherry tomatoes, halved

1) Cook the tortellini until tender. Drain, then immerse in cold water and drain again. Toss with the olive oil.

2) Meanwhile, soak the sun-dried tomatoes in very hot water. Let rest until softened, about 15 minutes.

3) Whisk the pesto with 1 to 2 teaspoons of the water in which the tomatoes are soaking to thin the pesto to a pourable consistency. Whisk in the vinegar and salt. Toss with the tortellini. Stir in the broccoli and cherry tomato halves. Drain the sun-dried tomatoes, chop, and add to the salad. Serve at room temperature.

Per Serving: Calories 208; Protein 9g; Fat 7g (Saturated 2g); Carbohydrates 29g; Fiber 3g; Sodium 114mg

Tuna and Shells Salad

Makes: 5 servings

Capers go well with all types of seafood, but especially tuna. For salads, use the smallest ones you can find.

4 cups cooked medium pasta shells (from about 1/2 pound dried), rinsed and cooled

One 6-ounce can water-packed albacore tuna, drained

1 cup peas, lightly cooked

1/2 red bell pepper, chopped, or 1/2 cup roasted pepper

1 rib celery, chopped

1/2 cup chopped red onions

2 tablespoons red wine vinegar

1 teaspoon Dijon mustard

2 teaspoons Worcestershire sauce

2 teaspoons olive oil

2 tablespoons reduced-fat mayonnaise

1/2 teaspoon kosher salt

1/4 teaspoon freshly ground pepper

1 tablespoon capers, drained

1 tablespoon chopped fresh parsley

1) Toss the pasta together with the tuna, peas, bell pepper, celery, and onions.

2) In another bowl, whisk together the remaining ingredients except the capers and parsley. Stir the dressing into the shells mixture. Toss in the capers and parsley.

Per Serving: Calories 242; Protein 14g; Fat 5g (Saturated 1g); Carbohydrates 34g; Fiber 3g; Sodium 470mg

Tropical Chicken and Pasta Salad

Makes: 9 servings

This is one of my favorite recipes to take to a potluck picnic or serve for a luncheon buffet. To save time on the day of the event, combine the pineapple, grapes, and mango the night before. The pasta can also be cooked the previous day. Toss the salad within a few hours of serving.

One 8-ounce can pineapple chunks packed in their own juice
1 cup red seedless grapes
1 ripe mango, peeled, seeded, and cut into cubes (if unavailable, use cantaloupe balls or cubes)
2 cups cooked and cubed skinless, boneless chicken breast
2 ribs celery, chopped
2 scallions, sliced
3 cups cooked rotini or other similar pasta shape, rinsed and cooled
2 tablespoons chopped fresh parsley
1/2 cup plain nonfat yogurt
1/4 cup reduced-fat mayonnaise
1 teaspoon kosher salt
1/4 teaspoon freshly ground pepper
1/4 cup sliced almonds, toasted (optional)

1) Drain the pineapple. Reserve 3 tablespoons of the juice and discard the rest.

2) In a large bowl, toss together the pineapple chunks, grapes, mango, chicken, celery, scallions, pasta, and parsley.

3) In another bowl, whisk together the yogurt, mayonnaise, salt, pepper, and reserved pineapple juice. Pour the dressing over the salad and stir to combine. If you wish, top with the almonds.

Per Serving: Calories 181; Protein 11g; Fat 4g (Saturated 1g); Carbohydrates 26g; Fiber 2g; Sodium 304mg

Japanese Noodle Salad

Makes: 6 servings

The Asian sesame oil brings a lot of flavor to this recipe. This dark oil is extracted from toasted sesame seeds. Other oils, or a smaller quantity, cannot be substituted.

One 8-ounce package Japanese noodles, either udon or soba
1 1/2 cups broccoli florets (sliced stems can also be used)
1 carrot, grated or thinly sliced
1 tablespoon vegetable oil
2 tablespoons Asian sesame oil
2 tablespoons sesame seeds
4 scallions, sliced on the diagonal
1 1/2 tablespoons soy sauce
1 teaspoon lemon juice

1) Cook the noodles, drain, run under cool water, drain again, and set aside.

2) Steam the broccoli and carrots until the color of the broccoli brightens, about 3 minutes. Stop the cooking process by immersing the vegetables in cold water.

3) Heat the vegetable oil in a pan until it is hot but not bubbling. Add the sesame seeds. Remove the pan from the heat as soon as the seeds turn light brown. Stir the scallions into the hot oil; they will wilt.

4) Combine the noodles, vegetables, sesame oil, and scallions. Add the soy sauce and lemon juice. Serve at room temperature.

Per Serving: Calories 231; Protein 9g; Fat 9g (Saturated 1g); Carbohydrates 33g; Fiber 3g; Sodium 351mg

Sesame Soba Salad

Makes: 6 servings

The Asian vegetables are important to this salad: the bean sprouts lighten the texture and the radishes give it a sharp bite. Daikon radish is a fat, long vegetable that is not quite as sharp as the small red radishes and is worth trying if you can find it.

One 8- to 9-ounce package soba noodles
6 scallions, sliced
1 1/2 cups fresh mung bean sprouts
6 radishes, sliced, or 1/2 cup grated daikon radish
1 tablespoon tahini
2 tablespoons soy sauce
2 tablespoons mirin or sweet sherry
1 1/2 teaspoons rice vinegar
1 1/2 tablespoons Asian sesame oil
1/16 teaspoon cayenne pepper, preferably Chinese
1 teaspoon sesame seeds, toasted, for garnish (optional)

1) Cook the soba noodles just as you would cook regular pasta for salads (see Cooking Pasta for Salads, page 86). However, before dropping them in the boiling water, break the noodles in half. This will make the salad easier to toss later.

2) Toss the noodles with the scallions, bean sprouts, and radishes.

3) Place the tahini, soy sauce, mirin, vinegar, sesame oil, and cayenne pepper in a blender and process until smooth. If the dressing is sticky and won't pour easily, add a tablespoon or two of water.

4) Pour the dressing over the salad. Toss to combine. Garnish with toasted sesame seeds, if desired.

Per Serving: Calories 206; Protein 9g; Fat 1g (Saturated 1g); Carbohydrates 34g; Fiber 3g; Sodium 432mg

Chinese Broccoli and Pasta Salad

Makes: 4 servings

Breaking the spaghetti in half before cooking will make it easier to toss and serve.

2 cups cooked spaghetti, rinsed and cooled
3 cups small broccoli florets, lightly steamed
1/2 red bell pepper, julienned
1 scallion, sliced
1 1/2 tablespoons soy sauce
1 1/2 teaspoons Asian sesame oil
1 teaspoon sugar
1 1/2 teaspoons rice vinegar
1/8 teaspoon crushed red pepper flakes (optional)

1) Place the spaghetti in a large bowl. Toss it with the broccoli, bell pepper, and scallion until the vegetables are evenly distributed among the strands.

2) Whisk together the soy sauce, sesame oil, sugar, vinegar, and red pepper flakes. Pour over the salad and toss again. Let rest 1 hour or up to 1 day to let the pasta absorb the flavors.

Per Serving: Calories 134; Protein 5g; Fat 2g (Saturated 0g); Carbohydrates 24g; Fiber 2g; Sodium 396mg

Chinese Chicken and Noodle Salad

Makes: 6 servings

Leftover roast chicken can be used here, or it can be poached especially for this salad (see page 103 for poaching directions).

8 ounces vermicelli or Chinese noodles
$1/2$ pound cooked and cubed skinless, boneless chicken breast
1 cucumber, peeled, seeded, and grated,or finely julienned
1 carrot, peeled and grated, or finely julienned
One 8-ounce can sliced water chestnuts, drained and rinsed
1 cup fresh mung bean sprouts, washed
3 scallions, sliced, divided
$1/3$ cup Chinese Vinaigrette (page 57)
2 tablespoons unsalted roasted peanuts, chopped

1) Break the vermicelli or noodles into thirds, then cook in a large pot of rapidly boiling water for about 6 minutes, until just done. Drain and immerse in cool water to bring to room temperature. Drain again.

2) Toss together the chicken, cucumber, carrot, water chestnuts, bean sprouts, and all but 2 tablespoons of the scallions in a large bowl. Toss in the vermicelli and combine until the the vegetables and chicken are distributed throughout the noodles.

3) Whisk the dressing just prior to pouring it on the noodles. Toss the dressing into the salad. The salad can be made several hours before serving and kept chilled in the refrigerator.

4) Arrange the salad on a serving platter or bowl and garnish with the reserved scallions and the peanuts.

Per Serving: Calories 281; Protein 19g; Fat 5g (Saturated 1g); Carbohydrates 40g; Fiber 3g; Sodium 499mg

Asian Beef and Noodle Salad

Makes: 3 servings

Deli roast beef is convenient, but a $1/2$ pound of boneless beef top sirloin steak, broiled until done, could also be used.

$1/3$ pound deli roast beef ($1/4$-inch-thick piece)
2 tablespoons fresh lime juice
2 tablespoons soy sauce
1 tablespoon sugar
2 teaspoons Asian sesame oil
1 clove garlic, minced
$1/8$ teaspoon crushed red pepper flakes
3 cups cooked Chinese noodles or spaghetti, rinsed and cooled
2 cups small broccoli florets, steamed until crisp-tender
$1/4$ cup chopped red onions
2 tablespoons chopped fresh cilantro (optional)

1) Cut the deli roast beef into thin strips. Whisk the lime juice, soy sauce, sugar, sesame oil, garlic, and pepper flakes and toss with the beef. Let marinate for 30 minutes, or up to several hours.

2) Arrange the noodles on a serving platter. Top with the broccoli. Take the beef out of the dressing and distribute the meat on the salad, then pour the marinade over the salad. Garnish with the onions and cilantro. Or toss together all the ingredients to serve as a mixed salad.

Per Serving: Calories 322; Protein 19g; Fat 6g (Saturated 1g); Carbohydrates 49g; Fiber 3g; Sodium 1206mg

Rice and Grain Salads

Salads are an excellent way to use leftover rice or other grains. Rice that has sat overnight in the refrigerator dries out slightly and the individual grains separate, perfect for salads. The grains then absorb the salad's dressings while maintaining their texture and shape.

Herbed Rice Salad

Makes: 8 servings

Save this recipe for the summer when fresh herbs and ripe tomatoes are abundant.

3 cups long-grain rice
1 cup cooked corn kernels (fresh or frozen)
1 cup peas, lightly steamed
1 cucumber, peeled, seeded, and diced
1 large ripe tomato, cored and diced, or 8 cherry tomatoes, halved
2 scallions, sliced
1 tablespoon minced fresh parsley
1 tablespoon minced fresh basil
1 tablespoon minced fresh dill
1 tablespoon minced fresh mint
2 tablespoons extra-virgin olive oil or Garlic Oil (page 607)
3 tablespoons lemon juice
1/2 teaspoon kosher salt
1/4 teaspoon freshly ground pepper, or more to taste

1) Toss the rice together with the vegetables and herbs in a large bowl.

2) In a small bowl, whisk together the oil, lemon juice, salt, and pepper. Pour over the salad and toss.

Per Serving: Calories 140; Protein 4g; Fat 4g (Saturated 1g); Carbohydrates 23g; Fiber 3g; Sodium 131mg

Indonesian Rice Salad

Makes: 4 servings

This is a great salad to bring to work because it is a complete meal in a bowl. For a vegetarian version, substitute firm tofu, cubed, for the chicken.

1 1/2 tablespoons fresh lime juice
2 tablespoons chunky peanut butter, unsalted and unsweetened
2 teaspoons soy sauce
1 tablespoon mustard
1 tablespoon honey
1 1/2 tablespoons water
1/4 teaspoon Tabasco sauce
Pinch cayenne pepper
1/2 pound skinless, boneless chicken breast or firm tofu, cut into cubes
1 cup cooked brown rice
2 scallions, sliced
1/2 red bell pepper, chopped
1/2 cup peas
One 8-ounce can pineapple chunks, packed in juice, drained
1/2 cup sliced water chestnuts
2 tablespoons orange juice
1/2 teaspoon soy sauce

1) Puree the lime juice, peanut butter, soy sauce, mustard, honey, water, Tabasco, and cayenne pepper. Reserve 2 tablespoons, and toss the remainder with the chicken or tofu. Marinate the chicken or tofu for at least an hour and up to one day.

2) Cook the chicken or tofu. If using tofu, bake at 425°F, on a baking sheet lined with parchment, for 15 minutes. Shake the pan several times during cooking to loosen the cubes. Then turn over the cubes and bake another 15 minutes, until the cubes get crispy. If using chicken, bake in a similar fashion, but at 350°F and for less time, about 20 minutes altogether.

3) Combine the rice with the scallions, bell pepper, peas, pineapple, and water chestnuts in a large bowl. When the tofu or chicken cools, add that as well.

4) Whisk together the reserved 2 tablespoons of marinade and the orange juice and soy sauce. Pour this dressing over the salad and stir gently to mix well.

Per Serving: Calories 223; Protein 18g; Fat 5g (Saturated 1g); Carbohydrates 27g; Fiber 3g; Sodium 308mg

Wild Rice, Corn, and Broccoli Salad

Makes: 4 servings

If you can't find wild rice, or if it is too pricy for you, use a packaged wild rice blend. Follow the directions on the package for cooking times, but don't add any fat and don't use the spice blend packet.

2 scallions, sliced
2 ribs celery, chopped
1 cup cooked corn kernels (from fresh or frozen)
1 cup cooked wild rice, cooled
2 cups broccoli florets, steamed until tender
1/4 cup chopped fresh parsley
1 1/2 tablespoons extra-virgin olive oil or Garlic Oil (page 607)
2 tablespoons lemon juice
1 teaspoon kosher salt
1/4 teaspoon freshly ground pepper, or more to taste
1 tablespoon chopped fresh basil, or 1 teaspoon dried

1) Toss together the scallions, celery, corn, rice, broccoli, and parsley.

2) In a small bowl, whisk together the oil, lemon juice, salt, pepper, and basil. Pour over the salad and stir to combine.

Per Serving: Calories 218; Protein 10g; Fat 5g (Saturated 1g); Carbohydrates 36g; Fiber 2g; Sodium 764mg

Wild Rice, Smoked Turkey, and Grape Salad

Makes: 4 servings

Turkey roasted at home or honey-baked deli turkey will each yield tasty though different results.

3 scallions, sliced
1 rib celery, chopped
3 cups cooked wild rice or wild rice blend, cooled
1/4 pound smoked turkey breast, cut into small cubes
1 cup seedless grapes
1/4 cup chopped fresh parsley
1 tablespoon extra-virgin olive oil or Garlic Oil (page 607)
2 tablespoons lemon juice
1 teaspoon kosher salt
1/4 teaspoon freshly ground pepper, or more to taste

1) Toss together the scallions, celery, rice, turkey, grapes, and parsley.

2) In a small bowl, whisk together the oil, lemon juice, salt, and pepper. Pour over the salad and stir to combine.

Per Serving: Calories 221; Protein 11g; Fat 5g (Saturated 1g); Carbohydrates 36g; Fiber 2g; Sodium 784mg

Curried Chicken, Fruit, and Rice Salad

Makes: 8 servings

On hot nights, serve this as a main course salad on a bed of greens, with Limeade (page 609) to drink and Chocolate Pudding (page 564) for dessert.

1 apple, cored and cut into cubes
3 teaspoons lemon juice, divided
1/2 cantaloupe or other orange-fleshed melon
3 cups cooked brown or white rice, preferably basmati, cooled
1 cup seedless grapes
2 cups cooked and cubed skinless chicken breast
1/2 cup plain nonfat yogurt
1 tablespoon white wine vinegar
1 tablespoon vegetable oil
1 1/2 teaspoons curry powder
1/2 teaspoon kosher salt
2 tablespoons chutney
1 tablespoon chopped nuts, lightly toasted, for garnish (optional)

1) Coat the cubed apple with 1 teaspoon of the lemon juice to prevent browning.

2) Scoop out the melon's seeds, then make melon balls. (Using a melon baller takes only a few minutes more than cutting the fruit into pieces.)

3) Combine the apple, melon, rice, grapes, and chicken.

4) Whisk or puree together the yogurt, the remaining 2 teaspoons of lemon juice, and the vinegar, oil, curry powder, and salt until the dressing is smooth. Stir in the chutney until it is evenly distributed throughout.

5) Stir the dressing into the rice mixture. Garnish with chopped nuts, if desired.

Per Serving: Calories 176; Protein 12g; Fat 4g (Saturated 1g); Carbohydrates 25g; Fiber 2g; Sodium 169mg

Spanish Rice Salad

Makes: 6 servings

Rice cooked in juice will be sticky, but much more flavorful than rice cooked in water. Also, cooking the rice in tomato juice colors it an appealing red.

1 cup long-grain brown rice
$3/4$ cup tomato juice
$1^1/2$ cups water
1 green bell pepper, chopped
1 red bell pepper, chopped
$1/4$ cup thinly sliced red onions
2 tomatoes, chopped
$1/4$ cup chopped fresh parsley
1 pound cooked chicken breast, cut into bite-size chunks
$1/4$ cup red wine vinegar
$1/4$ cup extra-virgin olive oil
$1/4$ cup tomato juice
$1/4$ teaspoon Tabasco sauce, or more to taste
1 teaspoon dried thyme
$1/4$ teaspoon paprika
1 small clove garlic, minced
$1/4$ teaspoon kosher salt

1) Cook the rice in the tomato juice and water. When done, fluff and let rest, covered, until room temperature. Then place the rice in a bowl and toss with the bell peppers, onions, tomatoes, parsley, and chicken.

2) Whisk together the remaining ingredients.

3) Pour the dressing over the salad. Toss.

Per Serving: Calories 305; Protein 21g; Fat 10g (Saturated 2g); Carbohydrates 32g; Fiber 2g; Sodium 286mg

Toasted Quinoa Salad

Makes: 6 servings

Quinoa is as fine-grained as millet and makes a light-textured grain salad.

$3/4$ cup uncooked quinoa
$1^1/2$ cups water
1 cup diced carrot
$1/2$ red bell pepper, chopped
$1/4$ cup minced fresh parsley
2 scallions, sliced
$1/2$ cup pepitas or sunflower seeds, toasted
$1^1/2$ tablespoons soy sauce
$1/4$ cup lemon juice
$1/4$ teaspoon Tabasco sauce
1 clove garlic, minced

1) Rinse the quinoa in a fine-meshed wire strainer under cool running water. Place the quinoa in a heavy-bottomed pot and dry toast until a few grains begin to pop. Add the water and bring to a boil. Cover, reduce heat, and simmer for 15 minutes, or until the quinoa has absorbed all the liquid. Remove from the heat and let stand for 10 minutes. Fluff with a fork.

2) Mix together the carrot, bell pepper, parsley, scallions, and pepitas in a large bowl. When the quinoa has cooled, add it to the bowl and combine.

3) Whisk together the soy sauce, lemon juice, Tabasco, and garlic. Pour over the other ingredients and toss to mix.

Per Serving: Calories 166; Protein 5g; Fat 8g (Saturated 1g); Carbohydrates 21g; Fiber 3g; Sodium 274mg

Bulgur Wheat Salad

Makes: 6 servings

Bulgur wheat varies in coarseness; the larger the grain, the longer it needs to soak. This salad can be served on a bed of romaine lettuce leaves.

2 cups hot water
1 cup uncooked fine bulgur wheat
$1/3$ cup lemon juice
$1/2$ to 1 teaspoon soy sauce, to taste
$1/8$ teaspoon cayenne pepper (optional)
2 cloves garlic, minced
1 large, ripe tomato, diced
1 cup scallions, minced
3 tablespoons chopped fresh parsley
2 tablespoons minced fresh mint leaves, or
    2 teaspoons dry
2 tablespoons extra-virgin olive oil

1) Pour the hot water over the bulgur wheat and let it rest until the bulgur softens and cools to room temperature. Once softened, drain in a fine mesh strainer to remove excess water.

2) Combine the remaining ingredients, then mix with the bulgur.

Per Serving: Calories 138; Protein 4g; Fat 5g (Saturated 1g); Carbohydrates 22g; Fiber 5g; Sodium 43mg

Bulgur and Feta Salad

Makes: 8 servings

This salad stays fresh for several days. Leftovers make good pita pocket sandwich lunches.

$1^1/2$ cups hot water
$3/4$ cup uncooked fine bulgur wheat
$1/2$ cup minced red onions
2 cucumbers, peeled, seeded, and diced
6 brine-cured olives, pitted and chopped
1 large ripe tomato, diced
1 cup chopped fresh parsley
2 tablespoons chopped fresh mint
3 tablespoons lemon juice
2 tablespoons extra-virgin olive oil
$1/2$ teaspoon kosher salt
$1/4$ teaspoon freshly ground pepper
$1/4$ cup crumbled feta cheese

1) Pour the hot water over the bulgur wheat and let it rest until the bulgur softens and cools to room temperature. Once softened, drain in a fine mesh strainer to remove excess water.

2) Combine the onions, cucumbers, olives, tomatoes, parsley, and mint. Toss with the bulgur. Whisk in the lemon juice, oil, salt, and pepper. Pour it over the salad and toss. Toss in the feta cheese, or serve with the cheese as a garnish on top.

Per Serving: Calories 118; Protein 3g; Fat 5g (Saturated 1g); Carbohydrates 16g; Fiber 4g; Sodium 229mg

About Wheat Berries

Wheat berries are wheat kernels cleaned of their husks but otherwise left whole. Their cooked exteriors are smooth, not starchy, and their interiors are chewy and sweet, so they provide a good texture for grain salads. If unavailable, use barley or other whole grains.

Sunburst Salad

Makes: 5 servings

Hearty enough for a winter lunch, this salad also tastes fresh and light enough for a summer meal.

3 cups cooked wheat berries
1 cucumber, peeled, seeded, and chopped
4 scallions, sliced
2 tablespoons chopped fresh parsley
1/2 cup dried fruit, such as apricots or peaches, soaked in hot water to soften, then sliced
1/2 cup nuts or pumpkin seeds, toasted
1 orange
3 tablespoons lemon juice
1 tablespoon Dijon mustard
2 tablespoons extra-virgin olive oil
1/4 teaspoon ground cinnamon
1 teaspoon chopped fresh mint, or
    1/2 teaspoon dried

1) Combine the wheat berries, cucumber, scallions, parsley, fruit, and nuts. Cut the orange in half and scoop out the segments, as you would a grapefruit. Stir in the orange segments and squeeze in any remaining juice from the halves.

2) Whisk together the lemon juice, mustard, oil, cinnamon, and mint and pour over the salad. Toss to combine.

3) Allow the salad to mellow for at least 1 hour before serving.

Per Serving: Calories 236; Protein 5g; Fat 14g (Saturated 2g); Carbohydrates 29g; Fiber 5g; Sodium 82mg

Wheat Berry and Barley Salad

Makes: 5 servings

In this salad, the textures of chewy grains and crunchy vegetables are well-balanced and the dressing pulls it all together.

1/2 cup uncooked wheat berries
1/2 cup uncooked barley
3 cups water
3 scallions, sliced
1/2 green bell pepper, chopped
1 carrot, peeled and chopped or grated
6 radishes, sliced
1/4 cup chopped fresh parsley
3 tablespoons extra-virgin olive oil
2 tablespoons red wine vinegar
2 tablespoons lemon juice
1/4 teaspoon dried dill, or 1 teaspoon fresh
1/8 teaspoon freshly ground pepper
6 drops Tabasco sauce
1/2 teaspoon soy sauce, or more to taste

1) In a covered pot, simmer the wheat berries and the barley together with the water for 1 hour, until all the water is absorbed and the grains are tender. Fluff with a fork and let cool.

2) Combine the scallions, green pepper, carrot, radishes, and parsley in a bowl with the grains.

3) Whisk together the remaining ingredients, pour over the salad, and mix well.

Per Serving: Calories 224; Protein 5g; Fat 9g (Saturated 1g); Carbohydrates 35g; Fiber 6g; Sodium 51mg

Pita Salad

Makes: 4 servings

If you don't like chopping, you can prepare the mint, parsley, onions, and scallions in a food processor. Chop the cucumber and tomatoes by hand because the bigger and tidier cubes you get with a knife are more appetizing in this salad.

1 pita pocket, preferably whole wheat
4 large romaine lettuce leaves
$1/2$ cup chopped red onions
3 scallions, chopped
1 cucumber, peeled, seeded, and chopped
2 medium tomatoes, cored and chopped
2 tablespoons minced fresh mint
3 tablespoons chopped fresh parsley
1 small clove garlic, minced
$1/4$ cup lemon juice
$1^1/2$ tablespoons extra-virgin olive oil
$1/2$ teaspoon kosher salt
$1/2$ teaspoon freshly ground pepper

1) Toast the pita pocket until crispy. Break it into pieces the size of large croutons.

2) Cut the lettuce leaves into pieces about 2 inches square. It's not necessary to tear the leaves; cutting them with a sharp knife is fine.

3) Combine the pita with the lettuce, onions, scallions, cucumber, tomatoes, mint, parsley, and garlic.

4) Whisk together the remaining ingredients. Pour the dressing over the salad and toss. Serve immediately.

Per Serving: Calories 117; Protein 3g; Fat 6g (Saturated 1g); Carbohydrates 16g; Fiber 3g; Sodium 313mg

Bean Salads

I've taught people how to make my Black Bean and Corn Salad in several communities at cooking classes and have heard that it shows up later at their potluck suppers (it even turned up at a library potluck in my own town!). This pleases but doesn't surprise me. The ingredients are readily available, the salad is easy to prepare, it can be made a day ahead of time, and it travels well—the very reasons why I love bean salads.

Because bean salads are often dense and filling, the portion size is smaller than for other salads. I like to fill the plate by serving a bean salad with a selection of other salads, such as a slaw and a pasta salad. In the summer, a plate of homemade salads is my ideal meal. In August, I am not likely to cook up a pot of beans from scratch; it would heat up the kitchen, so I use canned beans, rinsed very well.

Many-Bean Salad

Makes: 6 servings

Any combination of beans works here. Have fun varying the colors, textures, and flavors. If starting with dried beans, cook them separately, since different varieties of beans cook for different times.

1 cup cooked pinto beans, drained and rinsed
1 cup cooked chickpeas, drained and rinsed
1 cup cooked white beans, drained and rinsed
2 cups green beans, trimmed, cut into 1-inch pieces, and steamed
1/2 cup thinly sliced red onions
2 scallions, sliced
2 tablespoons minced fresh parsley
1 small clove garlic, minced
1/4 cup red wine vinegar
2 tablespoons extra-virgin olive oil
1 teaspoon sugar
1/2 teaspoon kosher salt
1/4 teaspoon freshly ground pepper

1) In a large bowl, combine all the beans with the onions, scallions, and parsley.

2) In a separate bowl, whisk together the remaining ingredients. Pour over the salad, and toss to coat.

Per Serving: Calories 190; Protein 8g; Fat 6g (Saturated 1g); Carbohydrates 29g; Fiber 8g; Sodium 167mg

All-Season Black Bean Salad

Makes: 6 servings

There are many opportunities to make this salad because the ingredients are available year-round and the flavors suit summer picnics as well as winter dinners.

3 cups cooked black beans, drained and rinsed
1 red bell pepper, chopped
1/2 green bell pepper, chopped
1/4 cup chopped red onions
2 scallions, sliced (use all the green tops if they're crisp)
1 rib celery, chopped
1 orange
1 1/2 tablespoons orange juice
1 1/2 tablespoons lemon juice
1 teaspoon extra-virgin olive oil
1/4 teaspoon Tabasco sauce
1/4 teaspoon kosher salt
1/2 teaspoon ground cumin
1/4 teaspoon ground coriander

1) In a large bowl, combine the beans, bell peppers, onions, scallions, and celery.

2) Cut the orange in half and scoop out the segments as you would a grapefruit. Place the segments into the bowl with the beans.

3) Squeeze the juice from the orange halves into a small bowl. Remove the seeds, if any. Whisk in the remaining ingredients. Pour over the salad and toss.

Per Serving: Calories 144; Protein 8g; Fat 1g (Saturated 0g); Carbohydrates 26g; Fiber 9g; Sodium 89mg

Black Bean and Corn Salad

Makes: 5 servings

The colors of black, yellow, red, and green are beautiful, the textures of the beans balanced by the crisp vegetables, and the spicy dressing holds it all together. This is the salad that I've taught in many cooking classes, and has now appeared in many homes and at numerous potluck dinners.

1 1/2 cups cooked black beans, drained and rinsed
2 cups cooked corn kernels
1 red bell pepper, fresh or roasted, chopped
3 scallions, sliced
2 tablespoons minced fresh parsley or cilantro
2 tablespoons diced canned mild green chilies
1 tablespoon olive oil
2 tablespoons red wine vinegar
1 1/2 tablespoons lemon juice
1/4 teaspoon kosher salt
1/8 teaspoon crushed red pepper flakes
1/2 teaspoon ground coriander
1/2 teaspoon ground cumin

1) In a large bowl, combine the beans, corn, bell pepper, scallions, parsley, and chilies.

2) Whisk together the remaining ingredients in a small bowl and stir the dressing into the salad.

Per Serving: Calories 175; Protein 7g; Fat 4g (Saturated 1g); Carbohydrates 32g; Fiber 7g; Sodium 132mg

Black Bean and Yellow Rice Salad

Makes: 8 servings

The yellow rice combined with the colorful vegetables gives this salad a festive look.

2 cups water
1 teaspoon ground turmeric
1 teaspoon kosher salt, divided
1 clove garlic, crushed
1 cup white rice
2 cups cooked black beans, drained and rinsed
1 roasted red bell pepper, diced
4 scallions, sliced
1/2 green bell pepper, diced
8 cherry tomatoes, halved
2 tablespoons chopped fresh parsley
1 tablespoon chopped fresh cilantro (optional)
3 tablespoons fresh lime juice
1 tablespoon lemon juice
1 1/2 tablespoons extra-virgin olive oil
1/8 teaspoon Tabasco sauce
1/4 teaspoon ground cumin
1/4 teaspoon freshly ground pepper

1) Bring the water, turmeric, 1/2 teaspoon of the salt, and the garlic to a boil. Reduce to a simmer, add the rice, cover, and cook for 15 minutes. Fluff with a fork, remove the garlic, and let stand, uncovered, until it reaches room temperature.

2) Combine the beans, roasted pepper, scallions, bell pepper, tomatoes, and herbs in a bowl. Stir in the cooled rice.

3) Whisk together the lime and lemon juices, oil, Tabasco, cumin, ground pepper, and remaining 1/2 teaspoon of salt. Pour over the salad and toss to coat.

Per Serving: Calories 177; Protein 6g; Fat 3g (Saturated 0g); Carbohydrates 32g; Fiber 5g; Sodium 247mg

Chickpea, Broccoli, and Pasta Salad

Makes: 6 servings

This hearty salad is easy to make, travels well, and stays fresh for days—all the reasons to make it early in the week and rely on it for brown-bag lunches or time-crunched dinners.

2 cups cooked corkscrew-shaped pasta
1¹/2 cups cooked chickpeas, drained and rinsed
2 cups small broccoli florets, steamed until
  crisp-tender
¹/4 cup diced red onions
¹/4 cup chopped fresh parsley
6 cherry tomatoes, halved
2 tablespoons red wine vinegar
2 teaspoons balsamic vinegar
1 teaspoon Dijon mustard
2 tablespoons extra-virgin olive oil
1 teaspoon dried marjoram
¹/2 teaspoon kosher salt, or more to taste
¹/4 teaspoon freshly ground pepper, or more
  to taste

1) Toss together the pasta, chickpeas, broccoli, red onions, parsley, and cherry tomatoes.

2) In a small bowl, whisk together the remaining ingredients and pour over the salad. Toss to coat. Taste and adjust the salt and pepper. Serve at room temperature.

Per Serving: Calories 189; Protein 7g; Fat 6g (Saturated 1g); Carbohydrates 28g; Fiber 3g; Sodium 192mg

Chickpea and Roasted Red Pepper Salad

Makes: 4 servings

Both the chickpeas and the roasted peppers can come from cans, so there is little preparation for this salad. Serve it as a side salad at dinner, or as one part of a meal made up of a selection of salads and spreads, such as Hummus (page 30) and Pita Salad (page 98).

2 cups cooked chickpeas, drained and rinsed well
1 roasted red pepper, chopped (¹/2 cup)
2 tablespoons chopped fresh parsley
2 tablespoons chopped red onions
1¹/2 teaspoons extra-virgin olive oil or Garlic Oil
  (page 607)
2 tablespoons lemon juice
1 teaspoon red wine vinegar
¹/8 teaspoon freshly ground pepper
¹/4 teaspoon kosher salt
¹/2 teaspoon ground coriander
¹/8 teaspoon Tabasco sauce

1) Stir together the chickpeas, red pepper, parsley, and onions.

2) Whisk together the remaining ingredients. Pour the dressing over the chickpeas. Stir to coat.

Per Serving: Calories 160; Protein 8g; Fat 4g (Saturated 0g); Carbohydrates 25g; Fiber 5g; Sodium 128mg

Red Lentil Salad

Makes: 6 servings

Red lentils (which are actually orange in color) are sold in many gourmet and ethnic markets. They are sweeter and milder in flavor and cook more quickly than brown lentils. Select red lentils the size of split peas. Very tiny red lentils are also available, but they turn to mush when cooked.

1 cup red lentils

3 cups water

3 scallions, sliced

2 cucumbers, peeled, cut lengthwise into 4 strips, then sliced

2 tablespoons extra-virgin olive oil

4 teaspoons red wine vinegar

1 tablespoon balsamic vinegar

1/2 teaspoon kosher salt

1/4 teaspoon freshly ground pepper

1/8 teaspoon Tabasco sauce, or more to taste

1) Rinse the lentils and check for stones. Bring the water to a boil and add the lentils. Reduce the heat and simmer for about 4 minutes. Keep an eye on the pot and test the lentils frequently; if allowed to cook for too long they turn to mush; too little and they will be hard. Don't worry about the that foam rises to the surface.

2) As soon as the lentils soften, pour them into a fine mesh strainer and rinse very gently with cold water until they cool. This step keeps them from becoming a sticky mass.

3) Combine the lentils, scallions, and cucumbers. In a small bowl, whisk together the remaining ingredients. Pour the dressing over the salad and toss.

Per Serving: Calories 166; Protein 10g; Fat 5g (Saturated 1g); Carbohydrates 23g; Fiber 5g; Sodium 167mg

White Bean and Tuna Salad

Makes: 4 servings

Serve this with crusty bread and a tossed green salad, or pack it (with some crackers) for a brown-bag lunch.

1 1/2 cups cooked cannellini or white navy beans, drained and rinsed

One 6-ounce can water-packed tuna (preferably albacore), drained

1/3 cup chopped red onions

1 rib celery, chopped

1 tablespoon chopped fresh basil

1/4 cup chopped fresh parsley

1/2 teaspoon kosher salt

1/4 teaspoon freshly ground pepper

2 tablespoons lemon juice

1 1/2 teaspoons extra-virgin olive oil

Red onion, for garnish (optional)

Sprigs of parsley, for garnish (optional)

1) Gently toss together the beans, tuna, onions, celery, basil, and parsley.

2) In a small bowl, whisk together the remaining ingredients, pour over the beans, and stir to combine. If desired, garnish with circles of red onion and parsley sprigs.

Per Serving: Calories 134; Protein 13g; Fat 3g (Saturated 0g); Carbohydrates 13g; Fiber 4g; Sodium 552mg

Poultry and Fish Salads

Poached Chicken for Salads

Makes: 1 pound cooked chicken, or about 3 1/2 to 4 cups

You can use leftover baked chicken for chicken salads, but by far the plumpest and juiciest chicken for chicken salads is poached chicken. Here is a recipe for one pound, though it can be adapted to any amount. Note that a recipe for poached turkey breast appears on page 431.

1 pound skinless, boneless chicken breast
1 1/4 cup water
1/4 cup white wine
2 bay leaves

1) Use a heavy pot with a tight-fitting lid in which the chicken can comfortably fit without crowding. Bring the water, wine, and bay leaves to a boil. Reduce to a simmer and add the chicken. The chicken should be covered with liquid by at least 1 inch. If not, add more water. Check the liquid after 2 minutes. A gentle simmer is desired, not a rolling boil or a still surface.

2) Cover the pan and simmer for 7 minutes. Turn the meat over, and simmer for another 10 minutes. If cooking a lot of chicken in one pan, or if the chicken has bones, cook for an additional 10 minutes. Then turn off the heat and let the chicken rest in the hot liquid for 20 minutes.

Per 1/4-pound Serving: Calories 125; Protein 26g; Fat 1g (Saturated 0g); Carbohydrates 0g; Fiber 0g; Sodium 74mg

Chicken and Artichoke Heart Salad

Makes: 6 servings

This is an excellent salad for a luncheon because it can be made the day before, yet still look fresh and extravagant plated on a bed of greens the day of the party.

1/2 pound cooked and cubed skinless, boneless chicken breast (about 2 cups)
One 8-ounce can artichoke hearts, packed in water (6 artichokes)
1/2 red bell pepper, julienned
1 rib celery, thinly sliced on the diagonal
1/4 cup thinly sliced red onions
1 cup cooked long-grain brown rice
1 tablespoon dried tarragon
1/2 cup Red Wine Vinaigrette (page 56)

1) Gently stir together the chicken, artichoke hearts, bell pepper, celery, onions, rice, and tarragon.

2) Pour on the dressing. Toss to coat. Refrigerate for several hours to allow the rice and chicken to absorb some of the dressing.

Per Serving: Calories 162; Protein 14g; Fat 6g (Saturated 1g); Carbohydrates 12g; Fiber 3g; Sodium 151mg

Curried Chicken Salad

Makes: 8 servings

Since no two curry powders are exactly alike, you might want to put half the curry into the dressing, taste it, and then decide how much more to mix in.

4 cups cooked and cubed skinless chicken breast
1 green bell pepper, chopped
$1/2$ cup diced celery
$2/3$ cup thinly sliced red onions
$1/2$ cup raisins
2 apples
2 teaspoons lemon juice
1 cup 1% lowfat cottage cheese
$3/4$ cup plain lowfat yogurt
$1/2$ teaspoon ground turmeric
1 to 2 tablespoons curry powder
$1/8$ teaspoon cayenne pepper (optional)
1 teaspoon sugar

1) Toss the chicken with the bell pepper, celery, onions, and raisins.

2) Cut the apples into cored wedges, then halve. Toss with the lemon juice to prevent browning. Add the apples to the chicken mixture.

3) In a food processor, puree the remaining ingredients until the dressing is smooth and thick.

4) Pour the dressing over the salad and toss to coat.

Per Serving: Calories 178; Protein 22g; Fat 2g (Saturated 1g); Carbohydrates 19g; Fiber 2g; Sodium 186mg

Turkey Salad

Makes: 6 servings

A recipe for poaching turkey breast appears on page 431.

4 cups cooked and cubed turkey breast, from the deli or home-cooked (about 1 pound)
3 scallions, sliced
2 ribs celery, chopped
2 tablespoons chopped fresh parsley
$1/2$ cup reduced-fat mayonnaise
$1/2$ cup plain nonfat yogurt (drain liquid off before measuring)
2 teaspoons lemon juice
1 teaspoon celery seed
$1/2$ teaspoon kosher salt
$1/4$ teaspoon freshly ground pepper

1) Toss together the turkey, scallions, celery, and parsley.

2) In a separate bowl, whisk together the remaining ingredients. Pour the dressing over the salad and stir to combine.

Per Serving: Calories 235; Protein 29g; Fat 10g (Saturated 2g); Carbohydrates 4g; Fiber 0g; Sodium 399mg

Turkey, Walnut, and Grape Salad

Makes: 7 servings

Adding grapes and nuts stretches the meat portion as well as turning this into a sophisticated main-course salad.

1 recipe Turkey Salad (opposite)
1 cup seedless grapes
1/3 cup toasted walnut pieces

Toss the grapes and walnuts in with the prepared Turkey Salad.

Per Serving: Calories 234; Protein 26g; Fat 13g (Saturated 3g); Carbohydrates 9g; Fiber 1g; Sodium 343mg

Tuna Salad with Capers and Artichoke Hearts

Makes: 4 servings

This is the sort of salad found at upscale gourmet shops, but it is not much trouble to prepare and is much more economical when made at home.

6 plum tomatoes, cut into large pieces
One 6-ounce can water-packed tuna, drained
1 rib celery, chopped
3 scallions, sliced
4 fresh or canned artichoke hearts, quartered
2 tablespoons drained capers
1 tablespoon minced fresh parsley
1 1/2 teaspoons extra-virgin olive oil or Garlic Oil (page 607)
1 tablespoon lemon juice
1 tablespoon red wine vinegar
1 teaspoon balsamic vinegar
1/4 teaspoon kosher salt
1/4 teaspoon freshly ground pepper

1) Stir together the tomatoes, tuna, celery, scallions, artichokes, capers, and parsley.

2) In a small bowl, whisk together the remaining ingredients. Pour the dressing over the salad. Stir to combine.

Per Serving: Calories 99; Protein 11g; Fat 2g (Saturated 0g); Carbohydrates 10g; Fiber 4g; Sodium 440mg

Blissful Tuna Salad

Makes: 6 servings

Potatoes, green beans, and tuna take to any number of dressings, which is why the vinaigrette choice is left to you.

2/3 pound red bliss potatoes, cut into
    1/2-inch cubes
1/2 pound green beans, trimmed and halved
1/2 cup thinly sliced red onions
2 tablespoons chopped fresh parsley
1 tomato, cut into wedges and then each
    wedge halved
One 6-ounce can water-packed tuna, drained
1/2 cup lowfat vinaigrette of choice

1) Steam the potatoes until tender, immerse in cold water, and drain. Steam the green beans, immerse in cold water, drain, and toss in with the potatoes. Stir in the onions, parsley, tomatoes, and tuna.

2) Pour the dressing over the salad and toss. Allow to rest at least 1 hour before serving to allow the potatoes to absorb some of the dressing.

Per Serving: Calories 128; Protein 8g; Fat 4g (Saturated 1g); Carbohydrates 15g; Fiber 3g; Sodium 322mg

Snow Pea and Shrimp Salad

Makes: 5 servings

This salad can make even the most inexperienced cook look like a seasoned pro. The combination of fresh ginger and lime juice is bright and intriguing, and the shrimp and snow peas give it a showy extravagance. All, however, is easy to put together and requires no special skills in the kitchen.

3 to 4 cups snow or snap peas, trimmed and
    strings removed if necessary
One 8-ounce can sliced water chestnuts, rinsed
    and drained
3 scallions, sliced
1 red bell pepper, julienned
14 to 16 ounces cooked small or medium
    shrimp, shelled
1 tablespoon Asian sesame oil
2 tablespoons rice or white wine vinegar
1 tablespoon soy sauce
3 tablespoons sherry
1 teaspoon finely grated fresh ginger
1 teaspoon fresh lime juice

1) Steam the snow peas a brief minute or two until they turn bright green. Immediately immerse in a bowl of cool water. Drain and pat dry.

2) Stir together the snow peas, water chestnuts, scallions, bell pepper, and shrimp.

3) Put the sesame oil, vinegar, soy sauce, sherry, and ginger into a small saucepan. Bring to a boil, then remove from the heat and let it come to room temperature. Stir in the lime juice. Pour the dressing over the salad and toss.

Per Serving: Calories 175; Protein 20g; Fat 4g (Saturated 1g); Carbohydrates 13g; Fiber 4g; Sodium 393mg

Ocean and Grape Salad

Makes: 4 servings

This salad looks lovely plated on a bed of leafy lettuce. Garnish each plate with two wedges of lemon so that each person can squeeze juice from the lemon wedges onto the salad.

1 pound white-fleshed fish (such as pollock or scrod)
1/2 cup lowfat sour cream
1/4 cup plain nonfat yogurt
1 tablespoon lemon juice
2 teaspoons sherry
1/2 teaspoon kosher salt
1/8 teaspoon freshly ground pepper
1 tablespoon fresh minced dill
1 1/2 cups seedless grapes

1) Poach the fish according to the directions on page 241. Allow the fish to cool in the poaching liquid. Remove the fish from the poaching liquid and break it into bite-size flakes.

2) In a medium bowl, whisk together the sour cream, yogurt, lemon juice, sherry, salt, pepper, and dill. Add the grapes and fish. Gently stir until all is coated with dressing.

Per Serving: Calories 195; Protein 24g; Fat 3g (Saturated 2g); Carbohydrates 16g; Fiber 0g; Sodium 381mg

Salmon Salad

Makes: 6 servings

Fresh salmon is a necessity for this elegant salad. Leftover salmon from the previous night's dinner is fine. Or you can poach the fish just for this recipe (page 241). For a pretty presentation, place the salad on lettuce leaves and top with shredded carrots.

1 pound salmon, cooked
1 tablespoon drained capers
1/2 teaspoon green peppercorns, lightly crushed
2 scallions, sliced
1 cup peas, lightly cooked
1 tablespoon minced fresh dill
1 tablespoon olive oil
2 tablespoons lemon juice
1 1/2 teaspoons white wine vinegar
1/4 teaspoon kosher salt

1) Break the salmon into large, bite-size flakes.

2) Gently combine the fish with the capers, peppercorns, scallions, peas, and dill.

3) In a small bowl, whisk together the remaining ingredients. Pour over the salmon and toss.

Per Serving: Calories 156; Protein 21g; Fat 6g (Saturated 1g); Carbohydrates 4g; Fiber 1g; Sodium 200mg

Soups

Broths
110

Vegetable Broth

Beef Broth

Chicken Broth

Chilled Soups
113

Chilled Cherry Soup

Strawberry Soup

Melon-Berry Swirl

Watermelon Soup

Gazpacho

Tropical Gazpacho

Corn Gazpacho

Cucumber Yogurt Soup

Garlic and Dill Tomato Soup

Chilled Carrot Soup

Borscht

Pureed Soups
119

Cauliflower Soup

Curried Tomato Soup

Carrot-Tomato-Orange Soup

Gingery Almond Carrot Soup

Curried Squash Soup

Gingery Pumpkin Soup

Pumpkin-Peanut-Apple Soup

Root Vegetable Soup

Potato Leek Soup

Leek and Corn Soup

Corn Chowder

Indian-Style Coconut Soup

Egg Drop Soup

Vegetable, Pasta and Grain Soups
126

Roasted Garlic Vegetable Soup

Minestrone

North African Vegetable Soup

Salad Bar Pesto Soup

Italian Vegetable Noodle Soup

Busy Day Tortellini Soup

Quick Vermicelli Soup

Vegetable Rice Soup

Barley Vegetable Soup

Mushroom Barley Soup

Quinoa Vegetable Soup

Bread Soup

Tortilla Soup

Tortilla Soup with Crab

Tortilla Soup with Chicken

Bean Soups
133

Lentil Soup

Ginger Lentil Soup

Spinach and Lentil Soup

*Lentil and Rice Soup
with Sausage*

Black Bean Soup

*Brazilian Black Bean and
Pumpkin Soup*

Split Pea Soup

*Split Pea and Smoked Turkey
Soup*

Two-Pea Soup

Housewarming Soup

*Smoked Turkey, Bean, and
Tomato Soup*

Pasta e Fagioli Soup

Broccoli, Bean, and Pasta Soup

Fish Soups
142

*Manhattan-Style
Fish Chowder*

Fish and Vegetable Soup

Italian Fish and Rice Soup

Chicken Soups
144

No-Bones Chicken Soup

Lemon Chicken Soup

Spanish Chicken Noodle Soup

Velvet Corn Soup

Chinese Chicken Noodle Soup

Mandarin Soup

Matzo Ball Soup

Chicken Corn Soup

Caribbean Corn Soup

Chicken Noodle Soup

It is hard to go wrong making soups. Soup recipes are usually very forgiving; you can add a little more of this and that until it is right. If a soup doesn't taste perfect, try adding salt. Often only a teaspoon more will make a substantial difference. Additional pepper can also brighten up a soup. On the other hand, if a soup tastes too spicy, add some cooked rice or leftover baked potato and a touch more broth. As with all recipes, start with the very best ingredients. Although wilted vegetables are often fine, don't use up vegetables that are starting to turn because bad ingredients will still taste off even after they are cooked.

Many soups freeze well, especially those with beans and rice. I like to freeze soups in single-serving containers that I use later for lunches. However, some ingredients, such as potatoes and fish, turn mealy when defrosted. For soups with such ingredients, freeze the base, then add the potatoes or fish after the soup has been defrosted.

For vegetarians, soup can become the main course, especially a hearty soup filled with beans and grains. Recipes that call for chicken broth can be cooked with vegetable broth instead. Even for nonvegetarians, having soup as a first or main course is a good idea. Soups can be as satisfying as a filled dinner plate, but with far fewer calories. Also, for those who have a hard time eating enough vegetables, soups are a way to sneak more into the diet.

Broths

Broth (also called stock) is a complexly flavored liquid that adds depth and character to recipes and is often the base for soups. Think of broth as a savory tea. Just as you steep water with a tea bag and then discard the bag, so do you infuse water with flavor from the broth's ingredients, then strain out the solids. Defatted broth is very low in calories and almost fat-free. It is easy to defat broths: when chilled, the fat rises and solidifies on the surface, where it is easily removed.

Making broth at home takes time and planning, but the results can be frozen and used for many months. I make broth several times each winter (when I don't mind having a simmering pot on my stove for hours), then use it

year-round. Broth can also be found in the supermarket. There are several excellent brands of reduced-sodium chicken broths available. (Purchase those without MSG and sugar.) But I've yet to find canned vegetable or beef broths that meet my standards. Commercial vegetable broths are often too sweet (even the ones sold at natural food stores) and beef broths tend to be too salty and taste like additives. I also avoid bouillon cubes because of their salty, unnatural flavors.

Vegetable Broth

Makes: 12 cups

Vegetable broth can be frozen, but because of its delicate flavors, it will be best if used within 4 months.

3 ribs celery, with leaves
1 leek
1 summer squash
3 carrots
3 cloves garlic, unpeeled, crushed
1 bunch parsley
2 yellow onions, unpeeled, quartered
4 peppercorns
2 bay leaves
1/2 teaspoon kosher salt
1/4 teaspoon dried thyme
3 quarts water

1) Wash all the vegetables well, especially the leek. Cut the celery, leek, squash, and carrots into chunks about 2 inches long.

2) Put all the ingredients in a big pot with water. Bring to a boil, then reduce to a simmer. Skim off and discard any sediment that foams to the surface.

3) Cover and cook for 40 minutes.

4) Discard the vegetables. Strain the stock through a fine sieve or cheesecloth.

Per Cup: Calories 128; Protein 1g; Fat 0g (Saturated 0g); Carbohydrates 1g; Fiber 0g; Sodium 87mg

Beef Broth

Makes: 16 cups

Many markets sell bones for stock or broth making. They are cut into 4-inch pieces and trimmed of most meat, but filled with marrow.

5 pounds beef bones for broth
1 Spanish onion, peeled and quartered
3 large carrots, peeled and cut into 2-inch lengths
3 ribs celery, preferably with leaves, cut into
    2-inch lengths
4 cloves garlic
1 1/2 gallons cool water
1 bunch fresh parsley, washed well
2 teaspoons kosher salt
8 peppercorns
2 bay leaves

1) Preheat the oven to 425°F. Put the bones in a roasting pan and place in the middle of the oven for 15 minutes, turning them frequently. Stir in the onion, carrots, celery, and garlic. Continue to roast for another 30 minutes, so that the bones and vegetables brown.

2) Using a slotted spoon, lift the bones and vegetables out of the beef fat and transfer to a stockpot. Pour in the water.

3) Bring to a gentle simmer. Skim off the brown foam that rises to the surface. Once the broth simmers clear, add the parsley, salt, peppercorns, and bay leaves. Continue to simmer for 3 to 5 hours. Strain out all solids and refrigerate until the fat solidifies on the surface. Remove the fat. The broth will freeze very well for up to 6 months or longer.

Per Cup: Calories 12; Protein 2g; Fat 0g (Saturated 0g); Carbohydrates 1g; Fiber 0g; Sodium 251mg

Chicken Broth

Makes: 16 cups

The best broth is made from a fowl, which is an older bird, very flavorful but too tough for much else. If you can't find a fowl use a whole roaster, but don't waste the good meat. After about 40 minutes of simmering, remove the meat from the bones and save it for another use. Put the bones back into the pot, where they will continue to add flavor to the broth. I've also made broth from bones I've saved after boning chicken breasts. Whenever I bone a chicken breast, I save the bones in the freezer and when I have at least 3 pounds, I make broth.

6 quarts water
One 3- to 4-pound fowl
3 cloves garlic, crushed
1 large Spanish onion, halved, peeled, and cut into big slices
1 small bunch parsley
1 rib celery, cut into 2-inch pieces
2 carrots, scrubbed and cut into 2-inch pieces
3 bay leaves
8 peppercorns
1 teaspoon kosher salt

1) Put the water and fowl in a big stockpot and bring to a boil. Reduce to a simmer. Skim off the brownish foam that rises to the surface.

2) Add the remaining ingredients. Simmer gently, uncovered, for 2 hours.

3) Let it rest until cool enough to handle safely (big pots are awkward, and you want to avoid splashing hot broth on yourself). With a slotted spoon, remove and discard the bones and vegetables. Then pour the broth through a fine wire mesh strainer, preferably lined with cheesecloth.

4) Chill the broth in the refrigerator for 1 day until the fat rises to the surface and solidifies. Skim off and discard the fat, then store the broth in the freezer. I put it in 2- and 4-cup containers. You can store broth in the refrigerator, but chicken broth is a magnet for bacteria and should not be kept for more than 2 days, and even then should be brought to a rolling boil before use. If you are in a rush to use the broth as soon as it is made and want to avoid the fat, use a turkey baster to suck up the broth from under the fat floating on the surface.

Per Cup: Calories 12; Protein 2g; Fat 0g (Saturated 0g); Carbohydrates 1g; Fiber 0g; Sodium 131mg

Chilled Soups

Chilled soups can be the most refreshing element of a summer menu. I like clear, distinctive flavors and pretty colors. Some chilled soups are also excellent when served hot; it's nice to have that flexibility in designing a menu. If a summer storm comes in and you are faced with a dinner party on an unexpectedly cold night, a warm soup is just the thing. I've indicated in the recipes which ones can serve double duty.

When making chilled soups, bear in mind that a recipe will taste different after it is refrigerated; for example, cold foods taste less sweet. So taste as you cook and sample again just prior to serving. Adjust the seasonings as necessary.

Chilled Cherry Soup

Makes: 4 servings

As a child I would eat fresh cherries until I thought I would burst. I still tend to overindulge, but now have other ways to consume one of my favorite fruits.

2 pounds sour cherries, pitted, or three
    14 ^{1}/$_2$-ounce cans unsweetened pitted sour
    cherries, drained
2 cups water
^{1}/$_2$ cup sugar
1 teaspoon lemon juice
1 cinnamon stick
^{1}/$_4$ cup quick tapioca
^{1}/$_4$ cup lowfat sour cream

1) Put the cherries, water, sugar, lemon juice, and cinnamon stick in a saucepan. Bring to a simmer, cover, and cook for 10 minutes. Remove the cinnamon stick. Taste and adjust the sugar.

2) Stir in the tapioca. Continue to cook over low heat until thickened. Puree or put though a food mill. Chill.

3) Put a dollop of sour cream in each serving.

Per Serving: Calories 260; Protein 3g; Fat 2g (Saturated 1g); Carbohydrates 63g; Fiber 3g; Sodium 26mg

Strawberry Soup

Makes: 4 servings

Because this soup is not cooked, it is important to use the best wine you have. Strawberry soup is a good way to use up the last of a bottle of fine dessert wine, or an excuse to buy one.

1 quart strawberries, washed and hulled
^{1}/$_4$ cup frozen orange juice concentrate, thawed
^{1}/$_3$ cup white wine, preferably a sweet dessert wine
^{1}/$_2$ cup lowfat sour cream
1 teaspoon sugar, or more to taste
^{1}/$_8$ teaspoon kosher salt
^{1}/$_4$ teaspoon freshly ground pepper
6 fresh mint leaves, finely sliced

1) Set 4 of the berries aside for garnish. Puree the remaining berries and the orange juice concentrate and wine until smooth. Add the sour cream, sugar, salt, and pepper. Puree until combined. Chill.

2) Taste and adjust the sugar. Slice the 4 berries. Serve garnished with the sliced berries and mint.

Per Serving: Calories 141; Protein 2g; Fat 3g (Saturated 2g); Carbohydrates 24g; Fiber 2g; Sodium 94mg

Melon-Berry Swirl

Makes: 4 servings

The dramatic two-colored presentation of this soup makes Melon-Berry Swirl an impressive start of a summer dinner party—and only the cook has to know how easy it was to prepare. Note that a 4-pound melon yields about 3 pounds of usable fruit.

2 pounds melon meat
1 teaspoon frozen apple juice concentrate, thawed, or sugar
$1/4$ teaspoon ground cinnamon
$1/8$ teaspoon ground cloves
4 teaspoons lemon juice, divided
3 tablespoons minced fresh mint
2 cups raspberries or strawberries
$1/3$ cup plain nonfat yogurt
Fresh mint leaves, for garnish

1) Puree the melon, apple juice concentrate, cinnamon, cloves, 2 teaspoons of the lemon juice, and the mint. Chill.

2) Puree the remaining 2 teaspoons of lemon juice, the berries, and yogurt. Chill separately from the melon puree.

3) Just prior to serving, pour the melon mixture into soup bowls, filling them no more than two-thirds of the way.

4) Pour the berry puree into the center of the soup bowls.

5) Create a swirling pattern by mixing the two purees using one circular motion with a spoon. Garnish with the mint leaves.

Per Serving: Calories 127; Protein 3g; Fat 1g (Saturated 0g); Carbohydrates 31g; Fiber 4g; Sodium 41mg

Watermelon Soup

Makes: 4 servings

Even though there is no way my family can eat it all, I can't resist buying a whole huge watermelon in the summer, so I've had to come up with creative ways to use up all of that fruit. This soup is one way I fit it into our menu.

6 cups watermelon (about 4 to 6 pounds)
1 orange
$1/4$ cup chopped fresh mint
3 tablespoons fresh lime juice
1 tablespoon Grand Marnier or other orange-flavored liqueur
$1/4$ teaspoon ground ginger
$1/4$ teaspoon ground allspice
$1/8$ teaspoon ground cinnamon

1) Seed the watermelon, then cut the flesh into chunks.

2) Peel the orange with a sharp knife to remove the skin and the white pith underneath. Cut the orange in half along its equator. Remove the seeds. Add the orange segments to the soup.

3) Puree all the ingredients together, then chill before serving.

Per Serving: Calories 112; Protein 2g; Fat 1g (Saturated 0g); Carbohydrates 24g; Fiber 2g; Sodium 8mg

Gazpacho

Makes: 7 servings

I used to make this soup when I was a cook at a small Harvard Square cafe. The highest compliment I received was from a customer who would order two bowls at a time. He said it was so good, he knew he'd want the second.

1 quart tomato juice
1 lemon, juiced
2 limes, juiced
2 tablespoons red wine vinegar
1 teaspoon frozen apple juice concentrate, thawed
3 ripe tomatoes, cored and diced
1/2 cup minced red onions
1 green bell pepper, minced
1 tablespoon dried basil
2 teaspoons dried tarragon
1/3 cup minced fresh parsley
2 tablespoons minced fresh chives
1/2 teaspoon paprika
1/8 teaspoon Tabasco sauce
2 teaspoons soy sauce
One 14 1/2-ounce can whole tomatoes, or 3 very
    ripe fresh tomatoes
2 cucumbers, peeled, seeded, and diced, divided
1 clove garlic

1) In a large bowl, combine all the ingredients except the whole tomatoes (canned or fresh), one of the cucumbers, and the garlic.

2) Pour the juice from the canned tomatoes into the bowl. Remove the seeds from the canned tomatoes by rinsing them under gently running water. Canned tomatoes are so soft that they don't need chopping; as you add them to the bowl of other ingredients, squeeze them so that they break into pieces.

3) Puree the second cucumber with the garlic. Add this to the soup. (It contributes body.)

4) Chill and then season to taste.

Per Serving: Calories 77; Protein 3g; Fat 1g (Saturated 0g); Carbohydrates 18g; Fiber 3g; Sodium 704mg

Tropical Gazpacho

Makes: 8 servings

This twist to gazpacho is made with tropical fruits and lime juice. Although the ingredients list is lengthy, there is little chopping. Once you try this, you may find yourself making it several times each summer.

1 quart tomato juice
One 20-ounce can crushed pineapple packed in its own juice
1/2 cantaloupe, peeled, seeded, and cut into large chunks
1 cucumber, peeled and seeded
1 green bell pepper, trimmed
1 papaya, peeled and seeded
1/4 cup fresh lime juice
1/4 cup lemon juice
2 teaspoons kosher salt
1/4 teaspoon freshly ground pepper
1/8 teaspoon Tabasco sauce
1 tablespoon minced fresh parsley or cilantro
1 1/2 teaspoons minced fresh mint

1) Puree the tomato juice, pineapple (including the juice from the can), and cantaloupe.

2) Dice the cucumber, green pepper, and papaya.

3) Put the puree, diced vegetables, and papaya in a large bowl. Stir in the remaining ingredients.

4) Let the soup rest for 1 hour, preferably in the refrigerator, before serving. You can serve this soup the next day, but the flavor will not hold more than 2 days.

Per Serving: Calories 102; Protein 2g; Fat 0g (Saturated 0g); Carbohydrates 26g; Fiber 2g; Sodium 927mg

Corn Gazpacho

Makes: 6 servings

Make this summertime soup when there is an abundance of sweet corn and fresh herbs. Leftovers still taste good the second day.

3 medium cucumbers, peeled and seeded, divided
3 cups corn kernels, cooked, divided
2 cups reduced-sodium, defatted chicken broth
1 cup plain nonfat yogurt
1 cup lowfat sour cream
1/2 red bell pepper, diced
2 tablespoons chopped fresh basil
1 tablespoon chopped fresh dill
2 teaspoons kosher salt
1 teaspoon freshly ground pepper

1) Cut 2 of the cucumbers into chunks. Place these pieces in a blender or food processor along with 2 cups of the corn kernels and all of the broth. Puree until smooth. If desired, put through a food mill to filter out the coarse bits of corn.

2) Finely chop the third cucumber. Stir this and the remaining ingredients into the soup. Chill, taste, and adjust the salt and pepper before serving.

Per Serving: Calories 187; Protein 9g; Fat 4g (Saturated 2g); Carbohydrates 34g; Fiber 4g; Sodium 889mg

Cucumber Yogurt Soup

Makes: 4 servings

Taste the cucumbers before you make this soup. Large yellowed cucumbers will make the soup bitter. But shiny green, firm, small cucumbers will make a refreshing soup with clear flavors.

4 cucumbers, peeled and seeded, divided
1 clove garlic
1/4 cup water
3 cups plain nonfat yogurt
1 1/2 tablespoons minced fresh dill
1 1/2 teaspoons minced fresh mint, plus additional
    for garnish
1/8 teaspoon kosher salt
1/8 teaspoon freshly ground pepper
3 scallions, minced, or 2 tablespoons fresh chives,
    plus additional for garnish

1) Cut 3 of the cucumbers into large chunks. With the food processor or blender running, drop in the garlic and mince. Add the chunks of cucumber. Pour in the water and puree.

2) Pour the soup into a large bowl. Whisk in the yogurt, dill, mint, salt, and pepper.

3) Finely dice the remaining cucumber. Stir it into the soup. Stir in the scallions. Chill. Serve garnished with more of the fresh mint and scallions.

Per Serving: Calories 146; Protein 13g; Fat 1g (Saturated 0g); Carbohydrates 23g; Fiber 2g; Sodium 209mg

Garlic and Dill Tomato Soup

Makes: 6 servings

This soup can be served hot or chilled. Garnish with nonfat yogurt and sliced scallions, or with sprigs of fresh dill.

1 1/2 cups minced onions
3 large cloves garlic, minced
2 tablespoons olive oil
6 cups drained canned tomatoes, coarsely chopped
2 cups liquid from the canned tomatoes or
    tomato juice
1 tablespoon frozen apple juice concentrate, thawed
1/4 teaspoon kosher salt
1/4 teaspoon freshly ground pepper
1 tablespoon minced fresh dill, or
    1 teaspoon dried

1) Over low heat, sauté the onions and garlic in the oil until the onions become translucent and slightly brown at the edges.

2) Put all the ingredients into a soup pot and simmer for 30 minutes.

Per Serving: Calories 124; Protein 3g; Fat 5g (Saturated 1g); Carbohydrates 19g; Fiber 3g; Sodium 767mg

Chilled Carrot Soup

Makes: 3 servings

Both fresh and crystallized ginger are used here. The zing of the two gingers is balanced by the sweetness of the maple syrup and the sour of the lemon juice. The end result is a sprightly soup that is the perfect start to a summer dinner.

1 tablespoon vegetable oil
4 shallots, minced
1 pound carrots, peeled and thinly sliced
  (about 3 cups)
1 tablespoon finely grated fresh ginger
$2^1/4$ cups water, divided
1 tablespoon maple syrup or honey
$1/2$ teaspoon kosher salt
$1/4$ teaspoon freshly ground pepper
2 tablespoons lemon juice
2 tablespoons minced crystallized ginger

1) Heat the oil in the bottom of $1^1/2$- to 2-quart pot. Cook the shallots over low heat, covered, until golden. Stir in the carrots, fresh ginger, and 2 tablespoons of the water. Keep the pot covered and cook slowly, for about 10 minutes, until softened and lightly golden. Slow cooking will develop the flavor.

2) Pour in the remaining water. Bring to a boil, then immediately reduce to a gentle simmer. Cover and cook for 30 minutes. Let rest until cool enough to handle.

3) Puree the contents of the pot. Stir in the maple syrup, salt, pepper, and lemon juice. Chill. Serve with some crystallized ginger on top of each portion.

Per Serving: Calories 173; Protein 2g; Fat 5g (Saturated 0g); Carbohydrates 33g; Fiber 4g; Sodium 382mg

Borscht

Makes: 6 servings

Wear rubber gloves when peeling beets to keep your hands from turning purple. Grating beets is easy with a food processor. If fresh beets are not available (or if the idea of working with fresh beets is too daunting), canned shoestring beets, no sugar added, can be substituted.

1 large all-purpose potato, peeled and cubed
$1^1/2$ pounds beets, peeled and grated
1 cup chopped onions
6 cups water
2 bay leaves
4 peppercorns
2 tomatoes, peeled and chopped
1 tablespoon tomato paste
2 tablespoons lemon juice
1 teaspoon apple cider vinegar
2 tablespoons honey
2 teaspoons kosher salt
Plain nonfat yogurt

1) Bring the potato, beets, onions, and water to a boil. Add the bay leaves and peppercorns. Simmer, covered, for 45 minutes.

2) Add the remaining ingredients except the yogurt and simmer for another 30 minutes. Serve hot or chilled, and top each bowl with a dollop of yogurt.

Per Serving: Calories 436; Protein 3g; Fat 0g (Saturated 0g); Carbohydrates 25g; Fiber 4g; Sodium 720mg

Pureed Soups

I know people who avoid pureed soups because their appearance reminds them of baby food. This is a shame, because smooth soups can be sophisticated, complex, and filling. And since you don't have to worry about chopping the vegetables into pretty pieces, they are easy to make. Full-fat recipes use cream to achieve smoothness and flavor. These healthier versions keep the rich texture, but use lowfat dairy and other ingredients, such as rice, for body, and a balance of ingredients for flavor. Pureed soups are improved by garnishes that add contrasting color (such as a fresh sprig of green dill on a red tomato soup), or some texture, such as croutons floated on top.

Blenders are better than food processors for pureeing. They hold more, leak less, and puree very smoothly. Do take care, however, to let the soup cool before pureeing in a blender. If you try to puree hot liquids in a blender the top will explode off (spoken from the personal experience of this impatient cook). Hand blenders will let you puree the soup right in the pot. Food mills also puree foods, as well as separate out all that is coarse. These tools take a little hand-cranking, but the results are velvety.

Cauliflower Soup

Makes: 5 servings

Athough caulifower's cousin broccoli wins all the "most popular" awards, cauliflower should win the "miss congeniality" title. Its flavor mellows nicely with dairy products and it becomes attractively rosy-colored with the addition of other vegetables. Here the carrot sweetens the cauliflower and lends an orange glow and the sour cream enriches and thickens the soup.

1 head cauliflower (about 1 1/2 pounds)
1 carrot, diced
1 tablespoon olive oil
1 cup chopped leeks or onions
1 rib celery, chopped
2 cloves garlic, minced
4 cups reduced-sodium, defatted chicken broth, divided
1 teaspoon kosher salt
1/4 cup 1% lowfat milk
1/4 cup lowfat sour cream

1) Trim and discard the leaves and tough stem ends of the cauliflower. Cut enough florets to fill 2 cups. Set these aside. Chop the rest of the cauliflower, stems, and florets. Steam the chopped cauliflower until very soft, about 10 minutes. Remove to a bowl. Using the same pot, steam the 2 cups of florets and the carrots until tender. Set aside.

2) In a heavy-bottomed soup pot, heat the oil and sauté the leeks, celery, and garlic until golden. Puree this sauté with the chopped cauliflower and 2 cups of the broth. Return the puree to the pot.

3) Stir in the remaining broth and the salt. Bring to a simmer and cook until hot, but no bubbles reach the surface. Stir in the milk, sour cream, and reserved steamed carrots and cauliflower florets.

Per Serving: Calories 94; Protein 5g; Fat 4g (Saturated 1g); Carbohydrates 11g; Fiber 2g; Sodium 819mg

Curried Tomato Soup

Makes: 6 servings

This soup can also be served chilled.

2 teaspoons olive oil
1 cup chopped onions
2 cloves garlic, peeled and crushed
$1/4$ cup raw white rice, preferably basmati
1 teaspoon kosher salt
1 teaspoon curry powder
$1/2$ teaspoon ground coriander
$1/2$ teaspoon ground cumin
Two 28-ounce cans whole tomatoes, with juice
4 cups reduced-sodium, defatted chicken broth
1 tablespoon chopped fresh cilantro (optional)

1) Heat the oil in a soup pot. Sauté the onions and garlic until the onions soften and turn golden. Stir in the rice and seasonings. Cook for 1 minute until the aromas intensify.

2) Pour the juice from the tomatoes into the pot. Remove and discard the seeds from the tomatoes. Chop the pulp and put it into the pot.

3) Stir in the broth and bring to a boil. Reduce to a simmer, cover, and cook for 30 minutes. Uncover, remove from the heat, and let cool until the soup can be handled.

4) Puree. Return the soup to the pot and heat through. Add the cilantro, if desired.

Per Serving: Calories 121; Protein 5g; Fat 2g (Saturated 0g); Carbohydrates 21g; Fiber 3g; Sodium 1073mg

Carrot-Tomato-Orange Soup

Makes: 5 servings

The complex flavors of this soup are deceptive, since it is very easy to make. Basmati rice will lend even more intrigue to the flavor because it adds a sweet, slightly exotic aroma to the soup.

1 tablespoon olive oil
1 cup chopped onions
4 large carrots, grated (about 2 cups)
$1/4$ cup raw white rice, preferably basmati
4 cups reduced-sodium, defatted chicken broth
One $14^1/2$-ounce can whole tomatoes, with juice
1 orange
$1/2$ teaspoon kosher salt
2 tablespoons chopped fresh mint, for garnish (optional)

1) Heat the oil in a soup pot. Sauté the onions and carrots until they soften and turn golden, about 10 minutes. Keep the pot covered between stirrings. Stir in the rice, broth, and tomatoes. Bring to a simmer and cook, covered, for 30 minutes. Let rest until cool enough to handle.

2) Using a vegetable peeler, peel a long strip of zest off of the orange (avoid the white pith beneath the surface). Mince and measure 1 tablespoon of the zest. Juice the orange and reserve $1/2$ cup for the soup.

3) Puree the cooled soup. Return the soup to the pot, add the zest, juice, and salt and heat through. Garnish with the mint, if desired.

Per Serving: Calories 382; Protein 5g; Fat 3g (Saturated 0g); Carbohydrates 22g; Fiber 3g; Sodium 723mg

Gingery Almond Carrot Soup

Makes: 6 servings

Ginger, curry, and carrots have a natural affinity for each other. Here they are thickened and enriched with finely ground almonds.

$1^1/2$ pounds carrots, peeled and shredded
1 cup white wine
3 cups water
1 tablespoon lemon juice
$1/2$ cup chopped onions
1 clove garlic, minced
1 teaspoon grated fresh ginger
2 tablespoons almonds or almond pieces
1 teaspoon vegetable oil
$1/4$ teaspoon curry powder
$1^1/2$ teaspoons kosher salt
$1/4$ teaspoon freshly ground pepper
3 tablespoons sliced almonds, lightly toasted, for garnish (optional)

1) Simmer the carrots, wine, water, and lemon juice until the carrots are tender, about 15 minutes. Allow to cool until safe to puree.

2) Meanwhile, sauté the onions, garlic, ginger, and almonds in the oil until the onions soften and the garlic turns golden. Take care not to scorch the ginger. Stir in the spices.

3) Put the sautéed mixture into a blender. Add a cup of the liquid from the cooked carrots and puree. Add the remaining carrot mixture and puree until blended and smooth.

4) Serve hot or chilled. Garnish with the sliced almonds, if desired.

Per Serving: Calories 107; Protein 2g; Fat 3g (Saturated 0g); Carbohydrates 14g; Fiber 4g; Sodium 526mg

Curried Squash Soup

Makes: 6 servings

Serve this soup with bowls of raisins, sliced apples, and yogurt on the side so that each person can garnish it according to personal preference.

1 large butternut squash (about $2^1/2$ to 3 pounds), peeled, seeded, and cut into large chunks
1 medium all-purpose potato, peeled and cubed
1 tart apple, peeled, cored, and quartered
1 leek, washed well and chopped
2 cloves garlic, peeled and crushed
1 teaspoon grated fresh ginger
1 tablespoon vegetable oil
$1/4$ teaspoon ground cardamom
1 teaspoon ground coriander
$1/4$ teaspoon ground turmeric
2 teaspoons curry powder
2 teaspoons soy sauce
$1/16$ to $1/8$ teaspoon cayenne pepper

1) Put the squash, potato, and apple into a pot, add enough water to cover by 1 inch, and bring to a boil. Reduce to a simmer, uncover, and cook until the squash is tender, about 20 minutes.

2) In a small sauté pan, sauté the leek, garlic, and ginger in the oil.

3) Stir the sautéed vegetables and the spices into the pot. Remove from the heat and cool until safe to handle, then puree and return it to the pot.

4) Simmer for 10 minutes. Taste and adjust the seasonings.

Per Serving: Calories 121; Protein 2g; Fat 3g (Saturated 0g); Carbohydrates 25g; Fiber 5g; Sodium 125mg

Gingery Pumpkin Soup

Makes: 4 servings

The sad truth is that pumpkin recipes are usually reserved for the fall season. I love pumpkin pie but I never make it in the summer, and the same is true for this soup. Although it is made with canned pumpkin and other ingredients found year-round, it fits an autumn menu.

2 teaspoons vegetable oil
2 shallots, minced (2 tablespoons)
1/2 cup chopped onions
1 1/2 teaspoons grated fresh ginger
2 cups canned pumpkin puree
1 cup orange juice
2 cups reduced-sodium, defatted chicken broth
1 teaspoon kosher salt
1 teaspoon minced orange zest
1/2 teaspoon freshly ground pepper
1/16 teaspoon ground cloves
2 tablespoons minced fresh parsley (optional)
1/4 cup toasted pumpkin seeds (optional)

1) Heat the oil in a soup pot over low heat. Sauté the shallots, onions, and ginger in the oil until the onions are soft and golden. Be careful not to scorch the ginger.

2) Add the pumpkin, orange juice, broth, salt, zest, pepper, and cloves. Simmer for 10 minutes over medium heat.

3) Garnish with parsley and pumpkin seeds, if desired.

Per Serving: Calories 117; Protein 4g; Fat 3g (Saturated 0g); Carbohydrates 21g; Fiber 4g; Sodium 731mg

Pumpkin-Peanut-Apple Soup

Makes: 5 servings

A garnish of chopped roasted peanuts is a nice final touch. My husband loves peanuts, and his garnish is usually more like a handful.

1 teaspoon vegetable oil
1 1/2 cups chopped onions
2 Granny Smith apples
1 to 2 tablespoons curry powder, to taste
1/4 teaspoon ground cardamom
4 cups reduced-sodium, defatted chicken broth, divided
One 15-ounce can pumpkin
1/4 cup unsalted, unsweetened peanut butter
1/4 teaspoon Tabasco sauce
1 1/2 teaspoons kosher salt

1) Heat the oil in a heavy-bottomed, preferably nonstick, saucepan. Sauté the onions over moderate heat until they begin to soften and change color, about 5 minutes. Cover between stirrings.

2) Meanwhile, core, peel, and coarsely grate the apples. Stir the grated apples in with the onions and sauté for 3 minutes more, until the apples wilt. Stir in the curry and cardamom and cook another minute.

3) Add 2 cups of the broth and the pumpkin, peanut butter, Tabasco, and salt. Stir until there are no lumps. Simmer for 15 minutes. Remove from the heat and pour in the remaining 2 cups of broth. Allow the soup to cool.

4) Puree the soup, then return it to the pot. Heat through and adjust the seasonings. Thin with water if desired.

Per Serving: Calories 180; Protein 7g; Fat 8g (Saturated 1g); Carbohydrates 23g; Fiber 5g; Sodium 969mg

Root Vegetable Soup

Makes: 8 servings

It is ironic how rutabagas and parsnips—vegetables associated with the hard life of peasants—can make such a sophisticated soup. If you haven't yet tried cooking these maligned vegetables, this soup is a good place to start.

2 teaspoons olive oil
1 rib celery, chopped
1 leek, washed well and chopped (about 1 cup)
3 cloves garlic, minced
3 parsnips, peeled and sliced (about $^1/_2$ pound)
2 carrots, peeled and sliced
1 rutabaga, peeled and cut into large chunks
8 cups reduced-sodium, defatted chicken broth
2 teaspoons kosher salt
1 teaspoon light brown sugar
$^1/_4$ teaspoon freshly ground pepper
2 tablespoons chopped fresh parsley

1) Heat the oil in a large, heavy-bottomed pot. Add the celery, leek, and garlic and sauté until the leek turns golden, about 7 minutes. Cover between stirrings to keep the vegetables moist.

2) Add the parsnips, carrots, rutabaga, broth, and salt. Bring to a boil, then reduce to a simmer. Cover and cook for 40 minutes, or until the vegetables are very soft.

3) Cool until safe to handle. Puree.

4) Return the soup to the pot, and add the sugar, pepper, and parsley. Heat through.

Per Serving: Calories 89; Protein 4g; Fat 1g (Saturated 0g); Carbohydrates 15g; Fiber 3g; Sodium 986mg

Potato Leek Soup

Makes: 7 servings

Serve hot or chilled.

3 cups chopped leeks, including the light green tops, washed well and chopped
4 cups peeled, shredded all-purpose potatoes
6 cups reduced-sodium, defatted chicken broth
1 teaspoon kosher salt
1 tablespoon minced fresh chives
1 tablespoon chopped fresh parsley
Freshly ground pepper to taste
$^1/_2$ cup plain lowfat yogurt or fromage blanc

1) Simmer the leeks, potatoes, broth, and salt in a pot for 30 minutes. Add the chives and parsley. Cook for 10 minutes more. Puree if a totally smooth soup is desired.

2) Season to taste. Chill or serve immediately, stirring in the yogurt or fromage blanc just prior to ladling out the soup.

Per Serving: Calories 123; Protein 6g; Fat 0g (Saturated 0g); Carbohydrates 24g; Fiber 3g; Sodium 712mg

Leek and Corn Soup

Makes: 6 servings

The red bell peppers make this soup a pretty salmon color.

1 tablespoon olive oil
2 cloves garlic, minced
1 large leek, washed well and chopped
1 red bell pepper, chopped
2 bay leaves
6 cups corn kernels (preferably fresh or frozen shoepeg), divided
4 cups reduced-sodium, defatted chicken broth
1 teaspoon kosher salt
$1/8$ teaspoon freshly ground pepper
Pinch cayenne pepper
1 teaspoon dried basil
$1/4$ teaspoon dried thyme
1 cup 1% lowfat milk
1 tablespoon minced fresh parsley

1) Heat the oil in a soup pot. Sauté the garlic and leek until the leek softens and turns golden.

2) Stir in the bell pepper, bay leaves, 5 cups of the corn (set 1 cup aside for later), the broth, salt, both peppers, basil, and thyme. Bring to a boil, reduce to a simmer, cover, and cook for 20 minutes. Uncover, remove from the heat, and let cool until the soup can be safely handled.

3) Discard the bay leaves and puree.

4) Return the soup to the pot, add the milk, parsley, and reserved corn and heat gently.

Per Serving: Calories 201; Protein 9g; Fat 5g (Saturated 1g); Carbohydrates 36g; Fiber 5g; Sodium 689mg

Corn Chowder

Makes: 4 servings

There isn't any milk in this creamy corn chowder. Use fresh or frozen shoepeg corn for the best results.

1 teaspoon unsalted butter
$1/2$ cup chopped onions
1 yellow bell pepper, diced
One 1-pound package frozen corn, or 3 cups fresh corn kernels
3 cups reduced-sodium, defatted chicken broth
1 medium potato, peeled and diced
$1/2$ teaspoon kosher salt
$1/4$ teaspoon freshly ground pepper
2 slices bacon, cooked crisp, then chopped
1 tablespoon chopped fresh chives or scallions

1) Heat the butter in a small nonstick sauté pan. Cook the onions in the butter until they turn golden. Stir in the bell pepper and cook over low heat for 5 minutes, until the diced pepper softens.

2) Put the sauté into a soup pot. Add the corn, broth, potato, salt, and pepper. Simmer, covered, until the potato is tender, about 20 minutes. Let rest until cool enough to handle, then puree half.

3) Put the pureed soup back into the pot, stir in the bacon, and gently simmer for 10 minutes. Stir in the chives.

Per Serving: Calories 204; Protein 8g; Fat 4g (Saturated 1g); Carbohydrates 35g; Fiber 5g; Sodium 719mg

Indian-Style Coconut Soup

Makes: 7 servings

Many gourmet stores and some supermarkets sell unsweetened lowfat coconut milk. The cauliflower added to this soup must be cooked because raw cauliflower gives the broth a strong cabbage flavor. Leftover steamed or roasted cauliflower can be used.

1 tablespoon vegetable oil
1 cup chopped onions
2 cloves garlic, minced
2 bay leaves
2 teaspoons kosher salt
1 teaspoon curry powder, or more to taste
1 teaspoon dried basil
1/2 teaspoon dried thyme
3 cups reduced-sodium, defatted chicken broth
One 1-pound package frozen corn (preferably shoepeg), thawed
1 cup unsweetened lowfat coconut milk
1 tablespoon fresh lime juice
2 cups cooked cauliflower florets
2 cups frozen peas, thawed
2 tablespoons chopped fresh cilantro

1) Heat the oil in a heavy-bottomed soup pot. Sauté the onions and garlic over moderate heat until softened and golden, about 7 minutes. Meanwhile, measure out the bay leaves, salt, curry powder, basil, and thyme in a small bowl. Add them to the sauté and cook until the aromas intensify, about 1 minute.

2) Pour the broth into the pot and bring to a boil. Immediately reduce to a simmer and add the corn. Simmer for 15 minutes. Discard the bay leaves. Let the soup sit until it is cool enough to handle. Puree and return the soup to the pot.

3) Stir the coconut milk and add it to the soup along with the lime juice, cauliflower, peas, and cilantro.

4) Bring the soup almost to a boil, then reduce the temperature and gently simmer for 5 minutes.

Per Serving: Calories 160; Protein 6g; Fat 5g (Saturated 1g); Carbohydrates 24g; Fiber 5g; Sodium 856mg

Egg Drop Soup

Makes: 5 servings

My children love this soup, and I love the fact that on a night of sparse leftovers all of the necessary ingredients are on hand to make it, so that I can fill out the menu and make everyone happy.

1 egg
2 egg whites
6 cups reduced-sodium, defatted chicken broth
1 tablespoon soy sauce
1 tablespoon oyster sauce
1 tablespoon sherry
1/2 teaspoon kosher salt
3 tablespoons cornstarch mixed with 1/4 cup water
2 scallions, chopped, for garnish

1) Put the egg and egg whites into a small bowl and set aside.

2) Bring the broth to a boil. Reduce to a simmer and add the soy sauce, oyster sauce, sherry, and salt. Slowly add the cornstarch paste until the soup thickens and clears.

3) Lightly beat the eggs until broken up but not bubbly. Remove the soup from the heat and immediately pour in the eggs in a slow and steady stream, stirring constantly. Garnish with the scallions and serve right away.

Per Serving: Calories 73; Protein 7g; Fat 1g (Saturated 0g); Carbohydrates 7g; Fiber 0g; Sodium 1202mg

Vegetable, Pasta, and Grain Soups

Roasted Garlic Vegetable Soup

Makes: 6 servings

Kale is a strongly flavored dark leafy green that, even when simmered at length, retains much of its texture. Spinach can be substituted but it will disintegrate if cooked too long, so add it during the last 5 minutes of cooking.

1 head Roasted Garlic (page 603)
5 cups reduced-sodium, defatted chicken broth, divided
1 1/2 teaspoons olive oil
1 cup chopped onions
1 small zucchini, chopped
2 ribs celery, with leaves, chopped
2 carrots, peeled and chopped
1/2 pound kale, deribbed and chopped
2 cups corn kernels
2 tablespoons chopped fresh parsley
1 teaspoon dried oregano
1 teaspoon kosher salt
1/4 teaspoon freshly ground pepper
Croutons and Parmesan cheese, for garnish (optional)

1) Squeeze the roasted garlic out of its skin and put the cloves in the blender along with 1 cup of the broth. Puree into a thin, smooth paste.

2) Heat the oil in a large soup pot. Cook the onions, zucchini, celery, and carrots in the oil. Keep the pot covered; the vegetables will sweat out liquid and become lightly browned over low heat. Stir occasionally.

3) Pour the remaining 4 cups of broth and the garlic puree into the soup pot. Add the remaining ingredients. Simmer, covered, for 15 minutes. Add more salt to taste if you wish.

4) If desired, serve with croutons and grated Parmesan cheese over each serving.

Per Serving: Calories 126; Protein 7g; Fat 2g (Saturated 0g); Carbohydrates 23g; Fiber 4g; Sodium 767mg

Minestrone

Makes: 6 servings

Minestrone tastes even better the second day and will still be good a few days after that. If it thickens up (as bean soups tend to do), it can be thinned with tomato juice.

2 tablespoons olive oil
1 cup chopped onions
2 ribs celery, chopped
2 cloves garlic, minced
One 28-ounce can whole tomatoes, with juice
1/2 cup chopped green cabbage
1 carrot, chopped
1 zucchini, chopped
2 tablespoons chopped fresh parsley
2 cups water or reduced-sodium, defatted chicken broth
4 cups tomato juice
2/3 cup cooked chickpeas (or any other leftover bean or pasta)
1 bay leaf
1 tablespoon dried basil
1 teaspoon dried oregano
1/2 teaspoon dried thyme
Freshly ground pepper to taste

1) Heat the oil in a large, heavy-bottomed pot. Add the onions and celery. Cover and cook on low heat for 15 minutes. If more cooking liquid is needed, add some juice from the canned tomatoes. Stir occasionally.

2) Add the garlic and cook for 5 minutes more.

3) Crush the tomatoes with your hands as you add them and the juice from the can to the sautéed vegetables.

4) Add the remaining ingredients and simmer, uncovered, for 45 minutes.

Per Serving: Calories 152; Protein 5g; Fat 6g (Saturated 1g); Carbohydrates 24g; Fiber 4g; Sodium 826mg

North African Vegetable Soup

Makes: 5 servings

Like minestrone, this soup is filled with vegetables and chickpeas, but there are no tomatoes and the spices originate from another culture.

6 cups reduced-sodium, defatted chicken broth
3 cloves garlic, minced
1 cup chopped leeks or onions
1 rib celery, chopped
1 small sweet potato, peeled and cubed (about 1^1/2 cups)
1 small zucchini, diced (about 1 cup)
1 large carrot, diced
One 16-ounce can chickpeas, drained and rinsed (2 cups)
1 cinnamon stick
^{1}/2 teaspoon ground cumin
^{1}/8 teaspoon ground cloves
^{1}/2 teaspoon chili powder
1 teaspoon kosher salt, or more to taste
2 tablespoons lemon juice
^{1}/4 cup chopped fresh mint, or 1^1/2 tablespoons dried
^{1}/4 cup chopped fresh parsley

1) Bring the broth to a simmer. Add all the ingredients except the salt, lemon juice, mint and parsley. Cover and simmer for 30 minutes.

2) Add the remaining ingredients and simmer for 10 minutes longer. Remove the cinnamon stick.

Per Serving: Calories 127; Protein 8g; Fat 2g (Saturated 0g); Carbohydrates 21g; Fiber 6g; Sodium 1120mg

Salad Bar Pesto Soup

Makes: 5 servings

This is a very fast soup to make since all of the vegetables can come from a salad bar and there is no sautéing—you just simmer it all together. If you can't get to a salad bar, pull peas, corn, and green beans out of the freezer.

6 cups reduced-sodium, defatted chicken broth (three 16-ounce cans)
2 cups mixed cut-up raw vegetables (try broccoli, cauliflower, carrots, or others)
1^1/2 cups chopped tomatoes, or one 15-ounce can diced tomatoes
1 cup cooked chickpeas, drained and rinsed
^{1}/4 cup Basil Pesto (page 589 or store-bought)
^{1}/4 teaspoon freshly ground pepper
About ^{1}/2 cup angel hair pasta
1 tablespoon grated Parmesan cheese (optional)

1) Bring the broth to a simmer. If necessary, cut the vegetables into pieces that can fit in a soup spoon. Add the mixed vegetables and stir in the tomatoes. Cover and simmer for about 10 minutes, until the vegetables soften.

2) Stir in the chickpeas, pesto, and pepper. Simmer 5 minutes. Break up the pasta and add it to the soup. Cook 5 minutes more, uncovered. Dust each serving with Parmesan, if desired.

Per Serving: Calories 178; Protein 10g; Fat 5g (Saturated 1g); Carbohydrates 24g; Fiber 3g; Sodium 619mg

Italian Vegetable Noodle Soup

Makes: 5 servings

Italian frying peppers are mild-tasting long, light green peppers. If unavailable, use half a green bell pepper.

1 tablespoon olive oil
1 cup chopped onions
3 cloves garlic, chopped
1 Italian frying pepper, chopped
1/2 cup vermicelli, broken into 1- inch pieces
6 cups reduced-sodium, defatted chicken broth
One 28-ounce can whole tomatoes, drained and chopped
2 small zucchinis, diced
1 carrot, diced
1 teaspoon kosher salt
1/2 teaspoon freshly ground pepper
1 teaspoon dried basil
2 tablespoons chopped fresh parsley

1) Heat the oil in large (3-quart) soup pot. Sauté the onions, garlic, and frying pepper over medium heat until the onions turn golden, about 10 minutes. Keep the pot covered between stirrings. Add the vermicelli and cook over high heat until slightly brown, about 2 to 3 minutes.

2) Stir in the remaining ingredients except the parsley. Bring to a boil, immediately reduce to a simmer, cover, and cook 15 minutes. Stir in the parsley and serve.

Per Serving: Calories 144; Protein 8g; Fat 3g (Saturated 0g); Carbohydrates 22g; Fiber 3g; Sodium 1155mg

Busy Day Tortellini Soup

Makes: 6 servings

Start to finish, this soup is ready to eat in less than 20 minutes and can be the centerpiece of a light meal.

6 cups reduced-sodium, defatted chicken broth
One 10- to 14-ounce package frozen cheese or chicken tortellini
1/3 cup chopped scallions (about 4 scallions)
1 carrot, diced (about 1/2 cup)
1 teaspoon dried basil
1/2 teaspoon kosher salt, or to taste
1/4 teaspoon freshly ground pepper
1 cup chopped fresh spinach or escarole
1 cup frozen peas

1) Bring the broth to a simmer. Stir in the tortellini, scallions, carrot, basil, salt, and pepper. Simmer, covered, for 7 minutes.

2) Stir in the remaining ingredients. Cook until the tortellini is tender, about 5 minutes more.

Per Serving: Calories 176; Protein 11g; Fat 2g (Saturated 1g); Carbohydrates 27g; Fiber 3g; Sodium 757mg

Quick Vermicelli Soup

Makes: 4 servings

Cooking the vermicelli in oil over high heat transforms plain white pasta into something dark and nutty. The other ingredients stay as they are, but simmered together these simple basics turn into an interesting and delicious soup.

1 tablespoon olive oil
1/2 cup chopped onions
2 cloves garlic, minced
1/2 cup vermicelli, broken into 1- to 2-inch pieces
1/2 pound frozen carrots and peas
One 14 1/2-ounce can whole tomatoes, drained, seeded, and chopped
4 cups reduced-sodium, defatted chicken broth
1 teaspoon dried basil
1 teaspoon kosher salt
1/4 teaspoon freshly ground pepper
1 tablespoon canned diced mild green chilies
1 tablespoon chopped fresh parsley

1) Heat the oil in a heavy-bottomed soup pot. Add the onions and garlic. Cook over medium to high heat for 3 minutes. Stir in the vermicelli. Stir continually and cook until the pasta turns light brown.

2) Add the remaining ingredients, bring to a boil, reduce to a simmer, and cook for 15 minutes.

Per Serving: Calories 155; Protein 8g; Fat 4g (Saturated 1g); Carbohydrates 23g; Fiber 4g; Sodium 1137mg

Vegetable Rice Soup

Makes: 6 servings

Vegetable Rice Soup is one of those comforting, calming recipes that nurtures as it nourishes. It freezes well, so put some aside in one-serving containers, so that you won't be caught without a steaming hot bowl of it on a cold day.

8 cups reduced-sodium, defatted chicken or beef broth, divided
1/4 teaspoon saffron threads, or 1/8 teaspoon ground saffron
1/3 cup uncooked medium-grain rice, preferably Arborio
1 cup diced carrots
1 cup green beans, trimmed and cut into 1/2-inch lengths (can use frozen beans)
2 cups chopped white-ribbed Swiss chard or spinach
1 1/2 cups diced tomatoes (drained, if canned)
1/8 teaspoon crushed red pepper flakes
1 teaspoon dried basil
2 tablespoons chopped fresh parsley
1 teaspoon kosher salt, or to taste

1) Bring 1/4 cup of the broth to a boil (you can do this quickly in the microwave). Stir in the saffron and let rest until the broth turns orange, about 15 minutes.

2) Pour the remaining broth into a soup pot and bring to a boil, then reduce to a simmer. Strain the saffron broth through a fine mesh sieve over the soup pot. Press against the saffron solids to extract as much flavor as possible. Add the remaining ingredients and cook, covered, until the rice is tender, about 20 to 30 minutes.

Per Serving: Calories 93; Protein 6g; Fat 0g (Saturated 0g); Carbohydrates 16g; Fiber 2g; Sodium 1001mg

Barley Vegetable Soup

Makes: 6 servings

Soups made with barley thicken to the consistency of stew by the second day. Thin with broth if desired. This soup freezes well.

1 1/2 teaspoons olive oil

2 cloves garlic, minced

1/2 cup chopped leeks or onions

1 rib celery, chopped

1 carrot, peeled and chopped

1/2 cup barley

6 cups reduced-sodium, defatted chicken broth

1 cup sliced mushrooms, preferably a dark variety such as cremini

1/2 cup green beans, trimmed and cut into 1-inch pieces

1 1/2 teaspoons kosher salt

1/2 teaspoon freshly ground pepper

1/2 teaspoon dried sage

1) Heat the oil in a soup pot over low heat. Sauté the garlic, leeks, and celery in the oil. Keep the pot covered. (While watching the pot and occasionally stirring it, this is a good time to chop the other vegetables.) Cook until the leeks are soft and golden.

2) Add the remaining ingredients. Bring the soup to a boil. Reduce to a gentle simmer and cook, covered, for 1 hour.

Per Serving: Calories 108; Protein 5g; Fat 1g (Saturated 0g); Carbohydrates 18g; Fiber 3g; Sodium 975mg

Mushroom Barley Soup

Makes: 7 servings

It is amazing how so few ingredients can become something so richly satisfying. This is a recipe for when the wind is howling and snow or freezing rain is rattling the house. It takes a while to cook, which on bad-weather days is a plus—your windows will steam up and the soup's wonderful aroma will fill the kitchen. You will feel warmed even before you sit down to the table.

1 1/2 cups sherry, divided

3 large cloves garlic, minced

3/4 cup chopped onions

1 pound mushrooms, sliced (about 4 cups)

8 cups reduced-sodium, defatted chicken broth

2/3 cup barley

3 tablespoons soy sauce

1/4 cup chopped fresh parsley

Freshly ground pepper to taste

1) Heat a heavy-bottomed soup pot, add a thin layer of sherry, and cook the garlic and onions over low heat, until the onions soften. Continue to add sherry as needed until the onions become translucent. Cover the pan between stirrings.

2) Add the mushrooms and remaining sherry. Cover and cook until the mushrooms are wilted and soft. Stir once or twice.

3) Pour in the broth and add the remaining ingredients. Simmer, covered, for 1 1/2 hours. This soup freezes well.

Per Serving: Calories 154; Protein 8g; Fat 1g (Saturated 0g); Carbohydrates 22g; Fiber 4g; Sodium 1000mg

Quinoa Vegetable Soup

Makes: 4 servings

If quinoa is not available, pasta or rice can be sub-
stituted Add these precooked and reduce the water
by 1 cup.

1 clove garlic, minced
1 carrot, diced
$1/2$ cup chopped onions
$1/4$ cup chopped green bell pepper
$1/2$ cup chopped or shredded green cabbage
1 tablespoon olive oil
$1/4$ cup quinoa, rinsed well
3 cups water or reduced-sodium, defatted
    chicken broth
1 cup corn kernels
One $14 1/2$-ounce can whole tomatoes, with juice
$1/4$ cup chopped fresh parsley
$1/4$ teaspoon dried thyme
1 bay leaf
$1/2$ teaspoon kosher salt
Freshly ground pepper to taste

1) Sauté the garlic, carrot, onions, bell pepper,
and cabbage in the oil over low heat until the
onions become translucent.

2) Add the quinoa and cook until the quinoa
grains begin to pop. Add the water, corn, tomatoes, herbs, and seasonings. Crush the tomatoes
with your hands to break them apart as you
drop them into the pot.

3) Simmer, covered, for 30 minutes. Remove
the bay leaf before serving.

Per Serving: Calories 144; Protein 4g; Fat 5g (Saturated 1g);
Carbohydrates 24g; Fiber 4g; Sodium 426mg

Bread Soup

Makes: 4 servings

This recipe, of peasant origin, turns scraps of stale
bread, herbs, and tomatoes into a wonderful meal.
The tomatoes must be in season and ripe. Canned
tomatoes, hard pink tomatoes, and even winter
plum tomatoes won't do.

1 tablespoon olive oil
2 cloves garlic, minced
2 shallots, minced (2 tablespoons)
2 bay leaves
2 to 3 large beefsteak-style tomatoes, peeled and
    seeded, then chopped ($3 1/2$ cups)
1 cup coarsely chopped fresh basil, lightly packed
$2 1/2$ cups reduced-sodium, defatted broth or water
1 teaspoon kosher salt
$1/4$ teaspoon freshly ground pepper
2 cups stale, hearty bread, cut into 1-inch cubes
2 cups fresh spinach, torn or cut into large pieces
Grated Parmesan cheese, for garnish (optional)

1) Heat the oil in a soup pot over low heat. Sauté
the garlic, shallots, and bay leaves in the oil.
Cover and cook over low heat for about 10 minutes, until the vegetables are soft and golden.

2) Add the tomatoes, basil, broth, salt, and pepper and simmer, covered, for 15 minutes. You
can store the soup prepared up to this point
until the next day.

3) Ten minutes before serving, remove the bay
leaves and bring the soup to a boil. Stir in the
bread cubes and spinach. Turn off the heat. If
you're using an electric stove, take the pot off
the burner. Cover the pot and let the soup rest
for 10 minutes. If desired, garnish with grated
Parmesan cheese.

Per Serving: Calories 133; Protein 6g; Fat 5g (Saturated 1g);
Carbohydrates 19g; Fiber 3g; Sodium 894mg

Tortilla Soup

Makes: 10 servings

For this soup, tortillas are crisped in the oven, then added to the soup at the last minute.

4 corn tortillas, halved and cut into thin strips
2 teaspoons vegetable oil
1 cup chopped onions
1 rib celery, chopped
3 cloves garlic, minced
One 14.5-ounce can whole tomatoes, with juice
One 24-ounce can tomato puree
6 cups reduced-sodium, defatted chicken broth
1 cup fresh or frozen corn kernels
2 teaspoons ground chili powder
2 teaspoons dried basil
2 teaspoons ground cumin
1 teaspoon kosher salt
2 tablespoons diced canned mild chilies
2 tablespoons fresh lime juice
1 cup cooked chickpeas, drained and rinsed
2 tablespoons chopped fresh cilantro (optional)
$1/2$ cup grated reduced-fat cheddar or jack cheese

1) Preheat the oven to 400°F. Coat a baking sheet with nonstick spray and spread the tortillas on it. You can make this soup ahead of time, or even freeze it, but wait to cook the tortillas until 10 minutes before ladling out the soup.

2) Heat the oil in a soup pot. Sauté the onions, celery, and garlic until the onions soften and turn golden. Stir frequently.

3) Pour the juice from the canned whole tomatoes into the pot. Chop the tomatoes, or break apart with your hands, and add them to the pot. Stir in the remaining ingredients except the cilantro, cheese, and tortillas. Bring to a simmer and cook, uncovered, for 15 minutes.

4) While the soup is simmering, put the tortillas in the oven. Bake until crisp, then immediately remove them from the baking sheet and put in a serving bowl.

5) Stir in the cilantro, if using, and cook the soup for 5 minutes longer.

6) Ladle the soup into bowls, top with the cheese, and pass the tortillas.

Per Serving: Calories 135; Protein 7g; Fat 3g (Saturated 1g); Carbohydrates 23g; Fiber 4g; Sodium 878mg

Tortilla Soup with Crab

Follow the Tortilla Soup recipe (opposite), but omit the chickpeas. During step 5, add one 6-ounce can crabmeat, picked over and cartilage removed.

Per Serving: Calories 122; Protein 9g; Fat 3g (Saturated 1g); Carbohydrates 18g; Fiber 3g; Sodium 924mg

Tortilla Soup with Chicken

Follow the Tortilla Soup recipe (opposite), but omit the chickpeas. During step 2, after the onions soften, add $1/2$ pound skinless, boneless chicken breast cut into small, thin strips. Cook until white on all sides, then proceed to step 3.

Per Serving: Calories 133; Protein 11g; Fat 3g (Saturated 1g); Carbohydrates 18g; Fiber 3g; Sodium 892mg

Bean Soups

Bean soups are not as time-consuming to make as some people fear. Canned beans work fine for many soup recipes, and dried beans aren't really that difficult to prepare. Once soaked, beans take only about an hour to cook, and lentils and split peas don't even need soaking. To tell when beans are thoroughly cooked, squish one between your fingers. It should feel smooth all the way through. Salt and acidic ingredients inhibit the softening of beans, which is why they are added late in the cooking. If the beans take much longer to cook than the times specified in the recipe, it is likely because they are old. If old, their flavor and texture will be lacking, and they may never soften completely. Old split peas lose their bright green color, but it is hard to tell when other beans have been stored too long. Beans stay fresh for about a year. When purchasing beans, buy from a natural food store with a fast turnover, or look for bags that are dust-free and check the sell-by date.

Lentil Soup

Makes: 4 servings

Lentil soup is totally satisfying on its own, or with a loaf of crusty bread, or a green salad, or a sandwich, or with a dollop of goat cheese on top.

2 teaspoons olive oil
3 small carrots, peeled and chopped
1 rib celery, chopped
1/2 cup chopped onions
3 cloves garlic, minced
1 cup lentils, rinsed and picked through
4 cups reduced-sodium, defatted chicken broth
1 tablespoon minced fresh parsley
One 14 1/2-ounce can whole tomatoes, with juice, broken up with your hands
1 teaspoon dried oregano
1 1/2 teaspoons dried basil
1/4 teaspoon freshly ground pepper
1 teaspoon balsamic vinegar
2 bay leaves
1/8 teaspoon Tabasco sauce
1/2 teaspoon kosher salt

1) Heat the oil in a soup pot over low heat. Sauté the carrots, celery, onions, and garlic in the oil. Keep the lid on between stirrings. Cook until the onions are soft and golden.

2) Add the remaining ingredients, except the salt, to the pot.

3) Bring to a boil, then simmer, covered, for about 45 minutes, until the lentils soften.

4) Add the salt and adjust the other seasonings to taste.

Per Serving: Calories 262; Protein 19g; Fat 3g (Saturated 0g); Carbohydrates 42g; Fiber 9g; Sodium 917mg

Ginger Lentil Soup

Makes: 5 servings

Sometimes it is a seemingly fussy technique that makes a recipe. For example, the spices for this soup are first cooked in the sauté pan before being added to the simmering soup. This step enhances both flavor and aroma and since it only takes a minute is not as much bother as it might first appear.

1 cup lentils, rinsed and picked through
6 cups water
2 teaspoons olive oil
1 cup chopped onions
1 carrot, chopped
4 cloves garlic, minced
$1^1/2$ tablespoons finely grated fresh ginger
1 teaspoon ground coriander
$1/2$ teaspoon ground cumin
One $14^1/2$-ounce can whole tomatoes, drained
   and chopped
$1/8$ teaspoon Tabasco sauce
2 teaspoons kosher salt
2 tablespoons chopped fresh parsley
1 tablespoon chopped fresh cilantro (optional)

1) Bring the lentils and water to a boil in a large saucepan. Reduce to a simmer and cook, uncovered, for about 20 minutes, or until the lentils begin to soften.

2) Meanwhile, heat the oil in a large nonstick pan. Sauté the onions, carrot, and garlic for about 5 minutes, until the onions begin to change color. Keep the lid on between stirrings.

3) Stir the ginger, coriander, and cumin into the onion mixture. Cook for 1 minute, then scrape it all into the pot with the lentils. Add the tomatoes, Tabasco, and salt to the pot.

4) Simmer the soup, covered, for 30 minutes. Stir in the parsley and cilantro, if using, and serve.

Per Serving: Calories 183; Protein 12g; Fat 3g (Saturated 0g); Carbohydrates 30g; Fiber 7g; Sodium 882mg

Spinach and Lentil Soup

Makes: 5 servings

I've watched spinach being washed and bagged at a packaging plant and although the process gets most of the grit off, the leaves are not really clean, so it prudent to wash the spinach at home too.

1 tablespoon vegetable oil
1 cup chopped onions
3 cloves garlic, minced
1 teaspoon ground cumin
1 teaspoon ground coriander
1 teaspoon paprika
One 10-ounce package fresh spinach, washed and
   trimmed of tough stems
$1/8$ teaspoon Tabasco sauce
1 teaspoon dried oregano
1 cup lentils, rinsed and picked through
7 cups reduced-sodium, defatted chicken broth
1 teaspoon kosher salt, or to more taste
$1/4$ teaspoon freshly ground pepper, or more
   to taste
1 tablespoon lemon juice
2 tablespoons tomato paste

1) Heat the oil in a soup pot over low heat. Sauté the onions and garlic in the oil until the onions are soft and golden. Add the cumin, coriander, and paprika. Stir and cook until the aromas intensify.

2) Coarsely chop the spinach. Add it to the sauté and cook until it wilts.

3) Add the Tabasco, oregano, lentils, and broth to the pot.

4) Bring the soup to a boil, then immediately reduce to a simmer. Cook, covered, for about 50 minutes until the lentils become very soft.

5) Stir in the salt, pepper, lemon juice, and tomato paste. Simmer for 10 minutes more. Add more salt and pepper to taste if desired.

Per Serving: Calories 157; Protein 13g; Fat 3g (Saturated 0g); Carbohydrates 22g; Fiber 5g; Sodium 803mg

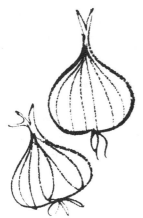

Lentil and Rice Soup with Sausage

Makes: 6 servings

It is amazing how the addition of a small amount of sausage can boost a recipe's appeal. Lentils pair especially well with sausage flavors.

2 teaspoons olive oil
1 cup chopped onions
2 cloves garlic, minced
1 carrot, diced
2 ounces sweet sausage, preferably lowfat, chopped
8 cups reduced-sodium, defatted chicken
   or beef broth
1 bay leaf
1/2 cup lentils, rinsed and picked over
1/2 cup brown rice
1 teaspoon kosher salt
1/4 teaspoon freshly ground pepper
1 tablespoon chopped fresh parsley
1/2 cup fat-free croutons

1) Heat the oil in a soup pot over low heat. Sauté the onions and garlic in the oil for 5 minutes. Keep the lid on between stirrings. Stir in the carrot and sausage. Continue to cook until the onions are soft and golden.

2) Add the broth and bay leaf to the pot. Bring to a boil, then reduce to a simmer. Add the lentils and rice and cook, covered, for about 45 minutes, or until the lentils are soft.

3) Add the salt, pepper, and parsley. Cook for 5 minutes longer. Remove the bay leaf. Serve garnished with croutons.

Per Serving: Calories 190; Protein 12g; Fat 3g (Saturated 1g); Carbohydrates 27g; Fiber 3g; Sodium 1040mg

Black Bean Soup

Makes: 7 servings

Some soups can be made with canned beans, but this one should start with dried so that the flavors cook into the beans.

3 cups dried black beans (about 1 pound), rinsed and picked over
8 cups water or reduced-sodium, defatted broth
2 bay leaves
2 ribs celery, chopped
2 carrots, chopped
1 cup chopped onions
6 cloves garlic, minced
2 limes, juiced
1 tablespoon ground coriander
$1^1/_2$ teaspoons kosher salt
1 tablespoon dried oregano
$^1/_2$ to 1 teaspoon Tabasco sauce
$^1/_4$ teaspoon cayenne pepper
2 teaspoons ground cumin
2 tablespoons chopped fresh parsley
$^1/_4$ cup sherry
Plain nonfat yogurt, for garnish (optional)
Sliced scallions, for garnish (optional)

1) Wash the beans. Soak them for at least 4 hours or up to a day in plenty of water to cover by several inches.

2) Drain the beans from the soaking liquid and put them in a large, heavy pot. Add the 8 cups of water or broth, the bay leaves, celery, carrots, onions, and garlic. Bring to a boil, reduce to a simmer, cover, and cook for 1 hour.

3) Add the lime juice, coriander, salt, oregano, Tabasco, cayenne, cumin, and parsley and simmer for 45 minutes longer, or until the beans are very soft. At this stage, half of the soup can be pureed if desired.

4) Fifteen minutes before serving, stir in the sherry.

5) Garnish with a spoonful of nonfat yogurt and sliced green scallions, if desired. Serve chilled in the summer and piping hot in the winter.

Per Serving: Calories 307; Protein 19g; Fat 2g (Saturated 0g); Carbohydrates 55g; Fiber 20g; Sodium 445mg

Brazilian Black Bean and Pumpkin Soup

Makes: 8 servings

This is a different take on the familiar black bean soup. The pumpkin smooths and sweetens the soup, while the lemon provides a bright contrast.

1 cup dried black beans, rinsed and picked over
8 cups reduced-sodium, defatted chicken broth
1 cup chopped onions
3 cloves garlic, minced
One 15-ounce can pumpkin or squash puree ($1^1/_2$ cups)
1 cup chopped tomato, or one 14.5-ounce can diced tomatoes, drained
1 teaspoon kosher salt
$^1/_2$ teaspoon freshly ground pepper, or to taste
$1^1/_2$ tablespoons lemon juice
1 teaspoon finely sliced lemon zest
2 scallions, thinly sliced, divided

1) Soak the beans in water for at least 4 hours or up to 1 day. Drain and put them in a soup pot with the broth, onions, and garlic and bring to a boil, then reduce the heat and simmer until the beans are soft, about an hour.

2) Add the remaining ingredients, reserving 2 tablespoons scallions for a garnish. Simmer for 15 minutes.

3) If desired, puree half or all of the soup. Garnish with the reserved scallions.

Per Serving: Calories 133; Protein 9g; Fat 1g (Saturated 0g); Carbohydrates 23g; Fiber 7g; Sodium 727mg

Split Pea Soup

Makes: 7 servings

This soup is tried and true. I've taught it in many cooking classes. Occasionally a student calls me to say that it wasn't as good as the one tasted in class. I've found that the problem is always the peas. Split peas should be a bright green color, never dull like olives. The color correlates with age, and that translates into flavor and texture. The older the bean, the poorer the quality. I know that it is hard to throw out a bag of beans; after all, even a bag three years old doesn't look as if it has deteriorated. But, trust me, bright green peas make a world of difference.

8 cups water or reduced-sodium, defatted
    chicken broth
2 cups split peas, rinsed and picked over
2 bay leaves
1 tablespoon vegetable oil
2 cloves garlic, minced
1 rib celery, chopped
2 carrots, chopped
1 leek, washed well and minced
1 medium all-purpose potato, peeled and cubed
2 tablespoons minced fresh parsley
1/4 teaspoon dried thyme
1/2 teaspoon dried marjoram
1 tablespoon soy sauce, or more to taste
Freshly ground pepper to taste

1) Bring the water or broth to a boil. Add the split peas and bay leaves. Cover and simmer for 30 minutes, stirring occasionally.

2) Meanwhile, heat the oil in a nonstick skillet. Sauté the garlic, celery, carrots, and leek over low heat until the vegetables soften and the onions turn slightly golden. Keep the pot covered between stirrings.

3) Add the sautéed vegetables and remaining ingredients to the pot with the split peas. Simmer, uncovered, for another 20 minutes, stirring occasionally.

Per Serving: Calories 255; Protein 15g; Fat 3g (Saturated 0g); Carbohydrates 45g; Fiber 6g; Sodium 181mg

Split Pea and Smoked Turkey Soup

Makes: 5 servings

The smoked turkey acts like a ham hock, bringing a salty, smoky, meaty flavor to the soup.

$1^1/2$ teaspoons vegetable oil
1 cup chopped onions
1 clove garlic, minced
2 ribs celery, chopped (preferably with leaves)
8 cups reduced-sodium, defatted chicken broth
2 cups split peas, rinsed
2 bay leaves
1 small carrot, finely chopped
$1/4$ pound smoked turkey breast, cut into
      small cubes
$1/4$ teaspoon freshly ground pepper
1 teaspoon kosher salt

1) Heat the oil in a heavy-bottomed soup pot and add the onions, garlic, and celery. Cook until the onions soften, about 5 minutes. Keep the pot covered between stirrings.

2) Add the remaining ingredients and bring to a boil. Reduce to a simmer and cook, uncovered, for $1^1/4$ hours.

Per Serving: Calories 357; Protein 29g; Fat 3g (Saturated 0g); Carbohydrates 55g; Fiber 8g; Sodium 1398mg

Two-Pea Soup

Makes: 4 servings

Usually found only on winter menus, split pea soup becomes appealing year-round with the addition of fresh peas and mint.

$1^1/2$ teaspoons olive oil
2 cups chopped onions
4 cloves garlic, minced
3 ribs celery, with leaves, chopped
3 carrots, chopped
4 cups reduced-sodium, defatted chicken broth
$1/4$ cup split peas, rinsed and picked through
One 10-ounce package frozen peas
1 teaspoon kosher salt
$1/2$ teaspoon freshly ground pepper
2 tablespoons minced fresh mint
Grated Parmesan cheese, for garnish (optional)

1) Heat the oil in a soup pot over low heat. Cook the onions, garlic, celery, and carrots in the oil for about 15 minutes, until the onions turn golden and the vegetables sweat out liquid. Keep the pot covered between stirrings.

2) Add the broth and split peas. Bring to a boil, then reduce to a simmer. Cover and cook for 30 minutes, until the peas are soft.

3) Add the frozen peas, salt, pepper, and mint. Simmer for 5 minutes longer.

4) Puree half the soup, then return it to the pot. Serve with grated Parmesan cheese, if desired.

Per Serving: Calories 196; Protein 12g; Fat 2g (Saturated 0g); Carbohydrates 33g; Fiber 8g; Sodium 1091mg

Housewarming Soup

Makes: 6 servings

White-ribbed—not red—Swiss chard is called for here because red chard would dye the soup a light purple color.

1 cup dried white beans, rinsed and picked over
1^1/2 teaspoons olive oil
1 cup chopped onions
2 cloves garlic, minced
3 small carrots, peeled and cubed (1^1/2 cups)
^{1}/2 pound white-ribbed Swiss chard, chopped
    (4 to 5 cups)
1 rib celery, chopped
6 cups reduced-sodium, defatted chicken broth
2 bay leaves
^{1}/2 teaspoon freshly ground pepper
2 tablespoons minced fresh parsley
^{1}/2 teaspoon dried sage
1 teaspoon kosher salt, or more to taste
2 tablespoons grated Parmesan or Romano cheese

1) Soak the beans in plenty of water for at least 4 hours or up to 12 hours. Drain.

2) Heat the oil in a soup pot over low heat. Sauté the onions and garlic in the oil until the onions are soft and golden. Keep the pot covered between stirrings.

3) Add the beans and the remaining ingredients, except the salt and cheese, to the pot. Bring the soup to a boil. Reduce to a simmer and cook, covered, for 45 minutes to 1 hour, until the beans are thoroughly cooked.

4) Stir in the salt. Add more salt to taste if desired.

5) Puree half of the soup and stir it all back together so that the soup is thick and lumpy.

6) Stir in the cheese or use it as a garnish on top of each serving.

Per Serving: Calories 196; Protein 13g; Fat 2g (Saturated 1g); Carbohydrates 32g; Fiber 9g; Sodium 944mg

Smoked Turkey, Bean, and Tomato Soup

Makes: 10 servings

The saltiness of the smoked turkey breast varies according to its maker, so taste and adjust the salt after the soup has simmered for a while.

2 teaspoons vegetable oil
1 cup chopped onions
2 cloves garlic, minced
One 14^1/2-ounce can whole tomatoes, with juice
1^1/2 cups cooked navy or white kidney beans, drained and rinsed
^{1}/2 cup corn kernels
1 teaspoon dried thyme
^{1}/2 teaspoon dried sage
1 teaspoon kosher salt, or more to taste
^{1}/4 teaspoon freshly ground pepper, or more to taste
6 cups reduced-sodium, defatted chicken broth
^{1}/2 pound skinless smoked turkey breast, diced (1^1/2 cups)
1 tablespoon chopped fresh parsley

1) Heat the oil in a soup pot and sauté the onions and garlic until golden, about 10 minutes. Keep the pot covered between stirrings.

2) Drain the juice from the canned tomatoes into the pot, then chop the tomatoes and add them to the pot.

3) Stir in the remaining ingredients. Bring to a boil, then reduce to a simmer. Cover and cook for 1 hour. Stir occasionally. Taste and adjust the salt and pepper.

Per Serving: Calories 103; Protein 9g; Fat 2g (Saturated 0g); Carbohydrates 13g; Fiber 3g; Sodium 761mg

Broccoli, Bean, and Pasta Soup

Makes: 8 servings

Many hearty soups have long lists of ingredients and take an equally long time to prep and cook. Not this soup. Start to finish, this will be ready in under an hour.

2 pounds broccoli
1^1/2 teaspoons olive oil
2 cups chopped onions
8 cups reduced-sodium, defatted chicken broth
1 tablespoon dried basil
1 tablespoon kosher salt
^{1}/4 teaspoon freshly ground pepper, or more to taste
1^1/2 cups cooked cannellini or navy beans, drained and rinsed
2 cups cooked small, shaped pasta

1) Cut off and discard the tough broccoli stems. Peel the remaining stalk. Cut the tops into small florets and finely chop the peeled stems.

2) Heat the oil in a heavy-bottomed soup pot. Add the onions and cook until softened and golden, about 10 minutes. Keep the pot covered between stirrings.

3) Add the broccoli, broth, basil, salt, and pepper and bring to a boil. Reduce to a simmer and cook, uncovered, for 15 minutes. Allow to cool.

4) Puree half of the soup. Return it to the pot, bring back to a simmer, and add the beans and pasta. Heat through for about 10 minutes.

Per Serving: Calories 157; Protein 10g; Fat 2g (Saturated 0g); Carbohydrates 26g; Fiber 7g; Sodium 1225mg

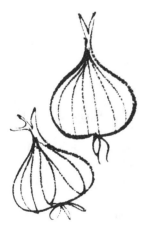

Pasta e Fagioli Soup

Makes: 4 servings

Many people who claim not to like beans are perfectly happy consuming bowls of this soup. In fact, soups are a terrific (and not too sneaky) way to get your family to eat more beans, one of nature's most healthful foods.

1 1/2 teaspoons olive oil
1 cup chopped onions
1 clove garlic, minced
1 rib celery, chopped
1 carrot, chopped
2 cups cooked white beans (such as cannellini), drained and rinsed
One 14 1/2-ounce can whole tomatoes, drained, seeded, and chopped
2 tablespoons chopped fresh parsley
4 cups reduced-sodium, defatted chicken broth
1/2 teaspoon dried rosemary
1/2 teaspoon dried sage
1/2 teaspoon kosher salt
1/4 teaspoon freshly ground pepper
1/3 cup uncooked small, shaped pasta

1) Heat the oil in a large heavy-bottomed soup pot. Add the onions, garlic, celery, and carrots. Cook over low to medium heat until the carrots soften, about 10 minutes. Keep the pot covered between stirrings.

2) Slightly crush the beans between your fingers as you drop them into the pot. Stir in the remaining ingredients except for the pasta. Bring to a simmer and cook, covered, for 10 minutes.

3) Stir in the pasta and continue to simmer until the pasta is cooked through, about 10 minutes more.

Per Serving: Calories 169; Protein 9g; Fat 2g (Saturated 0g); Carbohydrates 28g; Fiber 5g; Sodium 1016mg

Fish Soups

Often, the fishmonger has "chowder fish" for sale. These are oddly shaped pieces that cannot be sold as fillets. Although the price is usually half that of fillet fish, the quality and freshness should be as good; ask to smell it to make sure. Chowder fish is frequently a combination of several types of fish, which makes the soup even tastier.

Manhattan-Style Fish Chowder

Makes: 7 servings

Living in New England as I do, I am well aware of the belief of this region's chowder (or "chowdah") lovers that anything other than a cream-based chowder is sacrilegious. What's more, this recipe's very name reminds us of New York (home of the hated Yankees). So I must really believe in this recipe or I wouldn't offer it here.

1 tablespoon olive oil
1 cup chopped onions
3 cloves garlic, minced
1 rib celery, chopped
1/2 cup dry white wine
1 medium potato (about 1/2 pound), peeled and cubed
One 28-ounce can whole tomatoes, chopped, with juice
2 cups reduced-sodium, defatted chicken broth
1 cup water
1/2 teaspoon dried basil
1/2 teaspoon dried thyme
2 tablespoons chopped fresh parsley
1 teaspoon kosher salt
1/4 teaspoon freshly ground pepper, or more to taste
3/4 pound fish fillets or steaks, cut into 1- to 2-inch pieces

1) Heat the oil in a heavy-bottomed pot. Sauté the onions, garlic, and celery in the oil until golden. Pour in the wine and simmer for 1 minute. Add all the remaining ingredients except the fish. Bring to a simmer. Cook, covered, for 10 minutes.

2) Stir in the fish, then cover and cook for 6 to 10 minutes, until the fish cooks through.

Per Serving: Calories 130; Protein 12g; Fat 3g (Saturated 0g); Carbohydrates 13g; Fiber 2g; Sodium 632mg

Fish and Vegetable Soup

Makes: 8 servings

Adding salsa to soup is a quick way to add a lot of flavor for no extra work.

1 tablespoon olive oil
1 cup chopped onions
1 rib celery, chopped
1/2 cup chopped green bell pepper
2 cloves garlic, minced
1 large carrot, diced
2 medium potatoes (about 1 pound), peeled and cubed
8 cups reduced-sodium, defatted chicken broth
2 teaspoons kosher salt
1/4 teaspoon freshly ground pepper, or more to taste
1 pound fish fillets or steaks, cut into 1- to 2-inch pieces
1 cup Red Salsa (page 592 or store-bought)
1 cup Croutons (page 606 or store-bought)

1) Heat the oil in a heavy-bottomed pot. Sauté the onions, celery, and bell pepper in the oil for 5 minutes. Stir in the garlic and cook for 2 minutes longer. Add the carrot and potatoes and cook for 2 minutes more.

2) Pour in the broth, add the salt and pepper, and bring to a simmer. Cover and cook until the potatoes are tender, about 10 minutes.

3) Stir in the fish, then cover and cook for 5 to 7 minutes, until the fish cooks through. Stir in the salsa and heat through. Garnish with croutons.

Per Serving: Calories 151; Protein 15g; Fat 2g (Saturated 0g); Carbohydrates 16g; Fiber 3g; Sodium 1342mg

1) Soak the saffron in the hot water. The water will turn golden orange.

2) Heat the oil in a heavy-bottomed pot. Sauté the onions, leeks, and zucchini in the oil until golden. Stir in the rice and cook until shiny. Stir in the tomatoes, broth, bay leaves, cayenne, and salt. Add the saffron water. Bring to a simmer, cover, and cook 15 minutes.

3) Stir in the fish and cook for 5 minutes, until the fish is cooked through. Stir in the parsley. Remove the bay leaves (if you can find them).

Per Serving: Calories 172; Protein 16g; Fat 2g (Saturated 0g); Carbohydrates 21g; Fiber 2g; Sodium 1000mg

Italian Fish and Rice Soup

Makes: 8 servings

Saffron turns the soup a beautiful golden color and imparts that unmistakable saffron flavor. Expensive, but well worth it.

1 large pinch saffron threads, or $1/2$ teaspoon
    ground saffron
$1/2$ cup hot water
1 tablespoon olive oil
1 cup chopped onions
1 cup chopped leeks
2 medium zucchini, diced (about 3 cups)
$3/4$ cup long-grain rice
1 cup diced tomatoes, fresh or canned
8 cups reduced-sodium, defatted chicken broth
2 bay leaves
$1/16$ to $1/8$ teaspoon cayenne pepper
2 teaspoons kosher salt
1 pound fish fillets, cut into 1-inch pieces
3 tablespoons chopped fresh parsley

Chicken Soups

Scientific studies have proven what Grandma said for years—that chicken soup helps relieve the symptoms of colds. Scientists haven't been able to identify the exact mechanism or ingredient, but they confirm that the soup must be chicken; fish or vegetable just won't do. That is fine with me (and it would have pleased my Nana Rose). I'll take chicken soup over a pill any day.

No-Bones Chicken Soup

Makes: 4 servings

When I don't have the time or inclination to make chicken soup from a whole chicken, I pull out this recipe.

1 cup chopped onions
1 clove garlic, minced
2 ribs celery, including leaves, chopped
1 large carrot, cubed
1^1/2 teaspoons olive oil
^{1}/2 pound skinless, boneless chicken breast, cubed
1 tablespoon chopped fresh parsley
2 teaspoons minced fresh dill, or 1 teaspoon dried
4 cups reduced-sodium, defatted chicken broth
^{1}/2 teaspoon kosher salt
^{1}/2 teaspoon freshly ground pepper
1 cup cooked brown rice, or other cooked grain
    or pasta
^{1}/2 cup peas

1) Sauté the onions, garlic, celery, and carrot in the oil in a soup pot. Cook over low heat for about 10 minutes, until the onions soften and become golden. Keep the pot covered between stirrings. Add a touch of chicken broth if there's not enough oil to keep the vegetables from sticking.

2) Make sure that the chicken is trimmed of all fat, otherwise the soup will foam and need to be skimmed. Put the chicken in the pot and cook for about 2 minutes, until the outside of the chicken begins to turn white.

3) Stir in the parsley, dill, broth, salt, pepper, and rice and simmer for 30 minutes. If you are using pasta, put it into the pot 10 minutes before serving or it will become mushy. Add the peas during the last 5 minutes of cooking so that they remain bright green.

Per Serving: Calories 195; Protein 19g; Fat 3g (Saturated 1g); Carbohydrates 22g; Fiber 3g; Sodium 784mg

Lemon Chicken Soup

Makes: 7 servings

This soup takes only 25 minutes to cook, so it won't heat up the kitchen. That, and the fact that it is light and fresh-tasting, makes it a chicken soup suited to warm-weather menus.

1 tablespoon olive oil
1 cup chopped onions
4 cloves garlic, minced
2 large carrots, diced
1 rib celery, diced
8 cups reduced-sodium, defatted chicken broth
1 cup diced tomatoes (canned or fresh)
2 cups chopped fresh spinach or white-ribbed Swiss chard
$1/2$ teaspoon dried thyme
1 teaspoon honey
1 teaspoon kosher salt
$1/4$ teaspoon freshly ground pepper
$1/2$ pound skinless, boneless chicken breast, cut into tiny pieces
$1/3$ cup uncooked rice
$1/4$ cup chopped fresh parsley
2 tablespoons lemon juice

1) Heat the oil in a large pot, add the onions, garlic, carrots, and celery, and cook for about 10 minutes, until the onions turn golden and are lightly browned around the edges. Keep the pot covered between stirrings.

2) Add the remaining ingredients except for the parsley and lemon juice. Bring to a simmer, cover, and cook for 10 minutes.

3) Stir in the parsley and lemon juice. Cook for 5 minutes longer.

Per Serving: Calories 143; Protein 13g; Fat 3g (Saturated 0g); Carbohydrates 16g; Fiber 2g; Sodium 874mg

Spanish Chicken Noodle Soup

Makes: 6 servings

Cilantro gives this soup a Spanish flare and is important to the recipe. Parsley will do, but the recipe won't be the same.

$1^1/2$ teaspoons olive oil
1 cup chopped onions
3 cloves garlic, minced
1 cup diced chicken breast (from about $1/2$ pound)
$1/8$ teaspoon saffron powder
One $14^1/2$-ounce can whole tomatoes, drained and chopped, or 5 plum tomatoes
6 cups reduced-sodium, defatted chicken broth
$1^1/2$ teaspoons paprika
$1/2$ teaspoon ground cumin
2 teaspoons kosher salt
$1/4$ teaspoon freshly ground pepper
1 cup fettuccine, broken into 2-inch pieces
$1/4$ cup chopped fresh cilantro

1) Heat the oil in a heavy-bottomed soup pot. Add the onions and garlic. Cook over medium heat for 5 minutes. Stir in the chicken pieces. Cook until white on all sides.

2) Put the saffron in a small heatproof bowl. Pour the tomatoes and broth into the soup pot. Bring to a boil, then reduce to a simmer. Scoop out about $1/2$ cup of liquid and pour over the saffron, then return it to the pot.

3) Add the remaining ingredients except for the cilantro. Cover and cook for 15 minutes. Stir in the cilantro.

Per Serving: Calories 161; Protein 15g; Fat 2g (Saturated 0g); Carbohydrates 19g; Fiber 1g; Sodium 1225mg

Velvet Corn Soup

Makes: 5 servings

This soup is ever so easy to make, and is best when made right before serving.

1 tablespoon dry sherry
4 cups reduced-sodium, defatted chicken broth
One 16-ounce can cream-style corn
1 teaspoon finely grated fresh ginger
1/2 pound skinless, boneless chicken breast, finely chopped
1 teaspoon kosher salt
1 tablespoon cornstarch mixed with 2 tablespoons water
2 egg whites, lightly beaten but not frothy
1/2 teaspoon Asian sesame oil
1 scallion, chopped (about 2 tablespoons), for garnish

1) Bring the sherry, broth, corn, and ginger to a boil. Immediately reduce to a simmer. Add the chicken, stirring to break it up so that it does not clump together. Cook until the meat is white throughout, about 8 to 10 minutes.

2) Stir in the salt. Stir the cornstarch paste and pour it into the pot. Stir until the soup clears and thickens.

3) Remove the pot from the heat and immediately stir in the egg whites. Do this slowly in a steady stream. They will form cooked white strands. Stir the soup a few times so that they rise to the surface. Drizzle the soup with the sesame oil and garnish with the chopped scallions.

Per Serving: Calories 157; Protein 16g; Fat 1g (Saturated 0g); Carbohydrates 19g; Fiber 1g; Sodium 1126mg

Chinese Chicken Noodle Soup

Makes: 7 servings

Look in the international foods aisle of almost any supermarket and you'll find an array of Chinese noodles. Read the labels, though, as some ramen-style noodles are fried and high in fat. Chinese noodles, like mung bean threads, have a unique, chewy texture (my kids might say slimy, but that would be a compliment). Use whichever you choose. If preferred, vermicelli is also fine in this soup.

1 teaspoon cornstarch
1 tablespoon soy sauce
1 tablespoon dry sherry
6 cups reduced-sodium, defatted chicken broth
1 teaspoon finely grated fresh ginger
1 rib celery, sliced thinly on the diagonal
1 carrot, sliced thinly on the diagonal
1/2 pound skinless, boneless chicken breast, cut into tiny pieces
1/2 pound Chinese noodles or vermicelli, cooked, drained, and rinsed
1/2 teaspoon kosher salt
2 cups chopped fresh spinach

1) Combine the cornstarch, soy sauce, and sherry and set aside.

2) Bring the broth to a boil. Reduce to a simmer and add the ginger, celery, carrot, and chicken. Cook until the chicken is white through.

3) Add the noodles, salt, and cornstarch mixture. Simmer for 5 minutes, until the soup is slightly thickened. Stir in the spinach. Cook for about 2 minutes more, until the spinach wilts.

Per Serving: Calories 186; Protein 15g; Fat 1g (Saturated 0g); Carbohydrates 27g; Fiber 2g; Sodium 781mg

Mandarin Soup

Makes: 4 servings

The first step in making this soup not only makes the broth but also cooks the chicken. This takes time but not much effort.

4 large fresh shiitake mushrooms ($^1/_2$ cup)
2 cloves garlic, peeled and crushed
2 chicken thighs, skinned and fat removed
6 cups water
1 leek, washed well and chopped
$^1/_2$ cup snow peas
1 tablespoon minced fresh ginger
3 tablespoons soy sauce, or more to taste
5 scallions, sliced
$^1/_2$ cup fresh mung bean sprouts
$^1/_4$ teaspoon freshly ground pepper, or more to taste
1 tablespoon dry sherry
One 11-ounce can mandarin oranges packed in light syrup, drained

1) Snap the stems off the mushrooms. Reserve the caps. Put the stems in a pot with the garlic, chicken, water, and leek, and simmer for 45 minutes.

2) Strain the stock through a fine mesh colander and discard the vegetables. Set the chicken aside. Put the broth back in the pot. It will have been reduced by about one-third, to around 4 cups.

3) Take the chicken off the bones and cut it into small pieces. Add the meat to the pot.

4) Strip the strings off the snow peas, then cut the peas into thirds. Add the snow peas, ginger, soy sauce, scallions, bean sprouts, pepper, and sherry to the soup.

5) Slice the mushroom caps and add them to the soup.

6) Puree the mandarin oranges and stir into the soup.

7) Bring the soup to a gentle simmer. Cook for 10 minutes. Check the seasonings. Add more soy sauce and pepper if desired.

Per Serving: Calories 121; Protein 10g; Fat 2g (Saturated 0g); Carbohydrates 18g; Fiber 3g; Sodium 826mg

Matzo Ball Soup

Makes: 6 servings

In my family there were two opposing styles of matzo ball soup cookery, and this didn't have to do with how light or heavy the balls were—it had to do with the vegetables. The first style belonged to my Nana Rose, who left the vegetables almost entirely whole. I can remember pieces of carrot that were so large they didn't fit in the bowl. I loved those carrots, soft and sweet with homemade broth. The other school of soup cookery cut the vegetables into small pieces, easy to eat and easy to share (large pieces meant that some people had lots and others had none). This recipe is a compromise. The vegetables are large enough to have presence, but cut small enough to fit in the bowl. Of course, the matzo balls are light. There was no argument about that in our family.

Matzo Balls

2 eggs

1 egg white

1 1/2 teaspoons vegetable oil

3/4 cup matzo meal

1/8 teaspoon kosher salt

2 tablespoons sparkling water or plain seltzer

Broth

8 cups reduced-sodium, defatted chicken broth, preferably homemade

2 carrots, peeled and cut into 2-inch pieces

1 parsnip, peeled and cut into 2-inch pieces

1 rib celery, peeled and cut into 2-inch pieces

1 teaspoon kosher salt, or to taste

1/4 teaspoon freshly ground pepper

1) Beat the eggs and egg white with the oil. Stir in the matzo meal and salt. Stir in the sparkling water. Let rest 15 minutes.

2) Meanwhile, bring the broth ingredients to a boil. Reduce to a simmer. Cover.

3) Using your hands, roll the matzo batter into 1 1/2-inch-diameter balls (makes about 12). Wet your hands with water to keep the batter from sticking. As each is shaped, drop it directly into the simmering soup. When all are made, cover the pot and cook for 15 minutes. Do not lift the lid to peek, or the balls will not fluff up.

Per Serving: Calories 155; Protein 0g; Fat 3g (Saturated 1g); Carbohydrates 21g; Fiber 2g; Sodium 1047mg

Chicken Soups from Scratch

It is messy, time-consuming, and requires a large pot, but making chicken soup from scratch results in one of the most glorious foods to come out of a home kitchen. The messiest step is removing the chicken carcass and taking the meat off the bones. It helps to have a large colander that fits into an even larger bowl. That way the carcass drains as you work on it, and you don't lose the wonderful broth. The colander and large bowl are also useful when separating and discarding the flavor-giving but inedible broth ingredients from the finished soup.

If you can, set aside two days to make the soup so that there is time for the fat to rise to the surface and congeal (which is the easiest way to defat a soup). I live in the Northeast and wait until winter when I can leave my large pot out on the deck overnight in near-freezing temperatures. If you don't have the time, you can skim the surface of the soup or use a fat-separating cup.

Chicken Corn Soup

Makes: 10 servings

Cream-style corn adds sweetness and thickness to this chicken soup.

One 3- to 4-pound chicken
3 cloves garlic
2 carrots, peeled
4 quarts water
2 bay leaves
1 1/2 teaspoons olive oil
1 cup chopped onions
1 rib celery, chopped
2 carrots, chopped
1 red bell pepper, chopped (optional)
One 16-ounce package frozen corn, thawed,
    preferably white shoepeg
1 pound all-purpose potatoes, peeled and diced
    (about 2 medium potatoes)
Two 15-ounce cans cream-style corn
1/2 teaspoon dried thyme
1 teaspoon dried sage
1 tablespoon kosher salt
1/4 teaspoon freshly ground pepper

1) Put the chicken, garlic, carrots, water, and bay leaves in a large pot. Bring to a boil, then immediately reduce to a simmer. Skim the surface with a slotted spoon or other tool to remove the grayish foam that forms on the surface. Simmer, uncovered, for 1 hour. Allow to cool until the contents can be safely handled.

2) Meanwhile, heat the oil in a sauté pan and sauté the onions and celery in the pan until the onions turn golden, about 7 minutes. Set aside for use later.

3) Remove the chicken from the pot and take the meat from the bones. Discard the carcass and skin. Chop the meat and reserve it.

4) Strain the cooking liquid. Wipe out the pot and return the broth to it. Defat the broth (see "Chicken Soups from Scratch," opposite).

5) Stir in the chicken meat, sautéed onions and celery, and the remaining ingredients. Bring to a boil, reduce to a simmer, and cook, uncovered, for 20 minutes, or until the potatoes and carrots are tender. If necessary, skim the fat off the surface of the soup before serving.

Per Serving: Calories 240; Protein 18g; Fat 4g (Saturated 1g); Carbohydrates 34g; Fiber 4g; Sodium 964mg

Caribbean Corn Soup

Makes: 7 servings

The jalapeño pepper adds a lot of flavor, but this soup isn't mouth-burning hot. Of course, if you prefer it that way, you can use a hotter variety of chili pepper.

One 3- to 4-pound chicken

3 quarts water

1 fresh jalapeño pepper, cut into quarters and seeds scraped out

2 bay leaves

3 cloves garlic

1 medium yellow onion, quartered

1/2 red bell pepper, chopped

Two 15-ounce cans cream-style corn

1 teaspoon dried thyme

2 teaspoons kosher salt

1/4 teaspoon freshly ground pepper

1 tablespoon minced jalapeño pepper, fresh or canned

2 scallions, chopped

1) Put the chicken, water, jalapeño, bay leaves, garlic, and onion in a large pot. Bring to a boil, then immediately reduce to a simmer. Skim the surface with a slotted spoon or other tool to remove the grayish foam that forms on the surface. Simmer, uncovered, for 40 minutes. Allow to cool until the contents can be safely handled.

2) Remove the chicken from the pot and take the meat from the bones. Discard the carcass and skin. Chop the meat and reserve it.

3) Strain the cooking liquid through a fine mesh sieve or a colander lined with cheesecloth. Wipe out the soup pot, pour the broth back into it, and discard all else. Defat the broth (see "Chicken Soups from Scratch," page 148).

4) Stir in the chicken meat and bring to a boil. Reduce to a simmer and add the remaining ingredients except for the scallions. Cook, covered, for 15 minutes. Stir in the scallions and serve.

Per Serving: Calories 216; Protein 23g; Fat 4g (Saturated 1g); Carbohydrates 23g; Fiber 2g; Sodium 1046mg

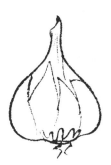

Chicken Noodle Soup

Makes: 10 servings

Here is my version of this traditional favorite. I like broad noodles, but this is something to personalize. Alphabet pasta or elbow noodles are equally welcome in this soup.

One 3- to 4-pound chicken
1 gallon water
3 ribs celery, cut into 3-inch pieces
1 medium onion, peeled and quartered
2 carrots, peeled and cut into 3-inch pieces
1 parsnip, peeled and cut into 3-inch pieces
2 bay leaves
8 peppercorns
8 parsley stems, with leaves
$1/2$ teaspoon dried thyme
$1/2$ teaspoon dried marjoram
1 cup diced carrots
2 tablespoons chopped fresh parsley
2 teaspoons kosher salt, or more to taste
2 cups egg noodles

1) Put the chicken and the water into a large pot. Bring to a boil and reduce to a simmer. Skim off any brown foam that rises to the surface. Stir in the celery, onion, carrots, parsnip, bay leaves, peppercorns, and parsley stems. Simmer, uncovered, for 30 to 40 minutes until the chicken is cooked through.

2) Remove the chicken from the pot and take the meat from the bones. Discard the carcass and skin. Chop the meat and refrigerate it until later. Put the chicken bones back into the pot, add the thyme and marjoram, and simmer for 1 hour, loosely covered.

3) Strain the broth through a fine mesh sieve or a colander lined with cheesecloth and discard all solids. Defat the broth (see "Chicken Soups from Scratch," page 148).

4) Put the defatted broth, chicken meat, carrots, chopped parsley, and salt into a soup pot. Bring to a boil. Reduce to a simmer and add the noodles. Simmer until the noodles are done, about 8 to 10 minutes. Taste and adjust for salt.

Per Serving: Calories 165; Protein 17g; Fat 2g (Saturated 1g); Carbohydrates 17g; Fiber 1g; Sodium 455mg

Entrées: Poultry and Meat

Breaded Chicken
155

Chicken Baked in Mustard

Honey-Mustard
Chicken Nuggets

Nutty Honey Chicken

Pecan Baked Chicken

Crusty Horseradish Chicken

Chicken Baked in Pesto Crust

Chutney Chicken

Grilled and Broiled Chicken
159

Fresh Herb Marinated Chicken

Maple-Mustard Glazed
Chicken

Tandoori Chicken

Turkish-Style Yogurt Chicken

Kebabs
162

Chicken Yakitori

Tropical Chicken Kebabs

Honey-Hoisin Kebabs

Honey-Teriyaki Chicken
Kebabs

Persian Lemon Chicken Kebabs

Curried Lime Chicken Satay

Garlic-Oregano Chicken
Kebabs

Baked Chicken
166

Red Currant and
Blackberry Chicken

Gingered Marmalade Chicken

Baked Hoisin Chicken

Apricot Glazed Chicken

Papaya Baked Chicken Breasts

Lemon-Rosemary Chicken

Pineapple Barbeque Chicken

Orange Barbeque Chicken

Sesame Buttermilk Chicken

Chicken in Orange and Tahini

Marmalade Chicken

Apricot Chicken

Chicken in Chili Tomato Sauce

Lemon-Thyme Chicken Rolls

Oriental Chicken in
Parchment

Roasted Chicken
176

Herb Roasted Chicken

Lemon Roasted Chicken

Orange and Lime Roasted Chicken

Garlic Chicken

Sweet Soy Roasted Chicken

Chicken Roasted with Red Rubbing Spices

Casseroles
181

Mexican Corn and Chicken Casserole

Greek Chicken Casserole

Moussaka

Lamb Moussaka

Frontier Pie with Cornbread Topping

Chicken Pot Pie

Chicken Enchiladas

Turkey Lasagna

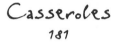

Stovetop Cooking
188

Apple and Cherry Chicken

Apple Cider Chicken Stew

Chicken and Apple Curry

Chili Pumpkin Chicken

Chicken and Rice

Country Chicken

Fragrant Chicken

Beef and Noodles

Chicken and Noodles

Turkey Picadillo

Southern Chicken Stew

Old-Fashioned Beef Stew

Lamb Stew

Easy Turkey Chili

White Chili

Mexican Mole Chili

Smoked Turkey Gumbo

Barbecued Hot Dogs

Chicken Fajitas

Balsamic Chicken and Broccoli

Chicken in Indonesian Sauce

Wok Cooking
201

Kung Pao Chicken

Hoisin Chicken and Broccoli Stir-Fry

Honey Teriyaki Chicken Stir-Fry

Spinach, Shiitake, and Turkey Stir-Fry

Beef with Broccoli

Stir-Fried Beef and Snow Peas

Moo Shu Beef

Hoisin Chicken Lo Mein

Turkey Cutlets
207

Pan-Fried Turkey Cutlets

Turkey Cutlets with Gremolata

Turkey Cutlets in Lemon-Caper Sauce

Turkey Cutlets with Rosemary-Caper Sauce

Five-Spice Turkey Cutlets

Cooking with Lean Ground Beef and Turkey
211

Muffin-Tin Meatloaves

Spinach-Stuffed Meatloaf

Turkey Meatloaf

Mexican Meatloaf

Stuffed Peppers

Ground Turkey Spaghetti Sauce

Porcupine Meatballs

Seasoned Meatballs

Turkey Meatballs

Turkey Meatball and Penne Casserole

Spaghetti and Tiny Meatballs in Creamy Tomato Sauce

Although most health experts agree that reducing the amount of meat consumed (especially fatty red meat) is essential to eating well, there is still a place for meat in the diet if it is lean and eaten in modest-size portions. One way to get the flavor of meat, while keeping the amount small, is to use it in stir-fries and stews. Even when meat is the focus of the meal, the portion size in these recipes is not more than 4 ounces. In all cases the meat is used for variety, not for bulk. Enjoy the meat, but fill up on other foods, like soup, good bread, and interesting vegetable side dishes.

One of the first changes people make when reducing their fat intake is to eat more chicken, especially skinless, boneless white meat. But it is a mistake to eat it the way you would a large piece of steak—boneless, skinless chicken breast is boring on its own. Yet it doesn't take much to make it tasty and this book offers many recipes for this lean, versatile meat that do not leave diners saying, "Oh, no, chicken again."

The biggest reduction in fat comes from removing the skin. If the chicken does not come skinned, it is not hard to do yourself. Slip your fingers under the skin to loosen it, then pull it off. One trick is to let frozen chicken thaw halfway, then pull off the skin—it will be very easy to do. (If a recipe calls for skinless chicken and you can only find the skin-on type, purchase 25 percent more than specified.)

Although white meat is the lowest in fat, dark meat is not off limits. Dark meat contributes much flavor to a recipe. Combining light and dark meat can keep the recipe interesting while keeping the fat content within reasonable limits. When a recipe calls for "chicken pieces," use a selection of both light and dark cuts.

Sometimes, too, cooking chicken with the bone in is a good idea. The bones help keep the chicken moist, give it shape, and lend a little more flavor. Although stews made with skinless bone-in chicken pieces can be messy to eat, they are full-flavored.

Chicken breasts come whole or split. "Split" means that they are halved down the middle along the breastbone. Each half of a small chicken breast is the right size for one serving. Some breasts are large and will need to be cut to make a 1/4-pound portion of edible meat.

There is a large difference in flavor between brands of chicken. The average 4-pound chickens are ready for slaughter when only a few months old, but how they were fed and handled during that time is evident in their flavor. When fattened on inexpensive feed like fish meal and kept in crowded, stressful buildings, the meat either lacks distinction or tastes slightly off. If, on the other hand, the birds were fed whole grains, given room to move, and were less stressed, the meat has a fuller, sweeter flavor and a firmer, more pleasing texture. Sometimes this chicken is termed "free range." There are several national brands available as well as some regional ones. I believe it is well worth the extra money both for the better quality and to support farmers who raise their stock with care. However, the differences between these types of chicken is most obvious with simple recipes, like roast chicken. For highly seasoned stews, the lesser-quality chicken is adequate.

Breaded Chicken

When chicken skin is removed fat is reduced by half. But since the skin protects, moistens, and adds flavor to chicken meat, something needs to replace it. One solution is to coat the chicken pieces with breading. The following recipes result in moist pieces of chicken, wrapped with flavor and an appetizing exterior texture. All are very easy to make and please both adults and children alike.

The amount of breading needed for the recipes varies depending on the size of the chicken pieces. Numerous small pieces of chicken have more surface area than a few larger ones and therefore need more breading. The coatings vary, too. Soft breadcrumbs crisp up a bit, while pieces rolled in dry breadcrumbs and nuts are crunchier. For the crispiest texture, spray the chicken lightly with nonstick spray.

Do not bread the chicken more than 15 minutes ahead of time or the coating will become soggy. Also, don't crowd the chicken pieces together or they will take longer to cook and won't brown. The chicken usually won't stick much to the baking pan, but a light coating of nonstick spray ensures easy removal. Breaded chicken doesn't take long to cook. A clear glass casserole will cause the chicken to dry out, so if using one be sure to reduce the oven temperature by 25°F. Bake until the chicken turns white throughout and springs back to the touch.

Chicken Baked in Mustard

Makes: 4 servings

This exceedingly easy recipe is probably the most popular dish that I have ever written or taught. Beginning cooks gain confidence making it and experienced cooks have a good time varying the mustard. It goes well with any side dish and can be served with any number of chutneys or salsas. All of my breaded chicken recipes take their cue from this one.

1 pound skinless, boneless chicken breast
1/4 cup mustard
1/2 cup soft breadcrumbs

1) Preheat the oven to 400°F.

2) Cut the chicken into 4 equal pieces and pat dry with a paper towel.

3) Brush the mustard onto both sides of the chicken. Roll each piece in breadcrumbs, coating thoroughly, and then gently shake off the excess. Place on a baking sheet coated with nonstick spray.

4) Bake for 20 minutes, or until done.

Per Serving: Calories 152; Protein 27g; Fat 2g (Saturated 0g); Carbohydrates 4g; Fiber 1g; Sodium 298mg

Honey-Mustard Chicken Nuggets

Makes: 4 servings

The coating with mayonnaise and milk keeps these nuggets exceptionally moist.

2 tablespoons honey mustard
1 tablespoon reduced-fat mayonnaise
1/2 cup nonfat milk
1 pound skinless, boneless chicken breast, cut into 1-inch pieces
1/2 cup dry breadcrumbs
1 cup cornflakes
1/4 teaspoon kosher salt

1) Preheat the oven to 425°F. Coat a baking pan with nonstick spray.

2) Whisk together the mustard, mayonnaise, and milk. Add the chicken and stir to coat.

3) Put the breadcrumbs, cornflakes, and salt in a food processor or blender. Process until fine and place on a dinner plate.

4) Using tongs, remove the chicken piece by piece from the milk mixture and dip in the crumbs. Turn to coat and place on the baking sheet.

5) Bake for 8 to 12 minutes.

Per Serving: Calories 237; Protein 29g; Fat 3g (Saturated 1g); Carbohydrates 19g; Fiber 1g; Sodium 417mg

Nutty Honey Chicken

Makes: 4 servings

My husband's family is from Alabama and so our preferred nuts are pecans. You can use whatever nut you like; just make sure they are finely chopped so that they can evenly coat the chicken.

1/4 cup honey
2 tablespoons Dijon mustard
1 tablespoon soy sauce
1/2 cup finely chopped pecans or other nuts
1/2 cup soft breadcrumbs, preferably whole wheat
2 pounds skinless chicken parts, cut as desired

1) Preheat the oven to 400°F. Lightly coat a baking pan with nonstick spray.

2) Combine the honey, mustard, and soy sauce in a bowl.

3) Toss the nuts and breadcrumbs together on a plate.

4) Brush each piece of chicken with the sauce, then roll it in the crumb mixture. Gently shake off the excess. Place the pieces on the baking pan.

5) Bake for 40 to 50 minutes for drumsticks and thighs, 20 to 25 minutes for large portions of boneless chicken, or 12 minutes for boneless strips.

Per Serving: Calories 387; Protein 40g; Fat 15g (Saturated 2g); Carbohydrates 24g; Fiber 1g; Sodium 605mg

Pecan Baked Chicken

Makes: 4 servings

Excess breading is gently shaken off of these breaded chicken recipes. Otherwise some of the breading would be too thick, with a resultant soggy texture.

1/2 cup finely chopped pecans
1/2 cup soft breadcrumbs, preferably whole wheat
1/4 teaspoon kosher salt
1/4 teaspoon freshly ground pepper
1/2 cup buttermilk
2 pounds skinless chicken parts, with or without bones

1) Preheat the oven to 400°F.

2) On a plate, mix together the pecans, breadcrumbs, salt, and pepper.

3) Pour the buttermilk into a bowl. Thoroughly coat the chicken with buttermilk.

4) Roll the chicken in the pecan mixture. Gently shake off the excess. Place the chicken pieces in a casserole or baking pan.

5) Bake, uncovered, for 20 to 45 minutes, depending on the thickness of the chicken.

Per Serving: Calories 324; Protein 40g; Fat 15g (Saturated 2g); Carbohydrates 7g; Fiber 1g; Sodium 310mg

Crusty Horseradish Chicken

Makes: 4 servings

The mustard and horseradish gives this chicken a kick. These can make great hors d'oeuvres if the chicken is cut into bite-size pieces before breading.

1 pound skinless, boneless chicken breast
3/4 cup dry breadcrumbs
1/4 teaspoon kosher salt
1/4 teaspoon freshly ground pepper
2 tablespoons store-bought bottled white horse-radish
1 tablespoon Dijon mustard
1/4 cup white wine

1) Preheat the oven to 400°F.

2) Trim the fat off the chicken. Cut the meat into 4 portions.

3) On a plate, mix together the breadcrumbs, salt, and pepper.

4) In a bowl, stir together the horseradish, mustard, and wine.

5) Dip the chicken in the horseradish mixture until it is well coated. (If you're not preparing the chicken immediately, at this stage you may leave it to marinate for up to 1 hour.)

6) Roll the chicken piece by piece in the breadcrumbs to form an even coating. Gently shake off any excess. Place the pieces in a casserole or baking sheet.

7) Bake, uncovered, for 20 to 30 minutes, or until done.

Per Serving: Calories 204; Protein 29g; Fat 2g (Saturated 1g); Carbohydrates 14g; Fiber 1g; Sodium 381mg

Chicken Baked in Pesto Crust

Makes: 4 servings

A jar of pesto in the refrigerator allows the cook to make a sophisticated meal out of a minimum of ingredients.

1 pound skinless, boneless chicken breast, or other skinless chicken parts
1 egg white
3 tablespoons nonfat milk
1/2 cup dry breadcrumbs
1/4 cup Basil Pesto (page 589 or store-bought)

1) Preheat the oven to 400°F. Coat a baking sheet with nonstick spray.

2) Cut the chicken into 4 portions. Pat dry with a paper towel.

3) Combine the egg white and nonfat milk in a shallow bowl. Put the breadcrumbs on a plate. Brush the pesto onto both sides of the chicken. Dip the chicken in the egg mixture, then place it in the breadcrumbs. Turn, coat thoroughly, and press the crumbs onto the chicken. Place on the baking sheet.

4) Bake for 25 to 30 minutes, until done.

Per Serving: Calories 229; Protein 30g; Fat 7g (Saturated 1g); Carbohydrates 10g; Fiber 1g; Sodium 232mg

Chutney Chicken

Makes: 4 servings

If using a chunky chutney, puree it first so that it can coat the chicken evenly.

1 pound skinless, boneless chicken breasts
1/4 cup dry or soft breadcrumbs
1 teaspoon kosher salt
1/4 teaspoon freshly ground pepper
1/3 cup chutney

1) Preheat the oven to 375°F. Coat a baking pan or sheet with nonstick spray.

2) Wash the chicken and pat dry with a paper towel. Mix the breadcrumbs, salt, and pepper on a plate.

3) Brush the chutney all over the chicken. Place the chicken in the breadcrumbs, turn, and coat. Place on the baking sheet.

4) Bake for 25 minutes, or until done.

Per Serving: Calories 185; Protein 27g; Fat 2g (Saturated 0g); Carbohydrates 14g; Fiber 1g; Sodium 659mg

Grilled and Broiled Chicken

As with all of my chicken recipes, I remove the skin in order to remove the fat. But a plain piece of skinless chicken becomes dry and tough when cooked on the grill. If cooked with the skin on with the intention of removing the skin before dining, either the chicken underneath tastes boring or the skin gets eaten. The solution is to use glazes and marinades that provide moistness and flavor. It also helps to have the chicken in small enough pieces that they cook fairly quickly and evenly. Big pieces dry out on the outside before they are cooked on the inside. Undercooked chicken is a health risk, so it is important to cook the chicken well. The following recipes cook chicken thoroughly in under 20 minutes.

Grilling Tips

Make sure your grill rack is clean. I prefer to get mine very hot, then scrub it off with a metal brush. If the rack has bits of previous meals clinging to it, the chicken will stick and tear. I also find it easier to oil the meat rather than the grill rack. If the marinade has oil in it, a brush with the marinade before grilling is usually all that is needed. If the marinade has little oil, the chicken can be lightly coated with a nonstick spray, preferably olive oil. Chicken should be grilled at a moderate temperatute.

Fresh Herb Marinated Chicken

Makes: 4 servings

Fresh herbs are a must. If you can't find one of the ones listed here, substitute others. Chicken breasts with or without bones can be used.

1 cup white wine
1 tablespoon olive oil
1 clove garlic, crushed
2 bay leaves
6 green peppercorns, crushed
$1/4$ teaspoon kosher salt
1 teaspoon minced fresh thyme
2 teaspoons minced fresh rosemary
2 tablespoons chopped fresh basil
2 skinless chicken breasts, split

1) Combine all the ingredients except the chicken. Pour the mixture over the chicken and let marinate for 1 hour.

2) Prepare the broiler or grill. Cook the chicken for 5 minutes, brush with the marinade, then turn and brush the top with the marinade. Continue to cook until done.

Per Serving: Calories 147; Protein 27g; Fat 2g (Saturated 1g); Carbohydrates 0g; Fiber 0g; Sodium 107mg

Maple-Mustard Glazed Chicken

Makes: 8 servings

This marinade stays fresh for weeks if stored in a glass jar in the refrigerator. Thus, although the recipe calls for 2 pounds of chicken, you could use just enough marinade for one serving and save the remaining, untouched glaze for another time. To avoid bacterial contamination, never save or reuse marinade that has had chicken soaking in it or that has been touched with the basting brush used on the chicken.

$1/2$ cup maple syrup
$1/3$ cup apple cider vinegar
$1/4$ cup water
3 tablespoons Dijon mustard
$1/2$ teaspoon kosher salt
1 tablespoon vegetable oil
2 pounds skinless, boneless chicken breast

1) In a small saucepan combine the maple syrup, vinegar, water, mustard, and salt. Bring to a boil, immediately reduce to a simmer, and cook for 15 minutes. Remove from the heat and whisk in the oil. Cool to room temperature.

2) Cut the chicken into pieces weighing about 4 ounces each. Put them in a shallow dish or sealable plastic bag and coat with enough sauce to cover. Let the chicken marinate for 30 minutes or up to 2 hours. Turn several times.

3) Preheat and prepare the grill. Grill the chicken for 4 minutes, then brush with the marinade, turn, and continue to cook until done, about 5 to 8 minutes longer. Although the dark grill marks look and taste wonderful, this recipe can also be broiled. Cover a baking sheet with foil and cook the chicken on it, about 6 inches from the heat source, basting and turning once.

Per Serving: Calories 144; Protein 26g; Fat 2g (Saturated 0g); Carbohydrates 4g; Fiber 0g; Sodium 140mg

Tandoori Chicken

Makes: 4 servings

Because this chicken requires at least several hours of marinating and is even better if left an entire day, it is a good choice when you want to give a fuss-free dinner party. Pair it with several do-ahead salads and all you'll have to do is heat up the grill as your guests arrive.

2 pounds skinless chicken pieces, bone-in
1 teaspoon kosher salt
2 tablespoons lemon juice, divided
$1/2$ cup plain lowfat yogurt
1 tablespoon apple cider vinegar
2 cloves garlic, minced (1 teaspoon)
2 teaspoons finely grated fresh ginger
2 to 3 teaspoons mild curry powder
$1/4$ teaspoon ground chili pepper (optional)

1) Wash the chicken, then pat it dry. Make $1/2$-inch-deep cuts on the surface of the chicken.

2) Sprinkle the chicken with the salt, then 1 tablespoon of the lemon juice. Rub the salt and juice into the meat.

3) In a glass or stainless-steel bowl, combine the yogurt, the second tablespoon of lemon juice, and the remaining ingredients. Marinate the chicken in this mixture. Turn the pieces several times to make sure they are well coated. Leave the chicken in the marinade for at least several hours, preferably an entire day. Keep covered and refrigerated.

4) Preheat the broiler or prepare the grill. Remove the chicken from the marinade and shake off any excess, allowing some marinade to cling to the meat.

5) Place the chicken in the broiler or directly on the grill. Cook for 7 to 10 minutes. Turn the chicken, then continue cooking for about 10 to 15 minutes more until done. Do not brush with the sauce.

Per Serving: Calories 204; Protein 38g; Fat 4g (Saturated 1g); Carbohydrates 1g; Fiber 0g; Sodium 615mg

Turkish-Style Yogurt Chicken

Makes: 4 servings

Like Tandoori Chicken, this recipe is a good one to do ahead because it requires marinating. However, the lemon juice tenderizes the chicken, and if left in the marinade too long, the meat proteins (and therefore the texture) will begin to break down. So don't leave it in the refrigerator for longer than the suggested 8 hours.

1/4 cup lemon juice
3 cloves garlic, minced
2 teaspoons paprika
1/4 teaspoon ground allspice
1 teaspoon ground cumin
1 teaspoon kosher salt
1/4 teaspoon freshly ground pepper
1 cup plain nonfat yogurt
8 skinless chicken thighs, trimmed of fat

1) In a glass or stainless-steel bowl, blend all of the ingredients except the chicken. Add the chicken and toss to coat. Cover and marinate in the refrigerator for 2 to 8 hours.

2) Preheat the broiler or prepare the grill. Coat a baking sheet with a nonstick spray or oil the grill.

3) Remove the chicken from the marinade and place on the baking sheet or directly on the grill. Don't wipe or shake off the marinade. Broil 4 to 6 inches from the heat source or over a moderate grill. After 10 minutes, turn the chicken over but do not baste with more marinade or the marinade already on the chicken will rub off. Cook another 10 minutes, or until the chicken is tender and the yogurt begins to bubble and brown.

Per Serving: Calories 176; Protein 28g; Fat 6g (Saturated 1g); Carbohydrates 2g; Fiber 0g; Sodium 251mg

Kebabs

Cooking meat on skewers has many advantages. Because the meat is cut into cubes, it cooks quickly and evenly. Basting first in a marinade insures flavor and moistness. A moderate portion of meat can be stretched by including vegetables and fruits on the skewers. Kebabs are perfect for an informal buffet party because they can be eaten while standing up. Some recipes, such as the Chicken Yakitori, can be served as hors d'oeuvres.

Skewers can be metal or wood. Metal skewers are sturdy and reusable, but they come off the grill dangerously hot. Wooden skewers can be held in the hand, but they must be soaked in water before use to prevent them from scorching while on the grill.

Keep at least an inch of space between the kebabs as they are cooking, and turn several times. They'll cook quickly so stay near the grill or broiler. Use long stainless-steel spring tongs to rotate the kebabs. Have a clean platter for the cooked kebabs next to the grill. (Never put cooked meat back on a plate that held raw).

Chicken Yakitori

Makes: 4 servings

The crisp water chestnuts balance the tender texture of the chicken.

1 pound skinless, boneless chicken breast, cut into
    1-inch cubes
1/2 cup Teriyaki sauce or Spicy Sesame Teriyaki
    Sauce (pages 588, 589)
3 scallions, cut into 1-inch pieces
One 5 1/2-ounce can whole water chestnuts

1) Toss the chicken pieces with the sauce in a bowl and marinate for 1 to 2 hours in the refrigerator. Stir twice while marinating to ensure that all of the chicken is in contact with the sauce.

2) Preheat the broiler or grill. If using the oven, line a baking sheet with foil to ease clean-up, and place the oven rack 4 inches from the heat source.

3) Divide the chicken pieces into 12 portions and thread on 12 skewers, placing a scallion between each piece and a water chestnut on each end. Set on the baking sheet and place in the oven, or place right on the grill. Cook for 3 minutes. Turn and cook another 2 minutes.

Per Serving: Calories 154; Protein 27g; Fat 2g (Saturated 0g); Carbohydrates 6g; Fiber 1g; Sodium 336mg

Tropical Chicken Kebabs

Makes: 6 servings

Serve this over rice, with wedges of lime for garnish.

2 cloves garlic, smashed
1/4 cup fresh lime juice
2 tablespoons honey
2 teaspoons vegetable oil
1 teaspoon soy sauce
1 teaspoon Asian sesame oil
One 8-ounce can pineapple chunks,
    packed in juice
1 1/2 pounds skinless, boneless chicken breast, cut
    into 2-inch cubes
1 papaya, peeled, seeded, cut into 2-inch pieces
2 green bell peppers, cut into 2-inch squares
4 scallions, cut into 2-inch lengths

1) Stir together the garlic, lime juice, honey, vegetable oil, soy sauce, and sesame oil. Pour in the juice from the pineapple can.

2) Thread 12 large skewers alternating chicken and the fruits and vegetables. Lay the skewers in a shallow dish, pour the dressing over, and turn to coat. Cover and refrigerate for 2 to 24 hours. Turn the kebabs several times while marinating to make sure that all of the chicken absorbs the flavorings.

3) These can be grilled or broiled. If broiling, line a baking sheet with foil to ease clean-up and place the oven rack 4 inches from the heat source. Preheat the broiler or prepare the grill.

4) Take the skewers out of the marinade and, if broiling, place them on the baking sheet. Don't crowd or they won't cook properly. If grilling, place directly on a hot grill.

5) Cook for 4 minutes, turn the kebabs, and continue to cook until done but still moist-looking, about 3 to 5 minutes more.

Per Serving: Calories 182; Protein 27g; Fat 2g (Saturated 0g); Carbohydrates 13g; Fiber 2g; Sodium 92mg

Honey-Hoisin Kebabs

Makes: 4 servings

Although this recipe only calls for 1 pound of chicken, it makes enough sauce to flavor 4 pounds. The extra marinade will remain fresh in the refrigerator for several weeks. Not only is it good on chicken, but it is also terrific on tofu, or as a flavor base for a stir-fry.

1/4 cup hoisin sauce
2 tablespoons Worcestershire sauce
2 tablespoons soy sauce
1 tablespoon vegetable oil
1/4 cup honey
1 tablespoon apple cider vinegar
1 pound skinless, boneless chicken breast, cut into large cubes

1) Whisk together all the ingredients except the chicken. Put the chicken in a bowl and pour on 1/4 cup of sauce. Toss to coat. Let rest for 30 minutes to 1 hour.

2) If broiling, line a baking sheet with foil to ease clean-up and place the oven rack 4 inches from the heat source. Preheat the broiler or prepare the grill.

3) Thread 8 skewers with the chicken. Leave a little space between each piece of chicken. Grill or broil the skewers, brushing twice with the marinade and turning each time. Total cooking time will be 8 to 10 minutes.

Per Serving: Calories 195; Protein 27g; Fat 3g (Saturated 0g); Carbohydrates 13g; Fiber 0g; Sodium 498mg

Honey-Teriyaki Chicken Kebabs

Makes: 4 servings

If the honey isn't easy to pour, warm it in the microwave (this usually takes less than 20 seconds). This will make it easier to blend with the other marinade ingredients.

1/4 cup soy sauce
1 tablespoon finely grated fresh ginger
1 clove garlic, minced
1/2 cup water
1 tablespoon lemon juice
1 1/2 tablespoons honey
6 scallions, sliced
1 pound skinless, boneless chicken breast, cut into strips

1) Whisk together all the ingredients except the chicken. Add the chicken and marinate for 1/2 hour.

2) If broiling, line a baking sheet with foil to ease clean-up and place the oven rack 4 inches from the heat source. Preheat the broiler or prepare the grill.

3) Remove the chicken from the marinade and thread the meat on 8 skewers. Set the kebabs on the baking sheet and place in the oven or right on the grill. Cook for 4 minutes. Turn and cook another 4 minutes, or until done.

Per Serving: Calories 133; Protein 26g; Fat 1g (Saturated 0g); Carbohydrates 2g; Fiber 0g; Sodium 331mg

Persian Lemon Chicken Kebabs

Makes: 6 servings

Offer a basket of flat breads, such as lavash or pita, along with this entrée.

1/8 teaspoon ground saffron, or 4 saffron threads

1 tablespoon hot water

1/4 cup lemon juice

1 tablespoon olive oil

1 teaspoon kosher salt

1/4 teaspoon freshly ground pepper

1 1/2 pounds skinless, boneless chicken breast, cut into 1/2-inch-wide strips

1) Crumble the saffron into the hot water (use a very small bowl or a glass). Let rest until the water turns golden orange, about 5 minutes.

2) Whisk together the lemon, oil, salt, and pepper. Stir in the saffron and water.

3) Put the chicken in a glass or stainless-steel bowl. Pour the marinade over the chicken and toss to coat. Cover and refrigerate for 12 to 24 hours. Stir the chicken several times while marinating.

4) If broiling, line a baking sheet with foil to ease clean-up and place the oven rack 4 inches from the heat source. Preheat the broiler or prepare the grill.

5) Remove the chicken from the marinade and thread onto 12 skewers. Place the skewers on the baking sheet and put in the oven, or place the kebabs directly on the grill. Cook for 4 minutes, turn the kebabs, and continue to cook until done but still moist-looking, about 2 to 3 minutes more.

Per Serving: Calories 136; Protein 26g; Fat 3g (Saturated 1g); Carbohydrates 0g; Fiber 0g; Sodium 234mg

Curried Lime Chicken Satay

Makes: 4 servings

Fresh lime juice is far superior to bottled. I buy bags of limes when they are on sale and squeeze the juice from all of them at one time. What isn't immediately used gets frozen so that I am never without fresh lime juice.

1 teaspoon finely grated fresh ginger

2 cloves garlic, minced

2 tablespoons fresh lime juice

1 tablespoon soy sauce

2 teaspoons vegetable oil

1 teaspoon curry powder

1 to 1 1/2 pounds skinless, boneless chicken breast, cut into 3×1/2-inch strips

1) Whisk together all the ingredient except the chicken. Stir in the chicken pieces and marinate, in the refrigerator, for 2 to 24 hours. Stir twice while marinating to ensure that all of the chicken comes in contact with the sauce.

2) If broiling, line a baking sheet with foil to ease clean-up and place the oven rack 4 inches from the heat source. Preheat the broiler or prepare the grill.

3) Remove the chicken from the marinade and thread the meat on 8 skewers. Set the kebabs on the baking sheet and place in the oven or place the chicken directly on the grill. Cook for 3 minutes. Turn and cook another 2 minutes, or until done (these cook very quickly).

Per Serving: Calories 138; Protein 26g; Fat 3g (Saturated 0g); Carbohydrates 1g; Fiber 0g; Sodium 202mg

Garlic-Oregano Chicken Kebabs

Makes: 6 servings

Sometimes fancy produce stores have fresh rosemary spears, which are woody, tough, and straight. For a special event, use these instead of skewers.

6 cloves garlic, sliced
1/4 cup lemon juice
3 tablespoons olive oil
1 teaspoon kosher salt
1/4 teaspoon freshly ground pepper
1 teaspoon dried oregano
1 1/4 pounds skinless, boneless chicken breast, cut into 2-inch cubes
3 tomatoes, quartered
18 large mushrooms (about 10 ounces)
2 green bell peppers, cut into 2-inch squares
1 Spanish onion, halved, then each half quartered

1) Stir together the garlic, lemon juice, oil, salt, pepper, and oregano. Marinate the chicken in this sauce for 2 to 24 hours.

2) Have 12 large skewers on hand. Thread the skewers alternating the chicken and the vegetables. Brush the kebabs with the marinade, being especially generous with the sauce on the vegetables.

3) If broiling, line a baking sheet with foil to ease clean-up and place the oven rack 4 inches from the heat source. Preheat the broiler or prepare the grill. If broiling, place the skewers on the baking sheet. If grilling, place the kebabs directly on the grill.

4) Cook for 4 minutes, turn the kebabs, and continue to cook until done but still moist, about 4 minutes more.

Per Serving: Calories 176; Protein 24g; Fat 5g (Saturated 1g); Carbohydrates 9g; Fiber 2g; Sodium 230mg

Baked Chicken

Baking is a slower form of cooking than grilling or broiling, yet it is just as easy to end up with tough, dried-out meat. To prevent that, I've created recipes that have sauces to keep the chicken moist and directions to ensure that the recipes come out right. It helps to have a heavy metal or ceramic baking pan for even heat distribution. I've found that using glass baking dishes causes the most problems. Always reduce the oven temperature by 25°F when baking in glass.

Chicken doesn't take very long to cook. Boneless white meat takes the least amount of time. Bones add a few more minutes and dark meat takes a bit longer. Professional chefs depend on their sense of touch to tell when the chicken is done. It should feel firm to the touch and spring back slightly when pushed. Undercooked chicken feels soft, like the flesh by the heel of your thumb, whereas perfectly cooked chicken feels like your wrist. Overcooked chicken feels hard, like a rubber ball. If in doubt, check the color, which should be white throughout. Once the chicken reaches the desired texture, it is done and should be removed from the oven immediately because the heat inside the chicken will continue to cook for a while longer. Except for roast chicken I don't use thermometers, since holes poked in chicken allow the juices to escape, and a thermometer is often inaccurate on small pieces.

Red Currant and Blackberry Chicken

Makes: 4 servings

Red currant jelly is more tangy than sweet. Combined with vinegars and blackberries, it makes an ideal savory sweet and sour glaze.

1/3 cup red currant jelly
1 tablespoon balsamic vinegar
1 tablespoon red wine vinegar
1/4 teaspoon kosher salt
1/4 teaspoon freshly ground pepper
2 small skinless chicken breasts, bone-in, split
1/2 cup blackberries, fresh or frozen

1) Put the jelly, vinegars, salt, and pepper into a small saucepan. Warm over low heat, whisking until smooth. Simmer for 5 minutes to thicken slightly. This can be made ahead of time and stored in a glass jar in the refrigerator.

2) Preheat the oven to 375°F. Line a baking dish with foil to ease clean-up.

3) Generously brush the chicken all over with the sauce. Place the chicken in the baking dish and bake for 25 to 30 minutes. Brush the chicken with the sauce every 10 minutes.

4) Bring the remaining sauce to a boil and cook for 2 minutes. Turn off the heat and stir in the blackberries. If the berries were frozen, heat gently until thawed.

5) Put the chicken on a serving platter and pour the sauce over and around the chicken.

Per Serving: Calories 212; Protein 25g; Fat 3g (Saturated 1g); Carbohydrates 21g; Fiber 1g; Sodium 193mg

Gingered Marmalade Chicken

Makes: 4 servings

This glaze bubbles, browns, and releases an enticing aroma as the chicken bakes.

1/2 cup orange marmalade
1/2 cup orange juice
1/2 teaspoon finely grated fresh ginger
1 tablespoon Dijon mustard
1/8 teaspoon Tabasco sauce
1/2 teaspoon kosher salt
1/4 teaspoon freshly ground pepper
2 small skinless chicken breasts, bone-in, split

1) Preheat the oven to 350°F.

2) Blend together all the ingredients except the chicken.

3) Brush the chicken all over with the marmalade mixture. Place in a heavy baking dish (not glass) and set in the center of the oven. Bake for 25 to 30 minutes. Baste with the sauce every 10 minutes. The basting sauce is also excellent on a whole roasted chicken.

Per Serving: Calories 242; Protein 27g; Fat 2g (Saturated 0g); Carbohydrates 30g; Fiber 0g; Sodium 432mg

Baked Hoisin Chicken

Makes: 6 servings

Obviously, the longer the chicken has to absorb the sauce, the deeper the flavor penetrates. I find, however, that soy marinades dry out chicken if left for more than 12 hours.

1 teaspoon soy sauce
1 teaspoon honey
3 tablespoons hoisin sauce
2 tablespoons sherry
1 teaspoon finely grated fresh ginger (optional)
2 cloves garlic, minced (optional)
3 pounds skinless chicken parts, bone-in

1) Combine all the ingredients except the chicken in a bowl.

2) Generously coat the chicken with the hoisin mixture. Place the pieces in a stainless-steel or glass bowl, cover, and refrigerate. Reserve any extra marinade for basting later. Let the chicken marinate a few minutes to several hours.

3) Preheat the oven to 350°F. Brush off the excess sauce. Place the chicken pieces in a baking dish. Bake for 35 to 40 minutes, depending on the type of chicken part. Brush the chicken with the reserved marinade every 10 minutes or so.

Per Serving: Calories 214; Protein 37g; Fat 4g (Saturated 1g); Carbohydrates 4g; Fiber 0g; Sodium 227mg

Apricot Glazed Chicken

Makes: 8 servings

Leftover glaze will last for several weeks in the refrigerator.

$1/4$ cup dried apricots
1 clove garlic
$1/2$ cup apricot jam
$1/4$ cup dry white wine
2 tablespoons light brown sugar
2 teaspoons Worcestershire sauce
$1 1/2$ teaspoons vegetable oil
$1/4$ teaspoon freshly ground pepper
$1/2$ teaspoon kosher salt
2 pounds skinless chicken pieces, bone-in

1) Preheat the oven to 375°F. Line a baking dish with foil to ease clean-up.

2) Soak the apricots in hot water until soft. Drain the water and puree the apricots, garlic, and jam. Add the remaining ingredients except the chicken and puree until smooth.

3) Brush the chicken all over with the glaze and place in the baking dish. Bake for 30 to 45 minutes, depending on the size and type of the chicken pieces, brushing once more halfway through baking.

Per Serving: Calories 183; Protein 19g; Fat 3g (Saturated 1g); Carbohydrates 19g; Fiber 1g; Sodium 209mg

Papaya Baked Chicken Breasts

Makes: 6 servings

Ripe papayas are slightly firm to the touch and mottled orange in color. They have far more flavor than the harder yellow ones. Papayas that have some orange color will ripen if left out on the counter.

1 ripe papaya
2 cloves garlic
1 shallot, peeled
1/4 cup orange juice
3/4 cup reduced-sodium, defatted chicken broth
2 tablespoons lemon juice
1/2 teaspoon dry thyme
1/4 teaspoon dry mustard
1/4 teaspoon kosher salt
1 teaspoon soy sauce
1/4 teaspoon freshly ground pepper
3 small skinless chicken breasts, split

1) Scoop out and discard the papaya's black seeds. Peel off the skin and cut the fruit into quarters.

2) In a food processor, mince the garlic and shallot. Add the papaya and pulse until chopped. Add all the remaining ingredients except the chicken. Puree until smooth.

3) Transfer the marinade to a glass or stainless-steel bowl. Add the chicken, turning the pieces until they are well coated. Marinate for 4 hours or up to 1 day. Turn the chicken occasionally. The marinade will solidify in the refrigerator.

4) Preheat the oven to 350°F.

5) Take the chicken out of the marinade and shake off the excess papaya. Place the breasts in a heavy casserole. Brush the marinade onto the chicken so that it covers the meat evenly with a 1/4-inch-thick coating. Bake until done. Boneless pieces will take about 25 to 30 minutes; those with the bones in will take 35 to 45 minutes, depending on the thickness.

Per Serving: Calories 163; Protein 28g; Fat 2g (Saturated 0g); Carbohydrates 8g; Fiber 1g; Sodium 276mg

Lemon-Rosemary Chicken

Makes: 4 servings

The lemon marinade and light breading prevent these chicken breasts from tasting dull or dried out.

2 skinless chicken breasts, bone-in, split
2 lemons
1/4 cup unbleached, all-purpose white flour
1/2 teaspoon paprika
1/4 teaspoon kosher salt
1/4 teaspoon freshly ground pepper
1 teaspoon honey
1/2 cup reduced-sodium, defatted chicken broth
1 tablespoon chopped fresh rosemary, or
       1 teaspoon dried

1) Halve the chicken breasts and put the 4 portions into a glass or stainless-steel bowl.

2) Peel a long strip of peel off one of the lemons and thinly slice the peel. (Avoid the white pith beneath the yellow peel.) Or use a zester to get fine strips of peel. You'll need 1 tablespoon of chopped peel.

3) Juice the lemons and pour the juice over the chicken. Cover with plastic wrap and store in the refrigerator for at least 4 hours but no longer than 12.

4) Remove the chicken from the marinade. Discard the lemon juice. Preheat the oven to 375°F.

5) Put the flour, paprika, salt, and pepper into a plastic bag. One at a time, shake the pieces of chicken in the bag until each is well coated with flour. Place the chicken in a baking pan or oven-proof casserole and bake for 20 minutes.

6) In a small bowl, combine the honey, broth, rosemary, and lemon peel. Pour this over the chicken and continue to bake for 15 minutes longer.

7) If a sauce is desired, put the chicken onto a warm plate and cover to keep warm. Put the baking pan, with its juices, on the stovetop (make sure that the casserole can safely be heated on the burner). Boil the liquid, at a high heat, for about 4 minutes, stirring frequently, until the volume is reduced by half. Pour over the chicken.

Per Serving: Calories 176; Protein 31g; Fat 2g (Saturated 0g); Carbohydrates 7g; Fiber 1g; Sodium 263mg

Pineapple Barbeque Chicken

Makes: 4 servings

Children love this dish. There's lots of pineapple and sauce to pour over rice.

1/2 cup barbeque sauce (see pages 587–588 for
       a selection)
One 20-ounce can pineapple chunks, packed in
       their own juice
2 pounds skinless chicken pieces, bone-in

1) Preheat the oven to 375°F.

2) Pour the barbeque sauce and the pineapple (with juice) into a baking dish. Stir to combine.

3) Place the chicken one layer deep in the dish. Turn once to coat with the sauce.

4) Cover and bake for 30 minutes. Turn the chicken pieces and continue to bake until done. Thighs will take about 50 minutes, breasts about 30. Uncover for the last 10 minutes.

Per Serving: Calories 290; Protein 29g; Fat 4g (Saturated 1g); Carbohydrates 35g; Fiber 2g; Sodium 414mg

Orange Barbeque Chicken

Makes: 4 servings

This is a recipe for those moments when you think that you don't have the time or the energy to cook. Actually, I first put this together when, with a new baby in the house, cooking was the last thing on my mind and all I had were some chicken breasts in the freezer. Since then it has remained a standard in my kitchen, because, despite being a food writer, I often don't have time to cook!

$1/2$ cup barbeque sauce (see pages 587–588 for a selection)
$1/4$ cup orange juice
2 pounds skinless chicken pieces, bone-in

1) Preheat the oven to 375°F.

2) Pour the barbeque sauce and the orange juice into a baking dish. Stir to combine.

3) Place the chicken one layer deep in the dish. Turn once to coat with the sauce. If necessary, add more orange juice so that the sauce reaches halfway up the chicken pieces.

4) Cover and bake for 20 minutes. Turn the chicken pieces over and continue to bake until done. Thighs will take about 50 minutes, breasts about 30. Uncover for the last 10 minutes.

Per Serving: Calories 196; Protein 25g; Fat 4g (Saturated 1g); Carbohydrates 15g; Fiber 1g; Sodium 374mg

Sesame Buttermilk Chicken

Makes: 8 servings

I make this recipe whenever I have buttermilk left over from baking.

2 pounds skinless, boneless chicken breast
$1/2$ teaspoon freshly ground pepper
$1/3$ cup sesame seeds, lightly toasted
$1/2$ cup dry or soft breadcrumbs
1 cup buttermilk
Paprika, for garnish (optional)

1) Preheat the oven to 375°F.

2) Cut the chicken into about 8 pieces. Wash, then pat dry. Rub on the pepper.

3) Mix together the sesame seeds and breadcrumbs. Dip the chicken in the buttermilk and then roll the pieces in the crumb mixture, coating well.

4) Place the chicken in a casserole dish and pour in enough buttermilk to reach halfway up the chicken. Depending on the size of the dish, you might need slightly more or less buttermilk.

5) Top the chicken with the remaining breadcrumb-sesame mixture.

6) Cover and bake for 20 minutes. Uncover and bake for 10 minutes more. If desired, dust with paprika to add color.

Per Serving: Calories 207; Protein 30g; Fat 5g (Saturated 1g); Carbohydrates 7g; Fiber 1g; Sodium 168mg

Chicken in Orange and Tahini

Makes: 4 servings

Sesame seeds lend a richness to otherwise pallid chicken breasts.

1 clove garlic, crushed
3/4 cup orange juice, divided
1 tablespoon frozen orange juice
    concentrate, thawed
1 tablespoon soy sauce
2 tablespoons tahini
1 pound boneless, skinless chicken breast, cut into
    4 portions
1 tablespoon sesame seeds

1) Combine the garlic, 1/2 cup of the orange juice, the orange juice concentrate, soy sauce, and tahini. Blend well. Marinate the chicken in this mixture for 1 hour in the refrigerator.

2) Preheat the oven to 375°F.

3) Remove the chicken from the marinade and place in a baking dish. Pour the remaining 1/4 cup of orange juice over the chicken and add as much of the marinade as is necessary to cover three-quarters of the chicken.

4) Sprinkle the sesame seeds on top.

5) Bake for 30 minutes.

Per Serving: Calories 216; Protein 29g; Fat 7g (Saturated 1g); Carbohydrates 9g; Fiber 1g; Sodium 333mg

Marmalade Chicken

Makes: 8 servings

Fruit and chicken have a natural affinity for each other, but recipes often err on the side of sweetness. Here it is kept from being too cloying by the addition of herbs, lemon zest, and soy sauce.

2 pounds skinless chicken pieces, bone-in
1/4 cup unbleached, all-purpose white flour
2 teaspoons olive oil
1/4 cup reduced-sodium, defatted chicken broth
1/2 teaspoon dried marjoram
1/2 teaspoon minced lemon zest
2 tablespoons sherry
1 teaspoon soy sauce
1/4 cup orange marmalade
1 orange

1) Preheat the oven to 375°F.

2) Dust the chicken with the flour. Heat the oil in a skillet and lightly brown the chicken. When done, arrange the chicken in a single layer in a casserole.

3) Combine the broth, marjoram, zest, sherry, and soy sauce. Pour over the chicken.

4) Brush the chicken with the marmalade.

5) Cut away the peel and white pith from the orange. Cut the segments away from the membranes. Do this over the casserole dish to catch the juice as you work. Arrange the orange segments over the chicken.

6) Bake for 30 to 40 minutes.

Per Serving: Calories 157; Protein 19g; Fat 3g (Saturated 1g); Carbohydrates 11g; Fiber 0g; Sodium 129mg

Apricot Chicken

Makes: 4 servings

One way to serve this is to have a big shallow serving bowl filled with hot, cooked couscous. Form a well in the center and pour in the Apricot Chicken.

2 pounds skinless chicken pieces, bone-in
1 Spanish onion, sliced
4 cloves garlic, thinly sliced
1/4 cup honey, warmed until pourable
1/4 cup lemon juice
1/2 cup reduced-sodium, defatted chicken broth
1/2 teaspoon ground cumin
1/2 teaspoon kosher salt
1/2 cup dried apricots, halved

1) Preheat the oven to 350°F.

2) If using large chicken pieces or whole breasts, cut into serving-size pieces.

3) Place the onion and garlic in a Dutch oven or casserole. Put the chicken on top.

4) Whisk together the honey, lemon juice, broth, cumin, and salt. Pour over the chicken.

5) Place the apricots on top of the chicken.

6) Cover and bake for 40 minutes. Turn the chicken over and bake for another 15 minutes, or until the chicken is done.

Per Serving: Calories 326; Protein 39g; Fat 4g (Saturated 1g); Carbohydrates 33g; Fiber 2g; Sodium 434mg

Chicken in Chili Tomato Sauce

Makes: 4 servings

I like wine, but rarely drink more than one glass at a meal, so I usually have an opened bottle of wine in my refrigerator. Wine that is good enough to drink is the best type for cooking. So-called "cooking wine" has poor flavor and contains added salt (to make it undrinkable). It should not be used for cooking. This recipe uses a small amount of white wine—just the amount to finish off that bottle.

2 teaspoons vegetable oil
1/2 cup chopped onions
4 ribs celery, chopped
1/2 green bell pepper, chopped
1/4 cup white wine
One 24-ounce can whole tomatoes, drained
    and seeded
1/4 cup tomato juice
2 tablespoons lemon juice
2 cloves garlic, chopped
1 teaspoon kosher salt
1 teaspoon pure ground chili or chili powder
1/8 teaspoon crushed red pepper flakes
1/8 teaspoon Tabasco sauce
2 small skinless chicken breasts, bone-in, split

1) Heat the oil in a saucepan and sauté the onions, celery, and bell pepper. As the vegetables begin to soften, add the wine.

2) Stir in the remaining ingredients except the chicken. Cover and simmer for 15 minutes. Allow to cool and then puree the mixture.

3) Preheat the oven to 375°F. Place the chicken in a baking dish, pour in enough sauce just to cover the chicken, and bake for 20 to 30 minutes, until done. Unused sauce can be frozen.

Per Serving: Calories 208; Protein 29g; Fat 4g (Saturated 1g); Carbohydrates 11g; Fiber 2g; Sodium 846mg

Lemon-Thyme Chicken Rolls

Makes: 4 servings

This recipe is suitable for formal dinner parties, when each meal is arranged on each dinner plate in the kitchen and brought to the table with a flourish, accompanied by impressed "ahhs" from the guests.

2 small skinless, boneless chicken breasts (about 1^1/$_4$ pounds)
^{1}/$_4$ cup lemon juice
5 tablespoons white wine, divided
2 cloves garlic, minced
1 teaspoon dried thyme
2 teaspoons olive oil
1 shallot, minced
^{1}/$_4$ pound mushrooms, sliced (about 1 cup), divided
1^1/$_2$ tablespoons minced fresh parsley
^{1}/$_8$ teaspoon kosher salt
^{1}/$_8$ teaspoon freshly ground pepper

1) Trim the chicken of fat. Cut the chicken into 4 portions, removing the cartilage. If there are tenderloins (those fingerlike pieces of meat inside the breast) remove them and save for another purpose. If the breast is very thick, slice in half horizontally. Place the chicken between 2 pieces of wax paper and, using a rolling pin, pound lightly on the breasts until they are about ^{1}/$_4$ inch thick.

2) Whisk together the lemon juice, 4 tablespoons of the wine, and the garlic and thyme. Pour over the chicken and marinate for 2 to 8 hours, refrigerated.

3) When the chicken has finished marinating, preheat the oven to 350°F. Heat the oil in a pan. Sauté the shallot until soft. Add all but ^{1}/$_4$ cup of the mushrooms, the remaining wine, and the parsley, salt, and pepper. Cook gently until the mushrooms soften and shrink in size.

4) Remove the chicken from the marinade onto a clean surface. Place a portion of the mushrooms in the center of each piece of chicken. Starting at the narrower end, tightly roll up the chicken and arrange in a casserole, seam side down, so the rolls are close but not touching.

5) Strain the marinade through a fine sieve and pour over the chicken.

6) Cover and bake for 20 minutes.

7) Place the cooked chicken on a serving plate and keep warm. Pour the baking liquid into a small saucepan, add the remaining ^{1}/$_4$ cup of mushrooms, and boil until the liquid cooks down to only a few tablespoons. Pour over the chicken and serve.

Per Serving: Calories 177; Protein 28g; Fat 4g (Saturated 1g); Carbohydrates 4g; Fiber 1g; Sodium 140mg

Oriental Chicken in Parchment

Makes: 2 servings

Each diner's meal is individually wrapped in parchment paper. Not only is it an impressive presentation at dinner, but, since the packets can be assembled well ahead of the baking time, this recipe allows the cook time to socialize with guests instead of fussing in the kitchen.

1/2 teaspoon Asian sesame oil
1 clove garlic, crushed
1 teaspoon finely grated fresh ginger
1 teaspoon soy sauce
2 tablespoons sherry
1 pound skinless, boneless chicken breast, cut into 2 portions
2 tablespoons julienned leeks
1/2 carrot, cut into matchsticks
1/4 cup julienned red bell peppers
2 slices fresh ginger, peeled

1) Combine the sesame oil, garlic, grated ginger, soy sauce, and sherry. Pour over the chicken, cover, and refrigerate for at least 2 hours.

2) Cut 2 pieces of parchment paper, each piece a little more than double the size of each piece of chicken. Fold the sheets of parchment in half.

3) Divide the ingredients into two equal portions and arrange as follows for both packets: put the leeks on one side of the folded parchment, arrange the carrots on top of the leeks, followed by the chicken. Crisscross the bell peppers over the chicken and place the ginger slice next to the chicken.

4) Fold the other half of the parchment paper over the chicken and with tight creases, seal the edges of the packets. These can be prepared several hours ahead of time to this point.

5) Place the closed packets in a baking dish and bake in a preheated 350°F oven for 30 minutes.

6) Remove the packets from the oven and place on dinner plates. Cut an X in each, being careful of escaping steam.

Per Serving: Calories 291; Protein 53g; Fat 4g (Saturated 1g); Carbohydrates 5g; Fiber 1g; 329mg

Roasted Chicken

A roasted chicken, with its crisp bronzed skin, is home cooking at its best. Although I don't eat the skin, I do roast the bird with it on. It keeps the meat moist and contributes to that rich aroma that welcomes your family into the dining room.

To prepare the chicken for roasting, take out the bag of organs and neckbone that is tucked inside, then wash the cavity well with warm water. To make the bird more attractive, cut off the triangular tail piece and the wing tips. Remove any large clumps of fat under the skin that sometimes appear near the tail. Pat the chicken dry with a paper towel.

Arrange the rack in the oven so that the chicken will bake in the middle. Preheat the oven to 425°F. Get out a roasting pan and a rack for the chicken to sit on. The rack keeps the chicken out of dripping fat and also allows hot air to circulate all around so that it cooks quickly and evenly.

Although stuffing might be part of the menu, I don't stuff the bird. Instead, I fill the chicken with ingredients that add flavor and aroma, like apples, lemons, and herbs. Not stuffing it reduces the cooking time and keeps the stuffing recipes low in fat (they absorb drippings from the skin if cooked in the cavity).

Nor do I truss the bird. Not only does this save time, but if trussed the dark meat takes too long to cook and so the white meat dries out (in the past, birds were "larded" or wrapped in fat to prevent this). I also find it unnecessary to turn the chicken as it cooks, so I start it breast side up and leave it there.

Prepare the chicken according to the recipe. Twenty minutes after the chicken is put in the oven, reduce the temperature to 375°and cook until done. Basting is an option, not a necessity. If the chicken is glazed and begins to scorch, tent loosely with foil. If the chicken browns unevenly, rotate the pan twice during roasting.

The chicken is done when a thermometer, inserted in the meaty part of the thigh, reads 165°F. (An instant-read thermometer is far better than a meat thermometer.). Another way to tell if the chicken is done is to wiggle the leg joint. It will move loosely in the socket and clear juices will pour out. A general rule is that small birds take 20 minutes per pound to cook, and chickens over 3 pounds need 15 minutes per pound to cook. After roasting, take the chicken out of the oven and let it rest for 15 minutes so that it is easier to carve. Remove the skin before serving.

Herb Roasted Chicken

Makes: 4 servings

I have a small herb garden in my backyard, and if the season is right, I'll snip a variety of herbs for the chicken. I haven't tried any combination of fresh herbs that hasn't been delicious.

One 3- to 4-pound whole chicken
$1/2$ cup fresh parsley leaves
1 sprig fresh thyme, or $1/2$ tablespoon dried
1 long sprig fresh rosemary, or 1 tablespoon dried
1 small yellow onion, peeled and cut in half
$1/2$ teaspoon paprika
Olive oil (optional)

1) Prepare the bird (see Roasted Chicken, opposite). Preheat the oven to 425°F.

2) Fill the cavity with the parsley, thyme, rosemary, and onion halves. Rub the paprika on the skin. If desired, brush with olive oil.

3) Place the bird on a rack in a roasting pan and follow the Roasted Chicken directions (opposite) for cooking.

Per Serving: Calories 202; Protein 36g; Fat 5g (Saturated 1g); Carbohydrates 0g; Fiber 0g; Sodium 131mg

Lemon Roasted Chicken

Makes: 4 servings

If you don't have a fresh lemon, use an orange. Once I had an excess of kumquats and stuffed those in the bird, and it was one of the best chickens I've ever roasted.

One 3- to 4-pound whole chicken
1 lemon wedge or slice
2 cloves garlic, peeled and crushed
Kosher salt
Freshly ground pepper
Olive oil

1) Prepare the bird (see Roasted Chicken, opposite). Preheat the oven to 425°F.

2) Rub the chicken with the lemon and garlic, then put the lemon and garlic in the cavity. Rub with the salt and pepper. Brush with a little olive oil to make the skin glisten.

3) Place the bird in a roasting pan and follow the Roasted Chicken directions (opposite) for cooking.

Per Serving: Calories 202; Protein 36g; Fat 5g (Saturated 1g); Carbohydrates 0g; Fiber 0g; Sodium 131mg

Orange and Lime Roasted Chicken

Makes: 4 servings

Placing the orange slices under the chicken skin transports the flavors deep into the meat so that when you take off the skin, you won't find the the meat lacking in taste. The sauce complements and confirms the good flavors.

One 3- to 4-pound whole chicken
2 oranges
1 lime
1/2 red onion, quartered
1 sprig fresh rosemary, or 2 teaspoons dried
1 teaspoon Worcestershire sauce
1 teaspoon soy sauce
2 tablespoons honey

1) Prepare the bird (see Roasted Chicken, page 176). Preheat the oven to 425°F.

2) Halve one of the oranges and squeeze out, and reserve the juice. Quarter the rinds. Do the same for the lime. Put the onion quarters and rosemary in the chicken's cavity. Add as many of the orange and lime quarters as the cavity can hold.

3) Thinly slice the remaining orange into rounds. Loosen the skin from the chicken. Slip the rounds under the skin. Leftover orange rounds can be used to garnish the dinner plates.

4) Whisk together the Worcestershire sauce, soy sauce, and honey. Pour in the reserved orange and lime juices.

5) Place the chicken on a rack in a roasting pan. Put it in the oven and cook for 20 minutes. Reduce the oven temperature to 350°F. Brush the chicken with the sauce. Baste every 10 minutes until the chicken is done, about 40 minutes

longer. Remove the bird from the oven and let it rest for 15 minutes before carving. Remove the skin and orange peels before serving.

6) Put the sauce in a small pot, bring to a boil, and cook for 3 minutes. Serve with the chicken.

Per Serving: Calories 256; Protein 37g; Fat 5g (Saturated 1g); Carbohydrates 14g; Fiber 0g; Sodium 231mg

Garlic Chicken

Makes: 4 servings

Garlic cooked under the skin and in the pan juices loses its sharpness and becomes as spreadable as butter.

One 3- to 4-pound whole chicken
Kosher salt
Freshly ground pepper
2 heads garlic
1/2 cup fresh parsley leaves
1 cup sliced onions, divided
1 teaspoon dried thyme
2 bay leaves
2 tablespoons red wine vinegar
1/2 cup white wine

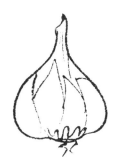

1) Prepare the bird (see Roasted Chicken, page 176). Preheat the oven to 425°F.

2) Rub the chicken with salt and pepper.

3) Break the garlic heads into cloves. Peel one head, but leave the skins on the other. Put the unpeeled garlic, the parsley, and half the onions in the cavity.

4) Slice 4 large cloves of peeled garlic. Cut small slits in the chicken skin and slide the slivers of garlic under the skin.

5) Put the chicken in a roasting pan (not on a rack). Surround the bird with the remaining onions and the peeled garlic and bay leaves. Pour in the vinegar and wine.

6) Put the pan in the oven. After 20 minutes, reduce the temperature to 350°F. Continue to cook, basting with the pan juices every 20 minutes, until done.

Per Serving: Calories 208; Protein 36g; Fat 5g (Saturated 1g); Carbohydrates 0g; Fiber 0g; Sodium 131mg

Sweet Soy Roasted Chicken

Makes: 4 servings

The marinade permeates the chicken before roasting so that flavor isn't lost when the skin is removed.

One 3- to 4-pound whole chicken
1/4 cup soy sauce
1/4 cup rice or white wine vinegar
2 tablespoons honey
2 tablespoons sherry
1 tablespoon minced garlic
1 tablespoon grated fresh ginger
1 teaspoon ground Sichuan peppercorns

1) Prepare the bird (see Roasted Chicken, page 176).

2) In a bowl large enough to hold the bird, combine the remaining ingredients. Place the chicken in the bowl and turn several times so that the color of the marinade darkens the entire bird. Cover the bowl and put it in the refrigerator. Marinate the chicken for 1 to 4 hours. Turn the chicken several times so that it absorbs the marinade evenly.

3) Preheat the oven to 425°F.

4) Remove the chicken from the marinade and with a pastry brush, brush off the bits of garlic and ginger sticking to the skin.

5) This marinade tends to stick to the roasting pan and burn, so to ease clean-up, either line the pan with foil or coat with a nonstick spray. Place the bird, breast side up, on a rack in the pan and put the pan in the oven. If the chicken browns unevenly, rotate the pan a few times during roasting.

6) After 20 minutes, reduce the temperature to 350°F. After the skin begins to crisp, tent with foil and brush with the marinade every 20 minutes to keep the skin from cracking and scorching. Cook until done.

Per Serving: Calories 215; Protein 37g; Fat 5g (Saturated 1g); Carbohydrates 3g; Fiber 0g; Sodium 400mg

Chicken Roasted with Red Rubbing Spices

Makes: 4 servings

This dry spice blend colors the chicken a warm brick red and gives it an equally warm flavor. Rub the spices both on the skin and under the skin (when you discard the skin you'll still have flavored meat). These spices can be used for roasting chicken parts as well as whole birds. Save any extra spice blend in a glass jar in your cupboard. The recipe makes enough for several roasters.

One 3- to 4-pound whole chicken
1 teaspoon paprika
1 teaspoon ground cumin
1 teaspoon ground coriander
1 tablespoon mild chili powder
1/4 teaspoon ground cinnamon
1/16 teaspoon cayenne pepper
1/4 teaspoon kosher salt
Olive oil (optional)

1) Prepare the bird (see Roasted Chicken, page 176). Preheat the oven to 425°F.

2) Stir all the spices together until the color is even throughout.

3) Loosen the chicken skin and rub the spice blend on the meat, then dust the chicken skin with the spice blend and rub it in with your fingers. If desired, rub a small amount of olive oil on the chicken to give the skin an attractive sheen.

4) Place the bird on a rack in a roasting pan and place in the oven. After 20 minutes, reduce the temperature to 350°F and cook according to the Roasted Chicken directions (page 176). After the chicken begins to crisp, tent with foil and baste with olive oil or pan juices every 20 minutes to prevent the spices from scorching.

Per Serving: Calories 205; Protein 37g; Fat 5g (Saturated 1g); Carbohydrates 0g; Fiber 0g; Sodium 166mg

Casseroles

Mexican Corn and Chicken Casserole

Makes: 4 servings

Since both my husband and I work at home, I love a casserole that makes leftovers so that we can have lunches from it later in the week. This one does just that, and since it can be doubled, it is especially welcome in my kitchen.

1 tablespoon vegetable oil
1 medium yellow onion, halved and sliced
2 cloves garlic, chopped
$1/2$ red bell pepper, chopped, or $1/2$ cup chopped roasted pepper
1 pound skinless, boneless chicken breast, cut into 8 pieces
One $14^1/2$-ounce can whole tomatoes, with juice
2 cups corn kernels
$1/2$ teaspoon ground cumin
2 tablespoons diced canned mild green chilies
$1/8$ teaspoon Tabasco sauce
1 teaspoon kosher salt
$1/4$ teaspoon freshly ground pepper
1 cup shredded reduced-fat jack cheese

1) Preheat the oven to 400°F.

2) Heat the oil in a Dutch oven or large skillet. Sauté the onion, garlic, and pepper for about 5 minutes over medium-high heat, until the onions turn golden brown. Push to the side. Add the chicken. Stir and cook until all sides turn white.

3) Pour the juice from the tomatoes into the pot. Break up the tomatoes and add them to the pot. Stir in the remaining ingredients except for the cheese. Simmer, covered, for 10 minutes.

4) Top with the cheese and place in the oven, uncovered, for 15 minutes. (If using a skillet, transfer to an ovenproof casserole before adding the cheese.)

Per Serving: Calories 312; Protein 36g; Fat 10g (Saturated 3g); Carbohydrates 24g; Fiber 4g; Sodium 888mg

Greek Chicken Casserole

Makes: 4 servings

This casserole requires little work to prepare, yet is attractive and full-flavored when it comes out of the oven. Serve with rice, salad, and crusty bread.

1¹/2 teaspoons olive oil
1 medium yellow onion, halved and sliced
2 cloves garlic, chopped
1 pound skinless, boneless chicken breast, cut into 6 pieces
1 zucchini, chopped
One 14¹/2-ounce can whole tomatoes, with juice
1 teaspoon dried oregano
2 bay leaves
1 teaspoon kosher salt
¹/4 teaspoon freshly ground pepper
2 ounces feta cheese, crumbled (about a 2-inch-square piece)

1) Preheat the oven to 400°F.

2) Heat the oil in a Dutch oven or large skillet. Sauté the onion and garlic for about 5 minutes over medium-high heat until the onion turns golden brown. Add the chicken and stir and cook until all sides turn white. Add the zucchini and cook for 2 minutes.

3) Pour the juice from the canned tomatoes into the pot. Break up the tomatoes and add them to the pot. Stir in the oregano, bay leaves, salt, and pepper. Simmer, covered, for 10 minutes.

4) Top with the feta and place, uncovered, in the oven for 15 minutes. (If using a skillet, transfer to an ovenproof casserole.)

Per Serving: Calories 221; Protein 31g; Fat 7g (Saturated 3g); Carbohydrates 9g; Fiber 2g; Sodium 875mg

Moussaka

Makes: 8 servings

Moussaka is a layered Greek casserole traditionally made with lamb. You can substitute ¹/2 pound of ground lamb for half the ground turkey.

1 pound lean ground turkey
2 teaspoons olive oil
2 cups sliced onions
2 cups sliced green bell peppers
¹/3 cup dry red wine
¹/2 cup currants
5 cups diced tomatoes (two 15-ounce cans)
1 tablespoon tomato paste
¹/4 teaspoon ground nutmeg
¹/4 teaspoon ground allspice
¹/4 teaspoon ground cinnamon
¹/2 teaspoon kosher salt
¹/8 teaspoon cayenne pepper
2 eggplants (1¹/2 pounds total)
2 large russet potatoes, peeled
1 cup plain nonfat yogurt
1 cup lowfat sour cream
1 egg yolk

1) Brown the turkey in a nonstick pan.

2) Heat the oil in a 3- to 4-quart heavy-bottomed pot. Sauté the onions and bell peppers until softened and lightly golden. Stir in the wine, currants, diced tomatoes and tomato paste, nutmeg, allspice, cinnamon, salt, and cayenne pepper. Transfer the cooked turkey to the pot. Stir. Cover and simmer on low for 1¹/2 hours, until cooked down into a thick sauce. If it is still watery after 1 hour, leave the lid off.

3) Meanwhile, slice the eggplants lengthwise into ¹/4-inch slices. Line a baking sheet with foil. Coat both sides of the eggplant slices with nonstick spray. Place in 1 layer on the baking sheet. Broil

for 4 minutes, until the eggplant begins to brown. Turn over and broil until brown. Set aside.

4) Boil the potatoes until a knife can be inserted into their centers. Remove, cool, and slice 1/4 inch thick.

5) Preheat the oven to 400°F. Coat a 13×9-inch pan with nonstick spray. Place half the eggplant in a layer, then top with half the potatoes and half the sauce. Repeat.

6) Whisk together the yogurt, sour cream, and egg yolk. Spread over the moussaka. Bake for 15 minutes, until the sauce is bubbling and the topping begins to brown. Remove from the oven and let rest 15 minutes before serving.

Per Serving: Calories 254; Protein 20g; Fat 5g (Saturated 2g); Carbohydrates 33g; Fiber 6g; Sodium 223mg

Lamb Moussaka

Makes: 8 servings

This Moussaka has a potato topping.

1 large eggplant (about 1 1/2 pounds), peeled and cubed
1 large zucchini, diced (about 3 cups)
4 cups diced tomatoes, fresh or canned (two 14 1/2-ounce cans)
1 cup diced onions
2 cloves garlic, minced
1 teaspoon dried oregano
1/2 teaspoon ground cinnamon
1/4 teaspoon freshly ground pepper
1/8 teaspoon ground nutmeg
1 pound lean ground lamb
2 pounds potatoes (about 4 large potatoes), peeled and quartered
1/2 cup nonfat milk
2 tablespoons feta cheese (about 1 1/2 ounces)
1 teaspoon kosher salt

1) Preheat the oven to 400°F. Coat a baking sheet with nonstick spray. Bake the eggplant and zucchini, in a single layer on the sheet, for 20 to 30 minutes, until softened. Set aside. Reduce the oven temperature to 350°F.

2) Simmer the tomatoes with the onions, garlic, oregano, cinnamon, pepper, and nutmeg, covered, for 15 minutes.

3) Brown the lamb in a nonstick pan. Drain and add to the cooked tomato mixture. Set aside.

4) Boil the potatoes. As soon as they are tender, drain them, and while still hot, mash with the milk, feta cheese, and salt. Set aside.

5) Coat a 9×13-inch baking dish or casserole with nonstick spray. Layer half the eggplant and zucchini, then half the meat mixture. Repeat with the vegetables and the rest of the meat. Top with the mashed potatoes, spreading as evenly as possible without disturbing the layers below. One way to do this is to form thin patties of potatoes in your hands, then place on top. Moussaka is supposed to look rustic, so don't worry about perfection. Place in the oven and bake for 45 to 50 minutes, until the potatoes begin to brown and the sauce bubbles.

Per Serving: Calories 277; Protein 16g; Fat 9g (Saturated 4g); Carbohydrates 34g; Fiber 6g; Sodium 358mg

Frontier Pie with Cornbread Topping

Makes: 6 servings

This recipe makes use of all of the traditional frontier ingredients—beef, bacon, beans, and chilies. It is even topped by classic Western cornbread. But you don't have to be having a themed party to enjoy this tried-and-true everyday fare.

1 teaspoon vegetable oil

1/2 pound beef top sirloin, cut into 1/2- to 1-inch cubes

1 cup chopped onions

1/2 green bell pepper, chopped

1 rib celery, chopped

One 15-ounce can corn, drained and rinsed

One 15-ounce can pinto beans, drained and rinsed

1 slice bacon, cooked and chopped

1 tablespoon chili powder

1/4 teaspoon sugar

One 4-ounce can diced mild green chilies (or hotter chili if desired)

One 14 1/2-ounce can stewed tomatoes

3/4 cup unbleached, all-purpose white flour

1/4 cup cornmeal

1 teaspoon baking powder

1/4 teaspoon salt

1/2 cup buttermilk

2 egg whites, lightly beaten

1) Preheat the oven to 400°F.

2) Heat the oil in the bottom of a 2- to 2 1/2-quart Dutch oven. (If you don't have a Dutch oven, do steps 2 and 3 in a skillet and then transfer the mixture to an oven casserole.) Stir in the beef, onions, bell pepper, and celery. Cook, covered, until the meat browns on all sides. Stir frequently.

3) Stir in the corn, beans, bacon, chili powder, sugar, chilies, and tomatoes. Simmer, covered, over medium-low heat for 15 minutes. Remove from the stovetop.

4) Sift together the flour, cornmeal, baking powder, and salt. Stir until well mixed. Stir in the buttermilk and egg whites until all is moist but still lumpy. Drop this batter on top of the stew and spread it out with a spatula. It will cover most but not all of the stew. Place the Dutch oven, uncovered, in the oven, and bake for 12 to 15 minutes, until the cornbread is firm and lightly brown.

Per Serving: Calories 268; Protein 18g; Fat 5g (Saturated 1g); Carbohydrates 40g; Fiber 7g; Sodium 746mg

Chicken Pot Pie

Makes: 6 servings

To save time, use frozen (and thawed) vegetables instead of the carrots and broccoli.

4 teaspoons vegetable oil, divided
1 cup chopped onions
2 cups reduced-sodium, defatted chicken broth
1 rib celery, chopped
2 carrots, cubed
1 cup chopped broccoli or cauliflower
1 cup frozen peas, thawed
3 cups cooked and cubed chicken breast
1 tablespoon unsalted butter
$^1/_2$ cup unbleached, all-purpose white flour
2 cups nonfat milk, divided
$^1/_2$ teaspoon dried thyme
1 teaspoon kosher salt
$^1/_4$ teaspoon freshly ground pepper
1 cup lowfat Bisquick mix, or other lowfat baking mix
1 egg

1) Put the oven rack in the center of the oven and preheat to 400°F.

2) Heat 1 teaspoon of the oil in a small nonstick pan. Cook the onions until softened.

3) Bring the broth to a simmer. Add the celery and carrots and simmer for 5 minutes. Remove the vegetables with a slotted spoon. Combine these with the sautéed onions, and stir in the broccoli, peas, and chicken. Set aside.

4) In a heavy saucepan, heat the remaining oil and the butter until melted. Stir in the flour and heat until it begins to turn golden. The texture will be crumbly. Stir $1^1/_2$ cups of the milk in with the broth, then whisk it into the flour. Add the thyme, salt, and pepper. Bring to a boil and whisk constantly until thickened, about 3 minutes.

5) Put the chicken and vegetables into a 9×13-inch baking pan and pour in the sauce. Combine the baking mix, the remaining milk, and the egg. Pour this batter over the casserole. (It won't cover it completely.)

6) Bake for 25 minutes, or until the top browns and the sauce is bubbly.

Per Serving: Calories 338; Protein 27g; Fat 10g (Saturated 3g); Carbohydrates 35g; Fiber 3g; Sodium 853mg

Chicken Enchiladas

Makes: 4 servings

Serve with Hot! Sauce (page 601) or a salsa on the side.

1 1/2 teaspoons vegetable oil

1 medium yellow onion, sliced

1 small zucchini, cut into french-fry-size strips

1 teaspoon ground chili powder

1 pound skinless, boneless chicken breast, cut into thin strips

2 tablespoons diced canned mild green chilies

8 corn tortillas

3 cups Fat-Free Enchilada Sauce (page 586), divided

1/2 cup shredded reduced-fat jack or mild cheddar cheese

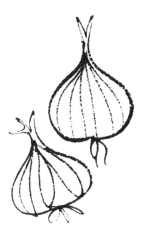

1) Preheat the oven to 375°F.

2) Heat the oil in a nonstick sauté pan. Add the onion and cook over moderate heat for 3 minutes. Stir in the zucchini and chili powder and cook until the zucchini wilts. Put the vegetables in a bowl and set aside. Put the chicken in the pan, stir, and cook until it turns white on all sides. Toss it in the bowl with the vegetables and stir in the chilies.

3) Put a small amount of water in a shallow dish. Place the stack of tortillas in this dish. Each time you need a new tortilla to fill with the chicken stuffing, take it from the bottom of the stack. The damp tortilla won't crack when rolled.

4) Spread 2 cups of the Enchilada Sauce on the bottom of an oblong baking dish. Put about 1/3 cup of chicken filling into the center of a tortilla. Roll it up and place seam side down in the pan. Repeat with each tortilla, leaving a little space between each because they expand during baking.

5) Pour the remaining cup of sauce in a stripe across the middles of the enchiladas and distribute the cheese on top.

6) Cover and bake 30 minutes. If foil is used to cover the pan, take care that it doesn't touch the sauce. Uncover and bake for 10 minutes more.

Per Serving: Calories 389; Protein 36g; Fat 7g (Saturated 2g); Carbohydrates 47g; Fiber 8g; Sodium 814mg

Turkey Lasagna

Makes: 9 servings

Perhaps the best thing about lasagna is the left-overs. By the second, third, or even fourth day this lasagna still tastes great. And it reheats perfectly in the microwave. A busy person can't hope for much more than that.

9 lasagna noodles
1 pound lean ground turkey
2 cups tomato sauce, or one 15-ounce can
One 14 1/2-ounce can whole tomatoes, chopped, with juice
1 teaspoon dried oregano
2 teaspoons dried basil
1 pound lowfat ricotta (about 2 cups)
1 cup shredded reduced-fat mozzarella
2 tablespoons grated Parmesan cheese

1) Bring a large pot of water to a boil. Cook the lasagna noodles until pliable but not soft. Drain and lay out on clean kitchen towels.

2) Meanwhile, cook the turkey in a large non-stick skillet until white throughout. As it cooks, break it apart. Pour off any fat or liquid. Stir in the tomato sauce, chopped whole tomatoes, oregano, and basil. Simmer gently, uncovered, for 15 minutes. Measure out 1 cup of sauce and set aside.

3) Preheat the oven to 350°F. Coat a 9×13-inch pan with cooking spray.

4) Place 3 noodles on the bottom the pan. Spread half the turkey sauce over the noodles, then dot with half the ricotta (don't try to spread the ricotta smooth; it will spread out as it cooks). Layer another 3 noodles. Repeat with the rest of the sauce and ricotta. Place the last 3 noodles on top. Spread the reserved cup of sauce on the noodles. Finish by distributing the mozzarella and Parmesan across the top.

5) Bake, uncovered, for 40 minutes. Remove from the oven and let it rest for 10 minutes before cutting.

Per Serving: Calories 236; Protein 23g; Fat 5g (Saturated 3g); Carbohydrates 23g; Fiber 1g; Sodium 533mg

Stovetop Cooking

Apple and Cherry Chicken

Makes: 6 servings

This recipe is not difficult to make but has several steps. It will all go smoothly if you have the ingredients prepared ahead of time. The sauce is wonderful over couscous or aromatic rice.

4 medium Granny Smith apples, peeled, cored, and sliced

1 tablespoon lemon juice

3 pounds skinless chicken parts

$1/2$ cup apple juice

$1/4$ cup white wine

1 teaspoon kosher salt

$1/4$ teaspoon freshly ground pepper

$1/2$ teaspoon ground cinnamon

1 tablespoon olive oil

2 cups sliced onions

One $14^1/2$-ounce can tart cherries packed in water, drained (about $1^1/2$ cups cherries)

$1/8$ teaspoon ground saffron, dissolved in 2 tablespoons hot water

2 tablespoons light brown sugar

1) Toss the apple slices with the lemon juice in a bowl. If the chicken parts are large, cut them into serving-size pieces (for example, cut whole legs into thighs and drumsticks) and set on a plate. Measure the apple juice, wine, salt, pepper, and cinnamon into a small bowl. Have the rest of the ingredients at hand.

2) Heat a large skillet or Dutch oven, preferably nonstick. Pour in the olive oil. Cook the onions over moderate heat until they turn golden brown, about 5 minutes. Add the apples and cook for a few minutes until the fruit begins to soften around the edges. Stir in the cherries, then put the contents of the skillet into a bowl. (Use the bowl the apples were in for one fewer dish to wash.) Set aside.

3) Cook the chicken in the skillet, turning frequently, until it turns white but remains raw in the center. If your pot is not nonstick you will have to add a little oil to keep the chicken from sticking. Add the apple juice mixture to the chicken, bring to a simmer, cover, and cook 20 minutes. Stir in the saffron water and brown sugar. Stir, cover, and continue to simmer for another 20 minutes. Gently stir in the apple mixture and simmer for 5 minutes longer.

Per Serving: Calories 337; Protein 39g; Fat 7g (Saturated 1g); Carbohydrates 29g; Fiber 3g; Sodium 458mg

Apple Cider Chicken Stew

Makes: 6 servings

Because I live within a few miles of apple orchards, I can get apple cider all year. This is fresh-pressed apple juice, darker in color, cloudy with solids, and with a bold apple flavor. If not available near you, bottled cider might be stocked in the juice aisle. Just don't confuse this apple cider with alcoholic hard cider.

1/4 cup unbleached, all-purpose white flour
1/2 teaspoon kosher salt
1/4 teaspoon freshly ground pepper
1 1/2 pounds skinless, boneless chicken breast, cut into large cubes
1 tablespoon olive oil
1 yellow onion, cut in half and thinly sliced, then cut in half once more
2 ripe tomatoes, chopped, or one 14 1/2-ounce can diced tomatoes
1 cup apple cider
1 tablespoon chopped fresh basil, or 1 teaspoon dried
1 teaspoon finely minced orange zest

1) Combine the flour, salt, and pepper in a plastic bag.

2) Heat a heavy-bottomed pan and coat with some of the oil.

3) Shake the chicken in with the flour until lightly coated.

4) Cook the chicken in the oil until white on all sides. This might have to done in several batches, depending on the size of the pan. Don't crowd the cooking chicken. Remove the chicken and set aside.

5) Sauté the onion in the pot. If needed, add a little cider or some broth to keep the onion from drying out.

6) Add the tomatoes and apple cider, along with the chicken. Simmer gently, covered, for 20 minutes.

7) Add the basil and orange zest. Cook for 10 minutes more.

Per Serving: Calories 199; Protein 27g; Fat 4g (Saturated 1g); Carbohydrates 13g; Fiber 1g; Sodium 240mg

Chicken and Apple Curry

Makes: 4 servings

You'll never find this curry in India. It isn't at all authentic, but it sure tastes good.

2 teaspoons vegetable oil, divided
1 pound skinless, boneless chicken breast, cut into 1/2-inch pieces
1 cup chopped onions
3 cloves garlic, minced
1 teaspoon finely grated fresh ginger
1/2 teaspoon ground coriander
1 to 2 teaspoons curry powder
1 cup diced tomatoes
2 apples, peeled, cored, and diced
1/2 cup reduced-sodium, defatted chicken broth
1/2 teaspoon kosher salt
1/4 teaspoon freshly ground pepper
1/2 cup raisins
2 tablespoons chutney
3 tablespoons lowfat sour cream

1) Heat 1 teaspoon of the oil in a large, nonstick skillet. Cook the chicken until white, and in some places brown, on all sides, but still pink in the center. Remove to a plate.

2) Add the remaining teaspoon of oil. Sauté the onions and cook, stirring frequently, until golden. Stir in the garlic, ginger, coriander, and curry powder and cook until the aromas intensify, about 2 minutes. Stir in the tomatoes and apples. Cook until the apples begin to soften.

3) Stir in the remaining ingredients except the sour cream. Return the chicken to the skillet, cover, and simmer for 10 minutes, until the chicken is cooked through. Stir in the sour cream and serve.

Per Serving: Calories 303; Protein 29g; Fat 5g (Saturated 1g); Carbohydrates 38g; Fiber 4g; Sodium 413mg

Chili Pumpkin Chicken

Makes: 6 servings

When winter squash season comes around, I look for ways to use this vegetable that taste like something other than pumpkin pie. This recipe combines hot spices, dried fruit, and chicken with the squash to make an unusual, savory dish.

1 tablespoon vegetable oil
$2^1/2$ cups chopped onions
3 cloves garlic, minced
$1/2$ green bell pepper, chopped
1 rib celery, chopped
1 pound skinless, boneless chicken breasts
4 to 5 cups cubed sugar pumpkin or other winter squash
2 cups reduced-sodium, defatted chicken broth
One $14^1/2$-ounce can whole tomatoes
$2/3$ cup pitted prunes
$1/2$ cup dried apricots
$1/8$ teaspoon ground chili pepper
$1^1/2$ tablespoons chili powder
1 teaspoon kosher salt
$1/2$ cup roasted pumpkin seeds, for garnish (optional)

1) Heat the oil in a sauté pan. Sauté the onions, garlic, bell pepper, and celery in the oil for 7 to 10 minutes. Cover so that the steam from the vegetables helps them to cook.

2) Add the chicken to the vegetables. Stir and cook until the meat is white on all sides.

3) Stir in the pumpkin, broth, tomatoes, dried fruit, and spices. Simmer, uncovered, for 20 minutes. Some chili powders are milder than others, so taste and adjust the seasonings.

4) Garnish with roasted pumpkin seeds, if desired.

Per Serving: Calories 237; Protein 22g; Fat 4g (Saturated 1g); Carbohydrates 30g; Fiber 7g; Sodium 826mg

Chicken and Rice

Makes: 6 servings

This recipe starts on the stovetop and ends up in the oven. If you have a large Dutch oven, you can use one pan for all the steps. Otherwise, use a separate saucepan for the first two steps, then transfer the mixture to a metal or ceramic (not glass) casserole for baking.

2 teaspoons olive oil
$2^1/2$ pounds skinless chicken pieces, bone-in
1 green bell pepper, cut into 1-inch pieces
1 cup chopped onions
2 cloves garlic, minced
1 cup uncooked brown rice
2 cups reduced-sodium, defatted chicken broth
One $14^1/2$-ounce can whole tomatoes, with juice
2 tablespoons minced fresh parsley
1 teaspoon paprika
$1/2$ teaspoon kosher salt
$1/4$ teaspoon freshly ground pepper
1 teaspoon dried thyme
2 teaspoons dried basil
$1/4$ teaspoon Tabasco sauce

1) Heat 1 teaspoon of the oil in the Dutch oven. Brown the chicken pieces in it, then remove them to a plate.

2) Add the remaining teaspoon of oil. Sauté the pepper, onions, and garlic in the oil until the onions are golden. Put all the remaining ingredients except the chicken in this pan. Cover and simmer for 25 minutes, stirring occasionally. Break the tomatoes into pieces as you stir.

3) Preheat the oven to 350°F.

4) Put the chicken into the Dutch oven and stir once through to combine. Cover and bake for 40 minutes.

Per Serving: Calories 330; Protein 36g; Fat 6g (Saturated 1g); Carbohydrates 31g; Fiber 3g; Sodium 542mg

Country Chicken

Makes: 4 servings

Serve this rustic stew over mounds of rice or noodles.

1 1/2 to 2 pounds skinless chicken breast, quartered
3 tablespoons unbleached, all-purpose white flour
3 cups reduced-sodium, defatted chicken broth
6 small white onions (pearl onions), peeled
2 cloves garlic, minced
10 large mushrooms, quartered
One 14 1/2-ounce can whole tomatoes, with juice
1 teaspoon dried thyme
1/4 cup fresh minced parsley
2 bay leaves
1 tablespoon soy sauce
Freshly ground pepper to taste

1) Lightly dust the chicken with the flour, then shake off the excess. Heat a thin layer of broth in a heavy-bottomed, nonstick pot. Brown the chicken, adding more broth as is necessary. Once browned, remove the chicken to a plate.

2) In the same pot, cook the onions and garlic in the remaining broth. Scrape up the flour from the bottom of the pan with a wooden spoon. This will form a gravy with the next ingredients.

3) Add the mushrooms and cook for a few minutes until they wilt. Add the tomatoes, barely crushing them with your hands as they go into the pot. Return the chicken to the pot and add the remaining ingredients. Simmer, covered, for 30 minutes.

Per Serving: Calories 227; Protein 37g; Fat 2g (Saturated 1g); Carbohydrates 13g; Fiber 2g; Sodium 873mg

Fragrant Chicken

Makes: 4 servings

Cinnamon and cloves aren't just for pies. Combine them with savory seasoings, onions, and capers and the resulting mixture will remind you not of dessert, but will instead transport you to the sunny Mediterranean, or at least a leisurely meal on the patio.

$1/2$ teaspoon kosher salt, divided
1 teaspoon freshly ground pepper
$1/2$ teaspoon ground cinnamon
$1/8$ teaspoon ground cloves
$1/2$ teaspoon ground turmeric
$1/4$ cup unbleached, all-purpose white flour
$1 1/2$ pounds skinless, boneless chicken breast, cut into large pieces
1 tablespoon olive oil
$1/2$ to 1 cup white wine or reduced-sodium, defatted chicken broth
1 cup chopped onions
2 cloves garlic, minced
1 cup orange juice
Pinch saffron
3 tablespoons golden raisins
1 tablespoon drained capers
1 orange

1) In a plastic bag, combine $1/4$ teaspoon of the salt with the pepper, cinnamon, cloves, turmeric, and flour. Put the chicken in the bag and shake until lightly coated.

2) Heat the oil in a large skillet. Cook the chicken in the oil until the meat turns white. Do not let pieces of chicken touch each other. Pour in a tablespoon or two of the wine as needed if more liquid is required to cook the chicken. Remove the chicken to a plate.

3) Pour the the remaining wine into the skillet. Cook the onions and garlic in this until the onions are cooked through. With a wooden spoon, scrape the flour from the bottom of the pan and stir constantly as the onions cook.

4) Return the chicken to the pot, along with the orange juice, saffron, raisins, and capers. Cover and simmer for 30 minutes. If necessary, add a little chicken broth so the sauce comes halfway up the chicken.

5) Cut the peel and white pith away from the orange, then slice the fruit. Add the orange slices to the skillet. Cook for 5 minutes longer.

Per Serving: Calories 349; Protein 42g; Fat 6g (Saturated 1g); Carbohydrates 27g; Fiber 2g; Sodium 434mg

Beef and Noodles

Makes: 5 servings

My teenage stepson would be happy if he had this to eat once a week, which is fine by me, as it doesn't require any special ingredients and can be ready in under half an hour. To spike up the flavor, use Mexican-style stewed tomatoes.

$1/2$ pound 10% fat ground beef

$1 1/2$ teaspoons olive oil

1 cup chopped onions

2 cloves garlic, minced

3 cups reduced-sodium, defatted beef or chicken broth

One $14 1/2$-ounce can stewed tomatoes

2 teaspoons Worcestershire sauce

$1/2$ pound egg noodles

$1/2$ teaspoon kosher salt

$1/4$ teaspoon freshly ground pepper

1 cup frozen peas, thawed

1) In a large Dutch oven, brown the beef. (Use a pot that is wider, rather than taller.) Remove the beef and wipe the fat out of the pot. Pour in the oil and sauté the onions and garlic until golden.

2) Add the broth, stewed tomatoes, Worcestershire sauce, and cooked beef. Bring to a boil and add the noodles. Reduce to a simmer, cover, and cook for 10 minutes, until the noodles are tender and most of the liquid is absorbed. Stir in the salt, pepper, and peas. Cook for 3 minutes more, uncovered.

Per Serving: Calories 333; Protein 20g; Fat 8g (Saturated 2g); Carbohydrates 46g; Fiber 4g; Sodium 779mg

Chicken and Noodles

Makes: 5 servings

Make this when you have leftover roast chicken. Or use raw chicken and sauté it in the oil before cooking the onions.

1 cup sliced onions

1 teaspoon olive oil

1 rib celery, chopped

2 cloves garlic, minced

3 cups reduced-sodium, defatted chicken broth

$1/2$ pounds egg noodles

$1 1/4$ pounds cooked skinless, boneless chicken meat, cut into $1/2$- to 1-inch pieces

One $14 1/2$-ounce can stewed tomatoes

1 teaspoon dried basil

1 teaspoon kosher salt, or more to taste

$1/2$ teaspoon freshly ground pepper

1 cup frozen peas, thawed

1) In a large Dutch oven, sauté the onions in the oil until golden. Stir in the celery and garlic. Cook until the garlic turns golden.

2) Stir in the remaining ingredients except the peas. Bring to a boil and immediately reduce to a simmer. Cover and cook about 10 minutes, until the noodles are tender. Stir in the peas and cook 2 minutes more.

Per Serving: Calories 460; Protein 43g; Fat 10g (Saturated 3g); Carbohydrates 47g; Fiber 4g; Sodium 1015mg

Turkey Picadillo

Makes: 4 servings

This dish comes from sunny Spanish-speaking regions. A picadillo is usually a flavorful pork or beef hash made with potatoes. It is served in flour tortillas or as a filling for chilies, although it is also wonderful served over rice. Here is a picadillo made with lean ground turkey.

1 pound lean ground turkey
2 teaspoons olive oil
1 cup chopped onions
1 clove garlic, minced
$1/2$ cup diced green bell peppers
   (about $1/2$ a pepper)
2 tablespoons diced canned mild green chilies
One $14^1/2$-ounce can whole tomatoes, chopped,
   with juice
$1/2$ cup raisins
1 large potato, peeled and cubed
2 tablespoons drained capers
1 teaspoon kosher salt
3 tablespoons barbeque sauce

1) Brown the turkey in a large nonstick skillet. Remove to a plate and wipe out the pan. In the same skillet, heat the oil and cook the onions, garlic, and bell peppers, covered, until golden. Stir frequently.

2) Stir the remaining ingredients into the pan and return the turkey to the skillet. Loosely cover and simmer for 20 minutes. While it is cooking, add water a tablespoon at a time if the sauce is too dry (this will depend on the type of barbeque sauce used).

Per Serving: Calories 302; Protein 31g; Fat 4g (Saturated 1g); Carbohydrates 37g; Fiber 4g; Sodium 980mg

Southern Chicken Stew

Makes: 4 servings

Frozen lima beans, like dried beans, are filling and full of fiber. But, unlike dried, they have a fresh vegetable texture and their flavor matches their bright green color. Lima beans make this stew filling without being heavy. No wonder a friend's husband calls this recipe his favorite "vegetarian" meal.

1 pound red bliss potatoes, scrubbed and cut into
   $1/2$-inch cubes
One $14^1/2$-ounce can whole tomatoes, with juice
1 cup chopped onions
1 cup reduced-sodium, defatted chicken broth
$1/2$ cup lima beans (frozen, not dried)
1 cup corn kernels (fresh or frozen)
1 pound skinless, boneless chicken breast, cut into
   large chunks
1 tablespoon molasses
$1/2$ teaspoon kosher salt
$1/4$ teaspoon freshly ground pepper
$1/8$ teaspoon cayenne pepper
1 tablespoon tomato paste (optional)

1) Simmer the potatoes, tomatoes, and onions in the broth until the potatoes start to soften, about 7 minutes.

2) Add the lima beans, corn, and chicken, and cook until the chicken turns white all the way through, about 12 minutes.

3) Add the remaining ingredients and simmer for at least 20 minutes. Like all stews, this will taste best if it is allowed a long, slow cooking time. If you do want to eat it right away, you may want to thicken it up with a tablespoon of tomato paste.

Per Serving: Calories 334; Protein 34g; Fat 2g (Saturated 1g); Carbohydrates 46g; Fiber 6g; Sodium 645mg

Old-Fashioned Beef Stew

Makes: 5 servings

Do all of the vegetable peeling and cutting before you start cooking.

2 teaspoons vegetable oil

1 pound lean beef chuck, trimmed of fat and cut into 1-inch pieces

2 tablespoons unbleached, all-purpose white flour

3 cups sliced onions

2 cloves garlic, chopped

1/4 cup red wine

3 ribs celery, cut into 1-inch pieces

3 large carrots, cut into 1-inch rounds

2 large potatoes (about 1 pound), cut into 2-inch pieces

1/2 small rutabaga (about 1 pound), peeled and cubed

2 cups reduced-sodium, defatted beef broth

2 teaspoons kosher salt

1/2 teaspoon freshly ground pepper, or to taste

1 bay leaf

One 10-ounce package frozen peas, thawed

One 10-ounce package frozen cut green beans, thawed

1) Heat the oil in a large, preferably nonstick pot. Dust the cubes of beef with the flour and brown them on all sides. Remove the beef to a plate. Add the onions and garlic to the pot. Stir and scrape up bits of flour. Cook until the onions begin to turn golden. Keep covered between stirrings to capture the vegetables' moisture, but if that is not enough to keep them from sticking add a little bit of the wine. Once the onions are golden, stir in any remaining flour.

2) Put the beef back in the pot, along with the celery, carrots, potatoes, and rutabaga. Pour in the wine and broth. Stir in the salt, pepper, and bay leaf. Pour in water to come just to the top of the vegetables. Bring to a boil, reduce to a simmer, cover, and cook for 1 hour. Remove the lid and continue to simmer for another 30 minutes.

3) Stir in the peas and beans and cook for 15 minutes longer. Remove the bay leaf.

Per Serving: Calories 385; Protein 30g; Fat 8g (Saturated 2g); Carbohydrates 49g; Fiber 11g; Sodium 1042mg

Lamb Stew

Makes: 6 servings

Use whatever lamb meat is available. I've made it with stewing pieces. Dress it up with fresh thyme for a garnish.

2 teaspoons vegetable oil
1 pound lamb, cut into 1- to 2-inch cubes
8 pearl onions, peeled and halved
One 1-pound bag baby-cut carrots
8 small red or white new potatoes
    (about 1 pound), scrubbed and halved
1/2 pound rutabaga or turnip, peeled and cubed
1 tablespoon red currant jelly
2 tablespoons unbleached, all-purpose white flour
1 1/2 cups reduced-sodium, defatted beef broth
    or water
4 cloves garlic, chopped
1/2 cup dry red wine
1 teaspoon kosher salt
1/2 teaspoon freshly ground pepper, or to taste
1 bay leaf
1 1/2 teaspoons dried thyme

1) Preheat the oven to 325°F.

2) Heat the oil in a 2 1/2- to 3-quart Dutch oven or large skillet. Brown the lamb, remove to a plate, and stir the onions, carrots, potatoes, rutabaga, jelly, and 1 tablespoon of water into the pot. Cook until the vegetables are brown in spots. Return the meat to the pot. Dust the flour into the pot and stir until it darkens in color.

3) Pour a small amount of broth into the pot while scraping the bottom with a wooden spatula or spoon. Then pour in the remaining broth and the remaining ingredients.

4) Cover and place in the oven (or transfer from the skillet to an ovenproof casserole). Bake for 45 minutes.

Per Serving: Calories 261; Protein 17g; Fat 8g (Saturated 2g); Carbohydrates 29g; Fiber 5g; Sodium 460mg

Easy Turkey Chili

Makes: 5 servings

Almost all you need to do to make this chili is to chop a few cloves of garlic and open some cans.

1 teaspoon vegetable oil
4 cloves garlic, chopped
1 1/4 pounds lean ground turkey
Two 16-ounce cans pinto or kidney beans, drained
    and rinsed
One 16-ounce can stewed tomatoes
Two 14 1/2-ounce cans diced tomatoes
One 4 1/2-ounce can diced mild green chilies
2 tablespoons chili powder
1 teaspoon paprika
1 teaspoon dried oregano
1/4 teaspoon crushed red pepper flakes
1/2 to 1 teaspoon Tabasco sauce

1) Heat the oil in a 4-quart pot. Add the garlic and turkey, and cook over moderate heat, stirring frequently to break up the turkey, until the turkey becomes lightly browned.

2) Add the remaining ingredients and bring to a simmer. Cook, uncovered, for 20 minutes.

Per Serving: Calories 370; Protein 40g; Fat 3g (Saturated 1g); Carbohydrates 46g; Fiber 15g; Sodium 653mg

White Chili

Makes: 6 servings

The long cooking of the dried beans in garlic, onions, and broth gives this recipe its flavor. Don't use canned beans.

1 pound dry white beans, such as navy beans (about 2^1/2 cups)
6 cups reduced-sodium, defatted chicken broth
1 cup chopped onions
2 cloves garlic, chopped
2 teaspoons ground cumin
1 teaspoon dried oregano
Two 4^1/2-ounce cans diced mild green chilies
^{1}/8 teaspoon ground cloves
1 pound skinless, boneless chicken breast, cubed
1 teaspoon kosher salt
2 tablespoons chopped fresh cilantro or parsley

1) Wash the beans and soak them for at least 4 hours in enough water to cover by 3 inches. Drain and proceed with Step 2. Or wash the beans and place them in a pot. Cover with water by 2 inches and put over high heat. Once boiling, cook for 2 minutes. Remove from the heat and let rest 1 hour. Drain.

2) Put the prepared beans in a pot with the broth, onions, and garlic. Bring to a boil, reduce to a gentle simmer, and cook, uncovered, until the beans are tender, about 1 to 1^1/2 hours. Pour in water as needed to keep the beans moist.

3) Stir in the cumin, oregano, chilies, cloves, and chicken. Cook for 30 minutes. Stir in the salt. Garnish with cilantro.

Per Serving: Calories 379; Protein 37g; Fat 2g (Saturated 0g); Carbohydrates 53g; Fiber 16g; Sodium 1017mg

Mexican Mole Chili

Makes: 7 servings

A mole sauce is made with cocoa. But there are so many complex seasonings in mole that the chocolate becomes transformed into a new, unique flavor.

2 pounds 10% fat ground beef
1 tablespoon vegetable oil
2 cups chopped onions
4 cloves garlic, minced
One 8-ounce can tomato sauce
2 cups cooked kidney beans, drained and rinsed
3 cups tomato juice
^{1}/4 teaspoon crushed red pepper flakes
2 teaspoons ground cumin
2 tablespoons ground chili powder
2 tablespoons unsweetened cocoa powder
1^1/2 teaspoons ground cinnamon
1^1/2 teaspoons kosher salt
2 teaspoons dried oregano
2 tablespoons cornmeal

1) Heat a large, heavy pot and cook the beef in it, stirring frequently, until the meat is cooked through. Pour off and discard the meat juices. Remove the beef to a plate.

2) Put the oil in the pot and cook the onions and garlic over moderate-high heat until the onions begin to change color, about 5 minutes. Cover between stirrings.

3) Return the meat to the pot and stir in the remaining ingredients except the cornmeal. Bring to a boil and immediately reduce to a gentle simmer. Cover and cook for 1 hour.

4) Stir in the cornmeal (this will thicken the chili) and cook uncovered for about 30 minutes longer.

Per Serving: Calories 370; Protein 34g; Fat 15g (Saturated 5g); Carbohydrates 27g; Fiber 7g; Sodium 1074mg

Smoked Turkey Gumbo

Makes: 6 servings

Filé powder, also called gumbo filé, is ground sassafras. Very mild in flavor, it thickens the gumbo and gives it a greenish tint. If you can't find filé powder, cook off the liquid until the dish is the thickness of a stew.

1 pound lowfat turkey sausage, sliced into
    1/2-inch rounds
2 tablespoons vegetable oil
1/4 cup unbleached, all-purpose white flour
1 green bell pepper, chopped
3 ribs celery, chopped
1 1/2 cups chopped onions
2 cups cubed smoked turkey breast
    (about 10 ounces)
4 cups water
1/4 teaspoon kosher salt
1/4 teaspoon freshly ground pepper
1/4 teaspoon Tabasco sauce, or more to taste
1 tablespoon filé powder

1) Cook the sausage in a nonstick pan. Put a little water in the pan to keep the meat moist. Remove and drain on paper towels.

2) Heat the oil in a heavy-bottomed pot. Add the flour and stir constantly until it turns copper-colored. This will take several minutes.

3) Add the bell pepper, celery, onions, cubed turkey, and cooked sausage. Pour in the water. Simmer, uncovered, for 1 1/2 to 2 hours, stirring occasionally. Stir in the salt, pepper, Tabasco, and filé powder. Taste and adjust the seasonings. Serve over mounds of plain rice.

Per Serving: Calories 258; Protein 22g; Fat 14g (Saturated 3g); Carbohydrates 10g; Fiber 1g; Sodium 1016mg

Barbequed Hot Dogs

Makes: 4 servings

This family favorite is a recipe I adapted from one my mother served to my brothers and me when we were little. I've cut the fat and dish it out over brown rice.

1 teaspoon oil
1/2 cup chopped yellow onions
1 recipe Very Quick Barbeque Sauce (page 587)
1/2 teaspoon paprika
1 tablespoon apple cider vinegar
1/4 cup water
10 lowfat hot dogs (no more than 1.5g fat each)

1) In a heavy-bottomed saucepan, heat the oil and sauté the onions until they turn golden and soften.

2) Stir in the barbeque sauce, paprika, vinegar, and water.

3) Cut the hot dogs into 1/2-inch-thick rounds. Stir into the pot and simmer, covered, for 20 minutes.

Per Serving: Calories 216; Protein 19g; Fat 4g (Saturated 1g); Carbohydrates 26g; Fiber 1g; Sodium 1917mg

Chicken Fajitas

Makes: 4 servings

Fajitas are chili-seasoned stir-fried strips of vegetables, and, in this case, chicken. Serve fajitas with salsa and sour cream (and guacamole if desired) and a platter of warmed tortillas to wrap it all up in.

1 pound skinless, boneless chicken breast, cut into long, thin strips
3 tablespoons fresh lime juice
1/2 teaspoon kosher salt
2 teaspoons chili powder
1/8 teaspoon Tabasco sauce
1 1/2 teaspoons vegetable oil
1 fresh or pickled jalapeño, seeded and minced (wear rubber gloves)
1 cup sliced red onions
1 green bell pepper, julienned
1 red bell pepper, julienned
8 medium flour tortillas

1) Put the chicken into a sealable plastic bag or in a glass bowl. Combine the lime juice, salt, chili powder, and Tabasco and pour in with the chicken. Toss until all is well coated. Let marinate for 15 minutes to 1 hour.

2) Heat the oil in a large nonstick skillet. Sauté the jalapeño, onions, and bell peppers over moderate heat, covered, for 10 minutes. Raise the heat under the skillet to moderate-high and add the chicken to the pan. Cook, uncovered, stirring and turning frequently until the chicken is white throughout.

3) Meanwhile, if serving all at once, wrap the tortillas in foil and place in a 325°F oven until warm. Or, just before dining, each tortilla can be heated in a hot, dry skillet, 1 minute on each side.

Per Serving: Calories 361; Protein 32g; Fat 7g (Saturated 2g); Carbohydrates 40g; Fiber 3g; Sodium 607mg

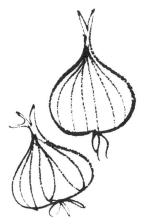

Balsamic Chicken and Broccoli

Makes: 4 servings

I like it with plenty of freshly ground pepper.

1/2 small yellow onion, thinly sliced, then slices cut into thirds
1 or 2 cloves garlic, minced
2 tablespoons minced shallots
1 tablespoon olive oil
1/4 cup white wine
1 pound skinless, boneless chicken breast, cut into strips
3 tablespoons balsamic vinegar
2 cups broccoli spears
1 cup sliced mushrooms, preferably fancy ones like oyster or shiitake
1/3 cup reduced-sodium, defatted chicken broth
1/4 teaspoon kosher salt
Pepper to taste, at the table
4 servings pasta or brown rice

1) In a large sauté pan, slowly cook the onion, garlic, and shallots in the oil until the vegetables turn light golden. Use a tablespoon or so of the wine if more liquid is needed. Keep the pan covered between stirrings.

2) Add the strips of chicken and enough of the wine to keep the meat from sticking to the pan. Cook until the chicken is white all the way through, about 5 to 7 minutes. When more liquid is needed, add more wine.

3) Remove the chicken and sautéed vegetables with a slotted spoon.

4) Add the vinegar to the pan, raise the heat, and scrape and stir the pan with a wooden spoon until the liquid is reduced down to about half its volume and is thickened.

5) Reduce the heat. Return the chicken, onions, shallots, and garlic to the pan. Add the broccoli, mushrooms, broth, remaining wine and salt. Cook at a gentle simmer until the the broccoli turns bright green. Add pepper to taste, and serve over the pasta or brown rice.

Per Serving: Calories 517; Protein 39g; Fat 6g (Saturated 1g); Carbohydrates 71g; Fiber 4g; Sodium 257mg

Chicken in Indonesian Sauce

Makes: 4 servings

Serve with rice and steamed vegetables.

1 1/2 tablespoons fresh lime juice
2 tablespoons chunky, unsalted, unsweetened peanut butter
2 teaspoons soy sauce
1 tablespoon mustard
1 tablespoon honey
1 1/2 tablespoons water
1/4 teaspoon Tabasco sauce
Pinch cayenne pepper
1 pound skinless, boneless chicken breast, cut into long strips
1 teaspoon sesame or vegetable oil

1) Puree all of the ingredients except the chicken and sesame oil.

2) Toss the chicken with the sauce until it is well coated.

3) Heat the oil in a large nonstick sauté pan or wok. Stir-fry the chicken until it is cooked through, about 5 to 7 minutes.

Per Serving: Calories 204; Protein 29g; Fat 7g (Saturated 1g); Carbohydrates 7g; Fiber 1g; Sodium 298mg

Wok Cooking

A wok is designed to cook foods fast at high temperatures. Because of its flared sides, a large volume of food can fit in a wok and all of it has contact with a hot surface as it is tossed. But because the bottom is only a few inches across, only a small amount of oil is needed, and small portions of food can be cooked in it as well (unlike a 13-inch skillet, which needs lots of fat for greasing and is too big for small sautés). My 13-inch nonstick wok is an indispensable tool in my kitchen. If you don't own a wok, consider purchasing one. Until then, for the stir-fries in this book, use the heaviest and largest sauté pan that you have.

For the best results when stir-frying, chop all ingredients into small pieces about the same size. This promotes fast, even cooking. Because the cooking time from start to finish is so brief, the ingredients not only need to be prepped ahead of time, but it helps to have them organized as well. For example, if four vegetables are to be added all at once, have them all in one bowl. Otherwise, by the time you've tossed in the last vegetable, the first one will be overcooked.

Also, have the rest of the dinner ready before you begin cooking in the wok so that you won't be distracted as you stir-fry and so that all will be ready to eat as soon as the stir-frying is done. Because all of the prep work is finished before cooking in the wok, I often do it up to a day ahead of time. Then when I am ready to make dinner all I have to do is pull a few bowls of ingredients from my refrigerator and heat up the wok. The only other bit of cooking is to cook up a pot of rice, since all of these stir-fries are best when eaten with a big mound of rice on the side.

Kung Pao Chicken

Makes: 4 servings

Unlike many other Asian recipes, this one calls for light, untoasted sesame oil. Although used infrequently in my kitchen, when specified, it is an essential ingredient. I buy a small bottle at a natural food store or Asian market and keep the opened container in my refrigerator. It solidifies in the cold, but, like olive oil, quickly becomes clear and liquid at room temperature.

1 pound skinless, boneless chicken breast, cut into small cubes
1 tablespoon finely grated fresh ginger
2 cloves garlic, minced
3 scallions, sliced
2 ribs celery, halved lengthwise and then sliced
1 green bell pepper, cut into 1/2-inch pieces
2 tablespoons sherry
2 tablespoons soy sauce
1 teaspoon light, untoasted sesame oil
1 tablespoon cornstarch
1 1/2 teaspoons sugar
1/4 teaspoon crushed red pepper flakes
1 tablespoon peanut oil, divided
1/4 cup roasted peanuts

1) First, organize your ingredients in several bowls. Have the chicken in one bowl, and the ginger, garlic, scallions, celery, and bell pepper in another. Combine the sherry, soy sauce, sesame oil, cornstarch, sugar, and pepper flakes in a small bowl.

2) Heat half the peanut oil in a nonstick wok. Add the chicken and cook over high heat, stirring constantly, until the chicken is white all the way through. This takes about 5 minutes. Remove to a plate.

3) Add the remaining oil to the wok. Toss in the vegetables and cook for about 3 minutes.

4) Pour in the sherry mixture and return the chicken to the wok. Stir in the peanuts. Cook until the sauce thickens, about 3 minutes.

Per Serving: Calories 255; Protein 30g; Fat 10g (Saturated 2g); Carbohydrates 9g; Fiber 2g; Sodium 609mg

Hoisin Chicken and Broccoli Stir-Fry

Makes: 3 servings

Any green vegetable, from asparagus to snap peas, would be as suitable as broccoli for this stir-fry. Use the best of what is in season.

1 teaspoon soy sauce
1 teaspoon honey
3 tablespoons hoisin sauce
2 tablespoons sherry
1 teaspoon finely grated fresh ginger
1/2 pound skinless, boneless chicken breast, cut into small, thin strips
1 pound broccoli
1 teaspoon peanut or canola oil
6 scallions, cut diagonally into 1/2-inch pieces
2 tablespoons water
2 teaspoons cornstarch

1) Whisk together the soy sauce, honey, hoisin, sherry, and ginger in a bowl. Put 2 tablespoons of this sauce in with the chicken and reserve the rest. Toss the chicken to coat it thoroughly.

2) Trim the broccoli into florets. Peel the stems and slice. Briefly steam or microwave the broccoli until it turns bright green.

3) Heat a nonstick wok or large sauté pan over high heat. Add the oil. Quickly cook the scallions. Stir the chicken into the wok. Toss constantly until all sides whiten. Stir in the broccoli and the hoisin marinade. In a small bowl, mix the water and cornstarch, then pour it into the wok. Stir and cook over high heat until the sauce thickens.

Per Serving: Calories 191; Protein 23g; Fat 3g (Saturated 1g); Carbohydrates 18g; Fiber 5g; Sodium 348mg

Honey Teriyaki Chicken Stir-Fry

Makes: 4 servings

Stir-fries have a repuation for requiring lots of fancy knife work. This recipe disproves that notion.

1/4 cup soy sauce
1 tablespoon finely grated fresh ginger
1 clove garlic, minced
1/2 cup water or reduced-sodium, defatted
    chicken broth
1 tablespoon lemon juice
3 tablespoons honey
1/2 pound skinless, boneless chicken breast, cut
    into thin strips
1 tablespoon cornstarch, dissolved in
    1 tablespoon water
One 4 1/2-ounce can sliced water chestnuts,
    drained and rinsed
1/2 pound snow peas, trimmed
6 scallions, sliced
1/2 cup fresh mung bean sprouts

1) Whisk together the soy sauce, ginger, garlic, water, lemon, and honey to make the sauce.

2) Heat a nonstick wok or large sauté pan and add a thin layer of the sauce. Sauté the chicken in this liquid until the pieces are cooked all of the way through, about 5 minutes. Because this has sugar and no oil, the sauce might blacken along the edges of the wok. If this happens, wipe it out with a paper towel.

3) Add the remaining sauce, pour in the cornstarch paste, and stir. Add the remaining ingredients except the sprouts and cook for about 5 minutes, or until the snow peas turn a brighter green. Use a lid during this step to trap steam and hasten cooking. Stir frequently. Toss in the bean sprouts and cook for 1 minute, until they begin to soften.

Per Serving: Calories 175; Protein 17g; Fat 1g (Saturated 0g); Carbohydrates 26g; Fiber 3g; Sodium 1076mg

Spinach, Shiitake, and Turkey Stir-Fry

Makes: 4 servings

If fresh shiitake mushrooms are not available, try portobello mushrooms.

1 teaspoon Asian sesame oil
1 teaspoon rice or white wine vinegar
1/4 cup reduced-sodium, defatted chicken broth
1 tablespoon dry sherry
2 tablespoons soy sauce
1/4 teaspoon kosher salt
1/8 teaspoon crushed red pepper flakes
1 teaspoon sugar
1 clove garlic, crushed
1/2 pound turkey cutlet or breast, cut into long, thin strips
2 teaspoons vegetable oil
8 shiitake mushrooms, stems discarded, caps sliced
1 teaspoon cornstarch
6 cups spinach, washed, tough stems trimmed off
2 scallions, sliced

1) Combine the sesame oil, vinegar, broth, sherry, soy sauce, salt, pepper flakes, sugar, and garlic. Toss the turkey in this marinade. Cover and refrigerate for 1 to 4 hours.

2) Heat the vegetable oil in a large nonstick wok. Remove the turkey from the marinade and sauté it until white on all sides. Stir in the mushrooms and cook until wilted.

3) Discard the garlic from the marinade. Stir the cornstarch into the marinade. Pour this liquid into the wok. Add the spinach. Cook, stirring frequently, until the sauce is thickened and bubbly and the spinach is wilted. Add the scallions and cook for 1 minute more.

Per Serving: Calories 131; Protein 17g; Fat 3g (Saturated 0g); Carbohydrates 10g; Fiber 3g; Sodium 260mg

Beef with Broccoli

Makes: 5 servings

If the broccoli stems are fresh and crisp, peel them, slice on the diagonal, and use along with the florets. If red bell peppers are very expensive, use julienned carrots that have been briefly steamed first.

1/4 cup light brown sugar
2 tablespoons dry sherry
2 tablespoons soy sauce
2 teaspoons Asian sesame oil
1 teaspoon finely grated fresh ginger
1/8 teaspoon crushed red pepper flakes (optional)
1 pound boneless beef top sirloin or flank steak, trimmed of fat
1 tablespoon vegetable oil
1 cup onions, sliced thick into 2-inch-long pieces
4 cups broccoli florets
1 red bell pepper, julienned
2 teaspoons cornstarch
1/4 cup water

1) Combine the sugar, sherry, soy sauce, sesame oil, and ginger. Add the pepper flakes, if desired. Slice the beef into thin 2-inch-long strips. Stir into the marinade and let rest for 1/2 hour.

2) Heat a large nonstick wok. Pour in the vegetable oil. Stir in the onions and cook about 1 minute. Put the meat and marinade into the wok and cook, stirring constantly, until the steak is browned on all sides. Stir in the broccoli and bell pepper. Cook about 3 minutes, covered, until the broccoli softens slightly and turns bright green. Shake the pan frequently.

3) Stir the cornstarch and water together until a paste forms and pour it into the wok. Stir constantly and cook over high heat until the sauce thickens.

Per Serving: Calories 257; Protein 23g; Fat 10g (Saturated 2g); Carbohydrates 19g; Fiber 3g; Sodium 481mg

Stir-Fried Beef and Snow Peas

Makes: 4 servings

A stir-fry is a great way to stretch a small amount of beef but still satisfy red meat lovers.

2 cloves garlic, crushed
2 tablespoons soy sauce
1/4 cup reduced-sodium, defatted chicken broth
1 tablespoon rice or white wine vinegar
2 teaspoons Asian sesame oil
1 tablespoon sugar
1/8 to 1/4 teaspoon crushed red pepper flakes
3/4 pound beef tenderloin steak, trimmed of fat, thinly sliced
1 teaspoon vegetable oil
1 red bell pepper, julienned
1 tablespoon cornstarch
5 cups snow peas or sugar snap peas, trimmed and strings removed
One 5-ounce can sliced water chestnuts, drained and rinsed
1/4 cup chopped scallions (about 2 scallions)
1 tablespoon finely grated fresh ginger

1) Combine the garlic, soy sauce, broth, vinegar, sesame oil, sugar, and pepper flakes in a bowl. Toss the beef in the marinade. Let it rest while preparing the rest of the recipe, or cover and refrigerate for up to 2 hours.

2) Heat a large nonstick wok. Take the meat out of the marinade and cook it over high heat, stirring constantly, for about 3 minutes, until the meat begins to brown. Remove it to a plate.

3) Pour the vegetable oil into the wok and add the bell pepper strips. Cook until the peppers begin to wilt. Meanwhile, stir the cornstarch into the marinade until dissolved.

4) Pour the marinade into the wok, add the snow peas, water chestnuts, scallions, and ginger. Return the meat to the wok. Stir and cover. Cook for 2 minutes, or until the sauce thickens.

Per Serving: Calories 288; Protein 24g; Fat 10g (Saturated 3g); Carbohydrates 25g; Fiber 7g; Sodium 597mg

Moo Shu Beef

Makes: 4 servings

Using a packaged coleslaw mix (shredded carrots and cabbage) is a real time-saver for this recipe. If you prefer, substitute thinly sliced Chinese cabbage.

2 tablespoons dry sherry, divided

2 tablespoons soy sauce

2 teaspoons sugar

1 teaspoon finely grated fresh ginger

2 cloves garlic, crushed

1 tablespoon cornstarch

1/3 cup water

1/2 pound boneless beef top sirloin or flank steak

8 large flour tortillas or Chinese pancakes

6 large mushrooms, sliced

3 cups packaged coleslaw mix

1/2 cup bean sprouts

3 scallions, sliced

One 8-ounce can bamboo shoots, drained and rinsed

1 egg, lightly beaten

1/3 cup hoisin sauce

1) Combine 1 tablespoon of sherry and the soy sauce, sugar, ginger, and garlic in a medium-size bowl. Remove 1 tablespoon of the marinade and put it in a small bowl with the cornstarch, water, and remaining tablespoon of sherry.

2) Trim away all of the fat from the beef. Cut the meat into small, thin slices. Stir it into the marinade.

3) Wrap the tortillas in foil and place in a warm oven.

4) Have the mushrooms, coleslaw mix, sprouts, and scallions in a bowl. Pile the bamboo shoots on a cutting board and, using a large chef's knife, slice across the pile to sliver, not chop, the shoots. Add these to the bowl with the vegetables.

5) Heat a large nonstick wok. Pour the egg along the rim so that it cooks as it runs into the bottom of the wok. Stir with a wooden spatula, cook through, and remove it to a plate.

6) Remove the beef from the marinade and put the meat into the wok, stirring constantly. When it is no longer pink, toss in the vegetables. Stir the cornstarch mixture and add it to the wok. Cook until the sauce thickens. Stir in the egg and remove the beef to a serving dish.

7) Serve with the warmed tortillas and a bowl of hoisin sauce. Each diner spreads a thin layer of hoisin sauce on a tortilla and puts about a 1/2 cup of Moo Shu Beef in a line along the center. Then the tortilla is rolled up, and it is eaten out of hand. This can be a messy meal, but it is always fun.

Per Serving: Calories 489; Protein 25g; Fat 12g (Saturated 3g); Carbohydrates 70g; Fiber 5g; Sodium 1077mg

Hoisin Chicken Lo Mein

Makes: 4 servings

Hoisin sauce is appealing to all, from toddlers to parents. It is available in most supermarkets, but if you have to make a special trip to get it, buy several jars. Unopened, it lasts indefinitely.

8 ounces vermicelli or Chinese noodles

1/3 cup hoisin sauce

1 1/2 tablespoons white wine vinegar or rice wine vinegar

1 1/2 teaspoons sugar

1 1/2 teaspoons Asian sesame oil

1 1/2 teaspoons vegetable oil

1 pound skinless, boneless chicken breast, cut into small cubes

3 cloves garlic, minced

4 scallions, sliced, divided

1) Cook the noodles according to the package directions. If they are ready before you need to add them in Step 4, rinse with cold water and set aside in a colander.

2) In a small bowl, whisk together the hoisin sauce, vinegar, sugar, and sesame oil. Set aside.

3) Heat the oil in a large nonstick wok. Add the chicken and stir constantly until it cooks through. Stir in the garlic and all but 2 tablespoons of the scallions and cook for 1 minute more, until the scallions wilt and the garlic turns golden but not brown.

4) Add the hoisin mixture and vermicelli to the wok. Toss until all is evenly coated with the sauce. Remove from the heat and garnish with the reserved scallions.

Per Serving: Calories 427; Protein 34g; Fat 7g (Saturated 1g); Carbohydrates 55g; Fiber 2g; Sodium 414mg

Turkey Cutlets

Turkey cutlets are such an easy entrée to prepare that I keep a package in the freezer especially for those times when I haven't planned a menu or gone shopping. The packages usually weigh about a pound and the cutlets are sliced about 1/3 inch thick. They can be cooked straight from the package, though lightly pounding them first makes for tenderer pieces of meat, as well as stretching the food dollar. One pound of flattened cutlets looks like a lot and can easily feed four people. Leftovers make great sandwich fillings.

Instead of a meat pounder, I use a wooden rolling pin because it accomplishes the job quickly, evenly, and will not tear or shred the cutlets. To use, put the cutlets—one layer deep and not crowded—between two sheets of wax paper. Then gently tap, tap with the rolling pin, first in one direction and then the other until the cutlets flatten and spread out to about 1/4 inch thick.

Pan-Fried Turkey Cutlets

Makes: 4 servings

If you bought a carton of buttermilk especially for this recipe, you will have some left over. Don't let it go to waste. Use it up by making Molasses Cornbread (page 486), and then have pancakes (pages 452–456) on the weekend.

1 cup buttermilk
1 teaspoon Worcestershire sauce
1 teaspoon dry mustard
1 teaspoon dried oregano
1/4 teaspoon kosher salt
1/4 teaspoon freshly ground pepper
1 pound turkey cutlets, lightly pounded
2 egg whites, lightly beaten
11/4 cup dry breadcrumbs
1 tablespoon vegetable oil, divided

1) Whisk the buttermilk, Worcestershire, mustard, oregano, salt, and pepper together. Place the cutlets in a shallow dish and pour this mixture over them. Turn to coat thoroughly, refrigerate, and let marinate for 30 minutes or up to 1 day.

2) Put the egg whites in a shallow dish, and the breadcrumbs in another. Heat half of the oil in a large, nonstick skillet over a moderate burner or on a nonstick electric griddle. Using tongs, take a cutlet out of the marinade, dip it in the egg whites, and then coat it with the breadcrumbs. Gently shake off the excess breading.

Cook 2 minutes on one side, then, using a flat spatula, turn and cook until done, about 2 to 4 minutes more. Repeat with all of the cutlets, adding more oil in a thin layer as necessary. If loose breadcrumbs in the skillet start to burn, wipe them out with a paper towel.

Per Serving: Calories 295; Protein 33g; Fat 6g (Saturated 1g); Carbohydrates 24g; Fiber 1g; Sodium 397mg

Turkey Cutlets with Gremolata

Makes: 4 servings

This is one of my favorite summer grilled recipes. It is especially useful when feeding a crowd. The recipe can be doubled or tripled, the cutlets themselves take little time to prepare or cook, and they taste good even when not piping hot. I put pile them on a platter, crisscrossed with Gremolata. The lemon, parsley, and garlic flavors are sharp and fresh, a perfect combination for summer dining.

2 tablespoons lemon juice
1 tablespoon olive oil
1/4 teaspoon kosher salt
1/4 teaspoon freshly ground pepper
1 pound turkey cutlets, lightly pounded
11/2 tablespoons Gremolata (page 591)

1) Combine the lemon juice, oil, salt, and pepper in a plastic bag. Add the turkey, seal the bag, toss to coat the meat well, and let rest for 30 minutes or up to 1 hour, but not longer.

2) Preheat a nonstick electric griddle or large skillet. Spray once with nonstick spray. Remove the turkey from the marinade and cook for 2 minutes per side. Top each portion with a dab of Gremolata and serve.

Per Serving: Calories 193; Protein 27g; Fat 8g (Saturated 1g); Carbohydrates 1g; Fiber 0g; Sodium 205mg

Turkey Cutlets in Lemon-Caper Sauce

Makes: 4 servings

The small amount of butter in this recipe gives body and smoothness to the sauce.

1/2 cup unbleached, all-purpose white flour
1/2 teaspoon kosher salt
1/2 teaspoon freshly ground pepper
1 tablespoon olive oil, divided
1 pound turkey cutlets, lightly pounded
2 teaspoons unsalted butter
1/4 cup dry white wine
1/4 cup lemon juice
1 1/2 tablespoons drained capers
2 tablespoons chopped fresh parsley

1) Combine the flour, salt, and pepper on a plate. Heat half the olive oil in a large sauté pan. Dredge the cutlets in the flour, shake off the excess, then place in the pan without crowding. You may need to do this in several batches. Cook cutlets for 2 minutes, then turn and cook another 2 to 3 minutes until done. Remove to a plate and cover to keep warm. Pour the remaining oil in the pan and cook the remaining cutlets. If the loose flour in the pan blackens, wipe it out with a paper towel. Remove all cooked cutlets to the plate and keep warm. Leave drippings and flour in the skillet.

2) Melt the butter in the pan. Add the wine, lemon juice, capers, and parsley. Boil for 2 minutes until slightly reduced. Pour over the cutlets and serve.

Per Serving: Calories 237; Protein 29g; Fat 7g (Saturated 2g); Carbohydrates 12g; Fiber 1g; Sodium 411mg

Turkey Cutlets with Rosemary-Caper Sauce

Makes: 4 servings

It is the rare kitchen that has a skillet large enough to cook all of the cutlets at once. Mine doesn't, and I have to remind myself to stay patient. The cutlets can't be dusted with flour ahead of time or the coating will become soggy. They can't be crowded or the edges won't brown properly. What I really need to remember is that they cook so quickly that I don't need all that much patience after all.

3 tablespoons unbleached, all-purpose white flour
1/4 teaspoon kosher salt
1/4 teaspoon freshly ground pepper
2 to 3 teaspoons olive oil, divided
1 pound turkey cutlets, lightly pounded
1/2 cup reduced-sodium, defatted chicken broth
1 tablespoon balsamic vinegar
1 tablespoon drained capers
1/2 teaspoon dried rosemary
1 teaspoon unsalted butter
1 tablespoon chopped fresh parsley, for garnish

1) Combine the flour, salt, and pepper on a sheet of wax paper or a dinner plate. Heat a teaspoon of oil in a large nonstick skillet. Dip a cutlet in the flour mixture and gently shake off the excess so that the cutlet is powdery dry and white. Drop it in the skillet and cook for 2 to 3 minutes on one side. Turn to finish cooking. Meanwhile, continue to dust the cutlets and add them to the pan. Do not crowd. When the cutlets are cooked through, remove to a serving platter and tent with foil to keep warm. Add more oil to the skillet as necessary.

2) Once all the cutlets are cooked, pour the broth and balsamic vinegar into the skillet. Add the capers, rosemary, and butter. Cook over high heat, scraping the bottom with a wooden spatula or spoon until all of the bits are stirred into the sauce. Cook for 1 to 2 minutes, until the sauce is slightly reduced. Pour it over the cutlets, garnish with the parsley, and serve.

Per Serving: Calories 179; Protein 28g; Fat 4g (Saturated 1g); Carbohydrates 5g; Fiber 0g; Sodium 311mg

Five-Spice Turkey Cutlets

Makes: 4 servings

Chinese five-spice powder is a blend of spices. It includes star anise that most people don't have as a single ground spice in a jar. The flavor is unique, and the first time guests taste this recipe they'll probably say, "This is great," quickly followed by "What is it?" Then they'll ask you to make it again.

3 tablespoons soy sauce
2 tablespoons light brown sugar
1/2 teaspoon Chinese five-spice powder
2 cloves garlic, sliced
1 teaspoon finely grated fresh ginger
1 teaspoon Asian sesame oil
1 pound turkey cutlets, lightly pounded
1 teaspoon vegetable oil
2 scallions, minced, for garnish
1 teaspoon sesame seeds, lightly toasted, for garnish

1) Combine the soy sauce, sugar, five-spice powder, garlic, ginger, and sesame oil. Marinate the cutlets in this mixture, turning several times so that all is evenly coated.

2) Heat the vegetable oil in a large nonstick skillet over medium-high heat. Remove the turkey from the marinade and cook in the skillet for 3 to 4 minutes. Turn and continue to cook, about 3 minutes longer, until done. It is okay if garlic and ginger clings to the meat. The cutlets will probably have to be cooked in two batches; put the cooked turkey on a serving platter and tent with foil to keep warm.

3) Strain the marinade through a fine mesh sieve directly into the pan. Cook for about 30 seconds to 1 minute, until it thickens and reduces to a few tablespoons. Pour over the cutlets. Garnish with the scallions and sesame seeds.

Per Serving: Calories 187; Protein 28g; Fat 4g (Saturated 1g); Carbohydrates 9g; Fiber 0g; Sodium 826mg

Cooking with Lean Ground Beef and Turkey

There is a large selection of ground meats on the market. They are labeled by the percent of fat by weight, not by calories (as are most other foods). To be "lean," ground meat needs to be less than 10 percent fat by weight. My market never carries such lean ground beef, but usually has 10 percent fat ground beef (4g fat per serving). To stretch the meat and lower the fat content, it can be combined with ground turkey. Take care, though, in selecting ground turkey. It is not necessarily lean. Some is ground with turkey skin and can be higher in fat than ground beef. Look for lean ground turkey and compare labels. Ground turkey breast is extremely low in fat, but cooks up dry and tasteless. It is best when used in concert with other ground meats.

Because lean ground beef contains little fat, it cooks up differently than regular ground meat. The exterior tends to get overcooked before the center is done. For this reason, I like to make small meatloaves, or even individual-portion-size loaves. The smaller sizes cook faster and moister. I also like to include vegetables and breadcrumbs or grains. This stretches the food dollar, improves the nutritional value, and enhances the texture.

Muffin-Tin Meatloaves

Makes: 6 servings

Not only is this a clever-looking way to serve meatloaf, but it is practical too. It can be prepared a day ahead of time, or the uncooked portions can be frozen, giving you readily available individual servings. Also, portion control is of no issue, as it is obvious how much is a serving. Mostly, though, I like this recipe because it looks so cute on the plate.

1 1/2 pounds lean ground turkey
1/2 pound 10% fat ground beef
1 cup shredded zucchini (about 1 small zucchini)
1/2 cup shredded carrots (about 1 small carrot)
2 egg whites
1 cup soft breadcrumbs (about 2 slices of bread)
1 tablespoon Worcestershire sauce
1 teaspoon poultry or Italian seasoning
1/4 cup ketchup

1) Combine the turkey, beef, shredded vegetables, egg whites, breadcrumbs, Worcestershire sauce, and poultry seasoning. Using your hands, squeeze together almost as if kneading bread, until evenly mixed.

2) Pack the meat mixture into 12 muffin cups. There is no need to grease the pans. These can be made up to one day in advance. If doing so, cover tightly and refrigerate. Just prior to baking, top with the ketchup.

3) Preheat the oven to 400°F. Bake 30 minutes. Unmold from muffin cups and serve.

Per Serving: Calories 235; Protein 37g; Fat 5g (Saturated 2g); Carbohydrates 9g; Fiber 1g; Sodium 286mg

Spinach-Stuffed Meatloaf

Makes: 6 servings

Although my family might dispute it, this meatloaf is not a sneaky way to get them to eat spinach (and eat it they do, when packaged like this). I use the spinach for flavor, to stretch the meat portion, and to keep the loaf moist. Besides, I like spinach and don't believe one has to be sneaky about it.

1 1/2 pounds 10% fat ground beef
2 egg whites
1 cup soft breadcrumbs (from about 2 slices of bread)
1 1/4 teaspoons kosher salt, divided
1 shallot, minced
1 clove garlic, minced
1 teaspoon Worcestershire sauce
1 teaspoon dried oregano
One 10-ounce package frozen chopped spinach, thawed
1/2 cup shredded reduced-fat mozzarella cheese
1/8 teaspoon ground nutmeg
1/4 teaspoon freshly ground pepper
1/4 cup ketchup (optional)

1) Combine the beef, egg whites, breadcrumbs, and 1 teaspoon of the salt. Add the shallot, garlic, Worcestershire sauce, and oregano. Using your hands, squeeze together almost as if kneading bread, until evenly mixed.

2) Put the spinach in a colander in the sink and squeeze out as much water as possible. Combine the spinach with the cheese, nutmeg, pepper, and remaining 1/4 teaspoon of salt.

3) On a piece of wax paper, shape the meat into a rectangle approximately 12×8 inches. Spread the spinach mixture on top, leaving about $1/2$ inch clear around the edges. Roll up, starting from a shorter side. Use the wax paper to help you do this, by bringing it up and pressing gently to form a firm loaf. Press the ends together. Up to this point the meatloaf can be wrapped tightly and refrigerated for a day before baking. Place the loaf on a rack in a roasting dish. Spread the ketchup on top, if desired.

4) Bake in a preheated 350°F oven for 1 hour.

Per Serving: Calories 251; Protein 29g; Fat 12g (Saturated 5g); Carbohydrates 7g; Fiber 2g; Sodium 599mg

Turkey Meatloaf

Makes: 4 servings

This makes one small loaf. Double if desired, but bake in two loaf pans.

$1^1/4$ pounds lean ground turkey
1 egg
1 teaspoon lemon juice
$1/2$ cup dry breadcrumbs
$1/2$ teaspoon kosher salt
$1/4$ teaspoon freshly ground pepper
2 tablespoons chopped fresh parsley
2 tablespoons grated onions
1 tablespoon Worcestershire sauce
$1/4$ cup ketchup

1) Preheat the oven to 375°F.

2) Put all the ingredients except the ketchup in a bowl and squeeze together with your hands until evenly mixed. Shape into a loaf.

3) Set the meatloaf into a small, ungreased, 4×8-inch loaf pan. Press the meat into the corners. Spread the ketchup on top. (If you don't have a small loaf pan you can bake this free-form in a loaf shape on a baking sheet.) Loosely cover with foil, taking care not to let the foil touch the ketchup.

4) Bake for 30 minutes, uncover, and bake for 15 minutes longer. Let rest 5 to 10 minutes before slicing.

Per Serving: Calories 247; Protein 37g; Fat 3g (Saturated 1g); Carbohydrates 15g; Fiber 1g; Sodium 651mg

Mexican Meatloaf

Makes: 8 servings

The salsa really perks up this meatloaf. You don't need fresh salsa; a high-quality jarred brand will work just fine.

1¼ pounds lean ground turkey
½ pound 10% fat ground beef
2 egg whites
⅔ cup dry breadcrumbs
1 tablespoon white wine vinegar
3 cloves garlic, minced
¼ cup chopped scallions
¼ teaspoon kosher salt
¼ teaspoon freshly ground pepper
½ teaspoon ground cumin
1 teaspoon paprika
½ teaspoon dried oregano
1 cup shredded zucchini
1 cup salsa

1) Combine all the ingredients except the salsa. Using your hands, squeeze together almost as if kneading bread, until evenly mixed.

2) Divide into two portions. Place each in an 8×4-inch loaf pan. Up to this point, the meatloaves can be made up to 1 day ahead of time if wrapped tightly and stored in the refrigerator.

3) Preheat the oven to 350°F. Top the meatloaves with salsa. Bake for 50 minutes to 1 hour.

Per Serving: Calories 181; Protein 25g; Fat 4g (Saturated 1g); Carbohydrates 10g; Fiber 2g; Sodium 519mg

Stuffed Peppers

Makes: 5 servings

Because the filling doesn't have to hold together like meatloaf, the meat mixture can be stretched with grains and vegetables. Here I've used couscous, but cooked rice would also be good.

5 green bell peppers
½ pound 10% fat ground beef
One 14½-ounce can diced tomatoes, drained
2 cups cooked couscous or bulgur wheat
3 tablespoons minced onions
2 tablespoons pine nuts, lightly toasted
3 tablespoons currants
1 teaspoon dried mint, or 1 tablespoon chopped fresh mint
½ teaspoon ground coriander
¼ teaspoon ground cinnamon
½ teaspoon kosher salt
¼ teaspoon freshly ground pepper
1 egg white
2 teaspoons olive oil

1) Preheat the oven to 350°F. Use a nonstick baking dish or coat one with nonstick spray.

2) Slice the tops off of the peppers. Reach inside and pull out the white membranes. Tap to shake out all seeds.

3) Brown the beef in a nonstick skillet. If necessary, drain off any liquid or fat. Stir in the tomatoes and cook until they soften. Lift out of the skillet with a slotted spoon and place in a bowl. Discard the pan's juices. Stir the remaining ingredients except the peppers into the beef and tomato mixture.

4) Stuff the filling into the peppers. Place upright in the baking dish. Fill the pan with 1/4 inch of water. Cover loosely with foil. Bake for 30 minutes, until the peppers begin to soften but don't collapse.

Per Serving: Calories 230; Protein 15g; Fat 8g (Saturated 2g); Carbohydrates 26g; Fiber 3g; Sodium 339mg

Ground Turkey Spaghetti Sauce

Makes: 6 servings

The fresh basil gives this recipe its flavor; please don't substitute dried.

1 pound lean ground turkey
1 teaspoon vegetable oil
1 cup chopped onions
2 cloves garlic, minced
1/4 cup chopped fresh basil
1 1/2 teaspoons kosher salt
1/2 teaspoon freshly ground pepper
One 28-ounce can crushed tomatoes

1) In a large, heavy-bottomed, nonstick skillet, cook the turkey over moderate heat until cooked through. Stir constantly. This will take about 5 minutes. Remove to a plate.

2) In the same skillet, heat the oil and cook the onions and garlic, covered, until the onions soften, about 5 minutes.

3) Put the turkey back in the skillet (taking care to lift it out of any fat that might be on the plate) and add the remaining ingredients. Bring to a simmer, cover, and cook for 15 minutes.

Per Serving: Calories 146; Protein 21g; Fat 2g (Saturated 0g); Carbohydrates 12g; Fiber 3g; Sodium 721mg

Porcupine Meatballs

Makes: 6 servings

Named for the "quills" of rice sticking out of the meatballs, this whimsical recipe is just right for a dinner with young children.

One 28-ounce can crushed tomatoes
One 28-ounce can whole tomatoes, chopped, with juice
1 tablespoon dried basil
2 teaspoons dried oregano
1/4 teaspoon freshly ground pepper
2 bay leaves
1 1/2 teaspoons kosher salt, divided
1 pound 10% fat ground beef
2 egg whites
2 cups cooked long-grain rice

1) Put the tomatoes, basil, oregano, pepper, bay leaves, and 1 teaspoon of the salt into a pot and bring to a boil. Immediately reduce to a simmer.

2) While waiting for the sauce to reach a boil, combine the beef, egg whites, rice, and remaining 1/2 teaspoon of salt. Squeeze together with your hands, almost as if kneading bread, until well mixed. Shape into about thirty-six 1-inch meatballs.

3) Add the meatballs to the simmering sauce. Cover and cook gently, about 25 minutes, stirring occasionally. Remove the bay leaves.

Per Serving: Calories 270; Protein 22g; Fat 7g (Saturated 3g); Carbohydrates 29g; Fiber 4g; Sodium 976mg

Seasoned Meatballs

Makes: 10 servings

These can be simmered with any tomato sauce and served over spaghetti.

1¹/₃ pounds lean ground turkey
¹/₂ pound 10% fat ground beef
1 cup minced or grated onions
1¹/₂ cups fresh breadcrumbs
2 egg whites
2 cloves garlic, minced
¹/₄ cup chopped fresh parsley
¹/₂ teaspoon kosher salt
¹/₂ teaspoon freshly ground pepper
2 tablespoons tomato paste

1) Combine all the ingredients and knead until well mixed. Roll into about 45 medium-size balls, each 1¹/₄ inches across.

2) Heat a nonstick pan over moderate heat. Brown the meatballs on all sides. For some dishes you will want to cook them all the way through in the pan. If so, after browning, add a small amount of chicken or beef broth to the pan, cover, and cook.

Per Serving: Calories 137; Protein 21g; Fat 3g (Saturated 1g); Carbohydrates 6g; Fiber 1g; Sodium 190mg

Turkey Meatballs

Makes: 6 servings

These meatballs are for the times when I want the lighter flavor of turkey instead of beef.

1 pound lean ground turkey
1 clove garlic, minced
¹/₄ cup grated onions
¹/₄ cup chopped fresh parsley
1 teaspoon kosher salt
¹/₂ teaspoon freshly ground pepper
¹/₂ teaspoon dried oregano
1 egg, lightly beaten
¹/₂ cup dry breadcrumbs
2 teaspoons vegetable oil, divided

1) Combine all the ingredients except the oil in a bowl. You can grate the onions in a food processor, but do the rest by hand or the meatballs will turn out rubbery. Shape into about 30 balls, each 1 inch across.

2) Heat 1 teaspoon of the oil in a large nonstick skillet. Add half of the meatballs and cook over moderate heat for about 4 to 5 minutes, shaking the pan and turning the meatballs as needed. Brown them slightly and cook through. Remove the first batch from the pan, cover, and keep warm. Heat the remaining teaspoon of oil in the pan and cook the rest of the meatballs.

Per Serving: Calories 147; Protein 20g; Fat 4g (Saturated 1g); Carbohydrates 7g; Fiber 1g; Sodium 438mg

Spaghetti and Tiny Meatballs in Creamy Tomato Sauce

Makes: 5 servings

The ricotta cheese in the sauce takes this recipe out of the realm of the ordinary.

1/2 pound ground turkey breast
1/2 pound 10% fat ground beef
2 cloves garlic, minced
1/2 cup minced or grated onions
1/4 cup dry breadcrumbs
1 egg white
2 tablespoons chopped fresh parsley
1 teaspoon dried oregano
1/4 teaspoon dried sage
1 teaspoon olive oil
1 pound spaghetti
2 1/2 cups tomato or spaghetti sauce
1/2 cup reduced-fat ricotta cheese
1/2 teaspoon kosher salt, or to taste
4 tablespoons grated Parmesan cheese (optional)

1) Mix the turkey, beef, garlic, onions, bread-crumbs, egg white, and herbs. Squeeze together with your hands and knead until evenly mixed. Roll into small balls, each about 1 inch across.

2) Heat the oil in a nonstick pan over moderate heat. Brown the meatballs in batches. Once browned on all sides, remove to a plate, cover, and keep warm.

3) Meanwhile, put up a large pot of water to cook the pasta. Put the tomato sauce into a medium saucepan and heat until hot but not simmering. Stir the ricotta into the tomato sauce, taste, and add salt as needed (ricottas vary greatly in salt content). Cover and keep warm.

4) Cook the pasta. Drain and put in a large serving bowl. Top with the meatballs and sauce.

Per Serving: Calories 558; Protein 37g; Fat 8g (Saturated 3g); Carbohydrates 81g; Fiber 3g; Sodium 1041mg

Turkey Meatball and Penne Casserole

Makes: 8 servings

Baked pasta casseroles, thick with cheese and pasta, are favorites for many families. There is nothing trendy here, just food that you know everyone will enjoy.

1 pound penne
1 cup shredded reduced-fat mozzarella cheese
2 tablespoons grated Parmesan cheese
2 tablespoons grated Romano cheese
1 pound lowfat ricotta cheese
6 cups tomato sauce (pages 583–585 or store-bought)
1 recipe Turkey Meatballs (opposite)

1) Preheat the oven to 350°F.

2) Cook the pasta according to the package directions. Drain and set aside.

3) In a bowl, combine the cheeses. Set aside.

4) Spread 2 cups of the tomato sauce on the bottom of a 3- or 4-quart casserole. Place half the meatballs on the sauce, then half the penne on top of the meatballs. Pour 2 cups of the tomato sauce in the casserole, followed by half of the cheese mixture, the remaining pasta, the remaining meatballs, the rest of the sauce, and the remaining cheese.

5) Place the casserole in the center of the oven and bake for about 40 minutes, until bubbly and the top begins to brown.

Per Serving: Calories 481; Protein 33g; Fat 11g (Saturated 4g); Carbohydrates 60g; Fiber 4g; Sodium 643mg

Entrées:
Fish and Shellfish

Baked Fish
222

Fish Sticks

Parmesan Fish Sticks

Pecan Catfish

Cajun Catfish

Fish Baked with Pesto

Fish Baked in
Almost Sour Cream

Chili-Seasoned Fish Steaks

Mustard and Honey Fish

Lime-Thyme Fish

Ginger and Lime Fish

Fish Baked with Mint

Orange-Herb Fish

Fish with Mustard and Apples

Fish with Golden Raisin Sauce

Spanish Fish

Golden Fish

Spicy Onion and
Tomato Baked Fish

Fish Baked in Creole Sauce

Creole Sauce for Seafood

Tuna Noodle Casserole

Fish en Papillote

Ginger Fish in a Packet

Salmon and Scallop Packets

Whole Trout
233

Whole Trout with Cornbread
Stuffing

Whole Trout Baked in Foil

Grilled and Broiled Fish
234

Grilling or Broiling Fish

Fresh Herb–Marinated Fish

Citrus-Marinated Fish

Garlic-Broiled Fish

Lemon-Ginger Fish

Fish Steak in
Raspberry Marinade

Maple Teriyaki Fish

Salmon Teriyaki

Fish Steak with
Tomato Caper Sauce

Grilled Fish with
Piri Piri Sauce

Grilled Fish with
Currant-Caper Relish

Swordfish and
Pineapple Skewers

Grilled Scallop Skewers

Poached Fish
241

Fish Poached in
Wine and Lemon Juice

Poached Fish with Herbs

Dill Poached Fish

Chilled Poached Salmon

Chilled Whole Poached Salmon

Chinese Steamed Fish

Stovetop Cooking
244

Pan-Cooked Fish Fillets

Fish in Curried Coconut Sauce

Moroccan Fish Stew

Cioppino

Fish in a Pot

Seafood Gumbo

Fish Steak and Asparagus
Stir-Fry

Sweet and Sour Fish
and Vegetables

Shrimp and Shellfish
250

Shrimp and Snow Peas

Shrimp and Broccoli

*Deep South
Boiled Shrimp Dinner*

Shrimp in Creole Sauce

*Spaghetti with
Fresh Clam Sauce*

Spaghetti with Clam Sauce

*Linguine with
Clam and Tomato Sauce*

*Four Peppers and Salmon
over Pasta*

Scallops Linguine

Scallops, Broccoli, and Pasta

*Spaghetti with Scallops and
Sun-Dried Tomatoes*

Peking Noodles and Scallops

Shrimp and Vegetable Lo Mein

Shrimp Fried Rice

Risottos
260

Mussels and Clams Risotto

Swordfish and Broccoli Risotto

Mussels
262

Mussels in Shallot Sauce

Spanish Mussels

Mussels in Spicy Tomato Broth

Fish, like many other foods, has become global. On any day you might find halibut from Alaska or tiger shrimp from Malaysia for sale, although most of the offerings at the supermarket (and those at the best prices) remain local and in season. However, freshness is more dependent on how the fish were handled in the boats and in the store than where they were caught. Buy fish that are moist but not wet, and those that look full and firm, not limp. They should smell clean, with only a light odor of fish. Seafood should be displayed on clean ice, never in melted ice water. If you can't find good fresh fish, you might be able to find excellent frozen fish. Some of the best fish I've eaten has come from the supermarket, flash-frozen and vacuum-packed.

At home, store fresh fish in the coolest part of the refrigerator (usually the back of the bottom shelf) and cook within twenty-four hours. Fish can be frozen. (When catfish goes on sale, I buy several pounds and freeze it for fish sticks.) Defrost fish in the refrigerator, never on the countertop. For fish sticks, fish can be cut into portions, breaded, and baked when still very cold and a bit icy

I cook almost exclusively with fillets and steaks, for several reasons. Fillets and steaks are the most widely available and it is easy to get the right portion size. (As a general rule, plan on 1/3 pound per person.) They require almost no preparation. Also, people who are squeamish about eating fish with skin, bones, and fins usually have no problem with fillets.

Many of my recipes do not specify exactly what type of fish to get, because most recipes will work with a number of varieties. I divide fish into three categories: dense fish steaks (such as swordfish), mild white-fleshed fish (such as haddock and flounder), and oily, flavorful fish (such as bluefish). If the type of fish is important to the dish, I note that in the recipe. Otherwise, buy what looks best at the market.

Checking for Doneness

Because fish cooks quickly, it is perfect for our time-crunched lives. As a general rule, each inch of fish takes 10 minutes to cook. But what about a fillet that is 3/8 of an inch? How to account for the fact that fish baked in a sauce takes longer to cook than fish on a metal sheet? And should oven temperatures vary according to fish type?

Don't worry. Cooking fish to perfection is not difficult. First, notice what the fish looks like when raw. As it cooks, the color changes. White-fleshed fish goes from gray to marble white. Salmon changes from orange to peach pink. When the fish is the same color throughout, it is done. Also notice the texture of the raw fish. Touch it. It yields to a finger. As it cooks, it firms up. When done, it will bounce back to the touch. Look at how the raw fish holds together. As it cooks, the muscles separate at the membranes. This is called "flaking." When done, a dull knife can separate a fillet into flakes almost all the way through.

So, use the 10-minute rule to give yourself a general idea as to how long the fish will take to cook, then use your senses of sight and touch to make the final decision. Check the fish frequently, since it goes from done to overcooked quickly. If in doubt, remove it from the oven and the retained heat will finish the cooking.

Baked Fish

Fish Sticks

Makes: 4 servings

I confess: I always eat fish sticks with ketchup and a side dish of peas.

1 1/3 pounds fish fillets, preferably a firm white fish such as catfish
1/3 cup nonfat milk
1/2 cup cornflakes
1/2 cup dry breadcrumbs
1/4 teaspoon kosher salt

1) Put the oven rack in the top third of the oven. Preheat the oven to 425°F. Coat a baking sheet with nonstick spray.

2) Cut the fish into pieces about 3 to 4 inches long and 1/2 inch around. Try to cut into similar-size pieces so that they bake evenly. Soak the fish sticks in the milk.

3) Finely chop the cornflakes, breadcrumbs, and salt in a food processor or blender and put on a dinner plate.

4) Dip the fish, wet from the milk, into the crumbs. Put the fish onto the baking sheet in one layer with space between the pieces. Spray very lightly with cooking spray. Bake for 8 to 10 minutes, until golden and firm.

Per Serving: Calories 212; Protein 27g; Fat 5g (Saturated 1g); Carbohydrates 13g; Fiber 1g; Sodium 335mg

Parmesan Fish Sticks

Makes: 4 servings

These are oh-so-much better than the fish sticks in the box, and almost as easy to make.

1 1/3 pounds fish fillets, preferably a firm white fish such as catfish
1/3 cup nonfat milk
1/4 teaspoon kosher salt
1/4 teaspoon freshly ground pepper
1/4 teaspoon dried thyme
1/2 teaspoon paprika
1/4 cup grated Parmesan cheese
1/4 cup cornflakes
1/2 cup dry breadcrumbs

1) Put the oven rack in the top third of the oven. Preheat the oven to 450°F. Coat a baking sheet with nonstick spray.

2) Cut the fish into pieces about 3 to 4 inches long and 1/2 inch around. Try to cut into similar-size pieces so that they bake evenly. Soak the fish sticks in the milk.

3) Finely chop the remaining ingredients in a processor or blender. Put on a dinner plate.

4) Dip the fish, wet from the milk, into the crumbs. Place the fish on the baking sheet in one layer with space between the pieces. Spray very lightly with cooking spray. Bake for 8 to 10 minutes, until golden and firm.

Per Serving: Calories 236; Protein 30g; Fat 7g (Saturated 2g); Carbohydrates 12g; Fiber 1g; Sodium 436mg

Pecan Catfish

Makes: 4 servings

Bread the fish just prior to baking. Don't do it ahead of time or the coating will become soggy and will not crisp up in the oven.

1/4 cup nonfat milk
3 tablespoons Dijon mustard
1 1/3 pounds catfish fillets
1/2 cup pecans
2/3 cup cornflakes
1/3 cup dry breadcrumbs

1) Preheat the oven to 425°F. Coat a baking sheet with nonstick spray.

2) Whisk together the milk and mustard and soak the fish in the mixture.

3) Finely chop the pecans, cornflakes, and breadcrumbs in a processor or blender. Put on a dinner plate.

4) Dip the fish, wet from the milk mixture, into the crumbs. Put the fish onto the baking sheet. Spray very lightly with cooking spray. Bake for 8 to 10 minutes, until golden and firm.

Per Serving: Calories 302; Protein 28g; Fat 15g (Saturated 2g); Carbohydrates 14g; Fiber 1g; Sodium 472mg

Cajun Catfish

Makes: 4 servings

Cajun has come to mean mouth-burning hot, but it doesn't have to. I don't like to hide the flavor of the fish, so this is highly seasoned but is not a test of your heat tolerance.

1/2 cup yellow cornmeal, preferably stone-ground
1 tablespoon cajun or creole spice blend
1/4 cup buttermilk
1 1/3 pounds catfish fillets
1 lemon, cut into wedges

1) Put the oven rack in the top third of the oven. Preheat the oven to 425°F. Place a wire cooling rack on a baking sheet (the smaller mesh of a cooling rack will support the fish). Coat with nonstick spray.

2) Combine the cornmeal and spices on a plate. Put the buttermilk in a shallow bowl.

3) Cut the fillets into 4 or more servings (depending on the shape of the fish). Dip the fish in the buttermilk so that it is completely covered. Lift the fish out and place in the cornmeal mixture. Press the cornmeal onto the fish, turning once to coat both sides. Lift the fish out and place on the wire rack. Repeat for each portion of fish. Lightly coat the fish pieces with baking spray.

4) Bake for 8 minutes to 10 minutes, until cooked through. Serve with lemon wedges.

Per Serving: Calories 222; Protein 27g; Fat 5g (Saturated 1g); Carbohydrates 16g; Fiber 2g; Sodium 437mg

Fish Baked with Pesto

Makes: 4 servings

Although basil pesto is the most common form of this herb paste and acceptable versions are available in jars or in a refrigerator in the market, pesto can have other flavors. See pages 589–591 for a selection.

1^1/$_3$ pounds fish steaks or fillets
^{1}/$_4$ teaspoon kosher salt
^{1}/$_8$ teaspoon freshly ground pepper
3 to 4 tablespoons pesto

1) Put the oven rack in the top third of the oven. Preheat the oven to 375°F. Lightly coat a baking sheet with nonstick spray.

2) If desired, cut the fish into 4 to 5 portions. Cut similar-size pieces so that they bake evenly. Rub them with the salt and pepper. Place on the baking sheet. Spread a layer of pesto on top of the fish.

3) Bake for 7 to 12 minutes, depending on the thickness of the fish, until the fish tests done.

Per Serving: Calories 168; Protein 30g; Fat 5g (Saturated 1g); Carbohydrates 1g; Fiber 0g; Sodium 246mg

Fish Baked in Almost Sour Cream

Makes: 4 servings

Years ago in college, I found a recipe similar to this in the old Joy of Cooking. *It was one of the first fish dishes I ever cooked. The original recipe called for sour cream, which covered the fish and helped to keep it moist. Here is my updated version. It is more healthful but still as accessible for someone unfamiliar with cooking fish.*

1^1/$_3$ pounds fish fillets
^{1}/$_4$ cup lemon juice
1 cup Almost Sour Cream (page 606)
1 tablespoon minced fresh herbs, such as tarragon and dill (optional)
Freshly ground pepper

1) Preheat the oven to 375°F.

2) Place the fish, skin side down, in a baking dish. Pour the lemon juice over the fish. If desired, combine the Almost Sour Cream and the herbs, then spread the Almost Sour Cream on top of the fish.

3) Cover and bake for 12 to 15 minutes. Uncover and bake for 5 more minutes, or until the fish tests done.

4) Grind pepper over the fillet before serving.

Per Serving: Calories 177; Protein 35g; Fat 2g (Saturated 1g); Carbohydrates 3g; Fiber 0g; Sodium 315mg

Chili-Seasoned Fish Steaks

Makes: 4 servings

This recipe utilizes the technique of the "dry rub," in which ground spices are rubbed onto fish (or chicken). Because there is no protective sauce, the fish can dry out. Restaurants use this method and cook quickly at high temperatures, then finish the recipe with butter. Here the fish is baked at moderately high heat, with lime juice for flavor and moisture.

1 1/2 teaspoons chili powder
1/2 teaspoon kosher salt
1 1/3 pounds thick fish steaks, such as swordfish or shark
2 tablespoons fresh lime juice

1) Preheat the oven to 425°F.

2) Combine the chili powder and salt in a small bowl.

3) Rub one side of the fish with some of the spices. Place seasoned side down in a baking dish. Pour the lime juice over the fish and then rub in more of the spices until the fish is an even rusty-brown color. Place in the oven and bake for 12 to 15 minutes, or until the fish is cooked through but still moist.

Per Serving: Calories 188; Protein 30g; Fat 6g (Saturated 2g); Carbohydrates 1g; Fiber 0g; Sodium 386mg

Mustard and Honey Fish

Makes: 4 servings

Baking fish in a small pool of liquid helps to keep the fillets moist, while also adding flavor.

1 tablespoon Dijon mustard
1 1/2 teaspoons honey
1 1/3 pounds fish fillets
1 tablespoon dry breadcrumbs
1/2 teaspoon paprika
1/4 cup dry white wine
1/4 cup water
2 teaspoons dried tarragon

1) Preheat the oven to 425°F.

2) Whisk together the mustard and honey until smooth. Place the fish in a 2-inch-deep baking dish. Brush the mustard mixture on the fillets. Dust on the breadcrumbs and garnish with the paprika.

3) Combine the wine, water, and tarragon in a measuring cup. Pour around, but not on top of the fish until it comes one-third of the way up the fillet.

4) Bake 7 to 10 minutes, until cooked through.

Per Serving: Calories 177; Protein 26g; Fat 5g (Saturated 1g); Carbohydrates 5g; Fiber 0g; Sodium 175mg

Lime-Thyme Fish

Makes: 4 servings

Although lemon is usually associated with fish, lime juice can bring even more zest to a recipe. Here it is paired with thyme and capers, which contribute flavor without overwhelming the fish itself.

2 tablespoons fresh lime juice
2 tablespoons white wine
1 tablespoon water
1 teaspoon drained capers
1/8 teaspoon kosher salt
1/8 teaspoon freshly ground pepper
1/4 teaspoon paprika
1/16 teaspoon Tabasco sauce
1 teaspoon chopped fresh thyme, or
   1/2 teaspoon dried
1 1/3 pounds fish fillets
1 lime cut into wedges, for garnish (optional)

1) Preheat the oven to 375°F.

2) Combine all the ingredients except the fish and lime wedges.

3) Put the fish in a baking dish, preferably a heavy ceramic casserole. Pour the baking liquid over the fish until it reaches halfway up the sides of the fillets. (Don't choose too large a baking dish or there won't be enough liquid. Too small a dish will crowd the fish against the sides.)

4) Bake until the fish is the same texture and color throughout. Dense haddock will take about 15 minutes, perch only 5 to 7 minutes.

5) Garnish the fillets with lime wedges, if desired.

Per Serving: Calories 139; Protein 29g; Fat 1g (Saturated 0g); Carbohydrates 1g; Fiber 0g; Sodium 190mg

Ginger and Lime Fish

Makes: 4 servings

This incredibly easy to make recipe is the perfect example of how painless and convenient cooking fish can be. How many main entrées call for so little time and so few ingredients? As long as the fish is fresh, dinner will be superb.

1 1/3 pounds thick fish fillets, such as cod or halibut
2 teaspoons finely grated fresh ginger, minced
1 tablespoon soy sauce
3 limes, juiced

1) Preheat the oven to 375°F. Place the fillet skin side down in a baking dish.

2) Combine the ginger, soy sauce, and lime juice. Pour over the fish. Add water if there isn't 1/4 inch of liquid covering the bottom of the pan. If time permits, marinate the fish for 30 minutes.

3) Bake for 20 to 25 minutes, or until the fish tests done.

Per Serving: Calories 130; Protein 27g; Fat 1g (Saturated 0g); Carbohydrates 2g; Fiber 0g; Sodium 339mg

Fish Baked with Mint

Makes: 4 servings

Keeping the flesh moist as the fish cooks is of utmost importance. One trick is to bake it on a bed of vegetables to provide moisture. Here, not only do the mint and onions keep the fish moist, but they also contribute an enticing aroma and look lovely. Serve this directly out of the baking dish.

$1/2$ cup fresh mint leaves
$1/2$ red onion, peeled and sliced into rounds
2 cloves garlic, minced
$1^1/3$ pounds thick fish fillets or steaks, such as swordfish
$1/16$ teaspoon kosher salt
$1/16$ teaspoon freshly ground pepper
$1/16$ teaspoon crushed red pepper flakes (optional)
1 tablespoon balsamic vinegar
2 tablespoons lemon juice
3 tablespoons white wine
1 tablespoon drained capers

1) Preheat the oven to 425°F.

2) Line the bottom of a baking dish with the mint leaves. Place the onion rounds on top of the mint. Scatter the garlic on top.

3) Rinse the fish in water, then pat dry with a towel. Rub on the salt, pepper, and pepper flakes. Place the fish in the baking dish.

4) Combine the vinegar, lemon juice, wine, and capers. Pour the mixture over the fish.

5) Bake for 10 to 20 minutes, depending on the thickness of the fish and type of baking dish used.

Per Serving: Calories 209; Protein 31g; Fat 6g (Saturated 2g); Carbohydrates 4g; Fiber 1g; Sodium 253mg

Orange-Herb Fish

Makes: 6 servings

Rosemary pairs well with fish, but too much can cancel out all of the other flavors. If you do have excess fresh rosemary, don't add it to the recipe (even an extra teaspoon will be too much). Instead, garnish the serving platter or save it for another use.

$1/2$ cup orange juice
$1/3$ cup white wine
$1/4$ cup lemon juice
1 large shallot, peeled and sliced
1 teaspoon fine strips of orange zest
$1/16$ teaspoon cayenne pepper
$1/2$ teaspoon paprika
1 tablespoon chopped fresh rosemary, or 1 teaspoon dried
2 tablespoons chopped fresh parsley
2 pounds fish fillets

1) Combine all the ingredients except the fish in a bowl.

2) Wash the fish, pat dry, then put it in the marinade. Turn it once or twice so that all sides come in contact with the liquid. If you have time and the fillet is thick, let the fish sit in the marinade for up to 30 minutes.

3) Preheat the oven to 350°F.

4) Place the fish in a baking dish. Pour the marinade over the fish until the liquid comes about halfway up the sides of the fillet.

5) Bake until done. Many fillets take only 7 minutes to cook, although a thick piece of haddock might require 15 minutes.

Per Serving: Calories 156; Protein 29g; Fat 1g (Saturated 0g); Carbohydrates 4g; Fiber 0g; Sodium 105mg

Fish with Mustard and Apples

Makes: 4 servings

The strong flavors of this sauce balance out the assertiveness of an oily fish like bluefish.

1 teaspoon olive oil
1 tablespoon minced shallots
1 1/3 pounds thick fish fillets, such as salmon or bluefish
1 tart, firm apple
1 teaspoon lemon juice
3 tablespoons Pommery or other coarse mustard
1/4 cup white wine
3 tablespoons water or fish broth

1) Preheat the oven to 375°F.

2) Heat the oil in a sauté pan and sauté the shallots until softened. Remove the shallots, leaving the oil in the pan. Place the shallots in a casserole dish and place the fish on top.

3) Core and thinly slice the apple. Cook it in the remaining oil plus the lemon juice until the apple softens but is not mushy. Toss or turn the slices several times during cooking.

4) Arrange the apple slices on top of the fish. I like to overlap them so they look like scales. All of the apple may not be needed.

5) Whisk together the mustard, wine, and water. Pour this sauce over and around the fish until it reaches halfway up the side of the fillet.

6) Bake until the fish is done, about 8 to 10 minutes for the average fillet.

7) If a sauce is desired, remove the fish to a serving platter, then strain the liquid through a sieve and into a saucepan. Boil, stirring constantly, until it is reduced to about 3 tablespoons and is a thick consistency. Pour over the fish.

Per Serving: Calories 268; Protein 30g; Fat 11g (Saturated 2g); Carbohydrates 6g; Fiber 1g; Sodium 338mg

Fish with Golden Raisin Sauce

Makes: 4 servings

A sweet and sour sauce is made when raisins are cooked with vinegar, one that is a lovely complement to a fish with flavor, like salmon.

1 1/3 pounds fillets with skin on, preferably salmon
2 teaspoons olive oil
1/2 cup onions, thinly sliced
1 red bell pepper, julienned
1/4 cup golden raisins
2 tablespoons red wine vinegar
1/3 cup white wine
1/4 teaspoon kosher salt
1/8 teaspoon freshly ground pepper
1 tablespoon chopped fresh parsley, for garnish

1) Preheat the oven to 425°F. Place the fish on a shallow baking pan that has been coated with nonstick spray. Set aside.

2) Heat the oil in a nonstick pan. Add the onions, pepper, raisins, vinegar, and wine. Bring to a boil, then reduce to a gentle simmer. Cover and cook for 25 minutes, or until the onions are soft. Season with the salt and pepper. Keep warm.

3) Bake the fish for about 8 to 10 minutes, or until done.

4) Put the fish on a serving platter, cover with the raisin sauce, and garnish with the parsley. Serve immediately.

Per Serving: Calories 179; Protein 22g; Fat 4g (Saturated 1g); Carbohydrates 12g; Fiber 1g; Sodium 169mg

Spanish Fish

Makes: 6 servings

The marinade is important—it imbues the fish with much flavor. However, if the fish is left in it for more than half an hour, the flesh will lose its firm texture.

4 cloves garlic, finely minced
1 shallot, finely minced
2 tablespoons fresh lime juice
1/2 cup orange juice
1 1/2 teaspoons olive oil
1/2 teaspoon kosher salt
1 teaspoon dried oregano
1/2 teaspoon dried rosemary, ground
1/2 teaspoon ground cumin
2 pounds fish fillets or steaks
1/2 cup pitted green olives
1 orange, peel and white pith cut away, chopped

1) Whisk together the garlic, shallot, juices, oil, salt, oregano, rosemary, and cumin. Marinate the fish in this mixture for 30 minutes.

2) Meanwhile, preheat the oven to 400°F. Place the fish in a baking dish. Pour in the marinade so that it comes halfway up the fish. Arrange the olives and orange pieces around and on the fish.

3) Bake for 8 to 15 minutes, until the fish is cooked through.

Per Serving: Calories 172; Protein 28g; Fat 1g (Saturated 0g); Carbohydrates 7g; Fiber 1g; Sodium 470mg

Golden Fish

Makes: 4 servings

Fish takes a little longer to cook when it is baked in a liquid bath in a covered casserole. This is partly because before the fish can begin to cook, the casserole and broth first have to heat up, and this varies with the type of baking dish. So start checking the fish at 15 minutes, then every few minutes after that until done.

Pinch saffron, or 1/4 teaspoon ground
1/4 cup white wine
1 1/3 pounds mild white-fleshed fish fillets, such as haddock
1/8 teaspoon kosher salt
1/8 teaspoon freshly ground pepper
3 plum tomatoes, cored, cut in half lengthwise and sliced into half rounds
1 clove garlic, peeled and crushed
1 shallot, minced, or 1 tablespoon minced red onions
1 teaspoon drained capers
2 tablespoons lemon juice

1) Crumble the saffron threads into the wine. Stir and let sit for 30 minutes until the saffron colors the wine.

2) Preheat the oven to 375°F.

3) Wash and dry the fish. Rub it with the salt and pepper and put it into a casserole.

4) Arrange the tomatoes, garlic, shallot, and capers around the fish.

5) Pour the saffron wine and lemon juice over the fish.

6) Cover the casserole and bake for 20 to 25 minutes, or until the fish tests done.

Per Serving: Calories 157; Protein 29g; Fat 1g (Saturated 0g); Carbohydrates 4g; Fiber 1g; Sodium 195mg

Spicy Onion and Tomato Baked Fish

Makes: 4 servings

Sometimes I like mild fish recipes, where the delicate flavors inherent in the fish come through. Other times I want a gutsily seasoned dish, when the fish is there as a vehicle for the flavors. This is for one of those times.

1¹/3 pounds fish fillets, such as catfish
1 tablespoon vegetable oil
2 cups sliced onions
3 cloves garlic, minced
1 jalapeño pepper, seeded and minced (use rubber gloves)
1 teaspoon ground coriander
¹/2 teaspoon kosher salt
1 tablespoon white wine vinegar
One 14¹/2-ounce can diced tomatoes
¹/8 teaspoon Tabasco sauce

1) Preheat the oven to 350°F. Place the fish in a baking dish.

2) Heat the oil in a nonstick pan. Add the onions, garlic, and jalapeño. Sauté until golden, about 10 minutes. Cover between stirrings. Stir in the coriander, salt, vinegar, tomatoes, and Tabasco. Simmer, uncovered, for 10 minutes. The sauce can be made a day ahead of time.

3) Cover the fish with the sauce. Bake for 15 minutes, or until the fish is done.

Per Serving: Calories 226; Protein 27g; Fat 8g (Saturated 1g); Carbohydrates 11g; Fiber 2g; Sodium 470mg

Fish Baked in Creole Sauce

Makes: 4 servings

Serve with a big bowl of rice and a loaf of French bread.

One 4-pound whole fish, cleaned, or 2 pounds thick fish fillets
¹/4 teaspoon kosher salt
¹/8 teaspoon freshly ground pepper
1 to 1¹/2 cups Creole Sauce (opposite)
1 tablespoon fresh lime juice

1) Preheat the oven to 400°F.

2) Rub the fish with the salt and pepper.

3) Spread the sauce in the bottom of a baking dish (the amount will vary depending on how large the dish is). Place the fish on the sauce. Pour the lime juice over the fish. Cover loosely with foil.

4) Bake in the oven for about 20 to 25 minutes, or until the fish is done.

Per Serving: Calories 256; Protein 47g; Fat 4g (Saturated 1g); Carbohydrates 5g; Fiber 1g; Sodium 487mg

Creole Sauce for Seafood

Makes: 4 cups

This freezes well, so make a double batch and store it in 2-cup containers to have on hand when you want a fast home-cooked meal.

1 tablespoon vegetable oil
1 cup chopped onions
1 rib celery, chopped
1/2 green bell pepper, finely chopped
3 cloves garlic, minced
One 28-ounce can whole tomatoes, with juice
1/4 cup tomato paste
1 tablespoon lemon juice
2 tablespoons fresh lime juice
1 teaspoon dried thyme
1/2 teaspoon dried oregano
1 teaspoon ground allspice
1/2 teaspoon Tabasco sauce
1 teaspoon kosher salt
1/4 cup fresh chopped parsley
1 teaspoon drained capers
1 cup water

1) Heat the oil in a nonstick saucepan. Add the onions, celery, bell pepper, and garlic. Cover and cook over medium heat, stirring frequently, until the vegetables soften and the onions begin to turn golden, about 10 minutes.

2) Pour the juice from the tomatoes into the pot. Put the tomatoes in a colander in the sink. Squeeze them to remove the seeds and to break them apart, then stir the tomato pulp into the saucepan. Add the remaining ingredients. Bring to a boil, reduce to a simmer, and cook, uncovered, for 15 minutes.

Per 1/2 Cup: Calories 56; Protein 2g; Fat 2g (Saturated 0g); Carbohydrates 9g; Fiber 2g; Sodium 444mg

Tuna Noodle Casserole

Makes: 4 servings

Years ago I never would have tampered with such an old-time favorite. However, the taste of lowfat sour cream has so improved that I believe that this version can hold its own with the original.

2 teaspoons olive oil, divided
1 cup sliced mushrooms
1 tablespoon minced onions
One 6-ounce can tuna, packed in water
3 cups cooked egg noodles
1 cup frozen peas
1 tablespoon unbleached, all-purpose white flour
1 cup lowfat sour cream
1/4 cup nonfat milk
1/2 teaspoon kosher salt
1/4 teaspoon freshly ground pepper
1/2 cup cornflake crumbs

1) Preheat the oven to 350°F. Coat a 2-quart casserole with nonstick spray.

2) Heat 1 teaspoon of the oil in a small nonstick pan. Sauté the mushrooms and onions until wilted. Put them in a bowl and toss with the tuna, noodles, and peas.

3) Add the second teaspoon of oil to the pan, and stir in the flour. Cook until lightly brown. Stir in the sour cream, milk, salt, and pepper and cook over high heat until bubbly, about 2 minutes. Stir this mixture into the bowl with the noodles.

4) Pour the mixture into the casserole. Top with the cornflake crumbs. Bake for 25 minutes.

Per Serving: Calories 367; Protein 20g; Fat 7g (Saturated 4g); Carbohydrates 57g; Fiber 4g; Sodium 615mg

Fish en Papillote

Makes: 2 servings

These can be prepared several hours before baking. Because the recipe can be multiplied to serve many, this is an excellent dinner party recipe.

1/4 cup thinly sliced carrots
1/2 red bell pepper, julienned
2/3 pound fish fillets
1 tablespoon lemon juice
1 tablespoon chopped fresh parsley
1/4 teaspoon ground coriander
1/8 teaspoon kosher salt
1/8 teaspoon freshly ground pepper
1 clove garlic, crushed

1) Preheat the oven to 375°F. Cut a circle of parchment twice the size of the fish, fold in half and crease, then open back up.

2) Put the carrots and bell peppers on half of the paper, leaving a 1/2-inch margin at the outside. Set the fish on top of the vegetables, close to the inside fold.

3) Distribute the lemon juice, parsley, coriander, salt, and pepper on top of the fish, and set the garlic to one side of the fillet.

4) Fold the parchment over the fish. Make small, tight folds inward around the circular edge of the packet to seal.

5) Place in an ovenproof dish and bake. Cook thin fillets 15 minutes, and thicker ones up to 30 minutes. Timing is not crucial because the moisture trapped in the paper packet will prevent a dried-out, overcooked fish disaster.

Per Serving: Calories 141; Protein 27g; Fat 1g (Saturated 0g); Carbohydrates 4g; Fiber 1g; Sodium 208mg

Ginger Fish in a Packet

Makes: 4 servings

The assembled packets, uncooked, can be refrigerated for several hours before baking. Once cooked, however, they must be served immediately or the steam in the packets will continue to cook the fish until it is quite overdone.

1 carrot
2 teaspoons grated fresh ginger
2 cloves garlic, minced
6 shiitake mushrooms, stems discarded and caps sliced
1 1/3 pounds skinless fish fillets, cut into 4 portions
2 scallions, cut into 1-inch pieces
2 tablespoons soy sauce
1 teaspoon Asian sesame oil
1 tablespoon dry sherry

1) Preheat the oven to 400°F. Fold four 20-inch-long pieces of foil or parchment in half.

2) Using a vegetable peeler, shave the carrot into long strips. Divide carrot into 4 portions, and mound each portion in the center of each piece of foil. Divide the ginger, garlic, and mushrooms equally among the packets and place on top of the carrots. Place a piece of fish on top of the vegetables. Arrange the scallions on top.

3) Combine the soy sauce, oil, and sherry. Pour over the portions of fish. Close the packets with tight folds.

4) Arrange, uncrowded, in a single layer on a baking sheet and bake A 3/4- to 1-inch-thick fillet will take about 12 minutes to bake. Cut an X in each packet to release steam and place on individual dinner plates.

Per Serving: Calories 178; Protein 30g; Fat 2g (Saturated 0g); Carbohydrates 8g; Fiber 1g; Sodium 626mg

Salmon and Scallop Packets

Makes: 2 servings

Bay scallops are the tiny scallops sold shucked and in plastic containers packed in ice at the fish counter. They should smell very fresh, with just a whiff of ocean air. Don't be shy about smelling the scallops before you decide to purchase them.

2/3 pound salmon fillets, cut into 2 portions
1/8 teaspoon kosher salt
4 ounces bay scallops
1 1/2 teaspoons lemon juice
1 tablespoon orange juice
2 teaspoons fine strips orange zest
1 teaspoon extra-virgin olive oil
2 scallions, cut into 1-inch pieces, including the green tops

1) Preheat the oven to 425°F. Cut 2 pieces of parchment paper or foil about 12 to 14 inches long. Fold each in half, then open back up.

2) Rub a fish fillet with the salt and place on one of the sheets of parchment, near the fold. Top with the half of the scallops, then arrange half the lemon and oranges juices, orange zest, oil, and scallions on top. Repeat for the second fillet.

3) Bring the parchment over the fish and seal the edges with small, tight folds. Start on one side and work around each packet. Put them on a baking sheet.

4) Bake for 8 to 10 minutes, depending on the thickness of the fish.

Per Serving: Calories 294; Protein 40g; Fat 12g (Saturated 2g); Carbohydrates 4g; Fiber 0g; Sodium 280mg

Whole Trout

Trout is now being farm-raised, which makes this delicious, mild fish more available to those of us who don't have trout streams in their backyards. Each small trout weighs about 1/2 pound and feeds one person. It comes cleaned and boned. It is your option whether to leave the head on or remove it before baking.

Whole Trout with Cornbread Stuffing

Makes: 4 servings

Baking whole fish can be intimidating, but not this recipe. Even the novice fish cook can make this perfectly on the first attempt.

4 whole trout, cleaned
1 1/2 cups store-bought cornbread stuffing mix
1/4 cup sliced almonds, lightly toasted
1/4 teaspoon freshly ground pepper
2 scallions, minced
3/4 cup reduced-sodium, defatted vegetable broth
1/2 teaspoon olive oil

1) Preheat the oven to 375°F. Line a baking sheet with foil and coat with nonstick spray. Place the fish, with at least 2 inches between them, on the foil.

2) Stir the stuffing, almonds, pepper and scallions together. Moisten with the broth. Divide into 4 portions and stuff each trout with the mixture. Brush the skin of the trout with the oil.

3) Bake for 20 to 25 minutes.

Per Serving: Calories 334; Protein 34g; Fat 13g (Saturated 3g); Carbohydrates 18g; Fiber 2g; Sodium 333mg

Whole Trout Baked in Foil

Makes: 4 servings

A subtle, elegant, and incredibly easy dish to make.

4 whole trout, cleaned
1 lemon
1/2 teaspoon kosher salt
1/8 teaspoon freshly ground pepper
2 cloves garlic, thinly sliced
4 sprigs fresh rosemary

1) Preheat the oven to 425°F. Tear off 4 pieces of foil in 12 inch lengths. Fold them in half, open back up and coat with nonstick spray.

2) Cut the lemon in half. Thinly slice a half and cut the other half into wedges.

3) Rub the trout inside and out with the salt and pepper. Place lemon slices, some garlic slices and a rosemary sprig inside each trout. Place the trout on the foil. Seal up the foil packets with tight folds. Place on a baking sheet and put in the oven.

4) Bake for 12 to 15 minutes. Take care opening the packets so that the steam exits away from you. Slip the fish on a serving platter or on individual plates, garnished with lemon wedges.

Per Serving: Calories 203; Protein 31g; Fat 8g (Saturated 2g); Carbohydrates 0g; Fiber 0g; Sodium 315mg

Grilled and Broiled Fish

Most recipes for grilling or broiling fish are interchangeable. I have a gas grill at home and use it in the summer. In the winter, I use the broiler or a stovetop grill. Following are basic directions for whenever you want to grill or broil fish. Such simply cooked fish can be served at the most elegant dinners, dressed up with salsas, relishes, or pestos.

Cooking time will vary according to the thickness of the fish and the heat of the grill. I like to get my gas grill very hot. As soon as I place the fish on the grill, I lower the temperature and close the lid. (Charcoal grills don't give you that ability to change temperature as quickly, so you have to start them at a more moderate temperature.)

Grilling or Broiling Fish

Makes: 4 servings

For simple recipes without a marinade, prepare fish by rubbing it with salt and brushing with oil.

1^1/3 pounds fish steaks or thick fillets
^{1}/4 teaspoon kosher salt
1 teaspoon olive oil

1) *To Grill:* Preheat the grill. When it is very hot, take the wire cleaning brush and give the grate a scrub—a hot grill is the easiest to clean, and a clean grill cooks with less sticking. Although some marinades contain enough oil to make greasing the grill unnecessary, most of the time you will need to oil the cooking surface. Use a grill brush specially designed for oiling the grill. Or lightly coat the food itself with a nonstick spray. Cook a 1-inch-thick piece of fish 4 minutes on one side, turn and continue to cook, 4 to 5 minutes, until barely cooked through and firm to the touch. Turn the fish only once or it will fall apart. If using a marinade, brush the fish before you turn it, then brush the top again.

2) *To Broil:* Put the oven rack about 4 inches from the heat source. Line a baking sheet with foil, then coat it lightly with nonstick spray. Rub the salt on the fish and then brush with the oil, or, if using a marinade, remove the fish from the marinade. Place it on the baking sheet. A 1-inch thick piece of fish will cook in about 10 to 12 minutes. If cooking a thick piece of fish and using a marinade, brush once with the marinade while broiling. Unless the fish fillet is very thick, do not turn it as it cooks.

Per Serving: Calories 86; Protein 16g; Fat 2g (Saturated 0g); Carbohydrates 0g; Fiber 0g; Sodium 176mg

Fresh Herb-Marinated Fish

Makes: 6 servings

Use only fresh herbs.

^{1}/2 cup white wine
1^1/2 teaspoons olive oil
1 teaspoon lemon juice
1 clove garlic, crushed
^{1}/4 teaspoon freshly ground pepper
^{1}/4 teaspoon kosher salt
1 teaspoon chopped fresh thyme
2 teaspoons chopped fresh tarragon
2 tablespoons chopped fresh dill
2 pounds fish fillets

1) Combine all of the ingredients except for the fish and let it sit for 1 hour. Place the fish in the marinade, turn to coat, and marinate for 15 minutes.

2) Preheat the broiler or grill. Remove the fish from the marinade, and follow the instructions for Grilling or Broiling Fish (opposite).

Per Serving: Calories 81; Protein 16g; Fat 1g (Saturated 0g); Carbohydrates 0g; Fiber 0g; Sodium 76mg

Citrus-Marinated Fish

Makes: 6 servings

Freshly squeezed juice is essential.

1/4 cup fresh lime juice (about 2 limes)
1/3 cup fresh pink grapefruit juice (1/2 grapefruit)
1/2 cup fresh orange juice (2 juice oranges)
1 1/2 teaspoons olive oil
1/4 teaspoon soy sauce
1 1/2 teaspoons finely grated fresh ginger
2 cloves garlic, crushed
1 shallot, peeled and quartered
1/8 teaspoon Tabasco sauce
2 pounds thick fish fillets

1) Combine all of the ingredients except the fish.

2) Pour the sauce around the fish and marinate, covered and refrigerated, for 1 hour.

3) Preheat the broiler. Place the fish in a baking dish, pour marinade around the fish to reach 1/4 inch up its sides, and place under the broiler. Cook until done. A 1-inch thick steak will take about 10 minutes.

Per Serving: Calories 147; Protein 29g; Fat 2g (Saturated 0g); Carbohydrates 3g; Fiber 0g; Sodium 111mg

Garlic-Broiled Fish

Makes: 4 servings

Have a loaf of French bread at the table, because the diners are sure to want to use it to sop up the juices.

3 tablespoons lemon juice
3 tablespoons olive oil
2 cloves garlic, crushed
1 shallot, peeled and crushed
1/4 teaspoon Tabasco sauce
2 teaspoons chopped fresh parsley
1 1/3 pounds thick fish fillets

1) Combine the lemon, olive oil and seasonings in a bowl. Marinate the fish in this mixture for at least 30 minutes, or as long as 6 hours.

2) Place the fish, skin side down, in a baking pan. Pour the marinade around the fillet. If necessary, pour in water until the liquid comes two-thirds of the way up the fish.

3) Broil the fish until done.

Per Serving: Calories 173; Protein 17g; Fat 11g (Saturated 1g); Carbohydrates 2g; Fiber 0g; Sodium 59mg

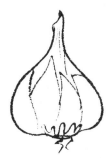

Lemon-Ginger Fish

Makes: 6 servings

When fresh ginger is used in a marinade, it must rest for at least an hour in order for the ginger's flavor to transfer to the liquid. It is best if this marinade is refrigerated for a day before use. Bring to room temperature before adding the fish.

1 teaspoon light brown sugar
1 tablespoon finely grated fresh ginger
2 cloves garlic, minced
$1/3$ cup lemon juice
$1/3$ cup dry white wine
1 teaspoon balsamic vinegar
$1/2$ teaspoon kosher salt
2 tablespoons olive oil
2 pounds salmon fillets

1) Combine all of the ingredients except for the fish and let this marinade rest for 1 hour or up to 1 day. Marinate the fish in this mixture for 30 minutes.

2) Follow the instructions for Grilling or Broiling Fish (page 235).

Per Serving: Calories 189; Protein 26g; Fat 10g (Saturated 1g); Carbohydrates 1g; Fiber 0g; Sodium 99mg

Fish Steak in Raspberry Marinade

Makes: 6 servings

I've made this many times as a last-minute dinner for guests. The color is a glorious deep mahogany red, the flavor is the perfect blend of tangy and sweet and it looks extravagant because of the fresh berries.

$1/4$ cup orange juice
3 tablespoons raspberry vinegar
2 tablespoons light brown sugar
1 tablespoon hoisin sauce
$1 1/2$ teaspoons vegetable oil
$1/2$ teaspoon kosher salt
$1/4$ teaspoon freshly ground pepper
$1/8$ teaspoon Tabasco sauce
2 pounds fish steaks
$1/4$ cup fresh raspberries

1) Whisk together all the ingredients but the fish and raspberries. Marinate the fish in this mixture for 30 minutes. Turn several times.

2) Meanwhile prepare the grill or broiler.

3) Remove the fish from the marinade and grill or broil according to the recipe for Grilling or Broiling Fish (page 235). Remove and keep warm.

4) Boil $1/2$ cup of the marinade for about 2 minutes, until slightly thickened. Stir in the raspberries and pour over the fish.

Per Serving: Calories 117; Protein 17g; Fat 2g (Saturated 0g); Carbohydrates 8g; Fiber 0g; Sodium 260mg

Maple Teriyaki Fish

Makes: 4 servings

Maple syrup and soy sauce combine to make a sophisticated sauce. Even my toddler loves it (though on rice, not fish).

1 teaspoon Asian sesame oil
2 tablespoons soy sauce
2 tablespoons maple syrup
1 teaspoon finely grated fresh ginger
1 clove garlic, minced
1 1/3 pounds fish fillets, salmon or tuna are
    good choices

1) Combine all of the marinade ingredients. Put the fish in a shallow dish, pour the sauce over, turn to coat, cover, and refrigerate 30 minutes to 2 hours.

2) Follow the instructions for Grilling or Broiling Fish (page 235).

3) Put the remaining marinade in a small pot and boil for 1 minute, until slightly thickened. It will yield about 1/4 cup. Pour over the fish or serve as a dipping sauce.

Per Serving: Calories 226; Protein 26g; Fat 9g (Saturated 1g); Carbohydrates 8g; Fiber 0g; Sodium 572mg

Salmon Teriyaki

Makes: 4 servings

When salmon is grilled with a teryaki sauce, the edges brown and crisp, adding to the overall appeal.

1 1/3 pounds salmon steaks or fillets
1 recipe Teriyaki Sauce (page 588)

1) Marinate the salmon in the sauce for 1/2 hour. Turn once to coat evenly.

2) Follow the instructions for Grilling or Broiling Fish (page 235).

Per Serving: Calories 244; Protein 30g; Fat 10g (Saturated 2g); Carbohydrates 4g; Fiber 0g; Sodium 586mg

Fish Steak with Tomato Caper Sauce

Makes: 4 servings

Capers appear frequently in this chapter because there are few seasonings that pair as well with fish. They come from a shrub that grows in the Mediterranean, and, not surprisingly combine well with other seasonings from that region, such as thyme and lemon. Here is a recipe that pulls them all together.

1 1/3 pounds fish steaks
1 tablespoon lemon juice
1/4 teaspoon kosher salt
1/4 teaspoon freshly ground pepper
2 teaspoons olive oil
1 cup sliced onions
1 clove garlic, minced
One 16-ounce can diced tomatoes
1/2 teaspoon dried thyme
1/4 cup white wine
1 tablespoon drained capers
2 tablespoons chopped fresh parsley

1) Preheat the broiler or grill. Rub the fish with 1 teaspoon of the lemon juice and the salt and pepper. Set aside until the sauce is almost ready.

2) Heat the oil in a nonstick pan. Add the onions and garlic. Sauté until softened. Stir in the tomatoes, thyme, wine, capers, and remaining 2 teaspoons of lemon juice. Simmer, uncovered, for 15 minutes. The sauce can be made a day ahead of time and reheated as the fish is cooking.

3) Halfway through simmering the sauce, start cooking the fish, following the instructions for Grilling or Broiling Fish (page 235).

4) Put the fish on a serving platter, cover with the sauce, garnish with the parsley, and serve immediately.

Per Serving: Calories 143; Protein 18g; Fat 3g (Saturated 0g); Carbohydrates 8g; Fiber 2g; Sodium 451mg

Grilled Fish with Piri Piri Sauce

Makes: 6 servings

The more hot peppers you use, the hotter the sauce. Peppers vary in size; about 2 tablespoons of the smallest peppers provide a moderate kick.

1/4 cup vegetable oil
2 to 3 dried whole red chili peppers, or to taste
4 cloves garlic, crushed
2 tablespoons lemon juice
1/2 teaspoon ground ginger
1/4 teaspoon ground cardamom
1/2 teaspoon kosher salt
2 pounds fish steaks or thick fillets

1) Heat the oil gently in a small saucepan. Drop in 1 pepper. The oil should bubble a bit around the edges, but not fry and pop. If the temperature is right, add the rest of the peppers and the garlic. Cook for 10 minutes, until the oil turns golden orange. Strain the liquid and discard the peppers and garlic. Let cool to warm before adding the lemon juice, ginger, cardamom, and salt.

2) Marinate the fish in the sauce for 30 minutes, then cook the fish according to Grilling or Broiling Fish (page 235).

Per Serving: Calories 157; Protein 29g; Fat 4g (Saturated 0g); Carbohydrates 0g; Fiber 0g; Sodium 151mg

Grilled Fish with Currant-Caper Relish

Makes: 4 servings

One of the easiest ways to prepare fish is to grill it plain, then adorn it with a relish or sauce. This Currant-Caper Relish can be made up to 8 hours in advance and kept refrigerated until needed, but for the fullest flavor, bring it to room temperature before use.

3 plum tomatoes, or 1 large tomato
$1/2$ cup pitted olives (any variety), chopped
2 scallions, minced
2 teaspoons extra-virgin olive oil
$1/3$ cup currants
1 tablespoon drained capers
1 tablespoon lemon juice
1 teaspoon minced lemon or orange zest
$1/8$ teaspoon Tabasco sauce
$1/4$ teaspoon freshly ground pepper
$1/4$ teaspoon kosher salt
1 tablespoon chopped fresh parsley
$1^1/3$ pounds fish steaks or thick fillets

1) Coarsely chop the tomatoes by hand (a food processor will make it too watery). However, the olives and scallions can be minced in the processor. Combine all of the ingredients except the fish. Let rest at least a half hour before serving, or up to 8 hours.

2) Follow the instructions for Grilling or Broiling Fish (page 235).

3) Put the fish on a serving platter and top with the relish.

Per Serving: Calories 136; Protein 17g; Fat 5g (Saturated 1g); Carbohydrates 5g; Fiber 2g; Sodium 385mg

Swordfish and Pineapple Skewers

Makes: 2 servings

You'll need 8 small or 4 large skewers. This is a good way to stretch an expensive piece of fish. Serve on a bed of rice.

$1/4$ cup soy sauce
1 tablespoon rice or white wine vinegar
1 teaspoon vegetable oil
$1/4$ teaspoon Tabasco sauce
1 teaspoon grated fresh ginger
3 cloves garlic, smashed
$1/2$ pound swordfish steak, cut into 8 cubes
16 cherry tomatoes
1 large green bell pepper, cut into 16 triangles
1 Spanish onion, cut in half and then quartered
One 8-ounce can unsweetened pineapple chunks

1) If using wooden skewers, soak them in water to prevent them from burning. Preheat the broiler or prepare the grill.

2) Combine the soy sauce, vinegar, oil, Tabasco, ginger, and garlic in a bowl. Marinate the swordfish in this for 10 minutes.

3) Thread each skewer in this order: pepper, onion, tomato, onion, pineapple, fish, pineapple, onion, tomato, onion, pepper.

4) Brush the vegetables and fish with the marinade. Place on a baking sheet coated with nonstick spray or directly on the grill. If broiling, place 3 inches from the heat source. Cook for 3 minutes on one side, brush with the marinade again, and cook for another 5 minutes, or until the swordfish is cooked through.

Per Serving: Calories 210; Protein 18g; Fat 4g (Saturated 1g); Carbohydrates 27g; Fiber 4g; Sodium 600mg

Grilled Scallop Skewers

Makes: 4 servings

Sea scallops are the largest scallops, just the right size for threading on a skewer. They can be costly, but one pound serves four people, and few who taste this would rue the expense.

1 teaspoon light brown sugar
2 tablespoons orange juice
3 tablespoons orange marmalade
2 teaspoons store-bought, bottled
    white horseradish
1/2 teaspoon kosher salt
1/8 teaspoon Tabasco sauce
1 pound sea scallops
1 pint cherry tomatoes
1 green bell pepper, cut into 2-inch pieces

1) You will need 8 skewers. If using wooden skewers, soak them in water to prevent them from burning. Preheat the broiler or prepare the grill. It should be moderately hot.

2) Combine the sugar, orange juice, marmalade, horseradish, salt, and Tabasco. Stir in the scallops and marinate for 30 minutes.

3) Remove the scallops from the marinade. Thread on skewers with pieces of bell pepper and cherry tomatoes. Grill on a baking sheet lined with foil and coated with nonstick spray, or grill on an oiled rack. Place the skewers on the cooking surface and brush them with the marinade. Cook 4 minutes, turn, and brush once more. Cook until done, about 4 minutes longer.

Per Serving: Calories 127; Protein 13g; Fat 3g (Saturated 0g); Carbohydrates 14g; Fiber 2g; Sodium 427mg

Poached Fish

This simplest approach to cooking fish has many benefits: there is little clean-up, there are no lingering fish odors in the kitchen, and it is a very lowfat method. Recipes can be expanded to feed many, or the same technique can be used for one. Cooking time will vary with the thickness of the fish—a thin fillet may take only 3 minutes, a thicker piece almost 10.

Fish Poached in Wine and Lemon Juice

Makes: 4 servings

Use wine that is good enough to drink. The flavor of the wine will come through and you'll notice the difference between fish poached in a fruity wine and that cooked in dry wine. Results from both, though, will be delicious.

2 parts white wine
1 part lemon juice
1 1/3 pounds fish fillet(s)
1/4 teaspoon kosher salt
1/4 teaspoon freshly ground pepper

1) The amount of poaching liquid depends on the thickness of the fish and the size of the pan. You need enough to cover three-quarters of the fish. Bring the wine and lemon juice to a simmer in a pan with a lid.

2) Rub the fish with the salt and pepper and place the fish fillets in the pan.

3) Cover and gently simmer until the fish is cooked through.

Per Serving: Calories 76; Protein 16g; Fat 1g (Saturated 0g); Carbohydrates 0g; Fiber 0g; Sodium 176mg

Poached Fish with Herbs

Makes: 2 servings

Tarragon is an herb that goes especially nicely with fish. However, its slight anise flavor can overwhelm a mild fish, so please use only the amount suggested.

2/3 pound white-fleshed fish fillets
1/8 teaspoon kosher salt
1/8 teaspoon freshly ground pepper
1/4 cup white wine
2 tablespoons lemon juice
1 tablespoon minced fresh chives
2-inch sprig fresh tarragon

1) Rub the fish with the salt and pepper.

2) Combine the wine and lemon juice. Pour enough in a pan so that it will reach halfway up the fish. The amount of liquid required is determined by the size of the pan and the thickness of the fish. If your pan is large, you might need more liquid.

3) Bring the wine and lemon juice to a simmer.

4) Add the fish, top with the chives, and put the tarragon to one side in the poaching liquid.

5) Cover the pan and simmer very gently (a few slowly rising bubbles) until the fish is done.

Per Serving: Calories 76; Protein 16g; Fat 1g (Saturated 0g); Carbohydrates 0g; Fiber 0g; Sodium 176mg

Dill-Poached Fish

Makes: 4 servings

Dill is often less expensive than other fresh herbs in the market and comes in large bunches. Wash the unused dill and dry very well in a salad spinner. It can then be frozen as is, or minced and frozen. It will remain bright green in the freezer for several months.

1 1/3 pounds fish fillets
1/4 teaspoon kosher salt
1/8 teaspoon freshly ground pepper
1/2 cup white wine
1/4 cup lemon juice
4-inch sprig fresh dill
1 shallot, peeled and crushed
1/2 teaspoon minced fresh dill, for garnish

1) Rub the fish with the salt and pepper.

2) Combine the wine and lemon juice. Pour enough in a pan so that it will cover two-thirds of the fish. If you have some of the liquid left over, save it for another dinner.

3) Put the dill sprig and the shallot in the poaching liquid. Bring the liquid to a simmer and let it cook, covered, for 5 minutes before adding the fish. This will infuse the cooking liquid with the herb and shallot flavors.

4) Before adding the fish, make sure the liquid is simmering gently. Place the fish on top of the dill. Cover the pan and simmer gently until the fish is done.

5) Remove to serving plates and garnish with minced fresh dill.

Per Serving: Calories 76; Protein 16g; Fat 1g (Saturated 0g); Carbohydrates 0g; Fiber 0g; Sodium 176mg

Chilled Poached Salmon

Makes: 3 to 9 servings

Serve with Cucumber Sauce or Sour Cream Lime Sauce (page 599) Or have both—I like to offer a selection.

1 cup dry white wine
4 cups water
1 tablespoon white wine vinegar
1 teaspoon kosher salt
1 to 3 pounds salmon fillets

1) Combine the wine, water, vinegar, and salt.

2) Use a heavy-bottomed pot that is wide and deep enough to accommodate the entire piece of fish without crowding, or cut the fillet in half and use 2 pans. Place the fish in the pan and pour in enough liquid just to cover the fish. Remove the fish and bring the liquid to a simmer. Reduce the heat so that the water moves but doesn't break into bubbles. Slip the fish back in. Cover and cook about 8 minutes, or until the center of the fish feels firm to the touch. Do not cook so long that it flakes apart.

3) Take the pan off the heat and uncover. Let the fish come to room temperature in the poaching liquid. If you're cooking an entire day ahead, chill it in the poaching liquid. Otherwise, put the fish on a serving platter and refrigerate until cold to the touch.

Per ¹/3 Pound: Calories 184; Protein 26g; Fat 8g (Saturated 1g); Carbohydrates 0g; Fiber 0g; Sodium 177mg

Chilled Whole Poached Salmon

This is a simple dish, but beautiful for a party.

1 whole salmon, cleaned and scaled
2 parts white wine
1 part lemon juice
¹/4 teaspoon kosher salt
¹/4 teaspoon freshly ground pepper

Follow instructions for Poached Fish (page 241). Cook about 10 minutes for each inch of thickness, measured at the thickest part. Let the salmon cool in the pan, then chill in the refrigerator. Remove the skin before placing on a serving platter.

Per ¹/3 Pound: Calories 212; Protein 30g; Fat 10g (Saturated 1g); Carbohydrates 0g; Fiber 0g; Sodium 177mg

Chinese Steamed Fish

Makes: 4 servings

I use a 13-inch wok and a steamer basket that opens flat to accommodate a whole fish.

2 tablespoons soy sauce
1 tablespoon dry sherry
1/2 teaspoon sugar
1 teaspoon Asian sesame oil
1 tablespoons finely grated fresh ginger
2 scallions, sliced
1 1/3 pounds fish fillets, or one 2-pound whole fish, cleaned and scaled
Minced cilantro, for garnish (optional)

1) Stir together all ingredients except the fish and cilantro.

2) Place the fish on a plate or a steamer rack. Bring water to a boil in a pot that will accommodate the steamer.

3) Place the fish in the steamer. Pour the sauce over the fish; it is okay if some of it drips into the boiling water. Cover and cook over medium heat for 7 to 10 minutes, or until fish is firm to the touch. Remove carefully from the steamer and place on a serving platter. If desired, garnish with cilantro.

Per Serving: Calories 98; Protein 17g; Fat 2g (Saturated 0g); Carbohydrates 2g; Fiber 0g; Sodium 572mg

Stovetop Cooking

Pan-Cooked Fish Fillets

Makes: 6 servings

Dredged in seasoned flour and lightly sautéed in a nonstick pan with just a trace of oil, thin, delicate white-fleshed fish fillets cook in only a few minutes on the stovetop. Here are three ideas on how to season the flour. This recipe is easily adaptable to serve one or many. If cooking for one, make the entire flour mixture, and store the excess for up to a month.

Blend 1
1/4 cup unbleached, all-purpose white flour
1/8 teaspoon kosher salt
1/8 teaspoon freshly ground pepper
1/4 teaspoon paprika

Blend 2
1/4 cup unbleached, all-purpose white flour
1/8 teaspoon kosher salt
1/8 teaspoon freshly ground pepper
1/2 teaspoon mild curry powder

Blend 3
1/4 cup unbleached, all-purpose white flour
1/8 teaspoon kosher salt
1/8 teaspoon freshly ground pepper
1/4 teaspoon paprika
1/4 teaspoon ground allspice
1/4 teaspoon ground cumin

For Each Blend
2 pounds thin, boneless fish fillets, such as turbot or flounder
1/2 to 2 teaspoons oil

1) Mix together the flour and spices until there are no spice streaks.

2) Wash the fish and pat it dry with a paper towel.

3) Heat a nonstick skillet over medium heat. Pour in the oil, spread it around, and pour off any excess.

4) Dredge the fish in the seasoned flour by placing one side and then the other in the flour blend. Shake gently to remove any excess.

5) Place the fish in the skillet. Turn only once. Very thin fillets will require about 2 minutes per side, a thicker fish perhaps 3 minutes.

Per Serving: Calories 158; Protein 29g; Fat 2g (Saturated 0g); Carbohydrates 4g; Fiber 0g; Sodium 163mg

Fish in Curried Coconut Sauce

Makes: 4 servings

This sauce can be made ahead and frozen. When ready to use, warm on the stove and then add the fish.

1 1/2 teaspoons vegetable oil
1 cup chopped onions
2 cloves garlic, minced
2 teaspoons curry powder
1 teaspoon finely grated fresh ginger
One 14 1/2-ounce can whole tomatoes, with juice
1 tablespoon lemon juice
1 teaspoon kosher salt
1/4 teaspoon freshly ground pepper
2 tablespoons shredded sweetened coconut
1 to 1 1/3 pounds thick fish fillets, cut into
     1-inch pieces

1) Heat the oil in a large nonstick skillet. Sauté the onions and garlic over medium heat until the onions soften and turn golden, about 5 minutes. Keep covered between stirrings. Stir in the curry powder and cook 1 minute. Add the ginger and juice from the tomatoes. Break up the tomatoes in your hands as you add them to the pot. Stir in the lemon juice, salt, pepper, and coconut. Bring to a simmer, cover, and cook for 5 minutes.

2) Stir in the fish and cook at a gentle simmer for 5 to 7 minutes, until the fish is cooked through. Serve with rice.

Per Serving: Calories 165; Protein 22g; Fat 4g (Saturated 1g); Carbohydrates 11g; Fiber 2g; Sodium 713mg

Moroccan Fish Stew

Makes: 4 servings

Monkfish or cod is perfect for this.

1¹/2 teaspoons olive oil
2 cloves garlic, minced
1 medium onion, halved and thinly sliced
2 carrots, cut into rounds
1 small zucchini, cut into rounds
¹/2 pound peeled butternut squash, cut into
   ¹/2- to 1-inch pieces
1 cup cooked chickpeas, drained and rinsed
One 14¹/2-ounce can whole tomatoes, drained
   and chopped
2 cups water
1 teaspoon paprika
1 teaspoon ground coriander
1 teaspoon kosher salt
¹/4 teaspoon freshly ground pepper
¹/8 teaspoon crushed red pepper flakes, or to taste
¹/2 pound skinless, boneless fish, cut into
   1-inch pieces
¹/2 cup golden raisins
2 tablespoons chopped fresh cilantro (optional)

1) Heat the oil in a 4-quart, heavy-bottomed saucepan. Sauté the garlic and onion over medium heat for about 5 minutes

2) Add the remaining ingredients except the fish, raisins, and cilantro. Bring to a boil. Reduce to a simmer, cover, and cook until the squash is tender, about 15 minutes.

3) Add the fish, raisins, and cilantro. Simmer 5 to 7 minutes, until the fish is cooked through.

Per Serving: Calories 268; Protein 17g; Fat 4g (Saturated 1g); Carbohydrates 45g; Fiber 7g; Sodium 698mg

Cioppino

Makes: 7 servings

The base without the fish can be made ahead of time and frozen.

2 ounces dried Italian mushrooms, such as porcini
1 cup warm water
2 tablespoons olive oil
2 cups chopped onions
4 cloves garlic, minced
1 green bell pepper, chopped
One 28-ounce can whole tomatoes, drained
¹/4 cup tomato paste
One 8-ounce bottle clam juice
1 cup white wine
2 tablespoons minced fresh parsley
2 tablespoons chopped fresh basil, or
   2 teaspoons dried
¹/4 teaspoon kosher salt
¹/4 teaspoon freshly ground pepper, or more
   to taste
¹/8 teaspoon crushed red pepper flakes
2 pounds fish pieces, cut into 1¹/2 inch chunks
1 pound fresh mussels or clams, or a combination

1) Rinse the mushrooms thoroughly, then soak them in the warm water until softened, about 15 minutes. Remove from the water and cut large ones in half. Strain the soaking water through cheesecloth to remove grit, and reserve the liquid.

2) Heat the olive oil in a large pot. Add the onions, garlic, and bell pepper. Sauté until the onions turn golden. Add the tomatoes, tomato paste, clam juice, wine, parsley, and basil. Pour in ¹/2 cup of the mushroom liquid and stir in the mushrooms. Simmer, covered, for 30 minutes.

3) Add the salt, pepper, pepper flakes, and fish pieces. Cover and simmer until the fish flakes done, about 5 minutes.

4) Scrub the mussels clean while the fish is cooking. Add them to the pot just prior to serving. They take only a few minutes to cook and if left in the pot too long will become rubbery. Discard any that don't open and serve the cioppino immediately.

Per Serving: Calories 266; Protein 31g; Fat 6g (Saturated 1g); Carbohydrates 15g; Fiber 3g; Sodium 616mg

Fish in a Pot

Makes: 4 servings

This fish stew can be served in a bowl, or over a bed of rice or pasta.

1 tablespoon olive oil
2 cups chopped onions
3 cloves garlic, minced
2 carrots, peeled and cut into rounds (cut the largest rounds in half)
2 ribs celery, with leaves, chopped
1 teaspoon kosher salt
$1/4$ teaspoon freshly ground pepper
1 bay leaf
3 tablespoons lemon juice
1 cup water
$1/2$ cup white wine
2 tablespoons chopped fresh parsley
1 teaspoon minced fresh thyme, or $1/2$ teaspoon dried
$1^1/2$ teaspoons chopped fresh rosemary, or $1/2$ teaspoon dried
$3/4$ teaspoon green peppercorns, crushed
$1/2$ teaspoon drained capers
$1/16$ teaspoon Tabasco sauce
$1/4$ teaspoon paprika
One $14^1/2$-ounce can whole tomatoes, drained
8 small new potatoes (1 pound), cut into large cubes
1 pound fish fillets, cut into 2-inch pieces

1) Heat the oil in a sauté pan. Sauté the onions, garlic, carrots, and celery in the oil. Cook, covered, until the vegetables sweat out liquid and the onions are golden.

2) Add the remaining ingredients except the fish. Cover and simmer for about 20 minutes, until the potatoes are cooked through.

3) Reduce the temperature so that the liquid is simmering gently. Stir in the fish. Cook for 7 to 10 minutes, until the fish is cooked through but not falling apart.

Per Serving: Calories 306; Protein 25g; Fat 5g (Saturated 1g); Carbohydrates 38g; Fiber 5g; Sodium 715mg

Seafood Gumbo

Makes: 5 servings

Filé powder, which is ground sassafrass, can be difficult to find in some regions. If you don't have any, it can be left out. The gumbo will not be as thick, but it will still taste great.

1 cup chopped onions
2 cloves garlic, minced
2 tablespoons vegetable oil
3 tablespoons unbleached all-purpose white flour
2 cups reduced-sodium, defatted chicken broth
2 ribs celery, chopped
1 green bell pepper, chopped
1 medium zucchini, thickly sliced
1 cup sliced okra, fresh or frozen
One 14^1/2-ounce can diced tomatoes
One 8-ounce can tomato sauce
1 teaspoon paprika
1 teaspoon kosher salt
^{1}/2 teaspoon freshly ground pepper
^{1}/2 teaspoon thyme
2 tablespoons chopped fresh parsley
2 bay leaves
^{1}/4 teaspoon Tabasco sauce, or more to taste
^{1}/2 pound fish fillets, cut into 1-inch pieces
^{1}/2 pound shrimp, peeled and deveined
2 tablespoons filé powder (optional)

1) In a heavy-bottomed soup pot, sauté the onions and garlic in the oil until the onions are lightly golden. Keep covered between stirring. Stirring constantly, add the flour a tablespoon at a time. Cook until it turns light brown. This step will take some time and is important because it adds a nutty flavor to the gumbo. Slowly stir in the broth, scraping the bottom of the pan with a wooden spatula or spoon.

2) Add the remaining ingredients except for the fish, shrimp, and filé powder. Bring to a boil, then immediately reduce to a simmer. Cover and simmer for 25 minutes.

3) Stir in the fish pieces, shrimp, and filé powder. Simmer, uncovered, until the fish is cooked through and the shrimp turn pink, about 5 minutes. Serve immediately over hot cooked rice.

Per Serving: Calories 224; Protein 22g; Fat 7g (Saturated 1g); Carbohydrates 19g; Fiber 3g; Sodium 1086mg

Fish Steak and Asparagus Stir-Fry

Makes: 4 servings

When thickening a stir-fry with cornstarch, the outcome will be smoother and clearer if the cornstarch is first well dissolved in the broth. Also, the thickening sauce should be stirred continually but not vigorously, or the finished dish will be rough with air bubbles.

1^1/3 pounds fish steaks
1/2 cup Teriyaki Sauce (page 588)
1 tablespoon vegetable oil
1 pound asparagus, ends trimmed, cut diagonally into 2-inch pieces
8 baby corn, halved (about half a 16-ounce can)
1 cup sliced mushrooms or canned straw mushrooms
1 scallion, cut into 2-inch pieces
2 teaspoons cornstarch
1/4 cup reduced-sodium, defatted chicken broth

1) Cut away the fish skin if necessary. Cut the steaks into 1-inch pieces. Stir into the Teriyaki Sauce. Let marinate for 1 hour.

2) Heat the oil in a large wok or nonstick skillet. Using a slotted spoon, remove the fish from the marinade and put into the wok. Stir-fry until the fish is cooked halfway through. Stir in the asparagus, corn, mushrooms, and scallions. Pour in the marinade. Cover and cook for 1 minute. Stir the cornstarch into the broth and pour into the wok. Cook until the sauce thickens.

Per Serving: Calories 318; Protein 37g; Fat 9g (Saturated 1g); Carbohydrates 21g; Fiber 6g; Sodium 1345mg

Sweet and Sour Fish and Vegetables

Makes: 4 servings

This recipe is gently seasoned. Spice it up with another teaspoon of ginger and a pinch of cayenne pepper if desired.

One 8-ounce can unsweetened pineapple chunks, with juice
1 teaspoon sugar
2 tablespoons honey
1^1/2 teaspoons lemon juice
1 tablespoon rice vinegar or white wine vinegar
1 tablespoon soy sauce
1 teaspoon finely grated fresh ginger
1 green bell pepper, cut into small triangles or squares
1 cup mushrooms, quartered
1 carrot, thinly sliced on the diagonal
2 teaspoons cornstarch dissolved in 1 tablespoon water
1^1/3 pounds fish steaks, cut into 4 or 5 portions
2 scallions

1) Drain the juice from the pineapple into a small bowl. Whisk in the sugar, honey, lemon juice, vinegar, soy sauce, and ginger. Put this sauce in a large skillet and bring to a simmer. Add the pineapple chunks, bell pepper, mushrooms, carrot, and scallions. Cover and cook for 5 minutes.

2) Stir the cornstarch paste into the sauce. Push the vegetables to the sides of the pan and place the fish in the center of the skillet. Cover and cook at a gentle simmer until the fish tests done, about 10 minutes. Serve over rice.

Per Serving: Calories 264; Protein 33g; Fat 4g (Saturated 1g); Carbohydrates 25g; Fiber 2g; Sodium 349mg

Shrimp and Shellfish

Once thought to contain too much cholesterol, shrimp are back on healthful menus. Although they do contain more cholesterol than other fish, their fat content—especially saturated fat—is minimal. For example, Shrimp and Snow Peas contains 172mg of cholesterol, but only 1g of saturated fat. Bivalves like mussels have both minimal fat and minimal cholesterol. So eat and enjoy.

Shrimp and Snow Peas

Makes: 4 servings

It is all too easy to overcook shrimp until shrunken and rubbery. Cook them only until they curl up and change color.

1 teaspoon finely grated fresh ginger
1 1/2 teaspoons soy sauce
1 tablespoon dry sherry
1/2 teaspoon kosher salt
1/2 cup reduced-sodium, defatted chicken broth
1 tablespoon cornstarch
1 tablespoon vegetable oil
1 pound shrimp, peeled and deveined
1 clove garlic, minced
3 tablespoons ketchup
2 cups snow peas, stem ends trimmed
8 baby corn (about half a 16-ounce can)

1) Combine the ginger, soy sauce, sherry, and salt in a bowl. Stir the broth and cornstarch into another small bowl.

2) Heat the oil a large wok. Toss in the shrimp and garlic. Cook over high heat until the shrimp turns pink, about 2 minutes. Add the soy mixture. Stir-fry 1 minute longer. Stir in the ketchup. Cook another minute. Stir the cornstarch and broth and pour into the wok. Add the snow peas and baby corn to the pan. Cover 1 minute to steam the snow peas. Uncover and stir until the sauce thickens. Serve immediately.

Per Serving: Calories 223; Protein 27g; Fat 6g (Saturated 1g); Carbohydrates 15g; Fiber 4g; Sodium 850mg

Shrimp and Broccoli

Makes: 4 servings

Not all stir-fries have a base of soy sauce. This one has no soy sauce at all.

1 head broccoli (about 1 1/4 pounds)
1 teaspoon finely grated fresh ginger
1 teaspoon dry sherry
1 teaspoon cornstarch
1 teaspoon kosher salt
1 pound shrimp, peeled and deveined
1 tablespoon vegetable oil
2 cloves garlic, sliced
1/8 teaspoon crushed red pepper flakes (optional)
1/4 cup defatted, reduced-sodium chicken broth
1 scallion, cut into 2-inch pieces

1) Cut the broccoli into florets. Trim the tough ends from the stalks, then peel the remaining stalk and slice it on the diagonal. Steam the broccoli florets and sliced stalks until barely cooked through, about 3 to 4 minutes. Immerse in cold water, then drain again. Set aside. (This step can be done up to 1 day ahead.)

2) Combine the ginger, sherry, cornstarch, and salt in a bowl and toss in the shrimp.

3) Heat the oil in a large wok. Over gentle heat, cook the garlic until golden but not brown. Remove with a slotted spoon to a paper towel.

4) Increase the heat to high. Stir in the shrimp mixture. Cook until the shrimp turns pink, about 2 minutes. Add the red pepper flakes, if desired. Pour in the broth and add the broccoli and scallions. Return the garlic to the wok. Cook until the shrimp is cooked through, about 2 minutes longer.

Per Serving: Calories 186; Protein 26g; Fat 6g (Saturated 1g); Carbohydrates 8g; Fiber 3g; Sodium 707mg

Deep South Boiled Shrimp Dinner

Makes: 6 servings

If crabs are available, add a few to the pot. This dinner has more vegetables than a traditional boil.

1¹/2 gallons water
One 3-ounce package crab and shrimp boil, or
    3 tablespoons Old Bay Seasoning
3 lemons, cut into quarters
4 bay leaves
¹/2 teaspoon cayenne pepper
2 tablespoons kosher salt
2 tablespoons peppercorns
6 cloves garlic
2 pounds new potatoes, if large, quartered
8 pearl onions, peeled
3 carrots, peeled, cut into 2-inch pieces
3 ribs celery, cut into 2-inch pieces
1 turnip or small rutabaga, peeled and
    cut into chunks
6 ears corn, shucked and silked, broken
    into halves
2 pounds raw, unpeeled shrimp (head on or off),
    thawed if frozen

1) Pour the water into a large stockpot. Add the crab boil, lemons, bay leaves, cayenne, salt, peppercorns, and garlic. Bring to a boil, then reduce to a simmer. Cover and cook 20 minutes to develop flavor. Stir in the potatoes, onions, carrots, celery, and turnip. Simmer 15 minutes, or until vegetables are tender.

2) Bring the pot to a full boil, add the corn and shrimp, and cook for 3 minutes, until the shrimp are pink through. Pour off the excess water, then drain the contents of the pot into a colander. Discard the crab and shrimp boil bag, if using. Serve immediately. Have bowls on the table for discarded corn cobs and shrimp shells.

Per Serving: Calories 326; Protein 26g; Fat 2g (Saturated 0g); Carbohydrates 54g; Fiber 7g; Sodium 2204mg

Shrimp in Creole Sauce

Makes: 4 servings

The Creole Sauce will take on the flavor of the shrimp.

1 recipe Creole Sauce (page 231)
1 pound raw shrimp, peeled and deveined

Bring the sauce to a full simmer in a saucepan. Add the shrimp. Cook until the shrimp turn pink, about 3 minutes. This can also be made in the microwave. As on the stovetop, heat the sauce first, then add the shrimp and cook about 3 minutes. Serve on a bed of boiled white rice.

Per Serving: Calories 233; Protein 26g; Fat 6g (Saturated 1g); Carbohydrates 19g; Fiber 3g; Sodium 1057mg

Spaghetti with Fresh Clam Sauce

Makes: 4 servings

When serving this with the clams still in their shells, arrange them around the perimeter of the platter. Not only is it a nice presentation, but it also makes it easier to serve the dish because the spaghetti can be plated first, and then the clams placed on top of each portion.

3/4 pound spaghetti
1 tablespoon olive oil
4 cloves garlic, minced
3/4 cup white wine
1/4 cup lemon juice
3 to 4 dozen littleneck clams, scrubbed
1/2 teaspoon kosher salt
1/4 to 1/2 teaspoon freshly ground pepper
1/4 cup chopped fresh parsley
1 tablespoon chopped fresh basil

1) Bring a large pot of water to a boil. You want the pasta ready just before or after the clams are cooked. Start cooking the pasta just before you begin to cook the clams in Step 2 and the timing should work. Once cooked, place the spaghetti in a pasta-serving bowl.

2) Heat the oil in a large, heavy-bottomed pot. Sauté the garlic over medium heat for 2 to 3 minutes, until the color changes slightly. Pour in the wine and lemon juice. Bring to a boil. Add the clams. Reduce to a simmer. Cover and cook until the clams open, about 7 to 10 minutes. Discard clams that remain closed. You can serve this dish with the clams shucked, or still in their shells. In either event, remove the clams from the pot and pour the sauce through a sieve lined with cheesecloth, leaving the last bit of liquid (and any sand) in the pot.

3) Toss the clams, salt, pepper, parsley, and basil with the pasta, or if using clams in their shells, arrange around the perimeter of the platter.

Per Serving: Calories 445; Protein 22g; Fat 6g (Saturated 1g); Carbohydrates 69g; Fiber 2g; Sodium 296mg

Spaghetti with Clam Sauce

Makes: 4 servings

This is one of those recipes that I call on when the refrigerator looks bare. Even if I don't have fresh parsley, I have some frozen and the rest of the ingredients are pantry staples. It is also great for time-crunched dinners, and if I haven't had time to shop, I probably haven't much time to cook dinner either. Spaghetti with Clam Sauce comes to the rescue because from start to finish it takes only as much time as required to boil a pot of pasta.

2/3 pound spaghetti or linguine
1 1/2 tablespoons olive oil
2 cloves garlic, minced
1/8 teaspoon crushed red pepper flakes
1/8 teaspoon freshly ground pepper
1/4 cup white wine
2 teaspoons lemon juice
One 10-ounce can baby clams
1/3 cup of water from cooking the pasta
3 tablespoons chopped fresh parsley

1) Bring a large pot of water to a boil. Break the pasta in half and add it to the pot. Cook according to the package directions.

2) Meanwhile, heat the oil in a saucepan. Sauté the garlic over medium heat for 2 to 3 minutes, until the color changes slightly. Add the red pepper flakes and cook for 1 minute more. Stir in the ground pepper, wine, lemon juice, and clams. When the pasta is almost fully cooked, use a glass heatproof measuring cup to scoop the pasta cooking water out of the pot and pour it into the saucepan. This liquid (with its starch) will add body to the sauce. Simmer the sauce for about 5 minutes, or until the pasta is ready. Do not cook the sauce for longer than 10 minutes or the clams will turn rubbery.

3) Drain the pasta and toss with the clam sauce. Toss in the parsley and serve immediately.

Per Serving: Calories 395; Protein 20g; Fat 7g (Saturated 1g); Carbohydrates 59g; Fiber 2g; Sodium 122mg

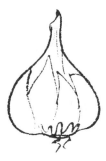

Linguine with Clam and Tomato Sauce

Makes: 6 servings

This is another pasta dish that relies on pantry staples. To round out the meal, buy a bag of salad greens and a loaf of bread, open a bottle of wine, light a candle, and relax.

3/4 pound spaghetti or linguine
1 teaspoon olive oil
1 clove garlic, minced
One 14 1/2-ounce can whole tomatoes, with juice
1/2 cup tomato juice
2 tablespoons tomato paste
1/4 cup white wine
1 tablespoon lemon juice
1 teaspoon kosher salt
1/4 teaspoon freshly ground pepper
3 tablespoons chopped fresh parsley
1 teaspoon dried oregano
1 teaspoon dried basil
One 10-ounce can baby clams

1) For this recipe, it is best if the pasta and the sauce are ready at the same time. To get the timing right, set a large pot of water to boil and begin cooking the pasta after you start simmering the sauce in Step 3.

2) In a medium saucepan, heat the oil and then cook the garlic over moderate heat until it turns golden, about 2 minutes. Drain the juice from the canned tomatoes into the pot. Squeeze the seeds out of the tomatoes (easily done over a sink in a colander—the idea is to get rid of most of the unsightly seeds and watery juice). Then break up the tomatoes with your hands as you add them to the pot.

3) Stir in the tomato juice, tomato paste, wine, lemon juice, salt, and pepper. Simmer for 7 minutes.

4) Stir in the herbs and clams and simmer for another 5 minutes, until the pasta is ready.

5) Once the pasta is ready, drain it in a colander, put it in a large bowl, pour the clam sauce over the pasta, toss, and serve immediately.

Per Serving: Calories 286; Protein 15g; Fat 2g (Saturated 0g); Carbohydrates 49g; Fiber 2g; Sodium 596mg

Four Peppers and Salmon over Pasta

Makes: 4 servings

This is equally good hot or served cold as a pasta salad.

8 ounces pasta (radiatore or other short, nubby shape)
2 tablespoons olive oil, divided
1 clove garlic, chopped
1 red bell pepper, julienned
1 green bell pepper, julienned
1/2 pound fresh poached salmon, or canned water-packed salmon, bones and skins removed
1 tablespoon green peppercorns, packed in water or vinegar, not dried
1/4 teaspoon kosher salt
1/4 teaspoon freshly ground pepper
2 tablespoons chopped fresh parsley

1) Cook the pasta. Try to time it so that the sauce is ready and hot at the same time that the pasta is drained. If the pasta is done early, drain it and toss with a little olive oil to keep it from sticking together.

2) Heat 1 tablespoon of the oil in a large sauté pan and cook the garlic until it turns golden. Add the bell peppers and sauté until they wilt.

3) Stir in the remaining olive oil and the salmon, peppercorns, salt, and pepper. Toss in the cooked pasta. Continue to heat until the salmon warms through. Toss in the parsley.

Per Serving: Calories 396; Protein 23g; Fat 12g (Saturated 2g); Carbohydrates 47g; Fiber 1g; Sodium 159mg

Scallops Linguine

Makes: 4 servings

White or wheat bread will work equally well.

3/4 pound linguine
1 1/2 tablespoons olive oil, divided
2 slices homemade-quality bread, in small cubes
2 tablespoons chopped fresh parsley
4 cloves garlic, minced
1 shallot, minced
One 28-ounce can whole tomatoes, drained and chopped
1/4 cup white wine
1 1/2 teaspoons kosher salt
1/8 to 1/4 teaspoon crushed red pepper flakes
1 pound scallops (if sea scallops, halve horizontally)

1) Have all of the ingredients prepped before you begin cooking. Bring a large pot of water to a rolling boil and cook the linguine.

2) Meanwhile, in a medium nonstick skillet, heat 1 tablespoon of the oil and toss in the bread cubes. Cook until they are lightly toasted, tossing frequently. Stir in the parsley, remove from the hot pan into a bowl, and set aside

3) In a nonstick saucepan or skillet, heat the remaining 1/2 tablespoon of oil. Over moderate-low heat, sauté the garlic and shallot for about 4 minutes, until the garlic is lightly golden. Stir in the tomatoes, wine, salt, and pepper flakes. Bring to a simmer and cook, uncovered, for about 5 minutes. Turn off the heat, cover, and keep warm until the pasta is almost ready. Then bring back to a simmer and stir in the scallops. Cook about 4 minutes, until the scallops are cooked through (they will turn white throughout). Toss with the cooked, drained pasta. Place in a serving bowl and top with the bread cubes.

Per Serving: Calories 550; Protein 33g; Fat 8g (Saturated 1g); Carbohydrates 82g; Fiber 4g; Sodium 1212mg

Scallops, Broccoli, and Pasta

Makes: 4 servings

Seashell-shaped pasta adds a whimsical touch to this recipe.

1/2 pound pasta (any shape)
1 tablespoon olive oil
2 shallots, minced
4 cloves garlic, minced
3 cups broccoli florets
One 14 1/2-ounce can whole tomatoes, drained, seeded, and chopped
1 teaspoon kosher salt, or more to taste
1/4 teaspoon freshly ground pepper, or more to taste
1/2 cup white wine
1 pound scallops (if sea scallops, cut in quarters)
1 tablespoon lemon juice
1 1/2 teaspoons chopped fresh basil

1) Begin cooking the pasta while sautéing the vegetables.

2) Heat the oil in a large, nonstick skillet. Sauté the shallots and garlic for 3 minutes, until golden. Stir in the broccoli, tomatoes, salt, pepper, and wine. Cover and cook until the broccoli turns bright green and gets tender, about 5 minutes.

3) Drain the cooked pasta and keep warm.

4) Add the scallops and lemon juice to the skillet. Cook over high heat until the scallops turn white throughout, about 3 minutes. Toss in the pasta and basil. Taste and adjust salt and pepper, if desired.

Per Serving: Calories 394; Protein 28g; Fat 5g (Saturated 1g); Carbohydrates 53g; Fiber 3g; Sodium 794mg

Spaghetti with Scallops and Sun-Dried Tomatoes

Makes: 2 servings

Sun-dried tomatoes and clam broth can be salty, so taste before adding the kosher salt.

3 plum tomatoes
1/2 cup sun-dried tomatoes, not packed in oil
1/2 pound spaghetti
1 teaspoon olive oil
2 cloves garlic, minced
1/2 pound scallops (if sea scallops, halve horizontally)
One 8-ounce bottle clam broth
2 tablespoons drained capers
1/8 teaspoon crushed red pepper flakes
2 tablespoons chopped fresh parsley
1/2 teaspoon kosher salt
1/4 teaspoon freshly ground pepper
1 tablespoon lemon zest in long, fine strips or finely minced

1) Bring a large pot of water to a boil, to use for several tasks. First, core the plum tomatoes and immerse them in boiling water for about 1 minute until their skins loosen. Remove from water with a slotted spoon, peel, and chop. Next, scoop out some water with a heatproof cup and soak the dried tomatoes in this until reconstituted, about 10 minutes.

2) Cook the pasta. Once the spaghetti is ready, drain, immerse in cold water, and drain again. Set aside.

3) Drain and slice the softened sun-dried tomatoes. Assemble all the remaining ingredients.

4) Heat the oil in a large nonstick wok or skillet. Briefly cook the garlic. Add the fresh and dried tomatoes and cook until the fresh tomatoes begin to soften. Stir in the scallops and cook about 3 minutes, until just done.

5) Add the remaining ingredients, including the spaghetti. Toss and heat through over medium-high heat.

Per Serving: Calories 611; Protein 37g; Fat 6g (Saturated 1g); Carbohydrates 102g; Fiber 6g; Sodium 1801mg

Peking Noodles and Scallops

Makes: 3 servings

My local supermarket sells fresh Chinese noodles in the produce case. Like all fresh pasta, it cooks in under 4 minutes. If unavailable, use spaghetti.

8 ounces Chinese noodles or spaghetti
8 shiitake mushrooms (about $1/4$ pound)
1 teaspoon Asian sesame oil
3 tablespoons hoisin sauce
2 tablespoon soy sauce
1 teaspoon sugar
1 teaspoon oil
2 cloves garlic, minced
2 tablespoon dry sherry
$1/2$ pound scallops (if sea scallops, halve horizontally)
6 scallions, cut into 1 inch pieces
$1/2$ cup frozen peas, thawed

1) Put a pot of water up to boil. Begin cooking the spaghetti now. Some Chinese noodles take only 3 to 4 minutes to cook, so if using those, wait to cook until you are halfway through Step 3.

2) Prepare the rest of the ingredients ahead of time before cooking. Discard the mushroom stems and slice the caps. Combine the sesame oil, hoisin sauce, soy sauce, and sugar.

3) Heat the oil in a large nonstick wok or skillet. Briefly cook the garlic until it begins to turn color. Add the sherry, scallops, and mushrooms. Cook for 2 to 3 minutes, until the scallops turn opaque all the way through. Stir in the scallions and peas and cook 1 minute more. Cover and remove from heat if the noodles are not yet ready.

4) Toss in the cooked noodles and the sauce. Heat through about 2 minutes more.

Per Serving: Calories 486; Protein 26g; Fat 6g (Saturated 1g); Carbohydrates 81g; Fiber 5g; Sodium 1096mg

Shrimp and Vegetable Lo Mein

Makes: 4 servings

Don't be deterred by the long list of ingredients. Once the components are assembled the cooking proceeds smoothly and quickly. I often prepare the ingredients in the morning (during those few undistracted moments when the kids are in school), as well as cook up a big pot of rice. When dinnertime comes around, the cooking takes only a few minutes (the rice reheats in the microwave.) To round out the meal, there is often a fast Chinese soup (try Egg Drop, page 125) and a steamed vegetable.

1 teaspoon finely grated fresh ginger

2 tablespoons dry sherry

3 tablespoons soy sauce

$1/2$ cup reduced-sodium, defatted chicken broth

2 teaspoons cornstarch

1 cup shredded cabbage (or coleslaw mix)

1 rib celery, cut diagonally

One 8-ounce can bamboo shoots, drained and rinsed

1 cup snow peas, ends and strings removed if necessary

2 scallions, sliced

1 cup fresh mung bean sprouts

1 tablespoon vegetable oil

1 pound shrimp, peeled and deveined

2 cloves garlic, minced

12 ounces Chinese noodles or spaghetti, cooked

1) Assemble the ingredients before you begin cooking. Combine the ginger, sherry, soy sauce, broth, and cornstarch in a small bowl. Have the cabbage, celery, and bamboo shoots in a bowl, and the snow peas, scallions, and bean sprouts in another bowl.

2) Heat the oil a large wok. Toss in the shrimp and garlic. Cook over high heat until the shrimp turns pink, about 3 minutes. Remove to a plate and keep warm by covering loosely with foil.

3) Add the cabbage, celery, and bamboo shoots to the wok. Stir-fry for about 2 minutes until the cabbage begins to wilt. Stir in the snow peas, scallions, and bean sprouts. Toss and cook 1 minute. Stir the sauce and pour it into the wok. Toss in the noodles. Cook until the sauce clears and thickens. Stir in the shrimp and serve immediately.

Per Serving: Calories 526; Protein 38g; Fat 7g (Saturated 1g); Carbohydrates 75g; Fiber 5g; Sodium 1025mg

Shrimp Fried Rice

Makes: 4 servings

Once all of the ingredients are in place, dinner can be cooked in less than 10 minutes.

4 cloves garlic, minced

$^1/_4$ cup chopped onions

1 egg

1 egg white

$^1/_2$ pound shrimp, peeled and deveined

2 scallions, sliced

One 8-ounce can water chestnuts, drained and chopped

1 red bell pepper, chopped

1 rib celery, chopped

1 tablespoon soy sauce

3 cups cooked long-grain rice

$^1/_4$ cup frozen peas, thawed

1 tablespoon vegetable oil

$^1/_4$ to $^1/_3$ cup reduced-sodium, defatted chicken broth

1) Assemble all of the ingredients first. Have the garlic and onions in separate small bowls. In another small bowl, lightly beat the egg and egg white. Put the shrimp, scallions, water chestnuts, bell pepper, celery, and soy sauce in a bowl. If the rice is in clumps, break it up; put it in a bowl with the peas. Chopping the vegetables and cooking the rice can be done a day ahead of time.

2) Heat the oil in a large, preferably nonstick, wok. Cook the garlic over moderate heat for a couple of minutes, until it begins to change color. Stir in the onions and cook for 2 minutes more. Raise the heat and add the contents from the bowl of shrimp. Stir-fry until the shrimp turn pink, keeping the wok covered and shaking the pan frequently. Stir in the rice and peas.

3) Pour the egg along the rim of the wok so that it cooks as it slides down. Stir the egg into the rice. Add as much broth as is necessary to moisten the rice without leaving a mushy puddle. The amount will vary depending on how dry the rice is. Cook until the rice is hot and the shrimp are cooked through, about 5 minutes.

Per Serving: Calories 299; Protein 19g; Fat 6g (Saturated 1g); Carbohydrates 41g; Fiber 4g; Sodium 427mg

Risottos

Mussels and Clams Risotto

Makes: 4 servings

Clams vary in size. You'll need from 6 to 12— however many will fill about the same volume as a dozen mussels. For more about risottos, please read Risottos (page 304).

1 cup dry white wine
1 pinch saffron threads, or $^1/4$ teaspoon powder
12 mussels, scrubbed and debearded
6 to 12 clams, scrubbed
2 cups reduced-sodium, defatted chicken broth
1 cup water
2 tablespoons olive oil
1 cup chopped onions
3 cloves garlic, minced
$1^1/2$ cups Arborio or other short-grain rice
3 plum tomatoes, chopped (about $1^1/2$ cups)
$^1/4$ teaspoon dried thyme
$^1/4$ teaspoon freshly ground pepper
$^1/2$ teaspoon kosher salt (optional)
$^1/4$ cup grated Parmesan cheese (optional)
2 tablespoons chopped fresh parsley, for garnish

1) In a large Dutch oven, heat the wine and saffron until boiling. Add the mussels and clams and cover and steam until they open. The clams will take longer to cook than the mussels. Discard any shellfish that remain closed. With a slotted spoon, remove the shellfish to a bowl. Cover loosely with foil. Strain the cooking liquid through a fine mesh sieve or coffee filter and reserve. Wipe out the pot.

2) Combine the broth, water, and shellfish cooking liquid in a small pot or microwavable measuring cup. Heat until very hot.

3) Heat the oil in the Dutch oven. Over moderate heat, cook the onions and garlic until golden, about 5 minutes. Add the rice, tomatoes, and thyme. Cook, stirring constantly, until all is shiny with oil.

4) Add about 1 cup of the hot liquid to the rice. Bring to a boil, reduce to a simmer, and stir. When almost all of the liquid is absorbed, stir in another cup. Continue to do this until all of the liquid is used and the rice is creamy on the outside but still a bit firm to the bite. This will take about 20 to 30 minutes.

5) Stir in the pepper, and the salt and Parmesan, if desired. Put the risotto in a serving bowl and top with the mussels, clams, and parsley.

Per Serving: Calories 485; Protein 20g; Fat 9g (Saturated 1g); Carbohydrates 69g; Fiber 3g; Sodium 406mg

Swordfish and Broccoli Risotto

Makes: 4 servings

If asparagus is in season, substitute it for the broccoli. Trim the ends and cut the spears into 2-inch pieces. For more about risottos, please read Risottos (page 304).

One 8-ounce bottle clam juice or fish broth
    (1 cup)
2 cups reduced-sodium, defatted chicken broth
1 cup dry white wine
1/2 cup water
2 tablespoons olive oil
1 cup chopped onions
1 clove garlic, minced
2/3 pound swordfish or catfish, cut into
    bite-size chunks
1 1/2 cups Arborio or other short-grain rice
2 cups small broccoli florets
2 tablespoons chopped fresh parsley
1/2 cup chopped red bell pepper
1/4 teaspoon kosher salt
1/4 teaspoon freshly ground pepper

1) Heat the clam juice, broth, wine, and water in either the microwave or a saucepan.

2) In a large, heavy-bottomed pot, heat the oil. Over moderate heat, cook the onions and garlic until golden, about 5 minutes. Add the swordfish and cook, stirring frequently, until it is seared on all sides. Add the rice and broccoli and cook, stirring constantly, until all is shiny with oil.

3) Using a ladle, add about 1 cup of the hot liquid to the pot. Bring it to a boil, reduce to a simmer, and stir. When almost all of the liquid is absorbed, stir in a cup of broth. Continue to do this until all of the liquid has been used and the rice is creamy on the outside, but still a bit firm to the bite. This will take about 20 to 25 minutes.

4) Stir in the parsley, bell pepper, salt, and ground pepper.

Per Serving: Calories 481; Protein 23g; Fat 10g (Saturated 2g); Carbohydrates 62g; Fiber 3g; Sodium 844mg

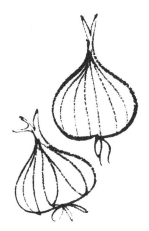

Mussels

I grew up on a tidal river on the New Jersey shore. If we had unexpected company, my mother would send my brothers and me down to the water to get mussels. These days I get farm-raised mussels at the market, but they are still one of the easiest foods to prepare for a crowd of people. Recipes can be doubled, or more. Serve with loaves of crusty bread, a salad, and a big bowl of spaghetti, and you have a feast.

Edible mussels are living mollusks, like clams. They are in good condition if they close up their shells when tapped, and if they open wide when steamed. Store them on ice. Refresh the ice frequently, as they will die if submerged in melted ice water. Mussels need to be scrubbed clean (use a vegetable brush). Do this right before cooking, as mussels can't survive rough handling. Most mussels have a tough green beard, which they use to anchor themselves in the water. Pull or cut this off as you clean the shells.

When mussels (and clams) cook, they give off a flavorful liquid. Most recipes make use of this as part of the sauce. Since it can be gritty, leave the last bit of liquid (and hopefully all of the sand) in the pot when pouring the sauce into a serving bowl.

Mussels in Shallot Sauce

Makes: 2 servings

Shallots are a relative of the onion, but they are different enough so that the two are not interchangeable. However, during the sweet onion season, when Vidalias, Walla Wallas, and the like appear, 3 minced tablespoons of these special onions can be used instead of the shallot.

2 teaspoons olive oil
1 large clove garlic, crushed
1 shallot, minced
$1/2$ cup white wine
1 leaf fresh basil, or 1 bay leaf
$2/3$ cup lemon juice
$1/4$ cup water
2 pounds mussels, scrubbed clean and debearded

1) Heat the oil in a pot large enough to hold all the mussels. Add the garlic and shallot and sauté.

2) Add the wine, basil, lemon juice, and water. If there is not enough liquid to cover the bottom of the pot by at least $1/4$ inch, add more water. When the liquid comes to a boil, reduce to a simmer and add the mussels. Cover and steam until the mussels open their shells, which will take less than 5 minutes. Discard mussels that do not open.

3) Put the mussels into a serving bowl and cover to keep warm.

4) Strain the cooking liquid through cheesecloth, put it into a saucepan, bring to a boil and reduce by half. This takes only a couple of minutes.

5) Pour the sauce over the mussels and serve.

Per Serving: Calories 295; Protein 27g; Fat 10g (Saturated 2g); Carbohydrates 16g; Fiber 0g; Sodium 653mg

Spanish Mussels

Makes: 2 servings

Fresh cilantro is essential here.

2 teaspoons olive oil
1/2 cup minced onions
1 rib celery, minced
4 cloves garlic, minced
4 plum tomatoes, cored, peeled and chopped
1/4 teaspoon Tabasco sauce
1/4 teaspoon ground coriander
1/2 teaspoon kosher salt
1/3 cup dry sherry
1/4 cup chopped fresh cilantro
1/2 cup chopped fresh parsley
2 pounds fresh mussels, scrubbed clean
   and debearded

1) Heat the oil in a saucepan large enough to accommodate the mussels. Cook the onions, celery, and garlic in the saucepan over moderate heat, until the vegetables soften and turn golden, about 7 minutes. Keep the pot covered between stirrings.

2) Stir in the tomatoes, Tabasco, coriander, salt, and sherry. Bring to a boil and then reduce to a simmer. Stir in the cilantro and parsley. Cook, covered, for 10 minutes. This recipe can be prepared up to this point and stored in the refrigerator for up to 2 days.

3) Put the mussels in the pot. Cover and simmer for 5 to 10 minutes, until the mussels open. Discard mussels that do not open.

4) Using a large spoon, transfer the mussels to a serving bowl. Carefully pour the sauce over the mussels, leaving the last bit in the pot. Eat immediately.

Per Serving: Calories 322; Protein 30g; Fat 10g (Saturated 2g); Carbohydrates 22g; Fiber 3g; Sodium 1175mg

Mussels in Spicy Tomato Broth

Makes: 4 servings

The spicy tomato broth, without the mussels, can be stored for up to 2 days. So make the sauce before weekend guests arrive, then relax and finish the meal in minutes. Serve with lots of crusty bread and a big green salad topped with croutons.

2 teaspoons olive oil
3 cloves garlic, minced
2 shallots, minced
1/2 cup chopped fresh parsley
2 teaspoons dried oregano
1/4 teaspoon crushed red pepper flakes (optional)
One 28-ounce can whole tomatoes, chopped,
   with juice
1 cup white wine
1/2 teaspoon kosher salt
3 1/2 pounds mussels, scrubbed clean and
   debearded

1) Heat the oil in a saucepan large enough to accommodate the mussels. Cook the garlic and shallots over moderate heat until they begin to change color, about 5 minutes.

2) Stir in the remaining ingredients except the mussels. Bring to a boil, then reduce to a simmer. Cook, covered, for 15 minutes. This recipe can be prepared up to this point and stored in the refrigerator for up to 2 days.

3) Put the mussels in the pot, cover, and simmer for 5 to 6 minutes, until the mussels open. Discard mussels that do not open.

4) Using a large spoon, transfer the mussels to a serving bowl. Carefully pour the sauce over the mussels, leaving the last bit in the pot. Eat immediately.

Per Serving: Calories 284; Protein 26g; Fat 7g (Saturated 1g); Carbohydrates 19g; Fiber 2g; Sodium 1139mg

Entrées: Vegetarian

Stuffed Vegetables
266

Rice and Pine Nut
Stuffed Eggplant

Bulgar and Feta
Stuffed Eggplant

Millet or Quinoa
Stuffed Squash

Wild Rice Stuffed Squash

From the Oven
269

Baked Pasta Casserole

Macaroni and Cheese

Macaroni and Cheese
with Vegetables

Oven-Baked Ratatouille

Tandoori Tofu

Vegetable Enchiladas

Bean Enchiladas

Spicy Tofu and
Green Chili Enchiladas

Southwest Torta

Bean and Tortilla Lasagna

Layered Tortilla Casserole

Lasagnas
277

Roasted Vegetable
Tortilla Lasagna

No-Pasta Vegetable Lasagna

Spinach Lasagna

Swiss Chard Lasagna

Broccoli and Carrot Lasagna

Mushroom Lasagna

Spinach Manicotti

Ravioli
282

Cheese Ravioli

Ricotta with Herb Ravioli

Spinach and
Mushroom Ravioli

Pumpkin Ravioli

Stovetop Cooking
285

Asparagus and Spaghetti

Basil and Broccoli Ziti

Broccoli and Garlic Pasta
for One

Walnut Linguine

Greens and Pasta

Pasta with Vegetables and Feta

Pasta with
Sun-Dried Tomato Pesto

Spinach and Friends

Shells with
Broccoli and Chickpeas

Mushroom and Tomato Sauce
over Pasta

Spaghetti all Puttanesca

Spaghetti with
Eggplant and Tomato Sauce

Penne with Mushrooms, Beans,
and Tomato Sauce

Penne with Vegetables
and Ricotta Sauce

Peanut Butter Noodles

Spaghetti Pie

Vegetable Fajitas

Stir-Fries and Dumplings
296

Ginger Greens Dumpling Rolls

Chinese Dumpling Rolls

Sweet and Sour Tofu Stir-Fry

Hoisin Tofu Stir-Fry

Stews and Chilis
298

Vegetables and Chickpeas over
Couscous

African Peanut Sauce

Vegetable Gumbo

Moroccan Vegetables

Belizean Bean and
Vegetable Stew

Chili

Black Bean Chili

Mexican Mole Vegetarian
Chili

Chickpea Curry

Curried Sweet Potatoes
and Greens

Risottos
304

Parmesan Parsley Risotto

Spinach Risotto

Asparagus Risotto

Mushroom Risotto

Vegetarian meals are no longer seen as something one consumes in penance. Vegetarian recipes do not lack for texture, flavor, or the ability to satisfy. Nutritionally, they can be at least as sound as meat-based meals. In fact, many health experts endorse eating several meals without meat every week and the United States government recently acknowledged that vegetarianism can be a healthy way to eat.

Fifteen percent of college students now say they are vegetarians, and more and more people across America are eating vegetarian meals. Many are not strict vegetarians but choose to eat some meals without meat. From a health perspective, this can be a good thing.

Some vegetarians eat no dairy products or eggs, others eat fish but no red meat. The recipes in this chapter are made without any meat or fish, but some do include dairy products and eggs. For strict vegetarians, vegetarian broth can be used in recipes calling for chicken broth.

This is not the cream- and cheese-filled diet of several decades past, nor is it a strict diet of rice and beans. Rather, it is adapted from cuisines from around the world that use meat as an occasional flavoring and not as the main source of calories.

Vegetarian dining can sometimes pose a problem for the cook in the family. Not only might he or she need to accommodate both vegetarians and meat-eaters at the same meal, but planning the menu and doing the shopping and preparation often take more thought, effort, and time than before. Turning raw vegetables into an entrée does require more work than putting a steak on the grill. However, if the family cook starts out with easy recipes, makes use of the freezer and leftovers, then vegetarian entrées can be welcome additions to the menu of even the busiest family.

Stuffed Vegetables

Although reminiscent of "crunchy-granola" food from the 1970s, stuffed vegetables have a long and venerable history as entrées in many cultures. If loaded with cheese and meat, they do not fit the criteria of healthy eating. But filled with grains, vegetables, seasonings, and perhaps a handful of nuts and a touch of cheese, they are very good eating—and very good for you. Stuffed vegetables are especially useful in households where some members of the family are vegetarians and others are not, for they can be side dishes for some and main courses for others.

Rice and Pine Nut Stuffed Eggplant

Makes: 3 servings

Pine nuts are also called pignolis. They are costly, but well worth the money.

1 large or 2 small eggplants
(about 1 1/4 pound total)
2 teaspoons olive oil
1 cup chopped onions
2 cloves garlic, minced
2 tablespoons pine nuts
1 tomato, diced
1 cup cooked rice
1 tablespoon chopped fresh parsley
1/4 teaspoon dried thyme
1/2 teaspoon kosher salt
1/2 teaspoon freshly ground pepper
1 tablespoon grated Parmesan cheese (optional)

1) Preheat the oven to 400°F. Cut the eggplant in half and place cut side down on a baking sheet lined with foil. Bake 15 to 35 minutes (depending on the size of the eggplant), until tender but not collapsed. Let rest until cool enough to handle. Scoop out the insides, leaving a ¹/₂ inch around the eggplant shell. Discard the strips of eggplant that are full of seeds and chop the rest of the flesh.

2) Heat the oil in a sauté pan. Cook the onions and garlic over moderate-low heat until golden. Stir in the pine nuts and cook until lightly toasted. Add the tomatoes and cook, covered, until they begin to wilt. Toss this sautéed mixture in a bowl with the rice, parsley, thyme, salt, pepper, and chopped eggplant.

3) Fill the eggplant shells with the stuffing. Place in a baking dish. They can be crowded together so as to keep each other upright. Dust with the Parmesan cheese, if desired.

4) Bake, loosely covered with foil, for 15 minutes. Remove the foil and bake for 10 minutes longer.

Per Serving: Calories 198; Protein 6g; Fat 6g (Saturated 1g); Carbohydrates 33g; Fiber 7g; Sodium 333mg

Bulgur and Feta Stuffed Eggplant

Makes: 3 servings

Bulgur is a grain that provides a nutty flavor and chewy texture. Soak or cook it according to package directions—the finer the bulgur, the less soaking or cooking it requires.

3 small eggplants, or 1 large (about 1¹/₄ pounds)
1 teaspoon olive oil
1 cup chopped red onions
2 cloves garlic, minced
2 tablespoons pine nuts
2 plum tomatoes, diced
³/₄ cup prepared bulgur wheat
2 tablespoons chopped fresh parsley
1 teaspoon dried mint, or 1 tablespoon fresh
¹/₂ teaspoon kosher salt
¹/₄ teaspoon freshly ground pepper
3 tablespoons crumbled feta cheese

1) Preheat the oven to 400°F. Cut the eggplant in half and place cut side down on a baking sheet lined with foil. Bake 15 to 35 minutes (depending on the size of the eggplant), until tender but not collapsed. Let rest until cool enough to handle. Scoop out the insides, leaving a ¹/₂ inch around the eggplant shell. Discard the strips of eggplant that are full of seeds and chop the rest of the flesh.

2) Heat the oil in a nonstick sauté pan. Cook the onions and garlic over moderate-low heat, covered, until golden. Stir in the pine nuts and cook until lightly toasted. Add the tomatoes and cook, covered, until they begin to wilt. Toss this sautéed mixture with the bulgar wheat, parsley, mint, salt, pepper, and chopped eggplant. Stir in 2 tablespoons of the feta cheese.

3) Fill the eggplant shells with the stuffing. Place in a baking dish. They can be crowded together so as to keep each other upright. Top with the remaining cheese.

4) Reduce the oven temperature to 350°F. Bake, loosely covered with foil, for 15 minutes. Remove the foil and bake for 10 minutes more.

Per Serving: Calories 180; Protein 7g; Fat 6g (Saturated 2g); Carbohydrates 29g; Fiber 9g; Sodium 414mg

Millet or Quinoa Stuffed Squash

Makes: 4 servings

Because squash don't come in consistent sizes, and because this recipe leaves open what type of squash to use (I prefer acorn in the winter and zucchini in the summer), you might have too much filling. Either hollow out the squash to accommodate the excess, or put the extra filling into whatever else is handy, such as a green bell pepper, and bake it along with the squash.

2 medium squash
1 cup cooked millet or quinoa
1 egg white, lightly beaten
1 cup 1% lowfat cottage cheese
1/4 cup minced fresh chives
1 clove garlic, minced
1/2 teaspoon dried marjoram
1/4 teaspoon freshly ground pepper
1 tablespoon grated Parmesan cheese
Paprika, chives, or minced parsley, for garnish
 (optional)

1) Cut the squash in half. Scoop out the seeds. Slice off a sliver of the squash from its bottom so that it will sit flat. Steam, bake, or microwave until tender. Baking will bring out the best flavor in winter squash. To bake, cut in half, put cut side down on a baking sheet, and place in a 375°F oven for about 30 minutes.

2) Combine the filling ingredients and spoon enough into the squash to form a nicely mounded top.

3) Put in a baking pan with 1/2 inch of water on the bottom (this will help cook the squash and keep it from drying out). Cover loosely and bake in a preheated 350°F oven for 30 minutes. Uncover and bake for 15 minutes more. Garnish with herbs, if desired.

Per Serving: Calories 203; Protein 12g; Fat 2g (Saturated 1g); Carbohydrates 36g; Fiber 7g; Sodium 279mg

Wild Rice Stuffed Squash

Makes: 2 servings

Serve this, stuffed in acorn squash, if you are having vegetarians to your Thanksgiving table.

1 recipe Wild Rice Stuffing (page 431)
1 tablespoon sherry
2 egg whites, lightly beaten
1 squash, halved, seeded, and softened by baking
 or steaming

1) Combine the stuffing, sherry, and egg whites.

2) If the squash rolls around, slice off a piece from the bottom so that it sits securely. Pack stuffing into the squash. At this point, the squash can be tightly wrapped and stored in the refrigerator for up to 1 day.

3) Bake in a preheated 375°F oven for 35 minutes. To keep them moist, put a little water in the bottom of the baking pan before baking.

Per Serving: Calories 510; Protein 17g; Fat 13g (Saturated 1g); Carbohydrates 88g; Fiber 18g; Sodium 918mg

From the Oven

Baked Pasta Casserole

Makes: 4 servings

This recipe can be doubled and baked in a large casserole. Also, it can be made through Step 2 in the morning and put in the oven that evening, which makes this just the recipe for when you're deciding what to feed a crowd.

1 tablespoon olive oil
1 cup chopped onions
2 cloves garlic, chopped
1 small yellow squash, diced
1 small zucchini, diced
6 plum tomatoes, chopped
1 tablespoon dried basil
1 1/2 teaspoons dried oregano
1 teaspoon kosher salt
1/4 teaspoon freshly ground pepper
4 cups cooked rotini pasta (from about
    3 cups dried)
1 cup lowfat ricotta cheese
1 slice homemade-quality white bread, cut into
    small cubes
2 tablespoons grated Parmesan cheese

1) Preheat the oven to 350°F.

2) Heat the oil in a sauté pan and cook the onions and garlic until they begin to change color and soften, about 5 minutes. Stir in the squash, zucchini, and tomatoes, and cover. Cook until wilted, about 5 minutes more. Stir in the herbs, salt, and pepper. Toss in the pasta and ricotta cheese. (Or, if your sauté pan isn't large enough to accommodate all of this, toss it in a bowl before putting it in the casserole.)

3) Put the pasta mixture into a 2- to 3-quart casserole. Top with the cubed bread and dust the Parmesan cheese on top. Bake 25 to 35 minutes, until the bread is toasted and the casserole is hot throughout.

Per Serving: Calories 378; Protein 16g; Fat 9g (Saturated 3g); Carbohydrates 59g; Fiber 5g; Sodium 647mg

Macaroni and Cheese

Makes: 6 servings

This has passed the kids' test in several homes, so I feel confident offering this version of the classic casserole here.

1 tablespoon unsalted butter
3 tablespoons unbleached, all-purpose white flour
1 teaspoon dry mustard
$1/2$ teaspoon paprika
$1/2$ teaspoon kosher salt
$1^1/2$ cups nonfat milk
1 cup nonfat sour cream
1 egg, lightly beaten
2 cups shredded reduced-fat cheddar cheese
4 cups cooked elbow macaroni (from about 2 cups dried)
$1/4$ cup cornflake crumbs or dried breadcrumbs

1) Coat a 2-quart casserole with nonstick spray. Preheat the oven to 350°F.

2) Melt the butter in a medium saucepan. Stir in the flour, mustard, paprika, and salt. Slowly pour in the milk, whisking all the while until there are no lumps of flour. Continue to stir with the whisk, raise the heat, and cook until the milk bubbles and thickens. Remove from the stovetop and stir in the sour cream, egg, and cheese.

3) Toss the macaroni and the cheese mixture together in a bowl and then pour it into the casserole. Top with the cornflake crumbs. Set in the oven and bake for 20 minutes, or until bubbly around the edges.

Per Serving: Calories 328; Protein 19g; Fat 8g (Saturated 5g); Carbohydrates 44g; Fiber 2g; Sodium 455mg

Macaroni and Cheese with Vegetables

Makes: 6 servings

The carrots are added raw to contribute crunch, but if your kids eat only soft vegetables, you can certainly cook them first.

1 tablespoon unsalted butter
3 tablespoons unbleached, all-purpose white flour
1 teaspoon dry mustard
$1/2$ teaspoon paprika
$1/2$ teaspoon kosher salt
$1^1/2$ cups nonfat milk
$3/4$ cup nonfat sour cream
$1/2$ cup lowfat sour cream
1 egg, lightly beaten
2 cups shredded reduced-fat cheddar cheese
4 cups cooked elbow macaroni (from about 2 cups dried)
1 cup frozen peas
1 cup diced carrots
1 cup chopped broccoli or small broccoli florets, lightly steamed
1 tablespoon minced onions
$1/4$ cup cornflake crumbs or dried breadcrumbs

1) Coat a $2^1/2$-quart casserole with nonstick spray. Preheat the oven to 350°F. (This recipe will proceed smoothly if all of the ingredients are measured before you start cooking. While the macaroni is boiling is a good time to do this.)

2) Melt the butter in a medium saucepan. Stir in the flour, mustard, paprika, and salt. Slowly pour in the milk, whisking all the while until there are no lumps of flour. Continue to stir with the whisk, raise the heat, and cook until the milk bubbles and thickens. Remove from the stovetop and stir in the sour creams, egg, and cheese.

3) Toss the macaroni with the cheese mixture in a bowl. Stir in the peas, carrots, broccoli, and onions. Put into the casserole and top with the cornflake crumbs. Bake for 30 to 35 minutes, or until bubbly and browning around the edges.

Per Serving: Calories 372; Protein 21g; Fat 10g (Saturated 6g); Carbohydrates 51g; Fiber 4g; Sodium 505mg

Oven-Baked Ratatouille

Makes: 4 servings

The vegetables are first roasted in the oven, then baked with wine and herbs. This technique, rather than simmering on the stovetop, brings a fuller, deeper flavor to the ratatouille.

1 large eggplant (about 1 pound), cut into 1-inch or smaller cubes
1 tablespoon olive oil
2 small yellow onions, coarsely chopped
4 large cloves garlic, minced
1 1/2 teaspoons kosher salt, divided
1 green, red, or yellow bell pepper, cut into large pieces
1 medium yellow summer squash (about 1/4 pound), cubed
1 medium zucchini, cubed
4 very ripe plum tomatoes, or 4 canned plum tomatoes, coarsely chopped
2 bay leaves
1/2 cup white wine
2 tablespoons chopped fresh parsley
1/4 cup chopped fresh basil, or 1 tablespoon dried
1/4 teaspoon freshly ground pepper, or more to taste
1 teaspoon lemon juice

1) Preheat the oven to 400°F.

2) Put the eggplant, oil, onions, garlic, and 1 teaspoon of the salt into a heavy casserole. Toss the ingredients so that the oil and salt coat the eggplant evenly. Bake, uncovered, for 35 minutes. Stir once or twice during cooking to keep the vegetables from sticking.

3) Reduce the oven temperature to 350°F. Add the remaining 1/2 teaspoon salt and the remaining ingredients, except the lemon juice, to the pot. Stir to combine. Cover the pot, leaving a small steam vent. Bake for 30 minutes.

4) Add the lemon juice. Adjust the salt and pepper to taste. Remove the bay leaves (if you can find them) before serving.

Per Serving: Calories 129; Protein 3g; Fat 4g (Saturated 1g); Carbohydrates 18g; Fiber 6g; Sodium 735mg

Tandoori Tofu

Makes: 8 servings

This recipe is similar to Tandoori Chicken (page 161). You can serve both, side by side, and please both vegetarians and meat eaters with little extra work for yourself. The recipe makes a generous amount, but leftovers are wonderful as a pita pocket filling.

2 pounds extra-firm or firm tofu
1/2 cup plain nonfat yogurt
2 tablespoons lemon juice
1 tablespoon apple cider vinegar
2 cloves garlic, minced
2 teaspoons finely grated fresh ginger
1 teaspoon kosher salt
2 to 3 teaspoons mild curry powder
1/4 teaspoon ground chili pepper (optional)

1) Wrap the tofu in a cloth towel and press out the excess water.

2) Cut the tofu into l-inch cubes or thickly slice.

3) Combine the remaining ingredients in a glass or stainless-steel bowl and stir the tofu into this mixture until it is evenly coated with the marinade. Marinate for 8 to 24 hours, keeping covered and refrigerated.

4) Preheat the broiler. As you place the tofu on a grill or broiler rack, shake off the excess marinade. Broil the tofu about 20 to 30 minutes, until the yogurt begins to bubble and brown. Turn the tofu every 5 to 7 minutes so that all sides are exposed to the heat.

Per Serving: Calories 170; Protein 18g; Fat 10g (Saturated 1g); Carbohydrates 6g; Fiber 0g; Sodium 142mg

Vegetable Enchiladas

Makes: 4 servings

The carrots and zucchini (and even broccoli stems) are cut into french-fry-size strips, which roll up tidier and look nicer than chopped vegetables.

1 tablespoon vegetable oil
1 small yellow onion, sliced
1 carrot, coarsely julienned
1 small zucchini, coarsely julienned
1/4 pound mushrooms, sliced (1 cup)
1 teaspoon ground chili powder
1/2 teaspoon ground coriander
1/2 teaspoon kosher salt
2 tablespoons chopped canned mild green chilies (optional)
2 cups broccoli florets, lightly steamed, chopped
1 cup reduced-fat jack or mild cheddar cheese, divided
8 corn tortillas
3 cups Fat-Free Enchilada Sauce (page 586 or store-bought)

1) Preheat the oven to 375°F.

2) Heat the oil in a nonstick sauté pan. Add the onion, carrot, zucchini, and mushrooms. Cover and cook over moderate heat until soft, about 4 minutes. Stir in the spices and chilies. Cook, uncovered, 2 minutes more. Stir in the broccoli. Allow to cool slightly and stir in 1/2 cup of the cheese.

3) To keep the corn tortillas pliable, put the stack of tortillas into a dish with a little water in the bottom. Starting with the one sitting in the water, take each tortilla from the bottom of the pile as you fill and roll.

4) Spread 2 cups of the sauce on the bottom of a shallow rectangular baking dish. Take a moistened tortilla from the bottom of the stack and put about 1/3 cup of the vegetables in its center. Roll it up and place seam side down in the pan of sauce. Repeat for each tortilla. Arrange the enchiladas in the pan leaving a little space between each tortilla (they will swell during baking).

5) Pour the remaining cup of sauce in a striped design across the enchiladas. Distribute the remaining cheese on top.

6) Cover and bake 30 minutes. If foil is used to cover the pan, take care that it doesn't touch the sauce. Uncover and bake for 10 minutes longer.

Per Serving: Calories 323; Protein 14g; Fat 9g (Saturated 3g); Carbohydrates 50g; Fiber 9g; Sodium 1031mg

Bean Enchiladas

Makes: 5 servings

The ingredients for enchiladas can be frozen separately. With containers of cooked beans, enchilada sauce, and tortillas in the freezer, this dish can be made in no time.

1 tablespoon vegetable oil
1/2 cup chopped onions
2 cloves garlic, minced
1/2 green bell pepper, minced
1 teaspoon ground coriander
1/2 teaspoon chili powder
1/8 teaspoon Tabasco sauce
6 cups cooked pinto beans, drained and rinsed
10 corn tortillas
4 cups Fat-Free Enchilada Sauce (page 586 or
    store-bought)

1) Preheat the oven to 375°F.

2) Heat the oil in a large sauté pan and cook the onions, garlic, and bell peppers until golden. As the vegetables cook, stir in the spices.

3) Mash half the beans and then stir them back in with the whole beans. Mix the sautéed ingredients in with beans.

4) To keep the corn tortillas pliable, put the stack of tortillas into a dish with a little water in the bottom. Starting with the one sitting in the water, take each tortilla from the bottom of the pile as you fill and roll.

5) Spread 3 cups of the enchilada sauce on the bottom of a shallow rectangular baking pan. Place 1/3 cup beans on a tortilla, and roll it up.

6) Set each tortilla into the baking pan with the seam side down. Leave a little space between each tortilla to ease removal after baking.

7) After all the tortillas are rolled and in the pan, drizzle the remaining cup of sauce over them.

8) Cover and bake for 45 minutes. If foil is used to cover the pan, take care that it doesn't touch the sauce.

Per Serving: Calories 526; Protein 23g; Fat 6g (Saturated 1g); Carbohydrates 99g; Fiber 25g; Sodium 684mg

Spicy Tofu and Green Chili Enchiladas

Makes: 6 servings

To make the tofu easier to mash, break it apart with your hands as you add it to the bowl.

One 1-pound package firm tofu
$1/2$ cup shredded lowfat jack cheese
One 4-ounce can chopped mild green chilies
2 cups Fat-Free Enchilada Sauce (page 586 or store-bought)
1 cup cooked black beans, drained and rinsed
$1/2$ teaspoon ground cumin
$1/2$ teaspoon kosher salt (optional)
1 green or red bell pepper, roasted and sliced
6 large corn or flour tortillas
Grated lowfat jack or cheddar cheese (optional)
2 plum tomatoes, chopped
2 scallions, chopped, for garnish

1) Heat the oven to 425°F. Coat a 13×9-inch pan with baking spray.

2) Mash the tofu, cheese, chilies, and $1/4$ cup of the enchilada sauce in a bowl. Stir in the black beans, cumin, and salt. Stir in the roasted pepper.

3) This step is messy but necessary. Pour the enchilada sauce onto a dinner plate. Dip both sides of a tortilla in the sauce. Fill with one-sixth of the tofu mixture. Roll up and place in the baking dish seam side down. Repeat with the remaining tortillas. Spoon any leftover sauce on top of the tortillas. If desired, top with grated cheese. Distribute the tomatoes over the enchiladas. Bake, uncovered, for 20 to 30 minutes, until bubbly and brown. Garnish with scallions.

Per Serving: Calories 275; Protein 20g; Fat 9g (Saturated 2g); Carbohydrates 33g; Fiber 7g; Sodium 416mg

Southwest Torta

Makes: 5 servings

Serve with Green Chili Sauce (page 600) and Red Salsa (page 592).

2 teaspoons vegetable oil
$1/2$ cup chopped red onions
$1/2$ cup red bell pepper, julienned
1 clove garlic, minced
One 4-ounce can chopped mild green chilies
1 medium zucchini, sliced into rounds (about 2 cups)
2 eggs
3 egg whites
$1/4$ cup lowfat sour cream
$1/2$ cup nonfat milk
$1/2$ teaspoon ground cumin
$1/2$ teaspoon kosher salt
2 scallions, sliced
8 corn tortillas, cut in halves
2 tablespoons shredded reduced-fat cheddar or jack cheese

1) Preheat the oven to 350°F. Coat a 2- to $2^1/2$-quart oblong casserole with nonstick spray.

2) Heat the oil in a nonstick sauté pan. Cook the onions until they begin to soften. Stir in the bell peppers and garlic and cook until the peppers wilt. Stir in the chilies and remove the mixture from the pan onto a plate. Put the zucchini into the skillet and cook a few minutes until they begin to soften and brown, stirring frequently. Remove from the heat.

3) In a bowl, whisk together the remaining ingredients except the tortillas and cheese.

4) Arrange 4 tortilla halves overlapping in the bottom of the casserole. Layer a third of the zucchini on the tortillas, then a third of the vegetable mixture. Pour in a quarter of the egg batter. Repeat with 4 more tortilla halves, a third more of the zucchini, the vegetables, and the batter. Layer one more time. Top with the remaining 4 tortilla halves and the remaining batter and then the shredded cheese.

5) Bake for 25 to 30 minutes, until the egg batter puffs and sets.

Per Serving: Calories 166; Protein 9g; Fat 6g (Saturated 2g); Carbohydrates 21g; Fiber 3g; Sodium 418mg

Bean and Tortilla Lasagna

Makes: 9 servings

Although pinto beans are specified, other varieties such as black beans would also taste great.

1 teaspoon vegetable oil
1/2 cup chopped onions
2 cloves garlic, minced
1 green bell pepper, chopped
3 cups cooked pinto beans, drained and rinsed
1/2 teaspoon kosher salt
1/4 teaspoon freshly ground pepper
1/8 teaspoon Tabasco sauce
2 cups Fat-Free Enchilada Sauce (page 586 or store-bought)
12 corn tortillas
1 cup shredded reduced-fat sharp cheddar cheese
1 1/2 cups sliced roasted peppers (2 to 3 peppers or one 12-ounce jar)
1 cup Red Salsa (page 592 or store-bought)

1) Preheat the oven to 350°F.

2) Heat the oil in a large sauté pan. Sauté the onions, garlic, and bell pepper until the vegetables soften.

3) Partially mash the beans until about half are smooth but some remain whole. Mix the beans with the sautéed vegetables, salt, ground pepper, and Tabasco.

4) Cover the bottom of an oblong pan, about 9×13-inches, with 1 1/2 cups of Fat-Free Enchilada Sauce. Place 4 tortillas on top. Spread on half the bean mixture, half the cheese, and half the roasted peppers. Place 4 more tortillas on top. Repeat the layers of beans, cheese, and peppers. Top again with tortillas. Then spread on the remaining sauce and the salsa. If the salsa is watery, drain it a bit first.

5) Cover with foil, taking care not to let the metal touch the tomatoes. You can make the casserole up to this point several hours ahead of time.

6) Bake for 45 minutes. Remove the foil for the last 5 minutes.

Per Serving: Calories 236; Protein 11g; Fat 4g (Saturated 1g); Carbohydrates 42g; Fiber 9g; Sodium 462mg

Layered Tortilla Casserole

Makes: 9 servings

For a hearty vegetarian recipe, this takes remarkably little time to prepare.

One 28-ounce can tomato puree
1 tablespoon ground cumin
1 tablespoon ground coriander
2 teaspoons chili powder
$1/2$ teaspoon kosher salt
One $14^1/2$-ounce can whole tomatoes, with juice
1 egg white
$1^1/2$ cups lowfat sour cream
$1^1/2$ cups shredded reduced-fat jack cheese
3 cups cooked pinto beans, drained and rinsed
2 tablespoons chopped canned mild green chilies
1 tablespoon canned jalapeño peppers, chopped (optional)
8 corn tortillas, sliced into wide strips
2 scallions, sliced, for garnish

1) Stir the tomato puree, cumin, coriander, chili powder, and salt into a medium saucepan. Add the juice from the whole tomatoes, then squeeze the tomatoes into the pot, breaking them apart into chunks. Bring to a simmer and cook the sauce, covered, for 15 minutes.

2) Preheat the oven to 400°F.

3) In a bowl, stir together the egg white, sour cream, and cheese. In another bowl, mix together the beans, chilies, and jalapeños.

4) When the tomato sauce is ready, pour half of it onto the bottom of a shallow rectangular baking dish, about 9×13 inches. Distribute half the bean mixture on the sauce, then half the cheese blend. Arrange half the tortillas on top. Repeat with the beans, cheese, and tortillas. Top with the rest of the sauce. Cover with foil, taking care not to let the metal touch the sauce.

5) Bake for 30 minutes, remove the foil, and bake for another 15 minutes. Take out of the oven and let rest 10 minutes. Garnish with the scallions.

Per Serving: Calories 249; Protein 14g; Fat 6g (Saturated 4g); Carbohydrates 40g; Fiber 9g; Sodium 709mg

Lasagnas

Making lasagna can seem like a daunting task, but despite the many steps and ingredients, it is hard to go wrong—lasagna recipes are very forgiving. Their very nature is rustic and messy; their flavors are a melange and rarely out of balance.

Most lasagnas are made with pasta, although other ingredients can be layered, such as tortillas or slices of vegetables. The pasta needs to be cooked before assembling the lasagna. It should be boiled until pliable but not soft. Cook the noodles in a very large pot, adding them one by one and crisscrossing them in the water. This keeps them from sticking together in the pot. Draining the noodles can cause them to lump or break, so I take them out with tongs and lay them flat on a clean dish towel. Letting them drain is important with a lowfat recipe, because it prevents the finished product from being loose (lowfat cheese doesn't bind as well as full-fat). The noodles can be cooked up to one hour ahead of time. No-boil lasagna noodles are also available. Although the texture isn't as good as regular pasta, it is convenient. You might have to add more liquid to the recipe. Follow package directions.

Most lasagnas are cooked in a tomato-based sauce. Which one you use depends on what you like and what you have. If there is time to plan ahead, use a homemade sauce; a selection appears on pages 583–585. In a pinch, store-bought sauce will do.

Lasagnas are held together with cheese. Lowfat cheeses have limitations. They give off more moisture and have a chewier texture than full-fat cheeses. Lowfat ricottas shrink more than they melt. My recipes take this into account. By using flavorful sauces, a combination of cheeses, and vegetable fillings, these homemade healthy lasagnas are as wonderful as their full-fat relatives. However, don't try to bring the fat content of these recipes down even further. Nonfat cheeses, cottage cheese, and salt-free products make chewy, tough, bland lasagnas.

Lasagna pans vary in both size and material. I have a glazed ceramic casserole from Italy that is just right, but any oblong pan is suitable. If baking in clear glass, reduce the oven temperature by 25°F. Pans do not have to be coated with nonstick spray.

Once the lasagna is put together, it can be tightly wrapped in plastic and frozen for about 2 months. Partially defrost (so that it is not rock hard, but is still icy) and bake. Lasagna is baked in a moderate oven, 350°F, which gives the cheese time to melt as the sauce bubbles. During baking, if the cheese browns too quickly, tent foil over the top. Never let foil touch a surface with tomato sauce, though, because the acid in the sauce will etch holes into the foil, and there will be flakes of metal on the food. Let the lasagna rest for 10 minutes on the counter to set. This will greatly ease cutting.

These lasagna recipes serve nine as part of a larger meal. However, since they are filled with vegetables, carbohydrates, and cheese, they can make a complete meal in themselves, and so would serve about five as a one-pot supper. Leftovers remain delicious for several days and single portions reheat in the microwave in about 2 minutes.

Roasted Vegetable Tortilla Lasagna

Makes: 9 servings

This recipe is quite flexible. Other vegetables can be used, even grilled vegetables. As a convenience, use store-bought enchilada or taco sauce, preferably mild or medium, not hot.

1 tablespoon vegetable oil
1 cup sliced red onions
4 cloves garlic, sliced
1 green bell pepper, sliced
1 medium zucchini, sliced into rounds
1 large carrot, cut into sticks
1 to 2 tablespoons sliced jalapeño peppers (fresh or pickled)
1 1/4 cup grated reduced-fat sharp cheddar cheese, divided
1 cup lowfat sour cream
1 cup nonfat sour cream
2 cups Fat-Free Enchilada Sauce (page 586 or store-bought)
12 corn tortillas, halved
2 cups cooked black or red kidney beans, drained and rinsed
1/2 cup Red Salsa (page 592 or store-bought)

1) Preheat the oven to 425°F.

2) Toss together the oil, onions, garlic, pepper, zucchini, carrot, and jalapeño in a roasting pan. Roast for 15 minutes, then stir. Continue to cook, about 10 minutes longer, until the vegetables soften and begin to brown in spots. Reduce the oven temperature to 375°F.

3) Set aside 1/4 cup of the cheddar cheese. Stir the remaining cup of cheddar cheese and the lowfat and nonfat sour creams together. Cover the bottom of an oblong dish, about 9×13 inches, with 1 1/2 cups of the Enchilada Sauce. Arrange 8 tortillas halves, overlapping each other, on top. Spread on half the roasted vegetables and half the beans. Drop dollops of half the sour cream mixture across the casserole. Place 8 more tortilla halves on top. Repeat the layers of vegetables, beans, and cheese. Top again with tortillas, then spread on the remaining sauce and the salsa.

4) Bake for 35 to 40 minutes.

Per Serving: Calories 283; Protein 13g; Fat 7g (Saturated 3g); Carbohydrates 45g; Fiber 7g; Sodium 384mg

No-Pasta Vegetable Lasagna

Makes: 9 servings

For people with wheat allergies, or for a buffet meal where many pasta dishes are being served, a lasagna made without pasta is not such a funny idea after all.

2 large eggplants
1 teaspoon kosher salt, divided
1/2 teaspoon freshly ground pepper, divided
1 pound reduced-fat ricotta
1 egg white
1 tablespoon minced fresh chives or scallions
2 1/2 cups tomato sauce (pages 583–585 or store-bought)
1 cup shredded reduced-fat mozzarella
1/4 cup grated Parmesan cheese

1) Preheat the oven to 425°F.

2) Slice the eggplants lengthwise into long, ¹/₄-inch strips. Use ¹/₂ teaspoon of the salt and ¹/₄ teaspoon of the pepper to season both sides. Place the strips on a nonstick or greased baking sheet. Bake for 5 to 7 minutes on each side. You also may grill the vegetable strips. Reduce the oven temperature to 350°F.

3) With a fork, mix together the ricotta, egg white, chives, and remaining salt and pepper.

4) Spread 1¹/₂ cups of the tomato sauce on the bottom of an oblong dish, about 9×13 inches. Then place a single layer of vegetables on top. Evenly spread half the ricotta mixture on top of the vegetables. Place another layer of vegetables on that, and the remaining ricotta, and top with the remaining vegetables. Cover with the remaining tomato sauce, then evenly distribute the mozzarella and Parmesan on top.

5) Cover with foil and bake for 1 hour. Remove the foil for the last 5 to 10 minutes.

Per Serving: Calories 144; Protein 1g; Fat 4g (Saturated 3g); Carbohydrates 15g; Fiber 4g; Sodium 768mg

Spinach Lasagna

Makes: 9 servings

Use any tomato sauce you like. Basic Basil Tomato Sauce (page 583) lends a light, fresh taste.

¹/₂ pound fresh spinach
1 pound lowfat ricotta
¹/₂ teaspoon kosher salt
¹/₂ teaspoon freshly ground pepper
1 tablespoon minced chives, fresh or frozen
1 egg white
3 cups tomato sauce (pages 583–585 or store-bought)
9 lasagna noodles, cooked until pliable
1¹/₂ cups shredded reduced-fat mozzarella
2 tablespoons grated Parmesan cheese (optional)

1) Preheat the oven to 350°F.

2) Wash the spinach well, then microwave or briefly steam until wilted. Squeeze out all the moisture and coarsely chop.

3) Using a fork, combine the spinach, ricotta, salt, pepper, chives, and egg white.

4) Spread half the tomato sauce in a shallow rectangular pan, about 9×13 inches. Lay down 3 noodles, top with half the ricotta mixture, lay down 3 more noodles and top with the remaining ricotta. Lay down the last 3 noodles, top with the remaining tomato sauce, and distribute the mozzarella and Parmesan (if using) on top.

5) Bake for 45 minutes. Let rest 5 minutes before serving.

Per Serving: Calories 190; Protein 13g; Fat 4g (Saturated 3g); Carbohydrates 23g; Fiber 1g; Sodium 730mg

Swiss Chard Lasagna

Makes: 9 servings

Although Swiss chard is a dark leafy green like spinach, it differs in flavor and the crispy texture of its stems.

1 pound lowfat or reduced-fat ricotta
$1/2$ teaspoon kosher salt
$1/4$ teaspoon freshly ground pepper
1 egg white
$1/2$ pound white-ribbed Swiss chard
3 cups tomato sauce (pages 583–585 or store-bought)
9 lasagna noodles, cooked until pliable
$1^1/2$ cups shredded reduced-fat mozzarella
2 tablespoons grated Parmesan cheese

1) Preheat the oven to 350°F.

2) Combine the ricotta, salt, pepper, and egg white.

3) Cut the ribs away from the leafy green parts of the Swiss chard. Finely chop the stalks and cook these for a few minutes until tender (they will retain a slight crunch). Slice the leafy parts into big pieces (remember, they'll shrink down just like spinach when cooked). Add the leaves to the stems and cook until wilted. Drain the chard well, then stir it into the ricotta mixture.

4) In a shallow, rectangular baking dish, about 9×13 inches, layer half the tomato sauce, 3 noodles, half the ricotta mixture, 3 more noodles, the remaining ricotta mixture, and the last 3 noodles. Top with the remaining tomato sauce, the mozzarella, and the Parmesan.

5) Bake for 1 hour. Let rest 5 minutes before serving.

Per Serving: Calories 195; Protein 14g; Fat 5g (Saturated 3g); Carbohydrates 23g; Fiber 1g; Sodium 789mg

Broccoli and Carrot Lasagna

Makes: 9 servings

Chopping the vegetables in the food processor saves a lot of time and trouble.

4 carrots, peeled and chopped ($1/2$ pound)
$1/2$ head broccoli, peeled and chopped ($1/2$ pound)
1 pound reduced-fat ricotta
2 cloves Roasted Garlic (page 603), or 2 cloves garlic, minced and sautéed in oil
$1^1/2$ teaspoons kosher salt
$1/4$ teaspoon freshly ground pepper
1 egg
1 tablespoon grated Parmesan cheese
$2^1/2$ cups tomato sauce (pages 583–585 or store-bought)
9 lasagna noodles, cooked until pliable
$1^1/2$ cups shredded reduced-fat mozzarella

1) Preheat the oven to 350°F.

2) Steam or microwave the carrots and broccoli in separate containers. Drain and set aside.

3) Combine the ricotta, garlic, salt, pepper, egg, and Parmesan. Divide this cheese mixture in half. Combine one half with the broccoli and the other with the carrots.

4) Spread 1 cup of the tomato sauce in the bottom of a shallow, rectangular baking dish, about 9×13 inches. Lay down 3 of the noodles and spread the carrot mixture over them. Lay down another 3 noodles and spread the broccoli mixture on top. Lay down the last 3 noodles, cover with the remaining tomato sauce, and sprinkle the mozzarella on top.

5) Bake for 45 minutes. Tent foil over the lasagna if the cheese browns before 30 minutes.

Per Serving: Calories 220; Protein 14g; Fat 6g (Saturated 3g); Carbohydrates 27g; Fiber 3g; Sodium 534mg

Mushroom Lasagna

Makes: 9 servings

Because mushrooms sweat out liquid as they cook, it is important for them to be cooked and drained before being added to the lasagna. Without that step the lasagna will be watery.

1¹/2 pounds lowfat ricotta

2 egg whites

¹/8 cup grated Parmesan cheese

1 tablespoon minced fresh chives

1 tablespoon minced fresh parsley

¹/4 teaspoon freshly ground black pepper

1 cup minced onions

¹/4 cup red wine

6 cups sliced mushrooms (about 1¹/2 pounds)

4 cups tomato sauce (pages 583–585 or store-bought)

One 10-ounce package lasagna noodles, cooked until pliable

¹/2 cup shredded reduced-fat mozzarella

1) Preheat the oven to 350°F. Mix together the ricotta, egg whites, and Parmesan. Stir in the chives, parsley, and pepper.

2) Simmer the onions in the wine until they are very soft. Keep the pot covered in between stirrings.

3) Add the mushrooms to the onions and cook, uncovered, until they wilt and are reduced by half. This step will take about 5 minutes. Drain the vegetables and discard the liquid.

4) Combine the cheese mixture and all but ¹/4 cup of the mushrooms.

5) Spread 2 cups of the tomato sauce in the bottom of a rectangular baking pan, about 9×13 inches. Layer in this order: noodles, cheese, noodles, cheese, noodles, remaining tomato sauce.

6) Distribute the reserved mushrooms on the top. Distribute the mozzarella across the lasagna.

7) Bake, tented with foil, for 1 hour. Uncover and cook for 5 minutes longer. Remove from the oven and let rest for 10 minutes before cutting.

Per Serving: Calories 274; Protein 15g; Fat 6g (Saturated 3g); Carbohydrates 37g; Fiber 3g; Sodium 228mg

Spinach Manicotti

Makes: 4 servings

Use a spaghetti sauce with lots of flavor.

9 manicotti noodles

One 10-ounce package frozen chopped spinach, thawed and drained

2 cups lowfat ricotta cheese

$1/2$ cup minced onions

1 teaspoon kosher salt

$1/2$ teaspoon freshly ground pepper

3 tablespoons grated Parmesan cheese

2 cups tomato or spaghetti sauce

$1/4$ cup shredded reduced-fat mozzarella cheese

1) Cook the manicotti noodles in a large pot of boiling water until flexible and cooked through but not soft. When ready, lift out of the boiling water and lay on a clean cloth kitchen towel. Preheat the oven to 350°F. Have a 9×13-inch pan on hand, either nonstick or coated with nonstick spray.

2) Squeeze all the excess moisture out of the spinach. Combine the spinach with the ricotta, onions, salt, pepper, and Parmesan.

3) Spoon the filling into the manicotti noodles, or use a pastry bag fitted with a large nib. Place the manicotti in the baking pan in one layer, touching each other but not crowded together. Pour the tomato sauce over the noodles. This amount will lightly cover most but not all of the pasta. Distribute the mozzarella on top.

4) Bake for 30 to 35 minutes until bubbly.

Per Serving: Calories 356; Protein 23g; Fat 8g (Saturated 5g); Carbohydrates 46g; Fiber 3g; Sodium 1480mg

Ravioli

Sheets or squares of fresh pasta are needed to make ravioli. But even if you don't make your own or can't find fresh pasta at a store, it doesn't mean that you can't have homemade ravioli. Won ton or eggroll wrappers, which are available in many produce departments, make excellent ravioli. They come in vacuum-packed packages of between 40 to 60 sheets. The eggroll wrappers will need to be cut in half but the won ton wrappers are already the right size.

Filling raviolis does take time, but the work will go smoothly if you set it up like a production line. Have the filling in a bowl and water in another. Get out a teaspoon, a fork, and a pastry brush. Generously flour 2 cookie sheets and set them near your work space. Won ton wrappers dry out quickly, so keep the opened package covered with a damp cloth towel.

Lay out 4 won ton wrappers in a line. Place about a teaspoon of filling in the center of each (or 2 teaspoons for large ravioli). Using the pastry brush, dampen the edges lightly with water. Fold the wrapper over to form a triangle, press the edges together with your fingers, and then seal them by pressing with the tines of the fork. Set each ravioli on a floured baking sheet, not touching each other. Keep covered with a damp towel to prevent dryness and cracking. Continue until the filling is used up.

Boil water in a large, wide-mouthed pot. Using a slotted spoon, drop in the ravioli one at a time. They will sink, then float up from the bottom. Don't crowd the ravioli; cook only a few at a time. In about 3 minutes, when they puff out, they are done. Serve immediately.

Uncooked ravioli can be frozen. First freeze, uncovered, on the cookie sheets until solid.

Then remove and store in a freezer bag. Boil frozen ravioli unthawed. Like fresh, they will take about 3 minutes to cook.

Top cooked ravioli with tomato sauce, toss with pesto, or serve in a bowl of homemade chicken broth.

Cheese Ravioli

Makes: 5 servings

These are your basic cheese ravioli. Funny, though, how I don't like the frozen ones but love these.

1 egg
1 egg white
1 pound reduced-fat ricotta cheese
1/4 cup goat's milk cheese
3 tablespoons grated Parmesan cheese
1/4 teaspoon freshly ground pepper
45 won ton wrappers or ravioli pasta squares

With a fork, mash together the filling ingredients. Follow directions in Ravioli, opposite.

Per Serving: Calories 366; Protein 20g; Fat 9g (Saturated 5g); Carbohydrates 47g; Fiber 1g; Sodium 264mg

Ricotta with Herb Ravioli

Makes: 5 servings

These ravioli have so much flavor that they are best paired with a light tomato sauce.

1 pound reduced-fat ricotta cheese
1/4 cup grated Parmesan cheese
2 tablespoons grated Romano cheese
2 egg whites
2 cloves garlic, minced
1 tablespoon dried basil
2 teaspoons dried oregano
1/2 teaspoon ground rosemary
1/2 teaspoon dried thyme
2 tablespoons fresh chopped parsley
2 tablespoons minced fresh chives or scallions
40 won ton wrappers or ravioli pasta squares

1) Combine the cheeses and egg whites. Stir until well blended. Mix in the remaining filling ingredients.

2) Follow directions in Ravioli, opposite.

Per Serving: Calories 321; Protein 18g; Fat 7g (Saturated 4g); Carbohydrates 43g; Fiber 2g; Sodium 267mg

Spinach and Mushroom Ravioli

Makes: 5 servings

You can reapeat the mushroom theme by topping these with Mushroom and Tomato Sauce (page 290).

1 tablespoon olive oil
2 cloves garlic, minced
4 shallots, minced ($1/2$ cup)
8 ounces mushrooms, stems discarded,
     finely chopped
One 10-ounce package frozen chopped spinach,
     thawed and squeezed dry
$1/2$ cup lowfat or reduced-fat ricotta cheese
2 tablespoons grated Parmesan cheese
$1/2$ teaspoon kosher salt
$1/4$ teaspoon freshly ground pepper
$1/8$ teaspoon ground nutmeg
2 egg whites
45 won ton wrappers or ravioli pasta squares

1) In a sauté pan, heat the oil and cook the garlic and shallots until golden. Stir in the mushrooms and cook until they wilt. Remove from the heat and let cool to room temperature.

2) Put the remaining ingredients, except the won tons, in a bowl and combine. Stir in the sautéed vegetables.

3) Follow directions in Ravioli, page 282.

Per Serving: Calories 311; Protein 15g; Fat 6g (Saturated 2g); Carbohydrates 50g; Fiber 4g; Sodium 373mg

Pumpkin Ravioli

Makes: 6 servings

Excellent served in a pool of homemade chicken broth and topped with a dab of pesto.

1 teaspoon vegetable oil
$1/2$ cup chopped onions
2 cloves garlic, minced
1 medium russet potato, cooked and peeled
One 15-ounce can pumpkin (about 2 cups)
1 teaspoon dried sage
$1/8$ teaspoon ground nutmeg
$1/2$ teaspoon kosher salt
$1/2$ cup grated Parmesan cheese
2 tablespoons chopped fresh parsley
54 won ton wrappers or ravioli pasta squares

1) In a small sauté pan, heat the oil and cook the onions and garlic until golden.

2) With a fork, mash the potato and pumpkin. Stir in the sautéed onions and garlic and blend in the remaining filling ingredients.

3) Follow directions in Ravioli, page 282.

Per Serving: Calories 310; Protein 12g; Fat 5g (Saturated 2g); Carbohydrates 55g; Fiber 4g; Sodium 366mg

Stovetop Cooking

Asparagus and Spaghetti

Makes: 3 servings

Snap off the tough ends of the asparagus so they'll be tender all the way through.

10 stalks asparagus

1/2 pound spaghetti (4 cups cooked)

1 tablespoon Garlic Oil (page 607), or 1 tablespoon vegetable oil plus 1/2 teaspoon minced garlic

One 8-ounce package fancy mushrooms, such as cremini or oyster, thickly sliced (about 2 cups)

1/3 cup reduced-sodium, defatted chicken broth

2 tablespoons minced fresh parsley

1 teaspoon lemon juice

1/2 teaspoon kosher salt, or more to taste

1/8 teaspoon freshly ground pepper, or more to taste

Grated Parmesan cheese, for garnish

1) Cut the asparagus on the diagonal into 1- to 2-inch pieces. Steam or microwave the asparagus pieces about 3 minutes, until they turn a brighter green and become slightly tender, then immerse in a bowl of cold water to stop the cooking. Drain. This can be done up to a day ahead of time.

2) Cook the pasta.

3) While the pasta is cooking, heat the oil in a sauté pan. Sauté the mushrooms in the oil. When they begin to wilt, add the broth. Cook for another 2 minutes at a temperature high enough that the broth bubbles.

4) Gently mix in the asparagus, parsley, lemon juice, salt, and pepper, then toss with the pasta. It can be difficult to distribute vegetables evenly among the spaghetti strands. I use spring-loaded tongs to pick up and separate the pasta. When putting the pasta on individual dinner plates, place a few asparagus nibs on top of each serving. Garnish with Parmesan cheese and serve immediately.

Per Serving: Calories 354; Protein 13g; Fat 6g (Saturated 1g); Carbohydrates 63g; Fiber 4g; Sodium 384mg

Basil and Broccoli Ziti

Makes: 3 servings

If you don't have a food processor, use a blender or mortar and pestle to make the basil puree.

1/2 pound ziti or other tubular or stubby pasta
    (4 cups cooked)
2 cloves garlic, peeled
2 tablespoons olive oil
2 tablespoons water
1 cup fresh basil, packed down
3 cups broccoli florets, lightly steamed
1 cup roasted red peppers, julienned
1/2 teaspoon kosher salt, or more to taste
1/4 teaspoon freshly ground pepper
Grated Parmesan cheese, for garnish (optional)

1) Cook the pasta.

2) Meanwhile, with the food processor running, drop in the garlic. Pour in the oil and water. Scrape down the sides. Add the basil. Process until the basil is finely minced.

3) Put the pasta, broccoli, roasted peppers, salt, and pepper in a large sauté pan and warm over medium heat.

4) Pour the basil puree over the pasta. Toss well. Heat until all is warm. Serve immediately. Garnish each plate with Parmesan cheese, if desired.

Per Serving: Calories 392; Protein 12g; Fat 11g (Saturated 1g); Carbohydrates 63g; Fiber 4g; Sodium 339mg

Broccoli and Garlic Pasta for One

Makes: 1 serving

This meal is perfect for a person dining alone and is a good way to use leftover pasta and steamed broccoli.

1 tablespoon chopped onions
1 to 2 cloves garlic, minced
1 teaspoon olive oil
1 tablespoon white wine
1/4 cup reduced-sodium, defatted chicken or
    vegetable broth
1 cup broccoli spears or florets
2 cups cooked pasta
1/4 teaspoon kosher salt
1/8 teaspoon freshly ground pepper
2 teaspoons grated Parmesan or Romano cheese

1) Sauté the onions and garlic in the oil over low heat until the onions become translucent.

2) Add the wine, broth, and broccoli. Cover and cook until the broccoli turns bright green.

3) Toss the pasta with the broccoli and cook until both are thoroughly hot and the broccoli is tender.

4) Season with the salt and pepper. Put on a dinner plate and dust with cheese.

Per Serving: Calories 473; Protein 17g; Fat 8g (Saturated 2g); Carbohydrates 81g; Fiber 5g; Sodium 694mg

Walnut Linguine

Makes: 6 servings

Walnuts are less expensive when purchased in bulk, but they go rancid quickly. Keep them fresh double-bagged in the freezer.

1 pound linguine
$1^1/2$ tablespoons olive oil
5 cloves garlic, minced
1 cup diced tomatoes (drained if canned)
$1/3$ cup chopped fresh parsley
$1/4$ cup chopped fresh basil
$1/2$ teaspoon kosher salt
$1/4$ teaspoon freshly ground pepper
$1/2$ cup chopped walnuts, lightly toasted
$1/3$ cup grated Parmesan cheese, divided

1) Cook the pasta in plenty of boiling water. Just before it is finished cooking, scoop out $1/4$ cup of the pasta cooking water. You will be adding this starchy water to the sauce later. Drain the pasta, but do not rinse. Put it in a large serving bowl.

2) While the pasta is cooking, heat the oil in a large skillet. Cook the garlic over moderate-low heat until golden. Stir in the tomatoes and cook until softened. Stir in the parsley and basil. Add the pasta cooking water, salt, and pepper. Pour this sauce over the cooked pasta.

3) Toss in the nuts and half the cheese. Dust the top of the pasta with the remaining cheese and serve immediately.

Per Serving: Calories 412; Protein 14g; Fat 13g (Saturated 2g); Carbohydrates 61g; Fiber 3g; Sodium 275mg

Greens and Pasta

Makes: 2 servings

Use any type of greens for this, but kale or Swiss chard are especially good. I cook this in my wok because it is large enough to hold the greens, which take up a lot of space when raw.

$1/2$ pound greens, finely chopped (4 cups)
$1^1/4$ cups reduced-sodium, defatted chicken or vegetable broth
3 whole canned tomatoes, with 1 tablespoon juice
1 teaspoon Garlic Oil (page 607)
3 cups cooked pasta
$1/8$ teaspoon crushed red pepper flakes
$1/4$ teaspoon kosher salt
Grated Parmesan cheese (optional)

1) Please read the note on preparing greens on page 337. Simmer the greens in the broth for about 15 minutes. (Large leaves of kale can be tough and might need to be cooked an extra 5 minutes.)

2) Using your hands, crush the tomatoes directly into the pot.

3) Stir in the oil. Toss in the pasta, pepper flakes, and salt. Stir until everything is heated through.

4) Dust with Parmesan cheese, if desired.

Per Serving: Calories 317; Protein 14g; Fat 4g (Saturated 1g); Carbohydrates 58g; Fiber 5g; Sodium 732mg

Pasta with Vegetables and Feta

Makes: 3 servings

Unlike many cheeses, feta does not melt or bind ingredients together. Instead, it is valued for its sharp flavor and is added at the end of the recipe, when it is heated through until the outside edges soften.

1/2 pound pasta, preferably a short, fat type like rigatoni (4 cups cooked)

1 tablespoon olive oil

1/2 cup sliced red onions

1 clove garlic, minced

1 small carrot, peeled and cut into matchsticks or thin half circles

1/4 cup reduced-sodium, defatted chicken or vegetable broth

1 small zucchini, cut into matchsticks or thin half circles

1/2 cup fresh or frozen peas (if frozen, defrost before using)

1 tablespoon minced fresh parsley

1 1/2 teaspoons dried basil

1/2 teaspoon dried oregano

1 teaspoon kosher salt

1/4 teaspoon freshly ground pepper

1/2 cup feta cheese, crumbled into small cubes (about 2 ounces)

1) Cook the pasta. If it is done at the same time as the sautéed vegetables, drain it and add it to the vegetables (in Step 4). If the pasta is ready early, to prevent it from sticking together, drain from the cooking water, immerse it in cold water, then drain again.

2) Heat the oil in a large nonstick sauté pan over low heat. Sauté the onions, garlic, and carrot in the oil. Cover between stirrings so that the steam helps to soften the carrots. Cook for about 5 minutes, until the carrots are tender.

3) Add the broth and zucchini. Continue to cook, covered, until the zucchini is tender but not mushy.

4) Stir in the pasta, peas, herbs, salt, and pepper. Increase the heat to medium. Stir constantly until all of the ingredients are hot. Toss in the feta and serve as soon as the outside edges of the cheese cubes begin to melt.

Per Serving: Calories 428; Protein 16g; Fat 10g (Saturated 4g); Carbohydrates 68g; Fiber 5g; Sodium 908mg

Pasta with Sun-Dried Tomato Pesto

Makes: 4 servings

A short, nubby pasta will be the easiest to toss with the pesto and broccoli. I've found that when spaghetti is used most of the florets end up in the bottom of the serving bowl.

12 ounces pasta
3 cups broccoli florets
2/3 cup Sun-Dried Tomato Pesto (page 591)
2 tablespoons chopped fresh parsley
Kosher salt, to taste
Freshly ground pepper, to taste
1 tablespoon grated Parmesan cheese

1) Cook the pasta. At the same time, lightly steam the broccoli.

2) Drain the pasta and immediately toss with the pesto, broccoli, and parsley. Taste and add salt and pepper, if desired. Garnish with Parmesan cheese.

Per Serving: Calories 378; Protein 14g; Fat 4g (Saturated 1g); Carbohydrates 71g; Fiber 4g; Sodium 210mg

Spinach and Friends

Makes: 2 servings

If you can find it, buy flat, broad-leafed spinach.

1/2 pound fresh spinach
1 1/2 tablespoons olive oil
2 cloves garlic, minced
1/2 pound fresh, very ripe tomatoes, peeled and thickly sliced
1/4 teaspoon kosher salt
1/4 teaspoon freshly ground pepper, or more to taste
4 ounces pasta (short and nubby is best)
Grated Parmesan cheese, for garnish (optional)

1) Wash the spinach well, but do not dry thoroughly. The water clinging to the leaves will be the liquid that it is cooked in. Remove the tough stems.

2) Heat the oil in a pot large enough to hold all of the spinach. Sauté the garlic until golden.

3) Put in the spinach, cover, and cook briefly until wilted. Stir once or twice during cooking.

4) Add the tomatoes and cook until softened. Stir in the salt and pepper and keep the sauce warm on a low heat.

5) Cook the pasta. As soon as it is done, drain and toss with the sauce.

6) Dust Parmesan cheese on top of each individual serving, if desired.

Per Serving: Calories 354; Protein 12g; Fat 12g (Saturated 2g); Carbohydrates 53g; Fiber 6g; Sodium 344mg

Shells with Broccoli and Chickpeas

Makes: 4 servings

Red onion is used here for its milder flavor and attractive color. Sometimes paying attention to these seemingly small details makes a world of difference to a recipe.

3 cups broccoli florets, lightly steamed or blanched
1/2 pound small pasta shells
1 tablespoon olive oil
1/2 cup sliced red onions
3 cloves garlic, minced
One 14 1/2-ounce can whole tomatoes, drained and chopped
1 cup cooked chickpeas, rinsed and drained
1/2 teaspoon kosher salt
1/4 teaspoon freshly ground pepper
1/8 teaspoon crushed red pepper flakes
1 tablespoon fresh chopped basil or 1 1/2 teaspoons dried
Crumbled feta cheese or grated Romano cheese, for garnish (optional)

1) Put a pot of water up to boil. This can be used first to blanch the broccoli and then to cook the shells. (I use a metal basket to hold the florets so they are easy to remove after their brief cooking.)

2) As the pot of water is coming to a boil, heat the oil in a large, heavy-bottomed pot and sauté the onions and garlic over moderate heat until the onions soften and turn golden. Keep covered between stirrings. Stir in the broccoli and remaining ingredients except the cheese. Simmer gently.

3) Just before the pasta is finished cooking, scoop out 1/4 cup of the boiling water (use a heat-proof glass measuring cup) and add it to the vegetables. When the pasta is ready, drain and put it in a large pasta serving bowl. Add the sauce and toss. Top with the feta cheese or Romano, if desired.

Per Serving: Calories 342; Protein 13g; Fat 6g (Saturated 1g); Carbohydrates 61g; Fiber 5g; Sodium 372mg

Mushroom and Tomato Sauce over Pasta

Makes: 4 servings

This is a thick and hearty tomato sauce. Make a double batch and freeze the extra (without the pasta) and use to top ravioli or for Mushroom Lasagna (page 281), or for another dinner of spaghetti and sauce.

1 tablespoon olive oil
1 cup chopped onions
2 cloves garlic, minced
4 cups thickly sliced mushrooms (about 1 pound)
1/3 cup red wine
1/4 cup chopped fresh parsley
One 28-ounce can whole tomatoes, coarsely chopped, with juice
2 bay leaves
1 tablespoon dried basil, or 3 tablespoons fresh
2 teaspoons drained capers
1 1/2 teaspoons soy sauce
Freshly ground pepper to taste
12 ounces rotini or other pasta

1) Heat the oil in a medium-size pot. Sauté the onions and garlic in the oil until the onions turn lightly golden. Add the mushrooms and wine, cover, and cook until the mushrooms soften. Stir occasionally.

2) Add the remaining ingredients except the pasta. Cover and simmer for 1 hour. Taste and adjust the pepper if desired.

3) Meanwhile, heat a large pot of water to boiling. About 10 minutes before serving, begin to cook the pasta. When cooked to desired consistency, drain, top with the sauce, and serve immediately.

Per Serving: Calories 439; Protein 15g; Fat 6g (Saturated 1g); Carbohydrates 81g; Fiber 6g; Sodium 518mg

Spaghetti alla Puttanesca

Makes: 6 servings

Puttanesca is spicy, with so much presence that you never notice that there isn't any meat in the sauce.

1 pound spaghetti
1 teaspoon olive oil
2 cloves garlic, minced
1/2 teaspoon crushed red pepper flakes
One 28-ounce can crushed tomatoes
1/4 cup brine-cured olives, pitted and chopped
1 tablespoon drained capers
1 teaspoon dried oregano
1 1/2 teaspoons anchovy paste
1 teaspoon dried basil
2 tablespoons chopped fresh parsley

1) Cook the spaghetti.

2) Meanwhile, heat the oil in a saucepan. Sauté the garlic until it turns golden, but not brown. Stir in the pepper flakes and cook for 1 minute longer. Add the remaining ingredients except the parsley. Simmer this sauce until the pasta is ready (but at least 10 minutes).

3) Drain the pasta, put it in a serving bowl, and toss in the sauce and the parsley. Serve immediately.

Per Serving: Calories 339; Protein 12g; Fat 4g (Saturated 1g); Carbohydrates 63g; Fiber 3g; Sodium 561mg

Spaghetti with Eggplant and Tomato Sauce

Makes: 6 servings

The eggplant flavor shines through here, so try to purchase eggplants that taste sharp yet sweet. It can be hard to tell without cutting one open and tasting, but the appearance of the eggplant yields clues to what is inside. Look for shiny skins with no soft or wrinkled spots. Also, it should feel heavy in the hand (lighter ones might be dried out or filled with seeds).

1 pound eggplant
1 1/2 tablespoons olive oil, divided
1 teaspoon kosher salt
1 cup chopped onions
3 cloves garlic, minced
One 28-ounce can whole tomatoes, with juice
1/8 teaspoon crushed red pepper flakes, or more to taste
1/4 teaspoon freshly ground pepper
1 pound spaghetti
Grated Parmesan or Romano cheese, for garnish

1) Preheat the oven to 400°F. Cut the eggplant into 1-inch cubes. Toss with 1 tablespoon of the oil and all of the salt. Place in a rimmed baking sheet, one layer deep. Bake for 15 minutes. Turn the eggplant cubes over with a metal spatula and bake for 5 minutes more, or until the eggplant is very tender and browned in places.

2) Meanwhile, bring a large pot of water to a boil, but don't begin cooking the spaghetti until the sauce is simmering.

3) In a large, nonstick skillet, heat the remaining oil. Sauté the onions and garlic over medium heat until it turns golden, about 5 to 7 minutes. Pour in the juice from the canned tomatoes, then squeeze the tomatoes with your hands, breaking them into chunks as you put them in the pot.

4) Add the pepper flakes and ground pepper, stir in the baked eggplant, and simmer, covered, for about 12 minutes, or until the pasta is cooked.

5) While the sauce is simmering, cook the spaghetti, then drain and place in a serving bowl. Toss in the sauce and serve immediately. Serve with grated Parmesan or Romano cheese, if desired.

Per Serving: Calories 369; Protein 12g; Fat 5g (Saturated 1g); Carbohydrates 70g; Fiber 5g; Sodium 544mg

Penne with Mushrooms, Beans, and Tomato Sauce

Makes: 6 servings

White beans have a milder flavor than the darker varieties (like pinto and kidney beans) and are necessary for this recipe.

2 teaspoons olive oil
1 cup chopped onions
4 cloves garlic, minced
8 ounces mushrooms (about 2 cups), sliced
One 28-ounce can whole tomatoes, with juice
2 cups cooked navy or cannellini beans, drained and rinsed
1 teaspoon dried sage
1 teaspoon kosher salt
1/4 teaspoon freshly ground pepper, or more to taste
1/4 cup chopped fresh parsley
1 pound penne

1) Heat the oil in a heavy-bottomed pot. Sauté the onions and garlic in the oil. Add the mushrooms and sauté until they wilt.

2) Break up the tomatoes with your hands as you add them to the pot. Stir in the beans, sage, salt, and pepper. Simmer over medium heat for 15 minutes. Add the parsley and cook for 5 minutes longer.

3) Meanwhile, cook the penne. Drain and top with the sauce. Serve immediately.

Per Serving: Calories 431; Protein 18g; Fat 4g (Saturated 1g); Carbohydrates 83g; Fiber 9g; Sodium 546mg

Penne with Vegetables and Ricotta Sauce

Makes: 4 servings

Health experts suggest that meat eaters should try to eat a couple of vegetarian meals a week. One-dish pasta suppers like this make it easy.

1 1/2 teaspoons olive oil
1/2 cup sliced onions
2 small zucchini or summer squash, julienned
    (about 2 cups)
1 clove garlic, minced
1 1/2 cups diced tomatoes, or one 16-ounce
    can, drained
1/2 pound reduced-fat ricotta cheese (about 1 cup)
1 tablespoon chopped fresh basil, or
    1 teaspoon dried
1 tablespoon chopped fresh parsley
1 teaspoon lemon juice
1/2 teaspoon kosher salt
1/4 teaspoon freshly ground pepper, or more
    to taste
12 ounces penne or other medium-size
    tubular pasta
2 tablespoons grated Parmesan cheese

1) Start heating a large pot of water to boiling. Meanwhile, heat the oil in a nonstick sauté pan. Sauté the onions, zucchini, and garlic until the onions turn golden. Stir in the tomatoes and cook 1 minute more. Set aside.

2) Stir together the ricotta, basil, parsley, lemon juice, salt, and pepper.

3) Cook the pasta. When almost done, scoop out 1/2 cup of the pasta water and stir it into the ricotta mixture.

4) Drain the pasta, then immediately put it back into the pot. Stir in the ricotta sauce and the vegetables. Put into a serving bowl. Dust with Parmesan cheese.

Per Serving: Calories 431; Protein 18g; Fat 7g (Saturated 2g); Carbohydrates 73g; Fiber 4g; Sodium 364mg

Peanut Butter Noodles

Makes: 4 servings

Because this recipe is tasty both warm or at room temperature, it is a good make-ahead meal for a busy summer evening.

1/2 pound spaghetti or Asian noodles
1 cup snow peas, trimmed and stringed
    if necessary
1 carrot, peeled and diced or grated
3 scallions, sliced
2 teaspoons soy sauce
1 teaspoon honey
1 1/2 teaspoons rice vinegar or white wine vinegar
1/4 cup unsalted, unsweetened peanut butter
1/4 cup water
1 clove garlic, peeled
1/16 teaspoon crushed red pepper flakes, or more
    to taste
2 tablespoons chopped dry roasted peanuts, for
    garnish (optional)

1) Cook and drain the pasta. Immerse in a bowl of cold water, then drain. (Rinsing the pasta is essential, otherwise the dish will be sticky and will quickly dry out.)

2) Blanch (immerse briefly in boiling water) the snow peas and carrot. Rinse them under cool water to stop the cooking. The vegetables should be crunchy and colorful, yet not taste or feel raw. Toss them with the pasta. Add the scallions.

3) In a blender, puree the soy sauce, honey, vinegar, peanut butter, water, garlic, and pepper flakes. Pour the sauce over the pasta and vegetables. Toss to combine. Serve at room temperature or warmed in the microwave. If desired, garnish with chopped peanuts.

Per Serving: Calories 338; Protein 13g; Fat 9g (Saturated 1g); Carbohydrates 53g; Fiber 4g; Sodium 186mg

Spaghetti Pie

Makes: 6 servings

Transform leftover spaghetti into a delicious meal with this simple recipe.

4 egg whites
1 whole egg
One 14 1/2-ounce can whole tomatoes, drained,
    seeded, and chopped
1/4 cup grated Romano cheese
1/4 cup chopped fresh parsley
1/2 teaspoon kosher salt
1/4 teaspoon freshly ground pepper
1 teaspoon dried basil
1/2 pound spaghetti, cooked

1) Preheat the oven to 400°F.

2) Lightly beat together the egg whites and egg. Add each remaining ingredient one at a time, stirring after each, to ensure that all is completely mixed.

2) Coat with cooking spray a 10- or 12-inch nonstick pan with an ovenproof handle. Place over moderate-high heat and pour in the spaghetti batter. Cook for about 4 to 6 minutes, until the bottom is lightly brown and the eggs set about halfway through.

3) Place the skillet in the oven and bake until the eggs set and the top lightly browns, about 4 minutes. Remove from the oven with very good oven mitts (the handle will be very hot). Slip onto a serving dish.

Per Serving: Calories 191; Protein 10g; Fat 3g (Saturated 1g); Carbohydrates 31g; Fiber 1g; Sodium 338mg

Vegetable Fajitas

Makes: 6 fajitas; serves 3

You can make this recipe even easier by purchasing sliced peppers and onions at a salad bar and buying the carrot sticks in bags. Also, since this recipe uses broccoli stalks, plan to make it the same week you prepare another dish that requires only florets.

1 large carrot, cut into sticks
1 large broccoli stalk, peeled and cut into sticks
1 tablespoon vegetable oil
2 cups sliced red onions
2 cloves garlic, minced
3 large bell peppers, preferably assorted
    colors, sliced
1 medium zucchini, cut into sticks
1 teaspoon chili powder
1 jalapeño (fresh or pickled), seeded and minced
$1/2$ to 1 teaspoon kosher salt
2 tablespoons lemon juice
2 tablespoons fresh lime juice
6 large flour tortillas

Toppings
Salsa
Guacamole
Reduced-fat sour cream
Shredded reduced-fat jack cheese

1) Blanch the carrot and broccoli until fork-tender.

2) Heat the oil in a large, nonstick skillet or large wok. Sauté the carrot, broccoli, onions, garlic, bell peppers, and zucchini until the onions turn golden. Keep covered while sautéing, but look in and stir frequently. Stir in the chili powder, jalapeño, and salt. Cook for 1 minute. Pour in the lemon and lime juices. Cook for 3 minutes more.

3) Meanwhile, warm the tortillas by cooking in a dry nonstick skillet for 1 minute on each side. Or wrap in foil and warm in a 300°F oven.

4) Serve all of the components of the fajitas in separate bowls and platters. Each person takes a tortilla, fills it with the sautéed vegetables, rolls it up, and tops it with the garnishes of choice.

Per Serving: Calories 370; Protein 10g; Fat 10g (Saturated 2g); Carbohydrates 62g; Fiber 8g; Sodium 696mg

Stir-Fries and Dumplings

Ginger Greens Dumpling Rolls

Makes: 4 servings

Serve with several other dishes, such as Velvet Corn Soup (page 146) and Shrimp Fried Rice (page 259).

1/2 cup cellophane or rice noodles

1 teaspoon vegetable oil

1/2 cup chopped shiitake mushroom caps (about 2 large)

2 cups finely chopped bok choy, including the green tops

1 egg, lightly beaten

2 teaspoons finely grated fresh ginger

2 scallions, thinly sliced

1/2 cup bean sprouts

1 tablespoon soy sauce

1/2 teaspoon mirin or sweet sherry

1/2 teaspoon Asian sesame oil

8 eggroll wrappers

1) Cook or soak the noodles according to the package directions. Drain. Chop into 1-inch lengths.

2) Heat the oil in a wok or sauté pan. Cook the mushrooms and bok choy over medium-high heat, covered, until the cabbage wilts. Stir frequently. Pour in the egg and stir until cooked. Add the ginger, scallions, and bean sprouts. Cook 2 minutes more. Put into a bowl and stir in the soy sauce, mirin, sesame oil, and noodles.

3) Open the package of eggroll wrappers, but keep it covered with a damp towel to prevent the wrappers from drying out as you work. Peel a wrapper from the block and set it on a clean, dry work surface, with one point toward you, like a diamond. Put 1/4 cup of filling in the center. Wet the edges of the wrapper. Fold the top point over the filling (but not all the way to the bottom point) then fold the 2 sides over the center (overlapping each other slightly), then roll the filled part down so that the bottom flap wraps around and the package becomes a tidy rectangle.

4) Line a steamer basket with parchment paper or lettuce or cabbage leaves. (This keeps the dumplings from sticking.) Set the filled dumplings in the basket over boiling water. Steam for 10 minutes. Or bake the dumplings on a baking sheet lined with parchment paper in a 350°F oven for 15 minutes.

5) They can be served at this point, or the wrappers can be crisped to a light brown by cooking them in a little oil (about a teaspoon) in a nonstick pan for 1 minute on each side.

6) Serve with a dipping sauce. (A selection of recipes appears on page 602.)

Per Serving: Calories 161; Protein 5g; Fat 3g (Saturated 1g); Carbohydrates 28g; Fiber 1g; Sodium 313mg

Chinese Dumpling Rolls

Makes: 4 servings

Although dumpling rolls take time to make, once you've tasted them, you'll agree that they are worth the trouble. Serve with a dipping sauce (see the selection on page 602), or a store-bought plum sauce.

1 teaspoon finely grated fresh ginger
2 scallions, thinly sliced
1/2 cup firm tofu, crumbled
1 cup shredded bok choy or other
    Chinese cabbage
1/2 cup fresh mung bean sprouts
1/2 cup sliced shiitake mushrooms,
    stems discarded
1 teaspoon Asian sesame oil
1/2 cup cooked brown rice
1 egg white, lightly beaten
1 tablespoon soy sauce
1/2 teaspoon mirin or sweet sherry
12 eggroll wrappers

1) Combine the ginger, scallions, tofu, bok choy, sprouts, and mushrooms. Heat a wok or skillet, add half the oil, and sauté until the cabbage softens.

2) Put the cooked vegetables into a bowl and stir in the remaining oil, rice, egg white, soy sauce, and mirin.

3) Using 3 tablespoons of filling per dumpling, fill and wrap as described in steps 3 through 6 of Ginger Greens Dumpling Rolls (opposite).

Per Serving: Calories 166; Protein 10g; Fat 5g (Saturated 1g); Carbohydrates 23g; Fiber 2g; Sodium 308mg

Sweet and Sour Tofu Stir-Fry

Makes: 4 servings

Even meat-loving teenagers love this recipe; just don't say a word about the tofu.

2 tablespoons honey
2 tablespoons ketchup
2 tablespoons rice vinegar or white wine vinegar
2 tablespoons soy sauce
One 8-ounce can pineapple chunks packed in
    juice, with juice
2 teaspoons cornstarch
2 tablespoons dry sherry
1 1/2 teaspoons vegetable oil
1/2 pound firm tofu, cut into small cubes
2 scallions, cut into 2-inch pieces
1 red bell pepper, cut into 1-inch pieces
3 cups broccoli florets, lightly steamed

1) In a small bowl, combine the honey, ketchup, vinegar, soy sauce, and pineapple. In another, small bowl, make a paste of the cornstarch and sherry.

2) Heat the oil in a large nonstick wok or sauté pan. Cook the tofu until it begins to brown on all sides. Add the scallions and bell pepper. Cook until the scallions wilt.

3) Pour the sauce ingredients into the wok. Stir the paste well and add to the wok. Add the broccoli. Simmer until the sauce thickens and clears and the broccoli softens a bit more. Serve over rice or noodles.

Per Serving: Calories (not including rice) 202; Protein 1g; Fat 7g (Saturated 1g); Carbohydrates 28g; Fiber 2g; Sodium 625mg

Hoisin Tofu Stir-Fry

Makes: 3 servings

As a time-saver, use a packaged slaw mix instead of the shredded cabbage.

1 tablespoon water
1 tablespoon soy sauce
2 tablespoons hoisin sauce
2 tablespoons dry sherry
1 teaspoon rice vinegar or white wine vinegar
1 teaspoon finely grated fresh ginger
2 cloves garlic, minced
1/4 teaspoon Tabasco sauce
1/2 pound firm tofu, cubed
1 1/2 teaspoons Asian sesame oil
2 cups shredded cabbage
1 cup snow peas, trimmed and strings removed
2 teaspoons cornstarch mixed with
    1 tablespoon water

1) Whisk together the water, soy sauce, hoisin, sherry, vinegar, ginger, garlic, and Tabasco. Toss in the tofu and marinate for at least 30 minutes or up to 1 day. (Keep refrigerated.)

2) Heat the oil in a wok. Remove the tofu from the marinade with a slotted spoon and put the tofu in the wok. Stir frequently and shake the pan to keep the cubes from sticking. When the tofu browns and becomes crispy in places, remove to a plate.

3) Stir in the cabbage and pour in the marinade. Stir-fry until wilted. Stir in the snow peas and cook 1 minute. Return the tofu to the wok and stir in the cornstarch. Cook until the sauce thickens, about 2 minutes more. Serve immediately over mounds of rice.

Per Serving: Calories 205; Protein 15g; Fat 10g (Saturated 1g); Carbohydrates 17g; Fiber 2g; Sodium 535mg

Stews and Chilis

Vegetables and Chickpeas over Couscous

Makes: 6 servings

This type of recipe—a vegetable stew—does not have to be followed exactly. If you're using a large, 19-ounce can of chickpeas, go ahead and use all 2 cups. If the head of cauliflower is small, add another vegetable or a sweet potato.

1 1/2 teaspoons kosher salt
1 teaspoon curry powder
1/2 teaspoon ground cumin
1 teaspoon ground coriander
1/4 teaspoon ground ginger
1 tablespoon olive oil
1 cup chopped onions
1 clove garlic, chopped
2 carrots, cut into 1/2-inch rounds
1 medium head cauliflower, cut into florets
1 1/2 cups cooked chickpeas, drained and rinsed
1 tablespoon lemon juice
3 cups reduced-sodium, defatted chicken broth
1/2 cup golden raisins
6 cups hot cooked couscous

1) Measure out the salt, curry powder, cumin, coriander, and ginger into a small bowl.

2) Heat the oil in a large, heavy-bottomed pot. Sauté the onions until they begin to change color. Stir in the spices and garlic and cook for 2 minutes longer.

3) Add the remaining ingredients except the raisins and couscous. Bring to a boil, reduce to a simmer, and cook, uncovered, for 10 minutes, or until the vegetables become tender. Stir in the raisins and cook for 5 minutes more. Serve over the couscous.

Per Serving: Calories 383; Protein 15g; Fat 4g (Saturated 1g); Carbohydrates 74g; Fiber 8g; Sodium 766mg

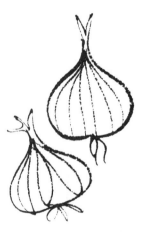

African Peanut Sauce

Makes: 5 servings

Because this recipe is made from pantry staples, and because it freezes well once prepared, it has become one of the standards in my kitchen.

1 1/2 teaspoons vegetable oil
1 cup chopped onions
2 cloves garlic, minced
2 teaspoons curry powder
1/2 teaspoon ground coriander
One 28-ounce can crushed tomatoes
1/2 teaspoon kosher salt
1/8 teaspoon crushed red pepper flakes
1/8 teaspoon Tabasco sauce
2 tablespoons unsalted, unsweetened
    peanut butter
1/4 cup unsalted roasted peanuts, coarsely
    chopped
6 cups cooked rice or pasta

1) Heat the oil in a heavy-bottomed pot. Sauté the onions and garlic in the oil until the onions are soft and golden.

2) Add the curry powder and coriander, and cook for 1 minute longer.

3) Stir in the tomatoes, salt, pepper flakes, and Tabasco. Cover and simmer over low heat for 15 minutes.

4) Stir in the peanut butter and peanuts. Cook for about 5 minutes longer, stirring frequently. The sauce is ready when it has thickened. Serve over rice or pasta.

Per Serving: Calories 461; Protein 11g; Fat 9g (Saturated 1g); Carbohydrates 84g; Fiber 4g; Sodium 454mg

Vegetable Gumbo

Makes: 5 servings

My husband, who grew up in New Orleans, declared, "Vegetable gumbo? No sausage, no meat?" It isn't traditional, but he did come back for second helpings. Filé powder, which is made of ground sassafras leaves, is a thickener that produces the gumbo texture. I get it in the South when we visit my husband's family. If filé powder is unavailable, leave it out. The results will be just as tasty, though a tad soupy.

1 cup chopped onions
2 cloves garlic, minced
2 tablespoons vegetable oil
3 tablespoons unbleached all-purpose white flour
2 cups reduced-sodium, defatted chicken or vegetable broth
3 ribs celery, chopped
1 green bell pepper, chopped
2 carrots, thickly sliced
1 small zucchini, thickly sliced
1 cup sliced okra (fresh or frozen)
1 cup corn kernels
One 14 1/2-ounce can diced tomatoes
One 8-ounce can tomato sauce
1 teaspoon paprika
1 teaspoon kosher salt
1/2 teaspoon freshly ground pepper
1/2 teaspoon dried thyme
1 teaspoon dried marjoram
2 bay leaves
1/4 teaspoon Tabasco sauce, or more to taste
2 tablespoons filé powder

1) In a heavy-bottomed soup pot, sauté the onions and garlic in the oil until the onions are lightly golden. Keep covered between stirrings.

2) Stirring constantly, add the flour into the pot, a tablespoon at a time. Cook until it turns light brown. Slowly stir in the broth, scraping the bottom of the pan with a wooden spatula or spoon.

3) Add the remaining ingredients except the filé powder. Bring to a boil, then immediately reduce to a simmer. Cover and simmer until the carrots are very soft, about 30 minutes.

4) Stir in the filé powder and simmer until thickened, about 2 minutes.

Per Serving: Calories 176; Protein 6g; Fat 7g (Saturated 1g); Carbohydrates 27g; Fiber 5g; Sodium 1010mg

Moroccan Vegetables

Makes: 4 servings

This recipe is flexible, and gives the cook a chance to use whatever vegetable is in the refrigerator. Green, leafy vegetables can be used, as well as harder veggies like broccoli, but if you use greens, you'll need 4 cups (not 1) because they shrink so much when cooked.

1 1/2 teaspoons olive oil
1 cup chopped onions
2 cloves garlic, minced
One 14 1/2-ounce can whole tomatoes
1 green bell pepper, cut into 1/2-inch pieces
1 teaspoon finely grated fresh ginger
3 tablespoons minced fresh parsley
2 carrots, cut into small pieces or rounds
1 cup cooked chickpeas, rinsed and drained
1 cup vegetable(s) of choice, such as broccoli or green beans
1 teaspoon paprika
1 cinnamon stick
1 teaspoon ground turmeric
1/2 teaspoon kosher salt
1/4 teaspoon freshly ground pepper
1 tablespoon lemon juice
1/16 teaspoon Tabasco sauce, or to taste
1 cup reduced-sodium, defatted chicken or vegetable broth or water

1) Heat the oil in a heavy-bottomed pot. Sauté the onions and garlic in the oil.

2) Add the tomatoes. Break them up with a spoon or spatula once they are in the pot.

3) Add the remaining ingredients. Bring the mixture to a boil, then simmer until the carrots are tender.

Per Serving: Calories 157; Protein 7g; Fat 3g (Saturated 0g); Carbohydrates 27g; Fiber 6g; Sodium 548mg

Belizean Bean and Vegetable Stew

Makes: 5 servings

Serve over rice or couscous, and pass bowls of raisins and toasted pine nuts as condiments.

2 teaspoons vegetable oil
1 cup chopped red onions
1 cup chopped onions
4 cloves garlic, minced
2 medium yellow squash, sliced into thick rounds
1 medium zucchini, sliced into thick rounds
1 cup baby-cut carrots, or 1 large carrot, cut into rounds
2 cups cooked red kidney beans, drained and rinsed
One 28-ounce can whole tomatoes, with juice
One 8-ounce can tomato sauce
1 teaspoon finely grated fresh ginger
2 teaspoons soy sauce
1 teaspoon dried oregano
1 teaspoon dried basil
1/2 teaspoon paprika
1 tablespoon honey
1/2 teaspoon Tabasco sauce, or more to taste
1 teaspoon kosher salt
1/4 teaspoon freshly ground pepper

1) Heat the oil in a heavy-bottomed pot. Sauté the onions and garlic in the oil.

2) Stir in the remaining ingredients. Bring the mixture to a boil, then simmer, covered, for 40 minutes.

Per Serving: Calories 230; Protein 11g; Fat 3g (Saturated 0g); Carbohydrates 44g; Fiber 11g; Sodium 1071mg

Chili

Makes: 5 servings

In some parts of the country, chili isn't considered authentic unless it is made with beef. But I'm not concerned with authenticity, just what tastes good—and this one is good.

1 cup chopped onions
2 cloves garlic, minced
2 tablespoons soy sauce
2 teaspoons vegetable oil
1/2 cup water
1 green bell pepper, chopped
3 tablespoons diced canned mild green
    chili peppers
1/2 teaspoon ground coriander
1 1/2 tablespoons chili powder, or more to taste
1/8 teaspoon cayenne pepper, or more to taste
1 teaspoon dried oregano
One 28-ounce can whole peeled tomatoes,
    with juice
4 cups cooked red kidney beans, drained and rinsed

1) In a medium saucepan, cook the onions and garlic in the soy sauce and oil. Add a little water if it begins to scorch. Stir in the bell pepper and the rest of the water and cook until soft. Stir in the chili peppers, spices, and oregano.

2) Pour the juice from the tomatoes into a bowl and reserve. Chop the tomatoes and add them to the pot. Add the beans.

3) Simmer for 45 minutes, or longer. After about 30 minutes of cooking, taste and adjust the seasonings. Chili powders vary greatly in strength; you might want to double the quantity suggested. If additional liquid is needed, use the juice from the canned tomatoes.

Per Serving: Calories 259; Protein 15g; Fat 3g (Saturated 0g); Carbohydrates 45g; Fiber 14g; Sodium 731mg

Black Bean Chili

Makes: 4 servings

One way to serve chili is on a tortilla, topped with salsa and lowfat sour cream.

2 teaspoons vegetable oil
1 medium yellow onion, chopped
2 cloves garlic, minced
2 carrots, peeled and chopped
1 green bell pepper, chopped
2 cups frozen or fresh corn kernels
4 cups black beans, drained and rinsed well
1 teaspoon ground coriander
1 tablespoon ground chili powder
3 tablespoons chopped canned mild green chilies
2 cups water

1) Heat the oil in a heavy-bottomed pot. Sauté the onions and garlic over moderate heat until the onions turn golden. Keep the pot covered between stirrings.

2) Stir in the carrots and bell pepper. Cook for 3 minutes.

3) Stir in the remaining ingredients and simmer, covered, over low heat for 30 minutes or up to 1 hour. Stir occasionally.

Per Serving: Calories 270; Protein 14g; Fat 5g (Saturated 0g); Carbohydrates 48g; Fiber 15g; Sodium 656mg

Mexican Mole Vegetarian Chili

Makes: 5 servings

The ingredient list is long, but that is mostly due to the spices. The preparation is easy.

1 tablespoon vegetable oil
2 cups chopped onions
4 cloves garlic, minced
1 large carrot, chopped
One 14^1/$_2$-ounce can tomato sauce
4 cups cooked kidney beans, drained and rinsed
4 cups tomato juice
1 cup fine bulgur wheat
^{1}/$_4$ teaspoon crushed red pepper flakes
1 tablespoon ground cumin
2 tablespoons ground chili powder
2 tablespoons unsweetened cocoa
1^1/$_2$ teaspoons ground cinnamon
2 teaspoons dried oregano
2 teaspoons kosher salt

1) Heat the oil in a large, heavy pot and sauté the onions, garlic, and carrot over moderate heat. Keep covered between stirrings. Cook until the onions soften and begin to change color, about 5 minutes.

2) Stir in the remaining ingredients. Bring to a boil and immediately reduce to a gentle simmer. Cover and cook for 1^1/$_2$ hours.

Per Serving: Calories 408; Protein 21g; Fat 5g (Saturated 1g); Carbohydrates 78g; Fiber 21g; Sodium 1982mg

Chickpea Curry

Makes: 5 servings

Have small bowls of condiments, such as raisins and nuts, Cucumber Raita (page 69) and a chutney (pages 594–596) on the table so diners may garnish their plates to their own liking. Always serve curry with rice.

2 teaspoons vegetable oil
3 cloves garlic, minced
2 teaspoons finely grated fresh ginger
1 to 2 leeks, white part only, washed well and minced
1^1/$_2$ cups peeled, grated butternut squash (easily grated in food processor)
1 carrot, shredded
2 medium all-purpose potatoes, peeled and cubed
2 cups water
4 cups cooked chickpeas, drained and rinsed
1^1/$_2$ to 2 teaspoons curry powder
^{1}/$_2$ teaspoon ground coriander
^{1}/$_8$ teaspoon cayenne pepper
^{1}/$_4$ teaspoon kosher salt
1 apple, peeled, cored, and chopped

1) Heat the oil in a large, heavy-bottomed pot. Sauté the garlic, ginger, and leeks in the oil over low heat until soft.

2) Add the squash, carrot, and potatoes. Pour in the water and simmer, covered, until the vegetables soften. If necessary, add more water so that the curry doesn't stick to the bottom of the pot.

3) Add the remaining ingredients except the apple and cook for 30 minutes longer.

4) Ten minutes before serving, add the apple. Taste and adjust the seasonings, if necessary.

Per Serving: Calories 359; Protein 15g; Fat 6g (Saturated 1g); Carbohydrates 66g; Fiber 11g; Sodium 125mg

Curried Sweet Potatoes and Greens

Makes: 4 servings

I prefer white-ribbed Swiss chard rather than red for this recipe because the red turns the dish light purple.

1¹/2 teaspoons vegetable oil

2 medium leeks, including the light green tops, washed well and chopped (1¹/2 cups)

3 cloves garlic, minced

¹/4 pound dark leafy greens, such as kale or Swiss chard

2 medium sweet potatoes, peeled and cubed (3 cups)

1 cup cooked chickpeas, rinsed and drained

4 cups reduced-sodium, defatted vegetable or chicken broth

2 teaspoons curry powder

¹/4 teaspoon ground coriander

¹/4 teaspoon turmeric

¹/2 teaspoon ground cumin

¹/16 teaspoon cayenne pepper

1¹/2 tablespoons soy sauce

1) Heat the oil in a sauté pan over low heat. Sauté the leeks and garlic in the oil. Keep the pan covered between stirrings. Cook for about 5 to 7 minutes, until the leeks are soft and turn a mellower color. Take care not to scorch the vegetables.

2) Meanwhile, wash the greens well. If you're using kale, cut out and discard the tough center rib. Chop the greens.

3) Add the remaining ingredients to the pot. Bring to a boil, then reduce to a simmer. Cover and cook for about 30 minutes, or until the sweet potatoes become soft.

Per Serving: Calories 285; Protein 11g; Fat 4g (Saturated 0g); Carbohydrates 54g; Fiber 9g; Sodium 900mg

Risottos

Risottos are Italian rice dishes that are simmered on the stovetop. They have a creamy texture that comes not from cream but from the rice itself. Risotto is made with Arborio rice, a short-grained Italian rice that cooks up starchy on the outside but has a chewy interior texture. American short-grain rices can be substituted, though they won't have the same feel.

Another difference between risotto and boiled rice is that twice as much liquid is used: four parts broth to one part rice, instead of two to one for boiled. The liquid, usually chicken broth, is added about a cup at a time and simmered until it cooks down before more is added. This contributes to the rich flavor and special texture. The broth is added hot. It can be warmed in a glass measuring cup in the microwave or heated on the stovetop.

Risottos have a reputation for being time-consuming, but the entire process takes only about 20 minutes. They do require stirring, but it is not constant and you can work on other recipes at the same time.

Risottos in restaurants are often filled with cheese and butter. Mine have a touch of these ingredients for flavor, but the fat numbers are still low. If desired, you can replace the butter with olive oil to reduce the saturated fat even further.

Parmesan Parsley Risotto

Makes: 3 servings

Risottos don't have to be filled with lots of different vegetables and ingredients. In this case, simple is sublime.

4 cups reduced-sodium, defatted chicken broth
1 1/2 teaspoons olive oil
1 tablespoon unsalted butter
2 shallots, chopped (about 2 to 3 tablespoons)
1 cup Arborio or other short-grain rice
2 tablespoons white wine
1/4 cup grated Parmesan cheese
1/2 teaspoon kosher salt
1/4 teaspoon freshly ground pepper
1/3 cup chopped fresh parsley

1) Heat the broth.

2) In a 2- or 3-quart heavy-bottomed pot, heat the oil and butter until the butter melts. Cook the shallots until golden, about 3 minutes. Add the rice and cook, stirring all the while, until the grains are shiny with oil. Pour in the wine.

3) Add about 1 cup of the broth, bring to a boil, reduce to a simmer, and stir until almost all of the liquid is absorbed. Pour in 1/2 cup of broth and stir and cook until the broth is absorbed. Continue to add the broth, 1/2 cup at a time, until all of the liquid is used up and the rice is creamy on the outside, but still a bit firm to the bite. This will take about 20 to 25 minutes.

4) Stir in the cheese, salt, pepper, and parsley and serve.

Per Serving: Calories 374; Protein 12g; Fat 9g (Saturated 4g); Carbohydrates 57g; Fiber 2g; Sodium 1122mg

Spinach Risotto

Makes: 3 servings

Frozen spinach is listed as a time-saver. Fresh spinach could be used, but it needs to be washed, trimmed of tough stems, wilted briefly in a sauté pan, chopped, and squeezed before adding to the risotto. Too much trouble for the average bagged spinach, but if baby spinach is at my grocer's I find it hard to resist, and use it here.

One 10-ounce package frozen spinach
4 cups reduced-sodium, defatted chicken broth
1 1/2 teaspoons olive oil
1 tablespoon unsalted butter
1 cup chopped onions
1 clove garlic, minced
1 cup Arborio or other short-grain rice
3 tablespoons white wine
1/4 cup grated Parmesan cheese
1/2 teaspoon kosher salt
1/4 teaspoon freshly ground pepper

1) Cook the spinach according to package directions. Drain, squeeze out as much water as possible, and chop.

2) Heat the broth.

3) In a 2 or 3 quart, heavy-bottomed pot, heat the oil and butter until the butter melts. Cook the onions and garlic until golden, about 3 minutes. Add the rice and cook, stirring all the while, until the grains are shiny with oil. Pour in the wine.

4) Add 1 cup of the broth, bring to a boil, reduce to a simmer, and stir until almost all of the liquid is absorbed. Pour in a 1/2 cup of broth and stir and cook until the broth is absorbed. Continue to do this, 1/2 cup at a time, until all of the liquid is used up and the rice is creamy on the outside, but still a bit firm to the bite. This will take about 20 to 25 minutes.

5) Stir in the cheese, salt, pepper, and spinach.

Per Serving: Calories 412; Protein 15g; Fat 9g (Saturated 4g); Carbohydrates 63g; Fiber 6g; Sodium 1189mg

Asparagus Risotto

Makes: 3 servings

This recipe heralds spring.

10 spears asparagus (about 1/2 pound), tough ends snapped off
1 red bell pepper, roasted
4 cups reduced-sodium, defatted chicken broth
1 1/2 tablespoons olive oil
1 cup chopped onions
1 clove garlic, minced
1 cup Arborio or other short-grain rice
3 tablespoons white wine
1/4 cup grated Parmesan cheese
1 tablespoon minced fresh basil
1/2 teaspoon kosher salt
1/4 teaspoon freshly ground pepper

1) Cut the asparagus on the diagonal into 1-inch long pieces. Steam briefly until bright green and just tender. Slice the roasted pepper, then cut into 1-inch lengths.

2) Heat the broth.

3) In a 2- or 3-quart heavy-bottomed pot, heat the oil. Cook the onions and garlic until golden,

about 3 minutes. Add the rice and cook, stirring all the while, until the grains are shiny with oil. Pour in the wine.

4) Add about 1 cup of the broth, bring to a boil, reduce to a simmer, and stir until almost all of the liquid is absorbed. Pour in a $1/2$ cup of broth and again stir and cook until the broth is absorbed. Continue to do this until all of the liquid is used and the rice is creamy on the outside, but still a bit firm to the bite.

5) Stir in the cheese, basil, salt, pepper, asparagus, and roasted pepper.

Per Serving: Calories 413; Protein 14g; Fat 10g (Saturated 3g); Carbohydrates 63g; Fiber 4g; Sodium 1120mg

Mushroom Risotto

Makes: 3 servings

Dried mushrooms are totally different from fresh. It is as if the mushroom's true earthy, musky essence has been trapped in a shriveled, dried shell. A small amount can bring a bit of the wildness of the woods into the kitchen.

1 cup hot water
$1/2$ ounce dried porcini (cèpes), or other dried mushrooms (about $2/3$ cup)
3 cups reduced-sodium, defatted chicken broth
2 tablespoons olive oil
3 shallots, chopped
1 clove garlic, minced
$1/2$ pound fresh shiitake or other flavorful mushrooms, stems discarded, sliced
1 cup Arborio or other short-grain rice
$1/4$ teaspoon dried sage
$1/3$ cup grated Parmesan cheese
$1/2$ teaspoon kosher salt
$1/4$ teaspoon freshly ground pepper

1) Soak the dried mushrooms in the hot water until soft, about 40 minutes to 1 hour. Remove them with a slotted spoon and wipe off any grit still clinging to them. Coarsely chop and set aside. Pour the soaking water through a fine mesh sieve or a coffee filter.

2) Combine the strained soaking water and the broth and heat it until almost boiling.

3) In a 2- or 3-quart, heavy-bottomed pot, heat the oil and cook the shallots and garlic until golden, about 3 minutes. Stir in the fresh mushrooms and cook until wilted. Add the rice and dried mushrooms and cook, stirring all the while, until the grains are shiny with oil. Stir in the sage.

4) Add about 1 cup of the broth, bring to a boil, reduce to a simmer, and stir until almost all of the liquid is absorbed. Pour in a $1/2$ cup of the broth and stir and cook until the broth is absorbed. Continue to do this, $1/2$ cup at a time, until all of the liquid is used and the rice is creamy on the outside, but still a bit firm to the bite. This will take about 20 to 25 minutes.

5) Stir in the cheese, salt, and pepper.

Per Serving: Calories 438; Protein 15g; Fat 13g (Saturated 3g); Carbohydrates 63g; Fiber 4g; Sodium 1017mg

Vegetables

Apples
311

Grilled Apples

Cinnamon Apples

Layered Apples and Turnips

Red Cabbage and Apples

Asparagus
313

Steamed Asparagus

*Asparagus with
Red Pepper Sauce*

*Asparagus in
Gingerly Citrus Dressing*

*Asparagus with
Warm Lemon Dressing*

Sautéed Asparagus

*Sautéed Garlic Asparagus
with Red Pepper*

Roasted Asparagus

Roasted Parmesan Asparagus

Beets
317

Baked Beets

Harvard Beets

*Raspberry and
Orange Glazed Beets*

Broccoli
319

Simply Steamed Broccoli

Broccoli and Roasted Peppers

Broccoli and Peanuts

Garlic and Lemon Broccoli

*Stir-Fried Broccoli with
Oyster Sauce*

Stir-Fried Garlic Broccoli

*Oven-Roasted Broccoli
with Parmesan*

*Oven-Roasted Broccoli
with Lemon*

Brussels Sprouts
323

Brussels Sprouts with Chestnuts

Roasted Chestnuts

Glazed Brussels Sprouts

*Oven-Roasted Brussels Sprouts
and Carrots*

Carrots
325

*Baby Carrots with
a Honey-Mustard Glaze*

Dilled Carrots

Orange Ginger Carrots

Italian Sweet and Sour Carrots

Carrots and Raisins

Rooted Carrots

Cauliflower
328

*Cauliflower with
Garlic Breadcrumbs*

Dressed Cauliflower Florets

Bayou Stewed Cauliflower

Curried Cauliflower and Peas

Roasted Cauliflower with
Rosemary and Garlic

Corn
330

Steamed Corn on the Cob

Microwaved Corn on the Cob

Grilled-in-the-Husk Corn
on the Cob

Roasted Corn on the Cob

Corn Confetti

Chili and Lime Corn

Corn Fried Rice

Green Beans
333

Steamed Green Beans

Green Beans and Almonds

Green Beans and Bacon

Green Beans Cooked
with Salsa

Gremolata Green Beans

Asian Green Beans

Great Green Beans

Creole Green Beans

Stewed Green Beans
and Potatoes

Greens
337

Spinach with Lemon
and Garlic

Spinach with Golden Raisins
and Almonds

African Spinach and Peanuts

Roasted Garlic and Greens

Steamed Beet Greens
with Sesame Oil

Sautéed Swiss Chard

Stir-Fried Bok Choy

Kale with Red Onion

Kale with Red Onion and Feta

Spinach Bake

Mushrooms
342

Herbed Broiled Mushrooms

Grilled Portobello Mushrooms

Exotic Mushroom Sauté

Pan-Fried Garlic Mushrooms

Thyme Mushrooms

Pearl Onions, Mushrooms,
and Peas

Peas
345

Buttered Peas

Carrots and Peas

Oriental Sugar Snap Peas

Snow Peas and
Water Chestnuts

Sugar Snap Peas with Mint

Potatoes
347

Perfect Baked Potato

Microwaved Baked Potato

Sour Cream and Chives for
a Baked Potato

Garlic Lovers' Potatoes

Onion and Herb Potatoes

Potato and Vegetable Gratin

Mushroom and Cheese
Scalloped Potatoes

Savory Potatoes

Confetti Potatoes

Dilled New Potatoes

Greek Stewed Potatoes
and Tomatoes

Greek Stewed Potatoes and
Tomatoes with Feta Cheese

Mashed Potatoes

Mashed Potatoes with
Roasted Garlic

Mashed Potatoes with Cheese

Curried Mashed Potatoes

Mashed Potatoes and
Balsamic Onions

Mashed Potato Timbales

Pan-Crisped
Sweet Potato Cubes

Candied Sweet Potatoes

Sweet Potato Spears

Sweet Potatoes
and Marshmallows

Not Your Traditional Tzimmes

Sweet Potato Bake

Root Vegetables
359

Sugar-Glazed Turnips

Parsnips and Pineapple

Mashed Rutabagas and Spuds

Squash
360

Baked Butternut Squash

Twice-Baked Butternut Squash

Baked Acorn Squash Rings

Cider-Roasted Squash
and Shallots

Winter Squash Gratin

Spiced Maple Pumpkin Mash

Lemony Squash and Carrots

Zucchini Spears with Pesto

Sautéed Summer Vegetables

Garlicky Zucchini and Corn

Zucchini Oven Fries

Zucchini Cheese Casserole

Mexican Zucchini Casserole

Parmesan
Summer Squash Packets

Grilled Zucchini

Tomatoes
368

Cheery Cherry Tomatoes

Sage Tomatoes

Turkish Tomatoes and Zucchini

Baked Tomatoes

Baked Tomato Jam

Vegetable Medleys
370

Southwestern Vegetable Sauté

Fall Vegetable Medley

Cider-Cooked Vegetables

Caponata

Ethiopian Vegetables

Succotash with Tomatoes
and Basil

Vegetables Under Wraps

Cowboy Foil-Wrapped
Vegetables

Vegetables deserve to be an important part of the menu, not merely an after-thought or a small garnish. When dining out, even if the main entrée is spectacular, if the vegetables aren't fresh and interesting, I'm disappointed. I also find the meal lacking when the vegetables are excellent but there are only two mouthfuls. Portion sizes for vegetables should be generous and the dish worthwhile on its own.

This chapter is organized alphabetically so that you can find a selection for each vegetable (vegetable medleys are at the end). Vegetable recipes don't have to be complicated, and there is nothing wrong with serving simply steamed vegetables, especially if the vegetables are fresh, tender, and flavorful. My family often eats steamed vegetables with salad dressing or Honey-Mustard Sauce (page 601). But don't hesitate to try the more involved recipes. Many are just as good when eaten at room temperature, so they can be made ahead. Not only does that ease the rush at dinnertime, but it means that leftovers will still be delicious the next day.

Although steaming vegetables until still crisp is trendy, there is nothing wrong with cooking vegetables until tender or even soft. In some cases it makes the proteins more available and starch more digestible (with a resultant benefit of causing less intestinal gas). Cooking does cause a loss of some nutrients, especially vitamin C, but that is far outweighed by the other benefits of cooked vegetables. One important reason to cook vegetables is that it is easier to eat large quantities of cooked vegetables than to crunch through a pile of raw ones. Also, some vegetables in the cabbage family, such as broccoli, taste bitter when partially cooked but sweeter when cooked until tender.

Microwaving, like steaming, cooks vegetables quickly in little water and so minimizes nutrient loss. But although this method cooks single portions well, larger recipes often come out of the microwave unevenly cooked and with poor texture.

Apples

Of course, apples aren't vegetables, but their sweet-tart flavor pairs well with many vegetables and savory dishes. Following is a selection of recipes in which apples are served as a side dish with the main course, in the capacity of a vegetable, and not as a dessert.

Grilled Apples

Makes: 6 servings

This simple recipe, with its sharp yet sweet flavor is the perfect accompaniment to roast chicken or spicy meats.

6 cups water
2 tablespoons lemon juice
2 Granny Smith apples

1) Combine the water and lemon juice in a container that can hold all the apple wedges.

2) Core and then peel the apples. Cut into thick wedges, about 8 per apple. Submerge them in the lemon-water bath until ready to use. Since the lemon juice prevents browning, you can prepare them a day ahead of time.

3) Get the grill hot. Using tongs, place the apples on the grill. Cook until dark lines sear the apples. Turn and cook until the apples are warm through but still firm, about 1 to 2 minutes per side.

Per Serving: Calories 24; Protein 0g; Fat 0g (Saturated 0g); Carbohydrates 6g; Fiber 1g; Sodium 0mg

Cinnamon Apples

Makes: 8 servings

I grew up eating macaroni-and-cheese TV dinners. The small square of cinnamon apples in the center of the tray was my favorite part. This recipe is even better than what I so fondly remember.

4 Granny Smith apples
1 tablespoon sugar
1/8 teaspoon ground cinnamon
1/4 teaspoon dried thyme
1/4 teaspoon kosher salt
2 teaspoons vegetable oil

1) Core and then peel the apples. Cut each apple into about 10 wedges. Toss with the sugar, cinnamon, thyme, and salt.

2) Heat the oil in a nonstick skillet. Sauté the apples over medium-high heat for 7 to 10 minutes, until the apples soften but still retain their shape. Add 2 tablespoons water if softer apples are desired.

Per Serving: Calories 53; Protein 0g; Fat 1g (Saturated 0g); Carbohydrates 1g; Fiber 1g; Sodium 60mg

Layered Apples and Turnips

Makes: 4 servings

A Macintosh apple will turn to mush when baked, but a baking variety, as specified here, will hold its shape.

2 apples, preferably a baking variety such as Rome or Cortland
6 small turnips (1/3 pound)
1/4 teaspoon ground coriander
1/2 cup apple juice or apple cider
1/4 cup walnut or pecan pieces

1) Preheat the oven to 350°F.

2) Core the apples, then slice them into rings. Scrub the turnips clean and cut off the ends, then cut the turnips into thin rounds.

3) Layer the apples and turnips in a 1 1/2- to 2-quart casserole. Dust on the coriander. Pour in the apple juice. Cover the casserole and bake for 30 minutes.

4) Uncover the casserole, top with the nuts, and bake for 10 minutes more.

Per Serving: Calories 114; Protein 2g; Fat 5g (Saturated 0g); Carbohydrates 18g; Fiber 3g; Sodium 27mg

Red Cabbage and Apples

Makes: 8 servings

Sometimes I really want a vegetable side dish that isn't green. This looks very pretty next to roast or grilled chicken.

1 tablespoon olive oil

2 cups sliced red onions

2 cloves garlic, minced

6 cups thinly sliced red cabbage
(about half a head)

1 teaspoon kosher salt

1/4 teaspoon freshly ground pepper

1/2 cup reduced-sodium, defatted chicken broth

2 tablespoons red wine vinegar

2 tablespoons honey

2 tablespoons sugar

3 apples, cored, peeled, and sliced, divided

1/4 cup chopped fresh parsley

1) Heat the oil in a large nonstick pan or wok. Sauté the onions, garlic, and cabbage over moderate heat until all is limp. Stir in the salt, pepper, broth, vinegar, honey, sugar, and all but 1 cup of the apple slices. Cover and cook for 7 minutes.

2) Uncover and cook another 7 to 10 minutes, until the cabbage is tender. Add the last cup of apples and the parsley. Cook, stirring, until the apples begin to soften and heat through. This can be made ahead of time and reheated. Leftovers remain good for several days.

Per Serving: Calories 80; Protein 1g; Fat 2g (Saturated 0g); Carbohydrates 17g; Fiber 2g; Sodium 222mg

Asparagus

Asparagus varies in thickness from pencil-thin to thick as a finger. Obviously the cooking time will vary according to the size. Some people have strong preferences about what type of asparagus they like best. As long as it is fresh, I like it all.

Choose asparagus that has tightly closed florets at the tips, with no gray or mushy parts. The stems should be full and bright green. If they have ridges or look dried out, they are inedible.

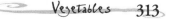

Steamed Asparagus

Makes: 4 servings

Store steamed asparagus layed flat on a paper towel in a covered container. Asparagus can be kept this way, in the refrigerator, for up to 2 days.

1 pound asparagus

1) Wash the asparagus well. To discard the woody bottoms, hold the asparagus near the middle with one hand, and at the bottom with the other hand. Bend until it snaps. A stalk will break where the unpalatable stem meets the fresh part. The jagged edge can be trimmed with a knife. (Very thick asparagus does not snap and should be trimmed with a knife.) Next, unless the asparagus are pencil-thin, pare the lower third of the stem with a vegetable peeler. This step allows the asparagus to steam evenly and makes the stems more palatable.

2) Traditionally, asparagus is steamed in a narrow, tall pot. This allows the tougher stems to cook thoroughly while the more tender tips are further from the heat. I don't own an asparagus steamer, but for large quantities I pour a few inches of water into a large, tall pot, insert a steamer basket, bring the water to a boil, and steam the asparagus upright. Smaller quantities (a pound or less) can be cooked in a skillet. Add about a 1/2 inch of water, bring to a boil, lay the asparagus in flat, and cover and steam until the asparagus reach the desired tenderness, about 4 to 7 minutes. Remove with tongs. I like to serve asparagus on a flat platter, with the bottoms of their stems together and their tips fanned out.

Per Serving: Calories 20; Protein 2g; Fat 0g (Saturated 0g); Carbohydrates 4g; Fiber 2g; Sodium 2mg

Asparagus with Red Pepper Sauce

Makes: 8 servings

This beautiful dish is perfect for a buffet party because it is equally good warm or at room temperature.

2 pounds asparagus
1 cup Red Pepper Sauce (page 586)

1) Prepare and steam the asparagus according to the directions opposite. Meanwhile, gently warm the Red Pepper Sauce.

2) Arrange the steamed asparagus on a platter. Pour the sauce over the vegetables in a pattern of crisscrossed lines, leaving the tips unadorned. Serve warm or at room temperature.

Per Serving: Calories 29; Protein 2g; Fat 1g (Saturated 0g); Carbohydrates 5g; Fiber 2g; Sodium 114mg

Asparagus in Gingerly Citrus Dressing

Makes: 4 servings

The ginger and orange zest are briefly boiled, which removes the sharp notes but leaves all the flavor.

1/2-inch piece fresh ginger
1 orange
1 tablespoon extra-virgin olive oil
2 teaspoons balsamic vinegar
1/4 teaspoon kosher salt
1/4 teaspoon freshly ground pepper
1/4 teaspoon soy sauce
1 pound asparagus

1) Peel the ginger. Cut it into thin rounds, then slice those pieces into very narrow strips of ginger.

2) Wash the orange well. Remove fine strips of orange zest using a zesting tool, or peel the orange skin, leaving all the white pith behind. Cut the peel into fine strips.

3) Boil the ginger and orange strips for 5 minutes, then drain through a wire mesh sieve and reserve.

4) Juice the orange. Measure $1/4$ cup juice. Whisk the oil, vinegar, salt, pepper, and soy sauce into the juice. Stir in the orange peel and ginger. You can make this dressing well ahead of time; it actually benefits from a few hours' rest.

5) Prepare and steam the asparagus according to the directions opposite.

6) Put the asparagus on a platter and pour the dressing over the asparagus while the stalks are still hot. Serve the asparagus hot or at room temperature.

Per Serving: Calories 63; Protein 2g; Fat 4g (Saturated 1g); Carbohydrates 7g; Fiber 2g; Sodium 144mg

Asparagus with Warm Lemon Dressing

Makes: 4 servings

A rectangular dish for serving asparagus is a useful platter to have. For this recipe, I arrange all of the asparagus tips facing toward one end, pour the dressing over the spears, and place the platter right on the dinner table.

1 pound asparagus
1 shallot, peeled and crushed
1 clove garlic, peeled and crushed
2 teaspoons olive oil
2 tablespoons white wine
1 tablespoon lemon juice
$1/4$ teaspoon freshly ground pepper

1) Steam the asparagus until just tender, about 5 minutes (opposite). Remove the asparagus to a platter.

2) Meanwhile, sauté the shallot and garlic in the oil and wine over low heat until the alcohol evaporates and the garlic turns a golden brown, about 10 minutes. Discard the garlic and shallot.

3) Whisk the lemon juice and pepper into the oil and wine. Pour over the steamed asparagus and serve immediately.

Per Serving: Calories 50; Protein 2g; Fat 2g (Saturated 0g); Carbohydrates 5g; Fiber 2g; Sodium 3mg

Sautéed Asparagus

Makes: 4 servings

The vinegar actually sweetens the dish.

1 pound asparagus
1 teaspoon olive oil
1/4 teaspoon kosher salt
1/8 teaspoon freshly ground pepper
1/2 to 1 teaspoon balsamic or raspberry vinegar

1) Prepare and steam the asparagus according to the directions on page 314. Pat the steamed asparagus dry and cut on the diagonal into 1-inch pieces.

2) Heat the oil in a large nonstick skillet. Toss in the asparagus and cook until warmed through. Remove from the heat and toss in the salt, pepper, and vinegar. Taste, adjust seasonings, and serve immediately.

Per Serving: Calories 30; Protein 2g; Fat 1g (Saturated 0g); Carbohydrates 4g; Fiber 2g; Sodium 122mg

Sautéed Garlic Asparagus with Red Pepper

Makes: 4 servings

Though they have a reputation for being an elegant vegetable, asparagus shouldn't be limited to gentle sauces. Don't hesitate to team them up with garlic or other strong flavors.

1 pound asparagus
2 teaspoons olive oil
1/2 red bell pepper, cut into thin 1-inch-long strips
2 cloves garlic, minced
1/4 teaspoon kosher salt (optional)
1/8 teaspoon freshly ground pepper
1/2 teaspoon balsamic vinegar

1) Prepare and steam the asparagus according to the directions on page 314. Pat the steamed asparagus dry and cut on the diagonal into 1-inch pieces.

2) Heat the oil in a large nonstick skillet. Toss in the bell pepper and garlic and cook over moderate heat until the pepper softens. Add the asparagus and cook until warmed through.

3) Remove from the heat and toss in the salt, pepper, and vinegar. Serve immediately.

Per Serving: Calories 45; Protein 2g; Fat 2g (Saturated 0g); Carbohydrates 5g; Fiber 2g; Sodium 2mg

Roasted Asparagus

Makes: 4 servings

Roasting browns the edges of the asparagus and changes their flavor from green and saladlike to rich and earthy.

1 pound asparagus
2 teaspoons olive oil
1/4 teaspoon kosher salt
1 lemon, cut into wedges

1) Place the oven rack in the top third of the oven and preheat to 450°F.

2) Trim and peel the asparagus. Place on a rimmed baking sheet. Drizzle on the oil. Dust on the salt. Roll the asparagus in the pan until the spears glisten with the oil.

3) Bake for 3 minutes and shake the pan. Continue to check the asparagus and turn them every 3 minutes. The asparagus will be done when they soften and begin to brown in spots, about 7 to 10 minutes. Serve with the lemon wedges.

Per Serving: Calories 44; Protein 2g; Fat 2g (Saturated 0g); Carbohydrates 5g; Fiber 2g; Sodium 122mg

Roasted Parmesan Asparagus

Makes: 4 servings

Squeeze the lemon directly onto your asparagus. The lemon juice will provide a bright contrast to the roasted flavor of the spears.

1 pound asparagus, steamed
1 teaspoon olive oil
1/4 teaspoon freshly ground pepper
2 tablespoons grated Parmesan cheese
1 lemon, cut into wedges

1) Place the oven rack in the top third of the oven and preheat to 475°F.

2) Place the asparagus on a rimmed baking sheet. Drizzle on the oil. Roll the asparagus in the pan until they glisten with oil. Dust on the pepper and distribute the cheese over the spears.

3) Bake for 5 minutes. Don't turn the asparagus or shake the pan. Serve with the lemon wedges.

Per Serving: Calories 48; Protein 3g; Fat 2g (Saturated 1g); Carbohydrates 5g; Fiber 2g; Sodium 60mg

Beets

Fresh beets often come with their green tops attached. These are delicious (see Greens, page 337, for cooking suggestions). Beets themselves can make a mess of the kitchen because anything they touch will be stained purple. I use disposable rubber gloves and work on a plastic cutting board, and I don't mind a bit because I love fresh beets. But some dishes are no trouble at all because they are just as good with canned beets, and this convenience is mentioned in the recipes.

Baked Beets

Makes: 4 servings

Beets can also be cooked in the microwave in about 15 minutes. They will be fine for some uses but won't be as sweet or buttery-textured as baked beets.

1 pound beets
1 tablespoon water
1/4 teaspoon ground nutmeg

1) Cut off the tops and tails of the beets. Large beets need to have their tough skins peeled but small ones only require a good scrubbing.

2) Place beets in a casserole dish, sprinkle with the water and nutmeg, and cover.

3) Bake in a preheated 350°F oven for 1 hour, until tender.

Per Serving: Calories 33; Protein 1g; Fat 0g (Saturated 0g); Carbohydrates 7g; Fiber 2g; Sodium 59mg

Harvard Beets

Makes: 8 servings

I serve these hot the day I make them, then save the leftovers in a glass jar for use on salads later.

3 tablespoons water
1/2 cup sugar
1/4 teaspoon kosher salt
1/2 cup white wine vinegar
1/4 teaspoon ground cloves
4 cups cooked beets (fresh or canned), sliced
2 teaspoons unsalted butter
2 teaspoons cornstarch mixed with
    1 tablespoon water

1) Put the water, sugar, salt, vinegar, and cloves in a saucepan. Bring to a boil and cook for 5 minutes.

2) Stir in the beets. Turn off the heat and let stand for 30 minutes.

3) Bring the beets back to a simmer and stir in the butter and the cornstarch paste. Cook until thickened.

Per Serving: Calories 105; Protein 1g; Fat 1g (Saturated 1g); Carbohydrates 23g; Fiber 1g; Sodium 126mg

Raspberry and Orange Glazed Beets

Makes: 6 servings

Beets are unusual for a root vegetable in that they are naturally elegant. Garnish this recipe with fresh raspberries and it will be impressive on even the most formal dinner table.

1 teaspoon cornstarch
1/3 cup orange juice
2 teaspoons fine strips orange zest
2 tablespoons packed light brown sugar
2 tablespoons raspberry vinegar
1/2 teaspoon kosher salt
1 teaspoon Worcestershire sauce
Two 15-ounce cans small whole beets, drained, or
    3 cups fresh cooked beets

1) Combine the cornstarch with 1 tablespoon of the orange juice and set aside.

2) In a medium saucepan, combine the remaining ingredients except for the beets. Bring to a boil. Stir in the beets. Simmer, uncovered, for 15 minutes.

3) Stir in the cornstarch mixture. Cook until clear and thickened.

Per Serving: Calories 53; Protein 1g; Fat 0g (Saturated 0g); Carbohydrates 13g; Fiber 2g; Sodium 404mg

Broccoli

Don't hesitate to cook the entire head of broccoli, even if only a portion will be eaten that evening. Cooked broccoli will almost always be eaten up quickly, whereas a stalk of raw, wilting broccoli in the vegetable bin becomes less and less appetizing until it is finally thrown out.

Simply Steamed Broccoli

Makes: 4 servings

Lightly steamed broccoli is the first step to other recipes, such as Oven-Roasted Broccoli with Parmesan (page 322), or it can be tossed in salads, added to soups, or used in stir-fries.

1 head broccoli

1) Prepare the broccoli by washing it well and then cutting off the bottoms of the stems that are dried out and woody. Peel the stems with a vegetable peeler. This step allows the broccoli to steam evenly and makes the stems more palatable. Cut the broccoli into florets or whatever size you prefer (my family likes "trees").

2) Place a steamer basket in a pot and pour a few inches of water into the pot so that it reaches the steamer insert. Bring it to a boil. Put the broccoli into the steamer, cover, and steam until the broccoli reaches the desired tenderness. Undercooked broccoli will be hard and have a strong cabbage flavor. Children tend to like broccoli soft. For most uses, broccoli is ready when it turns bright green and a fork can easily be inserted into a stem, which takes about 5 minutes.

3) If the broccoli is to be eaten later, immerse it in a bowl of cool water to stop the cooking process, then drain and chill.

Per Serving: Calories 24; Protein 3g; Fat 0g (Saturated 0g); Carbohydrates 4g; Fiber 3g; Sodium 23mg

Broccoli and Roasted Peppers

Makes: 2 servings

The bright green and red color combination makes this dish particularly attractive.

1 clove garlic, minced
1 teaspoon olive oil
1 roasted red bell pepper, julienned
2 large servings broccoli spears, lightly steamed
2 tablespoons reduced-sodium, defatted vegetable or chicken broth
1/4 teaspoon kosher salt
1/8 teaspoon freshly ground pepper

1) Sauté the garlic in the oil over low heat until the garlic turns light golden.

2) Stir in the roasted peppers and cook briefly. Add the broccoli. At this point more liquid will be needed both to heat the broccoli and to keep it moist. Add a few tablespoons of broth as needed. Cover and cook, stirring every few minutes, until the broccoli is hot and reaches the desired texture.

3) Season with salt and pepper and serve.

Per Serving: Calories 58; Protein 3g; Fat 3g (Saturated 0g); Carbohydrates 7g; Fiber 3g; Sodium 294mg

Broccoli and Peanuts

Makes: 5 servings

Serve this with any of the lo-mein or stir-fry selections.

1 head broccoli, trimmed and stalks peeled
1 teaspoon Asian sesame oil
2 cloves garlic, minced
1 tablespoon soy sauce
1 tablespoon dry roasted peanuts,
    coarsely chopped
1/16 teaspoon crushed red pepper flakes (optional)
1 tablespoon reduced-sodium, defatted chicken or
    vegetable broth

1) Slice the broccoli stalks and cut the head into large florets. Lightly steam the broccoli (see page 319) until it turns a brighter shade of green, then immediately stop the cooking by immersing it in cool water. Drain.

2) Heat the oil in a large pan or wok. Over low heat, sauté the garlic in the oil until it is golden. Raise the heat to medium-high. Toss in the broccoli. Add the remaining ingredients. Cover the pan. Toss the vegetables by shaking the pan, or lift the lid and stir. Cook until the broccoli becomes fork-tender, about 3 to 5 minutes.

Per Serving: Calories 42; Protein 3g; Fat 2g (Saturated 0g); Carbohydrates 5g; Fiber 2g; Sodium 230mg

Garlic and Lemon Broccoli

Makes: 5 servings

Although this calls for florets, broccoli "trees" (florets with long, peeled stalks attached) would also look and taste great.

4 cups broccoli florets
1 tablespoon olive oil
2 cloves garlic, minced
2 teaspoons fine strips lemon zest or minced
    lemon peel
1/4 teaspoon kosher salt
1/4 teaspoon freshly ground pepper

1) Steam the florets until tender. If you like, use peeled and sliced stems as well as crowns. Drain and put in a serving bowl and cover loosely to keep warm.

2) Heat the oil in a small sauté pan over moderate heat. Cook the garlic until golden but not brown. Stir in the zest. Pour this over the broccoli, toss with the salt and pepper, and serve immediately.

Per Serving: Calories 36; Protein 1g; Fat 3g (Saturated 0g); Carbohydrates 2g; Fiber 1g; Sodium 106mg

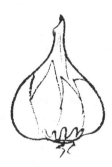

Stir-Fried Broccoli with Oyster Sauce

Makes: 4 servings

Recipes with cornstarch-thickened sauces like this should be eaten immediately because they do not reheat well.

1 head broccoli, trimmed and stalks peeled
1/2 red bell pepper
4 scallions, sliced
1 tablespoon cornstarch
1 tablespoon water
1 tablespoon oyster sauce
1/2 teaspoon soy sauce
1/2 teaspoon sugar
1 teaspoon vegetable oil
1 clove garlic, minced
1/2 cup reduced-sodium, defatted vegetable or chicken broth

1) Slice the broccoli stalks and cut the head into florets. Cut the bell pepper into small triangles. Put the broccoli, pepper pieces, and scallions in a bowl.

2) In a small bowl, whisk together the cornstarch, water, oyster sauce, soy sauce, and sugar. Set aside.

3) Heat a large nonstick wok and add the oil. Stir in the garlic and sauté briefly until the garlic begins to change color. Stir in the vegetables and pour in the broth. Cover and cook over high heat until the broccoli turns bright green and the stems become slightly tender.

4) Pour in the contents of the small bowl. Stir and toss the vegetables to coat. Cook, stirring constantly, until the sauce clears and thickens.

Per Serving: Calories 58; Protein 4g; Fat 1g (Saturated 0g); Carbohydrates 9g; Fiber 3g; Sodium 296mg

Stir-Fried Garlic Broccoli

Makes: 6 servings

This would be a welcome addition to any Asian menu.

1 large head broccoli, trimmed and stalks peeled
1 tablespoon sugar
2 tablespoons soy sauce
1 teaspoon cornstarch
1 teaspoon rice wine vinegar or white wine vinegar
1 teaspoon vegetable oil
1 tablespoon Asian sesame oil
4 cloves garlic, minced
1/8 teaspoon crushed red pepper flakes
1/2 cup reduced-sodium, defatted vegetable or chicken broth

1) Cut the broccoli into florets. Slice the stems if they are especially long.

2) In a small bowl, whisk together the sugar, soy sauce, cornstarch, and vinegar. Set aside.

3) Heat a large nonstick wok or skillet. Add in the vegetable and sesame oils. Stir in the garlic and sauté briefly until the garlic begins to change color. Stir in the broccoli and pepper flakes and cook for another 2 to 3 minutes. Pour in the broth. Cover and cook over high heat until the broccoli turns bright green and the stems become slightly tender.

4) Pour in the contents of the small bowl. Stir and toss the vegetables to coat. Cook, stirring constantly, until the sauce clears and thickens.

Per Serving: Calories 68; Protein 3g; Fat 3g (Saturated 0g); Carbohydrates 8g; Fiber 3g; Sodium 406mg

Oven-Roasted Broccoli with Parmesan

Makes: 4 servings

These are cooked to perfection when the edges begin to brown, though the broccoli remains moist. It is overcooked if the broccoli dries and shrinks.

1 head broccoli, cut into large florets, stalks peeled
$1/2$ teaspoon kosher salt
$1/4$ teaspoon freshly ground pepper
1 teaspoon olive oil
1 tablespoon grated Parmesan cheese

1) Lightly steam the broccoli (see page 319). This can be done up to a day ahead.

2) Preheat the oven to 400°F. Coat a rimmed baking sheet or casserole with nonstick spray.

3) On the baking sheet, toss the broccoli with the salt, pepper, and oil. Dust with the Parmesan and toss once more. Place in the oven and bake for 15 minutes.

Per Serving: Calories 41; Protein 3g; Fat 2g (Saturated 0g); Carbohydrates 5g; Fiber 3g; Sodium 292mg

Oven-Roasted Broccoli with Lemon

Makes: 4 servings

The refreshing tang of lemon juice enhances the deep roasted flavor of the roasted broccoli. But serve this immediately or the tang turns sour and the broccoli's color dulls.

1 head broccoli, trimmed, stalks peeled, and cut into large florets
$1/2$ teaspoon kosher salt
$1/4$ teaspoon freshly ground pepper
1 teaspoon vegetable oil
1 tablespoon lemon juice

1) Lightly steam the broccoli (see page 319). This can be done up to a day ahead.

2) Preheat the oven to 400°F. Coat a rimmed baking sheet or casserole with nonstick spray.

3) On the baking sheet, toss the broccoli with the salt, pepper, and oil. Place in the oven and bake for 15 to 20 minutes. Sprinkle with the lemon juice and serve immediately.

Per Serving: Calories 35; Protein 3g; Fat 1g (Saturated 0g); Carbohydrates 5g; Fiber 3g; Sodium 263mg

Brussels Sprouts

*I*t might not be a popular thing to admit, but I love Brussels sprouts. I like them straightforward and whole, like the bold little cabbages they are. Brussels sprouts are a cool-weather crop and taste best after the first frost. Trim them with a paring knife. First slice off the woody part of the stem, leaving enough intact so that the sprout doesn't fall apart. Then pull off any tough, evergreen-colored outer leaves. Bring water to a boil in a saucepan, drop in the prepared sprouts, and cook until the sharp tip of a knife can be inserted into the stem easily.

Brussels Sprouts with Chestnuts

Makes: 5 servings

This is the perfect side dish for a Thanksgiving meal.

1 pound Brussels sprouts, trimmed
1 teaspoon vegetable oil
1 cup Roasted Chestnuts (opposite), peeled and coarsely chopped
1/8 teaspoon kosher salt
1/8 teaspoon freshly ground pepper

1) Steam the Brussels sprouts until you can insert a fork through them easily.

2) Heat the oil in a nonstick pan. Add the Brussels sprouts, chestnuts, salt, and pepper. Toss until the Brussels sprouts are heated through and are coated with oil.

Per Serving: Calories 117; Protein 4g; Fat 2g (Saturated 0g); Carbohydrates 23g; Fiber 6g; Sodium 71mg

Roasted Chestnuts

Makes: 8 servings

Only about 6 percent of chestnuts' calories come from fat, which contrasts dramatically with other nuts, such as pecans and walnuts, which are 75 to 85 percent fat. Chestnuts taste rich and sweet, yet one chestnut contains less than 1 gram of fat.

2 pounds chestnuts in the shell

1) Preheat the oven to 425°F.

2) Cut an X into each shell to allow steam to escape as the chestnuts roast. (This is very important, as chestnuts not slashed will explode into a powdery dust.) To do this safely, place a chestnut on a cutting board, on the chestnut's flat side (if it has one) and pull a serrated knife across the shell.

3) Place the chestnuts in a single layer on a baking sheet and put them in the oven for 20 to 30 minutes, until the shells curl back from the X. Let them cool until you can handle them, but don't wait until they are room temperature because the bitter inner skin can be removed only while the nut is warm.

4) Use immediately or store peeled nuts in a container in the refrigerator. Use within 2 days of roasting.

Per Serving: Calories 180; Protein 2g; Fat 1g (Saturated 0g); Carbohydrates 41g; Fiber 5g; Sodium 2mg

Glazed Brussels Sprouts

Makes: 6 servings

Brussels sprouts are mellowed in this sweet-sour glaze. The carrots also bring sweetness to the dish, as well as a pretty contrasting color.

4 cups Brussels sprouts, trimmed
1 pound baby-cut carrots
3 tablespoons apple cider vinegar
1 tablespoon corn syrup
$1/2$ cup packed light brown sugar
$1/4$ teaspoon kosher salt
$1/2$ teaspoon ground ginger

1) Cook the Brussels sprouts and carrots in a steamer until fork tender. Drain and set aside.

2) Meanwhile, preheat the oven to 400°F. Combine the remaining ingredients in a bowl.

3) Put the vegetables in a casserole. Pour the sauce over and toss. Bake, uncovered, for 20 minutes.

Per Serving: Calories 114; Protein 3g; Fat 0g (Saturated 0g); Carbohydrates 28g; Fiber 5g; Sodium 139mg

Oven-Roasted Brussels Sprouts and Carrots

Makes: 4 servings

In this recipe the Brussels sprouts are first par-cooked, which cuts the roasting time by more than half and results in tender—but not soft—Brussels sprouts.

4 carrots, peeled and cut into rounds
     (or $1/2$ pound baby-cut carrots)
$1/2$ pound Brussels sprouts (about 12 to 16), trimmed
2 teaspoons olive oil
$1/4$ teaspoon kosher salt
$1/4$ teaspoon freshly ground pepper

1) Preheat the oven to 400°F.

2) Steam or microwave the carrots and Brussels sprouts together until they begin to soften. This will take about 6 minutes on high in the microwave. Put about $1/2$ inch of water in the dish or the vegetables will harden instead of soften.

3) Put the vegetables in a casserole and toss them with the oil, salt, and pepper. Bake for 20 minutes. Shake and stir once while roasting.

Per Serving: Calories 76; Protein 3g; Fat 3g (Saturated 0g); Carbohydrates 12g; Fiber 5g; Sodium 159mg

Carrots

I've always liked to eat carrots, both cooked and raw, but I find that I am eating more of them than ever because the market now sells bags of baby-cut carrots. These are small fingers of peeled carrots, rounded on both ends. Sometimes they are labeled "baby" carrots, but they are not really immature carrots. Rather they are full-grown carrots that have been trimmed to this size. They are perfect for raw munchies, perfect to steam and dress, perfect to toss in a vegetable soup or stew. I rarely pull out my vegetable peeler anymore.

Baby Carrots with a Honey-Mustard Glaze

Makes: 6 servings

The dressing is poured on the hot carrots so that it permeates the vegetables. They taste great right away but are just as good at room temperature. Leftovers remain tasty for up to 2 days.

1 pound baby-cut carrots
1 teaspoon Dijon or coarse mustard
1 teaspoon extra-virgin olive oil
1$^1/2$ teaspoons honey
1 teaspoon lemon juice

1) Steam or blanch the carrots until fork-tender.

2) Meanwhile, whisk together the remaining ingredients.

3) Toss the hot carrots with the dressing.

Per Serving: Calories 42; Protein 1g; Fat 1g (Saturated 0g); Carbohydrates 8g; Fiber 2g; Sodium 48mg

Dilled Carrots

Makes: 4 servings

Garlic oil provides garlic flavor without the texture of minced garlic, which would be obtrusive here.

1 pound baby-cut carrots or regular carrots
1$^1/2$ teaspoons Garlic Oil (page 607) or olive oil
$^1/4$ to $^1/2$ teaspoon kosher salt
$^1/8$ teaspoon freshly ground pepper
1 tablespoon minced fresh dill

1) If using regular carrots, slice into rounds. Steam or blanch until just tender.

2) Heat the oil in a large nonstick sauté pan. Toss in the carrots and cook for 1 to 2 minutes, until shiny with oil. Add the salt, pepper, and dill and cook for 2 minutes more.

Per Serving: Calories 58; Protein 1g; Fat 2g (Saturated 0g); Carbohydrates 9g; Fiber 4g; Sodium 160mg

Orange Ginger Carrots

Makes: 4 servings

This would complement a menu of meat, fish, or poultry and I've found that kids like it as much as adults.

1 pound carrots (about 8)
$^1/_4$ cup orange juice
$^1/_4$ teaspoon finely grated fresh ginger
1 to 2 teaspoons honey

1) Peel the carrots, then slice them Chinese-style—on the diagonal into thin ovals.

2) Combine the carrots with the orange juice, ginger, and 1 teaspoon of the honey.

3) Microwave on high for 4 minutes. Stir, then microwave for a few minutes more until the carrots are cooked through (timing will depend on your microwave). Or cook in a covered nonstick pan until the carrots soften.

4) You can serve the carrots like this or glaze them by putting them and the liquids into a pan, adding the remaining teaspoon of honey, and cooking them over medium-high heat until the orange juice evaporates and the carrots are shiny.

Per Serving: Calories 61; Protein 1g; Fat 0g (Saturated 0g); Carbohydrates 15g; Fiber 3g; Sodium 40mg

Italian Sweet and Sour Carrots

Makes: 6 servings

This is both good and different, which is hard to achieve with such a familiar vegetable.

2 pounds carrots, cut into $^1/_4$-inch rounds (about 5 cups)
1 tablespoon olive oil
1 shallot, chopped (about 1 tablespoon)
1 clove garlic, thinly sliced (optional)
3 tablespoons white wine vinegar
$1^1/_2$ teaspoons sugar
$^1/_2$ teaspoon kosher salt
$^1/_8$ teaspoon crushed red pepper flakes (optional)
1 tablespoon chopped fresh parsley

1) Steam or blanch the carrots until they are slightly tender but not fully cooked, about 3 to 4 minutes.

2) In a large nonstick skillet, heat the oil and stir in the shallot and garlic. Cook over medium heat until the shallot turns golden. Add the carrots.

3) Stir in the remaining ingredients except the parsley. Cook a few minutes until the liquid evaporates. Stir in the parsley.

Per Serving: Calories 93; Protein 2g; Fat 3g (Saturated 0g); Carbohydrates 17g; Fiber 4g; Sodium 214mg

Carrots and Raisins

Makes: 6 servings

If you like carrot salad, you are bound to like this warm version.

1 1/2 teaspoons vegetable oil
1 1/2 pounds carrots, peeled and sliced
    on the diagonal
1/2 teaspoon ground cumin
1/2 teaspoon ground cinnamon
1/2 teaspoon kosher salt
1/4 teaspoon freshly ground pepper
1/16 teaspoon cayenne pepper (optional)
1/2 cup orange juice
1/4 cup golden raisins
1 tablespoon packed light brown sugar
1 tablespoon chopped fresh parsley

1) Heat the oil in a large nonstick sauté pan. Add the carrots, cumin, cinnamon, salt, pepper, and cayenne. Stir and cook over medium heat until the aromas of the spices intensify, about 3 minutes.

2) Stir in the orange juice and raisins. Add the brown sugar. Simmer for 7 to 10 minutes, until the carrots become tender and the sauce thickens. Stir in the parsley and serve.

Per Serving: Calories 99; Protein 2g; Fat 1g (Saturated 0g); Carbohydrates 3g; Fiber 3g; Sodium 202mg

Rooted Carrots

Makes: 6 servings

Carrots bring sweetness to the sharper flavors of the root vegetables, and the root vegetables bring more complex, assertive flavors to the familiar taste of the carrots.

1 pound root vegetables, peeled and cut into
    chunks (parsnips, rutabaga, or turnips)
4 large carrots (about 1/2 pound), peeled and cut
    into 1-inch lengths
1/8 teaspoon freshly ground pepper
1/16 teaspoon ground nutmeg

1) Steam the vegetables until tender. This will take about 20 minutes, or less if cut into small cubes.

2) Mash or puree the vegetables with the spices, adding some of the steaming water if a thinner the consistency is desired.

Per Serving: Calories 66; Protein 1g; Fat 0g (Saturated 0g); Carbohydrates 16g; Fiber 4g; Sodium 20mg

Cauliflower

Cauliflower is not just pale broccoli and should be treated as the individual that it is. Cauliflower's florets and stems are very firm and yet they steam through to any tenderness desired and can handle long cooking. Its flavor is sharp and tangy without being overwhelming and combines wonderfully with other ingredients, from garlic to mild herbs. Not to mention that platters of crudités (raw vegetables) near dips are incomplete without this vegetable.

Cauliflower with Garlic Breadcrumbs

Makes: 5 servings

Herbs, garlic, and cauliflower are a wonderful combination.

1 large head cauliflower (about 1 1/2 pounds), cut into florets, stem discarded
1 slice bread, processed into soft breadcrumbs (about 1/2 cup)
1/2 teaspoon dried thyme
1 teaspoon dried basil
1/2 teaspoon dried marjoram
1/2 teaspoon kosher salt
1/4 teaspoon freshly ground pepper
1 1/2 tablespoons olive oil, divided
4 cloves garlic, minced

1) Steam the cauliflower. Once tender, drain and keep warm.

2) Meanwhile, combine the breadcrumbs with the herbs, salt, and pepper. Set aside. Heat 1 tablespoon of the oil in a large nonstick pan and cook the garlic over moderate heat until golden but not brown. Stir in the crumb mixture. Toss in the cauliflower and remaining oil. Toss until the cauliflower is well coated with oil and crumbs.

Per Serving: Calories 72; Protein 2g; Fat 4g (Saturated 1g); Carbohydrates 7g; Fiber 1g; Sodium 241mg

Dressed Cauliflower Florets

Makes: 6 servings

Serve hot or room temperature. Garnish with additional fresh chives for their bright color.

1 small head cauliflower, cut into florets, stem discarded
1 1/2 teaspoons olive oil
1 1/2 teaspoons honey
1/2 teaspoon Dijon mustard
1 tablespoon lemon juice
1/4 teaspoon kosher salt
1/8 teaspoon freshly ground pepper
1 1/2 teaspoons fresh tarragon (or 1/2 teaspoon dried)
1/2 teaspoon minced fresh chives

1) Steam the cauliflower until tender. Do not undercook.

2) Whisk together the remaining ingredients. Be sure to rub and crush the herbs between your fingers before adding them to the dressing. This releases their flavors.

3) Pour the dressing over the cauliflower while the florets are still warm.

Per Serving: Calories 26; Protein 1g; Fat 1g (Saturated 0g); Carbohydrates 4g; Fiber 1g; Sodium 102mg

Bayou Stewed Cauliflower

Makes: 6 servings

This is not a crisp vegetable dish! It stews for 1 hour and is all the better for the long time on the stove.

1 teaspoon vegetable oil
1/2 cup chopped onions
1 clove garlic, minced
1 small head cauliflower, cut into florets, stem discarded
One 14 1/2-ounce can stewed tomatoes
1 bay leaf
1/2 teaspoon dried thyme
1/2 teaspoon dried basil
1/8 teaspoon Tabasco sauce

1) Heat the oil in a large nonstick skillet. Brown the onions over high heat for 3 minutes. Stir in the garlic and cook 1 minute longer.

2) Add the remaining ingredients, reduce the heat to a simmer, and cook, uncovered, for 1 hour.

Per Serving: Calories 40; Protein 2g; Fat 1g (Saturated 0g); Carbohydrates 8g; Fiber 2g; Sodium 180mg

Curried Cauliflower and Peas

Makes: 6 servings

Cauliflower is frequently found on many Indian menus because it can handle long simmers, it doesn't get lost among the strong curry flavors, and its color is more attractive than green broccoli in the turmeric-yellow-tinged sauces.

1 tablespoon vegetable oil
1 jalapeño pepper, seeded and minced (wear rubber gloves)
1/4 cup chopped onions
1/2 teaspoon curry powder
2 teaspoons ground coriander
1 teaspoon ground cumin
1/4 teaspoon ground turmeric
1/2 teaspoon kosher salt
1 small head cauliflower, cut into florets, stem discarded
3/4 cup reduced-sodium, defatted chicken broth or water
1 cup diced red bell peppers
1 teaspoon finely grated fresh ginger
1 cup frozen peas
1/4 cup chopped fresh cilantro, for garnish (optional)

1) Heat the oil in a large nonstick skillet. Sauté the jalapeño and onions until golden. Stir in the dry spices and cook for 30 seconds and the aroma intensifies. Stir in the cauliflower and broth. Cover and cook until soft, about 15 to 20 minutes.

2) Stir in the bell peppers, ginger, and peas. Cook, uncovered, for 5 minutes. Garnish with the cilantro, if desired.

Per Serving: Calories 65; Protein 3g; Fat 3g (Saturated 0g); Carbohydrates 8g; Fiber 3g; Sodium 260mg

Roasted Cauliflower with Rosemary and Garlic

Makes: 6 servings

Garlic lovers can double the number of cloves.

1 large head cauliflower, cut into florets,
    stem discarded
3 tablespoons water
1 tablespoon olive oil
3 cloves garlic, crushed
1 teaspoon dried rosemary
1/2 teaspoon kosher salt

1) Preheat the oven to 450°F.

2) Toss together all the ingredients in a shallow casserole or rimmed baking sheet (a lasagna pan works well).

3) Place in the center of the oven and bake for 15 minutes. Stir and continue to bake, about 15 minutes longer, until the cauliflower is tender and brown in spots.

Per Serving: Calories 37; Protein 1g; Fat 2g (Saturated 0g); Carbohydrates 4g; Fiber 1g; Sodium 178mg

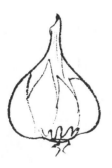

Corn

Every year new varieties of corn are introduced. Recently most of them have been "supersweet," which means that their sugar content remains high even after days of storage. This is in contrast to the older varieties, such as "sugar and butter" corn, that taste best within hours of picking. To my palate, the supersweet corn has a tough texture and the sweetness overwhelms the corn flavor; I'd go with the old-fashioned corn any day. There is nothing to compare to an ear of "Silver Queen" corn picked in the afternoon and eaten at dinner. All summer I go from farm stand to farm stand, trying each farmer's offerings. For those who live in the cities, farmer's markets are the place to buy fresh corn. Nonetheless, if you only have access to supersweet corn, it is a worthwhile seasonal pleasure. Cook it a minute or two longer than you would one of the more delicate varieties.

When corn is not in season it is not worth buying fresh. Fortunately, frozen corn kernels are excellent. I prefer the shoepeg variety because the kernels are smaller and sweeter than yellow corn. I rarely use canned corn kernels, since I'd rather do without the added sugars and salt. However, you'll find cream-style corn in several of my recipes (and often straight out of the can and on the dinner table, since it is one vegetable the kids never turn down).

Steamed Corn on the Cob

Makes: 6 servings

I like to steam, rather than boil, corn on hot days because it takes less time to bring the smaller amount of water to a boil. This saves a few minutes as well as keeps the kitchen and the cook cooler.

6 ears corn, husked and silked

Put a steamer basket in a large pot and pour in enough water to come up to the bottom of the basket. Bring to a boil. Add the corn, cover, and steam over high heat for 6 to 8 minutes, turning the ears once during cooking.

Per Serving: Calories 83; Protein 3g; Fat 1g (Saturated 0g); Carbohydrates 19g; Fiber 2g; Sodium 13mg

Microwaved Corn on the Cob

Makes: 1 serving

Microwaving is an excellent way to quickly cook a single ear of corn. It does so without the heat and bother of a pot of boiling water. However, the microwave is not a good choice for more than one ear, because the corn will cook unevenly and some kernels will toughen.

1 ear corn, husked and silked

Place the corn on a plate. Add 3 to 4 tablespoons water, cover with plastic wrap and microwave on high for 3 minutes. Let sit, wrapped, for 3 minutes before eating.

Per Serving: Calories 83; Protein 3g; Fat 1g (Saturated 0g); Carbohydrates 19g; Fiber 2g; Sodium 13mg

Grilled-in-the-Husk Corn on the Cob

Makes: 1 serving

When it is too hot to boil water, this is the way to cook corn on the cob.

1 ear corn

Prepare the grill. Place the corn, husk and all, directly on the grill. The corn will steam in its own wrapper and get some flavor from the grill. Turn several times during grilling, cooking about 10 minutes. Remove from the grill with tongs and let rest a few minutes until cool enough to handle. Husk, remove the silks, and eat.

Per Serving: Calories 83; Protein 3g; Fat 1g (Saturated 0g); Carbohydrates 19g; Fiber 2g; Sodium 13mg

Roasted Corn on the Cob

Makes: 4 servings

This is a good recipe for cookouts or camping trips. Put the foil-wrapped ears of corn in the hot ashes and turn frequently.

4 ears corn, husked and silked
1 1/2 teaspoons unsalted butter
1 1/2 teaspoons extra-virgin olive oil

1) Preheat oven to 450°F or prepare the grill.

2) Melt the butter with the oil and brush it onto the corn. Wrap each ear individually in foil.

3) Cook in the oven 30 minutes, or on the grill about 15 minutes. The corn should be cooked through and brown in places (though not burned).

Per Serving: Calories 111; Protein 3g; Fat 4g (Saturated 1g); Carbohydrates 19g; Fiber 2g; Sodium 13mg

Corn Confetti

Makes: 5 servings

This cheerful-looking dish is a good accompaniment for burgers or hot dogs.

1 1/2 teaspoons olive oil
1 red bell pepper, diced
1 clove garlic, minced
1/3 cup reduced-sodium, defatted chicken broth
4 cups corn kernels (thawed if frozen)
2 scallions, sliced
1/2 teaspoon kosher salt

1) Heat the oil in a medium nonstick sauté pan. Cook the bell pepper and garlic until wilted. Add the broth and corn. Cook, covered, over moderate-high heat until the corn is tender.

2) Toss in the scallions and salt. Cook 1 to 2 minutes, until the scallions wilt.

Per Serving: Calories 98; Protein 3g; Fat 2g (Saturated 0g); Carbohydrates 19g; Fiber 3g; Sodium 239mg

Chili and Lime Corn

Makes: 5 servings

This side dish has lots of flavor, but it won't overwhelm the main course.

2 teaspoons vegetable oil
2 cloves garlic, minced
1 jalapeño pepper (fresh or pickled), minced
3 scallions, sliced
1/2 teaspoon chili powder or pure ground mild chili powder
1/2 teaspoon kosher salt
1/4 teaspoon ground cumin
4 cups corn kernels (thawed if frozen)
1 teaspoon finely minced lime zest

1) Heat the oil in a large nonstick sauté pan. Cook the garlic over low heat until golden. Stir in the jalapeño and scallions and cook briefly. Stir in the chili powder, salt, and cumin and cook for about 30 seconds, until the aroma intensifies.

2) Stir in the corn and zest. Cover and cook until the corn is warmed through and no longer tastes raw. Add 1 tablespoon water if the mixture looks too dry.

Per Serving: Calories 109; Protein 4g; Fat 3g (Saturated 0g); Carbohydrates 21g; Fiber 3g; Sodium 179mg

Corn Fried Rice

Makes: 4 servings

Sichuan peppercorns impart a warm heat but are not as hot as cayenne pepper. They can be left out and the recipe will be less spicy yet still delicious.

1 teaspoon vegetable oil
1 tablespoon finely grated fresh ginger
1 clove garlic, minced
3 scallions, sliced
2 cups corn kernels (thawed if frozen)
1 cup cooked brown rice
1 tablespoon soy sauce
1/4 teaspoon freshly ground pepper
1/4 teaspoon crushed Sichuan peppercorns
2 tablespoons sherry
1 teaspoon Asian sesame oil

1) Heat the vegetable oil in a sauté pan over low heat. Sauté the ginger and garlic in the oil until they are golden. Keep the heat low because ginger tends to scorch.

2) Stir in the scallions. Cook for about 2 minutes, until the scallions wilt.

3) Add the corn, rice, soy sauce, pepper, peppercorns, sherry, and sesame oil. Increase the heat, cover, and cook about 5 minutes. Stir the rice a couple of times while cooking.

Per Serving: Calories 155; Protein 4g; Fat 4g (Saturated 0g); Carbohydrates 28g; Fiber 3g; Sodium 272mg

Green Beans

Pick green beans that are bright green, have tight, firm ends, and are smooth, not lumpy from being overmature.

Steamed Green Beans

Makes: 4 servings

1 pound green beans

1) Prepare the green beans by washing them well and then cutting off the tips at each end. To make this chore go quickly, put a handful onto a cutting board, line up the ends, and cut across many beans at one time. Haricots verts are fine, thin beans. Their tail end does not need trimming; only the stem end does.

2) Put a steamer insert in a pot, pour in a few inches of water, bring to a boil, and place the green beans in the steamer. Cover and cook for about 5 minutes, until the beans become pliable but still have a bit of a snap left to them. Remove from the steamer and eat immediately. If using in another recipe, chill in a bowl of cold water to stop the cooking, drain, and refrigerate until use. Beans can be steamed up to a day ahead of time.

Per Serving: Calories 35; Protein 2g; Fat 0g (Saturated 0g); Carbohydrates 8g; Fiber 4g; Sodium 7mg

Green Beans and Almonds

Makes: 6 servings

This classic combination is updated with garlic and olive oil.

1 1/2 tablespoons olive oil
1 clove garlic, minced
1/3 cup slivered almonds
1 1/2 pounds green beans, trimmed and steamed
1/4 teaspoon kosher salt
1/2 teaspoon dried marjoram

Heat the oil in a nonstick sauté pan. Add the garlic and almonds and cook until the almonds turn lightly golden. Toss in the beans, salt, and marjoram. Cook until the beans are warmed through.

Per Serving: Calories 110; Protein 4g; Fat 7g (Saturated 1g); Carbohydrates 10g; Fiber 5g; Sodium 88mg

Green Beans and Bacon

Makes: 4 servings

It is amazing how such a small quantity of bacon can make my family so happy. Even those not overly fond of green beans take heaping helpings when this appears at the table.

2 slices bacon
1 teaspoon olive oil
1/2 red bell pepper, julienned
1 pound green beans, trimmed and steamed
1/8 teaspoon kosher salt
1/8 teaspoon freshly ground pepper

1) Cook the bacon until crisp. Cut or crumble into small bits.

2) Heat the oil in a nonstick sauté pan. Sauté the bell peppers until they soften. Stir in the beans, then toss in the bacon, salt, and pepper and heat through.

Per Serving: Calories 66; Protein 3g; Fat 3g (Saturated 1g); Carbohydrates 9g; Fiber 4g; Sodium 118mg

Green Beans Cooked with Salsa

Makes: 4 servings

If you are tired of steamed vegetables, this is an easy way to jazz them up.

1 1/2 cups Red Salsa (page 592 or store-bought)
1 pound green beans, trimmed and steamed

Heat a nonstick sauté pan. Add the salsa and stir until warmed through. Add the beans and cook another 3 minutes, until all is hot and fragrant.

Per Serving: Calories 63; Protein 3g; Fat 0g (Saturated 0g); Carbohydrates 15g; Fiber 6g; Sodium 243mg

Gremolata Green Beans

Makes: 4 servings

Gremolata is a coarse mixture of garlic, parsley, and lemon. It does amazing things for green beans.

1 pound green beans, trimmed and cut into 2-inch pieces
2 tablespoons Gremolata (page 591)
1 teaspoon lemon juice

Steam the green beans until bright green and crisp-tender. While hot, toss with the gremolata and splash on the lemon juice. Serve immediately or at room temperature. The lemon juice will eventually cause the beans to brown, so do not make this too far ahead of time.

Per Serving: Calories 83; Protein 2g; Fat 5g (Saturated 1g); Carbohydrates 9g; Fiber 4g; Sodium 53mg

Asian Green Beans

Makes: 4 servings

Serve these hot or at room temperature. Leftovers continue to taste wonderful for several days.

1 pound green beans, trimmed

1 teaspoon Asian sesame oil

1 teaspoon vegetable oil

2 cloves garlic, minced

1 teaspoon finely grated fresh ginger

1/16 teaspoon crushed red pepper flakes, or to taste

1 1/2 teaspoons soy sauce

2 tablespoons water

1 teaspoon sesame seeds, toasted, for garnish (optional)

1) Lightly steam the beans, then immerse in cold water to stop them from cooking further. You can do this up to a day ahead of time.

2) Heat the oils in a sauté pan over low heat. Sauté the garlic and ginger in the oils until the garlic is golden and you can smell its sweetening aroma.

3) Add the beans, pepper flakes, soy sauce, and water. Stir to combine. Cook, covered, over high heat for a few minutes, until the water evaporates and the oil coats the beans and makes them shiny. Shake the pan and stir occasionally while the mixture is cooking.

4) Garnish with the sesame seeds, if desired.

Per Serving: Calories 59; Protein 2g; Fat 2g (Saturated 0g); Carbohydrates 9g; Fiber 4g; Sodium 136mg

Great Green Beans

Makes: 4 servings

Green beans keep their shape in vegetable stews. Here they provide texture to a melange of herbs and tomatoes.

2 teaspoons vegetable or olive oil
$1/2$ cup chopped onions
2 tablespoons white wine
1 teaspoon balsamic vinegar
3 plum tomatoes, seeded and chopped
$1/4$ teaspoon kosher salt
$1/4$ teaspoon freshly ground pepper
2 tablespoons minced fresh parsley
$1/4$ teaspoon dried oregano
$1/2$ pound green beans, trimmed and steamed

1) Heat the oil in a medium sauté pan. Add the onions and sauté until softened. Add the wine and vinegar and continue to cook over low heat, stirring frequently, until the onions begin to turn light golden and start to caramelize (this long cooking brings out the sweetness of the onions and thickens the vinegar).

2) Add the tomatoes and seasonings. Cook, covered, until the tomatoes are warmed through. If more liquid is needed, add another tablespoon or so of wine. Toss in the beans and heat through.

Per Serving: Calories 62; Protein 2g; Fat 3g (Saturated 0g); Carbohydrates 9g; Fiber 3g; Sodium 130mg

Creole Green Beans

Makes: 5 servings

In recent years there has been a growing though misguided belief that all vegetables should be served crisp and only lightly cooked. I don't agree. Sometimes stewed vegetables are just the ticket.

2 teaspoons vegetable oil
$1/2$ cup chopped onions
1 rib celery, chopped
$1/2$ green bell pepper, chopped
3 cloves garlic, minced
One $14 1/2$-ounce can stewed tomatoes
$1/2$ teaspoon dried thyme
$1/2$ teaspoon dried oregano
$1/4$ teaspoon ground allspice
$1/4$ teaspoon Tabasco sauce
$1/4$ teaspoon kosher salt
1 pound green beans, trimmed

1) Heat the oil in a medium saucepan or sauté pan and sauté the onions until translucent. Add the celery, bell pepper, and garlic. Sauté until the garlic turns golden.

2) Stir in the remaining ingredients and bring to a full simmer. Reduce to a gentle simmer and cook over medium-low heat, covered, until the beans are tender, about 10 to 15 minutes.

Per Serving: Calories 79; Protein 3g; Fat 2g (Saturated 0g); Carbohydrates 15g; Fiber 5g; Sodium 320mg

Stewed Green Beans and Potatoes

Makes: 6 servings

This is both a vegetable and a starch side dish. For a really easy dinner this is all you have to cook if it is served with a rotisserie chicken and a good loaf of bread.

1 tablespoon olive oil
1 cup chopped onions
2 cloves garlic, minced
1 pound green beans, trimmed
2 all-purpose potatoes, peeled and cubed (about 1 pound)
One 14$\frac{1}{2}$-ounce can whole tomatoes, drained and chopped
1 cup reduced-sodium, defatted chicken or vegetable broth
$\frac{1}{4}$ cup chopped fresh parsley
$\frac{1}{2}$ teaspoon kosher salt
$\frac{1}{4}$ teaspoon freshly ground pepper
1 teaspoon dried oregano

In a large skillet or Dutch oven, heat the oil and sauté the onions and garlic until golden. Stir in the remaining ingredients, reserving 1 tablespoon parsley for a garnish later. Bring to a full simmer, reduce to a gentle simmer, and cook over medium-low heat, covered, for 20 minutes.

Per Serving: Calories 133; Protein 5g; Fat 3g (Saturated 0g); Carbohydrates 25g; Fiber 5g; Sodium 359mg

Greens

Dark leafy greens are nutritional power-houses, high in iron, calcium, and folic acid among other nutrients, but unfortunately they are not often cooked in many kitchens. They have enough flavor to stand up to spices and meat entrées, so they can be an essential element in a menu.

All greens, even packaged spinach, need to be washed very well. Do this by immersing the leaves in a sink filled with cool water. If the bottom of the sink becomes gritty, lift out the greens, drain, and rinse out the sink and repeat the washing. Tear off any discolored, mushy leaves. Put the greens in a colander but don't dry (unless specified) because the clean wash water will help steam the greens.

Some leafy greens, like chard, have edible stems. Cut off the tough, ragged ends but save the rest. Red Swiss chard has ribs reminiscent of rhubarb and will leave a purple liquid in the pan. This is fine for a sauté, but if the chard is going into a recipe such as risotto, it is best to use the white-ribbed chard. Since the leaves cook more quickly than the stems, the ribs are often chopped and cooked first. Kale also has tough center ribs, but these are not good to eat and should be cut out and discarded. Sometimes spinach has tough ribs, which should be torn off. Small, tender leaves can be left whole.

Leafy greens start out taking up a lot of space but wilt down to less than one quarter of their original volume. For this reason, I use a large wok to cook greens because it can hold the entire amount. Use tongs to toss the greens constantly while cooking. Since they cook so quickly (they are done when wilted, which takes under 4 minutes), it is important to toss (not just stir) so that all the greens wilt at about the same time.

Spinach with Lemon and Garlic

Makes: 4 servings

Lemon zest provides a lot of lemon flavor. The recipe would be too sour if you tried to get all of that flavor from the juice alone.

2 teaspoons extra-virgin olive oil
2 cloves garlic, minced
2 teaspoons lemon juice
1 teaspoon lemon zest
$1/2$ teaspoon kosher salt
$1/8$ teaspoon freshly ground pepper
$1^1/2$ pounds fresh spinach, washed and trimmed

1) Heat the oil in a large sauté pan or wok. Sauté the garlic over low heat until golden but not browned.

2) Raise the heat to medium, add the lemon juice, zest, salt, pepper, and spinach. Stir until the spinach wilts. Immediately lift out of the pan using tongs (leaving the liquid in the pot) and place in a serving bowl.

Per Serving: Calories 61; Protein 5g; Fat 3g (Saturated 0g); Carbohydrates 7g; Fiber 5g; Sodium 375mg

Spinach with Golden Raisins and Almonds

Makes: 4 servings

Golden raisins—being milder and a prettier color than dark raisins—are best suited for this recipe.

2 tablespoons golden raisins
$1^1/2$ teaspoons olive oil
1 large shallot, minced (about 2 tablespoons)
2 tablespoons sliced or slivered almonds
1 pound fresh spinach, washed and trimmed
$1/8$ teaspoon ground nutmeg
$1/4$ teaspoon kosher salt
$1/4$ teaspoon freshly ground pepper

1) Soak the raisins in a small bowl of hot water to plump them.

2) Heat the oil in a large wok or sauté pan and cook the shallots about 3 minutes, until golden. Toss in the almonds and cook briefly until they change color. Drain the spinach and raisins (reserve the raisin water) and stir in. If you need to add some liquid to keep the greens moist, use the raisin water, a tablespoon at a time. Add the nutmeg, salt, and pepper and toss. Cover and cook until the greens wilt, about 4 minutes. Stir frequently. If there is liquid left in the wok when the spinach is done, lift out the greens, raisins, and nuts with tongs, leaving the liquid in the pot.

Per Serving: Calories 78; Protein 4g; Fat 4g (Saturated 0g); Carbohydrates 9g; Fiber 4g; Sodium 211mg

African Spinach and Peanuts

Makes: 8 servings

If you don't have a pot large enough to fit all the spinach, cook it in two batches.

2 pounds fresh spinach, washed and trimmed
2 cups thinly sliced onions
2 teaspoons vegetable oil
1/2 to 1 teaspoon kosher salt
1/8 teaspoon cayenne pepper
3/4 cup unsweetened lowfat coconut milk
3 tablespoons unsalted, unsweetened peanut butter
2 tablespoons chopped unsalted roasted peanuts,
    for garnish (optional)

1) Coarsely chop the spinach leaves.

2) Heat a large skillet or wok. Cook the onions in the oil until wilted. Stir in the spinach, a few handfuls at a time, and cook until all is wilted.

3) Stir in the salt, cayenne, coconut milk, and peanut butter. Keep stirring until the peanut butter is dissolved and no longer in one big lump. Cook until the sauce thickens. Garnish with peanuts, if desired.

Per Serving: Calories 95; Protein 5g; Fat 6g (Saturated 1g); Carbohydrates 9g; Fiber 4g; Sodium 219mg

Roasted Garlic and Greens

Makes: 4 servings

Raw garlic would be too sharp and bitter for this, but garlic mellowed and sweetened by roasting is just right.

10 to 12 cups dark leafy greens, washed
    and trimmed
1 teaspoon olive oil
4 large cloves Roasted Garlic (page 603), sliced
1/4 teaspoon kosher salt

1) Wash and trim the greens, then tear into medium-size pieces.

2) Heat the oil in a large saucepan or wok. Sauté the garlic over low heat until its aroma reaches you.

3) Add the greens and salt. Increase the heat and cook, covered, over high heat for 3 to 5 minutes, until the greens wilt. Shake the pan and stir frequently.

Per Serving: Calories 30; Protein 2g; Fat 1g (Saturated 0g); Carbohydrates 3g; Fiber 2g; Sodium 177mg

Steamed Beet Greens with Sesame Oil

Makes: 3 servings

Leaves with blemishes, brown spots, and those that are tough should be discarded. But tender beet greens are a summer delicacy.

1/2 pound fresh beet or other greens, washed
    and trimmed
1/4 teaspoon Asian sesame oil
1/8 to 1/4 teaspoon soy sauce
1/2 teaspoon toasted sesame seeds

1) Place the greens in a steamer basket set over rapidly boiling water. Cover and cook about 2 minutes, until they are wilted and a rich green color.

2) Toss the greens in a bowl with the sesame oil and soy sauce. Top with the sesame seeds and serve.

Per Serving: Calories 15; Protein 1g; Fat 1g (Saturated 0g); Carbohydrates 2g; Fiber 2g; Sodium 100mg

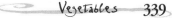

Sautéed Swiss Chard

Makes: 4 servings

Swiss chard has a slightly salty flavor. The leaves are often quite large and have holes in them. As long as they are unblemished and crisp, like fresh romaine lettuce, they are delicious.

3/4 to 1 pound red or white Swiss chard, washed
1 1/2 teaspoons olive oil
1 clove garlic, minced
1/4 teaspoon freshly ground pepper

1) Cut off and discard the tough bottoms of the stems. If the center rib is wider than 1 inch, cut it off and dice. Coarsely chop the leafy greens into pieces about 2 inches square.

2) Heat the oil in a large nonstick sauté pan or wok. Sauté the garlic over high heat for about 1 minute. Add the chard and cook for about 3 to 4 minutes more. Toss frequently until the chard is wilted and soft but still a bright, dark green. The wash water clinging to the leaves is usually enough liquid to cook and steam the greens. However, you might have to add 1 or 2 tablespoons more water to hasten cooking and make sure that the leaves wilt thoroughly.

3) Stir in the pepper and serve immediately.

Per Serving: Calories 31; Protein 1g; Fat 2g (Saturated 0g); Carbohydrates 3g; Fiber 1g; Sodium 167mg

Stir-Fried Bok Choy

Makes: 4 servings

Bok choy looks like a cabbage but is actually a dark leafy green. Purchase bok choy with crisp, dark leaves and pale green, almost white stems. All of it is edible.

1 to 1 1/2 pounds bok choy, washed
1 teaspoon vegetable oil
1 teaspoon Asian sesame oil
1 teaspoon finely grated fresh ginger
1 tablespoon sherry
1 1/2 teaspoons soy sauce
1 teaspoon toasted sesame seeds, for
    garnish (optional)

1) Slice the widest of the bok choy stems in half lengthwise, then cut all the stems Chinese-style, on the diagonal. Chop the leafy greens.

2) Heat the oils in a large nonstick sauté pan or wok. Add the ginger and cook for 1 minute. Stir in the bok choy and stir-fry for 3 minutes.

3) Pour in the sherry and soy sauce. Cover and cook until the greens are wilted, about 2 to 3 minutes more. Garnish with the sesame seeds, if desired, and serve.

Per Serving: Calories 39; Protein 2g; Fat 3g (Saturated 0g); Carbohydrates 3g; Fiber 1g; Sodium 203mg

Kale with Red Onion

Makes: 4 servings

I like plain, steamed kale only when the leaves are very young and very tender. (And if I can find them, I buy them, as they are a delicacy.) Otherwise, cooking kale with garlic and onions, as in this recipe, is the way to enjoy this strong green.

1 pound kale, washed and stems discarded
1 teaspoon olive oil
1 cup sliced red onions
2 cloves garlic, minced
1/4 teaspoon kosher salt
1/8 teaspoon freshly ground pepper
1/3 cup reduced-sodium, defatted chicken or
    vegetable broth

1) Bring a large pot of water to a boil. Immerse the kale in the boiling water and cook for about 4 minutes, until it turns bright green and wilts. Drain immediately. Once cool enough to handle, coarsely chop.

2) Heat the oil in a large sauté pan. Cook the onions and garlic about 5 minutes, until the onions wilt and the garlic turns golden. Stir frequently. Halfway through cooking, add a tablespoon of water. As it evaporates it will steam the onions, which will speed the cooking and keep the onions soft.

3) Add the chopped kale, salt, pepper, and broth to the pan. Stir and heat through.

Per Serving: Calories 67; Protein 3g; Fat 2g (Saturated 0g); Carbohydrates 11g; Fiber 3g; Sodium 189mg

Kale with Red Onion and Feta

Makes: 4 servings

This is a marvelous combination. All of the strong flavors balance each other.

1 recipe Kale with Red Onion (opposite)
1 ounce feta cheese (about 1/4 cup)

Follow the directions for Kale with Red Onion. During Step 3, crumble half the cheese into the kale right after adding the broth. Stir and heat through. Put in a serving bowl. Crumble the rest of the cheese over the kale. Serve immediately.

Per Serving: Calories 88; Protein 4g; Fat 3g (Saturated 1g); Carbohydrates 11g; Fiber 3g; Sodium 267mg

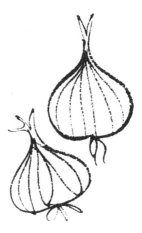

Spinach Bake

Makes: 8 servings

You'll need a food processor to mix this pie.

Two 10-ounce packages frozen spinach, thawed
1 cup 1% lowfat cottage cheese
3 cloves garlic
1 cup shredded reduced-fat mozzarella cheese
1 cup reduced-fat ricotta cheese
2 tablespoons grated Parmesan cheese
3 egg whites
1 teaspoon dried basil
1/4 teaspoon kosher salt
1/4 teaspoon freshly ground pepper

1) Preheat the oven to 350°F. Coat a 9-inch pie pan or round baking dish with nonstick spray.

2) Put the thawed spinach in a colander in the sink and squeeze out as much moisture as possible. Put the cottage cheese in a fine mesh sieve to drain out excess liquid.

3) With the food processor running, drop in the garlic to mince. Pulse in the cheeses, egg whites, basil, salt, and pepper until evenly mixed but not pureed. Pulse in the spinach.

4) Spread the mixture into the pie plate and place in the oven. Bake for 40 to 45 minutes, until the pie's center springs back to the touch. Wait 5 minutes for the casserole to set before serving.

Per Serving: Calories 110; Protein 13g; Fat 4g (Saturated 2g); Carbohydrates 6g; Fiber 2g; Sodium 358mg

Mushrooms

Mushrooms are often obviously dirty, with clumps of humus clinging to them. Mushrooms can be washed, but since they absorb water they should not be soaked. To get mushrooms clean, put them in a colander and toss under cool running water. Then take a damp paper towel and wipe the remaining dirt off. Do not wash mushrooms ahead of time or they will develop soft blotches. Large mushrooms with gilled undersides, such as portobellos, should not placed under water but wiped clean with a cloth.

Herbed Broiled Mushrooms

Makes: 6 servings

If you have a grilling rack for vegetables, cook these outside over moderate heat on the grill.

2 tablespoons olive oil
1 tablespoon white wine
1 tablespoon lemon juice
1 teaspoon dried tarragon
1 teaspoon dried basil
2 tablespoons chopped fresh parsley
1 clove garlic, crushed
1/2 teaspoon kosher salt
1/2 teaspoon freshly ground pepper
1 pound mushrooms, tough stem ends trimmed

1) In a medium bowl, whisk together all the ingredients except the mushrooms. Add the mushrooms and stir to coat evenly with the herbs. Let rest, stirring several times, until most of the liquid is absorbed, about 1/2 hour.

2) Coat a broiler pan with nonstick spray. Place the mushrooms on the pan and coat lightly with nonstick spray. Broil for about 3 minutes, until they sizzle and begin to brown. Serve immediately.

Per Serving: Calories 64; Protein 2g; Fat 5g (Saturated 1g); Carbohydrates 4g; Fiber 1g; Sodium 164mg

Grilled Portobello Mushrooms

Makes: 4 servings

Leftovers can be sliced and baked on a pizza.

1 pound portobello mushrooms (about 3 large)
2 teaspoons olive oil
Kosher salt
Freshly ground pepper

1) Preheat the grill to medium heat.

2) Snap out and discard the mushroom stems. Wipe the caps clean with a damp paper towel. Brush the caps with the oil.

3) Place the mushrooms on the grill. Cook until lines sear into the caps. Turn and continue to grill until the portobellos soften, about 5 minutes. Remove to a platter and dust with the salt and pepper.

Per Serving: Calories 48; Protein 2g; Fat 3g (Saturated 0g); Carbohydrates 5g; Fiber 1g; Sodium 5mg

Exotic Mushroom Sauté

Makes: 4 servings

Fancy mushrooms are showing up in markets. They have more pronounced mushroom flavor than the commercial white mushrooms and need little adornment beyond a touch of butter, salt, and pepper. The exotic mushrooms are costly, so I combine them with the standard white mushrooms; if you're feeling extravagant, splurge and use all fancy mushrooms.

1/2 pound white mushrooms
1/2 pound exotic mushrooms, such as oyster, enoki, or shiitake
1 1/2 teaspoons unsalted butter
1 1/2 teaspoons olive oil
1/4 teaspoon kosher salt
1/8 teaspoon freshly ground pepper

1) Clean the mushrooms and trim off and discard woody stems. Slice the mushrooms if they are large; otherwise halve them or leave whole.

2) Heat the butter and oil in a pan until the butter melts and begins to darken. Stir in the mushrooms and cook until wilted. Add the salt and pepper.

Per Serving: Calories 61; Protein 3g; Fat 4g (Saturated 1g); Carbohydrates 7g; Fiber 1g; Sodium 124mg

Pan-Fried Garlic Mushrooms

Makes: 6 servings

Instead of cooking off the mushroom juices, here it is absorbed by bread and so kept within the recipe.

1 pound mushrooms, preferably a dark variety such as crimini
2 tablespoons olive oil
4 cloves garlic, minced
2 tablespoons white wine
2 tablespoons chopped fresh parsley
1/2 teaspoon kosher salt
1/4 teaspoon freshly ground pepper
1 slice homemade-quality wheat or white bread, cut into tiny cubes

1) Clean the mushrooms and trim off the tough stem ends. Slice or quarter large mushrooms.

2) Heat the oil in a nonstick sauté pan. Sauté the garlic for about 3 minutes, until golden but not brown. Add the wine and mushrooms and cook for 4 to 5 minutes, until the mushrooms begin to wilt. Toss in the parsley, salt, pepper and bread. Continue to cook over medium-high heat until the bread absorbs the juices.

Per Serving: Calories 80; Protein 2g; Fat 5g (Saturated 1g); Carbohydrates 7g; Fiber 1g; Sodium 191mg

Thyme Mushrooms

Makes: 2 servings

Serve these with roasted chicken. Leftovers are super on a burger.

1/2 teaspoon olive oil
1/2 pound mushrooms, cleaned and stems trimmed, quartered if large
1/2 teaspoon dried thyme
1 tablespoon minced fresh parsley
1/8 teaspoon kosher salt
1/16 teaspoon freshly ground pepper

1) Heat the oil in a 10-inch nonstick sauté pan. Add the mushrooms. Cook, tossing frequently, until the caps brown.

2) Reduce the heat to medium-low, add the seasonings, and continue to cook until the mushrooms exude liquid, then increase the heat and cook off most of this liquid. Some very dry mushrooms won't give off any liquid; in that case simply cook until they begin to soften. The entire cooking time is no more than 7 minutes or so.

Per Serving: Calories 40; Protein 2g; Fat 2g (Saturated 0g); Carbohydrates 6g; Fiber 2g; Sodium 126mg

Pearl Onions, Mushrooms, and Peas

Makes: 5 servings

This isn't a trendy way to serve mushrooms, but I do like to see old favorites like this at the table. Roast a chicken, bake a winter squash, warm some dinner rolls, and put yourself in a Norman Rockwell picture.

1 1/2 teaspoons olive oil
12 to 16 pearl onions, peeled and ends trimmed (about 1 pound)
1/2 cup reduced-sodium, defatted chicken broth
1/2 pound mushrooms, cleaned and stems trimmed, quartered if large
1 pound frozen peas
1 teaspoon unsalted butter
1/2 teaspoon kosher salt
1/4 teaspoon freshly ground pepper

1) Heat the oil in a heavy nonstick pan and add the onions. Cook, stirring frequently, until the onions are lightly brown in spots. Pour in the broth, cover, and cook over moderate heat until the liquid is reduced and the onions are tender, about 5 to 7 minutes.

2) Melt the butter in the pan, add the mushrooms, and cook, uncovered, until they wilt, begin to brown, and exude liquid.

3) Meanwhile, cook the peas in the microwave or steamer. Drain and toss in with the mushrooms and onions. Add the salt and pepper.

Per Serving: Calories 128; Protein 7g; Fat 3g (Saturated 1g); Carbohydrates 21g; Fiber 6g; Sodium 346mg

Peas

There is always a bag of peas in my freezer. The season for fresh peas is so fleeting that peas would be a rare luxury if it weren't for the frozen. Luckily, frozen peas are of high quality, and if cooked briefly, they are sweet and retain much of their fresh texture.

Other peas available in the freezer are snap peas and snow peas. Snow peas are the familiar Chinese vegetable, and the entire flat pod is eaten. Fresh definitely hold up better when cooked, with a brighter color and crisper texture, though the frozen can be used in a pinch for stir-fries. Snap peas are crunchy, edible pods with full-size sweet peas inside. Fresh are delicious raw or cooked. Most fresh varieties need to have their tough strings pulled off before eating. Frozen versions are excellent and are convenient since they already have their strings removed.

Buttered Peas

Makes: 5 servings

Sometimes a food writer shouldn't tamper with the basics. Buttered peas can't be improved on.

2 teaspoons unsalted butter
1 pound frozen peas, thawed
1/4 teaspoon kosher salt
1 tablespoon minced fresh mint (optional)

Warm the butter in a nonstick pan. Add the peas, salt, and mint and toss over medium heat for about 2 minutes, until glistening with butter and heated through.

Per Serving: Calories 83; Protein 5g; Fat 2g (Saturated 1g); Carbohydrates 12g; Fiber 4g; Sodium 198mg

Carrots and Peas

Makes: 2 servings

I grew up in New Jersey and ate many meals at diners. (My dad still thinks that diner food is the height of culinary expertise. When it is done well, he is absolutely right.) So one thing that I ate a lot of as a child were little dishes of carrots and peas, which is the preferred side dish at such establishments. What I learned when I started to cook for myself was how good this humble dish is when the carrots are fresh, not frozen.

1 cup cubed carrots (about 2 carrots)
1/2 cup peas (fresh or frozen)
1/8 teaspoon freshly ground pepper
Minced fresh mint or dill (optional)

1) Place the carrots in a steamer over rapidly boiling water and steam for 5 minutes.

2) Add the peas to the steamer and heat through. Toss the peas and carrots in a bowl with the pepper, and the mint or dill, if desired.

Per Serving: Calories 60; Protein 3g; Fat 0g (Saturated 0g); Carbohydrates 13g; Fiber 4g; Sodium 27mg

Oriental Sugar Snap Peas

Makes: 6 servings

Snap peas go especially well with main course fish dishes.

1 pound sugar snap peas (fresh or frozen)
1 to 3 tablespoons water
1 teaspoon Asian sesame oil
1/2 teaspoon sesame seeds
1/4 teaspoon kosher salt

1) If the peas are frozen, thaw quickly under warm running water. If the peas are fresh it might be necessary to pull off their tough strings.

2) In a large sauté pan or wok, heat the water to boiling. Fresh peas will need the full amount, frozen only about 1 tablespoon. Toss in the peas and cook until they turn a brighter green and the water evaporates.

3) Stir in the oil, sesame seeds, and salt and cook for 2 minutes more.

Per Serving: Calories 42; Protein 2g; Fat 1g (Saturated 0g); Carbohydrates 6g; Fiber 2g; Sodium 88mg

Snow Peas and Water Chestnuts

Makes: 6 servings

Ever noticed how, at Chinese restaurants, the snow peas are eaten before the rest of the dish is polished off?

1/4 cup reduced-sodium, defatted chicken broth
1 pound snow peas, trimmed
1 teaspoon Asian sesame oil
One 5-ounce can sliced water chestnuts, drained and rinsed

1) Bring the broth to a boil in a large nonstick sauté pan or wok. Toss in the peas, cover, and cook for 3 minutes, until the peas turn bright green. Shake the pan frequently.

2) Add the sesame oil and water chestnuts and continue to cook for another 2 minutes. Serve immediately.

Per Serving: Calories 44; Protein 2g; Fat 1g (Saturated 0g); Carbohydrates 7g; Fiber 3g; Sodium 25mg

Sugar Snap Peas with Mint

Makes: 6 servings

Mint and peas are made for each other. But the mint must be fresh. Dried mint tastes like herbal tea leaves and is rarely successful in a recipe.

1 pound sugar snap peas (fresh or frozen)
1 to 3 tablespoons water
1 teaspoon olive oil
1 tablespoon chopped fresh mint
1/4 teaspoon kosher salt

1) If the peas are frozen, thaw quickly under warm running water. If the peas are fresh it might be necessary to snap off the stem end and pull off the tough strings.

2) In a large sauté pan or wok, heat the water to boiling. Fresh peas will need the full amount, frozen only about 1 tablespoon. Toss in the peas and cook until they turn a brighter green and the water evaporates.

3) Stir in the oil, mint, and salt and cook for 2 minutes more.

Per Serving: Calories 41; Protein 2g; Fat 1g (Saturated 0g); Carbohydrates 6g; Fiber 2g; Sodium 88mg

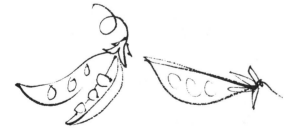

Potatoes

Potatoes are a healthful food. They contain potassium, vitamin C, and other important nutrients. But their positive qualities get lost when mashed with butter or filled with full-fat sour cream. Here are a selection of recipes that keep their beneficial reputation intact.

Before cooking potatoes it helps to know the differences between the major types. Baking potatoes, called russets (or sometimes Idahos) are usually a uniform, oblong size, with coarse brown skin and a white interior. Their moisture and starch content ensure that they bake up fluffy and dry. But these same qualities make the russet a poor choice for potato salads or skillet-cooked recipes.

When you need a potato to hold together, look for a waxy variety, like red bliss or white potatoes. These have thin skins, sometimes a golden interior, and a firm texture even when cooked. A special treat is when "new" potatoes are available. These are freshly dug, usually small and round waxy potatoes. I like to scrub them clean and roast them whole with garlic and rosemary.

All-purpose potatoes are starchy and boil up soft, which make them useful for stews and mashed potatoes. Another potato that is ideal for mashing is the Yukon Gold, or one called Yellow Finn. These are small, irregularly shaped potatoes with a creamy yellow interior that taste as if they have butter already in them.

In this country, the words *sweet potato* and *yam* are used interchangeably, but true yams (botanically speaking) are grown only in South and Central America and not at all like our sweet potatoes. There are many varieties of sweet potatoes, ranging from garnet red to light orange. All sweet potatoes are filled with beta-carotenes and other good things, but they vary in sweetness and moisture content and the recipes should be adjusted accordingly. When a recipe calls for a certain potato it is because the outcome will be best with that type. When a recipe doesn't specify, feel free to use whatever is on hand.

Perfect Baked Potato

Makes: 1 serving

Cook as many potatoes as needed. Leftovers are always welcome for hash browns, soups, and stuffed potatoes.

1 russet potato, scrubbed clean

1) Preheat the oven to 400°F. Bake the potato in the oven for 1 hour.

2) As soon as the potato is removed from the oven, slash it across its top and push it slightly open. This releases steam and prevents it from becoming soggy.

Per Serving: Calories 133; Protein 3g; Fat 0g (Saturated 0g); Carbohydrates 31g; Fiber 3g; Sodium 10mg

Microwaved Baked Potato

Makes: 1 serving

This is a useful shortcut but works best for single servings. If you want to cook two potatoes, you will have to almost double the cooking time and turn the potatoes several times.

1 russet potato, scrubbed clean
1/2 teaspoon vegetable oil (optional)

1) Prick the potato in several places with a fork. Place in the microwave oven and cook on high for 3 minutes. Turn over and cook for another 3 minutes. Let sit for 3 minutes before serving.

2) If you desire a crispy potato skin and an oven-baked appearance, before microwaving the potato, preheat the oven to 425°F. Once the potato is microwaved, rub the skin with the oil and place in the preheated oven for 7 minutes.

Per Serving: Calories 133; Protein 3g; Fat 0g (Saturated 0g); Carbohydrates 31g; Fiber 3g; Sodium 10mg

Sour Cream and Chives for a Baked Potato

Makes: 1 serving

Some people bake potatoes as an excuse to eat sour cream and chives. Here is a version to indulge in.

2 tablespoons lowfat sour cream
1/4 teaspoon chopped chives (fresh or frozen)
1/4 teaspoon kosher salt, or to taste
1/8 teaspoon freshly ground pepper, or to taste

Stir together all the ingredients to blend. Adjust the seasonings.

Per Serving: Calories 36; Protein 1g; Fat 2g (Saturated 2g); Carbohydrates 4g; Fiber 0g; Sodium 510mg

Garlic Lovers' Potatoes

Makes: 4 servings

Use the smallest new potatoes available.

1 pound new potatoes, scrubbed clean
1 teaspoon olive oil
4 cloves garlic, peeled and thickly sliced
1 tablespoon minced shallot
1/4 teaspoon kosher salt
1/8 teaspoon freshly ground pepper, or more
   to taste
Fresh chopped rosemary or parsley, for
   garnish (optional)

1) If large, cut the potatoes into thick slices. Steam for about 7 minutes, until they are firm but a knife can slip into the centers.

2) Coat a casserole dish with the oil. Add the steamed potatoes, garlic, shallot, salt, and pepper. Toss to mix well.

3) Bake, uncovered, in a preheated 350°F oven for 30 minutes. Stir a couple of times during baking.

4) Garnish with freshly chopped rosemary or parsley, if desired.

Per Serving: Calories 106; Protein 3g; Fat 1g (Saturated 0g); Carbohydrates 22g; Fiber 2g; Sodium 128mg

Onion and Herb Potatoes

Makes: 6 servings

Timing will depend on how deep the casserole is. Preferably, the potato cubes should be about three deep. Piled higher and they won't brown; in a single layer they'll dry out.

1 cup sliced onions
6 medium potatoes, peeled and cut into 1-inch
   chunks (2 pounds)
1 tablespoon olive oil
2 tablespoons water
1/2 teaspoon kosher salt
1/4 teaspoon dried thyme, or 1 teaspoon
   minced fresh
1/4 teaspoon dried rosemary, or 1 teaspoon
   minced fresh

1) Preheat the oven to 375°F.

2) Coat a casserole with nonstick spray.

3) Combine all the ingredients in a bowl, then transfer them to the casserole.

4) Place the casserole in the oven and bake for 45 minutes to 1 hour, until the onions begin to brown in spots. Stir the potatoes every 20 minutes to promote even cooking and browning.

Per Serving: Calories 147; Protein 3g; Fat 2g (Saturated 0g); Carbohydrates 29g; Fiber 3g; Sodium 170mg

Potato and Vegetable Gratin

Makes: 8 servings

If sweet onions are not in season, use a red onion.

1 slice white bread, cut into small cubes
1 tablespoon grated Parmesan or Romano cheese
6 medium potatoes (about 2 pounds)
3 cloves garlic, minced
1 red bell pepper, cut into 1/2-inch pieces
1 green bell pepper, cut into 1/2-inch pieces
1 cup sliced sweet onions, such as Vidalia
2 teaspoons kosher salt
1/4 teaspoon freshly ground pepper
2 teaspoons dried oregano
3 tablespoons olive oil

1) Preheat the oven to 400°F. Combine the bread cubes and cheese in a small bowl and set aside.

2) If you are using thin-skinned potatoes, they do not have to be peeled, but peel if using russet or all-purpose. Thickly slice the potatoes. There should be about 6 cups.

3) Toss the potatoes with the remaining ingredients except the bread and cheese. Put into a 3-quart casserole and place in the oven. Bake for 45 minutes, until the potatoes are tender. Top with the bread and cheese and continue to bake for about 10 minutes, until the bread begins to brown and the cheese melts.

Per Serving: Calories 170; Protein 4g; Fat 6g (Saturated 1g); Carbohydrates 27g; Fiber 3g; Sodium 523mg

Mushroom and Cheese Scalloped Potatoes

Makes: 6 servings

Slicing the potatoes can be quickly accomplished in a food processor.

2 pounds potatoes, peeled (about 4 large potatoes)
3 tablespoons unbleached, all-purpose white flour
1 teaspoon kosher salt
1/4 teaspoon freshly ground pepper
1 tablespoon grainy mustard
3/4 cup skim or 1% lowfat milk
1 cup lowfat sour cream
1/2 cup grated reduced-fat cheddar cheese
1 teaspoon unsalted butter
1 cup sliced mushrooms
1 tablespoon grated or minced onions

1) Preheat the oven to 375°F. Coat a 2- to 2 1/2-quart oblong pan with butter-flavored non-stick spray.

2) Slice the potatoes about 1/4 inch thick.

3) Whisk together the flour, salt, pepper, mustard, milk, and sour cream. Stir in all but 2 tablespoons of the cheddar cheese.

4) Melt the butter in a small nonstick sauté pan. Wilt the mushrooms and onions in the butter.

5) Place half the potatoes in the casserole, distribute all the mushrooms across the potatoes, and pour on half the milk mixture. Layer on the remaining potatoes and pour the rest of the sauce over them. Top with the reserved cheese.

6) Bake, covered, for 50 minutes. Uncover and bake for 10 minutes more, until the potatoes are tender when pierced with a fork.

Per Serving: Calories 197; Protein 8g; Fat 5g (Saturated 3g); Carbohydrates 33g; Fiber 2g; Sodium 487mg

Savory Potatoes

Makes: 6 servings

These soy sauce–darkened potatoes are cooked for a long time so that the flavors go all the way through.

5 medium all-purpose potatoes, sliced (about 1^1/2 pounds)
1 cup sliced onions
1 tablespoon minced fresh parsley
2 tablespoons soy sauce
^{1}/3 cup water or reduced-sodium, defatted chicken broth

1) Preheat the oven to 375°F.

2) Toss together all the ingredients and place in a covered casserole dish. Bake for 1^1/2 hours, stirring a couple of times while baking.

Per Serving: Calories 100; Protein 3g; Fat 0g (Saturated 0g); Carbohydrates 23g; Fiber 2g; Sodium 351mg

Confetti Potatoes

Makes: 6 servings

Someimes the color of diced red pepper in a recipe brightens an entire menu.

1 tablespoon olive oil
6 cups cooked potatoes (from about 6 medium potatoes)
^{1}/2 red bell pepper, diced
^{1}/2 green bell pepper, diced
2 tablespoons chopped fresh parsley
^{1}/8 teaspoon kosher salt
^{1}/4 teaspoon freshly ground pepper
Dash paprika for color

1) Heat the oil in a large skillet. Add the potatoes and bell peppers and cook until the potatoes begin to brown.

2) Add the parsley, salt, and pepper. Place in a serving bowl and dust with the paprika.

Per Serving: Calories 137; Protein 3g; Fat 2g (Saturated 0g); Carbohydrates 27g; Fiber 2g; Sodium 47mg

Dilled New Potatoes

Makes: 4 servings

Leftovers make a great potato salad.

1 pound waxy potatoes, such as red bliss
2 teaspoons olive oil
^{1}/4 teaspoon kosher salt
^{1}/4 teaspoon freshly ground pepper
1 teaspoon minced fresh dill

1) If potatoes are small, leave whole and unpeeled. Thickly slice large potatoes.

2) Steam the potatoes until just tender. (At this point they can be refrigerated for as long as 1 day.)

3) Heat the oil in a skillet and add the potatoes, salt, and pepper. Cook, stirring, until the potatoes begin to brown.

4) Toss in the dill and cook for 1 minute longer.

Per Serving: Calories 110; Protein 2g; Fat 2g (Saturated 0g); Carbohydrates 21g; Fiber 2g; Sodium 127mg

Greek Stewed Potatoes and Tomatoes

Makes: 4 servings

Waxy potatoes hold up during this long, slow cooking. All-purpose potatoes and russets would fall apart.

1 tablespoon olive oil
1 cup chopped onions
2 cloves garlic, minced
1 pound waxy potatoes, such as red bliss, thickly
  sliced
One 14^1/2-ounce can stewed tomatoes
1 cup water
1^1/2 teaspoons dried oregano
1 bay leaf
1 teaspoon kosher salt
^{1}/4 teaspoon freshly ground pepper

1) Heat the oil in a large nonstick skillet. Add the onions and garlic and cook about 4 minutes, until the onions soften and begin to change color. Add the potatoes and cook 2 minutes longer.

2) Stir in the remaining ingredients and bring to a full boil. Reduce to a simmer, cover, and cook for about 40 minutes, until the liquid has cooked down and the potatoes are very tender.

Per Serving: Calories 165; Protein 4g; Fat 4g (Saturated 1g); Carbohydrates 31g; Fiber 4g; Sodium 742mg

Greek Stewed Potatoes and Tomatoes with Feta Cheese

Makes: 4 servings

Adding feta cheese turns this into a richer, more complex side dish. Vegetarians can enjoy this for dinner along with a green salad and crusty bread.

1 recipe Greek Stewed Potatoes and Tomatoes
  (**opposite**)
^{1}/4 cup crumbled feta cheese

1) Prepare the Greek Stewed Potatoes and Tomatoes and place, very hot, in a serving dish.

2) Distribute the cheese on top and serve immediately.

Per Serving: Calories 185; Protein 5g; Fat 5g (Saturated 2g); Carbohydrates 31g; Fiber 4g; Sodium 820mg

About Mashed Potatoes

These mashed potato recipes are not made with butter, but they are still delicious and creamy. Cooking liquid, cheese, and seasonings take the place of butter. Using Yukon Gold potatoes will make the flavor even richer.

Mashed potatoes can be made with or without the skin. If the potato has a slight green cast or blemishes, peel it. But if the skin is thin and fresh-looking, leave it on. Red-skinned potatoes especially add an extra element of color, texture, and flavor when the skins are left on.

The best tool for mashing potatoes is a hand-held masher or ricer. Never use a food processor because the results will be as elastic as glue.

Mashed Potatoes

Makes: 6 servings

Cooking the potatoes in milk gives them a richer flavor and smoother texture than when water is used.

5 medium potatoes, scrubbed clean and quartered (1¹/2 pounds)
1¹/2 cups 1% lowfat milk
¹/4 teaspoon kosher salt, or more to taste
¹/8 teaspoon freshly ground pepper, or more to taste

1) Put the potatoes in a pot and pour in the milk. Add enough water just to cover the potatoes. Bring to a boil, then reduce the heat and simmer until the potatoes are soft and a dull knife can be inserted easily.

2) Using a slotted spoon, remove the potatoes and put them in a mixing bowl. Mash them, adding some cooking liquid if moisture is needed. Depending on the type and age of the potatoes, I've had to use anywhere from less than a cup to almost 2 cups of liquid. Mash in the salt and pepper. Taste and adjust the seasonings, if desired.

Per Serving: Calories 102; Protein 3g; Fat 0g (Saturated 0g); Carbohydrates 22g; Fiber 2g; Sodium 102mg

Mashed Potatoes with Roasted Garlic

Makes: 6 servings

Unlike raw or sautéed garlic, roasted garlic is as soft and spreadable as brie cheese. Most of it will mash smoothly with the potatoes, but flecks of intense flavor will remain studded throughout.

5 medium potatoes (about 1¹/2 pounds)
1¹/2 cups 1% lowfat milk
¹/4 teaspoon kosher salt, or more to taste
¹/8 teaspoon freshly ground pepper, or more to taste
5 cloves Roasted Garlic (page 603), peeled

Follow the directions for Mashed Potatoes (opposite). Add the roasted garlic along with the salt and pepper in Step 2.

Per Serving: Calories 105; Protein 3g; Fat 0g (Saturated 0g); Carbohydrates 23g; Fiber 2g; Sodium 103mg

Mashed Potatoes with Cheese

Makes: 6 servings

The type of cheese you choose will make a difference since both goat and feta are distinctive cheeses. Their salt contents vary greatly, so taste and adjust the seasonings before serving.

6 potatoes (about 2 pounds)
3 ounces goat or feta cheese (about 3 tablespoons)
1/2 cup nonfat milk, or more as necessary
1 teaspoon kosher salt, or to taste
1/4 teaspoon freshly ground pepper
1 tablespoon chopped chives (fresh or
    frozen; optional)

1) Peel the potatoes, cut into chunks, and put into a pot of boiling water. Cook for 10 minutes, until tender. Drain.

2) Mash the potatoes, cheese, and milk until smooth. Add more milk if the potatoes look dry. Stir in the salt, pepper, and chives.

Per Serving: Calories 178; Protein 7g; Fat 4g (Saturated 3g); Carbohydrates 29g; Fiber 2g; Sodium 413mg

Curried Mashed Potatoes

Makes: 6 servings

I love the combination of potatoes and peas. Remember mashing them together on your dinner plate when you were a kid? This version is a bit more adult, but no less fun.

2 teaspoons vegetable oil
1 cup chopped onions
2 cloves garlic, minced
1 small carrot, peeled and chopped
1/2 cup frozen peas, thawed
1/2 teaspoon kosher salt
2 teaspoons curry powder
1 pound potatoes, peeled and quartered (2 large)

1) Heat the oil in a small nonstick pan. Cook the onions, garlic, and carrot until they turn light golden. Cover between stirrings. Stir in the peas, salt, and curry powder and cook briefly until the curry aroma intensifies. Set aside.

2) Meanwhile, boil the potatoes until soft. Remove with a slotted spoon to a bowl. Mash, adding cooking liquid until the desired consistency is achieved. Stir in the sautéed vegetables.

Per Serving: Calories 101; Protein 3g; Fat 2g (Saturated 0g); Carbohydrates 20g; Fiber 3g; Sodium 184mg

Mashed Potatoes and Balsamic Onions

Makes: 6 servings

These are absolutely delicious.

1 tablespoon vegetable oil
1¹/2 cups chopped onions
2 teaspoons balsamic vinegar
2 cups nonfat milk
2 cups water
1¹/2 pounds potatoes, peeled and quartered (about 5 medium)
¹/2 teaspoon kosher salt, or to taste
¹/4 teaspoon freshly ground pepper, or to taste

1) Heat the oil in a nonstick sauté pan. Cook the onions until they turn golden, about 5 minutes. Stir in the balsamic vinegar and continue to cook until the onions are soft and sweet. Keep the pan covered between stirrings.

2) Meanwhile, bring the milk and water to a simmer in a saucepan. Add the potatoes and cook until soft. Using a slotted spoon, remove the tender potatoes to a bowl. Mash, adding cooking liquid until the desired consistency is achieved.

3) Stir in the sautéd onions, salt, and pepper. Taste and adjust for salt and pepper.

Per Serving: Calories 141; Protein 4g; Fat 3g (Saturated 0g); Carbohydrates 26g; Fiber 3g; Sodium 191mg

Mashed Potato Timbales

Makes: 2 servings

In this recipe, mashed potatoes rich with sour cream and cheese are baked in muffin cups to make elegant individual servings. Once the potato mixture is packed into the muffin cups, they can be covered with plastic wrap and refrigerated for up to 2 days.

1 tablespoon dry breadcrumbs
6 medium potatoes, cooked (about 2 pounds)
1 cup lowfat ricotta cheese
1 cup lowfat sour cream
1 egg white
6 cloves Roasted Garlic (page 603; optional)
1¹/2 teaspoons kosher salt
¹/2 teaspoon freshly ground pepper
1 tablespoon minced chives (fresh or frozen)

1) Coat 12 medium-size muffin cups with nonstick spray. Dust with the breadcrumbs. Preheat the oven to 375°F.

2) Peel the potatoes and mash them briefly until lumpy.

3) Using an electric mixer, beat the ricotta, sour cream, egg white, and garlic until smooth. Add the potatoes, salt, and pepper. Beat on low speed until almost smooth (small lumps are okay). Stir in the chives. Taste, and adjust the salt and pepper.

4) Pack the potato mixture into the muffin cups, filling each to its top, then smooth with a rubber spatula. Depending on the size of the potatoes and the muffin cups, you might need to prepare more cups or leave a few empty.

5) Bake for about 45 minutes, until cooked through and lightly brown.

Per Serving: Calories 104; Protein 4g; Fat 2g (Saturated 2g); Carbohydrates 17g; Fiber 1g; Sodium 290mg

Pan-Crisped Sweet Potato Cubes

Makes: 6 servings

Boiled sweet potatoes go mushy and lack the flavor of baked sweets. But parboiled and then crisped in a pan, they have it all—flavor, texture, and a cute shape.

2 to 3 large sweet potatoes, cut into $1/4$-inch cubes, about 6 cups
2 tablespoons vegetable oil
$1/2$ teaspoon kosher salt
$1/4$ teaspoon freshly ground pepper
2 tablespoons chopped fresh parsley

1) Drop the potatoes into the boiling water and cook for about 5 minutes, until they just begin to get tender on the outside but remain crisp inside. Immediately drain and turn out onto a clean kitchen cloth towel to dry.

2) Heat the oil over high heat in a large nonstick skillet. Add the cubes, shaking the pan and stirring frequently. Cook until the cubes crisp, about 15 minutes. (Cook them in two batches if they don't fit comfortably in the skillet.) Toss in the salt, pepper, and parsley and serve.

Per Serving: Calories 201; Protein 3g; Fat 5g (Saturated 0g); Carbohydrates 37g; Fiber 4g; Sodium 181mg

Candied Sweet Potatoes

Makes: 5 servings

Surprisingly, although sweet potatoes are very sweet on their own, they take well to added sugars.

4 medium sweet potatoes (about 2 pounds)
1 tablespoon unsalted butter
$1/4$ cup packed light brown sugar
1 tablespoon honey
$1/4$ cup hot water

1) Boil the potatoes whole in their skins until a fork can just be inserted. Don't boil until soft. This can be done up to 1 day ahead. Peel and cut into thick slices.

2) Melt the butter in a large nonstick pan. Brown the potato slices.

3) Meanwhile, dissolve the sugar and honey in the hot water. Pour over the browned potatoes. Cover and cook over low heat for 10 minutes.

Per Serving: Calories 267; Protein 3g; Fat 3g (Saturated 2g); Carbohydrates 59g; Fiber 4g; Sodium 29mg

Sweet Potato Spears

Makes: 6 servings

I make these a couple of times a month for my family and they are always on the Thanksgiving menu.

4 medium sweet potatoes, peeled
    (about 2 pounds)
1¹/2 tablespoons vegetable oil
¹/4 teaspoon kosher salt
¹/8 teaspoon freshly ground pepper

1) Preheat the oven to 425°F. A hot oven is required to crisp the potatoes. If you need the oven to be at a lower temperature because you are also baking something else at the same time, don't worry. The potatoes will still bake, but they won't be as firm. At the last minute, you can turn up the heat to crisp them.

2) Cut the sweet potatoes into pickle-size spears. If the potatoes are especially large around, cut the thickest spears in half lengthwise so that they look like steak fries, about ¹/2 inch thick.

3) Toss the spears with the oil, salt, and pepper until they are well coated.

4) Place the spears in one layer on a baking sheet. Bake for 40 minutes. While baking, turn them over with a metal spatula several times to prevent them from sticking to the pan and to ensure that they brown on all sides.

Per Serving: Calories 125; Protein 2g; Fat 4g (Saturated 0g); Carbohydrates 22g; Fiber 3g; Sodium 89mg

Sweet Potatoes and Marshmallows

Makes: 6 servings

This is sticky and sweet—a treat for kids and those who still have a soft spot for kid's food.

4 medium sweet potatoes (about 2 pounds)
¹/2 teaspoon kosher salt
¹/4 cup orange juice
2 tablespoons 1% lowfat milk
¹/4 teaspoon ground cinnamon
¹/4 teaspoon ground ginger
¹/2 cup tiny marshmallows

1) Bake or microwave the potatoes until soft. When cool enough to handle, halve and scoop out the pulp. Mash with all the ingredients except the marshmallows.

2) Preheat the oven to 350°F. Spray a 1¹/2-quart casserole with nonstick spray. Put in the potato mixture, then smooth the surface. Top with the marshmallows. This can be prepared up to 8 hours ahead of time, but if doing so, wait to top with the marshmallows.

3) Bake, covered, for 20 minutes, then uncover and bake for 10 minutes more. If the casserole was chilled when put into the oven, begin by cooking for an additional 10 minutes before adding the marshmallows.

Per Serving: Calories 114; Protein 2g; Fat 0g (Saturated 0g); Carbohydrates 27g; Fiber 3g; Sodium 174mg

Not Your Traditional Tzimmes

Makes: 4 servings

Tzimmes are part of the legacy of Eastern European Jewish cooking. These vegetable and fruit stews often feature carrots, chunks of meat, and chicken fat. I've left out the meat and fat and added my own surprise to this recipe, in the form of sweet yet tart chutney and a trace of curry powder.

1 large sweet potato, peeled and cut into small cubes (about 1 pound)
4 carrots, peeled and cut into small cubes (1/2 pound)
2 tablespoons chutney
1/2 cup pitted prunes, each cut in half
1/2 cup water
1/4 teaspoon kosher salt
1/2 teaspoon curry powder

1) Preheat the oven to 400°F.

2) Combine all the ingredients in a bowl and stir well.

3) Transfer the tzimmes to a 2-quart casserole. Cover and bake for 40 minutes. Uncover and bake for 20 minutes longer. You can make this dish up to 2 days ahead of time and reheat it in the microwave.

Per Serving: Calories 164; Protein 3g; Fat 0g (Saturated 0g); Carbohydrates 40g; Fiber 6g; Sodium 173mg

Sweet Potato Bake

Makes: 4 servings

This casserole can be put together a day ahead (through Step 3). When ready to bake, pour on the water and place in the oven. Be aware that because the casserole will be cold from storage in the refrigerator, it will take longer to cook.

1 pound sweet potatoes (about 1 large), peeled and cut into large chunks
1 tart apple, peeled, cored, and sliced
1/2 teaspoon finely grated fresh ginger
1/4 teaspoon ground cinnamon
1/8 teaspoon ground nutmeg
1/4 teaspoon ground cardamom
1 tablespoon maple syrup or honey
2 tablespoons raisins
6 walnut halves (optional)
1/4 cup water

1) Steam the sweet potatoes, apple, and ginger until the potato is soft, about 15 minutes.

2) Puree in a food processor fitted with a metal blade. While processing, add the spices and maple syrup.

3) Pour the mixture into a casserole dish. Top with the raisins and walnuts.

4) Pour the water over all, but do not stir it in. (It will keep the dish moist while forming a nice top as it bakes.)

5) Bake, uncovered, in a preheated 350°F oven for 40 minutes.

Per Serving: Calories 119; Protein 1g; Fat 0g (Saturated 0g); Carbohydrates 29g; Fiber 3g; Sodium 9mg

Root Vegetables

Turnips, rutabagas, and parsnips, like carrots, are root vegetables and grow underground. Unlike carrots, they are not very popular and are often difficult to find in the market. When faced with a thickly waxed, 2-pound rutabaga, most people are too intimidated to bring it home. But the assertive flavors and firm textures of these vegetables can be used to great advantage. Here are a few recipes to bring these underutilized vegetables into the home kitchen.

Sugar-Glazed Turnips

Makes: 4 servings

Sugar does not always make a recipe cloyingly sweet. Here it balances the sharp flavors of the turnips and the end product is savory, not something you'd serve for dessert.

3 cups diced peeled turnips or rutabagas
    (about 1 pound)
1/4 cup packed light brown sugar
1 tablespoon sugar
1/4 teaspoon kosher salt
1 1/2 teaspoons unsalted butter

1) Cook the turnips in a large pot of boiling water until just fork-tender, about 6 to 8 minutes. Drain well. Toss the turnips in a bowl with the brown and white sugars and the salt.

2) Melt the butter in a heavy skillet, then add the sugar-coated turnips. Cook over moderate-low heat until the sugars melt and glaze the turnips. Toss the turnips frequently as they cook.

Per Serving: Calories 103; Protein 1g; Fat 2g (Saturated 1g); Carbohydrates 23g; Fiber 2g; Sodium 191mg

Parsnips and Pineapple

Makes: 5 servings

Everyone who has tried this recipe has been surprised at how such an odd couple could get along so well together.

4 parsnips, peeled and cut into chunks (1 pound)
1 large carrot, peeled and cut into rounds
One 8-ounce can unsweetened pineapple chunks
    or crushed pineapple, packed in juice
1/2 cup water
1/2 teaspoon kosher salt
1/4 teaspoon freshly ground pepper

1) Preheat the oven to 350°F.

2) Put all the ingredients, including the pineapple juice, in a casserole. Stir to combine. Cover and bake for 30 minutes. Remove from the oven and puree or mash.

Per Serving: Calories 102; Protein 1g; Fat 0g (Saturated 0g); Carbohydrates 25g; Fiber 5g; Sodium 207mg

Mashed Rutabagas and Spuds

Makes: 6 servings

Simmering in milk mellows the rutabaga's bite while retaining its earthy flavor.

1 rutabaga (about 1 pound)
3 medium potatoes, preferably Yukon Gold (about 1 pound)
1¼ cups 1% lowfat milk, divided
1 to 1½ cups water
½ teaspoon kosher salt
½ teaspoon freshly ground pepper

1) To peel the rutabaga, cut off a slice so that the rutabaga sits securely flat on the board, which makes it easier and safer to prepare the vegetable. Cut off the peel and the wax by following the shape of the vegetable with a large chef's knife, always cutting down toward the cutting board. Cut the rutabaga into chunks.

2) Peel and cube the potatoes.

3) Put the rutabaga and potatoes in a saucepan. Pour in 1 cup of the milk. Add enough water to cover the vegetables.

4) Bring to a simmer. Cover the pot and cook for 20 to 30 minutes, until the rutabagas are soft all the way through.

5) Using a slotted spoon, remove the vegetables to a bowl. Pour the remaining milk over them. Mash in the salt and pepper. Leave the mixture a little lumpy.

Per Serving: Calories 84; Protein 3g; Fat 1g (Saturated 0g); Carbohydrates 20g; Fiber 2g; Sodium 191mg

Squash

Winter Squash

Winter squash, with their hard outer shells and irregular shapes, can be difficult to prepare. As a convenience, many markets offer peeled, cut winter squash. Check it closely for freshness. Cut squash should appear dry with no soft spots. Unfortunately, packaged squash is usually limited to butternut, so you'll be missing out on some wonderful vegetables if you don't face the challenge of a whole squash.

When cutting squash, always use a large knife with an inflexible blade. To peel a winter squash, cut slices off each end, then set a cut end flat on a large board and work the knife down, following the shape of the vegetable as you cut off the peel. Next, cut it in half and scoop out the seeds. Although winter squash is often baked with the skin on, the skin is usually too tough to be edible, except for delicata squash.

Baked Butternut Squash

Makes: 5 servings

There are many ways to serve baked squash. It can be sliced and served in the skin, or scooped out and mashed or used in other recipes.

1 butternut squash, any size

1) Preheat the oven to 375°F. To ease clean-up, line a baking sheet with foil or parchment paper.

2) Cut the squash in half lengthwise. Scoop out and discard the seeds and stringy flesh. Place cut side down on the baking sheet. Bake until tender, when the tip of a sharp knife can be easily inserted through the skin. This takes about 45 minutes to 1 hour, depending on the size of the squash.

Per Serving: Calories 44; Protein 1g; Fat 0g (Saturated 0g); Carbohydrates 11g; Fiber 3g; Sodium 4mg

Twice-Baked Butternut Squash

Makes: 5 servings

If you don't keep hard liquor in the house, you can buy one of those small "nips" at the package store.

1 butternut squash, about 2 pounds
1 tablespoon unsalted butter, softened
2 teaspoons brandy
1/2 teaspoon kosher salt
1/4 teaspoon freshly ground pepper
2 tablespoons packed light brown sugar
1/8 teaspoon ground nutmeg
1 tablespoon ground walnuts or pecans

1) Bake the squash until very soft (follow the preceeding recipe). Preheat the oven to 400°F. Coat a 1-quart casserole with nonstick spray.

2) Scoop out the squash and combine it with all the remaining ingredients except the nuts. Mash vigorously until fluffy. Spread it into the casserole. Dust the nuts on the surface.

3) Bake for about 30 minutes, until the casserole begins to brown.

Per Serving: Calories 99; Protein 1g; Fat 3g (Saturated 2g); Carbohydrates 17g; Fiber 3g; Sodium 199mg

Baked Acorn Squash Rings

Makes: 2 servings

Acorn squash's fluted edges and color contrast between the dark green skin and orange interior make rings of this vegetable particularly attractive.

1 acorn squash (about 1/2 pound)
1 apple, cored and sliced
1 teaspoon maple syrup
1/4 teaspoon ground cinnamon
1 teaspoon water

1) Preheat the oven to 375°F.

2) Wash the squash, then slice it crosswise into 1/4-inch rings. Remove the seeds and pulp.

3) Layer rings of squash and apple in a casserole dish, top with maple syrup, dust on the cinnamon, and sprinkle with the water.

4) Cover and bake for about 30 minutes, until the squash is tender.

Per Serving: Calories 89; Protein 1g; Fat 0g (Saturated 0g); Carbohydrates 23g; Fiber 4g; Sodium 3mg

Cider-Roasted Squash and Shallots

Makes: 4 servings

Use apple juice if apple cider is not in stock.

2 pounds butternut squash, peeled and cut into 1- to 2-inch pieces
6 shallots, peeled
2 teaspoons olive oil
1/4 cup apple cider
1/2 teaspoon kosher salt
1/4 teaspoon freshly ground pepper
1 tablespoon packed light brown sugar

1) Preheat the oven to 400°F.

2) Put the squash and shallots in a large roasting pan or casserole. It is best if the pieces are all about the same size and no larger than 2 inches across. If using a glass baking dish, reduce the oven temperature 25°F.

3) Whisk together the oil, cider, salt, pepper, and brown sugar in a small bowl and pour this over the vegetables. Toss to coat. Place in the oven and bake, uncovered. Shake the pan and turn the vegetables once during cooking. The sugars will begin to caramelize and the squash will be very soft when done. Test at 30 minutes and if not yet tender, bake for 15 minutes longer.

Per Serving: Calories 111; Protein 2g; Fat 2g (Saturated 0g); Carbohydrates 23g; Fiber 4g; Sodium 250mg

Winter Squash Gratin

Makes: 6 servings

Vegetarians might enjoy this as a main course.

2 tablespoons vegetable oil
3 pounds winter squash, peeled and cubed (5 cups)
1 cup chopped red onions
3 cloves garlic, minced
2 medium potatoes, peeled and cubed (3 cups)
1/2 teaspoon dried marjoram
1/2 teaspoon dried basil
1 tablespoon minced chives (fresh or frozen)
1/2 teaspoon kosher salt
1/2 teaspoon freshly ground pepper
1 1/2 cups nonfat yogurt (optional)
1/4 cup toasted pumpkin seeds or pepitas, for garnish

1) Preheat the oven to 350°F.

2) Stir together all the ingredients except the yogurt and pumpkin seeds. Transfer the mixture to a casserole. Cover and bake for 45 minutes.

3) Uncover and bake for 15 minutes longer.

4) If you like the tang of yogurt and a dairy flavor, stir in the yogurt. Broil the casserole until bubbly and the edges begin to brown. This takes only a couple of minutes.

5) Garnish with the toasted pumpkin seeds.

Per Serving: Calories 186; Protein 4g; Fat 6g (Saturated 1g); Carbohydrates 33g; Fiber 7g; Sodium 168mg

Spiced Maple Pumpkin Mash

Makes: 4 servings

Few pumpkins are good for eating. Most are purely decorative. But sugar pumpkins are bred for their baking qualities and rival the flavor of butternut squash. Always check with the produce manager to make sure that you are buying an eating pumpkin.

One 2- to 3-pound sugar pumpkin or winter
   squash, peeled and cubed (4 cups)
1 tablespoon maple syrup
1/4 teaspoon kosher salt
1/4 teaspoon freshly ground pepper
1 cup apple cider or apple juice
1/8 teaspoon ground cardamom

1) Simmer all ingredients except the cardamom over low heat until the pumpkin is soft. This will take about 15 minutes.

2) Using a slotted spoon, remove the pumpkin to a bowl. Add the cardamom. Mash the pumpkin until it is smooth (a few lumps are okay). Pour in a little of the cooking liquid if necessary.

Per Serving: Calories 58; Protein 1g; Fat 0g (Saturated 0g); Carbohydrates 14g; Fiber 2g; Sodium 63mg

Lemony Squash and Carrots

Makes: 4 servings

Hard winter squash usually takes more than an hour to bake, but when grated and sautéed it takes less than one-quarter of that time. You can grate the squash easily in a food processor. It can be grated a day ahead of time and stored in the refrigerator.

2 cups peeled and grated winter squash
1 small carrot, peeled and grated
1 tablespoon lemon juice
1/8 teaspoon kosher salt
1/8 teaspoon freshly ground pepper
2/3 cup reduced-sodium, defatted chicken or
   vegetable broth
1 tablespoon minced fresh parsley

1) Put everything but the parsley in a nonstick sauté pan. Cook, covered, over medium heat for about 10 minutes, until the vegetables soften. Stir occasionally.

2) Add the parsley and cook 1 minute longer.

Per Serving: Calories 33; Protein 1g; Fat 0g (Saturated 0g); Carbohydrates 7g; Fiber 2g; Sodium 267mg

Summer Squash

Zucchini and yellow squash are the two most popular of the summer squashes, though home gardeners are no doubt familiar with others. Summer squash have thin skins, mild flavors, and firm yet moist flesh. Usually the smaller they are, the sweeter. Also, small ones have immature seeds. Large squash have large seeds that are often tough; these can be scooped out and discarded.

Zucchini Spears with Pesto

Makes: 6 servings

This is the easiest way to dress up zucchini.

4 medium zucchini, halved crosswise and cut
    into spears
1 teaspoon olive oil
1/4 cup pesto (for a selection see pages 588–591)

1) Steam the zucchini until they are tender but not mushy, about 5 minutes. Remove from the pot.

2) Heat the oil in a large nonstick skillet. Add the spears and cook over high heat, tossing or stirring frequently until the edges begin to brown. Remove from the heat, add the pesto to the pan, and toss until the spears are coated.

Per Serving: Calories 56; Protein 2g; Fat 4g (Saturated 1g); Carbohydrates 4g; Fiber 2g; Sodium 24mg

Sautéed Summer Vegetables

Makes: 4 servings

This goes with nicely with many entrées but is especially good with grilled fish.

1/2 cup sliced onions
1 teaspoon olive oil
1/2 green bell pepper, julienned
1 yellow squash, thickly sliced
1 zucchini, thickly sliced
1 tomato, chopped
1/2 teaspoon dried oregano
1 teaspoon dried basil
1/4 teaspoon freshly ground pepper

1) Sauté the onions in the oil over low heat until soft and translucent.

2) Add the green peppers and cook until they wilt. Add the yellow squash, zucchini, and tomato, and cook, covered, for 10 minutes.

3) Stir in the herbs and pepper and serve.

Per Serving: Calories 43; Protein 2g; Fat 1g (Saturated 0g); Carbohydrates 7g; Fiber 2g; Sodium 6mg

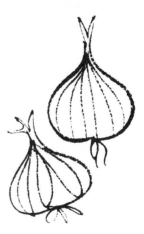

Garlicky Zucchini and Corn

Makes: 4 servings

When gardening friends bring over their excess zucchini and tomatoes this is the recipe to make, especially because it can be doubled.

2 teaspoons olive oil
1 cup chopped onions
3 cloves garlic, chopped
2 cups diced zucchini
1 cup corn kernels
2 plum tomatoes, diced
1/2 teaspoon dried oregano
1/2 teaspoon kosher salt
1/4 teaspoon freshly ground pepper

1) Heat the oil in a large nonstick skillet. Sauté the onions and garlic until golden. Add the zucchini and cook over high heat until the edges begin to brown.

2) Stir in the corn, tomatoes, and seasonings. Reduce the heat to moderate and cook until the tomatoes soften.

Per Serving: Calories 37; Protein 1g; Fat 2g (Saturated 0g); Carbohydrates 4g; Fiber 1g; Sodium 164mg

Zucchini Oven Fries

Makes: 6 servings

People who won't consider eating zucchini (especially children) can't resist these batter-baked fries.

1 tablespoon vegetable oil
3 medium zucchini
3 tablespoons 1% lowfat milk
1 egg white
1/2 cup dry breadcrumbs
1/2 teaspoon kosher salt
1/4 teaspoon freshly ground pepper
2 tablespoons grated Romano cheese

1) Place the oven rack in the top third of the oven and preheat it to 425°F. Coat a rimmed baking sheet with the oil.

2) Cut the zucchini in half lengthwise and if the seeds are large, scoop them out and discard. Cut the zucchini into spears the size of french fries.

3) Whisk together the milk and egg white. Toss the zucchini in this until well coated.

4) Combine the breadcrumbs, salt, pepper, and cheese. Dip the zucchini in this breading mixture a few pieces at a time, and remove with tongs and place on the prepared baking sheet. Leave a little space between the zucchini fries. If touching, they won't crisp.

5) Place in the oven and bake for 7 minutes, then turn over with a metal spatula (handle gently or some breading will slide off) and continue to bake until brown, another 6 to 10 minutes. Serve immediately.

Per Serving: Calories 81; Protein 4g; Fat 3g (Saturated 1g); Carbohydrates 9g; Fiber 2g; Sodium 273mg

Zucchini Cheese Casserole

Makes: 6 servings

One sure way to make a vegetable appealing is to bake it with cheese.

1 tablespoon olive oil
6 cups zucchini or yellow summer squash, cubed
    (from about 4 medium zucchini)
2 shallots, minced
2 cloves garlic, minced
1 egg
1 egg white
1 cup shredded lowfat cheddar cheese
1/2 teaspoon kosher salt
1/4 teaspoon freshly ground pepper
1 tablespoon chopped fresh basil or
    1 teaspoon dried
2 tablespoons chopped fresh parsley

1) Preheat the oven to 425°F. Toss the oil, squash, shallots, and garlic in a 2- to 2 1/2-quart casserole and bake for 15 minutes, stirring twice.

2) Lightly beat the remaining ingredients in a bowl. Take the casserole out of the oven and pour the cheese mixture over the vegetables. Return it to the oven and bake for another 12 to 15 minutes, until the cheese begins to bubble and brown.

Per Serving: Calories 95; Protein 7g; Fat 6g (Saturated 2g); Carbohydrates 6g; Fiber 2g; Sodium 272mg

Mexican Zucchini Casserole

Makes: 8 servings

This is a big hit with families with teenagers and young adults. The recipe makes a lot, but it's sure to be eaten.

6 medium zucchini, cubed (about 2 pounds)
2 cups corn kernels (fresh or frozen)
1/2 cup nonfat sour cream
1/2 cup nonfat yogurt
1 tablespoon unbleached, all-purpose white flour
One 14 1/2-ounce can whole tomatoes, drained
1/2 cup salsa
One 4-ounce can chopped mild green chilies
1 cup shredded lowfat cheddar or jack cheese

1) Steam or microwave the zucchini and corn until just tender. Set in a colander to drain.

2) Preheat the oven to 375°F. Coat a 2 1/2- to 3-quart casserole with nonstick spray.

3) Blend together the sour cream, yogurt, and flour. Put the tomatoes in a colander and squeeze the liquid out of them. Coarsely chop the tomato pulp and add to the sour cream mixture. Stir in the salsa, chilies, cheese, zucchini, and corn. Put into the casserole.

4) Bake for 20 to 25 minutes, until bubbly.

Per Serving: Calories 117; Protein 8g; Fat 2g (Saturated 1g); Carbohydrates 18g; Fiber 4g; Sodium 367mg

Parmesan Summer Squash Packets

Makes: 6 servings

If foil is used, these can be grilled, over low heat.

1 teaspoon olive oil
2 plum tomatoes, diced
1/2 cup chopped onions
1 clove garlic, sliced
4 cups diced zucchini or yellow summer squash
1/2 teaspoon kosher salt
1/4 teaspoon freshly ground pepper
1 teaspoon dried basil
1/2 teaspoon dried oregano
1/4 cup grated Parmesan cheese

1) Tear off six 12-inch pieces of foil or parchment paper. Fold in half and open back up.

2) Combine all the ingredients. Divide the mixture among the foil squares, placing each portion in the center to one side of the fold. Seal the packets with tight, narrow creases along the edges. Place in one layer on baking sheets. This can be done up to several hours ahead of time. Refrigerate if not using within the hour.

3) Preheat the oven to 425°F. Bake the packets for 20 minutes. Open carefully to avoid the outpouring of steam, and serve immediately.

Per Serving: Calories 49; Protein 3g; Fat 2g (Saturated 1g); Carbohydrates 5g; Fiber 2g; Sodium 243mg

Grilled Zucchini

Makes: 6 servings

Grilling puts this usually retiring vegetable into the spotlight. The zucchini slices are thick and long and don't get lost on the plate. The grill marks give it a hearty look and the seasonings bring out the flavor of the squash.

4 medium zucchini (about 1 1/2 pounds)
1 tablespoon olive oil or garlic oil
1 tablespoon minced fresh basil
1 teaspoon balsamic vinegar
1/2 teaspoon kosher salt
1/4 teaspoon freshly ground pepper

1) Prepare the grill. It should be hot enough to produce dark seared stripes, but not so hot that the vegetables burn. If using a gas grill, get it very hot and turn it down just prior to putting the zucchini on the grill. If using charcoal, cook over moderate heat.

2) Cut off the ends of the zucchini, then cut lengthwise into 1/2-inch-thick slices. Place on a baking sheet and lightly coat the zucchini on both sides with nonstick spray.

3) Combine the remaining ingredients and brush onto one side of the zucchini. Place this oiled side down on the grill. Cook 2 or more minutes, until grill stripes appear. Brush the tops with the oil mixture, turn, cover the grill, and cook until the vegetables are cooked through, about 5 minutes more (timing varies with the grill, so keep an eye on it).

Per Serving: Calories 37; Protein 1g; Fat 2g (Saturated 0g); Carbohydrates 4g; Fiber 1g; Sodium 164mg

Tomatoes

When tomato season is over, it is rare if not impossible to find flavorful tomatoes in the stores. That is when I turn to canned tomatoes for many of my recipes, and leave other recipes to wait until the next summer. But when ripe tomatoes are available, I never tire of them. Most of the time, ripe tomatoes need little embellishment, but there are times when cooked tomatoes are just the component a menu needs.

Some recipes ask for peeled and seeded tomatoes, so that only the pulp is used. This makes a smoother-textured, thicker recipe, and one free of the beige specks of seeds. That said, peeling and seeding tomatoes is rarely absolutely necessary and if in a rush, you can leave the step out.

Cheery Cherry Tomatoes

Makes: 6 servings

Cherry tomatoes are the one fresh tomato that tastes good year-round. Their flavor is improved by a brief cooking that cracks their skins but doesn't collapse them.

1 tablespoon olive oil
1 clove garlic, minced
1 tablespoon minced shallots
   (about half a large shallot)
1 pint cherry tomatoes, washed
1/4 teaspoon kosher salt
1/4 teaspoon freshly ground pepper

1) Heat a sauté pan, pour in the oil, and roll it around the pan so the surface is well coated.

2) Cook the garlic and shallots over low heat until golden.

3) Turn the heat to high and add the tomatoes, salt, and pepper. Toss continually until the skins pop open. This takes only about 1 minute.

Per Serving: Calories 38; Protein 1g; Fat 3g (Saturated 0g); Carbohydrates 4g; Fiber 1g; Sodium 87mg

Sage Tomatoes

Makes: 4 servings

These can hold their own on a plate of meat or grilled chicken.

1/2 medium leek, washed well, trimmed, and
   sliced (dark green tops discarded)
2 cloves garlic, minced
1 teaspoon olive oil
2 large beefsteak-style tomatoes, cored and cut
   into wedges (about 1 pound)
1/2 teaspoon dried sage
1/4 teaspoon kosher salt
1/8 teaspoon freshly ground pepper

1) Heat the oil in a sauté pan over medium heat. Sauté the leek and garlic in the oil until the leek is golden.

2) Add the tomatoes and seasonings. Cook about 4 minutes more, until the tomatoes soften, but not so long that they lose their shape and turn to mush.

Per Serving: Calories 41; Protein 1g; Fat 1g (Saturated 0g); Carbohydrates 7g; Fiber 1g; Sodium 132mg

Turkish Tomatoes and Zucchini

Makes: 5 servings

There is a farm a few miles from my house that sells tomato seconds for only fifty cents a pound, though these are wonderfully ripe and delicious tomatoes. When I come home (with far too many tomatoes), I pull out a recipe like this, where looks don't count.

1^1/2 teaspoons vegetable oil
1 cup chopped onions
4 beefsteak-type tomatoes, cored, seeded, and chopped (about 2 pounds)
1 medium zucchini, cut into ^{1}/4-inch-thick rounds
^{1}/3 cup chopped fresh basil
^{1}/8 teaspoon ground allspice
^{1}/4 teaspoon ground cumin
^{1}/4 teaspoon kosher salt
^{1}/8 teaspoon freshly ground pepper

1) Heat the oil in a sauté pan. Sauté the onions until they are soft and golden. Add the remaining ingredients. Cook, covered, over low heat until the vegetables exude moisture and the mixture looks soupy. Timing will vary with the ripeness of the tomatoes. Fresh beefsteaks will take less than 10 minutes, whereas plum tomatoes will require at least 15 minutes.

2) Uncover and cook for 10 minutes more; this will dry the dish out slightly and intensify the flavors.

Per Serving: Calories 62; Protein 2g; Fat 2g (Saturated 0g); Carbohydrates 11g; Fiber 3g; Sodium 112mg

Baked Tomatoes

Makes: 4 servings

Cutting off the tomato tops in a serrated pattern makes this an especially attractive side dish. This recipe is flexible on oven temperature and the tomatoes can go in the oven with anything else already baking.

4 ripe tomatoes
^{1}/8 teaspoon kosher salt
^{1}/8 teaspoon freshly ground pepper
^{1}/4 cup soft breadcrumbs
2 tablespoons minced fresh parsley
1 tablespoon sherry or sweet white wine
1 teaspoon olive oil

1) Preheat the oven to anywhere from 325 to 375°F. (Use whatever temperature is required for the rest of the meal.)

2) Use a paring knife to cut a line of connected V shapes about a fifth of the way down from the core of each tomato. Then pull the tops off, leaving the serrated edges. If necessary, slice a tiny bit off their bottoms so that the tomatoes do not roll around. Sprinkle the salt and pepper on the cut tomatoes.

3) Combine the breadcrumbs, parsley, wine, and oil. Divide the mixture into 4 portions, mound on top of each tomato, and lightly pack it down. Place the tomatoes on a baking sheet or shallow casserole. These can be made several hours ahead of time up to this point.

4) Bake the tomatoes until the skins start to crack and they are cooked through, about 20 minutes.

Per Serving: Calories 49; Protein 1g; Fat 2g (Saturated 0g); Carbohydrates 8g; Fiber 1g; Sodium 87mg

Baked Tomato Jam

Makes: 6 servings

This jam goes with almost anything—burgers, roast chicken, or fish.

3 pounds plum tomatoes
3 tablespoons sugar
1 teaspoon kosher salt

1) Preheat the oven to 350°F.

2) Slice the cores off the tomatoes, then cut in half. With your thumb, scoop out and discard the juice and seeds. Cut the tomatoes into strips (they don't have to be precisely sliced).

3) Place the tomatoes in a heavy ovenproof casserole (not glass) and toss with the sugar and salt. Bake, uncovered, for 1¹/₂ to 2 hours, until the tomatoes shrink in size and most of the liquid bakes off (timing will vary with the oven and ripeness of the tomatoes). Stir every 30 minutes.

4) Serve at room temperature.

Per Serving: Calories 72; Protein 2g; Fat 1g (Saturated 0g); Carbohydrates 17g; Fiber 2g; Sodium 340mg

Vegetable Medleys

Not all vegetable recipes need to showcase one vegetable. The following recipes succeed due to a group effort.

Southwestern Vegetable Sauté

Makes: 6 servings

If fresh jalapeños are not available, substitute canned.

1¹/₂ teaspoons vegetable oil
1 cup chopped onions
2 cloves garlic, minced
1 jalapeño pepper, seeded and minced
   (wear rubber gloves)
1 medium potato, peeled and cubed
¹/₂ cup water
1¹/₂ cups diced zucchini or yellow summer squash
¹/₂ cup corn kernels
8 cherry tomatoes
¹/₂ green bell pepper, chopped
¹/₂ teaspoon ground cumin
1 teaspoon ground coriander
¹/₂ to 1 teaspoon kosher salt
2 tablespoons chopped fresh cilantro (optional)

Heat the oil in a large nonstick pan. Sauté the onions, garlic, and pepper until the onions begin to turn golden. Stir frequently but keep covered between stirrings.

2) Add the potato and water, cover, and cook until a fork can be inserted into a potato, about 8 minutes. Stir in the remaining ingredients except for the cilantro. Cover between stirrings. Cook until the zucchini becomes tender but not yet soft, about 5 minutes. Stir in the cilantro, if desired, and serve.

Per Serving: Calories 73; Protein 2g; Fat 2g (Saturated 0g); Carbohydrates 14g; Fiber 2g; Sodium 169mg

Fall Vegetable Medley

Makes: 6 servings

Try to cut the vegetables into even, thin sticks. If the parsnip is large enough, cut that into sticks too. Not only will this make for a very attractive dish (yes, rutabagas can be beautiful), but the vegetables will cook quickly and evenly.

1/2 pound rutabaga, peeled and julienned (about 2 cups)
1 parsnip, peeled and sliced into rounds
1 small zucchini, julienned
2 carrots, peeled and julienned
1 tablespoon olive oil
Ground pepper to taste

1) Steam the vegetables until just tender, about 10 minutes.

2) Heat the oil in a heavy skillet, add the vegetables, and toss to coat with oil. When the edges of the vegetables start to brown slightly, remove from the heat, grind on the pepper, and serve.

Per Serving: Calories 65; Protein 1g; Fat 2g (Saturated 0g); Carbohydrates 10g; Fiber 3g; Sodium 20mg

Cider-Cooked Vegetables

Makes: 6 servings

Apple brandy is not a beverage that everyone has in their house. But it lasts indefintely in the liquor cabinet and I use it in several recipes. Very small "nips" bottles can be purchased, which are the most practical for those who cook with it but don't drink it.

1 tablespoon unsalted butter
1/2 pound parsnips (about 2 large), peeled and cut into thin rounds or sticks
1 pound baby-cut carrots
10 Brussels sprouts, trimmed
1 1/2 tablespoons honey, divided
1/2 cup apple cider
2 tablespoons apple brandy
1/4 teaspoon kosher salt

1) Melt the butter in a large nonstick sauté pan. Stir in the vegetables and toss until coated. Stir in 1 tablespoon of the honey and the remaining ingredients. Simmer, covered, for 15 minutes.

2) Uncover and continue to cook for 5 minutes. Stir in the remaining honey and continue to cook for about 5 more minutes, until the liquid is reduced to a glaze.

Per Serving: Calories 124; Protein 2g; Fat 3g (Saturated 1g); Carbohydrates 23g; Fiber 6g; Sodium 119mg

Caponata

Makes: 6 servings

I used to make this as a special at a cafe where I worked as a cook. At first no one ordered it, and I discovered that the waitresses were telling customers that it was "eggplant stew." I suggested that they say "spicy Sicilian eggplant casserole with basil and capers" and from then on, it always sold out.

1 cup chopped onions
3 cloves garlic, minced
1/3 cup red wine
1 rib celery, chopped
1 medium eggplant, cut into small cubes
One 28-ounce can whole tomatoes, with juice
2 tablespoons red wine vinegar
1 tablespoon honey
1 tablespoon dried basil
1 teaspoon drained capers
1/8 teaspoon Tabasco sauce
1/2 teaspoon kosher salt

1) Cook the onions and garlic in the wine over low heat until softened. Cover between stirrings.

2) Add the celery and eggplant and cook slowly until the eggplant softens. This will take at least 15 minutes. If more liquid is needed, add juice from the canned tomatoes.

3) Add the remaining ingredients and simmer 30 minutes, or longer if time permits. Serve hot or room temperature.

Per Serving: Calories 78; Protein 2g; Fat 1g (Saturated 0g); Carbohydrates 16g; Fiber 3g; Sodium 403mg

Ethiopian Vegetables

Makes: 5 servings

In the United States we tend to use one hot seasoning, like chili or Tabasco. Too much and the recipe has no flavor, it is just mouth-burning. In Ethiopia, they use many spices in a single recipe. Because there are so many intense and complex flavors, they can use far greater quantities of incendiary spices without the dish becoming incredibly hot. And always, the recipe has a deep flavor, much more interesting than a single note of one hot spice. This recipe is a mild introduction to Ethiopian cuisine.

1/2 cup minced onions
2 cloves garlic, minced
1 teaspoon finely grated fresh ginger
2 teaspoons vegetable oil
1 large potato, peeled and cubed, or 1/4 pound new potatoes, unpeeled
1 carrot, cut into rounds
1 pound spinach, washed and the coarse stems discarded
1/8 teaspoon ground cinnamon
1/8 teaspoon ground cardamom
1/4 teaspoon kosher salt
1/16 teaspoon cayenne pepper, or more to taste
1/8 teaspoon Tabasco sauce

1) Sauté the onions, garlic, and ginger in the oil in a heavy-bottomed pot. Slowly cook until the onions turn light golden.

2) Add the potatoes and carrots and pour in enough water to cover the vegetables halfway. Stir in the remaining ingredients.

3) Simmer, covered, until the potatoes and carrots start to fall apart. Stir occasionally, adding water as needed to cook the vegetables.

Per Serving: Calories 87; Protein 4g; Fat 2g (Saturated 0g); Carbohydrates 15g; Fiber 4g; Sodium 177mg

Succotash with Tomatoes and Basil

Makes: 4 servings

I don't know why succotash doesn't get more respect. Maybe it's the funny-sounding name. But succotash is pretty, flavorful, and easy to make and it deserves a place on the table.

One 14 1/2-ounce can no-salt-added whole tomatoes, with juice
1 cup corn kernels (fresh or frozen)
1 cup frozen baby lima beans
1 teaspoon dried basil, or 1 tablespoon chopped fresh
1/2 cup water
1 teaspoon kosher salt

1) Drain the juice from the canned tomatoes into a pot. Chop the tomatoes and add them to the pot.

2) Stir in the corn, lima beans, basil, and water and simmer gently, uncovered, for 20 minutes. Add the salt, raise the heat, and cook about 10 minutes longer, until the liquid cooks down and it no longer looks soupy.

Per Serving: Calories 117; Protein 6g; Fat 1g (Saturated 0g); Carbohydrates 24g; Fiber 6g; Sodium 557mg

Vegetables Under Wraps

Makes: 4 servings

If you don't have parchment paper use foil, but prick the top of each packet once with a fork so that some steam can escape.

1 medium zucchini, cut into rounds
1/4 cup thinly sliced onions
1/2 green bell pepper, cut into triangles
1 tomato, thickly sliced
1 cup mushrooms, quartered
1 1/2 teaspoons olive oil
1 bay leaf
1/4 teaspoon kosher salt
1/8 teaspoon freshly ground pepper
1/2 teaspoon dill seed

1) Cut a piece of parchment paper twice the size of all the vegetables. Fold it in half, then spread it open. Arrange the vegetables in layers on one side of the paper, beginning with the zucchini and then the onions, bell pepper, tomato, and mushrooms.

2) Drizzle the oil on top and add the bay leaf, salt, pepper, and dill seed.

3) Bring the parchment over the vegetables, sealing the edges together by making tight folds along the perimeter of the packet. This can be prepared several hours ahead of time.

4) Bake in a preheated 375°F oven for 45 minutes. Place the whole packet on a serving dish and cut an X into the top, being careful of the escaping steam.

Per Serving: Calories 39; Protein 1g; Fat 2g (Saturated 0g); Carbohydrates 5g; Fiber 1g; Sodium 125mg

Cowboy Foil-Wrapped Vegetables

Makes: 5 servings

Cook these packets at home or in the hot coals of a campfire.

2 teaspoons vegetable oil
2 medium russet potatoes, peeled and thickly
   sliced (about 1 pound)
2 carrots, cut into thick rounds
1 green bell pepper, cut into $1/2$-inch pieces
1 teaspoon paprika
1 teaspoon kosher salt
1 teaspoon dried oregano

1) Preheat the oven to 375°F. Have two 14-inch lengths of foil and a baking sheet ready.

2) Combine all the ingredients in a bowl and toss until all is evenly coated with the oil and seasonings.

3) Divide the vegetables in half and place one pile of vegetables in the center of one piece of foil. Fold up and crimp the edges closed. Repeat with the rest of the vegetables and foil. Place both packets on the baking sheet. Bake for 45 minutes.

Per Serving: Calories 93; Protein 2g; Fat 2g (Saturated 0g); Carbohydrates 18g; Fiber 2g; Sodium 399mg

Pastas, Grains, and Beans

Pasta
377

Buttered Egg Noodles

Garlic Oil Pasta

Garlic Oil Pasta with Broccoli

Vermicelli and Rice Pilaf

Spaghetti with Fresh Herbs

Lemon Garlic Angel Hair Pasta

Hot Pepper Pasta

Tiny Pasta with Almonds

Spinach and Orzo

Orzo with Parsley and Lemon

Orzo with Fresh Dill

Orzo with Peas and Mint

Far Eastern Ginger Noodles

Noodle Kugel

Spinach Noodle Kugel

Couscous
384

Basil and Tomato Couscous

Couscous with Peas and Dill

Apricot Couscous Pilaf

Summertime Couscous

Baked Couscous with Tomatoes

Rice
386

White Rice

Brown Rice

Lemon Rice

Orange Rice

Saffron Rice

Curried Rice

Rice with Peas and Mint

Raisins and Walnuts Pilaf

Basmati and Lentil Pilaf

Currant Pilaf

Curried Fried Rice

Vegetable Fried Rice

Dirty Rice

Shiitake Brown Rice

South of the Border Rice

Red Rice

Red Rice and Beans

Curried Pea Pilaf

Wild Wild Rice

Vegetable Paella

Other Grains
396

Portobellos and Grains

Basic Kasha

Kasha and Mushrooms

Barley with Mushrooms

Barley with Vegetables and Dill

Quinoa Pilaf

Beans
399

Basic Beans

Stewed Lentils

Carrots and Lentils

Brown Rice and Lentils

Spinach with Lentils

Dal Nepal

Baked Beans

Black Beans and Rice

Southwestern Black Beans

Black Beans and Pumpkin

White Bean Stew

Mediterranean Baked Beans

Cannellini and Corkscrew
Gratin

Hopping John

Chickpea Gratin

Polenta
707

Basic Polenta

Microwave Polenta

Vegetable Polenta

Double-Corn Polenta

Stuffing and Bread
709

Easy Stuffing

Cornbread Stuffing

Apple and Nut Stuffing

Sausage and Mushroom
Stuffing

Cranberry and Bread Stuffing

Wild Rice Stuffing

Pear Cornbread Pudding

Parmesan Toasts

Garlic Toast

American Garlic Bread

Dinner wouldn't be satisfying without bread, pasta, or rice. In all cultures throughout the world, these complex carbohydrates are used to satisfy hunger, balance protein, and stretch meat. Many carbohydrates, such as brown rice, are minimally processed and contain extra nutrients and fiber. Other carbohydrates, such as white pasta, are more refined, but still nutritionally sound, and their lighter flavors and textures make them very versatile.

Pasta

I rarely use whole wheat pasta, since it cooks up heavy and gummy. However, there are some excellent types of pasta, such as soba noodles, that are made from whole grains. Except for fresh Chinese noodles and frozen tortellini, I always purchase dried pasta. It is more economical and better than the packaged "fresh" noodles in the refrigerator case. One way to check quality is to read the label. Italian-style pasta should always be made from semolina flour. Of course, if you have access to real homemade pasta, use it. Fresh pasta weighs much more than dried, so purchase it by the serving size, not the weight. It also cooks in a short 2 to 3 minutes, so reduce the cooking time accordingly.

All pasta can be cooked the same way—in lots of boiling water. Pasta cooked in a too-small pot, with barely simmering water, will stick to the bottom and cook into a lump. Stir the pasta several times to keep it from sticking. If the pasta is going to be eaten immediately, do not rinse it. Not only does rinsing cool off the pasta but it removes the starch, which is necessary for sauces to cling to the noodles. If the pasta is to be made ahead and then held until later, it should be drained, rinsed, and drained again (see page 86 for more details).

Buttered Egg Noodles

Makes: 4 servings

There are times when I crave butter on noodles. Butter. Not margarine. Not olive oil. But the pasta doesn't have to be dripping with fat; it just needs the shine and flavor of real butter.

1/2 pound egg noodles
1 tablespoon unsalted butter
1/4 teaspoon kosher salt
1/8 teaspoon freshly ground pepper
1 tablespoon minced fresh parsley (optional)

1) Cook the noodles in a large pot of boiling water for about 8 minutes, until just tender. Drain into a colander, toss to shake out excess water, then return the pasta to the pot (both pot and noodles should still be quite hot).

2) Stir in the butter, salt, pepper, and parsley. Toss the noodles as the butter melts. Serve immediately.

Per Serving: Calories 242; Protein 8g; Fat 5g (Saturated 2g); Carbohydrates 40g; Fiber 2g; Sodium 132mg

Garlic Oil Pasta

Makes: 4 servings

Garlic oil contributes the flavor of garlic without the trouble of mincing and sautéing. You can make it yourself or purchase it at a gourmet shop.

1¹/2 teaspoons Garlic Oil (page 607)
3 cups cooked pasta
¹/2 cup roasted peppers, julienned
1 tablespoon chopped fresh parsley
¹/8 teaspoon kosher salt
¹/8 teaspoon freshly ground pepper

1) Heat the oil in a wok or large sauté pan over medium-high heat.

2) Toss in all the ingredients. Shake the pan and stir constantly, using a wooden spoon or spatula, for about 3 to 4 minutes, until heated through.

Per Serving: Calories 162; Protein 5g; Fat 2g (Saturated 0g); Carbohydrates 30g; Fiber 2g; Sodium 62mg

Garlic Oil Pasta with Broccoli

Makes: 6 servings

This is a vegetable and starch side dish all in one.

1 tablespoon Garlic Oil (page 607)
8 cherry tomatoes
¹/2 cup roasted peppers, julienned
4¹/2 cups cooked pasta (from about
    8 ounces dried)
1¹/2 cups broccoli florets, lightly steamed
¹/4 cup reduced-sodium, defatted chicken broth
2 tablespoons chopped fresh basil
1 teaspoon kosher salt
¹/4 teaspoon freshly ground pepper
1 tablespoon grated Parmesan cheese

1) Heat the oil in a wok or large sauté pan over medium-high heat.

2) Toss in the tomatoes. Heat until their skins begin to crack. Stir in the roasted peppers and cook for 1 more minute.

3) Toss in the remaining ingredients except the cheese. Shake the pan and stir constantly. A wooden spatula is the best tool for this job. Heat through. This will take 3 to 4 minutes.

4) Place in a serving bowl and dust the top with cheese.

Per Serving: Calories 179; Protein 6g; Fat 3g (Saturated 1g); Carbohydrates 31g; Fiber 2g; Sodium 366mg

Vermicelli and Rice Pilaf

Makes: 4 servings

Order rice in a Lebanese restaurant and it comes flecked with browned vermicelli. Traditionally this pilaf accompanies everything from lentil stews to chicken kebabs. You'll find it as versatile a side dish in your own kitchen.

2 cups reduced-sodium, defatted chicken broth
1 tablespoon olive oil
¹/2 cup vermicelli or other thin spaghetti, broken
    into 1- to 2-inch pieces
1 cup uncooked long-grain white rice
¹/2 teaspoon kosher salt

1) Bring the broth to a boil and turn off heat. (This can also be done in the microwave; the broth just needs to be hot when added in the next step.)

2) Heat the oil in a saucepan. Add the vermicelli and sauté until golden, about 1 minute. Pour in the broth, taking care not to get splattered when the liquid hits the hot pan. Stir in the rice and salt.

3) Bring to a boil, reduce to a simmer, cover, and cook until the liquid is absorbed, about 15 minutes. Remove from the heat and let rest 10 minutes. Fluff with a fork and serve.

Per Serving: Calories 257; Protein 6g; Fat 4g (Saturated 1g); Carbohydrates 47g; Fiber 1g; Sodium 483mg

Spaghetti with Fresh Herbs

Makes: 4 servings

This is what I make in the summer when my herb garden is full and green.

1 1/2 tablespoons extra-virgin olive oil
3 tablespoons minced fresh basil
2 tablespoons minced fresh parsley
2 teaspoons minced fresh rosemary
1 teaspoon minced fresh thyme
1 teaspoon kosher salt
1/4 teaspoon freshly ground pepper
1/2 pound spaghetti

1) In a small bowl, combine all the ingredients except the spaghetti.

2) Cook the spaghetti. Drain and put in a serving bowl. Top with the herb mixture and toss.

Per Serving: Calories 257; Protein 7g; Fat 6g (Saturated 1g); Carbohydrates 43g; Fiber 2g; Sodium 485mg

Lemon Garlic Angel Hair Pasta

Makes: 6 servings

Angel hair pasta cooks in less than two minutes, and it takes only a tad longer than that to put this entire dish together. The trick is to have all the ingredients measured out and next to the stovetop (as well as having the table set!), before you begin cooking.

1 tablespoon olive oil
3 cloves garlic, minced
1/4 cup dry white wine
1 teaspoon minced lemon zest
1 tablespoon lemon juice
1/2 cup reduced-sodium, defatted chicken or
    vegetable broth
1 teaspoon kosher salt
1/2 teaspoon freshly ground pepper
1/2 pound angel hair pasta
1/2 cup frozen peas, thawed
1/4 cup chopped fresh basil
2 tablespoons grated Parmesan cheese

1) Put a large pot of water up to boil. Meanwhile, measure out all your ingredients. When the water comes to a boil, begin Step 2.

2) Heat the oil in a nonstick sauté pan. Cook the garlic over low heat until lightly golden, about 3 minutes. Pour in the wine. Bring to a simmer and cook 3 minutes. Add the lemon zest, juice, broth, salt, and pepper. Keep it gently simmering as you go on to the next step.

3) Cook the pasta, stirring frequently to prevent it from clumping. Drain and put it in a large serving bowl. Pour in the simmering sauce, toss in the peas and basil, and pass a bowl of Parmesan around the table.

Per Serving: Calories 191; Protein 7g; Fat 4g (Saturated 1g); Carbohydrates 31g; Fiber 2g; Sodium 416mg

Hot Pepper Pasta

Makes: 4 servings

Pepperoncini are small, pale green spicy Italian peppers that are pickled in jars. They provide a kick to a recipe, but not the intense heat of jalapeños.

4 cloves garlic, minced
2 pepperoncini, chopped
2 tablespoons olive oil
One 16-ounce can whole tomatoes, chopped, with juice
$1/8$ to $1/4$ teaspoon crushed red pepper flakes
$1/2$ teaspoon kosher salt
$1/2$ pound penne

1) In a heavy-bottomed saucepan, sauté the garlic and pepperoncini in the oil over low heat until the garlic turns golden. Add the tomatoes, pepper flakes, and salt. Simmer, uncovered, for 20 minutes.

2) Meanwhile, cook the penne. Drain and toss with the sauce.

Per Serving: Calories 295; Protein 8g; Fat 8g (Saturated 1g); Carbohydrates 48g; Fiber 2g; Sodium 512mg

Tiny Pasta with Almonds

Makes: 4 servings

Tiny pasta often look nicer on a plate that bulky shells or spaghetti. The small shapes also toss well with other ingredients, as in this recipe, with almonds and parsley.

$1^1/2$ teaspoons olive oil
1 shallot, minced
2 tablespoons orange juice
1 teaspoon lemon juice
$1/2$ teaspoon kosher salt
$1/4$ teaspoon freshly ground pepper
2 tablespoons minced fresh parsley
2 tablespoons sliced almonds
3 cups cooked tiny pasta, such as orzo

1) Heat the oil in a sauté pan. Sauté the shallot in the oil.

2) In a small bowl, whisk together the orange juice, lemon juice, salt, and pepper. Using a rubber spatula, scrape the shallots and oil from the pan into the bowl. Add the parsley. Stir to combine. You can do this several hours ahead of time.

3) Toast the almonds in a sauté pan over medium heat until they become aromatic and start to darken.

4) Add the pasta to the almonds. Pour the sauce on top. Stir and heat thoroughly.

Per Serving: Calories 192; Protein 6g; Fat 4g (Saturated 0g); Carbohydrates 34g; Fiber 2g; Sodium 249mg

Spinach and Orzo

Makes: 5 servings

I like to add color to plain pasta. Here, the dark green of the spinach contrasts nicely with the ivory-colored orzo.

One 10-ounce package frozen chopped spinach, thawed, or 1-pound fresh
$1^1/2$ teaspoons olive oil
$2/3$ cup chopped onions
2 cloves garlic, minced
3 cups cooked orzo
$1/2$ teaspoon kosher salt
$1/4$ teaspoon freshly ground pepper
2 teaspoons lemon juice

1) Cook the spinach until warmed through (this can be done in the microwave). Squeeze out the excess water and set aside.

2) Meanwhile, heat the oil in a large nonstick skillet. Over medium-high heat, cook the onions and garlic until darkened but not brown. Stir in the orzo and cook about 2 minutes, until golden. Stir in the spinach, salt, pepper, and lemon juice. Warm through.

Per Serving: Calories 161; Protein 6g; Fat 2g (Saturated 0g); Carbohydrates 30g; Fiber 3g; Sodium 237mg

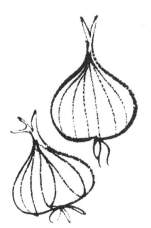

Orzo with Parsley and Lemon

Makes: 4 servings

This is lemony without being sour.

$1^1/2$ cups orzo
3 tablespoons chopped fresh parsley
$1/2$ teaspoon minced lemon zest
1 teaspoon kosher salt
1 tablespoon extra-virgin olive oil
1 teaspoon lemon juice

1) Cook the orzo in $1^1/2$ quarts of boiling water until done but not mushy, about 8 minutes. Drain and toss in a colander.

2) Put the hot orzo in a bowl and stir in the remaining ingredients. Serve immediately.

Per Serving: Calories 265; Protein 8g; Fat 4g (Saturated 1g); Carbohydrates 47g; Fiber 2g; Sodium 486mg

Orzo with Fresh Dill

Makes: 4 servings

The dill is not cooked in with the pasta but is added at the last minute so that it retains its bright green color and fresh flavor.

$1^1/2$ cups orzo
2 tablespoons minced fresh dill
1 teaspoon kosher salt
$1^1/2$ teaspoons extra-virgin olive oil

1) Cook the orzo in $1^1/2$ quarts of boiling water until done but not mushy, about 8 minutes. Drain and toss in a colander.

2) Put the orzo in a serving bowl, and stir in the dill, salt, and oil. Serve immediately.

Per Serving: Calories 249; Protein 8g; Fat 3g (Saturated 0g); Carbohydrates 47g; Fiber 2g; Sodium 485mg

Orzo with Peas and Mint

Makes: 5 servings

This really nice combination of flavors takes little time to put together.

1^1/2 cups orzo
1 teaspoon olive oil
^{1}/2 cup frozen peas, thawed
1 teaspoon minced lemon zest
1 teaspoon kosher salt
1^1/2 tablespoons minced fresh mint leaves

1) Cook the orzo in 1^1/2 quarts of boiling water until done but not mushy, about 8 minutes. Drain and toss in a colander.

2) Heat the oil in a large nonstick pan. Add the orzo. Cook for 2 minutes. Stir in the peas, zest, and salt. Continue to cook until the peas are warmed through, about 1 minute longer. Stir in the mint and serve.

Per Serving: Calories 207; Protein 7g; Fat 2g (Saturated 0g); Carbohydrates 40g; Fiber 2g; Sodium 405mg

Far Eastern Ginger Noodles

Makes: 2 servings

Don't substitute Italian spaghetti in this recipe, because part of the flavor comes from the Asian noodles themselves.

4 ounces udon or soba noodles, or ^{1}/2 pound fresh Chinese flat noodles
2 teaspoons vegetable oil
2 teaspoons finely minced fresh ginger
6 scallions (including crisp green tops), sliced diagonally into ^{1}/2-inch pieces
2 teaspoons soy sauce

1) Cook the noodles and drain well.

2) Heat the oil in a wok or heavy skillet and sauté the ginger until it starts to change color, but don't let it burn. Add the scallions and sauté until wilted.

3) Stir in the noodles and soy sauce and toss until the noodles are lightly coated.

Per Serving: Calories 264; Protein 12g; Fat 5g (Saturated 0g); Carbohydrates 48g; Fiber 3g; Sodium 475mg

Noodle Kugel

Makes: 12 servings

This is a somewhat sweet and rich noodle pudding. It tastes good warm or even at room temperature. It is quite firm and so is great for a buffet as it can be cut into squares and put on a platter. I've seen children reach out and happily take a piece in each hand.

1/2 pound egg noodles
1 pound 1% lowfat cottage cheese
1 pound lowfat sour cream
1/4 cup nonfat cream cheese
1 egg
2 egg whites
1/4 teaspoon kosher salt
1 teaspoon vanilla extract
1/4 cup sugar
1/2 cup golden raisins or currants
1/2 teaspoon ground cinnamon

1) Preheat the oven to 350°F. Coat a 9×13-inch baking dish with nonstick spray.

2) Cook the noodles until pliable but not soft. Drain, immerse in cold water, drain again, and set aside.

3) Beat the cottage cheese, sour cream, cream cheese, egg, and egg whites until well blended. The cottage cheese lumps will remain, but all else should be smooth. On low speed, mix in the salt, vanilla, and sugar. Stir in the raisins and noodles. Put the mixture into the baking dish. Dust with the cinnamon.

4) Bake for 50 to 60 minutes, until the pudding is set. Serve warm or at room temperature.

Per Serving: Calories 194; Protein 11g; Fat 4g (Saturated 2g); Carbohydrates 30g; Fiber 1g; Sodium 275mg

Spinach Noodle Kugel

Makes: 12 servings

This savory kugel reheats nicely the second day, which makes it useful for a party (or for someone like me who loves leftovers).

1/2 pound egg noodles
One 10-ounce package frozen chopped
    spinach, thawed
1 pound 1% lowfat cottage cheese
1 pound lowfat sour cream
1/4 cup nonfat cream cheese, softened
1 egg
2 egg whites
1/2 teaspoon kosher salt
1/2 teaspoon freshly ground pepper
1/4 teaspoon ground nutmeg
1 tablespoon finely minced or grated onions

1) Preheat the oven to 350°F. Coat a 9×13-inch baking dish with nonstick spray.

2) Cook the noodles until pliable but not soft. Drain, immerse in cold water, drain again, and set aside.

3) Squeeze the spinach to remove as much water as possible.

4) Beat the cottage cheese, sour cream, cream cheese, egg, and egg whites until well blended. The cottage cheese lumps will remain, but all else should be smooth. On the lowest speed, mix in the salt, pepper, nutmeg, spinach, and onions. Stir the noodles into the cheese mixture and then spread into the baking dish.

5) Bake for about 50 minutes, until the pudding is set. Serve hot.

Per Serving: Calories 162; Protein 11g; Fat 4g (Saturated 2g); Carbohydrates 21g; Fiber 1g; Sodium 332mg

Couscous

Couscous is a form of wheat pasta that originated in North Africa. Couscous looks like fine bulgur wheat. Originally it was made by hand and then steamed in special pots. But couscous has adapted to this country well, and it can now be found in boxes in supermarkets. It requires only a 5-minute soak in very hot water to cook. If a recipe calls for cooked couscous, follow the package directions but leave out the fat.

Basil and Tomato Couscous

Makes: 4 servings

Instead of mincing the basil leaves, here they are sliced into fine strips, which adds to the appearance of this recipe.

$1^{1}/4$ cup water
$1/2$ teaspoon kosher salt
1 cup couscous
$1/4$ cup thinly sliced fresh basil leaves
1 medium ripe tomato, chopped (1 cup)

1) Bring the water and salt to a boil in a small saucepan. Stir in the couscous and basil. Remove from the heat, cover, and let rest for 5 minutes.

2) Meanwhile, cook the tomato in a nonstick skillet until it softens and warms through. Stir the tomato into the couscous and serve.

Per Serving: Calories 211; Protein 7g; Fat 1g (Saturated 0g); Carbohydrates 43g; Fiber 2g; Sodium 249mg

Couscous with Peas and Dill

Makes: 4 servings

Cooking the couscous in broth instead of water lends a depth of flavor to this simple grain.

$1^{1}/2$ cups reduced-sodium, defatted chicken broth
$1/2$ teaspoon kosher salt
1 cup couscous
$2/3$ cup frozen peas (not thawed)
$1/2$ teaspoon dried dill, or $1/2$ tablespoon minced fresh dill

1) Bring the broth to a boil. Stir in the salt, couscous, peas, and dill.

2) Cover the pot, remove it from the heat, and let it rest about 5 minutes, until the couscous has absorbed all the liquid and becomes tender. Fluff with a fork before serving.

Per Serving: Calories 230; Protein 9g; Fat 1g (Saturated 0g); Carbohydrates 45g; Fiber 2g; Sodium 451mg

Apricot Couscous Pilaf

Makes: 4 servings

The carrots, apricots, and curry powder cast a pretty orange glow on this pilaf.

1 teaspoon vegetable oil
$1/2$ carrot, peeled and cut into small cubes ($1/2$ cup)
3 tablespoons sliced pecans or almonds
$1^{1}/2$ cups water
$3/4$ cup couscous
$1/2$ teaspoon curry powder
$1/4$ teaspoon kosher salt
$1/4$ cup dried apricots, sliced

1) Heat the oil in a nonstick pan. Cook the carrots in the oil for about 3 minutes, until they begin to soften, keeping the pan covered. Add the nuts, increase the heat to high, and cook, uncovered, for 1 minute, until the nuts begin to brown. You'll be able to smell the change in their aroma.

2) In another pot, bring the water to a boil. Stir in the couscous, curry powder, salt, apricots, and carrot mixture. Cover, remove from the heat, and let rest for 5 minutes.

Per Serving: Calories 224; Protein 6g; Fat 6g (Saturated 0g); Carbohydrates 38g; Fiber 2g; Sodium 130mg

Summertime Couscous

Makes: 3 servings

Fresh summer herbs, lemon zest, and balsamic vinegar combine to make a sprightly side dish that tastes good chilled as a salad the day after it is made.

2 cups cooked couscous
1 clove garlic, minced
1 1/2 teaspoons olive oil
1/4 cup chopped fresh mint
2 tablespoons chopped fresh parsley
1 tablespoon chopped fresh chives
Freshly ground pepper to taste
1/2 teaspoon minced lemon zest
1/4 teaspoon balsamic vinegar

1) Crumble the cooked couscous with a fork or your fingers.

2) Sauté the garlic in the olive oil over low heat until the garlic turns light golden.

3) Add the herbs, pepper, lemon zest, and vinegar. Stir in the couscous and heat through.

Per Serving: Calories 160; Protein 5g; Fat 3g (Saturated 0g); Carbohydrates 29g; Fiber 2g; Sodium 12mg

Baked Couscous with Tomatoes

Makes: 6 servings

Most couscous recipes, because of their quick cooking times and light flavors, tend to be warm-weather foods. But this recipe is hearty enough for a winter supper.

1 tablespoon olive oil
1/2 cup minced onions
One 14 1/2-ounce can diced tomatoes, drained
2 cups couscous
3 cups reduced-sodium, defatted chicken or
    vegetable broth
1 teaspoon kosher salt
1/4 teaspoon freshly ground pepper
1/2 teaspoon ground coriander

1) Preheat the oven to 375°F.

2) Heat the oil in a sauté pan. Sauté the onions in the oil about 5 minutes, until they are soft and golden.

3) In a bowl, combine the sautéed onions and the remaining ingredients. Transfer the mixture to a 2-quart casserole.

4) Bake for 20 minutes.

Per Serving: Calories 321; Protein 12g; Fat 4g (Saturated 1g); Carbohydrates 59g; Fiber 3g; Sodium 571mg

Rice

The last time I was at the Seattle farmer's market there was a booth selling no fewer than twenty varieties of rice, from the familiar long-grain white to a glutinous purple rice. Recently supermarkets have started to carry more than boxes of white rice. There is brown rice, Arborio rice (for risottos), wild rice, and aromatic rice. Aromatic rice might be called Texmati or basmati. It smells like popcorn when cooked and tastes slightly sweet and vaguely exotic. Kernels range from long- to short-grain (the shorter the grain, the stickier the rice cooks up). Some rice has been par-cooked, some has been fortified with nutrients. Follow package directions for cooking, but always leave out the fat and salt. Try an unfamiliar rice. Even an unadorned bowl of rice complements most menus.

White Rice

Makes: 4 servings

Not all white rice is cooked the same. Enriched rice should never be rinsed, because the nutrients are on the surface, but many Asian white rices require rinsing for cleansing and to prevent gumminess. If your rice comes in a package with directions, follow the cleaning directions and use the listed proportion of water to rice. (It is not necessary to add the suggested fats often found on labels.) Otherwise, use the directions here.

2¹/4 cups water
1 cup white rice

1) Bring the water to a boil and stir in the rice. Reduce to a simmer.

2) Cover tightly and cook until the water is absorbed, about 20 minutes. Remove from the heat and let steam with the cover still on for 5 to 10 more minutes. Fluff with a fork and serve.

Per Serving: Calories 169; Protein 3g; Fat 0g (Saturated 0g); Carbohydrates 37g; Fiber 1g; Sodium 5mg

Brown Rice

Makes: 4 servings

Brown rice comes out best if cooked liked pasta— in a lot of boiling water, then drained and allowed to rest and steam for a few minutes. Using this method, brown rice's individual grains cook up tender and distinct. If white rice was cooked like this, it would turn to mush.

1 quart water
1 cup brown rice

1) Bring the water to a boil. Add the rice. (Rice sold in supermarkets does not need rinsing. Rice sold in bulk at natural food stores benefits from a rinse in cool water.)

2) Reduce the heat and simmer, uncovered, for 25 to 30 minutes, until the rice is tender but not mushy. Rice from a natural food store will usually take longer to cook than supermarket rice.

3) Take the pot over to the sink, empty the contents into a mesh strainer, set the strainer on the pot, cover with a lid, and allow to sit for 10 minutes. Fluff with a fork and serve.

Per Serving: Calories 171; Protein 4g; Fat 1g (Saturated 0g); Carbohydrates 36g; Fiber 2g; Sodium 3mg

Lemon Rice

Makes: 4 servings

Lemon zest lightens and brightens the flavor of brown rice.

1 recipe Brown Rice (opposite)
2 teaspoons minced lemon zest
1/4 teaspoon freshly ground pepper
1/4 teaspoon kosher salt
1 tablespoon minced fresh parsley

1) Cook the rice according to the directions above.

2) Just prior to serving, stir in the remaining ingredients.

Per Serving: Calories 172; Protein 4g; Fat 1g (Saturated 0g); Carbohydrates 36g; Fiber 2g; Sodium 124mg

Orange Rice

Makes: 4 servings

Cooking the rice in orange juice brings the flavor of citrus to the core of each kernel.

1 orange
1 1/2 cups water
1/4 teaspoon kosher salt
1 cup long-grain brown rice

1) Peel the zest off the orange to mince and measure 1 1/2 teaspoons.

2) Juice the orange. Measure out 1/2 cup of juice. One orange should yield enough juice, but if it doesn't (sometimes navels are rather dry), squeeze another orange or add some store-bought juice.

3) Bring the orange juice, water, and salt to a boil. Rinse the rice, then stir it in.

4) Reduce the heat to a simmer. Cover and cook for about 45 minutes, until all the liquid is absorbed.

5) Remove the pot from the stove. Stir in the zest. Cover again and let the rice rest for 10 minutes before serving.

Per Serving: Calories 186; Protein 4g; Fat 1g (Saturated 0g); Carbohydrates 39g; Fiber 2g; Sodium 126mg

Saffron Rice

Makes: 4 servings

Saffron's color and aroma is unmistakable. Little more is necessary to turn basic white rice into something elegant and extravagant.

1/4 teaspoon saffron threads, or 1/8 teaspoon powdered saffron
2 tablespoons boiling water
3 cups reduced-sodium, defatted chicken broth
1 cup rice, preferably basmati or other aromatic variety
1/4 teaspoon kosher salt
1 clove garlic

1) Soak the saffron in the boiling water until the water turns orange.

2) Bring the broth to a boil and add the rice, salt, and garlic. Pour the saffron water through a fine mesh sieve and into the pot. Press down on the threads to extract as much flavor as possible. Discard the threads. Reduce to a simmer, cover, and cook for 20 minutes.

3) Remove from the heat, discard the garlic, strain the rice into a colander, and set the colander over the pot. Cover and let steam for 10 minutes.

Per Serving: Calories 188; Protein 6g; Fat 2g (Saturated 0g); Carbohydrates 38g; Fiber 2g; Sodium 484mg

Curried Rice

Makes: 4 servings

Sautéeing the rice and spices in oil heightens all of the flavors and keeps them prominent, even after boiling.

1 teaspoon vegetable oil
1 cup white rice
1 1/2 teaspoons curry powder
1/2 teaspoon turmeric
1/8 teaspoon cayenne pepper (optional)
One 16-ounce can reduced-sodium, defatted
    chicken broth
1 tablespoon chopped cashews, lightly toasted

1) Heat the oil in a saucepan. Stir in the rice, curry powder, turmeric, and cayenne pepper and cook for 1 minute, until the aromas heighten and the rice turns golden.

2) Pour in the broth, bring to a boil, reduce to a simmer, cover, and cook for 15 minutes, until all the liquid has been absorbed. Stir with a fork, cover again, and let rest for 10 minutes.

3) Put into a serving bowl and top with the cashews.

Per Serving: Calories 204; Protein 5g; Fat 3g (Saturated 0g); Carbohydrates 39g; Fiber 1g; Sodium 235mg

Rice with Peas and Mint

Makes: 4 servings

The peas are added frozen, during the last ten minutes. This gives them time to warm through and cook lightly, but not so long that they shrivel or turn dull.

2 cups water
1 cup long-grain white rice
1 cup frozen peas
2 tablespoons minced fresh mint leaves
1/4 teaspoon freshly ground pepper
1/2 teaspoon kosher salt

1) Bring the water to a boil. Stir in the rice, cover, and cook 20 minutes, until all the water has been absorbed.

2) Add the remaining ingredients and fluff the rice with a fork. Cover and let sit 10 minutes before serving.

Per Serving: Calories 198; Protein 5g; Fat 0g (Saturated 0g); Carbohydrates 42g; Fiber 2g; Sodium 288mg

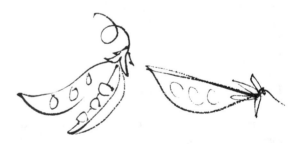

Raisins and Walnuts Pilaf

Makes: 4 servings

Walnuts enhance the natural nuttiness of brown rice.

1/4 cup walnut pieces
1/4 cup raisins
1/4 cup water
2 cups cooked brown rice, preferably short-grain

1) Heat a pan and toast the walnut pieces over dry heat to bring out their flavor.

2) Add the remaining ingredients and cook over low heat, covered, until hot. Shake the pan and stir occasionally to keep the rice from sticking. (Omit the water if using freshly cooked, still warm rice, or if reheating in a microwave, but you must still toast the nuts.)

Per Serving: Calories 189; Protein 4g; Fat 6g (Saturated 1g); Carbohydrates 33g; Fiber 2g; Sodium 3mg

Basmati and Lentil Pilaf

Makes: 10 servings

The lentils are first cooked separately, then with the rice. This insures that the lentils and rice are cooked for the appropriate times and neither becomes mushy. Also, by discarding the water that the lentils are first cooked in, the final color of the dish is attractive, not the murky brown of the bean liquid.

1/2 cup lentils, washed
1 teaspoon olive oil
1 clove garlic, minced
1 1/2 cups basmati (aromatic) rice
1/8 teaspoon ground saffron, or 1 pinch threads
    dissolved in 2 tablespoons hot water
2 3/4 cups reduced-sodium, defatted chicken broth
    or water
1/4 teaspoon ground cumin
1 teaspoon kosher salt
1 tablespoon chopped fresh mint

1) Put the lentils in a pot and fill with enough water to cover by 2 inches. Bring to a boil, reduce to a simmer, and cook for 10 minutes, until not quite tender. Drain and set aside.

2) Wipe out the pot, pour in the oil, and briefly cook the garlic over moderate heat until golden. Stir in the rice and cook for 1 minute.

3) Pour in the saffron, broth, cumin, and salt. Bring to a boil, add the lentils, and reduce to a simmer. Cover and cook until all the liquid is absorbed, about 15 minutes. Remove from the heat and let stand 10 minutes. Stir in the mint and serve.

Per Serving: Calories 146; Protein 6g; Fat 2g (Saturated 0g); Carbohydrates 29g; Fiber 3g; Sodium 327mg

Currant Pilaf

Makes: 6 servings

Currants are smaller and less sweet than raisins. The two are not interchangeable in this dish, as raisins would knock the flavors and textures out of balance.

2 teaspoons olive oil
2 carrots, grated or diced (1 cup)
1/4 teaspoon turmeric
1 1/2 cups long-grain brown rice, rinsed
3 cups reduced-sodium, defatted chicken broth
1/2 teaspoon kosher salt
1/4 teaspoon freshly ground pepper
1/3 cup currants

1) Heat the oil in a sauté pan over medium heat. Sauté the carrots in the oil for about 5 minutes.

2) Add the turmeric and rice, and continue to sauté until all the grains turn golden.

3) Add the broth, salt, and pepper. Bring to a boil, then reduce to a simmer. Cover and cook for 30 minutes.

4) Stir in the currants. Cover again and continue to cook for 10 to 15 minutes, until all the liquid is absorbed.

5) Turn off the heat. Fluff the rice with a fork, then let it rest, covered, for about 10 minutes.

Per Serving: Calories 209; Protein 6g; Fat 3g (Saturated 0g); Carbohydrates 40g; Fiber 3g; Sodium 412mg

Curried Fried Rice

Makes: 6 servings

This is a great use for leftover plain rice. In fact, fried rice is best made with day-old rice. I often boil up a double batch of rice, just so I'll have some on hand for fried rice later in the week.

4 cups cooked rice
1 cup diced carrots
1/4 cup reduced-sodium, defatted chicken broth
1/2 teaspoon kosher salt
1/4 teaspoon freshly ground pepper
1 tablespoon soy sauce
2 tablespoons vegetable oil
1/2 cup chopped onions
1 1/2 tablespoons curry powder, or more to taste
1/2 cup frozen peas
1 scallion, sliced

1) Cook the rice a day ahead of time to give the grains time to dry out and chill. Either steam or microwave the carrots briefly, then drain and set aside. Like the rice, they can be prepared the day before.

2) Combine the broth, salt, pepper, and soy sauce in a bowl. Set aside.

3) Over high heat, warm the oil in a large non-stick wok. Add the onions and cook, stirring constantly, until they soften. Add the curry and cook for about 30 seconds, until the aroma intensifies. Add the carrots and peas; heat thoroughly.

4) Stir in the rice, breaking it apart with a spatula. Pour in the broth mixture and add the scallions. Stir and heat through. Remove from the heat, cover, and keep warm until serving.

Per Serving: Calories 196; Protein 4g; Fat 5g (Saturated 0g); Carbohydrates 33g; Fiber 2g; Sodium 374mg

Vegetable Fried Rice

Makes: 5 servings

This can be served as one of several dishes with a Chinese meal, or eaten as a vegetarian main course.

3 cups cooked white or brown rice
1 cup snow peas, trimmed and stringed
    if necessary
1 tablespoon oil
1/2 red bell pepper, diced
1 cup mung bean sprouts, washed well
1 egg, lightly beaten
1 tablespoon soy sauce
1/4 teaspoon freshly ground pepper
1 scallion, sliced

1) If possible, cook the rice a day ahead of time to give the grains time to dry out and chill. Snap or cut off the stem ends of the snow peas, and if necessary pull off their strings (some peas are stringless). Cut them on the diagonal into thin strips.

2) Over high heat, warm the oil in a large non-stick wok. Add the snow peas, bell pepper, and sprouts. Cook for about 2 minutes. Add the rice. Break it apart and cook until it sounds as if it is popping.

3) Push the rice to the center of the wok and pour the egg along the rim so that it drips down into the wok and cooks as it reaches the rice. Stir the egg into the rice. Stir in the soy sauce, pepper, and scallion.

Per Serving: Calories 175; Protein 5g; Fat 4g (Saturated 1g); Carbohydrates 29g; Fiber 2g; Sodium 222mg

Dirty Rice

Makes: 4 servings

After a long day at work making rich foods, a catering friend of mine comes home and makes this for her supper.

1 tablespoon olive oil
1 clove garlic, minced
1 tablespoon minced leek or scallion
2 tablespoons pine nuts
1/4 pound mushrooms, chopped (about 1 cup)
2 1/2 cups cooked brown rice
1 tablespoon minced fresh parsley
1 teaspoon soy sauce

1) Heat the oil in a sauté pan. Add the garlic, leek, and pine nuts and cook until the nuts lightly toast. Add the mushrooms and cook, covered, until wilted.

2) Add the brown rice, parsley, and soy sauce. Heat until the rice is warmed through.

Per Serving: Calories 197; Protein 5g; Fat 6g (Saturated 1g); Carbohydrates 31g; Fiber 3g; Sodium 89mg

Shiitake Brown Rice

Makes: 3 servings

Although shiitake mushrooms vary in size, their flavor and texture are not linked to size, but to freshness and quality. Look for mushrooms that are evenly brown, with velvety caps. The stems can be dried out but not shriveled.

1 teaspoon vegetable oil
1 clove garlic, minced
1/2 small leek, cut into half rounds (1/2 cup)
6 medium shiitake mushrooms, stems discarded, caps sliced (about 1 cup)
2 teaspoons soy sauce, divided
2 tablespoons reduced-sodium, defatted chicken broth, divided
2 cups cooked brown rice

1) Heat the oil in a nonstick pan. Sauté the garlic and leeks in the oil until the leeks are golden. Be careful not to scorch the garlic.

2) Add the mushrooms along with 1 teaspoon of the soy sauce and 1 tablespoon of the broth. Cook until the mushrooms soften and wilt a bit.

3) Stir in the rice and the remaining soy sauce and broth. Heat through and serve.

Per Serving: Calories 160; Protein 4g; Fat 3g (Saturated 0g); Carbohydrates 32g; Fiber 3g; Sodium 259mg

South of the Border Rice

Makes: 6 servings

This goes well with any Southwestern or Mexican-inspired dish, from enchiladas to Tortilla Lasagna (pages 275, 278) to Chicken Roasted with Red Rubbing Spices (page 180).

2 cups reduced-sodium, defatted chicken broth or water
1 cup brown rice
1/2 cup chopped onions
1 tablespoon vegetable oil
1/2 green bell pepper, chopped
1/2 cup corn kernels (fresh or frozen)
1/2 teaspoon ground turmeric
1/8 teaspoon Tabasco sauce
1/8 teaspoon cayenne pepper
1/4 teaspoon kosher salt
1 tablespoon minced fresh parsley or cilantro

1) Bring the broth to a boil and add the rice to the pot. Cover and simmer.

2) Sauté the onions in the oil until they are translucent. Add the bell pepper and cook until wilted. Stir in the corn kernels (which can be added still frozen). Add the turmeric, Tabasco, cayenne pepper, and salt and cook until the onions turn yellow.

3) Add the sautéed vegetables to the pot of simmering rice, cover, and continue to simmer until all the liquid is absorbed. Total cooking time should be about 40 minutes.

4) Stir in the parsley. Remove the pot from the heat, keeping it covered, and let mixture steam for 10 minutes before serving.

Per Serving: Calories 160; Protein 4g; Fat 3g (Saturated 0g); Carbohydrates 28g; Fiber 2g; Sodium 246mg

Red Rice

Makes: 6 servings

Don't expect to see individual, fluffy grains of rice here. The vegetables make this dish moist, but also colorful and very flavorful.

1 teaspoon vegetable oil
$^1/_2$ cup chopped onions
2 cloves garlic, minced
1 rib celery, chopped
$^1/_2$ green bell pepper, chopped
2 medium tomatoes, peeled and chopped
2 bay leaves
1 cup brown rice
$1^3/_4$ cups water
$^1/_2$ teaspoon kosher salt
$^1/_4$ teaspoon freshly ground pepper
$^1/_8$ teaspoon cayenne pepper, or to taste

1) Heat the oil in a 2-quart saucepan. Sauté the onions, garlic, celery, and bell pepper in the oil. Keep the pan covered between stirrings. Cook for at least 5 minutes, until the vegetables are thoroughly softened and the onions are golden.

2) Add the tomatoes, bay leaves, and rice. Sauté for 2 minutes more.

3) Add the water and the remaining seasonings. Bring to a boil, then reduce to a simmer. Cook, covered, for about 50 minutes, until all the liquid is absorbed.

Per Serving: Calories 139; Protein 3g; Fat 2g (Saturated 0g); Carbohydrates 28g; Fiber 2g; Sodium 174mg

Red Rice and Beans

Makes: 8 servings

This can be a vegetarian's main entrée.

1 recipe Red Rice (opposite)
2 cups cooked kidney, pinto, or black beans, drained and rinsed

Prepare Red Rice according to directions above. Either heat the beans and then stir them into the hot rice, or heat the two together in the microwave.

Per Serving: Calories 160; Protein 6g; Fat 2g (Saturated 0g); Carbohydrates 31g; Fiber 5g; Sodium 132mg

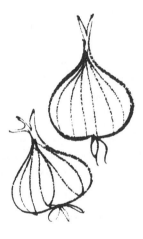

Curried Pea Pilaf

Makes: 6 servings

The sweetness and buttery texture of cashews makes them the nut of choice here.

2 teaspoons vegetable oil
$1/2$ cup chopped onions
2 cloves garlic, minced
1 teaspoon finely grated fresh ginger
1 teaspoon curry powder
$1/4$ teaspoon ground cinnamon
$1/2$ teaspoon kosher salt
$1/4$ teaspoon freshly ground pepper
2 cups peas (fresh or frozen)
$1/2$ cup water
3 cups cooked brown basmati or other
    aromatic rice
$1/2$ cup cashews, toasted (optional)

1) Heat the oil in a 10-inch nonstick pan. Sauté the onions and garlic in the oil. Keep the pan covered between stirrings. Cook over low heat until the onions are soft and golden.

2) Add the ginger, curry powder, cinnamon, salt, and pepper to the pan. Cook to release their aroma. You'll be able to smell the change as the spices get hot.

3) Add the peas and water. Gently cook until most of the liquid has evaporated.

4) Stir the rice into the curried peas. Heat through. Stir until the spices and peas are evenly distributed. Stir in the cashews, if desired.

Per Serving: Calories 169; Protein 5g; Fat 3g (Saturated 0g); Carbohydrates 31g; Fiber 5g; Sodium 169mg

Wild Wild Rice

Makes: 6 servings

This recipe combines two extravagant ingredients, wild rice and dried mushrooms. The earthy muskiness of the mushrooms complements the nutty flavor of the wild rice.

$1/2$ cup porcini or similar dried mushrooms
$2 1/2$ cups water
$1/4$ teaspoon kosher salt
$3/4$ cup long-grain brown rice
$1/2$ cup wild rice
$1/4$ teaspoon dried thyme
$1/4$ teaspoon dried sage
$1/8$ teaspoon freshly ground pepper
$1/2$ cup nuts, toasted and chopped (optional)
1 tablespoon minced fresh parsley, for garnish

1) Rinse the mushrooms thoroughly under cold running water, then soak them in hot water for about 5 minutes, until they become soft enough to slice. Cut them into thin strips.

2) Bring the water and salt to a boil. Stir in the rices and the sliced mushrooms. Reduce to a simmer, cover, and cook for 1 hour, until the rice is done.

3) Remove the pan from the stove. Stir in the herbs and pepper. Use a fork to stir and fluff. Cover the rice and let rest for 10 minutes before serving.

4) Just prior to putting the rice into a serving bowl, stir in the toasted nuts, if desired, and garnish with the parsley.

Per Serving: Calories 265; Protein 11g; Fat 2g (Saturated 0g); Carbohydrates 51g; Fiber 5g; Sodium 135mg

Vegetable Paella

Makes: 8 servings

Although appropriate for a dinner party, paella is also everyday fare. This recipe has been toddler tested. When a three-year-old (and his dad) ask for more, you know that you've had success in the kitchen.

$1/4$ teaspoon saffron threads, or $1/8$ teaspoon powdered saffron

$1/4$ cup dry white wine

1 tablespoon olive oil

1 cup chopped onions

3 cloves garlic, minced

1 cup chopped green bell pepper

1 cup chopped red bell pepper

1 bay leaf

$11/2$ cups short-grain or Arborio rice

$1/2$ teaspoon dried thyme

$1/2$ teaspoon kosher salt, or more to taste

$1/4$ teaspoon freshly ground pepper, or more to taste

$11/2$ cups chopped tomatoes, or one $141/2$-ounce can diced tomatoes

3 cups reduced-sodium, defatted chicken or vegetable broth

2 cups sliced zucchini or summer squash

1 cup small broccoli florets

1 cup green peas

1) Preheat the oven to 350°F. Steep the saffron in the wine and set aside.

2) Heat the oil in a Dutch oven. (If you don't have a Dutch oven, use a saucepan and transfer to an ovenproof casserole later.) Sauté the onions, garlic, bell peppers, and bay leaf until the onions become translucent. Stir in the rice, thyme, salt, and pepper. Stir until the grains of rice are coated and shiny from the oil.

3) Stir in the tomatoes, broth, and saffron-infused wine. Bring to a boil, take off the heat, and set the squash and broccoli on top. Cover and place in the oven for 25 minutes. Stir in the peas, and taste and adjust the salt and pepper. Remove the bay leaf.

Per Serving: Calories 206; Protein 6g; Fat 2g (Saturated 0g); Carbohydrates 39g; Fiber 4g; Sodium 308mg

Other Grains

Look next to the rice at the supermarket and you might be surprised at what you find. Other grains, in boxes and bags, are stocked on the shelves. There are the dark kernels of kasha, tiny grains of quinoa, and round pearls of barley. If your supermarket doesn't carry these items, the local natural food store will.

Portobellos and Grains

Makes: 5 servings

Although I specify kasha and brown rice, any two grains can be used in this recipe. It is a nice way to use up leftover grains.

1 to 2 large portobello mushrooms
   (about 4 ounces or 1 1/2 cups sliced)
1 tablespoon olive oil
1 cup chopped onions
1 cup cooked kasha
1 cup cooked brown rice
1/4 teaspoon kosher salt
1/4 teaspoon freshly ground pepper
2 tablespoons chopped fresh parsley

1) Remove and discard the mushroom stems. Halve the portobellos, then cut thinly crosswise.

2) Heat the oil in a sauté pan. Sauté the onions and mushrooms in the oil until the onions become translucent.

3) Stir in the remaining ingredients. Heat through. If the grains are too dry, add a tablespoon or more chicken broth.

Per Serving: Calories 120; Protein 3g; Fat 3g (Saturated 1g); Carbohydrates 21g; Fiber 2g; Sodium 100mg

Basic Kasha

Makes: 4 servings

Kasha, also called buckwheat, is not a member of the wheat family. Botanically it isn't even a grain, but it is considered and used as such by cooks throughout the world, especially in Eastern Europe. There are good reasons to cook with it—it is high in protein and potassium, has a unique flavor, and takes only a few minutes to cook. However, kasha can be heavy and dense; to improve the texture, cook it a day ahead of time. Storing kasha in the refrigerator dries out and separates the kernels.

2 cups water
1 cup kasha
1 egg white, lightly beaten

1) Bring the water to a boil.

2) Meanwhile, mix together the kasha and egg white. Heat the mixture in a small pan over medium heat until the egg white cooks and dries out. Stir constantly and break apart any clumps. This step helps to keep the kasha grains separate and not mushy.

3) Add the kasha to the boiling water. Cover and reduce to a simmer. Cook gently for about 10 minutes, until the kasha has absorbed all the liquid.

4) Remove the pot from the stove and allow the kasha to steam, with the lid on, for another couple of minutes.

Per Serving: Calories 150; Protein 7g; Fat 1g (Saturated 0g); Carbohydrates 30g; Fiber 4g; Sodium 18mg

Kasha and Mushrooms

Makes: 4 servings

Mushrooms and kasha have been paired together for centuries. I've added a carrot to bring color to this dish.

1 teaspoon olive oil
1/2 pound mushrooms, quartered (about 2 cups)
1 small carrot, peeled and chopped
2 cups cooked kasha (see Basic Kasha, opposite)
1/4 teaspoon kosher salt
1/4 teaspoon freshly ground pepper
2 tablespoons minced fresh parsley

1) Heat the oil in a 10-inch nonstick pan. Sauté the mushrooms and carrots in the oil until the mushrooms exude liquid.

2) Add the kasha, salt, pepper, and parsley. Break up any clumps of kasha as it warms through.

Per Serving: Calories 124; Protein 5g; Fat 2g (Saturated 0g); Carbohydrates 24g; Fiber 4g; Sodium 134mg

Barley with Mushrooms

Makes: 7 servings

Pearl barley has had the outer bran layer removed and thus is ivory-white. Unlike other grains, such as rice, barley's bran layer is tough and not particularly edible. Natural food stores have barley that has some of the bran remaining, but I don't see the need to buy it. It is a less attractive brown color and takes longer to cook. Besides, pearl barley is still very high in fiber (more than double that of brown rice), so I stick with the pearl.

1 teaspoon olive oil
2 tablespoons dry sherry
1/2 pound mushrooms, halved and thickly sliced (about 2 cups)
1 clove garlic, chopped
1 teaspoon kosher salt
1 1/3 cups pearl barley
3 cups reduced-sodium, defatted chicken broth
2 tablespoons chopped fresh parsley

1) Heat the oil and sherry in a saucepan. Add the mushrooms and garlic and cook until the mushrooms begin to shrink. Keep the pot covered between stirrings.

2) Add the remaining ingredients except the parsley. Bring to a boil, reduce to a simmer, cover, and cook for 30 minutes, until all the liquid is absorbed.

3) Stir in the parsley, cover, and let rest 10 minutes before serving.

Per Serving: Calories 160; Protein 6g; Fat 1g (Saturated 0g); Carbohydrates 32g; Fiber 6g; Sodium 486mg

Barley with Vegetables and Dill

Makes: 5 servings

Cooking barley in chicken broth really rounds out the flavor.

1¹/2 teaspoons vegetable oil
¹/2 cup chopped onions
1 clove garlic, chopped
1 small carrot, peeled and finely chopped
¹/2 pound mushrooms, halved and sliced
   (about 2 cups)
1 cup pearl barley
2 cups reduced-sodium, defatted chicken broth
1 teaspoon kosher salt
¹/4 teaspoon freshly ground pepper
1 tablespoon minced fresh dill
1 tablespoon chopped fresh parsley

1) Heat the oil in a saucepan. Sauté the onions, garlic, and carrot over medium heat for 5 minutes. Keep the pot covered between stirrings. Add the mushrooms and cook for another 3 minutes, until the mushrooms begin to shrink.

2) Add the remaining ingredients except the dill and parsley. Bring to a boil, reduce to a simmer, cover, and cook for 30 minutes, until all the liquid has been absorbed.

3) Stir in the herbs, cover, and let rest 5 minutes before serving.

Per Serving: Calories 186; Protein 7g; Fat 2g (Saturated 0g); Carbohydrates 37g; Fiber 7g; Sodium 588mg

Quinoa Pilaf

Makes: 4 servings

Quinoa is a South American grain. For more about it, see page 14.

1 cup uncooked quinoa
2 cups reduced-sodium, defatted chicken broth
1 cup finely diced carrot
1 tablespoon chopped fresh parsley
1 tablespoon chopped fresh chives
¹/4 teaspoon kosher salt
¹/4 teaspoon freshly ground pepper

1) Put the quinoa in a fine mesh strainer and wash it very well under cool running water.

2) Put the quinoa in a heavy-bottomed pot. Cook over moderately high heat until you hear or see a grain pop. Carefully pour in the broth (it will splatter on the hot surface). Stir in the carrot. Cover and simmer for 15 minutes.

3) Stir in the herbs, salt, and pepper. Cook for 3 minutes longer.

Per Serving: Calories 182; Protein 7g; Fat 3g (Saturated 0g); Carbohydrates 33g; Fiber 3g; Sodium 379mg

Beans

Beans are one of the most economical and versatile foods available. Their mild flavor pairs well with strong seasonings and their size and earthy colors allows them to blend in with other ingredients, especially stews and chilies. For many recipes, canned beans are as good as those cooked from scratch. Always rinse canned beans under cool running water, then drain. However, starting with dried beans allows you to control their texture. Whereas canned beans are always very soft, those cooked at home may be simmered until firm yet tender, which is the right texture for many recipes, especially salads.

Basic Beans

Makes: 4 servings

Starting with dried beans is easy, though time-consuming. One cup of dried beans weighs about 1/2 pound and will yield about 3 cups cooked.

1 cup dried beans

1) Wash the beans very well in plenty of water. Look for and discard clumps of dirt and pebbles. (This is what is meant by "wash and pick over.")

2) All beans, with the exception of lentils and split peas, should be soaked before cooking. This lessens the cooking time by at least 1 hour. To soak, put the beans in a bowl and cover with water by 2 inches. Discard beans that float to the surface. Let soak for 4 hours or up to 12. Beans that soak for a longer time might sprout. Or use the quick-soak method: Put the washed beans in a pot, cover with 2 inches of water, bring to a boil, then turn off the heat, cover, and let rest for 1 hour. This is the equivalent of a long cold soak. Regardless of which method you use, the beans, softened after absorbing the soak water, next need to be drained and rinsed.

3) Put the soaked, drained beans in a pot and again cover by 2 inches of water. Bring to a boil, then reduce to a simmer. Cook beans for salads until their skins just begin to break and they are tender through to their centers but still retain their shape. Those intended for casseroles and stews may be cooked until a bean turns to soft mush when squeezed between the fingers. If a bean is cooked for a long time and still feels gritty when pressed, it is probably old. It is best to discard these and start over. In fact, cooking times for dried beans will vary with the age of the bean. Although dried beans look as if they will last forever, after a year of storage they lose both flavor and texture. On average, dried beans that have been properly soaked will take from 50 to 80 minutes to simmer until tender.

Per Serving: Calories 181; Protein 11g; Fat 1g (Saturated 0g); Carbohydrates 35g; Fiber 10g; Sodium 6mg

Stewed Lentils

Makes: 4 servings

These are moist, but should not be soupy. Boil off excess liquid at the end of the cooking time.

1 cup dried lentils, washed and picked over
3 cloves garlic, sliced
2 bay leaves
One 14^1/2-ounce can whole tomatoes, drained, seeded and chopped
1^1/2 teaspoons lemon juice
^{1}/4 teaspoon dried ground rosemary
1 teaspoon dried basil
1 tablespoon chopped fresh parsley
1 teaspoon kosher salt
^{1}/4 teaspoon freshly ground pepper

1) Put the lentils in a pot with the garlic and bay leaves. Cover with water by 1 inch and bring to a boil. Reduce to a simmer and cook for 40 minutes, until the lentils are soft. Stir occasionally. By the end there will be little water left, but since cooking time varies, add water if necessary.

2) Stir in the remaining ingredients and gently simmer for 15 minutes more. Remove the bay leaves before serving.

Per Serving: Calories 182; Protein 14g; Fat 1g (Saturated 0g); Carbohydrates 32g; Fiber 7g; Sodium 601mg

Carrots and Lentils

Makes: 6 servings

Cooking the lentils with garlic, ginger, and cinnamon imbues the beans with a wonderful flavor.

4 cups water
1 cup dried lentils, washed and picked over
2 cloves garlic
One 1-inch piece fresh ginger, peeled
1 cinnamon stick
2 teaspoons olive oil
4 medium carrots, coarsely grated
1 cup chopped onions
^{1}/4 cup chopped fresh parsley
1 teaspoon kosher salt
^{1}/4 teaspoon freshly ground pepper

1) Bring the water to a simmer. Add the lentils, garlic, ginger, and cinnamon stick. Cook 12 to 18 minutes, until the lentils are tender on their outsides and slightly firm in their centers. Drain in a colander. Remove and discard the garlic, ginger, and cinnamon stick.

2) Meanwhile, heat the oil in a large nonstick sauté pan. Sauté the carrots and onions until golden brown around the edges. Toss in the lentils, parsley, salt, and pepper and warm through.

Per Serving: Calories 153; Protein 10g; Fat 2g (Saturated 0g); Carbohydrates 26g; Fiber 6g; Sodium 342mg

Brown Rice and Lentils

Makes: 5 servings

The parsley is added at the end so that it loses none of its bright color and flavor.

1/2 cup lentils, washed and picked over
2 1/4 cups reduced-sodium, defatted chicken broth
1/2 teaspoon kosher salt
1 cup long-grain brown rice
1 tablespoon chopped fresh parsley

1) Put the lentils in a pot and fill with enough water to cover the beans by 2 inches. Bring to a boil, reduce to a simmer, and cook for 10 minutes, until not quite tender. Drain and set aside.

2) Wipe out the pot, put in the broth and salt, and bring to a boil. Add the rice and lentils, then reduce to a simmer. Cover and cook until all the liquid is absorbed, about 35 to 40 minutes. Remove from the heat and let rest 10 minutes. Stir in the parsley and serve.

Per Serving: Calories 211; Protein 10g; Fat 1g (Saturated 0g); Carbohydrates 40g; Fiber 4g; Sodium 413mg

Spinach with Lentils

Makes: 6 servings

I've tested this with both fresh and frozen spinach and using the fresh made a big difference.

1 cup dried lentils, washed and picked over
2 bay leaves
1 1/2 teaspoons olive oil
1 small carrot, diced
3 cloves garlic, minced
1 pound fresh spinach, washed well, tough
    stems discarded
1 teaspoon kosher salt
1/4 teaspoon freshly ground pepper, or more
    to taste
1 tablespoon lemon juice

1) Put the lentils and bay leaves in a pot. Cover with 1 inch of water. Bring to a boil, reduce to a simmer, and cook until tender. Add water as necessary to keep the lentils covered; however, by the time they are soft, the water should be mostly cooked off. Cover and keep warm.

2) In a large skillet or wok, heat the oil and sauté the carrot and garlic over moderate heat until the garlic turns golden. Stir in the spinach and cook until wilted but not entirely shrunk down. (Cook the spinach in batches if the skillet is not large enough to hold it all comfortably.) Stir the spinach into the lentils. Stir in the salt, pepper, and lemon juice. Taste and adjust the pepper, if desired.

Per Serving: Calories 143; Protein 11g; Fat 2g (Saturated 0g); Carbohydrates 23g; Fiber 7g; Sodium 387mg

Dal Nepal

Makes: 4 servings

Red lentils have a sweet flavor and lovely salmon color and a softer cooked texture than brown lentils. They come in several sizes, from half that of split peas to the size of regular lentils. This recipe is written for the larger red lentils. The tiny ones cook as fast as instant oatmeal—and end up with the same porridgelike consistency.

2 teaspoons finely grated fresh ginger
1/2 cup minced onions
3 cloves garlic, minced
1 tablespoon vegetable oil
1 cup red lentils
3 cups water
1 teaspoon ground turmeric
2 teaspoons ground cumin
2 teaspoons chili powder
1/4 teaspoon Tabasco sauce

1) Sauté the ginger, onions, and garlic in the oil over low heat until thoroughly cooked.

2) Add the remaining ingredients and simmer, uncovered, for 20 minutes.

Per Serving: Calories 214; Protein 14g; Fat 4g (Saturated 0g); Carbohydrates 32g; Fiber 7g; Sodium 28mg

Baked Beans

Makes: 6 servings

Baked beans don't have to take six hours in a slow oven. This recipe takes less than 1 1/2 hours to make. Better yet, it works fine with canned beans, so you don't have to cook the beans from scratch.

1/2 teaspoon vegetable oil
1/2 cup chopped onions
4 cups cooked pinto or white beans, drained and rinsed
1 teaspoon dry mustard
2 tablespoons ketchup
1 tablespoon soy sauce
1/2 to 3/4 cup water
1/2 cup molasses, or more to taste

1) Preheat the oven to 350°F.

2) Heat the oil in a nonstick pan. Sauté the onions in the oil.

3) Combine the onions, beans, and remaining ingredients and put in a casserole, preferably ceramic. The water content of cooked beans varies a great deal, so gradually add up to 3/4 cup water until the mixture is loose but not soupy.

4) Cover the casserole and bake for 1 hour. Stir once while cooking to check the consistency. The end results are moist beans with a "gravy" around them. If they look dry, add a few tablespoons of water. After an hour, if the beans are too watery, take off the cover and cook until the liquid evaporates.

Per Serving: Calories 247; Protein 10g; Fat 1g (Saturated 0g); Carbohydrates 51g; Fiber 10g; Sodium 245mg

Black Beans and Rice

Makes: 9 servings

This is the popular side dish found in restaurants on Mexican meal combination plates. However, this version does without the saturated fats.

2 cups water
1 teaspoon kosher salt, divided
1 cup long-grain white rice
3 bay leaves
1 tablespoon vegetable oil
1 cup chopped onions
1 green bell pepper, chopped
1 chili pepper or jalapeño (fresh or canned), seeded and minced
2 cloves garlic, minced
2 cups cooked black beans, drained and rinsed

1) Bring the water and $1/2$ teaspoon of the salt to a boil. Add the rice and bay leaves, reduce to a gentle simmer, cover, and let cook for 20 minutes, until all the water is absorbed. Remove the bay leaves.

2) Meanwhile, heat the oil in a skillet. Add the onions, bell pepper, chili pepper, and garlic. Cook over moderate heat, stirring frequently, until the onions turn golden. Keep covered between stirrings. Stir in the black beans and remaining salt. Heat through.

3) Toss the beans with the rice and, if necessary, warm through.

Per Serving: Calories 151; Protein 5g; Fat 2g (Saturated 0g); Carbohydrates 28g; Fiber 4g; Sodium 217mg

Southwestern Black Beans

Makes: 4 servings

Make burritos out of leftovers.

1 teaspoon vegetable oil
$1/2$ cup chopped onions
2 cloves garlic, minced
$1 1/2$ teaspoons ground cumin
$1/2$ teaspoon ground coriander
$1/2$ teaspoon kosher salt
$1/4$ teaspoon Tabasco sauce, or to taste
1 tablespoon sherry
3 cups cooked black beans, drained and rinsed

1) Heat the oil in a sauté pan. Sauté the onions and garlic in the oil.

2) Add the cumin, coriander, and salt to the pan. Heat and stir until the aroma intensifies. Add the Tabasco, sherry, and beans. Cook, covered, until heated through.

3) Coarsely mash the beans. If the beans are too dry to mash, add a tablespoon or more water. Leftovers can be reheated in the microwave and also freeze well.

Per Serving: Calories 196; Protein 12g; Fat 2g (Saturated 0g); Carbohydrates 33g; Fiber 12g; Sodium 246mg

Black Beans and Pumpkin

Makes: 4 servings

Beans and pumpkin, both native to the Americas, come together in this dish.

1 teaspoon vegetable oil
1/2 cup chopped onions
1 clove garlic, minced
1 cup 1-inch cubes peeled sugar pumpkin or winter squash
1/4 cup sherry
1/4 cup reduced-sodium, defatted chicken broth or water
2 cups cooked black beans, drained and rinsed
1/2 teaspoon kosher salt
1/2 teaspoon ground cumin
1/2 teaspoon dried thyme
1 teaspoon red wine vinegar
1 scallion, sliced

1) Heat the oil in a nonstick pan. Sauté the onions, garlic, and pumpkin in the oil until the onions are golden.

2) Add the sherry and broth. Simmer until the pumpkin becomes fork-tender, about 15 minutes.

3) Add the beans, salt, cumin, thyme, and vinegar. Continue to simmer for 5 minutes more, until the beans are heated through. Stir in the scallions during the last minute of cooking.

Per Serving: Calories 159; Protein 9g; Fat 2g (Saturated 0g); Carbohydrates 26g; Fiber 9g; Sodium 274mg

White Bean Stew

Makes: 8 servings

This recipe requires a long simmer that starts with dried, soaked beans and an entire head of garlic. With time, the beans soften and the garlic mellows.

1 1/2 cups dried cannellini or navy beans, washed and picked over
1 head garlic
1 tablespoon olive oil
2 cups chopped onions
4 carrots, peeled and chopped
One 14 1/2-ounce can whole tomatoes, drained and seeded
2 1/2 cups water
1 teaspoon kosher salt
1/4 teaspoon freshly ground pepper
1 cup chopped fresh parsley
1 tablespoon lemon juice

1) Soak, drain, and rinse the beans (see Basic Beans, page 399).

2) Break the garlic head into cloves and peel.

3) Heat the oil in a heavy-bottomed pot over low heat. Cook the garlic, onions, and carrots in the oil until the onions are soft and golden. Keep covered between stirrings.

4) Add the beans to the pot. Then add the tomatoes, crushing large chunks into smaller pieces. Add the water. Cover the pot and simmer for about 1 1/2 hours, until the beans are very soft.

5) Stir in the salt and pepper. If you're serving the stew right away, add all the parsley and the lemon juice. If it is to be served later or at room temperature, add half the parsley, then add the remaining parsley and the lemon juice right before serving.

Per Serving: Calories 192; Protein 10g; Fat 2g (Saturated 0g); Carbohydrates 34g; Fiber 12g; Sodium 324mg

Mediterranean Baked Beans

Makes: 8 servings

Start this with dried, soaked beans, so that they have time to absorb the flavors from the broth and garlic.

2 cups dried navy or other white beans, washed and picked over
4 cups reduced-sodium, defatted chicken broth
2 bay leaves
3 cloves garlic, peeled and crushed
3 tablespoons chopped fresh parsley
2 teaspoons dried dill
1 teaspoon kosher salt
1 1/2 cups crushed tomatoes
1 cup tomato juice
1 cup chopped celery (about 2 ribs)
5 pepperoncini, rinsed and chopped
1/4 teaspoon freshly ground pepper

1) Soak, drain, and rinse the beans (see Basic Beans, page 399). Put the beans into a pot with the broth, bay leaves and garlic.

2) Simmer for about 45 minutes, until the skins on the beans burst. Add the remaining ingredients. If cooked in a Dutch oven, you will not have to transfer it to an ovenproof casserole and will have one fewer pot to wash.

3) Bake in a preheated 375°F oven for 2 hours. Stir the beans several times as they bake. If they start to dry out add more water.

Per Serving: Calories 202; Protein 14g; Fat 1g (Saturated 0g); Carbohydrates 36g; Fiber 14g; Sodium 747mg

Cannellini and Corkscrew Gratin

Makes: 6 servings

People who claim that they don't like beans will usually be willing to eat them in this.

2 teaspoons olive oil
1 cup chopped onions
2 cloves garlic, chopped
1 rib celery, chopped
One 14 1/2-ounce can whole tomatoes, drained and chopped
2/3 cup reduced-sodium, defatted chicken broth
4 cups cooked corkscrew pasta or other similar shape
2 cups cooked cannellini beans, drained and rinsed
1 1/2 teaspoons kosher salt
1/4 teaspoon freshly ground pepper
1/2 teaspoon dried sage
1/4 teaspoon dried oregano
1/4 cup soft breadcrumbs (from 2 slices bread)
2 tablespoons grated Parmesan cheese

1) Preheat the oven to 350°F.

2) Heat the oil in a 2- or 3-quart Dutch oven or a skillet. Sauté the onions, garlic, and celery over moderate heat for about 5 minutes, until the onions soften. Add the tomatoes to the pot. If using a skillet, transfer the vegetables to an ovenproof casserole.

3) Stir in the broth, pasta, beans, salt, pepper, sage, and oregano. Top with the breadcrumbs and cheese.

4) Cover and bake for 20 minutes, then uncover and bake 10 minutes longer.

Per Serving: Calories 246; Protein 10g; Fat 3g (Saturated 1g); Carbohydrates 43g; Fiber 6g; Sodium 846mg

Hopping John

Makes: 8 servings

A Southern tradition, this dish brings good luck when served on New Year's Day. Leftovers can be turned into a burrito filling by adding chopped jalapeño peppers, some corn, and a diced carrot.

1 pound dried black-eyed peas, washed and
    picked over
1 ham hock
2 bay leaves
1 cup chopped onions
1 tablespoon kosher salt
1/4 teaspoon freshly ground pepper
1 cup long-grain rice (3 cups cooked)

1) Soak the beans (see Basic Beans, page 399). Drain from the soak water, put the beans in a pot, add the ham hock, and pour in enough water to cover by 1 inch. Bring the water to a boil, reduce to a simmer, then add the bay leaves and onions. Simmer, uncovered, until the beans are tender, about 45 minutes to 1 hour. Add water if necessary to keep the beans from drying out. When the beans are soft, add the salt and pepper. Cook the beans for a total of 1 1/2 hours to develop the full flavor from the ham hock.

2) Meanwhile, cook the rice.

3) Remove and discard the ham hock and bay leaves. Serve the beans and rice side by side.

Per Serving: Calories 283; Protein 15g; Fat 1g (Saturated 0g); Carbohydrates 54g; Fiber 7g; Sodium 731mg

Chickpea Gratin

Makes: 8 servings

Italian frying peppers are long, light green, sweet peppers.

1 1/2 teaspoons olive oil
1 Italian frying pepper, seeded and chopped
1 cup chopped onions
2 cloves garlic, minced
One 8-ounce can stewed tomatoes
One 14 1/2-ounce can diced tomatoes
4 cups cooked chickpeas, drained and rinsed
1/2 teaspoon ground cumin
1/2 teaspoon dried oregano
1/2 teaspoon dried basil
1/2 teaspoon kosher salt
2 tablespoons dry breadcrumbs
1 tablespoon grated Parmesan cheese

1) Preheat the oven to 375°F.

2) Heat the oil in a sauté pan and cook the pepper, onions, and garlic over medium heat until softened.

3) Combine the sautéed vegetables and remaining ingredients, except the breadcrumbs and cheese, in a 2- to 2 1/2-quart casserole. Top with the breadcrumbs and then dust with the cheese.

4) Bake for 25 to 30 minutes, until bubbly and browned.

Per Serving: Calories 178; Protein 9g; Fat 4g (Saturated 1g); Carbohydrates 30g; Fiber 5g; Sodium 230mg

Polenta

Polenta is cooked cornmeal. It can be served as a warm porridge, but when left to cool it solidifies and then can be sliced and broiled or pan-fried. Polenta does take some effort (lots of stirring) to make; instant polenta can be difficult to find, though it is a convenient substitute.

Basic Polenta

Makes: 12 servings

This basic recipe makes a lot, but leftovers are so useful that it is unlikely the large amount will go to waste.

1 cup cornmeal
1/2 teaspoon kosher salt
4 cups water, divided

1) Combine the cornmeal and salt with 1 cup of the water to form a smooth, loose paste.

2) Bring the remaining water to a simmer.

3) Slowly pour the cornmeal slurry into the simmering water, stirring constantly with a wooden spoon until there aren't any lumps.

4) Warm over a medium-low heat so that the surface of the cornmeal bubbles gently. Polenta requires frequent stirring to prevent lumps and sticking and to develop the right texture. Spoon down the cornmeal that sticks to the sides of the pot. Cook until the cornmeal absorbs the water and the polenta becomes thick like oatmeal and hard to stir; coarse cornmeal, which is the type commonly available in natural food stores, will take up to 20 minutes to cook, finer cornmeal will take slightly less time.

5) Serve immediately, or pour onto an ungreased baking sheet to let the polenta solidify. Allow it to set until firm, about an hour. If you're going to refrigerate it, let it cool on the counter first or condensation will drip off the pan's cover and into the polenta. It can be made up to this point up to 2 days ahead of time.

6) Once solid, there are several ways to handle it. One way is to bake the entire pan at 400°F until the top begins to brown and bubble. I do not think that brushing oil on top (as is often suggested) improves the taste. You can also cut it into pieces and pan-fry it in a small amount of oil. If you have a grilling basket, oil it well and place squares of polenta in it, then grill over moderate heat.

Per Serving: Calories 42; Protein 1g; Fat 0g (Saturated 0g); Carbohydrates 9g; Fiber 1g; Sodium 83mg

Microwave Polenta

Makes: 5 servings

This is a quick and mess-free alternative to basic polenta.

1 cup cornmeal
2 cups reduced-sodium, defatted chicken broth
1/2 cup water
1/2 teaspoon kosher salt
1/3 cup grated Parmesan cheese

1) In a 2-quart microwave casserole, stir the cornmeal, broth, and water until smooth. Cook on high heat, covered, for 5 minutes. Lift the lid so that the steam escapes away from you, stir until smooth, cover again, and cook for 7 minutes longer.

2) Stir in the salt and Parmesan. Serve immediately or let set and follow suggestions in Step 6 of Basic Polenta (page 407).

Per Serving: Calories 139; Protein 6g; Fat 2g (Saturated 1g); Carbohydrates 22g; Fiber 2g; Sodium 510mg

Vegetable Polenta

Makes: 12 servings

To make a meal, all you need is to top this vegetable polenta with a homemade tomato sauce and some grated cheese. Bake in the oven until bubbly and serve with a green salad.

1 teaspoon vegetable oil
1 cup chopped onions
4 cups dark, leafy greens (such as spinach or white-ribbed Swiss chard), or 1 cup harder vegetables (such as green beans or broccoli), cut into bite-size pieces
1/2 teaspoon kosher salt
1/4 teaspoon freshly ground pepper
2 tablespoons grated Parmesan cheese (optional)
1 recipe Basic Polenta (page 407), still warm and in the pot

1) Heat the oil in a sauté pan over low heat. Sauté the onions in the oil for about 10 minutes, until golden.

2) Meanwhile, if using leafy greens, wilt them in a pan or the microwave, then squeeze out any excess moisture. Don't use red-ribbed Swiss chard or the polenta will have streaks of purple. If using harder vegetables, lightly steam or microwave them until tender but not soft.

3) Stir the onions, cooked vegetables, salt, pepper, and Parmesan into the polenta. Eat immediately, or follow suggestions in Steps 5 and 6 of Basic Polenta (page 407).

Per Serving: Calories 55; Protein 2g; Fat 1g (Saturated 0g); Carbohydrates 11g; Fiber 2g; Sodium 178mg

Double-Corn Polenta

Makes: 12 servings

Like going from a single note of music to a chord, the fresh corn flavor adds an extra dimension to this recipe.

4^1/$_2$ cups water, divided
1 teaspoon kosher salt
1^1/$_2$ cups cornmeal
1 cup cooked corn kernels

1) Bring 3^1/$_2$ cups of the water and the salt to a boil. Reduce to a simmer.

2) In a bowl, stir together the cornmeal and the remaining water until smooth.

3) Pour the cornmeal mixture slowly into the simmering water. Stir constantly to prevent lumps.

4) Simmer, uncovered, for 20 minutes, stirring frequently. Keep the heat very low to prevent scorching.

5) Stir in the corn kernels, then simmer for another 15 minutes, again stirring frequently. Eat immediately or follow suggestions in Steps 5 and 6 of Basic Polenta (page 407).

Per Serving: Calories 78; Protein 2g; Fat 0g (Saturated 0g); Carbohydrates 17g; Fiber 2g; Sodium 166mg

Stuffing and Bread

You don't have to cook a whole turkey to make stuffing; in fact, I rarely stuff birds, preferring to cook the stuffing separately. (If you do stuff a bird, plan on ^{1}/$_2$ cup per pound of bird.) Stuffing is usually pungent with herbs, broth, and sometimes sausage, so it can be used to balance a menu with plain meat or vegetables. However, on its own, it isn't the most attractive (being shades of brown and shapeless), so also serve a brightly colored vegetable or a colorful condiment, like rhubarb chutney.

Easy Stuffing

Makes: 5 servings

Stuffing is a great way to use up stale homemade bread, but if in a time-crunch, store-bought stuffing mix is a fine alternative.

2 tablespoons olive oil, divided
1 cup chopped onions
2 ribs celery, chopped
1/2 cup chopped walnuts or pecans
4 cups herb-seasoned stuffing mix
1 3/4 cups reduced-sodium, defatted chicken broth

1) Preheat the oven to 350°F. Coat a 1 1/2- or 2-quart casserole with nonstick spray.

2) Heat 1 tablespoon of the oil in a nonstick skillet, and sauté the onions and celery until the onions soften and begin to change color, about 5 minutes. Toss in the nuts and cook until they lightly toast.

3) Toss together the sautéed mixture and the stuffing in a bowl. Pour in the broth and toss once more.

4) Put the mixture into the casserole. Drizzle on the remaining oil. Place in the oven and bake, uncovered, for 35 to 40 minutes.

Per Serving: Calories 328; Protein 9g; Fat 15g (Saturated 1g); Carbohydrates 41g; Fiber 5g; Sodium 824mg

Cornbread Stuffing

Makes: 8 servings

The amount of bacon specified might seem so small as to be inconsequential, but it really is important to this recipe.

1 slice bacon
1 teaspoon vegetable oil
1 cup chopped onions
1 cup chopped celery
1 scallion, chopped
1/2 teaspoon dried ground sage
3 slices stale homemade-quality white
    bread, cubed
4 cups cornbread, crumbled into large chunks
    (from half an 8×8-inch pan)
1/2 cup buttermilk
1 cup reduced-sodium, defatted chicken broth

1) Preheat the oven to 350°F.

2) Cook the bacon until crisp. Pat dry with a paper towel and crumble into bits.

3) Heat the oil in a small nonstick pan. Add the onions and celery and cook, covered, over moderate heat, until the onions turn golden. Stir in the scallion and cook until wilted.

4) In a bowl, combine the bacon and sautéed vegetables. Stir in the sage, bread cubes, and cornbread. Pour in the buttermilk and stir. Add enough of the broth to moisten the bread, but not so much that it gets soggy.

5) Put stuffing into a 2 1/2-quart casserole or an 8×8-inch pan. Bake, uncovered, for 35 to 40 minutes.

Per Serving: Calories 123; Protein 4g; Fat 3g (Saturated 1g); Carbohydrates 19g; Fiber 2g; Sodium 312mg

Apple and Nut Stuffing

Makes: 8 servings

This goes just as nicely with meatloaf as it does with chicken.

1 pound homemade-quality white bread or Italian bread

2 tablespoons vegetable oil, divided

2 cups chopped onions

3 cloves garlic, chopped

2 ribs celery, chopped

2 large apples, cored and chopped

2 teaspoons dried sage

1 teaspoon dried thyme

1/2 teaspoon ground cinnamon

2 teaspoons kosher salt

1/2 teaspoon freshly ground pepper

1/2 cup chopped nuts, such as walnuts or pecans

2 cups reduced-sodium, defatted chicken or vegetable broth

1 tablespoon unsalted butter

1) Cut the bread into 1/2- to 1-inch cubes. Lay out on a baking sheet and allow to stale until dried out but not hard. This can be accomplished in a warm oven.

2) Heat 1 tablespoon of the oil in a large non-stick skillet, and sauté the onions, garlic, and celery until the onions soften and begin to change color, about 5 minutes. Keep the pan covered between stirrings. Add the apples and continue to cook until they wilt. Stir in the sage, thyme, cinnamon, salt, and pepper and remove from the heat. Meanwhile, preheat the oven to 350°F.

3) Toss together the sautéed mixture, the bread cubes, and the nuts in a large bowl. Pour in the broth and toss once more.

4) Put into a 2 1/2- to 3-quart casserole. Drizzle on the remaining oil and dot with the butter. Place in the oven and bake, uncovered, for 30 to 35 minutes.

Per Serving: Calories 304; Protein 8g; Fat 12g (Saturated 2g); Carbohydrates 43g; Fiber 4g; Sodium 891mg

Sausage and Mushroom Stuffing

Makes: 10 servings

This tastes great the second day. Try it for breakfast with some scrambled eggs.

1 pound homemade-quality bread
2 1/2 tablespoons vegetable oil, divided
2 cups chopped onions
2 cloves garlic, chopped
1 rib celery, chopped
1 carrot, chopped
1/2 pound mushrooms, sliced (about 4 cups)
1/2 teaspoon dried thyme
1/2 teaspoon dried sage
1/2 teaspoon dried crushed rosemary
1/2 teaspoon kosher salt
1/4 teaspoon freshly ground pepper
4 ounces lowfat sausage, chopped
1 1/2 cups reduced-sodium, defatted chicken broth

1) Cut the bread into 1/2- to 1-inch cubes. Lay out on a baking sheet and allow to stale until dried out but not hard. This can be accomplished in a warm oven.

2) Heat 1 tablespoon of the oil in a large non-stick skillet, and sauté the onions, garlic, celery, and carrot until the onions soften and begin to change color, about 7 minutes. Keep covered between stirrings. Add the mushrooms and cook until they wilt, about 2 minutes. Stir in the herbs, salt, and pepper. Put the contents of the pan into a bowl. Meanwhile, preheat the oven to 350°F.

3) Heat the sausage in the pan until it is cooked through. Drain off any fat and add the meat to the bowl of stuffing. Stir in the bread cubes.

4) Toss the ingredients and pour in the broth, stirring quickly. (If you don't stir quickly, some of the bread will become totally soggy while the rest will remain dry.) Stir in 1 more tablespoon of the oil.

5) Put into a 2 1/2- to 3-quart casserole. Drizzle on the remaining 1/2 tablespoon of oil. Bake, uncovered, for 30 to 35 minutes.

Per Serving: Calories 200; Protein 8g; Fat 6g (Saturated 1g); Carbohydrates 28g; Fiber 2g; Sodium 494mg

Cranberry and Bread Stuffing

Makes: 4 servings

Cranberries keep the raisins and brown sugar from making this stuffing too sweet.

1/2 pound homemade-quality white bread or Italian bread
2 tablespoons vegetable oil
1 cup chopped leeks (about 1 medium leek)
2 ribs celery, chopped
2 shallots, minced
1 1/2 cups cranberries
1 teaspoon dried crushed rosemary
1/2 teaspoon dried sage
1/4 teaspoon kosher salt
1/4 teaspoon freshly ground pepper
1/2 cup golden raisins
1 tablespoon packed light brown sugar
3/4 cup reduced-sodium, defatted chicken or vegetable broth

1) Cut the bread into 1/2- to 1-inch cubes. Lay out on a baking sheet and allow to stale until dried out but not hard. This can be accomplished in a warm oven.

2) Preheat the oven to 350°F. Heat the oil in a large nonstick skillet, and sauté the leeks, celery, and shallots until the vegetables soften and begin to change color, about 5 minutes. Keep covered between stirrings.

3) Toss together the sautéed mixture, the bread cubes, cranberries, rosemary, sage, salt, pepper, and raisins in a large bowl. Add the brown sugar, crumbling it to get rid of lumps. Pour in the broth and toss once more.

4) Put into a 2- to 2 1/2-quart casserole. Bake, uncovered, for 30 to 35 minutes.

Per Serving: Calories 339; Protein 7g; Fat 9g (Saturated 1g); Carbohydrates 59g; Fiber 4g; Sodium 518mg

Wild Rice Stuffing

Makes: 6 servings

Some varieties of wild rice come partially cooked and need less liquid, so if your rice came in a box, read the directions and add as much broth as they suggest. (But if it also comes with a spice packet, discard it.)

1 cup wild rice
2 1/2 cups reduced-sodium, defatted chicken broth
2 teaspoons olive oil
3 cloves garlic, chopped
1 tablespoon chopped shallots
1 medium leek, washed well and minced
  (about 1 1/2 cups)
2 ribs celery, including leaves, chopped
1/2 teaspoon minced orange zest
1/2 cup pecans, toasted and chopped
1 teaspoon kosher salt
1/2 teaspoon freshly ground pepper
2 oranges

1) Cook the wild rice in the the broth until all the liquid is absorbed. Meanwhile, preheat the oven to 375°F.

2) Heat the oil in a small sauté pan and cook the garlic, shallots, and leek until golden. Add the celery and sauté for a few more minutes.

3) Combine the cooked rice, sautéed vegetables, orange zest, pecans, salt, and pepper.

4) Cut the oranges in half and cut out the segments as you would a grapefruit. Add these to the stuffing.

5) Place the stuffing in a 2- to 2 1/2-quart casserole and bake for 30 minutes.

Per Serving: Calories 222; Protein 7g; Fat 9g (Saturated 1g); Carbohydrates 32g; Fiber 4g; Sodium 538mg

Pear Cornbread Pudding

Makes: 8 servings

This is a cross between a pudding and a stuffing. It is sweet and savory and goes nicely with chicken or fish steaks.

2 eggs
2 egg whites
1 cup reduced-sodium, defatted chicken broth
1 teaspoon kosher salt
1/4 teaspoon freshly ground pepper
1/2 teaspoon sage
1 cup canned corn kernels, drained
1 large firm pear, peeled, cored, and diced
3 cups cubed cornbread (about half an 8×8-inch pan)

1) Preheat the oven to 375°F. Spray a 1 1/2-quart casserole with nonstick spray. Have ready a larger baking dish that the casserole can fit into with at least an inch clearance all around for the water bath.

2) Whisk together the eggs, egg whites, broth, salt, pepper, and sage. Stir in the corn kernels, diced pear, and cornbread. Pour into the casserole. Place the casserole in the larger pan and put in the oven. Pour very hot water in the larger pan so that it comes about halfway up the sides of the casserole. (If the water is not very hot to begin with, the pudding will take longer to bake.) Bake for 40 to 45 minutes, until set and lightly brown in places.

Per Serving: Calories 118; Protein 5g; Fat 3g (Saturated 1g); Carbohydrates 18g; Fiber 2g; Sodium 544mg

Parmesan Toasts

Makes: 6 servings

The quantities don't have to be followed exactly. The type of bread will dictate how much oil and cheese it needs for flavor and texture. I often make a snack using one slice of bread.

1 long loaf Italian or French bread, sliced
1 tablespoon extra-virgin olive oil
1 tablespoon grated Parmesan cheese

Brush one side of each slice of bread with a touch of olive oil. (I have a pastry brush reserved for this and other savory tasks.) Dust with Parmesan cheese. Toast, grill, or broil until lightly browned.

Per Serving: Calories 230; Protein 7g; Fat 5g (Saturated 1g); Carbohydrates 38g; Fiber 2g; Sodium 461mg

Garlic Toast

Makes: 6 servings

This is the way Italians make garlic bread.

1 long loaf crusty bread, sliced
2 large cloves garlic, crushed
About 1 tablespoon olive oil (depending on size of loaf)

1) Just before you are ready to eat, toast or grill the slices of bread.

2) As soon as they come out of the oven or off the grill, rub one surface of each slice with a clove of garlic. As the garlic falls apart, switch to the next clove.

3) Lightly brush the garlicked side of the bread with olive oil and serve immediately.

Per Serving: Calories 229; Protein 7g; Fat 5g (Saturated 1g); Carbohydrates 40g; Fiber 2g; Sodium 461mg

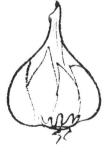

American Garlic Bread

Makes: 8 servings

This is as irresistible as the garlic bread sold at pizzerias. It is soft, warm, and redolent of garlic. But instead of oozing fat, it has a modest amount of butter and oil, which is plenty for flavor and moisture but not excessive.

1 pound Italian bread
1 1/2 teaspoons unsalted butter
1 tablespoon olive oil
3 cloves garlic, finely minced
2 tablespoons minced fresh parsley
1 tablespoon grated Parmesan cheese

1) Preheat the oven to 350°F. Cut the bread into slices about 1/2 inch thick, cutting down to, but not through, the bottom crust.

2) Melt the butter (this can be done in the microwave) and stir in the oil and garlic. Combine the parsley and Parmesan in a small bowl.

3) Brush the oil and butter onto the cut sides of the bread. Dust the parsley and cheese between the slices. Wrap the loaf in foil. Place in the oven for 15 minutes.

Per Serving: Calories 181; Protein 5g; Fat 5g (Saturated 1g); Carbohydrates 29g; Fiber 2g; Sodium 346mg

Casual Meals

Stuffed Potatoes
p18

Cheddar Stuffed Potatoes

Ricotta and Broccoli
Stuffed Potatoes

Salsa and Beans
Stuffed Potatoes

Chicken and Pesto
Stuffed Potatoes

Quesadillas
p23

Basic Quesadilla

Whole Wheat Cheddar
Quesadilla

Turkey and Zucchini
Quesadillas

Thick-with-Vegetables
Quesadillas

Sandwiches
p25

Crispy Tofu Pita Pockets

Mushroom, Garlic, and Onion
Open-Faced Sandwich

Topped Polenta

Greek Pita Pocket Sandwiches

Spicy Shredded Chicken
Roll Ups

Turkey Barbeque Sandwiches

Bayshore Meatball Subs

Sloppy Joes

Quick Confetti Sloppy Joes

Burritos
p20

Chicken Burritos

Beef Burritos

Fish Steak Burritos

Black Bean and Veggie Burritos

Vegetable Burritos

Sandwich Fillings
729

Egg Salad

Vinaigrette Tuna Salad

Apple and Tuna Salad

*Tuna Salad with
Almost Sour Cream*

Tuna and Vegetable Salad

Tofu Sandwich Spread

Poached Turkey Breast

Burgers
732

Turkey Burgers

Mushroom and Beef Burgers

Greek-Style Burgers

Barbeque Burgers

Tuna Burgers

Salmon Burgers

Fish Burgers

Tofu Burgers

Pizza
736

Pizza Dough

Whole Wheat Pizza Dough

Classic Red Pizza

Veggies and Cheese Pizza

Ricotta and Spinach Pizza

Sausage and Mushroom Pizza

Southwest Chicken Pizza

Hawaiian Pizza

Broccoli and Garlic Pizza

Aegean Pizza

Goat Cheese Pizza

Deep-Dish Rustica Pizza

Deep-Dish Vegetable Pizza

Some foods are meant for casual dining, either because they are eaten out of hand, or because they are associated with lunches, or because they are sloppy to eat. Stuffed potatoes, sloppy joes, sandwiches, and the like are foods that are obviously appropriate for lunches, but they also make fine dinners for relaxed gatherings.

Stuffed Potatoes

Beware of stuffed potatoes at restaurants. Filled with cheese and butter, they can use up a day's fat quota in one serving. The recipes here, however, are all lowfat yet are still satisfying and filling, the way a stuffed potato should be. Start with russet potatoes that have a uniform oblong shape and can sit without rolling. Scrub them well before baking. Once stuffed, they can be wrapped in plastic and refrigerated for up to 1 day. Bring these chilled potatoes to room temperature before baking.

Cheddar Stuffed Potatoes

Makes: 6 servings

Unlike a baked potato, which is slit open, potatoes to be stuffed have their tops cut off.

6 medium russet potatoes (about 2 to
    2¹/2 pounds), baked
1 cup lowfat sharp cheddar cheese
1 cup lowfat sour cream
¹/2 teaspoon kosher salt
¹/4 teaspoon freshly ground pepper
¹/4 cup minced fresh chives or scallions
Paprika, for garnish

1) Use a serrated knife to cut about ¹/4 inch off the top of each baked potato (on the long side). Scoop out the pulp, leaving a thick wall intact.

2) Put the pulp in a bowl and mash it with the cheese, sour cream, salt, and pepper. Stir in the chives. Stuff the potato skins with this mixture. Use all of the stuffing, mounding up the extra on top of each potato.

3) Preheat the oven to 425°F. Place the potatoes on a baking sheet, dust with the paprika, and cook for 15 minutes, until heated through.

Per Serving: Calories 216; Protein 8g; Fat 5g (Saturated 4g); Carbohydrates 37g; Fiber 3g; Sodium 297mg

Ricotta and Broccoli Stuffed Potatoes

Makes: 6 servings

As a time-saver, frozen broccoli can be used.

6 medium russet potatoes (about 2 to 2¹/2
    pounds), baked
1¹/2 cups reduced-fat ricotta
2 cups broccoli florets, lightly steamed and
    coarsely chopped
1¹/2 teaspoons kosher salt
¹/4 teaspoon freshly ground pepper
¹/2 teaspoon dried basil

1) Use a serrated knife to cut about ¹/4 inch off the top of each baked potato (on the long side). Scoop out the pulp, leaving a thick wall intact.

2) Put the pulp in a bowl and mash it with the ricotta, broccoli, salt, pepper, and basil. Stuff the potato skins with this mixture. Use all of the stuffing, mounding up the extra on top of each potato.

3) Preheat the oven to 425°F. Place the potatoes on a baking sheet and cook for 15 minutes, until heated through.

Per Serving: Calories 198; Protein 8g; Fat 3g (Saturated 2g); Carbohydrates 35g; Fiber 3g; Sodium 549mg

Salsa and Beans Stuffed Potatoes

Makes: 6 servings

I prefer using a fresh salsa for this, with its chunky pieces of fresh tomatoes and fresh-tasting herbs, but if I don't have any made up I will use salsa from the market's refrigerator case. Whether it is mild or hot is up to you.

6 medium russet potatoes (about 2 to $2^1/2$ pounds), baked

$1^1/4$ cups cooked pinto beans (from a 15-ounce can), rinsed and drained

1 cup salsa (homemade or store-bought)

$1/4$ cup shredded reduced-fat jack cheese

1) Use a serrated knife to cut about $1/4$ inch off the top of each baked potato (on the long side). Scoop out the pulp, leaving a thick wall intact.

2) Put the pulp in a bowl and mash it with the beans and salsa. Stuff the potato skins with this mixture. Use all of the stuffing, mounding up the extra on top of each potato. Top each potato with a portion of the cheese.

3) Preheat the oven to 425°F. Place the potatoes on a baking sheet, top each potato with the cheese, and cook for 15 minutes, until heated through.

Per Serving: Calories 204; Protein 7g; Fat 1g (Saturated 0g); Carbohydrates 43g; Fiber 7g; Sodium 459mg

Chicken and Pesto Stuffed Potatoes

Makes: 6 servings

Vegetarians can leave out the chicken.

6 medium russet potatoes (about 2 to $2^1/2$ pounds), baked

$1^1/2$ cups lowfat ricotta

$1^1/2$ cups diced cooked chicken breast

$1^1/2$ teaspoons kosher salt

$1/4$ teaspoon freshly ground pepper

$1/3$ cup Basil Pesto (page 000 or store-bought)

1) Use a serrated knife to cut about $1/4$ inch off the top of each baked potato (on the long side). Scoop out the pulp, leaving a thick wall intact.

2) Put the pulp in a bowl and mash it with the ricotta, chicken, salt, pepper, and pesto.

3) Stuff the potato skins with this mixture. Use all of the stuffing, mounding up the extra on top of each potato.

4) Preheat the oven to 425°F. Place the potatoes on a baking sheet and cook for 15 minutes, until heated through.

Per Serving: Calories 282; Protein 18g; Fat 8g (Saturated 3g); Carbohydrates 34g; Fiber 3g; Sodium 593mg

Burritos

Like enchiladas, burritos are filled tortillas. But because they are larger than enchiladas, one is a full serving. And because they are not topped with a warm and messy sauce, they can be eaten like a rolled-up sandwich. Salsa and sour cream are served with burritos, and the diner can put them either inside or on top of the tortillas. Burritos are always made with flour—not corn—tortillas. Flour tortillas vary in fat content. Sometimes instead of tortillas, I buy round flat bread called "Mountain Bread" and other times I purchase Middle Eastern flat bread. These are lower in fat than most tortillas and are available in whole wheat versions.

In order to avoid tearing the tortilla while wrapping the burrito, the tortilla must first be warmed. There are two ways to do this. If you are making many burritos, wrap the tortillas in foil and place in a 300°F oven for about 10 minutes. If making only a few burritos, place each tortilla in a dry, warm skillet. Heat for 30 seconds, then turn over and heat for about 30 seconds more until warm and pliable.

Leftover filling can be turned into a quick meal for one by filling a tortilla and microwaving it for about 1 1/2 minutes.

Chicken Burritos

Makes: 6 servings

If someone in your family doesn't like beans, use corn kernels instead.

1 tablespoon vegetable oil
1 cup chopped red onions
1/2 pound skinless, boneless chicken breast, cut into long, thin strips
1/2 teaspoon kosher salt
1 teaspoon chili powder
1 cup cooked black beans, rinsed and drained
1 tablespoon fresh lime juice
2 tablespoons diced canned mild green chilies or jalapeños
1 tablespoon chopped fresh cilantro (optional)
6 large flour tortillas

1) Heat the oil in a large nonstick skillet. Toss together the onions, chicken, salt, and chili powder and put into the skillet. Cook over high heat, stirring constantly, until the chicken is cooked through, about 6 to 8 minutes.

2) Stir in the beans, lime juice, chilies, and cilantro and warm through. Remove from the stove, cover and keep warm.

3) Warm the tortillas. Fill each tortilla with 1/2 cup of the chicken mixture. Roll and place seam side down on a serving dish. Repeat with the remaining tortillas and filling.

Per Serving: Calories 228; Protein 15g; Fat 5g (Saturated 1g); Carbohydrates 29g; Fiber 4g; Sodium 377mg

Beef Burritos

Makes: 6 servings

Draining the recipe after Step 1 isn't just to reduce fat. It also helps to keep the burritos from becoming soggy.

1 pound 10% fat ground beef
1 cup chopped onions
2 cloves garlic, chopped
1/2 green bell pepper, chopped
2 cups cooked pinto beans, rinsed and drained
One 4-ounce can diced mild green chilies
2 teaspoons chili powder
One 8-ounce can tomato sauce
1/8 teaspoon Tabasco sauce
6 large flour tortillas

1) Heat a large large nonstick skillet and add the beef, onions, garlic, and bell pepper. Brown the beef, stirring frequently. Cover the skillet so that the onions sweat as the beef browns. Drain off liquid or fat if necessary.

2) Stir in the beans, chilies, chili powder, tomato sauce, and Tabasco. Simmer, covered, for 10 minutes.

3) Warm the tortillas. Place one-sixth of the filling in a strip along the equator of a tortilla. Roll and place seam side down on the serving dish or individual dinner plates. Repeat for each tortilla.

Per Serving: Calories 349, protein 24g; Fat 10g (Saturated 3g); Carbohydrates 40g; Fiber 7g; Sodium 511mg

Fish Steak Burritos

Makes: 6 servings

Lime juice and cilantro give a tropical flavor to these unusual burritos.

1 teaspoon chili powder
1/2 teaspoon kosher salt
1/2 pound firm fish steaks, such as swordfish or halibut
1/4 cup chopped red onions
2 tablespoons chopped fresh cilantro or fresh parsley
1 tablespoon fresh lime juice
1 tablespoon diced canned mild green chilies or jalapeños
1 cup shredded mild reduced-fat cheese
6 large flour tortillas

1) Preheat the oven to 425°F.

2) Put the chili powder and salt in a small bowl. Rub both sides of the fish with the spice mixture. You might not need all of it. Place the fish in an ungreased baking dish. Bake for about 12 to 18 minutes, until the fish tests done. Remove from the oven. Reduce the oven temperature to 350°F. When the fish is cool enough to handle, cut into small cubes.

3) Toss the fish with the onions, cilantro, lime juice, chilies, and cheese.

4) Warm the tortillas. Put about 1/3 to 1/2 cup of the filling on each tortilla. Roll and place seam side down in a baking dish coated with nonstick spray. Bake for about 7 minutes, until the cheese has melted.

Per Serving: Calories 187; Protein 12g; Fat 6g (Saturated 3g); Carbohydrates 21g; Fiber 1g; Sodium 453mg

Black Bean and Veggie Burritos

Makes: 6 servings

The filling for these burritos (minus the cheese) can be made up to two days in advance.

1 tablespoon vegetable oil
1 cup chopped onions
2 cloves garlic, chopped
1 cup frozen corn, thawed
1 carrot, diced
$1/4$ cup water
One 10-ounce package frozen chopped spinach, thawed and drained
$1/2$ cup enchilada sauce (mild or medium)
2 scallions, sliced
2 cups cooked black beans, drained and rinsed
$1/2$ teaspoon kosher salt (optional)
$1/2$ cup shredded lowfat pepper jack cheese
6 large flour tortillas

1) Heat the oil in a large nonstick skillet. Sauté the onions and garlic over moderate heat for about 5 minutes; keep covered between stir-rings. Add the corn, carrots, and water. Cover and cook 5 minutes more, until the carrots soften. Squeeze the excess water out of the spinach, then put the spinach in the pan along with the enchilada sauce, scallions, beans, and salt. Heat through. Stir in the cheese and cook until it melts.

2) Warm the tortillas. Place one-sixth of the filling in a strip along the equator of a tortilla. Roll and place seam side down on the serving dish. Repeat for each tortilla.

Per Serving: Calories 308; Protein 13g; Fat 9g (Saturated 3g); Carbohydrates 46g; Fiber 9g; Sodium 286mg

Vegetable Burritos

Makes: 6 servings

Served with a bean side dish, this will make a complete and nutritious vegetarian meal.

1 tablespoon vegetable oil
$1/2$ cup sliced onions
1 clove garlic, chopped
1 cup carrot sticks
2 cups broccoli florets, cut into small pieces
$1/2$ red bell pepper, julienned
$1/4$ pound mushrooms, sliced (1 cup)
1 small zucchini, cut into sticks
1 teaspoon kosher salt
$1/4$ teaspoon freshly ground pepper
$1/2$ teaspoon ground cumin
1 teaspoon ground coriander
2 tablespoons chopped mild green chilies
1 teaspoon lemon or lime juice
6 large flour tortillas

1) Heat the oil in a large nonstick skillet. Sauté the onions and garlic over moderate heat for about 5 minutes; keep covered between stir-rings. Add the carrots and broccoli and about 2 tablespoons of water. Cover and cook 5 minutes more. Stir in the bell pepper, mushrooms, and zucchini and continue to cook until the mushrooms begin to wilt. Stir in the remaining ingredients except the tortillas. Cover and cook until vegetables are tender but not mushy.

2) Warm the tortillas. Place about $2/3$ cup filling in a strip along the equator of the tortilla. Roll and place seam side down on the serving dish.

Per Serving: Calories 165; Protein 5g; Fat 5g (Saturated 1g); Carbohydrates 26g; Fiber 3g; Sodium 520mg

Quesadillas

Quesadillas are like grilled cheese sandwiches made with tortillas. The quesadilla recipes can be multiplied to make as many as needed.

Basic Quesadilla

Makes: 1 serving

1/3 cup shredded reduced-fat jack cheese
2 tablespoons salsa
2 large flour tortillas

1) Heat a 10-inch (or larger) nonstick skillet over medium-high heat. Meanwhile, arrange the cheese and salsa on a tortilla. Place the tortilla in the pan and top with the second tortilla. Cook until the bottom tortilla begins to brown, about 2 to 3 minutes. Flip over and continue to cook until the second tortilla browns as well and the cheese is melted, about 2 minutes more.

2) Cut into 8 pieces. Serve immediately.

Per Serving: Calories 311; Protein 15g; Fat 9g (Saturated 4g); Carbohydrates 43g; Fiber 2g; Sodium 591mg

Whole Wheat Cheddar Quesadilla

Makes: 1 serving

Cheddar cheeses vary in flavor and that is especially true for lowfat varieties. It is important for this dish that the cheese tastes like a good sharp cheddar. I've found it worthwhile to taste all of the brands for sale in my area so that I'm sure to purchase the best one available.

2 large whole wheat flour tortillas
1/3 cup grated lowfat cheddar cheese
2 tablespoons salsa
2 tablespoons diced canned mild green chilies

1) Use a medium-high setting to heat a 10-inch (or larger) nonstick skillet. Meanwhile, arrange the cheese, salsa and chilies on a tortilla. Place the tortilla in the pan and top with the second tortilla. Cook until the bottom tortilla begins to brown, about 2 to 3 minutes. Flip over and continue to cook until the bottom tortilla browns as well and the cheese is melted, about 2 minutes more.

2) Cut into 8 pieces. Serve immediately.

Per Serving: Calories 233; Protein 14g; Fat 6g (Saturated 3g); Carbohydrates 44g; Fiber 6g; Sodium 946mg

Turkey and Zucchini Quesadillas

Makes: 4 servings

If turkey cutlets are too costly or not in stock, use chicken breasts and cut them into strips the size of fast-food french fries.

2 teaspoons vegetable oil
1 pound turkey cutlets, cut into thin strips
2 cups julienned zucchini
1 cup sliced red onions
1/2 teaspoon kosher salt
1/4 teaspoon freshly ground pepper
1 teaspoon lemon juice
1 cup cooked corn kernels
1/4 cup chopped fresh cilantro or parsley
8 large flour tortillas
1 cup shredded reduced-fat pepper jack cheese

1) Heat the oil in a nonstick pan. Over high heat, cook the turkey until white on all sides. Reduce the heat and stir in the zucchini, onions, salt, pepper, lemon juice, and corn. Cover and cook until the zucchini is tender. Stir in the cilantro.

2) Place a tortilla in a dry nonstick skillet. Fill with one-quarter of the filling, top with 1/4 cup of cheese and cap with another tortilla. Cook for a few minutes until the tortilla begins to brown and the cheese begins to melt. Turn and cook until toasty and golden brown. Repeat with the remaining tortillas.

Per Serving: Calories 499; Protein 42g; Fat 12g (Saturated 4g); Carbohydrates 56g; Fiber 4g; Sodium 770mg

Thick-with-Vegetables Quesadillas

Makes: 5 servings

If some vegetables fall out of the quesadilla when you are turning them in the skillet, just tuck them back inside.

1 cup broccoli florets, steamed until tender
2 cups julienned zucchini, steamed until tender
1 cup roasted pepper strips
1/2 cup chopped scallions
1 cup cooked corn kernels
1/2 cup cooked black beans, drained and rinsed
1/2 teaspoon kosher salt
1/4 teaspoon freshly ground pepper
1 teaspoon lemon juice
1/4 cup chopped fresh cilantro or parsley (optional)
2 tablespoons diced canned mild green chilies
10 large flour tortillas
1 1/3 cup shredded reduced-fat jack cheese

1) If the vegetables are moist from steaming, dry them on a towel. Toss together all the ingredients except the cheese and tortillas.

2) Put a tortilla in a dry nonstick skillet. Top with 1 cup of the filling, one-fifth of the cheese, and another tortilla. Cook for a few minutes until the bottom tortilla begins to brown and the cheese begins to melt. Turn and cook until thoroughly toasty and golden brown. Repeat for each quesadilla.

Per Serving: Calories 368; Protein 17g; Fat 9g (Saturated 4g); Carbohydrates 57g; Fiber 6g; Sodium 704mg

Sandwiches

H ere are some recipes for complete sandwiches. Round out the meal with a selection of side salads or a bowl of soup.

Crispy Tofu Pita Pockets

Makes: 5 servings

Some of the other tofu recipes in this book use only half a pound of tofu. This is a good way to use up the rest. To reduce this recipe, halve the tofu but keep the same amount of soy sauce, mustard, and oregano.

1 pound firm tofu
1 1/2 tablespoon soy sauce
1/4 teaspoon dry mustard
1 teaspoon dried oregano
3 large pita pockets, preferably whole wheat
1/2 cup alfalfa sprouts
1/2 cup sliced cucumbers
1/3 cup nonfat or lowfat salad dressing of choice

1) Cut the block of tofu into small cubes.

2) Toss the tofu in a bowl with the soy sauce, mustard, and oregano. Marinate for at least 15 minutes or as long as 1 day.

3) Line a baking sheet with parchment paper. Put the tofu cubes on the sheet in one layer, close together but not touching.

4) Bake in a preheated 450°F oven for 10 minutes, then shake the pan to loosen the cubes from the paper. Continue to bake, about 10 to 15 minutes more, until the outside of the tofu browns and crisps but the insides remain soft. Let cool.

5) Cut the pita pockets in half and fill with the tofu, sprouts, and cucumbers. Moisten with the salad dressing.

Per Serving: Calories 220; Protein 16g; Fat 8g (Saturated 1g); Carbohydrates 26g; Fiber 3g; Sodium 599mg

Mushroom, Garlic, and Onion Open-Faced Sandwich

Makes: 2 servings

The type of bread you use is of great importance. A crusty loaf, chewy and filled with flavor, is ideal.

2/3 cup Caramelized Onions (page 597)
1 recipe Thyme Mushrooms (page 344)
2 thick slices good-quality crusty bread
6 cloves Roasted Garlic (page 603)

1) The onions and mushrooms must be hot when constructing these sandwiches. If you're using leftovers (all the ingredients can be made ahead of time), reheat them. You can warm the onions in the microwave, but the texture of the mushrooms will be better if you heat them on the stovetop.

2) Toast or grill the bread. Put the slices on the dinner plates. (You won't be able to transfer these messy sandwiches from a serving platter to a dinner plate.)

3) Squeeze the garlic out of the peels and spread it onto the toasted bread with a knife. Top the bread with the onions and then the mushrooms. Serve immediately.

Per Serving: Calories 208; Protein 8g; Fat 4g (Saturated 1g); Carbohydrates 37g; Fiber 4g; Sodium 340mg

Topped Polenta

Makes: 1 serving

This recipe makes a sophisticated lunch for one person. All the ingredients can come from previous meals.

One 3×4-inch square Polenta (page 407)
1 1/2 teaspoons olive oil
3 mushrooms, sliced
1/4 cup chopped onions
1/2 cup tomato sauce
1 ounce grated mozzarella, Parmesan, or feta cheese (optional)

1) Place the polenta square on a greased baking sheet and bake at 425°F for 5 minutes on each side. A toaster oven is perfect for this.

2) While the polenta is browning, heat the oil in a sauté pan and sauté the mushrooms and onions. Warm the tomato sauce.

3) The polenta is done when it is bubbling and the edges look crisp. Using a metal spatula, slip it onto a dinner plate. Top with the mushrooms and onions, then the tomato sauce.

4) If you wish, grate cheese on top.

Per Serving: Calories 160, protein 5g; Fat 7g (Saturated 1g); Carbohydrates 21g; Fiber 2g; Sodium 806mg

Greek Pita Pocket Sandwiches

Makes: 4 servings

Olive lovers can toss in pitted olives of their choice.

4 cups romaine lettuce leaves, washed, dried, and chopped (1/2 medium head)
1 large tomato, cored and chopped
1 cucumber, peeled and diced
1/2 green bell pepper, chopped
1/2 medium red onion, halved and sliced (1/2 cup)
1/2 cup pitted, sliced olives (optional)
2 tablespoons Greek Oregano Vinaigrette (page 57)
2 ounces feta cheese, crumbled (about 1/2 cup), divided
4 large pita pockets, top third cut off

1) In a large bowl, combine the lettuce and vegetables. Toss with the dressing and 1 tablespoon of the feta.

2) Divide the salad into 4 portions, fill the pitas, and top each with the remaining feta.

Per Serving: Calories 248; Protein 9g; Fat 7g (Saturated 3g); Carbohydrates 37g; Fiber 3g; Sodium 519mg

Spicy Shredded Chicken Roll Ups

Makes: 4 servings

Cardamon and cinnamon are versatile spices. They add sweet aromas to desserts, but also combine wonderfully with savory and hot spices in recipes such as this.

1/4 teaspoon ground cardamom
1/4 teaspoon ground cinnamon
1/2 teaspoon kosher salt
1/4 teaspoon freshly ground pepper
1/8 teaspoon cayenne pepper
1/4 teaspoon ground coriander
2 cloves garlic, minced
1 tablespoon lemon juice
1 pound skinless, boneless chicken breasts
1 1/2 teaspoons vegetable oil
1/2 cup chopped onions
4 large flour tortillas

1) In a glass or stainless-steel bowl, combine the cardamom, cinnamon, salt, pepper, cayenne, coriander, garlic, and lemon juice.

2) Cut the chicken into narrow strips 1 1/2 inches long.

3) Toss the chicken with the spices until all of pieces are evenly coated. Marinate, covered and refrigerated, for 1 to 24 hours.

4) Heat the oil in a 10-inch nonstick pan over low heat. Cook the onions for about 10 minutes, until they are soft and golden. Add the chicken, increase the heat to medium-high, and cook for about 5 to 7 minutes, until the meat is white all the way through and the outside begins to brown, stirring frequently.

5) Warm the tortillas. Divide the chicken mixture among them and roll up.

Per Serving: Calories 267; Protein 30g; Fat 6g (Saturated 1g); Carbohydrates 23g; Fiber 1g; Sodium 484mg

Turkey Barbeque Sandwiches

Makes: 4 servings

Here is a good use for leftover Thanksgiving turkey. Thick, spongy bread works best for these.

1 1/2 teaspoons vegetable oil
1 cup sliced onions
2 cups cooked shredded or diced skinless turkey breast
2/3 cup barbeque sauce of choice, such as Very Quick Barbeque Sauce (page 587)
1/4 cup water
8 slices bread

1) Heat the oil in a heavy nonstick pan. Sauté the onions until golden.

2) Add the turkey, barbeque sauce, and water. Heat through until the sauce bubbles and thickens. If the sauce is too thick, add more water.

3) Divide among the bread to make sandwiches.

Per Serving: Calories 373; Protein 29g; Fat 6g (Saturated 1g); Carbohydrates 55g; Fiber 5g; Sodium 1186mg

Bayshore Meatball Subs

Makes: 6 servings

When I was a child, my family used to go to a shack on the Jersey shore and eat subs like these. It was a clever idea, to serve what is usually a messy sandwich in hollowed-out torpedo rolls. We kids loved it, and were always surprised to find meatballs in what looked like an uncut roll. Our parents appreciated how most of the sub made it into our mouths and not onto the floor.

1/2 recipe Seasoned Meatballs (page 216)
4 cups tomato sauce (homemade or store-bought)
6 torpedo rolls (about 6 inches long)

1) Follow the meatball recipe through the browning step. Then simmer the meatballs in the tomato sauce until the meat is cooked through, about 15 minutes.

2) Cut off the ends of the rolls, then pull out the bread to hollow out the rolls. Fill with 3 or 4 meatballs and sauce and plug the end with some of the bread.

Per Serving: Calories 546; Protein 32g; Fat 7g (Saturated 2g); Carbohydrates 88g; Fiber 4g; Sodium 1901mg

Sloppy Joes

Makes: 6 servings

My family likes intriguing, unusual recipes (and living with a food writer, they try plenty), but they are never so satisfied as when I serve them something like this.

1 pound lean ground turkey
2 teaspoons vegetable oil
1 cup chopped onions
2 cloves garlic, minced
1 green bell pepper, chopped
1 rib celery, chopped
One 15-ounce can tomato sauce
1 1/2 tablespoons Worcestershire sauce
1/2 teaspoon dry mustard
1 teaspoon kosher salt
1 teaspoon ground chili powder
1/8 teaspoon cayenne pepper (optional)
6 bulkie or hamburger rolls, split

1) In a heavy-bottomed pot, cook the turkey until no pink remains. Drain off any fat or water and remove the turkey from the pot.

2) In the same pot, heat the oil and sauté the onions until they begin to soften and change color. Add the garlic, bell pepper, and celery. Cover and cook until the vegetables soften, stirring occasionally.

3) Stir in the turkey, tomato sauce, and seasonings with the vegetables. Simmer, uncovered, for 15 minutes, until the sauce thickens slightly.

4) Divide into 6 portions and serve on the rolls.

Per Serving: Calories 264; Protein 24g; Fat 5g (Saturated 1g); Carbohydrates 31g; Fiber 2g; Sodium 1070mg

Quick Confetti Sloppy Joes

Makes: 6 servings

Not only are these very fast and easy to make, but they are also a way to stretch meat with vegetables.

1 pound 10% fat ground beef or lean
　　ground turkey
1 scallion, chopped
1 cup corn kernels (thawed if frozen)
1/2 cup chopped green bell pepper
1 cup diced zucchini
1/2 teaspoon kosher salt (optional)
1 teaspoon ground chili powder
1 cup barbeque sauce
1/2 cup water
6 bulkie or hamburger rolls, split

1) In a heavy-bottomed pot, cook the beef until no pink remains. Drain off any fat or water. Add all the remaining ingredients except the rolls and simmer, covered, until the zucchini is tender. Add more water if the mixture looks dry; this will depend on the thickness of the barbeque sauce.

2) Divide into 6 portions and serve on the rolls.

Per Serving: Calories 317; Protein 21g; Fat 11g (Saturated 3g); Carbohydrates 34g; Fiber 3g; Sodium 643mg

Sandwich Fillings

Here is a selection of sandwich fillings. I leave it up to you to select the bread and the garnishes. Lettuce and tomato are always appropriate, but if I have cole slaw, roasted peppers, or onion relish in the refrigerator, they are as likely to dress the sandwich as that leaf of iceberg.

Egg Salad

Makes: 4 servings

When I was pregnant with my first son, one of the few foods I could bear to eat was egg salad sandwiches—with hot pickle relish. This is good even if you don't have food cravings, and the relish is optional.

6 hard-boiled eggs, peeled
1/3 cup lowfat mayonnaise
1 rib celery, minced
2 scallions, sliced
1/4 teaspoon freshly ground pepper
1/2 teaspoon kosher salt
1 tablespoon hot red or green pickle
　　relish (optional)
1 teaspoon curry powder (optional)

Cut the eggs in half. Discard 4 of the yolks. Coarsely chop the eggs. Stir in the remaining ingredients.

Per Serving: Calories 153; Protein 10g; Fat 9g (Saturated 2g); Carbohydrates 7g; Fiber 0g; Sodium 529mg

Vinaigrette Tuna Salad

Makes: 4 servings

Many people don't like mayonnaise but still want tuna salad. This is for them.

One 6-ounce can tuna, packed in water
1 rib celery, chopped fine
1 tablespoon store-bought nonfat vinaigrette salad dressing
1 tablespoon sweet pickle relish

Drain and flake apart the tuna. Add the remaining ingredients and mash all together with a fork.

Per Serving: Calories 59; Protein 10g; Fat 1g (Saturated 0g); Carbohydrates 3g; Fiber 0g; Sodium 206mg

Apple and Tuna Salad

Makes: 3 servings

This is the favorite way to make tuna salad in my house, introduced to me by my stepson.

One 6-ounce can tuna, packed in water, drained
2^1/$_2$ tablespoons plain nonfat yogurt
2 tablespoons sweet pickle relish
1 medium apple, cored and chopped
^{1}/$_4$ teaspoon kosher salt

Put all the ingredients in a bowl and mix together with a fork.

Per Serving: Calories 103 protein 13g; Fat 1g (Saturated 0g); Carbohydrates 11g; Fiber 1g; Sodium 402mg

Tuna Salad with Almost Sour Cream

Makes: 5 servings

If you don't want to make Almost Sour Cream, you can use lowfat mayonnaise. Don't use yogurt; it is too sour.

One 12-ounce can tuna, packed in water, drained
1 rib celery, diced
^{1}/$_3$ cup Almost Sour Cream (page 606)
1^1/$_2$ teaspoons lemon juice
1 teaspoon minced chives, fresh or dried
^{1}/$_4$ teaspoon freshly ground pepper

Mash together all the ingredients with a fork.

Per Serving: Calories 79; Protein 16g; Fat 1g (Saturated 0g); Carbohydrates 1g; Fiber 0g; Sodium 255mg

Tuna and Vegetable Salad

Makes: 6 servings

Vegetables are used here to decrease tuna salad's fat and calories, as well as to add crunch and flavor.

1 recipe Tuna Salad with Almost Sour Cream (page above) or Vinaigrette Tuna Salad (page opposite)
1 carrot, peeled and diced
^{1}/$_2$ green bell pepper, diced
^{1}/$_2$ cup frozen peas, thawed
^{1}/$_4$ teaspoon dill
^{1}/$_4$ teaspoon kosher salt

Combine the Tuna Salad with the remaining ingredients.

Per Serving: Calories 82; Protein 14g; Fat 1g (Saturated 0g); Carbohydrates 4g; Fiber 1g; Sodium 311mg

Tofu Sandwich Spread

Makes: 6 servings

Like the egg in egg salad or the tuna in tuna salad, tofu is a main component of this filling and I don't try to hide it, only enhance it with some herbs and seasonings.

1 pound firm tofu
1 tablespoon lemon juice
1 tablespoon apple cider vinegar
$1/2$ teaspoon honey
2 teaspoons soy sauce
1 tablespoon vegetable oil
$1/8$ teaspoon freshly ground pepper
$1/8$ teaspoon Tabasco sauce
1 teaspoon dried dill
1 tablespoon minced onions
1 tablespoon minced fresh parsley
1 carrot

1) Combine the tofu and all the remaining ingredients except the parsley and carrot in a food processor fitted with a metal blade. Process until semi-chunky. Add the parsley, processing only 1 or 2 seconds to prevent the spread from turning green.

2) Replace the metal blade with the shredder blade. Grate the carrot into the work bowl.

3) Empty the contents into a container and stir until well blended.

Per Serving: Calories 139; Protein 12g; Fat 9g (Saturated 1g); Carbohydrates 6g; Fiber 1g; Sodium 131mg

Poached Turkey Breast

Makes: 16 servings

Cooking turkey at home is more economical and better tasting than turkey from the deli. Six pounds will cook down to about 4 pounds of edible meat. Note that there is a recipe for poaching chicken on page 103.

One 6- to 7-pound bone-in turkey breast
1 large onion, peeled and quartered
3 carrots, peeled and cut into large pieces
2 bay leaves
4 peppercorns
$1/4$ cup white wine vinegar
1 clove garlic
1 tablespoon kosher salt

1) If the turkey is frozen, defrost it in the refrigerator for about 24 hours. You will need enough water to cover the turkey by 1 inch. To determine this amount, put the turkey in a large pot and fill with enough water. Then remove the turkey to a plate. Add the remaining ingredients to the pot, bring to a boil, reduce to a simmer and return the turkey to the pot. Cover and simmer for $1^1/4$ hours. Let cool in the pot, uncovered, for 15 minutes.

2) Remove the turkey from the pot. Discard the contents of the pot, or serve the vegetables as a side dish. Peel the skin off the turkey and discard. The turkey can now either be sliced or pulled away from the bone and cut as desired.

Per Serving: Calories 159; Protein 34g; Fat 1g (Saturated 0g); Carbohydrates 0g; Fiber 0g; Sodium 154mg

Burgers

Burgers are favorite meals for many families. Each person at the table can dress up his or her burger according to personal taste. My husband uses a spicy barbeque sauce, my stepson goes the classic route with ketchup and pickles, I put on sautéed peppers and mushrooms, and the baby eats just the roll. Lots of flexibility for very little work!

The fat content of my burger recipes is brought down by using lean ground meats with fillers, such as breadcrumbs and vegetables. But they are not a compromise. Even cooked to well-done, these recipes are still juicy and flavorful.

Don't halve the recipe if it makes too much for you. Instead, freeze what you don't need. Individually wrap raw burgers and store in the freezer for up to several months.

Turkey Burgers

Makes: 6 servings

I don't see turkey burgers as the lesser cousin of beef burgers. There are times when I like the lighter flavor of turkey better than beef.

1 pound lean ground turkey (not ground turkey breast)
2 cloves garlic, minced
1 egg white
1/4 to 1/2 cup fresh or dry breadcrumbs
1 teaspoon dried basil
1/2 teaspoon kosher salt
1/4 teaspoon freshly ground pepper

1) Thoroughly combine all the ingredients. Add enough breadcrumbs to firm up the mixture.

2) Divide into 6 portions and form into patties.

3) Grill, broil, or cook in a nonstick pan on the stovetop until the burgers lose their pink color. Turn once while cooking.

Per Serving: Calories 94; Protein 19g; Fat 1g (Saturated 0g); Carbohydrates 2g; Fiber 0g; Sodium 212mg

Mushroom and Beef Burgers

Makes: 8 servings

The mushrooms can be chopped in a food processor.

1/2 pound 10% fat ground beef
1/2 pound lean ground turkey
1 egg white
2 tablespoons Italian-seasoned breadcrumbs
8 ounces mushrooms, finely chopped (2 cups)
1/2 cup chopped onions
1 tablespoon Worcestershire sauce
1/2 teaspoon kosher salt

1) Mix together all the ingredients by squeezing with your hands. Shape into 8 burgers.

2) Grill, broil, or cook in a nonstick pan on the stovetop until the burgers lose their pink color. Turn once while cooking.

Per Serving: Calories 101; Protein 14g; Fat 3g (Saturated 1g); Carbohydrates 4g; Fiber 1g; Sodium 204mg

Greek-Style Burgers

Makes: 6 servings

To continue the Greek theme, top these with yogurt or feta cheese and serve with Greek Cucumber Yogurt Salad (page 69) and tabouli.

1/2 pound ground lamb or 10% fat ground beef
1/2 pound lean ground turkey
1/4 cup cooked white rice
1/4 cup chopped fresh parsley
1 teaspoon dried oregano
2 tablespoons nonfat plain yogurt
1/2 teaspoon kosher salt
1/4 teaspoon freshly ground pepper
1 clove garlic, minced (optional)

1) Mix together all the ingredients by squeezing with your hands. Shape into 6 burgers.

2) Grill, broil, or cook in a nonstick pan on the stovetop until the burgers lose their pink color. Turn once while cooking.

Per Serving: Calories 130; Protein 16g; Fat 5g (Saturated 2g); Carbohydrates 3g; Fiber 0g; Sodium 203mg

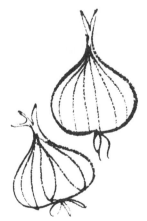

Barbeque Burgers

Makes: 6 servings

Cook these burgers on the stovetop; don't grill because they will crack.

1/4 cup water
1/2 cup barbeque sauce (for a selection see pages 587–588)
1/4 cup couscous
1/2 pound 10% fat ground beef
1/2 pound lean ground turkey
1 egg white
2 cloves garlic, minced (optional)

1) Heat the water and barbeque sauce until bubbling (I do this in the microwave in a glass measuring cup). Stir in the couscous. Cover and let rest 10 minutes.

2) Mix in the remaining ingredients by squeezing with your hands. Shape into 6 large burgers.

3) Broil or cook in a nonstick pan on the stovetop until the burgers lose their pink color. Turn once while cooking.

Per Serving: Calories 158; Protein 19g; Fat 4g (Saturated 2g); Carbohydrates 10g; Fiber 0g; Sodium 217mg

Tuna Burgers

Makes: 6 servings

Serve with thin rounds of red onion, lettuce, and Tartar Sauce (page 598).

3 tablespoons lowfat mayonnaise
1 egg white
Two 6-ounce cans albacore tuna, drained and
    flaked apart
1 medium potato, peeled, boiled, and mashed
2 scallions, minced
1/4 to 1/3 cup dry breadcrumbs, divided

1) Combine the mayonnaise, egg white, tuna, potato, scallions, and 2 tablespoons of the breadcrumbs. Shape into 6 burgers.

2) Dust with and then press in enough of the remaining breadcrumbs so the burgers are lightly coated.

3) Coat a nonstick skillet with nonstick spray and place over moderate heat. Cook the burgers for about 3 minutes, turn once, and cook until done, about 3 minutes more, until golden and cooked through.

Per Serving: Calories 121; Protein 14g; Fat 2g (Saturated 0g); Carbohydrates 11g; Fiber 1g; Sodium 303mg

Salmon Burgers

Makes: 6 servings

Discard the skin in canned salmon because it is unappealing and not very tasty, but leave the bones because they are so soft that they mash up inconspicuously and are an excellent source of calcium.

1 slice white bread
One 15-ounce can salmon, drained, skin (not
    bones) removed
2 egg whites
1 tablespoon lowfat mayonnaise
1/4 teaspoon paprika
1 1/2 teaspoons drained capers
1 teaspoon dried dill

1) Tear the slice of bread into several pieces. Put it in a processor fitted with a steel blade and pulse until coarsely chopped. Add the remaining ingredients and pulse until all is well mixed.

2) Form the salmon mixture into 6 patties.

3) Coat a nonstick skillet with nonstick spray and place over moderate heat. Cook the burgers for about 5 minutes on a side, turn once, and cook until done.

Per Serving: Calories 96; Protein 16g; Fat 3g (Saturated 0g); Carbohydrates 4g; Fiber 0g; Sodium 288mg

Fish Burgers

Makes: 5 servings

Only the light green and white parts of the scallions are added because the dark green shoots turn these burgers an unappetizing green.

3 scallions, white and light green parts only
1 pound white-fleshed fish, skinned and cut into 2-inch chunks
1 teaspoon Dijon mustard
1 egg
1 egg white
1 teaspoon kosher salt
1 russet potato, cooked, peeled and mashed
1 to 2 tablespoons dry breadcrumbs
1/2 cup cornmeal

1) In a processor, mince the scallions. Pulse in the fish until it is finely ground.

2) Remove the fish to a bowl. Blend in the mustard, egg, egg white, and salt. With a fork, mash in the cooked potato. Add just enough breadcrumbs to firm up the mixture without drying it out.

3) Divide the fish mixture into 5 portions and form into patties. Put the cornmeal on a dinner plate and turn each burger in it to coat lightly.

4) Coat a nonstick skillet with nonstick spray and place over moderate heat. Cook the burgers for about 5 minutes on a side, turn once, and cook until done, about 7 minutes more.

Per Serving: Calories 181; Protein 20g; Fat 2g (Saturated 0g); Carbohydrates 19g; Fiber 2g; Sodium 496mg

Tofu Burgers

Makes: 4 servings

I eat tofu burgers because I like them, not just because they're good for my health.

1 pound extra-firm or firm tofu
1 clove garlic, peeled
1 egg
1 1/2 teaspoons minced chives, fresh or frozen
1/2 teaspoon dried oregano
1 tablespoon soy sauce
1/2 cup rolled oats
1 teaspoon sesame seeds
1/4 teaspoon freshly ground pepper

1) Preheat the oven to 450°F. Coat a baking sheet with a nonstick spray or line with parchment paper.

2) Wrap the tofu in a clean kitchen towel. Squeeze out all the excess moisture. Twist the towel hard around the tofu because the less water, the better the texture of the burgers.

3) All the ingredients can easily be mixed in a food processor using the steel blade. Mince the garlic first, then pulse in the rest of the ingredients. If you're mixing the ingredients by hand, make sure the garlic is finely minced and the egg is lightly beaten before putting it all together. Handle it as you would meatloaf, kneading it with your hands.

4) Using your hands, form the mixture into 4 patties. Place them on the baking sheet.

5) Bake for 10 minutes, turn over, and bake for 5 minutes more.

Per Serving: Calories 230; Protein 22g; Fat 12g (Saturated 2g); Carbohydrates 13g; Fiber 1g; Sodium 290mg

Pizza

The first thing you need to make pizza is the dough. I have two recipes here, both very easy and quick to make. But when homemade dough it isn't fast enough, there are options. Most markets sell pizza dough in bags in the refrigerated case. Bring it home, let it come to room temperature, shape it, and proceed with your recipe. When my first son was a baby (who never napped), even that wasn't convenient enough, so I used pizza shells (and packaged, shredded cheese, and jarred sauce). That's the nice thing about pizza: whatever way you make it, it's always good.

Baking Tips

Some people have baking bricks or stones that preheat in the oven and simulate a brick-oven pizza at home. I use a perforated pizza pan. By allowing air to come into contact with the bottom of the dough it produces a crisp crust. But I also make pizzas on a rectangular baking sheet with great success. Coat the pan with nonstick spray (preferably olive oil), and/or dust with cornmeal.

Regardless of the pan, the most important thing is to preheat your oven until it is very hot with no cool spots. I leave mine on for a half hour before baking. Set your oven rack in the lowest third of the oven.

Cook the pizza until the crust's edges brown, the sauce bubbles, and the cheese turns golden. After removing it from the oven, let it rest for 5 minutes to firm up. Slip it onto a large cutting board and cut with a pizza wheel (a large knife will also do the job).

Serving Size

The serving sizes I have listed are for two large slices of pizza per person. This is plenty if you are also serving salad, bread, and maybe pasta. If making a meal of just pizza, or feeding someone who is used to eating an entire large pizza, adjust the serving size accordingly.

Pizza Dough

Makes: 8 servings

I have made this dough in the food processor, in the stand mixer, and by hand. (I have a nifty attachment for the processor: a large funnel that lets me add the flour while the machine is on.) All three methods are easy to do since, unlike bread dough, pizza dough rises only once. I've also experimented with the length of rising time. If using rapid-rise yeast, a 30-minute rise will suffice, but a 45-minute rise will make a softer crust. For active dry yeast, anywhere from 45 minutes to several hours will yield the sort of crust that looks like it came from a pizza parlor. (See page 493 for more information about yeast baking.)

1 package active dry or rapid-rise yeast
1 1/2 cups warm water
1 teaspoon sugar
3 1/2 to 4 1/2 cups unbleached, all-purpose
   white flour
1 teaspoon kosher salt
1 teaspoon olive oil

1) With the food processor: Combine the yeast, water, and sugar in a bowl. Put 3 1/2 cups of the flour and the salt into a food processor fitted with a plastic blade. Pour in the yeast mixture and oil, pulsing as you add it. Once the dough begins to stick together, let the machine run for 45 seconds. If the dough is very sticky, pulse in a little more flour until the dough forms a ball that pulls away from the sides of the machine.

2) With the stand mixer or by hand: Combine the yeast, water, and sugar in a bowl. Once the yeast begins to foam, mix in the oil, salt, and 1 cup of the flour. Gradually add the rest of the flour until a ball of dough forms. Stir in the flour until it is too stiff to use a spoon, then knead the dough on a floured surface until it is smooth and springy.

3) Place the dough in an oiled bowl, or on a piece of waxed paper, cover with a damp towel, and allow to rise for as long as desired, but at least 30 minutes.

4) Punch down the dough and divide it into 2 or 4 balls (for either 2 large, 16-inch pizzas or 4 small, 10-inch pizzas). Let rest 5 to 10 minutes, then roll or stretch each ball into a pizza pie shape. Proceed with a pizza recipe. Dough can be frozen, tightly wrapped, for about 2 months. Defrost it in the refrigerator (this can take 12 hours or more), then bring it to room temperature, allow to rise 30 minutes or longer, and proceed with the pizza recipe. (If freezing dough, use the active dry yeast, not the rapid-rise.)

Per Serving: Calories 183; Protein 6g; Fat 1g (Saturated 0g); Carbohydrates 37g; Fiber 1g; Sodium 242mg

Whole Wheat Pizza Dough

Makes: 8 servings

This dough has the same good elasticity as the regular version, but the whole wheat flour gives it that nutty whole wheat flavor.

1 package active dry or rapid-rise yeast
1 1/2 cups warm water
1/2 teaspoon sugar
2 teaspoons olive oil
1 teaspoon kosher salt
1 cup whole wheat flour
2 to 3 cups unbleached, all-purpose white flour

1) With the food processor: Combine the yeast, water, and sugar in a bowl. Put the oil, salt, and whole wheat flour into a food processor fitted with a plastic blade. Pulse until mixed. Pour in the yeast mixture and pulse. Gradually pulse in the white flour until a ball of dough forms. Let the machine run for about 1 minute but no longer. Take the ball of dough out of the machine, place on a floured surface, and knead until springy.

2) With the stand mixer or by hand: Combine the yeast, water, and sugar. Let stand until foamy. Stir in the oil, salt, and whole wheat flour. Continue to stir (or mix using the dough hook) while adding the white flour, 1/2 cup at a time, until a dough ball forms. Knead in the mixer or by hand until smooth and springy.

3) Divide the dough into 2 or 4 balls (for either 2 large, 16-inch pizzas or 4 small, 10-inch pizzas). Place in an oiled bowl or on wax paper, cover with a damp towel or plastic wrap, and allow to rise for as long as desired, but at least 30 minutes. If your kitchen is chilly or drafty, place the dough in an oven with the oven light turned on for warmth.

4) Punch the dough down and roll or stretch it into a pizza pie shape. Proceed with a pizza recipe. Dough can be frozen, tightly wrapped, for about 2 months. Defrost it in the refrigerator (this can take up to 12 hours), then bring it to room temperature, allow to rise 30 minutes or longer, and proceed with the pizza recipe. (If freezing dough, use the active dry yeast, not the rapid-rise.)

Per Serving: Calories 139; Protein 5g; Fat 2g (Saturated 0g); Carbohydrates 27g; Fiber 2g; Sodium 243mg

Classic Red Pizza

Makes: 4 servings

Although pizzas at cutting-edge restaurants have numerous exotic ingredients, a good pizza (and often a better pizza) can still be as basic as this.

1/2 recipe Pizza Dough (page 437), or 1 large pizza shell
1 cup tomato sauce (homemade or store-bought)
1 teaspoon dried oregano
1 cup shredded reduced-fat mozzarella
1 tablespoon grated Parmesan cheese

1) Put the oven rack on the lowest rung in the oven and preheat the oven to 450°F. If necessary, coat the pizza pan or baking sheet with nonstick spray.

2) Roll or stretch the dough into a 12-inch pie, or shape it to fit your pan. Place the dough on the baking sheet. Spread the sauce on the pizza dough and dust on the oregano. Distribute the cheeses on top.

3) Bake on the bottom rack of the oven for 15 minutes, until the cheese is bubbly.

Per Serving: Calories 260; Protein 14g; Fat 4g (Saturated 2g); Carbohydrates 41g; Fiber 2g; Sodium 739mg

Veggies and Cheese Pizza

Makes: 4 servings

This is one of those flexible recipes where as long as you have your proportions right, you can't go wrong. Most vegetables will taste great, from broccoli spears to artichoke hearts. Many vegetables benefit from a light steaming or they will taste uncooked even after their time in the oven. For example, wilt spinach and squeeze out its moisture; cook broccoli spears until fork-tender. However, vegetables such as onion slices, bell peppers, mushrooms, and canned artichoke hearts can be used without precooking.

2 cups vegetables of choice
1/2 recipe Pizza Dough (page 437), or 1 large pizza shell
1 cup tomato sauce (homemade or store-bought)
1 cup shredded reduced-fat mozzarella
1 tablespoon grated Parmesan cheese

1) Put the oven rack on the lowest rung in the oven and preheat the oven to 450°F. If necessary, coat the pizza pan or baking sheet with nonstick spray.

2) Roll or stretch the dough into a 12-inch pie, or shape it to fit your pan. Place the dough on the baking sheet. Spread the sauce on the pizza dough and then the vegetables. Top with the cheeses.

3) Bake on the bottom rack of the oven for 15 minutes, until the cheese is bubbly.

Per Serving: Calories 265; Protein 14g; Fat 4g (Saturated 2g); Carbohydrates 42g; Fiber 2g; Sodium 753mg

Ricotta and Spinach Pizza

Makes: 4 servings

A pizza doesn't have to have oozing strings of melted cheese to be good. The ricotta doesn't spread, but it does taste light and luscious.

One 10-ounce package frozen chopped spinach
$1^1/2$ cups reduced-fat or part-skim ricotta cheese
$1/4$ cup chopped fresh parsley
1 teaspoon dried basil
1 teaspoon dried oregano
$1/4$ teaspoon kosher salt
$1/4$ teaspoon freshly ground pepper
$1/2$ recipe Pizza Dough (page 437), or 1 large
 pizza shell
$1^1/2$ teaspoons extra-virgin olive oil
$1^1/2$ cups chopped tomatoes (or one 15-ounce can
 diced tomatoes), drained
$3/4$ cup tomato sauce (homemade or store-bought)
1 tablespoon grated Parmesan cheese

1) Put the oven rack on the lowest rung in the oven and preheat the oven to 450°F. If necessary, coat the pizza pan or baking sheet with nonstick spray.

2) Cook the spinach. Let cool and squeeze out as much moisture as possible. Combine the ricotta, parsley, basil, oregano, salt, and pepper.

3) Roll or stretch the dough into a 12-inch pie, or shape it to fit your pan. Place the dough on the baking sheet. Brush the dough with the olive oil. Top with the spinach, tomatoes, tomato sauce, and cheese mixture. The cheese will not spread like mozzarella, so drop small teaspoonfuls of the mixture on the pizza. Dust with the Parmesan.

4) Place the pizza on the bottom rack of the oven and reduce the temperature to 375°F. Bake for 25 minutes or longer, until the cheese is bubbly and the crust browns.

Per Serving: Calories 341; Protein 18g; Fat 8g (Saturated 3g); Carbohydrates 51g; Fiber 5g; Sodium 805mg

Sausage and Mushroom Pizza

Makes: 4 servings

If your sausage is very lean, leave out the turkey and use all sausage.

$1/2$ recipe Pizza Dough (page 437), or 1 large
 pizza shell
$1/3$ pound ground turkey breast
$1/3$ pound lowfat sausage, chopped
1 cup tomato sauce (homemade or store-bought)
$1^1/2$ cups sliced mushrooms (about $1/4$ pound)
$1/2$ to 1 cup reduced-fat mozzarella

1) Put the oven rack on the lowest rung in the oven and preheat the oven to 450°F. If necessary, coat the pizza pan or baking sheet with nonstick spray.

2) Cook the turkey and sausage in a large non-stick pan until cooked through, breaking pieces into small lumps as they cooks. Drain the fat.

3) Roll or stretch the dough into a 12-inch pie, or shape it to fit your pan. Place the dough on the baking sheet. Spread on the tomato sauce and top with the meats and mushrooms. Distribute the cheese on top.

4) Bake for about 15 minutes, until the crust begins to brown and the cheese bubbles.

Per Serving: Calories 339; Protein 26g; Fat 7g (Saturated 3g); Carbohydrates 42g; Fiber 2g; Sodium 907mg

Southwest Chicken Pizza

Makes: 4 servings

Offer lowfat sour cream and Guacamole (page 28) at the table as extra toppings for the finished pizza.

$1/2$ recipe Pizza Dough (page 437), **or** 1 large pizza shell

1 cup diced cooked chicken breast

3 tablespoons diced canned mild green chilies

$1/2$ cup roasted red bell pepper, patted dry and julienned (jarred peppers are okay)

$1/2$ cup corn kernels, thawed if frozen

$1/2$ cup cooked black beans, drained and rinsed

1 cup salsa

$1/2$ cup shredded reduced-fat jack or cheddar cheese

1) Put the oven rack on the lowest rung in the oven and preheat the oven to 450°F. If necessary, coat the pizza pan or baking sheet with nonstick spray.

2) Roll or stretch the dough into a 12-inch pie, or shape it to fit your pan. Place the dough on the baking sheet.

3) Distribute all the toppings on the pizza in the order listed, finishing with the cheese.

4) Bake in the lower third of the oven until the crust is done and the cheese melts and begins to brown, about 15 minutes.

Per Serving: Calories 328; Protein 20g; Fat 4g (Saturated 2g); Carbohydrates 52g; Fiber 6g; Sodium 1014mg

Hawaiian Pizza

Makes: 4 servings

The recipe tester who made this for her family says that now they ask for it once a week. In our household, too, when given a choice of toppings, pineapple is always at the top of the list.

$1/2$ recipe Pizza Dough (page 437), **or** 1 large pizza shell

$1/4$ pound cooked skinless turkey breast (home-cooked or from the deli)

1 cup tomato sauce (homemade or store-bought)

One 8-ounce can pineapple tidbits, drained

$1/2$ cup thin slices red onions

$1^1/2$ cups shredded part-skim mozzarella

1) Put the oven rack on the lowest rung in the oven and preheat the oven to 450°F. If necessary, coat the pizza pan or baking sheet with nonstick spray.

2) Roll or stretch the dough into a 12-inch pie, or shape it to fit your pan. Place the dough on the baking sheet. If using deli turkey, cut the slices into long strips. If using home-cooked turkey, cut it into cubes. Spread the sauce on the pizza dough and distribute the turkey, pineapple, and onions on the pizza. Arrange the cheese on top.

3) Bake for 15 minutes, until the cheese is bubbly.

Per Serving: Calories 356; Protein 25g; Fat 6g (Saturated 3g); Carbohydrates 50g; Fiber 2g; Sodium 781mg

Broccoli and Garlic Pizza

Makes: 4 servings

Instead of tomato sauce, this recipe uses fresh tomatoes and fresh basil.

2 teaspoons olive oil
4 cloves garlic, minced
1/2 recipe Pizza Dough (page 437), or 1 large
   pizza shell
1/2 teaspoon kosher salt
1/4 teaspoon freshly ground pepper
4 plum tomatoes, sliced lengthwise
1/4 cup coarsely chopped fresh basil
3 cups broccoli florets, blanched or steamed
   until tender
2 tablespoons grated Parmesan cheese
1 cup shredded reduced-fat mozzarella

1) Put the oven rack on the lowest rung in the oven and preheat the oven to 450°F. If necessary, coat the pizza pan or baking sheet with nonstick spray.

2) Heat the oil in a small nonstick pan. Cook the garlic over medium-low heat until it begins to turn golden.

3) Roll or stretch the dough into a 12-inch pie, or shape it to fit your pan. Place the dough on the baking sheet. Spread the garlic on the dough. Use a rubber spatula to scrape all the oil out of the pan and onto the pizza. Dust with the salt and pepper. Arrange the tomato slices in one layer on the dough (concentric circles make an attractive design), then place the basil and broccoli on top and distribute the cheeses over the pizza.

4) Bake for 12 to 15 minutes, until the crust begins to brown and the cheese bubbles.

Per Serving: Calories 299; Protein 15g; Fat 7g (Saturated 3g); Carbohydrates 44g; Fiber 3g; Sodium 663mg

Aegean Pizza

Makes: 2 servings

Pizza isn't always tomato sauce and mozzarella. Here capers and feta contribute the flavors of Greece.

1/2 cup sun-dried tomato halves
1 teaspoon olive oil
1 green bell pepper, julienned
1/2 cup sliced red onions
1/4 recipe Pizza Dough (page 437), or 1 small
   pizza shell
1 1/2 teaspoons drained capers
1/2 cup crumbled feta cheese

1) Soak the dried tomatoes in very hot water for 5 minutes, then drain and slice.

2) Put the oven rack on the lowest rung in the oven and preheat the oven to 450°F. If necessary, coat the pizza pan or baking sheet with nonstick spray.

3) Heat the oil in a small nonstick pan. Sauté the bell pepper and onions until the onions wilt. Set aside.

4) Roll or stretch the dough into a 10-inch pie, or shape it to fit your pan. Place the dough on the baking sheet. Place in the lower third of the oven and bake for 5 minutes. Prick with a fork where it balloons out.

5) Place the onions and peppers on the pizza. Use a rubber spatula to scrape all the oil out of the pan and onto the pizza. Arrange the tomatoes and capers on top. Dot with small pieces of the cheese.

6) Bake until the crust is done and the cheese softens, about 6 to 8 minutes. This cheese will not spread or bubble like mozzarella.

Per Serving: Calories 351; Protein 14g; Fat 10g (Saturated 6g); Carbohydrates 52g; Fiber 4g; Sodium 636mg

Goat Cheese Pizza

Makes: 2 servings

Often, what was once daring and trendy becomes passé. Not so goat cheese pizza. It is a worthwhile addition to the pizza repertoire and so has become welcome standard fare.

1/4 recipe Pizza Dough (page 437), or 1 small pizza shell

1 teaspoon olive oil

1/2 cup sliced sweet or red onions

2 cloves garlic, minced

1/4 cup sliced fresh basil leaves

1 teaspoon dried rosemary

1/4 teaspoon freshly ground pepper

1 ripe tomato, cored and sliced

3 ounces goat cheese (also called chèvre)

1) Put the oven rack on the lowest rung in the oven and preheat the oven to 450°F. If necessary, coat the pizza pan or baking sheet with nonstick spray.

2) Roll or stretch the dough into a 10-inch pie, or shape it to fit your pan. Place the dough on the baking sheet.

3) Heat the oil in a small nonstick pan. Sauté the onions and garlic briefly until the onions wilt and the garlic turns golden, about 5 minutes.

4) Place the onion mixture on the dough. Use a rubber spatula to scrape all the oil out of the pan and onto the pizza. Arrange the basil, rosemary, and pepper on top, and then the tomato slices. Dot with small pieces of the cheese.

5) Bake on the bottom rack of the oven until the crust is done and the cheese is melting, about 8 to 12 minutes. This cheese will not spread or bubble like mozzarella.

Per Serving: Calories 389; Protein 16g; Fat 17g (Saturated 9g); Carbohydrates 45g; Fiber 3g; Sodium 469mg

Deep-Dish Rustica Pizza

Makes: 4 servings

This is as much a vegetable pie as it is a pizza.

1 tablespoon olive oil
1 cup diced zucchini (1 small)
1 cup chopped green bell pepper (1 pepper)
1 cup chopped red bell pepper (1 pepper)
1 cup peeled and diced eggplant
1/2 pound lean ground turkey breast
1 teaspoon dried oregano
1 tablespoon dried basil
1/2 recipe Pizza Dough (page 437), or 1 large
    pizza shell
3/4 cup tomato sauce (homemade or store-bought)
1/2 cup shredded reduced-fat mozzarella cheese
2 tablespoons grated Parmesan cheese

1) Put the oven rack on the lowest rung in the oven and preheat the oven to 450°F. Coat a 9×13-inch pan or a large pizza pan with nonstick spray. If desired, dust with cornmeal.

2) Heat the oil in a nonstick pan. Cook the vegetables until tender, about 10 minutes. Keep covered between stirrings so the steam will keep them moist after they absorb the oil. Remove the vegetables from the pan and cook the turkey, breaking it apart with a spatula, until cooked through. Drain. Stir together the vegetables, turkey, oregano, and basil.

3) Roll or stretch the dough into a shape to fit your pizza pan. Place it in the pan so that it comes up and over the sides. Press the dough into the corners if necessary. Spread the vegetable and turkey mixture into the pan. Pour on the tomato sauce. Distribute the cheeses over the top. Roll the excess dough into an attractive rim to keep the filling from spilling out.

4) Put the pizza in the oven, reduce the temperature to 400°F, and bake until the crust browns and the cheese bubbles, about 25 to 30 minutes.

Per Serving: Calories 355; Protein 26g; Fat 8g (Saturated 2g); Carbohydrates 46g; Fiber 4g; Sodium 653mg

Deep-Dish Vegetable Pizza

Makes: 4 servings

Once you try this, feel free to choose different vegetables. Just make sure that they are thoroughly drained of moisture so that the crust doesn't become soggy.

2 teaspoons olive oil

4 cloves garlic, minced (optional)

1 green bell pepper, sliced

2 cups sliced mushrooms

1 cup sliced onions

$1/2$ recipe Pizza Dough (page 437), or 1 large pizza shell

2 cups small broccoli florets, lightly steamed

$1^1/2$ cups chopped tomatoes (or one 15-ounce can diced tomatoes), drained

1 teaspoon dried oregano

$1/2$ teaspoon dried basil

$1/8$ teaspoon crushed red pepper flakes (optional)

$1/2$ cup shredded reduced-fat mozzarella cheese

$1/2$ cup shredded reduced-fat cheddar cheese

1 tablespoon grated Parmesan cheese

1) Put the oven rack on the lowest rung of the oven and preheat the oven to 450°F. Coat a 10-inch diameter, 2-inch-deep pan with non-stick spray. If desired, dust with cornmeal.

2) Heat the oil in a nonstick pan. Cook the garlic, bell peppers, mushrooms, and onions over medium-low heat until they begin to wilt.

3) Roll or stretch the dough into a circle and place it in the pan, bringing the dough up and onto the rim. Flute the edges as you would a pie crust. Place in the oven for 7 minutes. Remove from the oven and prick any air bubbles with a fork. Use a rubber spatula to scrape all the vegetables and oil out of the sauté pan and onto the pizza. Top with the broccoli, tomatoes, oregano, basil, and pepper flakes. Distribute the cheeses over the top.

4) Put the pizza in the oven, reduce the temperature to 375°F, and bake until the crust begins to brown and the cheese bubbles, about 20 minutes.

Per Serving: Calories 310; Protein 15g; Fat 3g (Saturated 3g); Carbohydrates 48g; Fiber 4g; Sodium 405mg

Breakfasts

Bread Spreads
778

*Smoked Salmon
Cream Cheese Spread*

Cream Cheese and Chives

Cereal
779

Simply Oatmeal

Rich Old-Fashioned Oatmeal

Cinnamon-Raisin Oatmeal

Breakfast Polenta

Granola

Fruity Granola

Pancakes
752

Buttermilk Pancakes

Pecan Buttermilk Pancakes

Blueberry Pancakes

Oatmeal Pancakes

Wheat Germ Pancakes

Orange Nut Pancakes

Pumpkin Pancakes

Gingerbread Pancakes

Waffles
756

Buttermilk Waffles

Orange Nut Waffles

Gingerbread Waffles

French Toast
758

Basic French Toast

Banana French Toast

*Strawberry-Stuffed
French Toast*

Banana-Stuffed French Toast

Maple-Stuffed French Toast

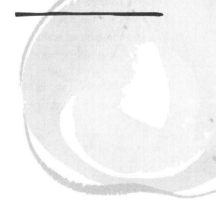

Frittatas
462

Broccoli Frittata

Asparagus Frittata

Tomato Frittata

Sausage and Cheese Egg Casserole

Chili Egg Casserole

Fruits and Vegetables
466

Shredded Hash Browns

Breakfast Potatoes

Applesauce

Peachy Applesauce

Dried Fruit and Ginger Compote

Stewed Apricots and Prunes

Honey and Ginger Broiled Grapefruit

Sugar and Rum Broiled Grapefruit

Very Berry Dairy Shake

Banana Yogurt Smoothie

Orange Mango Smoothie

Fruit and Yogurt Smoothie

Dairy-Free Fruit Smoothie

Breakfast is my favorite meal, and I bet that a majority of people would agree with me. I don't mean cold cereal and a slice of toast eaten on the run—I'm talking about breakfasts of abundance, leisure, and family time. A morning filled with pancakes, fruit syrups, juice, hot oatmeal with brown sugar, egg casseroles, bagels and cream cheese. All of that is possible with lowfat, healthy foods. And if you do have to eat breakfast on the run, there are muffins, granola, and drinks to soothe and nourish you on your way.

Bread Spreads

Whether it is a leisurely weekend affair or a meal on the run, breakfast usually includes some form of bread. The bread chapter contains many recipes suitable for breakfasts, from muffins to quick breads. Coffee cakes, found in the dessert chapter, are also good morning fare. Some breads are best when topped with a spread. I love to find homemade jams at farmstands and find that I don't miss butter when I have a great preserve. When I want something savory and not sweet, I like cream cheese. The following two recipes take that plain white spread and make it special.

Smoked Salmon Cream Cheese Spread

Makes: 1 1/3 cups

Smoked salmon varies in saltiness and depth of flavor. If yours is delicately flavored, add a few tablespoons more salmon.

8 ounces reduced-fat cream cheese
2 ounces chopped smoked salmon (about 1/4 cup)
1 tablespoon minced scallions, green tops only
1/4 teaspoon freshly ground pepper

Using an electric mixer, blend together all the ingredients until bright pink.

Calories per tablespoon 30; Protein 2g; Fat 2g (Saturated 2g); Carbohydrates 0g; Fiber 0g; Sodium 68mg

Cream Cheese and Chives

Makes: 1 1/4 cups

If fresh chives aren't available, don't use dried; use finely minced green scallion tops instead.

8 ounces reduced-fat cream cheese
2 tablespoons minced fresh chives
1/4 teaspoon freshly ground pepper
2 teaspoons prepared white horseradish

Using an electric mixer, blend together all the ingredients until smooth.

Calories per tablespoon 29; Protein 1g; Fat 2g (Saturated 2g); Carbohydrates 0g; Fiber 0g; Sodium 49mg

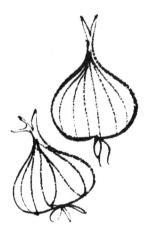

Cereal

Simply Oatmeal

Makes: 2 servings

Oatmeal is so simple to make and yet it can be made so badly. I've had oatmeal as dense as sticky glue, and oatmeal more like soup than porridge. Follow these directions and you will get the "just right" breakfast of Goldilocks's dreams.

2 cups water
1/4 teaspoon kosher salt
1 cup old-fashioned rolled oats

Bring the water and salt to a simmer. Stir in the oats and cook, stirring frequently, for about 5 minutes, until the oatmeal is creamy.

Per Serving: Calories 156; Protein 6g; Fat 3g (Saturated 0g); Carbohydrates 27g; Fiber 4g; Sodium 249mg

Rich Old-Fashioned Oatmeal

Makes: 5 servings

The nonfat dry milk gives this the richness of cream without the fat.

4 cups 1% lowfat milk
1/2 teaspoon kosher salt
2 cups old-fashioned rolled oats
2 tablespoons nonfat dry milk
1/4 cup packed light brown sugar

1) Bring the milk and salt to a simmer. Stir in the oats and continue to cook, stirring frequently, for about 5 to 7 minutes, until the oatmeal is creamy.

2) Stir in the nonfat milk and brown sugar. Continue to simmer until the cereal is the desired consistency.

Per Serving: Calories 254; Protein 12g; Fat 4g (Saturated 2g); Carbohydrates 43g; Fiber 3g; Sodium 305mg

Cinnamon-Raisin Oatmeal

Makes: 2 servings

Cooking raisins in with the oats imparts a sugary, fruity flavor to this cereal.

1 cup water
1 cup 1% lowfat milk
1/4 teaspoon kosher salt
1 cup old-fashioned rolled oats
1/2 teaspoon ground cinnamon
1/3 cup raisins
2 tablespoons packed light brown sugar

Bring the water, milk, and salt to a simmer. Stir in the oats, cinnamon, raisins, and brown sugar and cook, stirring frequently, for about 5 minutes, until the oatmeal is creamy.

Per Serving: Calories 342; Protein 11g; Fat 4g (Saturated 1g); Carbohydrates 68g; Fiber 5g; Sodium 316mg

Breakfast Polenta

Makes: 12 servings

This is a very attractive dish for a buffet brunch.

4 cups 1% lowfat milk
1 cup cornmeal (preferably finely ground)
1/2 teaspoon kosher salt
2/3 cup golden raisins
1/2 teaspoon ground cinnamon
1/8 teaspoon ground ginger

1) Gently heat the milk to hot but not quite simmering. Slowly pour in the cornmeal and stir until smooth. Stir in the remaining ingredients and bring to a slow simmer. Cook over moderate heat for 12 to 18 minutes, until thickened. Stir frequently during cooking.

2) Pour the polenta into a bowl. Let rest for 1 hour, until set but still warm. Unmold from the bowl onto a serving plate. It should slip out easily. If not, run a flexible rubber spatula between the bowl and the polenta.

3) Serve using a large spoon or cake server and have pitchers of warm milk and maple syrup on the side.

Per Serving: Calories 104; Protein 4g; Fat 1g (Saturated 1g); Carbohydrates 20g; Fiber 1g; Sodium 123mg

Granola

Makes: 20 servings (1/2 cup each)

If you can't find raw sunflower seeds, use roasted ones and add them at the end with the dried fruit.

1/4 cup nonfat dry milk
4 cups old-fashioned rolled oats
1/2 cup raw sunflower seeds
1/2 cup toasted wheat germ
1/4 cup sesame seeds
1 cup coarsely chopped almonds or other nuts
1 1/2 teaspoons ground cinnamon
1 teaspoon vanilla extract
3 tablespoons orange juice
1/2 cup honey or maple syrup
2 teaspoons vegetable oil
1 cup dried fruit bits or chopped dried fruit
1 cup raisins

1) Preheat the oven to 350°F. Line a large rimmed baking sheet with foil. Coat it with nonstick spray. Combine the milk, oats, sunflower seeds, wheat germ, sesame seeds, nuts, and cinnamon.

2) Warm the vanilla, orange juice, honey, and oil in a small saucepan. When it is thin and pourable, stir it into the oats mixture. When all is moistened, spread into the pan, about 1/2 inch thick.

3) Bake for 15 minutes. With a flat spatula, turn over the granola (it will be in large pieces). Continue to bake until lightly browned, another 7 to 10 minutes. Let cool in the pan. Break up and stir in the fruit. Stored in an airtight container it will last several weeks in the cupboard or a few months in the refrigerator.

Per Serving: Calories 219; Protein 7g; Fat 8g (Saturated 1g); Carbohydrates 33g; Fiber 4g; Sodium 10mg

Fruity Granola

Makes: 18 servings ($^1/_2$ cup each)

The color and flavor of golden raisins are appropriate here, but dark Thompson raisins could be used instead.

$^1/_4$ cup nonfat dry milk

4 cups old-fashioned rolled oats

$^1/_4$ cup packed light brown sugar

$^1/_2$ cup raw sunflower seeds

$^1/_2$ cup toasted wheat germ

$^1/_2$ cup coarsely chopped pecans or other nuts

$1^1/_2$ teaspoons ground cinnamon

$^1/_8$ teaspoon salt

2 teaspoons vanilla extract

$^1/_2$ cup frozen apple juice concentrate, thawed

2 tablespoons frozen orange juice concentrate, thawed

2 teaspoons vegetable oil

$^1/_2$ cup sweetened dried cranberries

1 cup golden raisins

$^1/_2$ cup chopped prunes or dried fruit bits

1) Preheat the oven to 350°F. Line a large rimmed baking sheet with foil or parchment paper. Coat foil with nonstick spray. Combine the milk, oats, brown sugar, sunflower seeds, wheat germ, nuts, cinnamon, and salt in a bowl.

2) Blend the vanilla, juice concentrates, and oil. Stir into the oats mixture. When all is moistened, spread into the pan, about $^1/_2$ inch thick.

3) Bake for 10 minutes. With a flat spatula, turn over the granola (it will be in large pieces). Continue to bake until lightly browned, another 7 to 10 minutes. This tends to brown around the edges, so watch carefully. Remove from the oven and let cool in the pan. Break up and stir in the dried fruit. Stored in an airtight container it will last several weeks in the cupboard or a few months in the refrigerator.

Per Serving: Calories 213; Protein 6g; Fat 6g (Saturated 1g); Carbohydrates 35g; Fiber 4g; Sodium 26mg

Pancakes

My family loves pancakes and we sometimes have them for dinner. We don't need butter. Along with the real maple syrup, there's always homemade applesauce or perhaps a fruit compote, maybe even Chocolate Syrup (page 576). When feeding a finicky toddler, add a little shredded carrot and ground nuts to the batter for an extra dose of nutrition.

Cooking Pancakes

To speed preparation in the morning, mix the dry ingredients in one bowl and the wet ingredients in another the night before. Cover and refrigerate the bowls. When ready to make the pancakes, all you'll have to do is stir the contents of the bowls together.

When mixing pancake batter, take care to stir the flour until moistened, but don't beat or the pancakes will be tough. The batter should be pourable, but not so thick that it sticks to the spoon, nor so thin that it runs. Add a little more liquid or flour as necessary. Once mixed, the batter can rest up to a half hour before cooking.

The best surface to cook pancakes on is a large, flat nonstick skillet. If using an electric skillet, preheat it to 350°F. The pan should be so hot that a drop of water sizzles on the surface. If you haven't seasoned the pan for a while, use a little oil or some nonstick spray. Pour the batter onto the skillet. One-quarter cup makes pancakes about 4 inches across. One serving is three to four pancakes.

It is time to turn the pancakes when they bubble in their middles and turn golden on their bottoms, in about 3 to 4 minutes. If turned too early they will not cook properly, and if turned more than once they lose their light inner textures. After flipping, cook until the centers feel firm to the touch and the pancakes turn light brown.

Pancakes are best if eaten immediately, but they can be cooled on a wire rack and then frozen in a sealable plastic bag. Pancakes can be reheated in a microwave or toaster oven.

Buttermilk Pancakes

Makes: 3 servings

Buttermilk lightens the batter and gives it a pleasantly sour taste.

2/3 cup whole wheat flour
1 cup unbleached, all-purpose white flour
1/4 teaspoon kosher salt
1 teaspoon baking soda
1 egg white
1 whole egg
2 cups buttermilk

1) Sift together the dry ingredients. Stir until you no longer see streaks of whole wheat flour.

2) In a separate bowl, whisk together the egg white, egg, and buttermilk.

3) Pour the wet ingredients into the dry. With a rubber spatula, stir the two together quickly until moist but still lumpy.

4) Preheat a skillet or griddle and spray with a nonstick spray or brush lightly with oil. Pour 1/4 cup of batter per pancake onto the pan, making sure the pancakes don't touch, and cook until bubbles start to burst on the surface. Turn and cook until golden.

Per Serving: Calories 319; Protein 16g; Fat 4g (Saturated 2g); Carbohydrates 55g; Fiber 4g; Sodium 792mg

Pecan Buttermilk Pancakes

Makes: 4 servings

Nuts make pancakes seem like a substantial meal.

1 recipe Buttermilk Pancakes (opposite)
1/2 cup chopped pecans

Follow the directions for Buttermilk Pancakes, adding the pecans to the dry ingredients before adding the wet.

Per Serving: Calories 338; Protein 14g; Fat 13g (Saturated 2g); Carbohydrates 44g; Fiber 4g; Sodium 594mg

Blueberry Pancakes

Makes: 4 servings

Small, wild blueberries appear in the markets during an all-too-short season at the end of the summer. But take a look in the freezer section of the supermarket. I've found them there throughout the year, although the supply is sporadic. These smaller berries have intense blueberry flavor without adding too much sweetness.

1 cup blueberries (fresh or frozen)
2 cups unbleached, all-purpose white flour
4 teaspoons baking powder
1 teaspoon salt
2 tablespoons sugar
1 egg
1 egg white
2 cups 1% lowfat milk

1) If using frozen blueberries, thaw, drain, and discard the juice. If using fresh berries, wash and sort through to discard stems and bruised berries.

2) Sift together the flour, baking powder, salt, and sugar.

3) In a separate bowl, lightly beat the egg, egg white, and milk. Pour this into the flour mixture and stir until smooth.

4) Gently stir in the berries.

5) Preheat a skillet or griddle and spray with a nonstick spray or brush lightly with oil. Pour 1/4 cup of batter per pancake onto the pan, making sure the pancakes don't touch, and cook until bubbles start to burst on the surface. Turn and cook until golden.

Per Serving: Calories 319; Protein 13g; Fat 3g (Saturated 1g); Carbohydrates 60g; Fiber 2g; Sodium 715mg

Oatmeal Pancakes

Makes: 4 servings

The flakes of rolled oats give these a sturdy, slightly chewy texture, which is a great base for stewed fruit or sliced strawberries.

1 cup unbleached, all-purpose white flour
1/4 cup sugar
1 teaspoon baking powder
1 teaspoon baking soda
1 cup old-fashioned rolled oats
1 egg
1 egg white
2 cups buttermilk

1) Sift together the flour, sugar, baking powder, and baking soda. Stir in the oats.

2) In a separate bowl, whisk together the egg, egg white, and buttermilk.

3) Pour the liquid ingredients into the dry. Stir until the batter is moist throughout. Let the batter rest at least 1 hour or as long as overnight.

4) Preheat a skillet or griddle and spray with a nonstick spray or brush lightly with oil. Pour 1/4 cup of batter per pancake onto the pan, making sure the pancakes don't touch, and cook until bubbles start to burst on the surface. Turn and cook until golden.

Per Serving: Calories 298; Protein 13g; Fat 4g (Saturated 1g); Carbohydrates 53g; Fiber 3g; Sodium 596mg

Wheat Germ Pancakes

Makes: 5 servings

Wheat germ provides a nutty, sweet flavor and a beautiful golden color to these pancakes (not to mention an extra dose of nutrition).

1/2 cup whole wheat flour
1 cup unbleached, all-purpose white flour
2 tablespoons sugar
1 teaspoon baking soda
1/4 teaspoon salt
1/2 cup toasted wheat germ
1 egg
1 egg white
2 cups buttermilk

1) Sift together the flours, sugar, baking soda, and salt. Stir in the wheat germ.

2) In a separate bowl, whisk together the egg, egg white, and buttermilk.

3) Pour the liquid ingredients into the dry. Stir until the batter is moist but still lumpy. Let the batter rest 15 minutes before cooking.

4) Preheat a skillet or griddle and spray with a nonstick spray or brush lightly with oil. Pour 1/4 cup of batter per pancake onto the pan, making sure the pancakes don't touch, and cook until bubbles start to burst on the surface. Turn and cook until golden.

Per Serving: Calories 240; Protein 13g; Fat 4g (Saturated 1g); Carbohydrates 41g; Fiber 4g; Sodium 486mg

Orange Nut Pancakes

Makes: 4 servings

These pancakes are so nutty, sweet, and fruity that the only accompaniment needed is a little maple syrup, or perhaps a dollop of yogurt.

1^1/$_2$ cups unbleached, all-purpose white flour
1 teaspoon baking powder
1 teaspoon baking soda
^{1}/$_2$ teaspoon salt
1 egg
1 egg white
1^1/$_4$ cups orange juice
^{1}/$_4$ cup sweetened condensed nonfat milk
1^1/$_2$ teaspoons minced orange zest
^{1}/$_3$ cup chopped nuts, such as pecans or walnuts

1) Sift together the flour, leaveners, and salt.

2) In a separate bowl, whisk together the egg, egg white, orange juice, and milk.

3) Pour the liquid ingredients into the dry. Stir until the batter is moist but still lumpy.

4) Gently stir in the zest and nuts.

5) Preheat a skillet or griddle and spray with a nonstick spray or brush lightly with oil. Pour ^{1}/$_4$ cup of batter per pancake onto the pan, making sure the pancakes don't touch, and cook until bubbles start to burst on the surface. Turn and cook until golden.

Per Serving: Calories 333; Protein 10g; Fat 9g (Saturated 2g); Carbohydrates 53g; Fiber 2g; Sodium 754mg

Pumpkin Pancakes

Makes: 4 servings

These are filling but not heavy.

^{1}/$_2$ cup whole wheat flour
1 cup unbleached, all-purpose white flour
^{1}/$_2$ teaspoon ground cinnamon
^{1}/$_4$ teaspoon ground nutmeg
1 tablespoon baking powder
^{1}/$_2$ teaspoon salt
1 egg
One 12-ounce can unsweetened evaporated nonfat milk
1 cup canned pumpkin
^{1}/$_2$ teaspoon vanilla extract

1) Sift together the flours, spices, baking powder, and salt.

2) In a separate bowl, whisk together the egg, milk, pumpkin, and vanilla.

3) Pour the liquid ingredients into the dry. Stir until the batter is moist throughout.

4) Preheat a skillet or griddle and spray with a nonstick spray or brush lightly with oil. Pour ^{1}/$_4$ cup of batter per pancake onto the pan, making sure the pancakes don't touch, and cook until bubbles start to burst on the surface. Turn and cook until golden.

Per Serving: Calories 268; Protein 15g; Fat 2g (Saturated 1g); Carbohydrates 49g; Fiber 4g; Sodium 762mg

Gingerbread Pancakes

Makes: 5 servings

The ginger, both ground and crystallized, is a wake-up call in the morning.

1 1/2 cups unbleached, all-purpose white flour
1/3 cup whole wheat flour
1/2 teaspoon salt
1 teaspoon baking soda
1 teaspoon ground ginger
1 teaspoon ground cinnamon
1 tablespoon vegetable oil
1/4 cup molasses
1 egg
1 egg white
1 3/4 cups buttermilk
2 tablespoons chopped crystallized ginger

1) Sift together the flours, salt, baking soda, ground ginger, and cinnamon. Stir until the spices blend into the flour and there are no dark streaks.

2) In a separate bowl, beat together the oil, molasses, egg, egg white, and buttermilk.

3) Pour the wet ingredients into the dry. Stir until the batter is moist but still lumpy. Stir in the crystallized ginger.

4) Let the batter rest 10 minutes before cooking. Preheat a skillet or griddle and spray with a nonstick spray or brush lightly with oil. Pour 1/4 cup of batter per pancake onto the pan, making sure the pancakes don't touch, and cook until bubbles start to burst on the surface. Turn and cook until golden.

Per Serving: Calories 288; Protein 10g; Fat 5g (Saturated 1g); Carbohydrates 52g; Fiber 2g; Sodium 586mg

Waffles

Waffles should not be made with the same batter as pancakes. Because they steam as they cook, they need more oil or they won't crisp properly. Each waffle iron is different, so cook according to its directions. But one thing is true for all waffle irons: the less opening and peeking, the better.

Buttermilk Waffles

Makes: 4 servings

Because waffles should be served immediately, it is best to transfer them right from the iron onto the eater's plate. If it looks like there will be leftovers, cool them on a wire rack to prevent sogginess, then freeze in a zipper bag. Warm frozen waffles in a toaster oven.

2/3 cup whole wheat flour
1 cup unbleached, all-purpose white flour
1/4 teaspoon salt
1 teaspoon baking soda
1 egg white
1 large egg
1 3/4 to 2 cups buttermilk
1/4 cup vegetable oil

1) Sift the dry ingredients into a bowl and stir until the flours are well combined and there are no dark streaks.

2) In another bowl, beat the egg, egg white, buttermilk, and oil until frothy.

3) Pour the wet ingredients into the dry. Stir until the flour is moist but still lumpy. If the batter looks too thick, stir in a bit more buttermilk.

4) Cook according to your waffle iron's directions.

Per Serving: Calories 353; Protein 12g; Fat 17g (Saturated 2g); Carbohydrates 41g; Fiber 3g; Sodium 591mg

Orange Nut Waffles

Makes: 4 servings

I like to use orange juice with pulp for added texture and fresh orange flavor.

1¹/2 cups unbleached, all-purpose white flour
1 tablespoon sugar
1 teaspoon baking powder
1 teaspoon baking soda
1/2 teaspoon salt
2 large eggs
1/4 cup vegetable oil
1¹/4 cups orange juice
1¹/2 teaspoons minced orange zest
1/2 cup chopped nuts, such as pecans or walnuts

1) Sift together the flour, sugar, leaveners, and salt.

2) In a separate bowl, beat the eggs, oil, and orange juice.

3) Pour the liquid ingredients into the dry. Stir until the batter is moist but still lumpy. Gently stir in the zest and nuts.

4) Cook according to your waffle iron's directions.

Per Serving: Calories 454; Protein 10g; Fat 27g (Saturated 3g); Carbohydrates 46g; Fiber 2g; Sodium 736mg

Gingerbread Waffles

Makes: 4 servings

Instead of a bagel for breakfast, try one of these spread with cream cheese.

1¹/2 cups unbleached, all-purpose white flour
1/3 cup whole wheat flour
1/2 teaspoon salt
1 teaspoon baking soda
1 teaspoon ground ginger
1 teaspoon cinnamon
1/4 cup vegetable oil
1/4 cup molasses
1 large egg
1 egg white
1¹/3 cups buttermilk
2 tablespoons chopped crystallized ginger

1) Sift together the flours, salt, baking soda, ground ginger, and cinnamon. Stir until the spices blend into the flour and there are no dark streaks.

2) In a separate bowl, beat together the oil, molasses, egg, egg white, and buttermilk.

3) Pour the wet ingredients into the dry. Stir until the batter is moist but still lumpy. Stir in the crystallized ginger.

4) Let the batter rest 10 minutes before cooking, then cook according to your waffle iron's directions.

Per Serving: Calories 440; Protein 11g; Fat 16g (Saturated 2g); Carbohydrates 64g; Fiber 3g; Sodium 705mg

French Toast

Bread for French toast cannot be soft and airy (like white sandwich bread) because it absorbs the batter too quickly and falls apart. Instead, a dense loaf is best. Although I specify white bread, whole wheat can be used. The whole wheat might mask the delicate flavors of vanilla and cinnamon, but it can make terrific French toast. Make sure that you use the size of loaf that the recipe specifies.

French toast is cooked to perfection when it is lightly browned and the center springs back to the touch.

Basic French Toast

Makes: 4 servings

The more batter the bread absorbs, the longer it will take to cook the toast. To tell if the toast is cooked through, push gently with a finger. Take French toast off the griddle when it springs back to the touch, but don't wait until it feels firm with no give.

1/2 teaspoon vanilla extract
1 egg
3 egg whites
1 cup 1% lowfat milk
1/2 teaspoon ground cinnamon
8 slices homemade-quality white bread

1) Combine all the ingredients except the bread. Preheat the griddle. If using an electric skillet, preheat it to 375°F.

2) Place the bread in an oblong pan and pour the batter over it. Turn the slices of bread so they absorb the batter evenly.

3) The skillet should be hot enough that a drop of water dances on the surface, but not so hot that the toast burns on contact. A nonstick pan does not have to be greased; otherwise, use nonstick spray. Cook the bread in the skillet until lightly browned on one side. Turn and cook until done.

Per Serving: Calories 240; Protein 12g; Fat 4g (Saturated 1g); Carbohydrates 37g; Fiber 2g; Sodium 414mg

Banana French Toast

Makes: 4 servings

This is an even easier way to use up overripe bananas than making banana bread. Here they are pureed in with the batter.

2 large ripe bananas
1/2 teaspoon vanilla extract
1 egg
3 egg whites
3/4 cup 1% lowfat milk
8 slices homemade-quality white bread
1/2 teaspoon ground cinnamon

1) Puree the bananas, vanilla, egg, egg whites, and milk. Preheat the griddle. If using an electric skillet, preheat it to 375°F.

2) Place the bread in an oblong pan and pour the batter over it. Turn the slices of bread so the batter is absorbed evenly. Soak the bread until soft and almost falling apart. You can do this step in two batches.

3) A nonstick pan does not have to be greased; otherwise, use a nonstick spray. Using a spatula, slip the bread onto the skillet and cook until lightly browned on one side. Turn and cook until done. Dust with the cinnamon and serve.

Per Serving: Calories 286; Protein 12g; Fat 5g (Saturated 1g); Carbohydrates 49g; Fiber 3g; Sodium 407mg

Strawberry-Stuffed French Toast

Makes: 5 servings

For this recipe, bread is sliced thickly and then each slice is cut almost all the way through to make pockets. Since it can be difficult to find good unsliced bread, I give directions for a sliced loaf as well.

One 1-pound loaf homemade-quality white bread
One 8-ounce package reduced-fat cream cheese, softened
1 tablespoon confectioners' sugar
1 pint strawberries, thickly sliced, divided
1/2 teaspoon vanilla extract
4 egg whites
2 whole eggs
1 cup 1% lowfat milk
Confectioners' sugar (optional)

1) Preheat the oven to 450°F and coat a large cookie sheet with a nonstick spray. (Do not use the insulated type of cookie sheet, which prevents browning.)

2) If using an unsliced loaf, cut off the crusty ends of the bread and discard or reserve for another use. Slice the loaf into 10 thick slices. Form a pocket in each slice by cutting up from the bottom crust, almost, but not quite, all the way through to the top. If using presliced bread, you'll need 20 slices.

3) In a small bowl, beat the cream cheese and sugar until creamy. Stir in all but 1 cup of the sliced berries, reserving the rest for garnish. If using bread pockets, fill them with the cheese mixture. If using presliced bread, spread the filling onto 10 slices of bread and press another slice on top.

4) Whisk together the vanilla, egg whites, eggs, and milk and pour over the bread. (I use the same bowl that the cream cheese was in to save washing another dish.) The bread will not be completely immersed, so turn it several times to allow it to absorb the batter evenly. In about 5 minutes the bread will be almost soggy with the batter. Transfer to the baking sheet, leaving space between each piece.

5) Bake for 5 minutes on one side, then turn and bake for 5 to 7 minutes longer, until the bread browns. Top with the reserved strawberries. Dust with confectioners' sugar, if desired.

Per Serving: Calories 451; Protein 20g; Fat 16g (Saturated 8g); Carbohydrates 55g; Fiber 3g; Sodium 737mg

Banana-Stuffed French Toast

Makes: 5 servings

These taste rich and are very filling.

One 1-pound loaf homemade-quality white bread
One 8-ounce package reduced-fat cream
     cheese, softened
1/4 cup honey
2 large ripe bananas, sliced
3 tablespoons chopped walnuts
1/2 teaspoon vanilla extract
4 egg whites
2 whole eggs
1 cup 1% lowfat milk

1) Preheat the oven to 450°F and coat a cookie sheet with a nonstick spray. (Do not use the insulated type of cookie sheet, which prevents browning.)

2) If using an unsliced loaf, cut off the crusty ends of the bread and discard or reserve for another use. Slice the loaf into 10 thick slices. Form a pocket in each slice by cutting up from the bottom crust, almost, but not quite, all the way through to the top. If using presliced bread, you'll need 20 slices.

3) In a small bowl, beat the cheese and honey until creamy. Stir in the bananas and walnuts. Fill the bread pockets with this mixture or spread the filling on 10 slices of bread, then press another on top of each. Place the stuffed bread in an oblong dish.

4) Whisk together the vanilla, egg whites, eggs, and milk. (I use the same bowl that the cream cheese was in to save washing another dish.) Pour this over the bread. The bread will not be completely immersed, so turn it several times to allow it to absorb the batter evenly. In about 5 minutes the bread will be almost soggy with the batter. Once all the batter has been absorbed, transfer to the baking sheet, leaving space between each piece.

5) Bake for 5 minutes on one side, then turn and bake for 5 to 7 minutes longer, until the bread browns.

Per Serving: Calories 550; Protein 21g; Fat 19g (Saturated 9g); Carbohydrates 75g; Fiber 3g; Sodium 738mg

Maple-Stuffed French Toast

Makes: 5 servings

Grade B maple syrup has a more pronounced maple flavor than grade A, yet is delicate enough to pour on pancakes. It can be difficult to find, especially outside New England. I buy a gallon each March at the end of the maple syrup run and hope that it will last until the next year (but it never does). Use either grade A or B here, but please use real maple syrup.

One 1-pound loaf homemade-quality bread
One 8-ounce package reduced-fat cream
    cheese, softened
$1/4$ cup maple syrup
$1/2$ teaspoon vanilla extract
4 egg whites
2 whole eggs
1 cup 1% lowfat milk

1) Preheat the oven to 450°F and coat a cookie sheet with a nonstick spray. (Do not use the insulated type of cookie sheet, which prevents browning.)

2) If using an unsliced loaf, cut off the crusty ends of the bread and discard or reserve for another use. Slice the loaf into 10 thick slices. Form a pocket in each slice by cutting up from the bottom crust, almost, but not quite, all the way through to the top. If using presliced bread, you'll need 20 slices.

3) In a small bowl, beat the cream cheese and maple syrup until creamy. Fill the bread pockets with the cheese mixture or spread the filling on 10 slices of bread, then press another slice on top of each. Place in an oblong dish.

4) Whisk together the vanilla, egg whites, eggs, and milk. (I use the same bowl that the cream cheese was in to save washing another dish.) Pour this over the bread. The bread will not be completely immersed, so turn it several times to allow it to absorb the batter evenly. In about 5 minutes the bread will be almost soggy with the batter. Once all the batter has been absorbed, transfer to the baking sheet, leaving space between each piece.

5) Bake for 5 minutes on one side, then turn and bake for 5 to 7 minutes longer, until the bread browns.

Per Serving: Calories 469; Protein 20g; Fat 16g (Saturated 8g); Carbohydrates 60g; Fiber 2g; Sodium 738mg

Frittatas

Frittatas are similar to omelets, but there are some differences. Rice is often stirred into the egg batter and the frittata is cooked longer and more slowly than an omelet, making it denser and more filling. Because of this, the frittata can be sliced into wedges and can be eaten hot or at room temperature, which makes it a good choice for a brunch buffet.

Broccoli Frittata

Makes: 6 servings

The broccoli florets must be small but still recognizable as florets and must not look chopped. Too large and they stick out of the batter, turn brown, and toughen.

1¹/2 cups broccoli florets, cut into small pieces
1/2 cup shredded carrot
3 eggs
4 egg whites
1/2 cup cooked rice, cooled to room temperature
1 teaspoon dried basil
1/2 teaspoon dried oregano
1/2 teaspoon dried marjoram
1/4 teaspoon kosher salt
1/4 teaspoon freshly ground pepper
2 tablespoons grated Parmesan cheese

1) Steam the broccoli for about 5 minutes, until tender but not soft. During the last 2 minutes, add the shredded carrot to the steamer. Drain and cool to room temperature.

2) In a medium bowl, lightly beat the eggs and egg whites. Stir in the rice, basil, oregano, marjoram, salt, pepper, and cheese.

3) Place the oven rack in the top third of the oven and preheat the oven to 400°F. Coat a 10-inch nonstick pan with an ovenproof handle with nonstick spray. Place it over medium heat on the stovetop.

4) Stir the vegetables into the eggs. Pour the batter into the pan and cook on the stovetop for 5 to 7 minutes, until it sets about halfway through. Do not stir as if scrambling eggs, but do occasionally lift the edges and tilt the pan to let the uncooked egg slide under the cooked. Place the pan in the oven and bake until the top sets and browns, about 8 to 10 minutes. Using insulated oven mitts (the handle will be extremely hot), remove from the oven and run a flexible spatula along the edge and under the frittata to loosen the eggs from the pan. Slip the frittata out of the pan and onto a serving plate.

Per Serving: Calories 82; Protein 7g; Fat 3g (Saturated 3g); Carbohydrates 1g; Fiber 6g; Sodium 193mg

Asparagus Frittata

Makes: 6 servings

Pencil-thin asparagus can be left whole and placed in the frittata in a pattern like spokes on a wheel.

10 slender asparagus stalks
$1/2$ cup chopped roasted red bell pepper
3 eggs
4 egg whites
1 cup cooked rice, cooled to room temperature
1 teaspoon dried basil
$1/2$ teaspoon dried thyme
$1/2$ teaspoon kosher salt
$1/4$ teaspoon freshly ground pepper
1 tablespoon grated Parmesan cheese

1) Trim off the tough ends of the asparagus. Cut the stalks into 1-inch pieces. Steam for about 5 minutes, until tender but not soft. Cool to room temperature. If using jarred roasted pepper, dry on a paper towel. Set the peppers and asparagus aside.

2) In a medium bowl, lightly beat the eggs and egg whites. Stir in the rice, basil, thyme, salt, pepper, and cheese.

3) Place the oven rack in the top third of the oven and preheat the oven to 400°F. Coat a 10-inch nonstick pan with an ovenproof handle with nonstick spray. Place it over medium heat on the stovetop.

4) Stir the asparagus and roasted pepper into the eggs. Do this at the last minute or the vegetables will color the eggs green and red. Pour the batter into the pan and cook on the stovetop for 5 to 7 minutes, until it sets about halfway through. Do not stir as if scrambling eggs, but do occasionally lift the edges and tilt the pan to let the uncooked egg slide under the cooked. Place the pan in the oven and bake until the top sets and browns, about 8 to 10 minutes. Using insulated oven mitts (the handle will be extremely hot), remove from the oven, and run a flexible spatula along the edge and under the frittata to loosen the eggs from the pan. Slip the frittata out of the pan and onto a serving plate.

Per Serving: Calories 94; Protein 7g; Fat 3g (Saturated 1g); Carbohydrates 10g; Fiber 1g; Sodium 249mg

Tomato Frittata

Makes: 6 servings

The tomato must have the seeds and juices removed so that only the pulp remains. Otherwise there would be too much water in the egg batter and it wouldn't set properly.

1 ripe medium tomato (about $^1/2$ pound)
3 eggs
4 egg whites
$^1/2$ cup cooked rice, cooled to room temperature
$^1/2$ cup shredded reduced-fat mozzarella cheese
1 tablespoon grated Parmesan cheese
1 tablespoon fresh chopped basil, or
    1 teaspoon dried
$^1/2$ teaspoon kosher salt
$^1/4$ teaspoon freshly ground pepper

1) Core the tomato and then cut it in half across its equator and squeeze out the seeds. Cut the tomato into $^1/4$-inch slices.

2) In a medium bowl, lightly beat the eggs and egg whites. Stir in the rice, cheeses, basil, salt, and pepper. Place the oven rack in the top third of the oven and preheat the oven to 400°F. Coat a 10-inch nonstick pan with an oven-proof handle with nonstick spray. Place it over medium heat on the stovetop.

3) Stir the tomatoes into the eggs. Pour the batter into the pan and cook on the stovetop for 5 to 7 minutes, until it sets about halfway through. Do not stir as if scrambling eggs, but do occasionally lift the edges and tilt the pan to let the uncooked egg slide under the cooked. Place the pan in the oven and bake until the top sets and browns, about 8 to 10 minutes. Using insulated oven mitts (the handle will be extremely hot), remove from the oven and run a flexible spatula along the edge and under the frittata to loosen the eggs from the pan. Slip the frittata out of the pan and onto a serving plate.

Per Serving: Calories 91; Protein 8g; Fat 4g (Saturated 2g); Carbohydrates 5g; Fiber 0g; Sodium 285mg

Sausage and Cheese Egg Casserole

Makes: 10 servings

Very high-quality and delicious lowfat sausages are showing up not only in gourmet stores but also in supermarkets. They run the gamut of flavors, from smoked chicken and apple to pesto and tomato, and are fun to cook with. That said, old-fashioned breakfast sausage is not likely to be run out of the kitchen anytime soon and its tried-and-true flavor is just right here.

$^1/3$ pound reduced-fat turkey sausage
$1^1/2$ pounds russet potatoes (3 medium), peeled
    and sliced
3 eggs
6 egg whites
1 pound 1% lowfat cottage cheese
$^1/4$ cup grated Parmesan cheese
$^1/2$ cup lowfat sour cream
$^1/4$ teaspoon kosher salt
$^1/4$ cup unbleached, all-purpose white flour
4 scallions, sliced
1 cup grated reduced-fat cheddar cheese

1) Spray a 9×13-inch baking dish with nonstick spray, or use a nonstick pan. Preheat the oven to 350°F.

2) Cook the sausage. If bulk sausage, it can be cooked in a nonstick pan until brown, then drained on paper towels. If link sausage, cook in a small saucepan with about 1/2 inch of water. Cover until browned and cooked through. Then drain and chop. Set aside.

3) Bring a large pot of water to a boil and simmer the potatoes until crisp-tender. Drain, rinse, and place on a clean cloth kitchen towel to absorb the moisture.

4) Whisk together the eggs, egg whites, cottage cheese, Parmesan, sour cream, salt, flour, and scallions.

5) Layer half the potatoes on the bottom of the baking dish. Top with half the sausage. Pour half the egg batter on top. Repeat with the rest of the potatoes, sausage, and egg batter. Distribute the cheddar cheese across the top.

6) Bake in the center of the oven for 40 to 45 minutes, until puffy and set.

Per Serving: Calories 193; Protein 18g; Fat 7g (Saturated 3g); Carbohydrates 16g; Fiber 1g; Sodium 492mg

Chili Egg Casserole

Makes: 6 servings

This casserole puffs up beautifully.

2 eggs
2 egg whites
1 cup nonfat milk
1 cup lowfat sour cream
4 scallions, sliced
1/2 teaspoon kosher salt
ten 6-inch corn tortillas
1 cup shredded reduced-fat jack or cheddar cheese
One 4-ounce can diced mild green chilies
1 1/2 cups cooked black beans, rinsed and drained

1) Spray a shallow or oblong 2 1/2-quart casserole with nonstick spray. Preheat the oven to 375°F.

2) Whisk together the eggs, egg whites, milk, sour cream, scallions, and salt. Cut the tortillas into large wedges.

3) Place one-third of the tortillas on the bottom of the casserole. Top with one-third of the cheese and half the chilies and beans. Arrange one-third of the tortillas on top. Top with the another third of the cheese and the remaining chilies and beans. Spread the rest of the tortilla wedges on top. Pour the egg batter over the casserole. Distribute the remaining cheese on top.

4) Bake in the center of the oven for 25 to 30 minutes, until puffy and set.

Per Serving: Calories 253; Protein 16g; Fat 8g (Saturated 4g); Carbohydrates 33g; Fiber 6g; Sodium 465mg

Fruits and Vegetables

Each meal should include fruits and vegetables, and breakfast is no exception. Along with juice, there are plenty of ways to serve these at the beginning of the day. Potatoes are welcome at breakfast in many forms. Often vegetables are included in frittatas or breakfast casseroles. Dishes like ratatouille are excellent brunch fare.

Fruits are especially easy to include at breakfast. There are breakfast drinks made with fruits in the blender, fruit sauces to top pancakes, and fruit compotes to serve on the side. In some farm communities, fruit pies and cobblers are breakfast fare, which is an old-fashioned country idea that would be welcome at any city breakfast table.

Shredded Hash Browns

Makes: 2 servings

This recipe can be multiplied to feed a crowd.

1 russet potato, peeled ($1/2$ pound)
1 teaspoon vegetable oil
Kosher salt (optional)
Freshly ground pepper (optional)

1) Trim green areas, blemishes, and eyes off the potato. Grate (easily accomplished in a food processor), then wrap the grated potato in a cloth kitchen towel and squeeze out excess moisture.

2) Heat the oil in a 10-inch nonstick pan. Add the potato, distributing it evenly and patting it down with a spatula.

3) Cover and cook over medium-low heat for 10 minutes. Shake the pan occasionally to keep the hash browns from sticking.

4) Flip the patty. Cook for 5 minutes, covered. Then remove the lid and cook for a few minutes more, until the hash browns crisp up.

5) Slip the potatoes out of the pan and onto a serving dish. Cut the patty in half or into wedges. Season with salt and pepper at the table, if desired.

Per Serving: Calories 110; Protein 2g; Fat 2g (Saturated 0g); Carbohydrates 20g; Fiber 2g; Sodium 7mg

Breakfast Potatoes

Makes: 4 servings

The crispy brown edges of sautéed potatoes are where all the flavor is. Oil is necessary, and just enough is used here to get the job done.

$1^1/2$ tablespoons vegetable oil
3 cups cooked cubed potatoes
2 tablespoons minced onions
$1/4$ teaspoon kosher salt
$1/8$ teaspoon paprika

Heat the oil in a pan over moderate-high heat. Stir in all the ingredients and cook until lightly browned, about 5 to 7 minutes, stirring frequently.

Per Serving: Calories 148; Protein 2g; Fat 5g (Saturated 0g); Carbohydrates 24g; Fiber 2g; Sodium 126mg

Applesauce

Makes: 5 servings

Each variety of apple brings its own unique flavor to the sauce. If you are used to supermarket applesauce, you'll be amazed at how distinctive and delicious homemade applesauce can be.

3 pounds apples, cored and quartered
1 cup water (less if the apples are fresh, more if old and dry)
1 cinnamon stick

1) Put the ingredients in a heavy pot, cover, and simmer for 30 minutes. Remove the cinnamon stick.

2) After the apples are cooked, there are several options. The peels can be picked out and discarded. (I like to leave them in during the cooking since they add a nice pink color and thicken the sauce.) Or the peels can be left in and the sauce pureed or run through a food mill. The sauce can also be left chunky, peels and all.

Per Serving: Calories 148; Protein 0g; Fat 1g (Saturated 0g); Carbohydrates 38g; Fiber 5g; Sodium 1mg

Peachy Applesauce

Makes: 6 servings

Almost all fruits, including apricots and strawberries, combine with apples to make delicious fruit sauce. Fruit used for sauce can be blemished but not discolored, and should always be ripe and juicy.

$1^1/2$ pounds peaches
2 pounds apples
$1/2$ cup honey
2 cinnamon sticks
$1/16$ teaspoon ground cloves
$1/8$ teaspoon ground cardamom
$1/4$ to $1/2$ cup water

1) Wash the peaches and remove the pits. This is an easy task if the peaches are a freestone variety, but a bit tedious if the flesh sticks to the pits. You can pit freestone peaches by running a knife around the equator, twisting lightly to pull the halves apart, and then removing the pit. To pit other peaches, you have to cut the flesh from the stone. Use a sharp paring knife and do this over a bowl to catch the juice.

2) Quarter and core the apples.

3) Put the fruit and the remaining ingredients in a pot. Drier, older fruit will need the full $1/2$ cup water. Otherwise, $1/4$ cup will be plenty. Simmer gently, covered, for 30 minutes. Stir once or twice.

4) Remove the cinnamon sticks. Put the sauce through a food mill or puree in a machine.

Per Serving: Calories 205; Protein 1g; Fat 1g (Saturated 0g); Carbohydrates 54g; Fiber 4g; Sodium 1mg

Dried Fruit and Ginger Compote

Makes: 6 servings

Although this is in the breakfast chapter, I also like it for dessert, warmed and topped with vanilla ice cream.

1 pound assorted dried fruit, such as apricots, pears, raisins, and prunes
1 cinnamon stick
2 slices fresh ginger, each about the size of a quarter
1/16 teaspoon ground cloves

1) Put the fruit, cinnamon stick, ginger, and cloves in a saucepan. Pour in enough water to cover. Simmer, covered, for about 1 hour. Stir occasionally.

2) Remove the cinnamon stick and ginger before serving. Serve hot or at room temperature.

Per Serving: Calories 184; Protein 2g; Fat 0g (Saturated 0g); Carbohydrates 48g; Fiber 3g; Sodium 14mg

Stewed Apricots and Prunes

Makes: 4 servings

This lasts for at least a week in the refrigerator, and once it's there you'll be surprised at how often you have a reason to eat stewed fruits.

1/2 pound dried apricots
1/2 pound dried pitted prunes
1 cinnamon stick
1 3/4 cups water
1/2 teaspoon vanilla extract (optional)

Put the fruit, cinnamon stick, and water into a saucepan. Bring to a boil, immediately reduce to a simmer, and cook, uncovered, for 15 minutes. Stir several times. Take off the heat, remove the cinnamon stick, and stir in the vanilla, if desired. Serve warm or at room temperature.

Per Serving: Calories 270; Protein 4g; Fat 1g (Saturated 0g); Carbohydrates 71g; Fiber 10g; Sodium 11mg

Honey and Ginger Broiled Grapefruit

Makes: 2 servings

This is best with a flavorful honey. My favorite comes from bees that pollinate a local cranberry bog.

1 grapefruit, halved
1 tablespoon honey
2 teaspoons minced crystallized ginger

1) Preheat the broiler and set the oven rack 6 inches from the heat source. Line an ovenproof baking dish with foil.

2) Halve the grapefruit. If necessary, cut a slice off of the bottom so that the grapefruit sits flat. Using a serrated grapefruit knife, cut to loosen the segments.

3) Drizzle on the honey and sprinkle with the ginger.

4) Place the grapefruit halves in the broiler, about 4 inches from the heating element, and cook for about 4 minutes, until the edges begin to brown.

Per Serving: Calories 85; Protein 1g; Fat 0g (Saturated 0g); Carbohydrates 22g; Fiber 2g; Sodium 0mg

Sugar and Rum Broiled Grapefruit

Makes: 2 servings

Broiled grapefruit is a wonderful way to start a leisurely brunch.

1 grapefruit, halved
2 tablespoons packed light brown sugar
1 tablespoon rum

1) Preheat the broiler.

2) Halve the grapefruit. Using a serrated grapefruit knife, cut to loosen the segments.

3) Dust with the sugar and drizzle on the rum.

4) Place the grapefruit halves in the broiler, about 4 inches from the heating element, and cook for 4 to 6 minutes, until the edges begin to brown.

Per Serving: Calories 105; Protein 1g; Fat 0g (Saturated 0g); Carbohydrates 23g; Fiber 2g; Sodium 5mg

Very Berry Dairy Shake

Makes: 2 servings

The recipe can be halved or doubled, so make exactly as much as is needed and serve this immediately because it will separate and become grainy with time.

1 cup 1% lowfat milk
1/2 cup plain nonfat yogurt
1 cup frozen blueberries
1 cup other berries of choice, such as raspberries or strawberries
2 to 4 tablespoons honey

Puree all the ingredients in a blender. Add more milk if you want a thinner consistency. Start with 2 tablespoons honey and add more if desired.

Per Serving: Calories 219; Protein 8g; Fat 2g (Saturated 1g); Carbohydrates 45g; Fiber 5g; Sodium 110mg

Banana Yogurt Smoothie

Makes: 2 servings

The confectioners' sugar makes a smoother smoothie than granulated sugar.

2 ripe bananas
1/4 cup confectioners' sugar
1 1/2 cups plain nonfat yogurt
1/4 teaspoon vanilla extract
1/8 teaspoon ground nutmeg

1) Peel the banana, slice into thick coins, then freeze until firm.

2) Puree the bananas, sugar, and yogurt in a blender until smooth. Stir in the vanilla, pour into glasses, and dust with the nutmeg. Serve immediately.

Per Serving: Calories 268; Protein 12g; Fat 1g (Saturated 0g); Carbohydrates 56g; Fiber 2g; Sodium 142mg

Orange Mango Smoothie

Makes: 2 servings

Play with the flavors of yogurt. Peach yogurt would also be marvelous.

1/4 cup frozen orange juice concentrate
8 ounces nonfat mango yogurt
1 cup nonfat vanilla frozen yogurt

Puree all the ingredients in a blender. Serve immediately.

Per Serving: Calories 265; Protein 11g; Fat 0g (Saturated 0 g) carb 55g; Fiber 0g; Sodium 135mg

Fruit and Yogurt Smoothie

Makes: 4 servings

When you start with frozen fruit, the smoothie is as cool and thick as a milk shake.

2 bananas
2/3 cup frozen raspberries
1/3 cup frozen apple juice concentrate
1/3 cup frozen pineapple juice concentrate
1/2 teaspoon lemon juice
2 1/2 cups plain nonfat yogurt

1) Peel the banana, slice into thick coins, then freeze until firm.

2) Puree all ingredients except the yogurt in a blender or food processor. Add the yogurt and blend until smooth, about 30 seconds. Serve immediately.

Per Serving: Calories 230; Protein 10g; Fat 1g (Saturated 0g); Carbohydrates 48g; Fiber 2g; Sodium 124mg

Dairy-Free Fruit Smoothie

Makes: 2 servings

Unlike smoothies made with dairy products, this can be made and then chilled up to 2 hours before serving.

1 ripe banana
4 large strawberries
1/2 cup orange juice
1 cup drained canned pineapple or fresh pieces
1 nectarine or peach, pitted and peeled
1 teaspoon honey, or more to taste

Puree all the ingredients in a blender.

Per Serving: Calories 228; Protein 3g; Fat 1g (Saturated 0g); Carbohydrates 57g; Fiber 5g; Sodium 4mg

Yeast Breads, Quick Breads, and Muffins

Muffins
473

100% Whole Wheat Muffins

Berry-Good Muffins

Blueberry Lemon Muffins

Apple Muffins

Honey Banana Muffins

Cranberry Maple Muffins

Sweet Potato Muffins

Ginger Carrot Muffins

Crystallized Ginger Muffins

Raisin Bran Cereal Muffins

Corn Muffins

Orange–Poppy Seed
Corn Muffins

Jam-Filled Muffins

Maple Cream Cheese–Filled
Muffins

Cottage Cheese–Dill Muffins

Sausage Surprise Muffins

Turkey and Cheese Muffins

Broccoli Cheddar Muffins

Scones
482

Orange Scones

Currant Scones

Lemon Oat Drop Scones

Corn Bread
486

Molasses Corn Bread

Vegetable Corn Bread

Chili Corn Bread

Quick Breads
488

Banana Bread

Blueberry Bran Bread

Orange Cranberry Bread

Pumpkin Bread

Irish Soda Bread

Basic Popovers

Basil Garlic Parmesan Popovers

Whole Wheat Cheddar
Popovers

Biscuits

Skillet Drop Bread

Yeast Breads
723

White Bread

Whole Wheat Bread

Anadama Bread

Oatmeal Bread

Cinnamon Raisin Swirl Bread

Wheat Germ Bread

French Bread

Focaccia
502

Basic Focaccia

Romano and Olive Focaccia

Red Onion and Rosemary
Focaccia

Herb and Garlic Focaccia

Corn Focaccia

It is hard to imagine life without bread in some form. From earliest times grains ground into flour have been transformed into life-giving foods. Although most people rely on professional bakers to supply their breads, making them at home does not require much in the way of skill or special equipment. The effort is worthwhile, if only for the aroma that fills your home.

Muffins

I love muffins, but I also know that a muffin bought at a bakery or from a fast-food chain might contain over 400 calories and 18 grams of fat. Many commercial lowfat versions, though contributing very little fat, still pack in the calories, often topping 250. Luckily, I love making muffins at home.

It is not hard to make excellent lowfat muffins. To make the project go quickly, get organized. Prepare the muffin tins, put the oven rack in the center of the oven, and preheat the oven. Get out your tools: most muffin recipes require only two bowls, a sifter, a whisk, and a spatula. Get out your ingredients. Once all is ready, you are set to cook. From start to finish, fresh muffins can be had in less than 45 minutes (25 of which is spent in anticipation, waiting for them to bake).

One trick to making excellent muffins is to mix the batter by hand, with wide strokes, only until moist. To avoid overbeating but to make sure that the ingredients are evenly distributed in the batter, stir the dry ingredients until the flour mixture is an even color. That way, once the wet and dry ingredients are combined, only a few stirrings with a flexible rubber spatula are necessary to mix the batter. As with most quick breads, lumps are all right, but dry patches are not.

Sizes of muffin cups vary. I prefer not to use the jumbo size, as the muffins' centers don't bake through properly. Fill the muffin cups three-quarters full (you might have a muffin more or less than the recipe specifies).

There are several ways to test if they are done. Color and aroma are good indicators; they will smell cooked and look golden brown. Touch is also a good indictor. If they feel firm and bounce back a bit, they are done.

Once baked, let the muffins sit in their cups for about 3 minutes before removing and cooling on wire racks. Muffins stale fast. What won't be consumed the first day should be frozen. Individual frozen muffins can be warmed in the microwave, but then must be eaten immediately.

100% Whole Wheat Muffins

Makes: 12 muffins

This recipe proves that muffins made from all whole wheat flour don't have to be heavy and dense. If using frozen berries, do not thaw them.

2 cups whole wheat flour
1 teaspoon baking soda
$1^1/4$ cups buttermilk
2 egg whites, lightly beaten
$1/3$ cup vegetable oil
$1/2$ cup honey
1 cup blueberries (fresh or frozen)

1) Preheat the oven to 350°F. Coat 12 muffin cups with nonstick spray.

2) Sift together the flour and baking soda.

3) In a separate bowl, whisk together the buttermilk, egg whites, oil, and honey until creamy, then stir in the blueberries.

4) Pour the wet ingredients into the dry. Fold together with a rubber spatula until the batter is moist yet remains slightly lumpy.

5) Pour into the muffin cups and bake for 30 to 35 minutes.

Per Serving: Calories 184; Protein 4g; Fat 7g (Saturated 1g); Carbohydrates 29g; Fiber 3g; Sodium 143mg

Berry-Good Muffins

Makes: 12 muffins

Any berry, fresh or frozen, can be used here. Do not thaw frozen berries, but, since they chill the batter, add an extra 5 minutes to the cooking time.

1 egg white
1 cup plain nonfat yogurt
1/4 cup vegetable oil
1/4 teaspoon vanilla extract
1/4 cup maple syrup or honey
1 cup whole wheat flour
1 cup unbleached, all-purpose white flour
1/4 cup sugar
1/4 teaspoon salt
1/2 teaspoon baking soda
1 1/2 teaspoons baking powder
1 1/2 cups berries

1) Preheat the oven to 350°F. Coat 12 muffin cups with nonstick spray.

2) Whisk together the egg white, yogurt, oil, vanilla, and maple syrup.

3) In a separate bowl, sift together the flours, sugar, salt, baking soda, and baking powder. Stir.

4) Pour the wet ingredients into the dry, and fold together with a rubber spatula until moist but still slightly lumpy. Fold in the berries.

5) Pour into the muffin cups and bake for 25 to 30 minutes.

Per Serving: Calories 164; Protein 4g; Fat 5g (Saturated 0g); Carbohydrates 27g; Fiber 2g; Sodium 180mg

Blueberry Lemon Muffins

Makes: 12 muffins

I use two sweeteners here, honey and sugar. The honey contributes flavor, but if only honey were used the muffins would be tough. The sugar adds sweetness and a soft crumb texture.

1 egg white
1 whole egg
1 cup plain nonfat yogurt
1/4 cup vegetable oil
1/2 teaspoon vanilla extract
1/4 cup honey
1/3 cup sugar
1 tablespoon minced lemon zest
1 cup unbleached, all-purpose white flour
1 cup whole wheat flour
1/4 teaspoon kosher salt
1 teaspoon baking soda
1 teaspoon baking powder
1 cup blueberries (fresh or frozen)

1) Preheat the oven to 350°F. Coat 12 muffin cups with nonstick spray.

2) Beat together the egg white, egg, yogurt, oil, vanilla, honey, sugar, and lemon zest.

3) In a separate bowl, sift together the dry ingredients and stir until well blended.

4) Pour the wet ingredients into the dry. Fold together with a rubber spatula until the batter is moist but still lumpy. Stir in the blueberries (if frozen, do not thaw).

5) Pour into the muffin cups and bake for 25 to 30 minutes.

Per Serving: Calories 177; Protein 5g; Fat 5g (Saturated 1g); Carbohydrates 29g; Fiber 2g; Sodium 213mg

Apple Muffins

Makes: 12 muffins

The apples are grated, not chopped, because the grated fruit is easy to distribute evenly throughout the batter and it doesn't sink to the bottom as the muffins bake.

2 cups whole wheat flour
1/2 cup unbleached, all-purpose white flour
1 teaspoon ground cinnamon
1/8 teaspoon ground allspice
1 1/2 teaspoons baking soda
1/2 teaspoon baking powder
2 egg whites
1 cup buttermilk
1/4 cup vegetable oil
1/2 cup honey
2 apples, peeled and grated (about 1 1/2 cups)

1) Preheat the oven to 350°F. Coat 12 muffin cups with nonstick spray.

2) Sift together the dry ingredients.

3) In another bowl, beat the egg whites, buttermilk, oil, and honey until creamy. Stir in the apples.

4) Pour wet ingredients into the dry. Stir until moist.

5) Pour into the muffin cups and bake for 25 to 30 minutes.

Per Serving: Calories 191; Protein 5g; Fat 5g (Saturated 1g); Carbohydrates 34g; Fiber 3g; Sodium 210mg

Honey Banana Muffins

Makes: 18 muffins

Because the batter is heavy with bananas, the eggs are beaten to a soft peak and then folded in. This gives the muffins a stonger though lighter structure than if the eggs where just whisked in with the rest of the wet ingredients.

1 cup unbleached, all-purpose white flour
2 cups whole wheat flour
2 teaspoons baking soda
1/4 teaspoon salt
1/4 teaspoon ground nutmeg
2/3 cup honey
1 1/3 cups buttermilk
1/3 cup vegetable oil
3 egg whites, beaten to a soft peak
2 ripe bananas, mashed (about 1 cup)

1) Preheat the oven to 350°F. Coat 18 muffin cups with nonstick spray.

2) Sift together the dry ingredients.

3) Whisk together the honey, buttermilk, and oil. Gently stir in the egg whites. Stir in the the bananas.

4) Pour the wet ingredients into the dry. Fold together with a rubber spatula until the batter is moist but remains lumpy.

5) Pour into the muffin cups and bake for 25 to 30 minutes.

Per Serving: Calories 163; Protein 4g; Fat 5g (Saturated 0g); Carbohydrates 29g; Fiber 2g; Sodium 199mg

Cranberry Maple Muffins

Makes: 12 muffins

You can tell that I come from New England and not California. I rarely see the plethora of interesting produce found on the West Coast, like baby artichokes, so you won't find them in this book, but I still have plenty of regional foods to cook with. Here are two favorites, cranberries and maple syrup, both of which are grown right in the town where I live (and I'm only 30 miles from Boston). They travel well, though, so you should be able to find them in your hometown, too.

2 cups whole wheat flour
1 teaspoon baking soda
$1/4$ teaspoon salt
1 cup buttermilk
2 egg whites
$1/4$ cup maple syrup
$1/4$ cup vegetable oil
2 tablespoons honey
1 cup cranberries (fresh or frozen), sorted
    and rinsed

1) Preheat the oven to 350°F. Coat 12 muffin cups with nonstick spray.

2) Sift together the flour, baking soda, and salt. Stir.

3) In another bowl, whisk together the buttermilk, egg whites, maple syrup, oil, and honey.

4) Pour the wet ingredients into the dry. Fold with a rubber spatula until the batter is moist but remains lumpy. Fold in the cranberries (if frozen, do not thaw).

5) Pour into greased muffin cups and bake for 25 to 30 minutes, until lightly browned on top.

Per Serving: Calories 151; Protein 4g; Fat 5g (Saturated 1g); Carbohydrates 24g; Fiber 3g; Sodium 182mg

Sweet Potato Muffins

Makes: 18 muffins

When my son was very young he rejected baby food (too mushy!). These muffins were how I fed him sweet potatoes. The rest of the family was pleased to see muffins on the table instead of jars of baby food, so all were happy.

$2 1/4$ cups unbleached, all-purpose white flour
1 tablespoon baking powder
1 teaspoon baking soda
$1/2$ teaspoon salt
$1/2$ teaspoon ground cinnamon
$1/2$ teaspoon ground allspice
1 tablespoon unsalted butter
$1/2$ cup packed light brown sugar
2 egg whites
2 cups buttermilk
3 tablespoons vegetable oil
1 cup mashed, cooked sweet potato (from about
    1 large potato)

1) Preheat the oven to 375°F. Coat 16 muffin cups with nonstick spray.

2) Sift together the dry ingredients. Stir until no brown streaks of spices remain.

3) In another bowl, beat the butter and brown sugar until no lumps remain. Then beat in the egg whites, buttermilk, oil, and sweet potato. Pour the wet ingredients into the dry. Gently fold the two together until an evenly moist batter forms.

4) Pour into the muffin cups and bake for 25 minutes, until done.

Per Serving: Calories 123; Protein 3g; Fat 3g (Saturated 1g); Carbohydrates 21g; Fiber 1g; Sodium 249mg

Ginger Carrot Muffins

Makes: 12 muffins

For an extra ginger boost, top with chopped crystallized ginger before baking.

1 teaspoon ground ginger
1 cup whole wheat flour
1¼ cups unbleached, all-purpose white flour
¼ teaspoon kosher salt
½ teaspoon ground cinnamon
1½ teaspoons baking powder
½ teaspoon baking soda
¾ cup buttermilk
3 tablespoons vegetable oil
½ cup honey
1 egg white
1 whole egg
1 large carrot, grated (1 cup)

1) Preheat the oven to 350°F. Coat 12 muffin cups with nonstick spray.

2) Sift together the dry ingredients. Stir until no brown streaks of spices remain.

3) Beat together the buttermilk, oil, honey, egg white, and egg. Stir in the carrot.

4) Stir the wet ingredients into the dry. Fold together until the batter is moist but still lumpy.

5) Pour into the muffin cups and bake for 25 to 30 minutes.

Per Serving: Calories 167; Protein 4g; Fat 4g (Saturated 1g); Carbohydrates 30g; Fiber 2g; Sodium 184mg

Crystallized Ginger Muffins

Makes: 12 muffins

I love crystallized ginger and can buy very good, inexpensive bags of it at a local Asian food market. If all you can find are small expensive bottles, you might want to make your own.

2 cups unbleached, all-purpose white flour
1 cup whole wheat flour
½ teaspoon salt
1½ teaspoons baking soda
1 teaspoon baking powder
¼ teaspoon ground nutmeg
¼ teaspoon ground ginger
1½ cups buttermilk
¼ cup vegetable oil
1 teaspoon vanilla extract
2 egg whites
½ cup honey
¼ cup finely chopped crystallized ginger

1) Preheat the oven to 350°F. Coat 12 muffin cups with nonstick spray.

2) Sift together the flours, salt, baking soda, baking powder, nutmeg, and ground ginger.

3) In another bowl, whisk together the buttermilk, oil, vanilla, egg whites, and honey.

4) Pour the wet ingredients into the dry. Gently fold the two together until an evenly moist batter forms. Stir in the crystallized ginger.

5) Spoon into the muffin cups. Bake for 25 minutes, until done.

Per Serving: Calories 215; Protein 5g; Fat 5g (Saturated 1g); Carbohydrates 39g; Fiber 2g; Sodium 329mg

Raisin Bran Cereal Muffins

Makes: 16 muffins

The zucchini moistens what might otherwise be a dry muffin.

2 cups unbleached, all-purpose white flour
$1/2$ cup sugar
$1/2$ teaspoon salt
2 teaspoons baking soda
$1^1/2$ teaspoons baking powder
3 cups raisin bran cereal
2 cups buttermilk
$1/4$ cup vegetable oil
1 egg white
1 egg
1 cup shredded zucchini

1) Preheat the oven to 400°F. Coat 16 muffin cups with nonstick spray.

2) Sift together the flour, sugar, salt, baking soda, and baking powder. Stir in the cereal.

3) In another bowl, whisk together the buttermilk, oil, egg white, and egg. Put the zucchini in a colander in the sink and squeeze the vegetable in your hand until most of the water comes out. Stir the zucchini into the wet ingredients.

4) Pour the wet ingredients into the dry. Gently fold the two together until an evenly moist batter forms. Spoon the batter into the muffin cups.

5) Bake for 20 to 25 minutes, until done.

Per Serving: Calories 156; Protein 4g; Fat 4g (Saturated 1g); Carbohydrates 26g; Fiber 2g; Sodium 368mg

Corn Muffins

Makes: 12 muffins

Toasted corn muffins with jam are a great way to start the day (or have an afternoon break, or a late-night snack).

$1/2$ cup whole wheat flour
$1^1/2$ cups unbleached, all-purpose white flour
1 cup cornmeal
1 tablespoon baking powder
$1/4$ teaspoon salt
$1/3$ cup vegetable oil
$1^1/2$ cups 1% lowfat milk
2 tablespoons molasses
$1/4$ cup honey
1 egg white, beaten

1) Preheat the oven to 375°F. Coat 12 muffin cups with nonstick spray.

2) Sift together the dry ingredients and stir.

3) In a separate bowl, whisk together the oil, milk, molasses, and honey.

4) Pour the wet ingredients into the dry and fold with a rubber spatula until moist. Fold in the egg white.

5) Pour into the muffin cups and bake for 30 minutes, until the edges just start to brown.

Per Serving: Calories 202; Protein 4g; Fat 7g (Saturated 1g); Carbohydrates 32g; Fiber 2g; Sodium 192mg

Orange–Poppy Seed Corn Muffins

Makes: 12 muffins

These are very pretty and full of flavor, though not very sweet.

1 cup whole wheat flour
1 cup unbleached, all-purpose white flour
$^1/_2$ cup cornmeal
1 teaspoon baking powder
2 teaspoons baking soda
$^1/_2$ teaspoon salt
$1^1/_2$ teaspoons poppy seeds
1 orange
1 cup plain nonfat yogurt
2 egg whites
3 tablespoons vegetable oil
$^1/_3$ cup honey

1) Preheat the oven to 350°F. Coat 12 muffin cups with nonstick spray.

2) Sift together the dry ingredients and stir.

3) Zest the orange until you have 1 tablespoon of zest, and then squeeze out $^1/_3$ cup of juice. Put the zest, juice, yogurt, egg whites, oil, and honey in a bowl. Beat until slightly foamy.

4) Pour the wet ingredients into the dry. Gently but quickly fold the two together until an evenly moist batter forms.

5) Fill the muffin cups about three-quarters full.

6) Bake for 25 minutes, until the muffins are golden and firm to the touch.

Per Serving: Calories 164; Protein 5g; Fat 4g (Saturated 0g); Carbohydrates 29g; Fiber 2g; Sodium 367mg

Jam-Filled Muffins

Makes: 10 muffins

Finding a mouthful of warm jam inside a muffin is a delightful surprise.

$1^1/_2$ cups unbleached, all-purpose white flour
$^1/_2$ cup whole wheat flour
$^1/_4$ teaspoon salt
$^1/_2$ teaspoon baking soda
2 teaspoons baking powder
$1^1/_4$ cups buttermilk
$^1/_4$ cup vegetable oil
2 egg whites
$^1/_4$ cup sugar
$^1/_4$ cup jam

1) Preheat the oven to 375°F. Coat 10 muffin cups with nonstick spray.

2) Sift together the flours, salt, baking soda, and baking powder.

3) In another bowl, whisk together the buttermilk, oil, egg whites, and sugar.

4) Pour the wet ingredients into the dry. Gently fold together until an evenly moist batter forms.

5) Spoon into the muffin cups until they are one-quarter full. Drop a teaspoon of jam in the center of each muffin, then finish filling the muffin cups with batter.

6) Bake for 20 to 25 minutes, until the muffins are golden and firm to the touch.

Per Serving: Calories 183; Protein 4g; Fat 6g (Saturated 1g); Carbohydrates 29g; Fiber 1g; Sodium 261mg

Maple Cream Cheese–Filled Muffins

Makes: 10 muffins

Instead of jam, these are oozing with sweet, soft cheese. They are excellent both warm and at room temperature.

1/4 cup reduced-fat cream cheese
2 tablespoons maple syrup
1 recipe Jam-Filled Muffins, without the jam (page 479)

1) Beat the cream cheese and maple syrup together until smooth.

2) Follow directions for Jam-Filled Muffins. In Step 5, instead of spooning in the jam, drop in a teaspoon of the sweetened cream cheese.

Per Serving: Calories 188; Protein 5g; Fat 7g (Saturated 1g); Carbohydrates 26g; Fiber 1g; Sodium 282mg

Cottage Cheese–Dill Muffins

Makes: 12 muffins

These savory muffins could be put a basket of rolls at dinner, or eaten at breakfast with an egg casserole.

1 2/3 cups unbleached, all-purpose white flour
1/2 teaspoon salt
4 teaspoons sugar
1 tablespoon baking powder
1 teaspoon baking soda
1 1/2 teaspoons dried dill, or 1 tablespoon minced fresh
2 egg whites
1 egg
1 3/4 cups 1% lowfat cottage cheese, not drained
3 tablespoons vegetable oil
1/4 cup lowfat sour cream

1) Preheat the oven to 375°F. Coat 12 large muffin cups generously with nonstick spray.

2) Sift together the flour, salt, sugar, baking powder, and baking soda. Stir in the dill.

3) In another bowl, using an electric mixer, beat the egg whites, egg, and cottage cheese until blended but still lumpy. Beat in the oil and sour cream on low speed. Gently fold the wet ingredients into the dry until a moist batter forms. Spoon into the muffin cups.

4) Bake for 25 minutes, until the muffins are golden and firm to the touch.

Per Serving: Calories 130; Protein 7g; Fat 5g (Saturated 1g); Carbohydrates 15g; Fiber 0g; Sodium 269mg

Sausage Surprise Muffins

Makes: 12 muffins

For health reasons, many people are forgoing rashers of bacon, but small amounts of breakfast meats placed in recipes like this (or the Sausage and Cheese Egg Casserole, page 464) keep those favorite foods on the table.

2 cups unbleached, all-purpose white flour
$1/4$ cup cornmeal
1 teaspoon salt
4 teaspoons sugar
1 tablespoon baking powder
$1^1/2$ teaspoons baking soda
2 egg whites
1 egg
$1^1/2$ cups buttermilk
3 tablespoons vegetable oil
2 ounces breakfast sausage links (preferably
    lowfat), cooked and sliced into 12 pieces

1) Preheat the oven to 375°F. Coat 12 muffin cups with nonstick spray.

2) Sift together the flour, cornmeal, salt, sugar, baking powder, and baking soda and stir.

3) In another bowl, whisk together the egg whites, egg, buttermilk, and oil. Pour the wet ingredients into the dry. Gently fold the two together until an evenly moist batter forms. Spoon into the muffin cups until they are two-thirds full. Put a piece of sausage in the center of each muffin. Top with the remaining batter.

5) Bake for 20 to 25 minutes, until the muffins are golden and firm to the touch.

Per Serving: Calories 142; Protein 5g; Fat 5g (Saturated 1g); Carbohydrates 19g; Fiber 1g; Sodium 543mg

Turkey and Cheese Muffins

Makes: 12 muffins

Home-cooked turkey or turkey from the deli can be used, but each produces different results. Deli turkey makes muffins with a stronger, sometimes smoked, often saltier flavor than mild home-cooked.

2 cups unbleached, all-purpose white flour
$1/4$ teaspoon salt
1 tablespoon sugar
1 tablespoon baking powder
$1^1/2$ teaspoons baking soda
1 egg
1 egg white
$1^1/2$ cups plain nonfat yogurt
$1/4$ cup vegetable oil
1 cup shredded reduced-fat cheese
$1/2$ cup chopped cooked turkey breast

1) Preheat the oven to 375°F. Coat 12 muffin cups with nonstick spray.

2) Sift together the flour, salt, sugar, baking powder, and baking soda, and stir.

3) In another bowl, whisk together the egg, egg white, yogurt, and oil. Stir in the cheese and turkey, then pour the wet ingredients into the dry. Gently fold the two together until an evenly moist batter forms. Spoon into the muffin cups.

4) Bake for 25 minutes, until the muffins are golden and firm to the touch. Remove the muffins from the tin and cool them on a rack.

Per Serving: Calories 160; Protein 8g; Fat 6g (Saturated 1g); Carbohydrates 18g; Fiber 0g; Sodium 403mg

Broccoli Cheddar Muffins

Makes: 12 muffins

This is a good use for leftover steamed broccoli. Frozen broccoli, lightly cooked, can also be used.

2 cups unbleached, all-purpose white flour
2 teaspoons baking powder
1¹/2 teaspoons baking soda
1 tablespoon sugar
¹/2 teaspoon salt
1 egg white
1¹/2 cups buttermilk
¹/4 cup vegetable oil
¹/2 cup reduced-fat cheddar cheese
1 cup chopped steamed broccoli

1) Preheat the oven to 375°F. Coat 12 muffin cups with nonstick spray.

2) Sift together the flour, baking powder, baking soda, sugar, and salt and stir.

3) In another bowl, whisk together the egg white, buttermilk, and oil. Pour the wet ingredients into the dry. Gently fold the two together until an evenly moist batter forms. Stir in the cheese and broccoli.

4) Pour into the muffin tins and bake for 25 minutes, until the muffins are golden and firm to the touch.

Per Serving: Calories 137; Protein 5g; Fat 6g (Saturated 1g); Carbohydrates 17g; Fiber 1g; Sodium 390mg

Scones

Scones have arrived on the scene as an alternative to muffins. Like muffins, traditional versions are packed with fat—one national chain has a scone that weighs in with 26 grams of fat and 530 calories! I've greatly lightened my scones, but retained the texture and flavor of the originals. I've done this by using a very small amount of butter and by handling them quickly and gently. Unlike full-fat scones, these cannot be made in the food processor.

Orange Scones

Makes: 12 scones

To make lemon scones, substitute lemon peel for the orange.

1/2 cup sugar, divided
2 1/4 cups unbleached, all-purpose white flour
2 teaspoons baking powder
1 teaspoon baking soda
1/2 teaspoon salt
2 teaspoons minced orange zest
2 tablespoons unsalted butter, kept firm and cold until use
1 tablespoon vegetable oil
1 cup buttermilk
2 tablespoons nonfat milk

1) Preheat the oven to 375°F. Coat a baking sheet with nonstick spray.

2) Set aside 1 teaspoon of the sugar, then sift the rest with the flour, baking powder, baking soda, and salt. Stir in the zest until all is well mixed.

3) Cut the butter into tiny pieces and add it to the dry ingredients. Blend it with your fingertips so that it forms tiny balls with the flour.

4) Pour in the oil and buttermilk and stir with a stiff spatula until a ball of sticky dough forms.

5) Put the dough onto a floured flat surface. Knead quickly into a lumpy ball. Turn over in the flour once or twice to keep it from sticking to you or the surface. Flatten into a 1/2-inch-thick rectangle. Use a drinking glass or other circle cutter about 3 inches in diameter to cut out the scones. Place them on the baking sheet; don't crowd because they will expand. Quickly and gently combine and flatten the dough scraps to cut again. Alternatively, the rectangle can be cut into 12 triangles.

6) Brush the scones with the milk and dust with the reserved sugar. Bake for 15 minutes, until they begin to turn golden. Remove from the oven and cool on a wire rack.

Per Serving: Calories 143; Protein 3g; Fat 4g (Saturated 1g); Carbohydrates 25g; Fiber 1g; Sodium 298mg

Currant Scones

Makes: 12 scones

Currants look like tiny raisins, but their small size and unique flavor sets them apart. If currants are not available, don't use raisins, which are too plump and large for this recipe. Instead, try dried cranberries, blueberries, or diced dried fruit.

$1/2$ cup sugar, divided
$2^1/4$ cups unbleached, all-purpose white flour
$1/2$ teaspoon ground cinnamon
2 teaspoons baking powder
1 teaspoon baking soda
$1/2$ teaspoon salt
2 tablespoons unsalted butter, kept firm and cold until use
1 tablespoon vegetable oil
1 cup buttermilk
$1/2$ teaspoon vanilla extract
$1/2$ cup currants
2 tablespoons nonfat milk

1) Preheat the oven to 375°F. Coat a baking sheet with nonstick spray or line with parchment paper.

2) Set aside 1 teaspoon of the sugar, then sift the rest with the flour, cinnamon, baking powder, baking soda, and salt. Stir well.

3) Cut the butter into tiny pieces and add it to the dry ingredients. Blend it with your fingertips so that it forms tiny balls with the flour.

4) Pour in the oil, buttermilk, and vanilla and stir with a stiff spatula until a sticky dough ball forms. Stir in the currants.

5) Put the dough onto a floured flat surface. Knead quickly into a lumpy ball. Turn over in the flour once or twice to keep it from sticking to you or the surface. Flatten into a $1/2$-inch-thick rectangle. Use a drinking glass or other circular cutter about 3 inches in diameter to cut out the scones. Place them on the baking sheet; don't crowd because they will expand. Quickly and gently combine and flatten the dough scraps to cut again. Alternatively, the rectangle can be cut into 12 triangles.

6) Brush the scones with the milk and dust with the reserved sugar. Bake for 15 minutes, until they begin to turn golden. Remove from the oven and cool on a wire rack.

Per Serving: Calories 147; Protein 3g; Fat 4g (Saturated 1g); Carbohydrates 26g; Fiber 1g; Sodium 298mg

Lemon Oat Drop Scones

Makes: 14 scones

These scones have a sticky, wet batter and so are dropped onto the baking sheet, not cut into shapes. The end result, though, is light and flavorful, with universal appeal. I brought a batch to my toddler's preschool and the little ones ate them, crystallized ginger and all.

1/3 cup sugar, divided
2 tablespoons unsalted butter
1 3/4 cups unbleached, all-purpose white flour
2 teaspoons baking powder
1 teaspoon baking soda
1/2 teaspoon salt
3/4 cup old-fashioned rolled oats
2 teaspoons minced lemon zest
2 tablespoons finely minced crystallized ginger
1 tablespoon vegetable oil
1 cup buttermilk
2 tablespoons nonfat milk

1) Preheat the oven to 375°F. Line one large baking sheet with parchment paper.

2) Set aside 1 teaspoon of the sugar, then, using a mixer, beat the rest with the butter until the texture becomes evenly granular like coarse sand. Sift the flour, baking powder, baking soda, and salt into the bowl. Add the oats, zest, and ginger. Stir with a rubber spatula until well mixed.

3) Pour in the oil and buttermilk and stir with a stiff spatula until a sticky dough forms.

4) Drop large portions of dough onto the baking sheets. Leave room between the scones because they will spread. Use a spatula to shape the scones into rough circles about 3 inches in diameter.

5) Brush the scones with the milk and dust with the reserved sugar. Bake for 15 minutes, until they begin to turn golden. Remove from the oven and cool on a wire rack.

Per Serving: Calories 123; Protein 3g; Fat 3g (Saturated 1g); Carbohydrates 21g; Fiber 1g; Sodium 256mg

Cornbread

ach region has its own taste in cornbread. In New England corn bread tends to be sweet; in the South it is saltier and more savory. Whichever way you like it, always start with the best cornmeal. If you have access to stone-ground cornmeal that includes the corn kernel's germ, buy it. Its flavor is rich and it is dense with nutrients. Such cornmeal needs to be kept refrigerated because it goes rancid quickly. Stoneground cornmeal is available through mail order and at many natural food stores. However, these recipes are still worth baking with super-market cornmeal.

1) Preheat the oven to 400°F. Coat an 8×8-inch pan with nonstick spray.

2) Combine the dry ingredients until well blended.

3) Whisk together the wet ingredients, then stir them into the dry.

4) Pour into the pan and bake for 20 minutes, until the center springs back when depressed. Be careful not to overcook or the corn bread will be heavy and dry. If cooked properly it will be light and moist and will remain that way for 2 days.

Per Serving: Calories 160; Protein 3g; Fat 7g (Saturated 1g); Carbohydrates 22g; Fiber 1g; Sodium 193mg

Molasses Cornbread

Makes: 12 servings

The molasses brings a mellow, not pronounced, sweetness to this recipe.

1 cup cornmeal
1 cup unbleached, all-purpose white flour
2^1/$_2$ teaspoons baking powder
^{1}/$_2$ teaspoon baking soda
^{1}/$_3$ cup vegetable oil
^{1}/$_4$ cup molasses
1^1/$_4$ cups buttermilk
2 egg whites

Vegetable Cornbread

Makes: 12 servings

For a less spicy version, use canned mild green chilies instead of jalapeños.

1^1/$_4$ cups cornmeal
1 cup unbleached, all-purpose white flour
1 tablespoon sugar
1 tablespoon baking powder
^{1}/$_2$ teaspoon baking soda
^{1}/$_2$ teaspoon salt
1^1/$_4$ cups buttermilk
^{1}/$_4$ cup vegetable oil
2 egg whites, lightly beaten
1 cup shredded zucchini, excess water
    squeezed out
^{1}/$_2$ cup chopped fresh or roasted red bell pepper,
    patted dry
^{1}/$_2$ cup corn kernels, thawed if frozen
1 tablespoon chopped canned jalapeño peppers

1) Preheat the oven to 450°F. Coat an 8×8-inch pan with nonstick spray.

2) Combine the cornmeal, flour, sugar, baking powder, baking soda, and salt. Stir until well blended.

3) Stir in the buttermilk, oil, and egg whites until all is moist but still lumpy. Stir in the remaining ingredients.

4) Pour the batter into the pan.

5) Bake for 30 minutes, until the center feels firm to the touch.

Per Serving: Calories 152; Protein 4g; Fat 5g (Saturated 1g); Carbohydrates 23g; Fiber 2g; Sodium 311mg

Chili Cornbread

Makes: 12 servings

This savory, spicy cornbread would suit many menus, but you might want to try it for lunch along with a bean salad.

1 cup cornmeal
1 cup unbleached, all-purpose white flour
1 teaspoon baking powder
1/2 teaspoon baking soda
1/4 teaspoon kosher salt
2 tablespoons vegetable oil
1 cup buttermilk
1 egg
1/4 cup sugar
One 4-ounce can chopped mild green
    chilies, drained

1) Preheat the oven to 400°F. Coat an 8×8-inch pan with nonstick spray.

2) Sift together the cornmeal, flour, baking powder, baking soda, and salt. Toss in any cornmeal that's too coarse for the sifter. Stir the dry ingredients until there are no streaks of white and yellow.

3) Whisk together the oil, buttermilk, and egg. Beat in the sugar. Stir in the chilies.

4) Make a depression in the center of the dry ingredients and pour the wet ingredients into it. Stir with a rubber spatula until the batter is evenly wet but still lumpy.

5) Pour into the pan. Gently spread the batter evenly across the pan.

6) Bake for 30 minutes, until the top begins to brown and the center is firm. Cool the bread in the pan for about 10 minutes before turning it out onto a wire rack, or it can be left in, and served from, the baking pan.

Per Serving: Calories 127; Protein 3g; Fat 3g (Saturated 0g); Carbohydrates 21g; Fiber 1g; Sodium 186mg

Quick Breads

Banana Bread

Makes: 1 loaf (12 slices)

Bananas are still good for baking when their skins turn darkly mottled, but they are past their prime when their sweet smell is sharp, or the fruit is bruised and mushy.

1$^1/_2$ cups mashed banana (about 3 bananas)
2 egg whites
1 cup sugar
1 teaspoon vanilla extract
$^1/_4$ cup vegetable oil
$^1/_2$ cup plain nonfat yogurt
2$^1/_4$ cups unbleached, all-purpose white flour
$^1/_4$ teaspoon salt
1$^1/_2$ teaspoons baking powder
$^1/_2$ teaspoon baking soda

1) Preheat the oven to 375°F. Coat a large loaf pan (about 9×4 inches) with nonstick spray.

2) With an electric mixer on medium speed, beat the banana, egg whites, sugar, vanilla, oil, and yogurt. Sift the flour, salt, baking powder, and baking soda into another bowl. Stir until well mixed. Then, beating at low speed, add the dry ingredients to the banana batter. Stop beating as soon as the batter is moist.

3) Spread into the loaf pan and bake for 50 to 60 minutes, until a toothpick inserted in the center comes out clean. Cool in the pan for 10 minutes before turning onto a wire rack.

Per Slice: Calories 214; Protein 4g; Fat 5g (Saturated 0g); Carbohydrates 40g; Fiber 1g; Sodium 175mg

Blueberry Bran Bread

Makes: 1 loaf (12 slices)

Although it is tempting, don't cut into this bread until it has cooled to almost room temperature. The cooling helps a fine, crumbly texture to develop. If cut while still hot, the loaf won't ever achieve that desired texture.

$^1/_4$ cup sugar
1$^1/_3$ cups unbleached, all-purpose white flour
$^1/_4$ teaspoon salt
2 teaspoons baking powder
$^1/_2$ cup wheat bran
$^1/_4$ cup wheat germ
2 egg whites
1 egg
$^1/_4$ cup vegetable oil
$^1/_4$ cup maple syrup
$^1/_4$ cup buttermilk
$^1/_2$ cup packed light brown sugar
1 teaspoon vanilla extract
1 cup blueberries (fresh or frozen)

1) Preheat the oven to 375°F. Coat a large loaf pan (about 9×4 inches) with nonstick spray.

2) Sift together the sugar, flour, salt, and baking powder into a bowl. Stir in the bran and wheat germ and mix well. With an electric mixer on medium speed, beat the egg whites, egg, oil, maple syrup, buttermilk, brown sugar, and vanilla. If the brown sugar is lumpy, crumble it between your fingers before using. If the lumps are hard, soften very briefly in the microwave before adding to the wet ingredients.

3) Stir the wet ingredients into the dry. Stir in the blueberries.

3) Spread the batter into the loaf pan and bake for 50 to 60 minutes, until a toothpick inserted in the center comes out clean. Tent with foil if the top browns too quickly. Cool in the pan for 10 minutes before turning onto a wire rack.

Per Slice: Calories 184; Protein 4g; Fat 6g (Saturated 1g); Carbohydrates 32g; Fiber 2g; Sodium 151mg

Orange Cranberry Bread

Makes: 1 loaf (12 slices)

Even though I bake quick breads in the center of my oven, I still need to rotate them once during cooking because the back right corner of my oven runs hot. Get to know your oven. This is especially important with lowfat recipes because they lack the fat to conduct heat evenly throughout the batter.

2 egg whites
1 egg
1/4 cup vegetable oil
1/4 cup orange juice
1/4 cup buttermilk
3/4 cup packed light brown sugar
1 teaspoon vanilla extract
1/4 cup sugar
2 cups unbleached, all-purpose white flour
1/4 teaspoon salt
2 teaspoons baking powder
1 cup cranberries
2 teaspoons finely minced orange zest

1) Preheat the oven to 375°F. Coat a large loaf pan (about 9×4 inches) with nonstick spray.

2) With an electric mixer on medium speed, beat the egg whites, egg, oil, juice, buttermilk, brown sugar, and vanilla. Sift the sugar, flour, salt, and baking powder into another bowl. Stir until well mixed. Blend the wet ingredients into the dry. Stir in the cranberries and orange zest.

3) Spread the batter into the loaf pan and bake for 60 minutes, until a toothpick inserted in the center comes out clean. Tent with foil if the top browns too quickly. Cool in the pan for 10 minutes before turning onto a wire rack.

Per Slice: Calories 193; Protein 3g; Fat 5g (Saturated 1g); Carbohydrates 34g; Fiber 1g; Sodium 151mg

Pumpkin Bread

Makes: 1 loaf (12 slices)

Slather thick slices with cream cheese.

$1/2$ cup unbleached, all-purpose white flour
2 cups whole wheat flour
$1/2$ teaspoon salt
$1^1/2$ teaspoons ground cinnamon
$1/8$ teaspoon ground cloves
$1/4$ teaspoon ground nutmeg
$1/2$ teaspoon ground ginger
1 teaspoon baking powder
1 teaspoon baking soda
1 cup pumpkin puree
3 tablespoons vegetable oil
1 cup honey
$1/2$ cup buttermilk
1 whole egg
1 egg white

1) Preheat the oven to 350°F. Coat 2 small loaf pans or 1 large one with nonstick spray.

2) Sift together the dry ingredients until there are no dark spice streaks.

3) In a separate bowl, beat together the remaining ingredients.

4) Pour the wet ingredients into the dry. Gently but quickly fold the two together until a moist batter forms. Pour the batter into the pan(s).

5) Bake the smaller loaves for 35 to 40 minutes and the large one for 50 minutes to 1 hour. If your oven heats unevenly, turn the pan(s) once during baking. The bread is done when the color becomes an even golden brown, the loaves feel firm to the touch, and the crack along the top looks baked, not raw. Let the bread cool in the pans for 5 minutes, then turn out onto a cooling rack.

Per Slice: Calories 221; Protein 5g; Fat 4g (Saturated 1g); Carbohydrates 44g; Fiber 3g; Sodium 258mg

Irish Soda Bread

Makes: 1 loaf (20 slices)

This is excellent with apple butter or thick jam.

1 cup whole wheat flour
$1^1/4$ cups unbleached, all-purpose white flour
1 teaspoon baking soda
$1/2$ teaspoon salt
1 teaspoon sugar
$1/4$ cup old-fashioned rolled oats
1 teaspoons caraway seeds
1 cup buttermilk

1) Preheat the oven to 375°F and set the baking rack in the oven's center. Coat a baking sheet with nonstick spray or line with parchment paper.

2) Sift together the flours, baking soda, salt, and sugar. Stir in the oats and caraway seeds. Make a well in the center and pour in $1/2$ cup of the buttermilk. Stir until the flour is moist and then pour in the remaining buttermilk. Stir.

3) Flour your hands and form the dough into a rough ball about 5 to 6 inches in diameter. It is okay if some dry flour is left behind in the bowl. Place the loaf on the baking sheet. Score an X across the top about 1/4 inch deep. Bake for 40 to 45 minutes, until the loaf browns and sounds hollow when tapped. Cool at least 10 minutes before slicing. Serve the day it is baked—this bread stales fast.

Per Slice: Calories 55; Protein 2g; Fat 0g (Saturated 0g); Carbohydrates 11g; Fiber 1g; Sodium 130mg

Basic Popovers

Makes: 6 popovers

Popovers are incredibly easy to make. They taste buttery but contain little fat. Although popover pans give them a dramatic tall shape, they are just as good when made in muffin tins or custard cups.

2 eggs
1 cup 1% lowfat milk
1 tablespoon unsalted butter, melted
1 cup unbleached, all-purpose white flour
1/2 teaspoon salt

1) Coat 6 popover cups or muffin cups with butter-flavored nonstick spray. Preheat the oven to 400°F.

2) Whisk together the eggs and milk. Stir in the butter, flour, and salt. Mix thoroughly but don't beat. Pour into the popover cups, filling halfway.

3) Bake for 25 minutes, reduce the oven temperature to 350°F, and bake for 10 to 15 minutes longer.

Per Serving: Calories 125; Protein 6g; Fat 4g (Saturated 2g); Carbohydrates 16g; Fiber 0g; Sodium 220mg

Basil Garlic Parmesan Popovers

Makes: 6 popovers

Consider serving these instead of garlic bread at your next Italian meal.

2 eggs
1 cup 1% lowfat milk
1 tablespoon unsalted butter, melted
1 teaspoon basil
1 clove garlic, minced
1 cup unbleached, all-purpose white flour
3 tablespoons grated Parmesan cheese, divided

1) Coat 6 popover cups or muffin or custard cups with butter-flavored nonstick spray. Preheat the oven to 400°F.

2) Whisk together the eggs and milk. Stir in the butter, basil, garlic, flour, and 2 tablespoons of the Parmesan. Mix thoroughly but don't beat. Pour into the popover cups, filling halfway. Top with the remaining Parmesan.

3) Bake for 25 minutes, reduce the oven temperature to 350°F, and bake for 10 to 15 minutes longer.

Per Serving: Calories 140; Protein 7g; Fat 5g (Saturated 3g); Carbohydrates 16g; Fiber 1g; Sodium 100mg

Whole Wheat Cheddar Popovers

Makes: 6 popovers

Cheddar cheese and whole wheat make these rich and nutty.

2 eggs
1 cup 1% lowfat milk
1 tablespoon unsalted butter, melted
1/2 cup whole wheat flour
1/2 cup unbleached, all-purpose white flour
1/2 teaspoon salt
1/4 cup shredded reduced-fat cheddar cheese

1) Coat 6 popover cups or muffin cups with butter-flavored nonstick spray. Preheat the oven to 400°F.

2) Whisk together the eggs and milk. Stir in the butter, flours, and salt. Mix thoroughly but don't beat. Pour into the popover cups, filling halfway. Top with the cheese.

3) Bake for 25 minutes, reduce the oven temperature to 350°F, and bake for 10 to 15 minutes longer.

Per Serving: Calories 135; Protein 7g; Fat 5g (Saturated 2g); Carbohydrates 16g; Fiber 1g; Sodium 242mg

Biscuits

Makes: 12 biscuits

Making biscuits can be tricky. The dough is sticky and it needs rolling out. But they sure are good.

1 cup unbleached, all-purpose white flour
1 cup whole wheat flour
1 teaspoon baking powder
1/4 teaspoon salt
1/4 cup vegetable oil, chilled
3/4 cup buttermilk, still cold from the refrigerator

1) Preheat the oven to 450°F. Line a baking sheet with parchment paper, or use a nonstick pan.

2) Sift together the dry ingredients and mix well. Make a well in the center. Pour in the oil and, using your fingers, quickly mix the two together until small clumps of dough form. Add the buttermilk, again mixing by hand until a large, rough dough ball forms.

3) Knead the dough in the bowl with the palm of your hand, using about 15 quick strokes.

4) Place the dough on a generously floured board and roll out to 1/2-inch thickness, then cut with a 2-inch biscuit cutter. Place the biscuits on the baking sheet.

5) Bake for 10 to 12 minutes.

Per Biscuit: Calories 113; Protein 3g; Fat 5g (Saturated 0g); Carbohydrates 15g; Fiber 1g; Sodium 102mg

Skillet Drop Bread

Makes: 6

The trick to having these little breads come out right is to handle the soft dough as little as possible. The batter will be workable but sticky. Dust your hands with flour before kneading. If more flour is needed (flour varies as to how much moisture it absorbs), add a teaspoon at a time.

1 cup whole wheat flour
1/4 cup unbleached, all-purpose white flour
1/4 teaspoon salt
1 teaspoon baking soda
1/2 cup buttermilk

1) Sift together the dry ingredients, then stir to mix well.

2) Make a well in the center of the dry mixture, pour in the buttermilk, and fold together until a soft ball forms.

3) With floured hands, knead the ball about 5 times, using the heel of your palm, not your fingers.

4) Heat a heavy skillet, preferably well-seasoned cast-iron, which will retain heat and cook evenly at a low temperature.

5) Divide the dough into 6 pieces, quickly forming each into the shape of a hamburger patty. Place them on the skillet (no shortening is necessary if using an iron or nonstick skillet) and cook for 10 minutes on one side and 7 minutes on the other. Use heat hot enough to brown the bread, but not so hot that it scorches.

Per Serving: Calories 93; Protein 4g; Fat 1g (Saturated 0g); Carbohydrates 19g; Fiber 2g; Sodium 321mg

Yeast Breads

Yeast baking is not an exact art. Almost every aspect is variable. Flour absorbs different amounts of moisture depending on its percentage of protein, the coarseness of the grind, and the weather. The dough rises at different rates depending on the weather, the type of bowl it is in, the age and brand of yeast, and the other ingredients in the recipe. The bread browns more or less depending on the oven temperature, ingredients in the dough, and the material the loaf pan is made of. Instead of discouraging prospective bakers, this flexibility should be seen as encouraging, as bread dough is very forgiving. The baker can keep working with it, adding and kneading and letting it rise until it feels right. Learning when the bread dough "feels right" does take time and experience, but each step along the way is fun to do and makes the house smell wonderful. Even if the bread doesn't look perfect, it tastes great.

Yeast and Proofing

Yeast are one-celled organisms, dormant in their refrigerated packages, but once in contact with warm water and a little food (usually sugar), they start to multiply. As they do so, they give off carbon dioxide. This gas gets trapped in the stretchy strands of gluten in the dough and expands, making the bread rise. Commercial yeasts are specifically designed for bread baking and each company holds the rights to its own unique yeast strains.

Of the yeasts available, those stocked in the supermarket are of two types. One is active dry yeast, which comes in packages or a jar (the jarred yeast is far more economical and easy to measure). Dough made from this yeast usually requires two rises of about an hour each, and then the loaf expands again in the oven. The second type of yeast in the supermarket is quick, or rapid-rise, yeast, which requires only half the rising time. Although this is useful for some recipes, others will be lacking in flavor or texture because of the shortened rise.

The first step when using either of these yeasts is to "proof" it. This means that the yeast is stirred into warm water with a touch of sugar. After a few minutes, a brown foam rises to the surface. This lets the baker know that the yeast is alive and ready to work. My favorite yeast is rarely available in supermarkets, but can be found in baking catalogs. It is an instant dry yeast that does not require proofing. It can be used in any recipe calling for active dry yeast. The baker leaves out the proofing step and stirs the yeast directly into the flour, which saves time and trouble. This yeast also makes the bread rise slowly and steadily, which creates the best flavor.

Regardless of what yeast you use, check the sell-by date on all packages because they lose their leavening powers as they age. Store yeast in the refrigerator.

Kneading Equipment

The springy texture of dough comes from the gluten (protein) in the flour. As it is kneaded, the gluten forms elastic strings. Once the dough is shaped, these strings stretch as the yeast's gases push them out, causing the bread to rise. Kneading can be done by hand, in a food processor, or in a stand mixer. When kneading by hand, it is hard to ruin the bread, but machines can overknead, causing the gluten strands to break, which ultimately yields a

tough, heavy loaf. I combine machine and hand kneading. I start the bread in a machine and have it do most of the work, then before there is a danger of harming the bread, I finish it by hand. (Bread machines are another story, and since recipes need to be adapted to each brand of machine, I don't include them here.)

For all methods, always add slightly less than the minimum of flour that the recipe calls for. As the dough ball begins to form, add more, a little at a time. This prevents the loaf from being heavy and dried-out.

The food processor mixes dough very quickly, in under 2 minutes. The plastic blade is used, which is gentler on the dough than the steel blade. The yeast is first proofed in another bowl, and then poured into the machine. Then the flour and other ingredients are pulsed together until a ball of dough forms. This takes less than a minute. Then the machine runs for another minute. The dough is then removed from the machine and placed on a floured surface and is kneaded briefly by hand until smooth and elastic. Since the food processor's capacity for dough can be small, some recipes will not fit in the machine.

A stand mixer is a terrific tool and is what almost every bakery and restaurant uses. The yeast can be proofed in the mixer's bowl. The dough hook is used and the ingredients are added as the machine runs on low speed. Once a ball of dough forms, the dough is kneaded for about 10 minutes. If a dough ball forms then loses its shape and looks wet, add a tablespoon of flour at a time. If in doubt, finish it by hand so that you don't dry out the dough with too much flour. At the most, bread kneaded in a machine requires only a couple of minutes of hand kneading.

You can follow these recipes and not use a machine. I learned to bake bread by hand, and

I believe that it is the only way to develop a baker's touch and feel for the bread. When doing a recipe by hand, begin by proofing the yeast in a large bowl, then stir in the other ingredients and the flour, 1 cup at a time, using a strong wooden spoon. When the dough becomes too sticky and dense to stir, generously flour a clean surface, place the dough on it, and begin kneading.

Kneading Technique

For me, there are few activities more pleasurable than taking a sticky, lumpy mass of dough and turning into an elastic, smooth loaf of bread ready for baking. Having the right baking surface helps. It should be at a comfortable height. Let your arms hang at your shoulders, then bend your elbows. The baking counter should be at your hand level. If you have to lift or twist your shoulders to reach the dough, it is too high and kneading will be painful work. The kitchen table is often a better height than the counter.

A soft dough is better than a stiff dough, and one mistake that beginning bakers often make is to add too much flour to the dough in an effort to keep it from sticking to every surface. To avoid this pitfall, put a generous amount of flour on the work surface, but never add it to the top of the dough. Keep your hands floured. If they become sticky, clean them off and start again. (Wash with cold water, not warm, to get the flour off.)

Knead using the base of your hands, not your fingers. As you work the dough, press only hard enough to push the dough, not so deeply that you expose the moist interior. Each kneading motion with the hand is followed by picking up the dough and moving it slightly or turning it over (this prevents the dough from sticking to the board). As the dough is worked, the baker can handle it with an increasingly firm touch. Dough should not be handled gently. Pick it up, turn it over, slap it onto the counter, and knead it energetically (this is the fun part) until the entire ball is smooth, feels almost silky to the touch, and springs back with each motion. This process will take about 15 minutes if kneading entirely by hand, or only a few minutes if most of the kneading was begun in a machine.

Rising Dough and Keeping the Bread Happy

Yeast prefers to do its work in warm (though not hot), moist environments. After the bread is kneaded, place it in an oiled bowl for its first rise. It is best to use a ceramic bowl, because glass and metal do not hold an even temperature. Choose a bowl that is large, since the dough will rise to double its size. Cover the bowl with a damp cloth kitchen towel and set in a warm place to rise. An oven with the oven light turned on is draft-free and a good temperature. Dough is very sensitive to temperature and the same recipe might take twice the time to rise on a cold day, or might overflow the bowl on a hot, humid day. A very fast rise is not preferred as the dough doesn't have time to develop texture and flavor and the bread will taste yeasty.

For a slow rise, which develops more flavor, put the dough in the refrigerator for 1 to 2 days, covered with plastic wrap. Whenever the dough looks as if it is peeking out of the top of the bowl, punch it down to deflate it and put it back in the fridge. This is a great trick if your bread baking day suddenly gets interrupted and you don't know what to do with the rising dough. When you are ready to bake, bring the dough to room temperature and continue with the recipe. However, such a long rise does not work with doughs made with instant yeast.

Storing and Freezing Bread

Fresh bread stales quickly but dries out even more rapidly in the refrigerator, so store it tightly wrapped on the counter, and eat it within 2 days. Bread can be frozen, and should be wrapped in plastic, then foil. Defrost loaves on the counter. The best way to store bread is to freeze the dough. Freeze dough after the first rise, wrapped tightly and put in a freezer bag. Defrost overnight in the refrigerator, then put the dough in an oiled bowl and proceed with the second rise. This might take a while, since the dough needs to come to room temperature before rising.

White Bread

Makes: 2 loaves (16 slices each)

If you are an inexperienced baker, white bread is a good recipe to start with. The dough is elastic and easy to work and the bread rises quickly, soft and pillowy, which is an immediate positive reinforcement for the beginning baker.

Some people knock white bread, but there are times when a homemade loaf of basic white bread is more appealing than a crusty sour loaf that has taken days to make. I am thinking of an egg salad sandwich on soft white bread. Or a piece of buttered white toast eaten just before bedtime. I am sure you can think of foods and moments that are made for white bread, too.

4 teaspoons active dry yeast
1 tablespoon sugar
1 cup warm water
5 1/2 cups unbleached, all-purpose white flour
2 teaspoons kosher salt
2 tablespoons vegetable oil
1 cup 1% lowfat milk

1) Dissolve the yeast and sugar in the water and let rest until the surface begins to foam.

2) Please read about bread techniques (page 493) and follow the directions there if using a stand mixer or making the bread by hand. If using a food processor, combine 5 cups of flour and the salt in the food processor bowl. Add the oil and milk. Pour in the water and yeast mixture and mix until moist, using the pulse button. Add the remaining flour 1 to 2 tablespoons at a time, while the machine is running, until a moist ball forms. It is better to have it sticky than dry. Once the ball forms, let the processor run 45 seconds.

3) Remove the dough from the machine and knead by hand until smooth and elastic.

4) Place the dough in an oiled bowl. Turn it once, cover with a damp cloth towel, and let it rest for 1 hour, until double in bulk.

5) After the dough is doubled in bulk, punch it down to deflate it, divide in half, and let it rest 5 minutes before shaping.

6) Coat 2 loaf pans (about 8 1/2×4 1/2 inches each) with nonstick spray.

7) Shape the dough into 2 loaves. This can be accomplished by using a rolling pin to flatten each dough ball into 2 rectangles, which are then tightly rolled up to form loaves. They can also be shaped by hand. Place the loaves in the loaf pans. Let rise, covered with a damp towel, until double in bulk, about 45 minutes to an hour in a warm, though not hot, space.

8) Put the oven rack in the center of the oven. Preheat the oven to 400°F. Preheat it for a long time, at least a half hour before baking.

9) Slash the tops of the loaves and place them in the oven. Bake for 35 to 40 minutes, until golden brown. Remove from the pans and cool on a wire rack.

Per Serving: Calories 81; Protein 3g; Fat 1g (Saturated 0g); Carbohydrates 15g; Fiber 1g; Sodium 124mg

Whole Wheat Bread

Makes: 2 loaves (16 slices each)

This recipe has enough white flour in it to make it easy to knead and shape.

4 teaspoons active dry yeast
1³/4 cups warm water
¹/4 cup honey
2 tablespoons vegetable oil
2 cups whole wheat flour
2¹/2 to 3 cups unbleached, all-purpose white flour
2 teaspoons kosher salt
¹/4 cup wheat germ

1) Dissolve the yeast in the water. Stir in the honey and oil and let rest until the surface begins to foam.

2) Please read about bread techniques (page 493) and follow the directions there if using a stand mixer or making the bread by hand. If using a food processor, combine the whole wheat flour, 2 cups of the white flour, the salt, and the wheat germ in the food processor bowl fitted with the plastic blade. Pour in the yeast mixture and pulse until moist. Add enough white flour 1 to 2 tablespoons at a time, while the machine is running, to form a moist ball. Once the ball forms let the processor run 45 seconds.

3) Remove the dough from the machine and knead by hand until smooth and elastic.

4) Place the dough in an oiled bowl. Turn it once, cover with a damp cloth towel, and let it rest for 1 hour, until double in bulk.

5) After the dough is doubled in bulk, punch it down to deflate it, divide in half, and let it rest 5 minutes before shaping.

6) Coat 2 loaf pans (about 8¹/2×4¹/2 inches each) with nonstick spray.

7) Shape the dough into 2 loaves. This can be accomplished by using a rolling pin to flatten each dough ball into 2 rectangles, which are then tightly rolled up to form loaves. Or they can be shaped by hand. Place the loaves in the loaf pans. Let rise, covered with a damp towel, until double in bulk, about 45 minutes to 1 hour in a warm, though not hot, space.

8) Meanwhile, put the oven rack in the center of the oven and preheat to 375°F.

9) Slash the tops of the loaves and place them in the oven. Bake for 40 to 45 minutes, until golden brown.

Per Serving: Calories 82; Protein 3g; Fat 1g (Saturated 0g); Carbohydrates 16g; Fiber 1g; Sodium 121mg

Anadama Bread

Makes: 2 large loaves (16 slices each)

Anadama is an old-fashioned bread made with cornmeal and molasses. The dough is dense, but as it rises it lightens and softens. The finished loaves slice perfectly for sandwiches. This recipe makes too much dough and it is too heavy to mix in a food processor, but Anadama bread can be kneaded in a stand mixer or by hand.

1$\frac{1}{2}$ tablespoons active dry yeast
2$\frac{1}{4}$ cups warm water
1$\frac{1}{2}$ cups cornmeal
$\frac{1}{3}$ cup molasses
$\frac{1}{3}$ cup honey
1 tablespoon vegetable oil
$\frac{1}{4}$ cup wheat germ
2 teaspoons kosher salt
2 cups whole wheat flour
2$\frac{1}{2}$ to 3 cups unbleached, all-purpose white flour

1) In a large bowl, dissolve the yeast in the water. Add the cornmeal. Beat in the molasses, honey, and oil by hand or in a mixer fitted with a bread hook.

2) Stir in the wheat germ, salt, and whole wheat flour. Stir in the white flour, $\frac{1}{2}$ cup at a time, until a soft dough ball forms. Knead until smooth and elastic.

3) Place the dough in an oiled bowl. Turn it once, cover with a damp cloth towel, and let it rest for 1 hour or longer, until double in bulk.

4) Punch the dough down to deflate it, divide it in half, and let it rest 5 minutes.

6) Coat 2 loaf pans (about 8$\frac{1}{2}$×4$\frac{1}{2}$ inches each) with nonstick spray.

7) Shape the dough into 2 loaves. This can be accomplished by using a rolling pin to flatten each dough ball into 2 rectangles, which are then tightly rolled up to form loaves. Or they can be shaped by hand. Place the loaves in the loaf pans. Let rise, covered with a damp towel, until double in bulk, about 45 minutes to an hour in a warm, though not hot, space.

8) Meanwhile, put the oven rack in the center of the oven and preheat it to 375°F.

9) Slash the tops of the loaves and place them in the oven. Bake for 35 to 40 minutes, until golden brown and the loaves sound hollow when tapped. Remove the bread from the pan and cool on wire racks.

Per Serving: Calories 114; Protein 3g; Fat 1g (Saturated 0g); Carbohydrates 24g; Fiber 2g; Sodium 123mg

Oatmeal Bread

Makes: 2 medium loaves (10 slices each)

Oats lend a chewy texture and pleasant flavor to yeast bread. The dough starts out sticky, but will be light and elastic by the final shaping.

2$1/2$ teaspoons active dry yeast
1$3/4$ cups warm water
$1/4$ cup packed light brown sugar, divided
1 tablespoon vegetable oil
1 teaspoon kosher salt
$1/4$ teaspoon ground cardamom
1$1/2$ cups old-fashioned rolled oats, divided
$1/4$ cup nonfat dry milk
3$1/2$ to 4$1/2$ cups unbleached, all-purpose white flour

1) Dissolve the yeast in the water. Stir in 1 teaspoon of the brown sugar and let rest until the surface begins to foam, about 5 minutes. Stir in the remaining sugar and the oil, salt, and cardamom. Stir in (don't vigorously beat) 1 cup of the oats and all of the dried milk.

2) Put the oats and yeast mixture in the bowl of a stand mixer fitted with a dough hook, or continue to stir by hand (don't use a food processor). Add the flour, $1/2$ cup at a time, until the dough becomes a wet ball (this should take about 3$1/2$ cups of flour). If using a machine, knead for about 10 minutes, adding a little flour at a time so that the dough ball holds its shape. If kneading by hand, lightly flour a work surface and turn the dough onto it. Knead until smooth and elastic.

4) Place the dough in an oiled bowl. Turn it once, cover with a damp cloth towel, and let it rest for 1 hour, until double in bulk.

5) After the dough is doubled in bulk, punch it down, divide it in half, and let rest 5 minutes before shaping.

6) Coat 2 loaf pans (about 8$1/2$×4$1/2$ inches each) with nonstick spray.

7) Shape the dough into 2 loaves. This can be accomplished by using a rolling pin to flatten each dough ball into 2 rectangles, which are then tightly rolled up to form loaves. Or they can be shaped by hand. Place the loaves in the loaf pans. Let rise, covered with a damp towel, until double in bulk, about 45 minutes to an hour in a warm, though not hot, space.

8) Meanwhile, put the oven rack in the center of the oven and preheat the oven to 375°F.

9) Slash the tops of the loaves and place them in the oven. Bake for 40 to 45 minutes, until golden brown.

Per Serving: Calories 123; Protein 4g; Fat 1g (Saturated 0g); Carbohydrates 24g; Fiber 1g; Sodium 103mg

Cinnamon Raisin Swirl Bread

Makes: 2 loaves (16 slices each)

Save one loaf to use for French toast.

4 teaspoons active dry yeast
1 cup warm water
2 tablespoons vegetable oil
1 tablespoon unsalted butter, melted
3 to 4 cups unbleached, all-purpose white flour
1 cup whole wheat flour
1 teaspoon kosher salt
3/4 cup nonfat milk
1 1/2 teaspoons ground cinnamon
1/2 cup packed light brown sugar
1 cup raisins

1) Dissolve the yeast in the warm water and let rest until the surface begins to foam. Stir in the oil and butter.

2) Combine 3 cups of white flour, all of the whole wheat flour, and the salt in a bowl, stand mixer bowl, or food processor. Pulse or mix in the yeast mixture. Add the milk. (If using a processor, do this while the machine is running.) Add more of the white flour, a tablespoon at a time, until a dough ball forms.

3) Knead until smooth and elastic

4) Place the dough in an oiled bowl. Turn it once, cover with a damp cloth towel, and let it rest for 1 hour, until double in bulk.

5) After the dough is doubled in bulk, punch it down, divide in half, and let it rest 5 minutes before shaping.

6) Coat 2 loaf pans (about 8 1/2×4 1/2 inches each) with nonstick spray.

7) Lightly dust the work surface with flour. Roll out one of the portions of dough into a rectangle, about 8×12 inches. Dust with half the cinnamon and spread on half the brown sugar and half the raisins, leaving a 1-inch margin all around. Starting from a short side, tightly roll up the rectangle, pinch the ends to seal, and place seam side down into the loaf pan. Repeat with the second ball of dough. Let the loaves rise, covered with a damp towel, until double in bulk, about 45 minutes to an hour in a warm, though not hot, space.

8) Put the oven rack in the center or bottom third of the oven and preheat the oven to 375°F.

9) Slash the tops of the loaves and place them in the oven. Bake for 40 to 50 minutes, until golden brown. Remove from the pans and cool on a wire rack.

Per Serving: Calories 105; Protein 3g; Fat 2g (Saturated 0g); Carbohydrates 21g; Fiber 1g; Sodium 66mg

Wheat Germ Bread

Makes: 2 loaves (16 slices each)

This makes a slightly sweet soft bread, ideal for sandwiches or toast.

1 package rapid-rise yeast
1 cup 1% lowfat milk, warmed to
    room temperature
1 cup warm water
2 tablespoons honey
2 tablespoons unsalted butter, melted
1/2 cup toasted wheat germ
1/3 cup wheat bran
1 teaspoon kosher salt
4 1/2 cups unbleached, all-purpose white flour

1) Mix together the yeast, milk, water, honey, and butter in a bowl, stand mixer bowl, or food processor. Let stand until proofed (see page 493). Add the wheat germ, bran, and salt.

2) Add the flour, 1 cup at a time, until a soft ball of dough forms.

3) Knead until smooth and elastic.

4) Place the ball of dough in an oiled bowl and cover with a damp towel. Let rise until double in bulk, about 45 minutes.

5) Preheat the oven to 350°F and put a pan of water in the oven. Coat 2 loaf pans (about 8 1/2×4 1/2 inches each) with nonstick spray.

6) Punch down the dough, divide in half, shape into loaves, and place in the pans. Let rise again until almost double in bulk, about 40 minutes longer.

7) Slit the tops, place in the oven, and bake for 50 minutes, until done.

Per Serving: Calories 78; Protein 3g; Fat 1g (Saturated 1g); Carbohydrates 14g; Fiber 1g; Sodium 65mg

French Bread

Makes: 2 loaves (8 slices each)

Since this bread has no fat at all, it goes stale very quickly and should be eaten the day it is made.

4 teaspoons active dry yeast
1 1/4 cups warm water
3 to 3 1/2 cups unbleached, all-purpose white flour
1 teaspoon kosher salt
Cornmeal

1) Dissolve the yeast in the water and let rest until the surface begins to foam.

2) Combine 3 cups of the flour and the salt in a bowl, stand mixer bowl, or food processor. Pour in the water and yeast mixture, then pulse or mix until moist. Add the remaining flour 1 to 2 tablespoons at a time until a moist ball forms.

3) Knead until smooth and elastic.

4) Place the dough in an oiled bowl. Turn it once, cover with a damp cloth towel, and let rest for 1 hour, until double in bulk.

5) After the dough is doubled in bulk, punch it down to deflate it, divide in half, and let it rest 5 minutes. At this point it benefits from a few minutes of kneading on a lightly floured surface.

6) Coat 2 baking sheets or baguette pans with nonstick spray. Dust with cornmeal.

7) Shape the dough into 2 long loaves by using a rolling pin to flatten each portion of dough into 2 rectangles, each about 8×11 inches. Tightly roll these up, pinch the seams, and taper the ends. Or roll each portion of the dough back and forth by hand until a long cigar shape is formed, about 12 inches long and 1 inch in diameter. Once the loaves are shaped, place onto the baking sheets. Let the loaves rise, covered with a damp towel, until almost double in bulk, about 45 minutes in a warm, though not hot, space.

8) Meanwhile, put the oven rack on a low rung and preheat the oven to 400°F. Preheat it a good long time, at least a half hour before baking. Put a bowl of water in the oven.

9) Slash the tops of the loaves and place them in the oven. Bake for 20 minutes, until golden brown.

Per Serving: Calories 78; Protein 3g; Fat 0g (Saturated 0g); Carbohydrates 16g; Fiber 1g; Sodium 121mg

Focaccia

Focaccia is an Italian yeast dough, similar to a thick-pizza crust, that is easy to make and versatile. It can be served in a bread basket at dinner or be dressed up like pizza and served as a light meal. Because it is not expected to be high and light, a beginning bread baker can feel confident making it.

Basic Focaccia

Makes: 8 servings

This recipe uses the quick-rising yeast, which cuts preparation time almost in half. If desired, use active dry yeast and double the rising time.

1 package rapid-rise yeast
1 cup warm water, divided
1 teaspoon sugar
1 tablespoon plus 1 teaspoon olive oil
1 teaspoon kosher salt
2 to 2 1/2 cups unbleached, all-purpose white flour
Cornmeal

1) Proof the yeast by combining it with 1/4 cup of the warm water and the sugar in a small bowl (metal and plastic do not maintain the temperature favored by yeast). When the water becomes foamy (1 or 2 minutes), stir in the rest of the water, 1 tablespoon of oil, and the salt.

2) Combine 1/2 cup of the flour with the proofed yeast in a bowl, stand mixer bowl, or food processor. Keep adding flour and mixing until a dough ball forms.

3) Lightly flour a clean counter and turn the dough ball onto it. Using your palms (not your fingertips), knead the dough until it is smooth and elastic.

4) Place the dough in an oiled bowl. Turn it once, cover with a damp cloth towel, and place it in a warm, draft-free place. Let rise for 1/2 hour, until double in bulk. Punch down the dough.

5) Preheat the oven to 400°F. Coat a rimmed baking sheet with nonstick spray, then dust lightly with cornmeal. (Do not use an insulated baking sheet because it will prevent a crust from forming.)

6) Put the dough on a lightly floured counter and roll out into a rectangle approximately the size of your baking sheet. The nice thing about focaccia is that it isn't supposed to look perfect, so if you can't get a geometrically correct rectangle, don't worry about it. Place the dough in the pan and press down into the corners so that it won't spring back into the center of the baking sheet. Loosely cover with the towel and allow to rise until double in bulk, about 1/2 hour.

7) Make indentations with the handle of a wooden spoon or your fingertips. Brush with the remaining teaspoon of oil. Place in the oven and bake for 30 to 40 minutes, until golden brown. Remove to a cooling rack. This is best if served hot, but it will still be wonderful the next day.

Per Serving: Calories 123; Protein 3g; Fat 3g (Saturated 0g); Carbohydrates 22g; Fiber 1g; Sodium 242mg

Romano and Olive Focaccia

Makes: 8 servings

Both the Romano and the olives are salty and sharp, which makes a nice flavor contrast to the chewy bread base.

1 recipe Basic Focaccia (opposite)
2 tablespoons grated Romano cheese
1/4 cup calamata or other brine-cured olives, pitted and chopped

Follow the directions for Basic Focaccia. Just prior to baking, after the olive oil is brushed on the dough, dust on the Romano and distribute the olives across the dough. Bake as directed.

Per Serving: Calories 139; Protein 4g; Fat 4g (Saturated 1g); Carbohydrates 22g; Fiber 1g; Sodium 318mg

Red Onion and Rosemary Focaccia

Makes: 8 servings

For added flavor, warm focaccia over a grill.

1 recipe Basic Focaccia (opposite)
1/2 teaspoon kosher salt
1 teaspoon dried rosemary, or 1 tablespoon fresh
1/2 cup thinly sliced red onions

Follow the directions for Basic Focaccia. Just prior to baking, after the olive oil is brushed on the dough, sprinkle on the salt and rosemary. Distribute the onion slices on the dough. Bake as directed.

Per Serving: Calories 127; Protein 4g; Fat 3g (Saturated 0g); Carbohydrates 22g; Fiber 1g; Sodium 362mg

Herb and Garlic Focaccia

Makes: 8 servings

1 recipe Basic Focaccia (opposite)
2 cloves garlic, minced
1 teaspoon dried rosemary, crumbled, or 1 tablespoon minced fresh
1/2 teaspoon ground sage, or 1 teaspoon minced fresh

Follow the directions for Basic Focaccia. After the water foams in Step 1, add the garlic, rosemary, and sage to the bowl, then proceed with the focaccia recipe.

Per Serving: Calories 125; Protein 4g; Fat 3g (Saturated 0g); Carbohydrates 22g; Fiber 1g; Sodium 242mg

Corn Focaccia

Makes: One 14×8 bread; serves 12

This recipe is written for the food processor but can be done by hand (follow the directions for Basic Focaccia, page 502).

1 package rapid-rise yeast
1 cup warm water, divided
1 teaspoon sugar
1 clove garlic
1 teaspoon dried rosemary
1 teaspoon kosher salt
2 cups unbleached, all-purpose white flour
1/2 cup cornmeal
1 tablespoon plus 1 teaspoon olive oil
1/2 cup corn kernels (if frozen, thawed)
2 tablespoons grated Parmesan cheese
1/4 teaspoon freshly ground pepper

1) Combine the yeast, 1/4 cup of the water, and the sugar in a measuring cup. Let proof.

2) In the food processor, mince the rosemary and garlic. Pulse in the salt, flour, and cornmeal. Pour in the yeast mixture. Pulse in the remaining water and 1 tablespoon of the oil and let run until a ball forms. If the dough is too wet, add flour, while pulsing, 1 tablespoon at a time.

3) Remove from the processor and knead briefly until smooth. Put in an oiled bowl. Cover with a damp cloth towel and let rise 1/2 hour. Punch down.

4) Preheat the oven to 400°F. Coat a rimmed baking sheet with nonstick spray, then dust lightly with cornmeal. (Do not use an insulated baking sheet because it will prevent a crust from forming.) Put the dough on a lightly floured counter and roll out into a rectangle approximately 14×8 inches. Place the dough in the pan. Loosely cover with a towel and let rise until double in bulk, about 1/2 to 1 hour.

5) Using your fingers or the end of a wooden spoon, press indentions into the dough. Brush with the remaining teaspoon of oil. Top with the corn, Parmesan, and pepper. Place in the oven and bake for 30 to 40 minutes, until golden brown. Remove to a cooling rack. This is best if served hot the day it is made.

Per Serving: Calories 172; Protein 5g; Fat 3g (Saturated 1g); Carbohydrates 30g; Fiber 2g; Sodium 273mg

Desserts

Fruit Desserts
508

Surprising Strawberries

Balsamic Berries with Mint

Grand Oranges

Five-Spice Orange Slices

Melon Ball Compote

Strawberry and Melon
Compote

Honeydew, Mango, and
Ginger Compote

Fruit Salad in a Jar

Fruit Salad with Yogurt
and Mint Sauce

Fruit Kebabs

Dessert Fruit Plates

Strawberry-Yogurt
Fruit Salad Dressing

Honeyed Pineapple

Broiled Fruit Kebabs

Baked Peaches with Ginger

Baked Apples

Microwaved Baked Apple
for One

Spiced Baked Apples
with Applejack

Brandy Baked Apples
with Jelly Glaze

Glazed Baked Pears

Pears as Blintzes

Poached Pears
in Raspberry Sauce

Pears with
Red Currant Jelly Sauce

Pies
521

Double Pie Crust

Graham Cracker Crust

Press-in Pie Crust

Meringue Shell

Apple Pie

Cranberry Apple Pie

More Than Apple Pie

Strawberry Rhubarb Pie

Peach Pie

Berry Pie

Pumpkin Pie

Blueberry and Banana
Sour Cream Pie

Cappuccino Mud Pie

Lemon Meringue Pie

Banana Meringue Pie

Strawberry Tart

Strawberry-Filled
Meringue Torte

Lemon Curd–Filled
Meringue Torte

Meringue for Pie

Italian Meringue

Cakes
530

Yellow Layer Cake

Cupcakes

Cocoa Cake

Zucchini Cocoa Cake

Apple Cake

Carrot Cake

Pineapple Upside-Down Bake

Lemon Poppy Bundt Cake

Rhubarb Bundt Cake

Pear and Spice Coffee Cake

Angel Food Cake

Cocoa Angel Food Cake

Orange Angel Food Cake

Almond Angel Food Cake

Mousselike Cheesecake

Chocolate Marble Cheesecake

Ginger Cheesecake

Frostings
577

Orange Icing Glaze

Lemon Icing Glaze

Seven-Minute Frosting

Seven-Minute Almond Frosting

Honey Fudge Frosting

Cream Cheese Frosting

Chocolate Cream Cheese
Frosting

Marshmallow Fluff

Cherry Topping

Cookies
577

Chocolate Chip Biscotti

Orange Biscotti

Oatmeal Drop Cookies

Apple and Date Cookies

Applesauce Cookies

Carrot Cookies

Banana Cookies

Cocoa Cookies

Chocolate Nut Crackle Cookies

Gingersnaps

Almond Loves

Chocolate Meringue Kisses

Brownies and Bars
556

Basic Brownies

Butterscotch Chip Brownies

Marbled Brownies

Hermits

Gingerbread

Chocolate Apricot Squares

Apricot and Oat Bars

Sour Cherry Nut Bars

Jam Squares

Cobblers
561

Cherry Cobbler

Blackberry-Pear Cobbler

Blueberry-Peach Cobbler

Puddings
564

Vanilla Pudding

Chocolate Pudding

Lemon Curd

Vanilla Cream

Pumpkin Custards

Rice Pudding

Banana Rice Pudding

Flan

Apple Cinnamon
Raisin Bread Pudding

Peach Bread Pudding

Cocoa Bread Pudding

Lemon Bread Pudding

Frozen Desserts
571

Chocolate-Covered
Banana Bites

Purple Pops

Pineapple Popsicles

Strawberry Banana Popsicles

Lemon Sorbet

Watermelon Sorbet

Berry Sorbet

Peach Sorbet

Pineapple Sherbet

Strawberry Frozen Yogurt

Banana Vanilla Frozen Yogurt

Honey Vanilla
Frozen Ice Cream

Strawberry Milk Shake

Ice Cream Pie

Syrups and Sauces
576

Chocolate Syrup

Marshmallow Sauce
for Ice Cream

Orange Grand Marnier Sauce

Blueberry Syrup

Blueberry Sauce

Berry Sauce

Caribbean Pineapple Topping

Pineapple-Mango Sauce

Maple Bananas

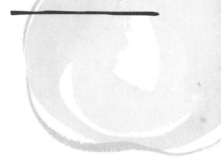

Desserts are definitely not off limits when eating a healthful diet. Many desserts are filled with good things such as fruits, whole grains, and nutrients. Others are lowfat and low-calorie. Even rich, decadent foods can occasionally be indulged in. Dessert is a problem when it becomes the main filler of the meal (or the meal itself), but presented as the final element of a good, healthful dinner, desserts are welcome at the table.

Note that unlike other recipes in this book, baked goods use regular table salt rather than kosher salt, because the smaller crystals dissolve into the batter.

Fruit Desserts

These recipes take basic, familiar fruits and make them more intriguing. Although you can get away with less than perfect specimens for the cooked recipes, the end results will be much better if ripe and flavorful fruits are used. Uncooked fruit desserts absolutely need to be made from the best fruits available. It might be difficult to tell if the fruit in the market has flavor and the right texture. Look for fruit free of blemishes, full of color and aromatic. A peach should smell sweetly peachy. Most ripe fruits should have a little give; a gentle touch will tell you what you need to know. Don't squeeze softfleshed fruits as they bruise easily. If in doubt don't be shy about asking for a sample.

Surprising Strawberries

Makes: 4 servings

Italians have long known that the flavor of strawberries is sweetened by a few drop of balsamic vinegar. Here the balsamic flavor marries nicely with the maple syrup.

1 pint strawberries
1 teaspoon balsamic vinegar
1 teaspoon maple syrup

1) Gently wash and dry the strawberries. Leave the stems on if fresh and green; they make convenient handles for picking up and eating the strawberries later.

2) Arrange the berries on a serving plate. Splash the balsamic vinegar over the berries as evenly as possible, then drizzle with maple syrup, making sure that each one gets a few drops.

3) Let berries sit for at least 1 hour or up to a day before serving.

Per Serving: Calories 27; Protein 0g; Fat 0g (Saturated 0g); Carbohydrates 6g; Fiber 1g; Sodium 1mg

Balsamic Berries with Mint

Makes: 6 servings

If desired, have a bowl of confectioners' sugar to roll berries in just prior to eating. (If dipped earlier, it dissolves on the fruit.)

1 tablespoon sugar
1 teaspoon balsamic vinegar
1 quart strawberries, hulled
2 tablespoons chopped fresh mint leaves

1) Combine the sugar and vinegar.

2) Toss the berries with the mint, then gently stir in the sugar and vinegar mixture.

Per Serving: Calories 39; Protein 1g; Fat 0g (Saturated 0g); Carbohydrates 9g; Fiber 2g; Sodium 2mg

Grand Oranges

Makes: 10 servings

Serve this on its own, or in a parfait glass with ice cream.

8 seedless oranges
1/2 cup orange juice
1/2 cup water
2 tablespoons sugar
1 tablespoon honey
2 tablespoons Grand Marnier or other orange-flavored liqueur
1/2 teaspoon vanilla extract
1 cup fresh raspberries (optional)

1) Peel the oranges, removing the bitter white pith as well as the peel. Slice the oranges into circles. Remove the seeds, if any.

2) Bring the orange juice, water, sugar, and honey to a boil. Add the oranges. Bring the mixture back to a boil, then immediately take the pot off the burner. Let it sit for 2 minutes. Do not stir.

3) Using a slotted spoon, remove the orange slices to a bowl.

4) Stir the Grand Marnier and vanilla into the pot. Return the liquid to a full boil and cook until the liquid reduces down to about 1/2 cup and becomes a thicker syrup. This will take about 20 minutes.

5) Cool the syrup to lukewarm. Pour it over the oranges and chill. Just prior to serving, add the raspberries, if desired.

Per Serving: Calories 84; Protein 1g; Fat 0g (Saturated 0g); Carbohydrates 20g; Fiber 2g; Sodium 2mg

Five-Spice Orange Slices

Makes: 6 servings

Chinese meals rarely end with a heavy dessert, but they don't have to end with plain quartered fruit either. Relax at the end of a meal with these orange slices and a pot of tea.

5 navel oranges
1/4 cup honey
1/2 teaspoon ground cinnamon
1/4 teaspoon Chinese five-spice powder
1 tablespoon slivered crystallized ginger

1) Using a sharp knife, cut away the peel and white pith from the oranges. Slice the oranges into thick circles and put into a large bowl.

2) In a small saucepan or a microwave, warm the honey until thin and pourable. Stir the cinnamon and five-spice powder into the honey, then pour over the oranges. Gently stir until the oranges are coated with the syrup. Arrange the oranges on a platter and top with the ginger.

Per Serving: Calories 105; Protein 1g; Fat 0g (Saturated 0g); Carbohydrates 27g; Fiber 2g; Sodium 2mg

Choosing a Melon

There are a number of wonderful-tasting melons besides canteloupes and honeydews. When deciding which to purchase, first determine which is ripe and has the most flavor. The stem end should have a little give when pressed, but the rest of the melon should feel firm. Hold the fruit up to your nose. A ripe melon will have a melon aroma; but take care, if the smell is strong (especially in the cold supermarket aisle), the melon is likely overripe. If several varieties of melons look ripe, then make your purchase based on color and flavor. I like contrasting colors in a fruit salad, such as orange mangoes paired with a green honeydew. Some melons, like crenshaws, are very sweet and soft and would pair well with citrus in a salad.

Melon Ball Compote

Makes: 6 servings

If you don't have time to use a melon baller, simply peel the melon and cut it into cubes.

1 cantaloupe
1 honeydew
1/4 cup honey
1 tablespoon lemon juice
1 tablespoon fresh lime juice
2 tablespoons chopped fresh mint

1) Cut the melons in half, scoop out and discard the seeds, and use a melon baller to remove the flesh.

2) Stir together the honey, lemon juice, and lime juice, then pour over the fruit. Add the mint and toss. The compote can be kept in the refrigerator for up to 2 days, but it is best if allowed to warm to room temperature before serving

Per Serving: Calories 152; Protein 2g; Fat 0g (Saturated 0g); Carbohydrates 0g; Fiber 39g; Sodium 31mg

Strawberry and Melon Compote

Makes: 6 servings

The lime juice perks up the flavor of the melon, even if it isn't perfectly ripe.

1 pint strawberries, hulled
1 canteloupe, scooped into balls (4 cups)
1 tablespoon orange-flavored liqueur, such as
    Grand Marnier
2 tablespoons fresh lime juice
1 tablespoon orange juice
1 to 2 tablespoons sugar
1 tablespoon fine strips lemon zest

1) Combine the strawberries and melon.

2) Whisk together the liqueur, juices, and sugar (use the lesser amount of sugar if the melon is sweet and ripe). Pour in with the fruit and gently stir in the zest. Serve chilled.

Per Serving: Calories 65; Protein 1g; Fat 0g (Saturated 0g); Carbohydrates 15g; Fiber 2g; Sodium 9mg

Honeydew, Mango, and Ginger Compote

Makes: 4 servings

The ripeness of honeydew melon is hard to gauge because the skin is thick and it is hard to smell a sweet aroma. The stem ends of ripe melons should have some give when pressed, and the melon's skin should feel firm but not rock hard. Also, look for melons that have a golden glow to their light green exterior. This recipe contains sugar, but it can be adjusted either way depending on the sweetness of the melon used.

1 honeydew or other melon
1 mango, peeled, seeded, and cubed
2 tablespoons minced crystallized ginger
2 teaspoons sugar
2 tablespoons fresh lime juice

1) Cut the melon in half, scoop out and discard the seeds, and use a melon baller to remove the flesh. (It should total about 4 to 5 cups.) Toss in the mango and ginger.

2) Dissolve the sugar in the lime juice. Pour in with the melon and stir. Serve chilled.

Per Serving: Calories 181; Protein 2g; Fat 0g (Saturated 0g); Carbohydrates 47g; Fiber 3g; Sodium 33mg

Fruit Salad in a Jar

Makes: 6 servings

My family and I eat at least twice as much fruit if it is cut up and put in a jar than if it is left whole, unwashed and unpeeled, in the fruit bin of the refrigerator. So once a week I buy a melon and whatever else is in season and looks good at the market. It takes about 10 minutes to fill up a 2-quart wide-mouth jar with fruit salad. Fruit salad will keep for up to 4 days as long as you use harder fruits like apples, grapes, and melons. Soft or delicate fruits, such as berries, kiwis, and bananas, can be added at the last minute. Always include a grapefruit or orange if you're using apples or pears. The citrus juice will prevent discoloration.

2- to 3-pound melon (about 3 to 4 cups)
1 pound seedless grapes (about 3 cups)
2 oranges
2 apples or pears

1) Cut the melon in half, scrape out the seeds, and use a melon baller to remove the flesh. Or peel the melon, cut it in half, scoop out the seeds, and cut the melon into cubes. Put the melon pieces in a large bowl. Watermelon is excellent in fruit salads, although the seeds can be annoying. To get rid of watermelon seeds, cut the watermelon off its rind. If it is a big piece of melon, do this in chunks. The seeds are not dispersed throughout the fruit, but grow in a line. Cut the melon straight through that line, exposing the seeds. Then cut off the section with the seeds. You can discard this or you take the time to pick the out the seeds.

2) Wash the grapes well, then pluck them off the stems and add them to the bowl.

3) Peel the oranges with a sharp knife, removing the bitter white pith along with the peel. Slice the oranges into rounds or cut them into cubes. Pick out the seeds, if any. Add the orange pieces to the bowl.

4) Wash the apples or pears, then cut them into 4 or 8 segments. Remove the core from each piece. Cut the segments into cubes. Toss them with the fruit salad. Put the salad in a large, wide-mouthed jar.

Per Serving: Calories 129; Protein 2g; Fat 1g (Saturated 0g); Carbohydrates 32g; Fiber 3g; Sodium 9mg

Fruit Salad with Yogurt and Mint Sauce

Makes: 8 servings

The grapefruit, melon, and orange can be prepared a day ahead of time, but add the berries and dress the salad just prior to serving.

1 grapefruit
2- to 3-pound melon, scooped into balls
1 orange, segments removed from the membranes
1 pint berries
2 cups plain nonfat yogurt
2 tablespoons minced fresh mint
1/4 teaspoon vanilla extract
1 tablespoon honey

1) Cut the grapefruit in half and scoop out the segments. Put the segments into a bowl. Squeeze the juice from the grapefruit into the bowl.

2) Add the melon, orange segments, and berries. Toss and chill.

3) Whisk together the yogurt, mint, vanilla, and honey, combine with the chilled fruit, and serve.

Per Serving: Calories 92; Protein 5g; Fat 0g (Saturated 0g); Carbohydrates 19g; Fiber 2g; Sodium 53mg

Fruit Kebabs

Makes: 4 servings

It takes time to thread these, but in the long run it can save labor. Serve these at a buffet and you won't need to put out (or later clean up) fruit salad bowls and spoons. The recipe can be expanded to feed many.

8 grapes
8 strawberries, hulled
8 melon balls or cubes
8 pineapple chunks
1 teaspoon lemon juice
1 teaspoon minced fresh mint

Toss the fruit with the lemon juice and mint. Thread 1 piece of each fruit onto a skewer, for a total of 8 eight skewers.

Per Serving: Calories 50; Protein 1g; Fat 0g (Saturated 0g); Carbohydrates 12g; Fiber 2g; Sodium 4mg

Dessert Fruit Plates

Makes: 6 servings

This can be a beautiful end to a formal dinner party. The fruits can be arranged ahead of time, the plates chilled, and then dressed just prior to serving.

1 papaya
1 kiwi
1/2 pint blueberries
1/2 pint raspberries
1 cup plain nonfat yogurt
1 tablespoon minced fresh mint
2 teaspoons honey
1 teaspoon fruit liqueur of choice, such as cassis

1) Peel the papaya and scoop out and discard the seeds. Cut the fruit into long, thin slices.

2) Peel the kiwi and slice into rounds.

3) Gently wash the blueberries. Avoid washing the raspberries if possible, since they turn mushy easily.

4) Arrange the fruit on 6 dessert plates.

5) Whisk the yogurt, mint, and honey until smooth.

6) Pour the sauce over the fruit in a narrow stream so there is a little on each type of fruit, but none is completely covered by the sauce. Garnish with mint if desired.

Per Serving: Calories 84; Protein 3g; Fat 0g (Saturated 0g); Carbohydrates 18g; Fiber 3g; Sodium 35mg

Strawberry-Yogurt Fruit Salad Dressing

Makes: 9 servings

For the best texture, use within a few hours of pureeing.

1 pint strawberries, hulled
1/4 cup orange juice
1/3 cup honey
8 ounces plain nonfat yogurt

Coarsely chop the strawberries in a food processor or by hand. Pulse or blend in the orange juice and honey. Remove from the machine and gently stir in the yogurt.

Per Serving: Calories 65; Protein 2g; Fat 0g (Saturated 0g); Carbohydrates 15g; Fiber 1g; Sodium 20mg

Honeyed Pineapple

Makes: 8 servings

Greater than the sum of its parts, this simple recipe is truly delicious.

1 pineapple
1/4 cup honey

1) Peel the pineapple, cut it into 4 wedges, and slice off and discard the core from each piece. Cut each section into narrower wedges or triangles. The pineapple triangles can be threaded onto skewers.

2) Put the pineapple in a glass or stainless-steel bowl. Coat it with the honey. Let it rest for at least 15 minutes, or up to several hours.

3) Preheat the broiler. Line a baking pan with parchment paper or foil coated with nonstick spray. (This greatly eases cleanup—broiled honey can really stick to a pan.)

4) Place the pineapple on the baking pan, then put it under the broiler. Cook for about 5 minutes, until the edges turn light brown. Turn thick pieces once during cooking, using long-handled metal tongs.

Per Serving: Calories 61; Protein 0g; Fat 0g (Saturated 0g); Carbohydrates 16g; Fiber 1g; Sodium 1mg

Broiled Fruit Kebabs

Makes: 4 servings

Make this when a light dessert is desired, but plain fresh fruit isn't enough.

8 grapes
8 strawberries, hulled
8 melon balls or cubes
8 pineapple chunks
1 tablespoon lemon juice
1 tablespoon fresh lime juice
1 tablespoon orange juice
1 teaspoon chopped fresh mint
2 tablespoons sugar

1) Toss the fruit with the fruit juices and mint. Let rest for 15 minutes.

2) Soak 8 wooden skewers in water. Preheat the broiler and line a baking sheet with foil.

3) Thread 1 of each fruit onto each skewer. Place them on the baking sheet. Dust generously with the sugar. Broil for about 3 to 5 minutes, until the sugar begins to brown.

Per Serving: Calories 78; Protein 1g; Fat 1g (Saturated 0g); Carbohydrates 19g; Fiber 2g; Sodium 4mg

Baked Peaches with Ginger

Makes: 4 servings

Use freestone peaches for pretty peach halves and less waste; their fruit is easily twisted away from the pit. Unfortunately, peaches are rarely labeled "freestone" or, their opposite, "cling" in the market. Ask to have one cut to make sure.

4 large or 8 medium freestone peaches
  (about 2 pounds)
2 tablespoons honey
3 tablespoons chopped crystallized ginger

1) Preheat the oven to 350°F.

2) Peel the peaches by immersing them for 30 to 60 seconds in a pot of boiling water. Their skins will slip right off. If after boiling you still have to peel the skins off with a knife, then the peaches weren't ripe (though they will still be okay for this recipe). Cut the peaches in half and twist off from the pit.

3) Place the peach halves in a baking dish or casserole. Drizzle on the honey and distribute the ginger on top. Cover and bake for 20 to 25 minutes. Serve hot or at room temperature.

Per Serving: Calories 143; Protein 1g; Fat 0g (Saturated 0g); Carbohydrates 37g; Fiber 3g; Sodium 0mg

Baked Apples

Makes: 6 servings

If you peel a strip of skin off the equators of the apples, they won't burst in the oven.

6 apples
6 cinnamon sticks
1/3 cup raisins, divided
1/2 cup frozen apple juice concentrate, thawed
1/2 cup water
1/4 teaspoon ground nutmeg
1/8 teaspoon ground cloves

1) Preheat the oven to 375°F.

2) Wash and core the apples. Peel a strip of skin off the apples' equators. Set them in a baking pan.

3) Put a cinnamon stick and 1 tablespoon of the raisins into each core.

4) Combine the apple juice concentrate and water and pour over the apples. There should be at least 1/4 inch of liquid on the bottom of the pan. If not, add a little more water.

5) Dust the nutmeg and cloves on top of the apples. The apples can be made up to this point and held for several hours before baking.

6) Bake, covered, for 30 to 40 minutes, until the apples soften.

Per Serving: Calories 148; Protein 1g; Fat 1g (Saturated 0g); Carbohydrates 38g; Fiber 3g; Sodium 8mg

Microwaved Baked Apple for One

Makes: 1 serving

A very firm apple like a Granny Smith might take a few minutes more to cook.

1 apple
1 tablespoon golden raisins
Dash ground cinnamon
Dash ground nutmeg
2 tablespoons apple juice

1) Wash and core the apple. Peel a strip from around its middle and another off the top. Set the apple in a microwavable bowl.

2) Put the raisins into the core. Dust with cinnamon and nutmeg. Pour the juice around the apple. Cover.

3) Microwave on high for 5 to 7 minutes, until the skin begins to crack.

Per Serving: Calories 128; Protein 1g; Fat 1g (Saturated 0g); Carbohydrates 33g; Fiber 3g; Sodium 2mg

Spiced Baked Apples with Applejack

Makes: 4 servings

These are not your typical baked apples.

4 large baking apples, such as Cortland
1/4 cup applejack or calvados
1/4 cup honey
1/4 cup packed light brown sugar
1/2 cup orange juice
1 tablespoon orange zest, finely minced or in fine strips
8 whole cloves
4 whole star anise
4 cinnamon sticks

1) Preheat the oven to 375°F.

2) Core the apples and peel a strip of skin from around their equators. Place them in a baking pan.

3) Combine the applejack, honey, and brown sugar. Warm the honey if it does not pour easily. Stir in the orange juice and zest. Pour this mixture into the cores of the apples and over their tops. Let it run into the pan. Distribute the cloves and anise in the pan and put a cinnamon stick in the core of each apple. The apples can be prepared up to this point and held for several hours before baking.

4) Place the apples in the oven and bake until soft, about 40 to 50 minutes. Baste every 15 minutes with the liquid from the pan.

Per Serving: Calories 289; Protein 1g; Fat 1g (Saturated 0g); Carbohydrates 67g; Fiber 4g; Sodium 7mg

Brandy Baked Apples with Jelly Glaze

Makes: 4 servings

Red currant jelly is often used for glazes because it is sweet but not too sweet, and it lends an attractive rosy shine to baked goods.

4 large baking apples, such as Cortland
1/4 cup packed light brown sugar
1 tablespoon brandy or cognac
1/4 cup raisins
3 tablespoons fresh breadcrumbs
2 tablespoons red currant jelly, melted

1) Preheat the oven to 375°F.

2) Core the apples and peel their top thirds.

3) Combine the sugar, brandy, raisins, and breadcrumbs. Stuff this mixture into each apple's core.

4) Using a pastry brush, coat the apples with some of the jelly.

5) Place the apples in a baking dish and pour 1/2 inch of water in the pan. Bake 40 to 45 minutes, until soft. Baste with jelly twice more during baking.

Per Serving: Calories 246; Protein 1g; Fat 1g (Saturated 0g); Carbohydrates 62g; Fiber 5g; Sodium 22mg

Glazed Baked Pears

Makes: 6 servings

Pears are one of the few fruits that can be bought concrete-hard from the supermarket, then left to ripen on the counter to a juicy sweetness.

6 pears
1/2 cup apple juice
1 cup honey
1/2 teaspoon ground allspice
1 1/2 teaspoons vanilla extract

1) Preheat the oven to 375°F.

2) Slice the pears in half lengthwise. For a pretty presentation I like to leave the stem on one of the halves. With a spoon (a grapefruit spoon works especially well), scrape out the core and tough string.

3) Place the pears cut side down in a casserole. The type of baking dish will make a big difference in the outcome of this recipe. When I baked this in an enameled cast-iron casserole, the sauce caramelized into a sticky candy. But in a white porcelain baking dish, which reflects heat, the sauce bubbled and thickened slightly. The pears in the white dish also took about 7 minutes longer to bake. (Both versions were yummy; just keep an eye on things.)

4) Whisk together the apple juice, honey, allspice, and vanilla. Pour the sauce over the pears.

5) Baking time varies with the ripeness of the pears. Rock-solid pears will take up to 45 minutes. For such pears, cover the casserole for the first 30 minutes. Ripe pears will take only 20 to 25 minutes and can be cooked uncovered. The pears are done when a knife can be inserted easily. (Try to do this test in an inconspicuous spot on the underside of the pear.) Or wait until their skins begin to crack.

6) Serve hot, with sauce poured over each portion. Leftovers are wonderful.

Per Serving: Calories 282; Protein 1g; Fat 1g (Saturated 0g); Carbohydrates 74g; Fiber 4g; Sodium 3mg

Pears as Blintzes

Makes: 4 servings

Blintzes are crepelike desserts filled with sweet cheese or fruit. Based on the concept of the blintz, I developed this whimsical dessert that uses whole poached pears instead of crepe wrappers to surround a filling. Serving cheese blintzes with jam is traditional, so here a sauce is with made fruit preserves and poured around the baked pears.

4 firm pears

Poaching Liquid
3 cups water
1 teaspoon ground cinnamon
1/2 cup frozen apple juice concentrate
1 teaspoon vanilla extract

Filling
2/3 cup farmer's cheese or dry-curd cottage cheese
2 tablespoons honey
1/4 teaspoon vanilla extract
1 egg white

Sauce
1 tablespoon cornstarch
1 tablespoon water
1 cup poaching liquid
1 cup fruit preserves

1) Core the pears, all the way through, from top to bottom, then peel. Combine the ingredients for the poaching liquid and bring to a simmer. Add the pears and cook over low heat until they soften, about 20 to 35 minutes, or until a knife can be slipped into the fruit without resistance. Turn the pears over several times while poaching so that all sides cook evenly. When done, remove the pears and discard all but 1 cup of the poaching liquid.

2) Preheat the oven to 350°F.

3) Combine the filling ingredients and blend until smooth. Fill the cored pears with this mixture.

4) Set the pears upright in a baking dish. Cover and bake 30 minutes.

5) In a small bowl, stir the cornstarch and water into a paste.

6) While the pears bake, prepare the sauce by boiling the reserved cup of poaching liquid and the fruit preserves for 5 minutes. Reduce the heat to a simmer and stir in the cornstarch paste, stirring until the sauce thickens and clears.

7) Pour half the sauce onto a serving platter or into individual bowls, place the pears upright in this, then drizzle the remaining sauce over them. Serve warm.

Per Serving: Calories 417; Protein 5g; Fat 5g (Saturated 3g); Carbohydrates 95g; Fiber 5g; Sodium 150mg

Poached Pears in Raspberry Sauce

Makes: 6 servings

The pears can be poached a day ahead of time. The sauce, too, can be made earlier, but cannot be reheated.

2 cups dry red wine
3 1/4 cups water, divided
1 1/2 cups frozen apple juice concentrate, thawed, divided
1 slice fresh ginger
2 cinnamon sticks
1/4 teaspoon ground nutmeg
6 firm pears, peeled and cored from the bottom, stems left intact
1 1/2 cups raspberries (fresh or frozen, without syrup)
2 tablespoons cornstarch
Fresh mint leaves, for garnish (optional)

1) Bring the wine, 3 cups of the water, and 1 cup of the apple juice concentrate to a boil. Add the ginger, cinnamon sticks, and nutmeg. Reduce the heat to a simmer.

2) Drop in the pears and poach until tender, about 20 to 35 minutes depending on their ripeness. The pears are done when a knife can be slipped into the fruit without resistance. (Do this from the core end so that no marks will show.) If the pears are overcooked, they will fall apart.

3) Remove the pears from the poaching liquid and set onto a serving platter or individual plates.

4) Discard the ginger, cinnamon sticks, and all but 3 cups of the poaching liquid. Add the remaining apple juice concentrate to the poaching liquid and boil until it is reduced to half its original volume (just under 2 cups). This will take less than 15 minutes.

5) Reduce the heat to a simmer and add the raspberries (reserving a few for garnish if using fresh fruit).

6) In a small bowl, stir together the remaining water and the cornstarch. Slowly add the cornstarch paste to the simmering liquid and stir constantly until the sauce thickens and clears.

7) Pour the sauce around the pears. If desired, insert a mint leaf near the stem and place a few fresh whole raspberries in the sauce. Serve warm or chilled.

Per Serving: Calories 230; Protein 1g; Fat 1g (Saturated 0g); Carbohydrates 51g; Fiber 5g; Sodium 16mg

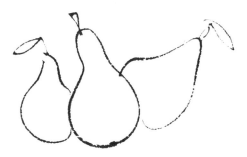

Pears with Red Currant Jelly Sauce

Makes: 8 servings

Don't serve these chilled. They are best when served warm.

1 cup red wine
1 cup water
2 cups apple juice
1 cinnamon stick
1 whole star anise
4 whole cloves
1 teaspoon vanilla extract
$^1/_4$ cup sugar
4 firm pears
$^1/_2$ cup red currant jelly
1$^1/_2$ tablespoons cornstarch mixed with
    1 tablespoon water

1) Bring the wine, water, apple juice, cinnamon, anise, cloves, vanilla, and sugar to a simmer.

2) Meanwhile, core and peel the pears. Once the liquid is simmering, add the pears and cook over low heat until they soften, about 20 to 35 minutes, until a knife can be slipped into the fruit without resistance. (Test the fruit from inside the core so that the outsides of the pears remain whole and pretty.) Very firm pears might take 45 minutes, softer pears only 20 minutes. Turn the pears over several times while poaching so that all sides are cooked evenly. When done, put the pears on a plate.

3) Strain the poaching liquid and discard all but 1 cup. Place the 1 cup of poaching liquid in a pot and add the jelly. Bring to a simmer and stir until the jelly is dissolved.

4) Stir the cornstarch paste into the pot and continue to gently stir until the sauce thickens and clears, about 2 to 3 minutes.

5) Cut the pears in half and place, cut side down, in a serving dish. Pour the sauce over and around the pears.

Per Serving: Calories 130; Protein 0g; Fat 0g (Saturated 0g); Carbohydrates 32g; Fiber 2g; Sodium 12mg

PIES

Pies are classic American fare. I have friends who love pie so much that they served apple pie at their wedding. Many pies, especially fruit pies, start out with healthful ingredients. The crust is usually what contains the majority of the fat. In these fruit pies, the crust is the only fat in the pie, and my crusts are lighter than most. Cream pies have also been lightened up by using lowfat pudding fillings and meringues instead of whipped cream toppings.

Double Pie Crust

Makes: two 8- to 10-inch crusts

I've worked on dozens of recipe tests for pie crusts. Although oil works fine for a pat-in crust, I found that butter was essential for a rolled crust. I finally came up with a recipe that met my standards. It has less saturated fat than a traditional crust, but all of the flakiness.

2 cups unbleached, all-purpose white flour
1/2 teaspoon salt
4 tablespoons chilled unsalted butter
5 tablespoons vegetable oil
1/4 cup water

1) Put the flour and salt in a food processor fitted with a steel blade. Cut the butter into pieces and drop it into the machine. Pulse until it is in bits the size of coarse sand. Slowly pour in the oil, pulsing the entire time, but do not let the machine run steadily. Pulse in the water 1 tablespoon at a time. This mixture will be crumbly. Take it out of the machine, press into a large ball, wrap in plastic, and let rest 15 minutes. Do not refrigerate.

2) To roll out the dough, first divide it into 2 portions and flatten each into a disk. Next, put a disk between 2 pieces of wax paper and, using a rolling pin, press from the center out. In order to get an evenly rolled crust, do not attempt to flatten it in a few hard passes. Instead, push moderately on the rolling pin and rotate the crust after each stroke. After several passes the dough will be evenly pressed into a circle. If the bottom sheet of wax paper wrinkles, pull it taut again as you work.

3) To place the crust in the pie pan, remove the bottom sheet of wax paper, center the crust over the pie pan, drop it in, press down lightly, and peel off the top piece of paper. After the pie is filled, repeat with the top crust, if necessary. Trim the edges with scissors or a knife, leaving a little extra for shrinkage. Press the crusts together along the rim and use your fingers to flute the edge, or decorate by pressing down with the tines of a fork. Top crusts benefit from being brushed with lowfat milk and dusted with sugar before baking.

4) To prebake a crust, lay it loosely in the pie pan, then trim the edges and flute them if desired. Bake in a preheated 425°F oven for 12 to 14 minutes, until golden and lightly brown along the edges.

Per Serving: Calories 180; Protein 3g; Fat 12g (Saturated 3g); Carbohydrates 17g; Fiber 1g; Sodium 108mg

Graham Cracker Crust

Makes: one 9-inch pie crust

The nice thing about making this crust is that it forces you to buy a box of graham crackers. Once they are in the pantry, you'll remember how good they are with a glass of milk.

1¹/2 cups ground graham cracker crumbs (from 12 large rectangles)
1 tablespoon butter
1¹/2 tablespoons vegetable oil
1 tablespoon nonfat milk
1 tablespoon sugar
1 egg white

1) Using a food processor, pulse the crumbs and butter until the butter is evenly distributed. Quickly pulse in each additional ingredient, one at a time in the order listed. Do not let the machine run continuously. The crust should be crumbly, not a smooth paste.

2) Pat the crust into a 9-inch pie pan, bringing it up the sides to the rim.

3) If a prebaked shell is desired, bake in a pre-heated 350°F oven for 8 minutes.

Per Serving: Calories 139; Protein 2g; Fat 6g (Saturated 2g); Carbohydrates 19g; Fiber 1g; Sodium 159mg

Press-in Pie Crust

Makes: one 9-inch crust

This is perfect for one-crust pies and for cooks who worry about making pastry. It is easy because no rolling is required, and the crust is made right in the pie pan.

1 cup unbleached, all-purpose white flour
¹/4 teaspoon salt
1 teaspoon sugar
¹/4 cup vegetable oil
2 to 3 tablespoons 1% lowfat milk

1) Combine the flour, salt, and sugar in a 9-inch pie pan. Drizzle in the oil, all the while tossing with your fingertips. Mix until crumbly. Pour in the milk, 1 tablespoon at a time, until small soft balls form and when pressed the dough stays together.

2) Pat the dough into the pan, bringing it up along the sides to the rim.

3) Refrigerate 15 minutes before filling. This can also be partially baked at 425°F. Line with foil and top with weights. To completely pre-bake, remove the weights and foil after 10 minutes, reduce the oven temperature to 350°F, and bake 10 minutes longer, until golden.

Per Serving: Calories 91; Protein 1g; Fat 6g (Saturated 0g); Carbohydrates 9g; Fiber 0g; Sodium 55mg

Meringue Shell

Makes: 8 servings

Meringues are very easy to make, but should only be attempted when the weather is very dry. Made on a damp day, the meringue will be chewy and tough, but baked during dry weather it will be crispy and light. Use this shell for any pie that does not need baking, such as lemon curd, chocolate, or ice cream.

1 cup sugar
1/8 teaspoon salt
2 teaspoons cornstarch
4 egg whites, at room temperature
1/4 teaspoon cream of tartar
1 teaspoon vanilla extract

1) Combine the sugar, salt, and cornstarch. Preheat the oven to 225°F. Line a baking sheet with parchment paper. Draw a 9-inch circle on it (use a pie pan for a stencil), or draw four 4-inch circles.

2) In a very clean bowl (a touch of fat will ruin a meringue), beat the egg whites until foamy. Add the cream of tartar and beat until soft peaks form. Gradually add the sugar mixture a few tablespoons at a time and beat until stiff peaks form. With a rubber spatula, fold in the vanilla.

3) Mound the meringue in the center of the circle and spread it out to form a pie shell, making it thicker toward the outside of the circle. Or spread some of the meringue evenly about 1/2 inch thick, then pipe a decorative ridge along the outside edge using a pastry bag.

4) Bake 1 hour. Turn off the oven, open the oven door, and let cool in the oven until crispy and dry. Shells will stay fresh for 1 day in a tightly sealed container.

Per Serving: Calories 109; Protein 2g; Fat 0g (Saturated 0g); Carbohydrates 26g; Fiber 0g; Sodium 61mg

Apple Pie

Makes: 10 servings

Because apple juice concentrate, not sugar, is used as a sweetener, this pie has a deep apple flavor.

6 baking apples
1 teaspoon lemon juice
1 1/2 tablespoons cornstarch
1/4 teaspoon ground nutmeg
1 1/2 teaspoons ground cinnamon
1/2 cup frozen apple juice concentrate, thawed
1/4 cup honey or maple syrup
1 recipe Double Pie Crust, rolled out for a 9-inch pan (page 521)

1) Preheat the oven to 425°F.

2) Peel and core the apples. Slice into fairly large wedges and toss with the lemon juice to prevent browning.

3) Add the cornstarch, nutmeg, and cinnamon to the apples. Toss until the apples are well coated. Pour in the apple juice concentrate and honey and stir.

4) Place the bottom crust in the pie pan. Press down and trim the edges. Fill the crust with the apples, piling them highest in the center.

5) Top the pie with the upper crust and crimp the two crusts together. Slice a steam vent in the top.

6) Bake for 20 minutes, then reduce the temperature to 375°F and bake for another 30 minutes.

Per Serving: Calories 279; Protein 3g; Fat 12g (Saturated 3g); Carbohydrates 42g; Fiber 2g; Sodium 112mg

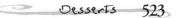

Cranberry Apple Pie

Makes: 10 servings

Look over the cranberries and discard mushy or shriveled berries and any stems. A few berries can be lighter in color or even have a tinge of green but most should be bright, shiny red.

1 recipe Press-in Pie Crust (page 521)
1 1/2 cups cranberries, washed and picked over
1/2 cup raisins
1/2 teaspoon ground cinnamon
1 tablespoon finely minced orange zest
2/3 cup packed light brown sugar
1/2 cup water
2 tablespoons cornstarch
2 medium apples, cored, peeled, and thinly sliced

1) Preheat the oven to 425°F. Line a baking sheet with foil to ease clean-up.

2) Prepare the crust in a 9-inch pie pan. Refrigerate the crust during the next step.

3) In a small pot, bring the cranberries, raisins, cinnamon, orange zest, brown sugar, and water to a boil. Reduce to a simmer and cook for about 6 minutes, until the cranberries split. Remove from the heat and stir in the cornstarch.

4) Arrange the apple slices on the crust in one overlapping layer. You might not need all the apples. Pour the cranberry mixture into the pie. Place the pie pan on the baking sheet and bake in the center of the oven for 15 minutes. Reduce the oven temperature to 350°F and cover lightly with a piece of foil. Continue to bake for another 25 minutes.

5) Cool on a wire rack.

Per Serving: Calories 199; Protein 2g; Fat 6g (Saturated 0g); Carbohydrates 37g; Fiber 2g; Sodium 62mg

More Than Apple Pie

Makes: 10 servings

Raisins and walnuts make this a dense, rich pie.

1 recipe Double Pie Crust, rolled out for a 9-inch pan (page 521)
6 baking apples (about 1 1/2 pounds)
1 1/2 teaspoons lemon juice
1/4 cup honey
1 teaspoon ground cinnamon
1/8 teaspoon ground cloves
1/3 cup walnuts
1/3 cup raisins

1) Preheat the oven to 425°F. Place the bottom crust in a pie pan. Prick the bottom of the crust and chill while preparing the pie filling.

2) Peel, core, and slice the apples. Toss with the lemon juice to prevent browning and to enhance flavor.

3) Stir the honey, cinnamon, cloves, walnuts, and raisins in with the apples.

4) Pour the apple mixture into the pie pan, mounding it in the center.

5) Place the upper crust on top and pinch the edges of the crusts together. Cut steam vents into the top.

6) Bake for 20 minutes, until the crust starts to brown. Reduce the heat and bake at 375°F for 30 minutes longer.

Per Serving: Calories 289; Protein 3g; Fat 14g (Saturated 4g); Carbohydrates 40g; Fiber 2g; Sodium 109mg

Strawberry Rhubarb Pie

Makes: 10 servings

I adore the combination of sour and sweet in this pie.

2 cups strawberries
3 cups 1-inch rhubarb pieces
3 tablespoons cornstarch
1 cup sugar
1 recipe Double Pie Crust, rolled out for a 9-inch pan (page 521)
1 tablespoon nonfat milk

1) Preheat the oven to 425°F. Line a baking sheet with foil to catch drips.

2) Wash the berries and remove the hulls and any bruised parts. Dry gently on paper towels. Place in a bowl and toss with the rhubarb, cornstarch, and sugar.

3) Place a crust in the pie pan. Put the pie filling in the pan. Place the second crust on top. Trim the edges and crimp the rim where the two crusts meet. Cut a decorative vent at the peak. Brush with the milk. Dust with additional sugar, if desired.

4) Place the pie pan on the baking sheet and bake in the center of the oven. After 10 minutes, reduce the temperature to 350°F and bake for another 35 minutes. Cool on a wire rack until the pie's juices set, at least 2 hours.

Per Serving: Calories 284; Protein 3g; Fat 12g (Saturated 3g); Carbohydrates 43g; Fiber 2g; Sodium 111mg

Peach Pie

Makes: 10 servings

Sometimes the less you do to fruit pies, the better they are. This recipe is a case in point. All that's needed are ripe peaches and a little honey. Anything more would detract from the inherent goodness of the fruit.

10 ripe peaches (about 5 cups peeled and pitted fruit)
1/3 cup maple syrup or honey
1 1/2 tablespoons cornstarch
1 recipe Double Pie Crust, rolled out for a 9-inch pan (page 521)

1) Preheat the oven to 425°F.

2) Drop the peaches in a pot of boiling water for 15 seconds. Remove immediately and peel. Cut in half and remove the pits, then cut the halves in half. If peaches are "cling" varieties, you'll have to cut the fruit away from the pit.

3) Toss the peaches with the maple syrup and cornstarch.

4) Set the bottom crust in a pie pan and prick the bottom. Fill the pie crust with the peaches. Place the upper crust on the pie and flute the edges, or seal them with the tines of a fork. Cut a steam vent in the top crust.

5) Bake for 20 minutes, then reduce the temperature to 350°F and bake for 30 to 40 minutes longer, until the crust browns and the pie bubbles.

Per Serving: Calories 250; Protein 3g; Fat 12g (Saturated 3g); Carbohydrates 35g; Fiber 2g; Sodium 109mg

Berry Pie

Makes: 10 servings

Although fresh berries in summer are excellent here, when bags of frozen berries are on sale, I make this pie, regardless of the time of year.

6 cups berries of choice (fresh or frozen)
1/4 cup cornstarch
3/4 to 1 cup sugar
1 recipe Double Pie Crust, rolled out for a 9-inch pan (page 521)
1 tablespoon nonfat milk (optional)

1) Preheat the oven to 350°F. Line a baking sheet with foil to ease clean-up, since berry pies ooze out sticky syrup.

2) If fresh, wash and sort through the berries. Put the berries, cornstarch, and sugar in a saucepan. If the berries are fresh, add 2 tablespoons water. Set over medium heat and cook until the sugar melts.

3) Place the bottom crust in the pie pan. Pour in the berry mixture. Place the top crust on top. Trim the edges and crimp the rim where the two crusts meet. Cut a decorative vent at the peak. Brush with milk and dust with additional sugar, if desired.

4) Place the pie pan on the baking sheet and bake in the center of the oven for 55 to 60 minutes. Cool on a wire rack until the fruit sets, at least 2 hours.

Per Serving: Calories 287; Protein 3g; Fat 12g (Saturated 3g); Carbohydrates 43g; Fiber 4g; Sodium 108mg

Pumpkin Pie

Makes: 10 servings

Make sure you're using unsweetened evaporated nonfat milk for this recipe, not sweetened condensed nonfat milk.

1/2 recipe Double Pie Crust (page 521), rolled out, or Press-in Crust (page 522)
One 15-ounce can pumpkin (2 cups)
1 cup evaporated nonfat milk
1/3 cup maple syrup
1/2 cup honey
1 teaspoon ground cinnamon
1/4 teaspoon ground ginger
1/8 teaspoon ground cloves
1/8 teaspoon allspice
1 tablespoon cornstarch
2 egg whites

1) Preheat the oven to 375°F. Prepare the crust in a deep pie dish.

2) Combine all the ingredients except the egg whites in a food processor fitted with a metal blade. Transfer to a bowl.

3) Beat the egg whites to a soft peak and fold into the pumpkin mixture.

4) Pour the batter into the pie pan and bake for about 1 hour, until a knife inserted into the center comes out clean.

Per Serving: Calories 211; Protein 4g; Fat 6g (Saturated 2g); Carbohydrates 37g; Fiber 2g; Sodium 98mg

Blueberry and Banana Sour Cream Pie

Makes: 8 servings

A store-bought reduced-fat graham cracker crust can be used, both to save time and to minimize calories from fat.

1 Graham Cracker Crust recipe (page 522)
1 banana
Two 13-ounce bags frozen blueberries (about 4 cups), thawed and drained
1/2 teaspoon lemon zest
3 tablespoons unbleached, all-purpose white flour
1/2 cup sugar
1 1/2 teaspoons vanilla extract
8 ounces lowfat sour cream
1/4 cup instant plain oatmeal
2 tablespoons packed light brown sugar
1 tablespoon unsalted butter, melted

1) Preheat the oven to 375°F.

2) Slice the banana into the pie crust. Arrange in one layer.

3) Stir together the blueberries, lemon zest, and flour. Spread over the bananas.

4) Combine the sugar, vanilla, and sour cream until smooth. Pour over the blueberries so that all the fruit is covered with a thin layer.

5) Mix together the oatmeal, brown sugar, and butter until crumbly. Distribute this topping over the pie.

6) Bake for 40 minutes, until set. Cool 1 hour to let set before serving.

Per Serving: Calories 323; Protein 5g; Fat 10g (Saturated 5g); Carbohydrates 53g; Fiber 4g; Sodium 180mg

Cappuccino Mud Pie

Makes: 10 servings

This pie, which looks and tastes so decadent, is one of the easiest pies to make. You don't have to have any crust-rolling skills. All that is needed is a food processor and an electric mixer.

12 chocolate wafer cookies
1 teaspoon cornstarch
1 tablespoon vegetable oil
One 8-ounce package reduced-fat cream cheese, softened
1/4 cup nonfat sour cream
2 teaspoons instant espresso powder
1 1/2 tablespoons coffee-flavored liqueur, such as Kahlua
2 tablespoons Dutch-process cocoa
2 tablespoons sugar
One 14-ounce can lowfat sweetened condensed milk
3 egg whites

1) Preheat the oven to 375°F.

2) In a food processor, grind the cookies into crumbs, then mix in the cornstarch. Pulse in the oil. Press the crumbs into a 10-inch pie pan, bringing the crust halfway up the sides.

3) Beat the cream cheese and sour cream until smooth. Add the espresso powder, liqueur, cocoa, and sugar. Continue to beat until all is evenly mixed. On low speed, beat in the milk and eggs whites.

4) Pour the batter into the crust. Bake for 40 to 45 minutes, until the center sets.

Per Serving: Calories 258; Protein 8g; Fat 9g (Saturated 5g); Carbohydrates 35g; Fiber 1g; Sodium 208mg

Lemon Meringue Pie

Makes: 8 servings

Use an 8- or 9-inch pie pan for this; a 10-inch pan is too large.

1 recipe Graham Cracker Crust (page 522)
1 recipe Lemon Curd (page 565)
1 recipe Meringue for Pie (opposite)

Prepare and bake the crust according to the recipe's directions. Fill with the curd and top with the meringue. Bake meringue as the recipe directs.

Per Serving: Calories 262; Protein 5g; Fat 8g (Saturated 2g); Carbohydrates 45g; Fiber 1g; Sodium 230mg

Banana Meringue Pie

Makes: 8 servings

Serve as soon as possible because meringue quickly weeps out liquid and loses its light texture.

1 recipe Graham Cracker Crust (page 522) in a
    9-inch pie pan
2 medium-size ripe bananas
1 recipe Vanilla Pudding (page 564), chilled
1 recipe Meringue for Pie (opposite)

1) Partially prebake the crust.

2) Preheat the oven to 350°F.

3) Slice the bananas and arrange on the crust in a single layer. Fill with the vanilla pudding. Top with the meringue, spreading it on so that it touches the crust.

4) Bake the pie for about 20 minutes, until the meringue lightly browns. Cool on a rack.

Per Serving: Calories 307; Protein 7g; Fat 9g (Saturated 3g); Carbohydrates 51g; Fiber 1g; Sodium 301mg

Strawberry Tart

Makes: 10 servings

Make this in a tart pan, which is a shallow dish with fluted edges and a removable bottom. If you don't own a tart pan, use a pretty pie pan.

1 recipe Press-in Pie Crust (page 522)
1/2 recipe Vanilla Cream (page 565)
1 pint fresh strawberries, washed, hulled,
    and halved
2 teaspoons unflavored gelatin (2 packages)
1/3 cup water
1/3 cup strawberry jam

1) Prebake the tart crust according to the recipe's directions. Let cool to room temperature. Spread the Vanilla Cream on the crust.

2) Reserve one perfect strawberry to be displayed in the center of the tart and arrange the other berries radiating out from that center.

3) In a small saucepan, sprinkle the gelatin over the water and let it sit for 1 minute, until dissolved. Stir in the jam. Heat gently until the jam softens and blends with the water. Bring to a strong simmer, bubbling but not a full boil. Cook for 5 minutes. Let cool to room temperature.

4) Slowly pour the gelatin mixture over the berries, taking care not to dislodge the berries. Use a pastry brush to spread the glaze and ensure that the berries are all glistening.

5) Refrigerate until set.

Per Serving: Calories 165; Protein 3g; Fat 7g (Saturated 2g); Carbohydrates 22g; Fiber 1g; Sodium 93mg

Strawberry-Filled Meringue Torte

Makes: 8 servings

I like vanilla frozen yogurt best for this, but you can try your favorite flavor.

1 pint frozen nonfat yogurt, any flavor
1 recipe Meringue Shell (page 523)
1 pint strawberries, sliced

Allow the yogurt to thaw out of the freezer until it is softened enough to handle. Spread it in the meringue shell. Top with the strawberries, arranged decoratively in a starburst pattern. Serve immediately.

Per Serving: Calories 167; Protein 4g; Fat 0g (Saturated 0g); Carbohydrates 38g; Fiber 1g; Sodium 94mg

Lemon Curd–Filled Meringue Torte

Makes: 8 servings

Lemon Curd is spread on a light, crispy, sweet meringue shell and topped with strawberries for an ethereal combination. Serve it within an hour of construction because the texture deteriorates fairly quickly.

1 cup Lemon Curd (page 565)
1 recipe Meringue Shell (page 523)
1 pint strawberries, sliced

Spread the curd in the meringue shell. Top with the strawberries, arranged decoratively in a starburst pattern.

Per Serving: Calories 187; Protein 3g; Fat 1g (Saturated 0g); Carbohydrates 43g; Fiber 1g; Sodium 64mg

Meringue for Pie

Makes: 8 servings

A meringue topping is a light, white alterative to whipped cream. Do not attempt making meringue on a hot, humid day because the meringue will sweat and be chewy.

4 egg whites, at room temperature
$1/8$ teaspoon salt
$1/4$ teaspoon cream of tartar
$1/4$ cup sugar

1) Preheat the oven to 350°F.

2) Combine the egg whites and salt in a mixing bowl. Beat until foamy. Add the cream of tartar. While beating, add the sugar about 1 tablespoon at a time. Continue to beat until stiff peaks form.

3) Slip the meringue onto the center of the filled pie of choice. With a rubber spatula, spread it out until it touches the crust. (This will keep it from shrinking back in as it browns in the oven.)

4) Bake in the top third of the oven about 15 to 20 minutes, until golden.

Per Serving: Calories 33; Protein 2g; Fat 0g (Saturated 0g); Carbohydrates 6g; Fiber 0g; Sodium 68mg

Italian Meringue

Makes: 8 servings

This meringue is sturdier, sweeter, and glossier than the regular meringue. A candy thermometer is useful for making it but not essential.

3 egg whites, at room temperature
1 cup sugar
$^1/_2$ cup water
1 teaspoon vanilla extract

1) Beat the egg whites until stiff.

2) In a small saucepan, bring the sugar and water to a boil. Do not stir. Once it is boiling, cover and cook for exactly 3 minutes. Remove the lid and continue to boil for 15 to 20 minutes until a candy thermometer reads 230°F, or when a shiny, thin thread spools off a spoon that has been dipped in the pot.

3) Slowly pour the hot sugar liquid into the egg whites, beating continuously until it cools to room temperature. Beat in the vanilla.

4) If using for pie, spread the meringue onto the dessert, taking care to have it touch the crust all the way around (this prevents it from shrinking in during baking).

5) Put the pie in the oven and broil less than a minute, until golden. Take care—this meringue burns quickly.

Per Serving: Calories 104; Protein 1g; Fat 0g (Saturated 0g); Carbohydrates 25g; Fiber 0g; Sodium 21mg

Cakes

My family loves desserts, especially cakes. Every birthday is greeted with a cake, though we often also have cake for no special reason. However, I am not a professional pastry chef and do not labor over elaborate desserts. All of these recipes are easy to prepare, even by those whose only prior baking experience has been opening a packaged mix.

Lowfat Baking

Unlike many recipes in this book that allow the cook to be flexible, baking recipes need to be followed exactly. Leaveners react precisely with other ingredients. If one is changed, all else must be adjusted. Technique is also crucial. Full-fat baked goods rely on butter for texture, and there is margin for error. The recipes here rely on the correct, timely beating of the small amount of fat and careful handling of the batter. Since there is so little fat, the cook must carefully scrape out every last bit off the spoons and the mixing bowl when putting the batter in the pan.

Ingredients have been chosen carefully. For example, the cheesecakes have a combination of reduced-fat and nonfat cream cheese. If entirely fat-free, the flavor and texture would not have met anyone's standards for cheesecake. (Note that cream cheese is softened by letting it come to room temperature. Softened cream cheese beats up smoothly.) Small touches, such as using a butter-flavored nonstick spray, make a big difference in the final outcome. Buttermilk needs to be fresh, not powdered, in order to give soft-ness and height to the recipe. Also remember that unlike other recipes in this book, baked goods use regular table salt so the smaller crystals will dissolve into the batter.

Equipment isn't elaborate. I've tested the recipes with a hand-held electric mixer, though a stand mixer can also be used. Many recipes don't need electric appliances at all, just a whisk and a couple of bowls. Do, though, make sure that the bowls are large enough. Stirring in a cramped space is not only annoying but will also adversely affect the batter.

Also, in all cases, add the ingredients in the order listed. For example, I am careful to list oil before honey. That way, the measuring cup is greased for the honey and it will slip right out. To measure dry ingredients, use cups made specifically for them—ones on which a knife can smooth off the surface so that the contents are measured exactly. Flour can be measured by scooping it out of its storage container, but if the flour has settled or is packed in, stir with a knife before scooping, or use a large spoon to transfer it into the measuring cup. Notice that the flours and leaveners are almost always sifted *after* measuring, to ensure that there are no lumps in the batter. I use a basic fine mesh sieve for sifting.

Because the batters are lowfat, recipes cannot be doubled or they will not bake through to the center. To assure perfect baking, many cakes require a Bundt pan, which has a tube in the center to conduct heat evenly throughout the batter. In a regular pan the outside of the cake would blacken before the inside was done.

Yellow Layer Cake

Makes: 10 servings

This is your basic cake. If you've been using cake mixes, try this and you'll be amazed at the difference.

1 3/4 cups unbleached, all-purpose white flour
1/2 teaspoon baking soda
2 teaspoons baking powder
1/4 teaspoon salt
2 tablespoons unsalted butter, softened
1 cup sugar
1 teaspoon vanilla extract
1 whole egg
2 egg whites
1/2 cup plain nonfat yogurt
Icing of choice (pages 544–547)

1) Preheat the oven to 375°F. Coat two 8-inch cake pans with nonstick spray, then lightly dust with flour.

2) Sift together the flour, baking soda, baking powder, and salt. In a separate bowl, using an electric mixer, beat the butter and sugar until the consistency of coarse sand. Beat in the sifted ingredients. On low speed, beat in the remaining ingredients. Pour half the batter into each cake pan.

3) Bake 25 to 30 minutes. Let cool to lukewarm in the pan, then invert onto wire racks. Top with the icing of your choice.

Per Serving: Calories 186; Protein 4g; Fat 3g (Saturated 2g); Carbohydrates 36g; Fiber 0g; Sodium 241mg

Cupcakes

Makes: 12 cupcakes

I brought these to my toddler's school for his birthday and all the teachers (who see a lot of cupcakes) raved about them. Cooking from scratch, especially with simple baked goods, really does make a flavor difference.

2 tablespoons unsalted butter, softened
1 cup sugar
1/4 cup vegetable oil
1 3/4 cups unbleached, all-purpose white flour
1/2 teaspoon salt
1 egg
1 egg white
1 teaspoon vanilla extract
1/2 teaspoon baking powder
1/2 teaspoon baking soda
1/2 cup plain nonfat yogurt
Icing of choice (pages 544–547)

1) Preheat the oven to 350°F. Coat 12 muffin cups with nonstick spray or line with paper cups.

2) Beat the butter and sugar. Add the oil, flour, salt, egg, egg white, and vanilla.

3) Sift the baking powder and baking soda into the bowl. Stir the leaveners and the yogurt into the batter. Pour into the muffin cups, filling halfway.

4) Bake 20 minutes, until the tops turn golden. Top with the icing of your choice.

Per Serving: Calories 193; Protein 3g; Fat 7g (Saturated 2g); Carbohydrates 30g; Fiber 0g; Sodium 180mg

Cocoa Cake

Makes: 12 servings

Make sure you sift together the dry ingredients in the order shown, so that the cocoa doesn't waft all over your kitchen in a brown dust cloud.

1/2 cup sugar
2 teaspoons instant coffee or instant espresso, dissolved in 2/3 cup hot water
1/2 cup vegetable oil
1 1/2 cups honey
3/4 cup buttermilk
3/4 cup cocoa
1 1/2 teaspoons baking soda
1 teaspoon baking powder
1/2 cup whole wheat flour
1 1/2 cups unbleached, all-purpose white flour
3 egg whites, beaten to a soft peak
Icing of choice (pages 544–547)

1) Preheat the oven to 350°F. Coat a 9×13-inch baking pan with nonstick spray.

2) Dissolve the sugar in the hot coffee. Add the oil and the honey and combine. Whisk in the buttermilk.

3) Sift together the dry ingredients.

4) Fold the wet ingredients into the dry using a rubber spatula. The cocoa resists incorporation into the liquid and tends to float in dry lumps, but don't beat it. Stir briskly in a circular motion, then slowly fold the batter over and over until moist and almost—but not entirely—smooth. Fold in the egg whites until only thin white streaks show.

5) Bake for about 45 minutes. Take care not to overcook the batter. The cake is done when it feels firm in the center and a toothpick comes out a bit moist but not coated. Let cool in the pan for 10 minutes, then turn onto a wire rack. Spread on the icing when the cake is cool.

Per Serving: Calories 331; Protein 5g; Fat 10g (Saturated 1g); Carbohydrates 61g; Fiber 3g; Sodium 231mg

Zucchini Cocoa Cake

Makes: 10 servings

If not using walnuts for decoration, place a paper lace doily on the cake and dust confectioners' sugar over it. Carefully remove the doily and you'll have a delicate design.

1 cup grated zucchini (about 1 small zucchini)
2 cups unbleached, all-purpose white flour
1/4 cup Dutch-process cocoa
1 teaspoon baking soda
1 teaspoon baking powder
1 teaspoon salt
1 cup sugar
1 cup buttermilk
1/3 cup vegetable oil
1 egg
1/4 cup chopped walnuts (optional)

1) Preheat the oven to 375°F. Coat a 9-inch round or square cake pan with nonstick spray.

2) Put the zucchini in a colander over the sink. With your hands, squeeze the liquid out of the zucchini. Let it drain in the sink while preparing the remaining ingredients.

3) Sift together the flour, cocoa, baking soda, baking powder, salt, and sugar. In a separate bowl, whisk together the buttermilk, oil, and egg. Stir the zucchini into the wet ingredients. Pour the wet mixture into the dry and fold the two together with a rubber spatula. Do not beat vigorously or the cake will toughen.

4) Spread the batter into the pan. If desired, top with the walnuts. Place in the oven and bake for 40 to 45 minutes, until the center tests dry with a toothpick and the top springs back to a finger's touch.

5) Allow to cool for 10 minutes, then remove from the pan and let cool on a wire rack.

Per Serving: Calories 245; Protein 4g; Fat 9g (Saturated 1g); Carbohydrates 40g; Fiber 1g; Sodium 421mg

Apple Cake

Makes: 10 servings

The size of the pan makes a huge difference in low-fat baking. With little fat in the batter, a taller cake heats through much more slowly. For example, in a 9-inch pan, this cake normally takes 40 minutes to bake, but if put in an 8-inch pan, it requires an additional 30 minutes.

1 tablespoon butter, softened
$1/2$ cup sugar
2 cups unbleached, all-purpose white flour
1 teaspoon baking soda
1 teaspoon baking powder
$1/4$ teaspoon salt
2 tablespoons vegetable oil
1 egg
1 egg white
1 cup nonfat plain yogurt
$1/3$ cup applesauce
1 teaspoon vanilla extract
$1^{1}/2$ cups peeled, diced apples
2 tablespoons finely ground nuts
1 tablespoon packed light brown sugar
$1/2$ teaspoon ground cinnamon
$1/8$ teaspoon ground allspice

1) Preheat the oven to 375°F. Coat a 9-inch springform pan with nonstick spray.

2) Using an electric mixer, beat the butter and sugar until the consistency of coarse sand. Sift the flour, baking soda, baking powder, and salt into this mixture. Beat until evenly combined.

3) On low speed in a separate bowl, beat together the oil, egg, egg white, yogurt, applesauce, and vanilla. Pour this into the dry mixture and stir with a rubber spatula until all is moistened. Do not beat vigorously or the cake will toughen. Pour the batter into the pan.

4) Distribute the apples, nuts, and brown sugar across the top of the batter. Dust on the cinnamon and allspice.

5) Bake for 40 minutes, until the cake is firm to the touch in the center. Cool in the pan, on a wire rack, for 10 minutes. Unmold onto a cake plate.

Per Serving: Calories 201; Protein 5g; Fat 5g (Saturated 1g); Carbohydrates 34g; Fiber 1g; Sodium 271mg

Carrot Cake

Makes: 12 servings

Icing is not essential (and an uniced cake is easier to pack in lunches), but Marshmallow Fluff (page 546) is wonderful spread thickly on this cake.

1 cup whole wheat flour
2 cups unbleached, all-purpose white flour
2 teaspoons baking soda
2 teaspoons ground cinnamon
$1/2$ teaspoon ground nutmeg
$1/4$ teaspoon ground cloves
$1/4$ teaspoon salt
3 egg whites
1 egg
$2/3$ cup vegetable oil
$2/3$ cup buttermilk
$1^1/4$ cups honey
2 cups shredded carrots
One 8-ounce can crushed pineapple, well drained
1 cup currants

1) Preheat the oven to 375°F. Grease a 10-inch Bundt pan.

2) Sift together the dry ingredients.

3) In a separate, large bowl, beat together the egg whites, egg, and oil. Whisk in the buttermilk, then add the honey, and beat until creamy.

4) Stir the carrots, pineapple, and currants into the wet ingredients.

5) Add the dry ingredients to the wet and stir gently until the batter is mixed but not totally smooth. If overmixed, the cake will be dense and tough.

6) Pour the batter into the Bundt pan. Tap the pan on the table to remove air pockets and smooth out the top.

7) Bake for 1 hour, turning the cake pan twice during baking to promote even browning. The cake is done when it feels firm to the touch.

8) Cool on a wire rack for 10 minutes before removing it from the Bundt pan, and then invert the cake onto a wire rack. Transfer to a cake plate only after it is thoroughly cooled or the bottom will become soggy.

Per Serving: Calories 355; Protein 6g; Fat 13g (Saturated 1g); Carbohydrates 57g; Fiber 3g; Sodium 297mg

Pineapple Upside-Down Bake

Makes: 10 servings

This is a sticky, sweet dessert. Warm up a portion in the microwave (less than 20 seconds will do) and top with frozen vanilla yogurt.

One 20-ounce can crushed pineapple, packed in juice
One 20-ounce can pineapple chunks, packed in juice
2 tablespoons pineapple juice from the can
$1/2$ cup honey
1 tablespoon cornstarch
1 egg
$1/4$ cup vegetable oil
$1/4$ cup plain nonfat yogurt
$1/2$ cup 1% lowfat milk
$1/2$ teaspoon vanilla extract
$1 1/4$ cups unbleached, all-purpose white flour
$3/4$ cup whole wheat flour
$1/4$ cup packed light brown sugar
$1 1/2$ teaspoons baking powder
1 teaspoon baking soda
$1/8$ teaspoon kosher salt
$1/2$ teaspoon ground cinnamon

1) Preheat the oven to 400°F. Coat a 2-quart casserole or baking pan with nonstick spray.

2) Drain both cans of pineapple. Discard all but 2 tablespoons of the juice.

3) Combine the pineapple, juice, and honey. Add the cornstarch by sifting to break up lumps. Distribute the pineapple mixture evenly on the bottom of the casserole.

4) Put the egg, oil, yogurt, milk, and vanilla in a mixing bowl. Beat until foamy.

5) In another bowl, sift together the flours, sugar, baking powder, baking soda, salt, and cinnamon and stir well.

6) Make a well in the flour, pour in the wet mixture, and fold the two together until there aren't any dry pockets and it is evenly moist.

7) The batter will be too thick to pour, so drop it by large tablespoonsful onto the pineapple. Spread it with a plastic spatula until it covers the pineapple.

8) Bake for 30 minutes.

Per Serving: Calories 270; Protein 5g; Fat 7g (Saturated 1g); Carbohydrates 51g; Fiber 2g; Sodium 244mg

Lemon Poppy Bundt Cake

Makes: 10 servings

This is a classic tea party cake.

2 tablespoons unsalted butter
1 cup sugar
2 tablespoons vegetable oil
$3/4$ cup buttermilk
1 egg
2 egg whites
1 tablespoon lemon juice
1 teaspoon minced lemon zest
1 teaspoon vanilla extract
$1 1/2$ cups unbleached, all-purpose white flour
$1/2$ teaspoon salt
2 teaspoons baking powder
1 teaspoon baking soda
$1 1/2$ teaspoons poppy seeds
1 recipe Lemon Icing Glaze (page 544)

1) Preheat the oven to 350°F. Spray an 8-inch (6-cup-capacity) Bundt pan with nonstick spray, then dust with flour.

2) Beat the butter and sugar until fluffy as snow. In a separate bowl, stir together the oil, buttermilk, egg, egg whites, lemon juice, lemon zest, and vanilla. Pour this into the sugar mixture and beat until well combined but not frothy.

3) Sift together the flour, salt, baking powder, and baking soda and slowly blend into the batter while beating on low speed. Stop when all is moist. Stir in the poppy seeds.

4) Bake for 40 minutes. Cool in the pan for 5 minutes before removing the cake to a wire rack. Glaze while still warm.

Per Serving: Calories 263; Protein 4g; Fat 6g (Saturated 2g); Carbohydrates 49g; Fiber 1g; Sodium 368mg

Rhubarb Bundt Cake

Makes: 12 servings

If rhubarb is not in season, you might find it at the supermarket in the frozen food case next to the frozen berries. If the pieces are large, chop them first (while still frozen) in the food processor and do not thaw before baking.

2 tablespoons unsalted butter, softened
1 cup sugar
1 1/2 cups unbleached, all-purpose white flour
2 teaspoons baking powder
1 teaspoon baking soda
1/2 teaspoon salt
2 tablespoons vegetable oil
3/4 cup buttermilk
1 egg
2 egg whites
1 teaspoon vanilla extract
1 cup chopped rhubarb
1 tablespoon sugar
1/2 teaspoon ground cinnamon

1) Preheat the oven to 350°F. Spray an 8-inch (6-cup-capacity) Bundt pan with nonstick spray, then dust with flour.

2) Beat the butter and sugar until fluffy as snow. Sift the flour, baking powder, baking soda, and salt into the bowl. Beat until well combined.

3) In a separate bowl, beat together the oil, buttermilk, egg, egg whites, and vanilla on low speed until mixed but not frothy. Stir this into the dry ingredients.

4) Pour the batter into the Bundt pan. Distribute the rhubarb across the top of the batter. Top with the sugar and cinnamon. Bake for 40 minutes. Cool for 10 minutes before removing the cake to a wire rack.

Per Serving: Calories 179; Protein 3g; Fat 5g (Saturated 3g); Carbohydrates 31g; Fiber 1g; Sodium 307mg

Pear and Spice Coffee Cake

Makes: 12 servings

To prevent the bottom of the cake from becoming soggy, leave this on a wire rack to cool thoroughly before putting it on a cake plate.

2 tablespoons unsalted butter, softened

1 cup sugar

1 1/2 cups unbleached, all-purpose white flour

2 teaspoons baking powder

1 teaspoon baking soda

1/2 teaspoon salt

1/4 teaspoon ground cloves

1/2 teaspoon ground ginger

1 teaspoon ground cinnamon

2 teaspoons minced orange or lemon zest

2 tablespoons vegetable oil

3/4 cup buttermilk

1 egg

2 egg whites

1 teaspoon vanilla extract

2 cups finely chopped pears (from 1 to 2 peeled and cored pears)

1/4 cup ground pecans or walnuts

2 tablespoons sugar

1/2 teaspoon ground cinnamon

1) Preheat the oven to 350°F. Spray an 8-inch (6-cup-capacity) Bundt or angel food pan with nonstick spray, then dust with flour.

2) Beat the butter and sugar until as granular and fine as sand. Sift the flour, baking powder, baking soda, salt, cloves, ginger, and cinnamon into the bowl. Beat until well combined. Stir in the zest.

3) In a separate bowl, beat together the oil, buttermilk, egg, egg whites, and vanilla on low speed until mixed but not frothy. Stir this into the dry ingredients. Add the chopped pears and stir gently until all is evenly mixed.

4) Pour the batter into the Bundt pan. Top with the nuts, sugar, and cinnamon. Bake for 45 minutes. Cool for 10 minutes in the pan, then turn upside down onto a cake rack and remove the pan. Leave upside down on the rack until cool.

Per Serving: Calories 203; Protein 4g; Fat 6g (Saturated 2g); Carbohydrates 35g; Fiber 1g; Sodium 306mg

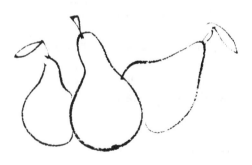

Angel Food Cake

Makes: 12 servings

Although the directions must be followed precisely, angel food cake is not difficult to make.

1 cup unbleached, all-purpose white flour
1 1/2 cups sugar, divided
12 egg whites
1/4 teaspoon salt
1 teaspoon vanilla extract
1 teaspoon cream of tartar

1) Place the oven rack in the bottom third of the oven and preheat the oven to 325°F. Get out your angel food cake pan, but do not grease. Make sure that all your bowls are dry and grease-free. The littlest bit of fat will defeat your cake.

2) Sift the flour with 1/2 cup of the sugar and then set it aside. Put the remaining sugar in a small bowl or measuring cup and set aside.

3) Use chilled eggs from the refrigerator. Separate each egg over a small bowl, then transfer the white into a large mixing bowl. This way, if any yolk gets into the egg whites, it won't ruin the whole batch. I like to separate eggs in my hand, letting the whites strain through my fingers.

4) Add the salt and vanilla to the egg whites. Beat until frothy (light and bubbly but no structure yet), then add the cream of tartar. Beat on high speed until the egg whites are almost stiff (the peaks will be soft and will fall over like the tip of a soft-serve ice cream cone). Add the 1 cup of sugar, shaking in a few tablespoons at a time. Continue to beat on high speed until the egg whites are stiff and shiny. Don't overprocess or the cake will weaken and not rise properly.

5) Using a rubber spatula in slow, sweeping motions, fold in the flour and sugar mixture. Run the spatula along the bottom of the bowl and fold the egg whites over and through the flour and sugar. Continue to do this until there are no longer any dry streaks. Vigorous stirring will deflate the cake, so be gentle.

6) Pour the batter into the pan. Smooth the top and tap the pan on the counter once to fill in any air pockets. Bake for 40 to 45 minutes, until the top turns golden and springs back when touched. If your oven tends to operate a few degrees cool, increase the temperature to 350°F.

7) The cake must cool completely, upside down, for 1 1/2 hours before being removed from the pan. Many angel food cake pans have feet on their tops so that they can be turned over, or you can invert a pan without feet onto a narrow-necked bottle so the cake's top isn't crushed.

8) Run a knife between the cake and the pan. Turn upside down and remove the cake from the pan. If desired, finish with icing, such as Seven-Minute Frosting (page 544), or a glaze.

9) When serving, cut gently with a serrated knife using a sawing motion, or pull waxed dental floss through the cake. A regular knife will just crush it down.

Per Serving: Calories 147; Protein 5g; Fat 0g (Saturated 0g); Carbohydrates 32g; Fiber 0g; Sodium 119mg

Cocoa Angel Food Cake

Makes: 12 servings

Guests will love this cake and say that the flavor is wonderfully interesting, but they probably won't be able to figure out that it is a small amount of cinnamon that does the trick.

3/4 cup unbleached, all-purpose white flour
1/4 cup cocoa
1/2 teaspoon ground cinnamon
1 1/2 cups sugar, divided
12 egg whites
1/4 teaspoon salt
1 teaspoon vanilla extract
1 teaspoon cream of tartar
1 recipe Honey Fudge Frosting (page 545) or
    other icing of choice

1) Place the oven rack in the bottom third of the oven and preheat the oven to 325°F. Get out a 10-inch angel food cake pan. Do not grease. Make sure that all your bowls are dry and grease-free. The littlest bit of fat will defeat your cake.

2) Sift the flour, cocoa, and cinnamon with 1/2 cup of the sugar and set aside. Put the remaining sugar in a small bowl or measuring cup and set aside.

3) Separate each egg over a small bowl, then transfer the white into a large mixing bowl. This way, if any yolk gets into the egg whites, it won't ruin the whole batch. I like to separate eggs in my hand, letting the whites strain through my fingers.

4) Add the salt and vanilla to the eggs. Beat until frothy (light and bubbly but no structure yet), then add the cream of tartar. Beat on high speed until the egg whites are almost stiff (the peaks will be soft and fall over like the tip of a soft-serve ice cream cone). Add the 1 cup of sugar, shaking in a few tablespoons at a time. Continue to beat on high speed until the egg whites are stiff and shiny. Don't overprocess or the cake will weaken and not rise properly.

5) Using a rubber spatula in slow, sweeping motions, fold in the cocoa mixture. Run the spatula along the bottom of the bowl and fold the egg whites over and through the flour and sugar. Continue to do this until there are no longer any dry streaks. Vigorous stirring will deflate the cake, so be gentle.

6) Pour the batter into the pan. Smooth the top and tap the pan on the counter once to fill in any air pockets. Place in the oven. Bake for 40 to 45 minutes, until the top turns golden and springs back when touched. If your oven tends to operate a few degrees cool, increase the temperature to 350°F.

7) The cake must cool completely, upside down, for 1 1/2 hours before being removed from the pan. Many angel food cake pans have feet on their tops so that they can be turned over, or you can invert a pan without feet onto a narrow-necked bottle so the cake's top isn't crushed.

8) Run a knife between the cake and the pan. Turn upside down and remove the cake from the pan. Decorate with the frosting.

9) When serving, cut gently with a serrated knife using a sawing motion, or pull waxed dental floss through the cake. A regular knife will just crush it down.

Per Serving: Calories 181; Protein 5g; Fat 1g (Saturated 0g); Carbohydrates 41g; Fiber 1g; Sodium 125mg

Orange Angel Food Cake

Makes: 12 servings

Continue the orange theme by serving this with Grand Oranges (page 509).

1 recipe Angel Food Cake (page 539)
1 tablespoon finely minced orange zest
1 teaspoon orange extract
1 recipe Orange Icing Glaze (page 544)

1) Follow the directions for Angel Food Cake, but stir the orange zest in with the flour and sugar in Step 3 and add the orange extract when you add the vanilla in Step 5.

2) Top with Orange Icing Glaze.

Per Serving: Calories 211; Protein 5g; Fat 0g (Saturated 0g); Carbohydrates 48g; Fiber 0g; Sodium 119mg

Almond Angel Food Cake

Makes: 12 servings

This cake is decorated by pressing almonds around the sides. This small step, which requires no skill, transforms a basic Angel Food Cake into something that looks like it came from a professional's kitchen.

1 recipe Angel Food Cake (page 539)
1 recipe Seven-Minute Almond Frosting (page 545)
1/2 cup sliced almonds, lightly toasted

1) Follow the directions for Angel Food Cake, but replace the vanilla extract with 1 teaspoon almond extract.

2) Frost with the Almond Frosting, then press the almonds around the sides of the cake.

Per Serving: Calories 265; Protein 6g; Fat 3g (Saturated 0g); Carbohydrates 54g; Fiber 1g; Sodium 151mg

Mousselike Cheesecake

Makes: 12 servings

The more a cheesecake batter is beaten, the lighter and fluffier the end result. If you want a denser, more "New York style" cheesecake, beat the batter at low speed, and stop as soon as it is smooth.

1/2 cup graham cracker crumbs
    (about 4 full-sized crackers)
1 teaspoon cornstarch
One 8-ounce package reduced-fat cream
    cheese, softened
One 8-ounce package nonfat cream
    cheese, softened
1 cup lowfat sour cream
One 14-ounce can skim or lowfat sweetened
    condensed milk
1/2 teaspoon vanilla extract
4 egg whites

1) Place the rack in the center of the oven and preheat to 300°F. Coat an 8- or 9-inch spring-form pan with nonstick spray. Cut a circle of parchment paper to line the bottom and a collar for the sides and place them in the pan.

2) Combine the crumbs and cornstarch and cover the bottom of the springform pan with this mixture.

3) Beat the cream cheeses and sour cream until smooth. Beat in the milk on low speed until all is smooth. Stir in the vanilla.

4) Beat the egg whites to a soft peak. Fold into the cheese mixture.

5) Bake for 1 hour, until almost set. Loosen the cake from the sides of the pan with a knife. Turn off the oven, leave the door open, and let the cake rest for 1 hour. This will prevent the cheesecake from cracking.

6) Remove from the oven, cool completely, and remove from the pan. Keep refrigerated. This cake stays fresh for several days.

Per Serving: Calories 209; Protein 10g; Fat 6g (Saturated 4g); Carbohydrates 29g; Fiber 0g; Sodium 275mg

Chocolate Marble Cheesecake

Makes: 12 servings

You can make this cake several days ahead of a party and it will stay fresh in the refrigerator.

1/2 cup chocolate-wafer cookie crumbs
    (about 10 cookies)
1 teaspoon cornstarch
One 8-ounce package reduced-fat cream
    cheese, softened
One 8-ounce package nonfat cream
    cheese, softened
1 cup lowfat sour cream
One 14-ounce can lowfat sweetened
    condensed milk
4 egg whites
1/2 teaspoon vanilla extract
1 ounce bittersweet chocolate, melted
2 tablespoons cocoa

1) Preheat the oven to 325°F and place the rack in the center of the oven. Coat an 8- or 9-inch springform pan with nonstick spray. Cut a circle of parchment paper to line the bottom and a collar for the sides and place them in the pan.

2) Combine the crumbs and cornstarch and cover the bottom of the springform pan with this mixture.

3) Beat the cream cheeses and sour cream until smooth. Beat in the milk, egg whites, and vanilla on low speed until all is smooth. Vigorous beating will make the cake airy.

4) Measure out 1 cup of the batter. Beat the chocolate and cocoa into this batter. Set aside.

5) Pour three-quarters of the plain batter into the pan. Spoon the chocolate mixture in, then top with the remaining plain batter. Run a knife through the batter so that chocolate swirls appear on the surface.

6) Bake for 50 to 60 minutes, until almost set. Turn off the oven, leave the door open, and let the cake rest for 1 hour. This will prevent the cheesecake from cracking.

7) Remove from the oven, cool completely, and remove from the pan. Keep refrigerated. This cake stays fresh for several days.

Per Serving: Calories 230; Protein 10g; Fat 8g (Saturated 5g); Carbohydrates 29g; Fiber 1g; Sodium 279mg

Ginger Cheesecake

Makes: 12 servings

The heaviness of the cheesecake is offset by the sprightly ginger flavor.

1/2 cup gingersnap crumbs (about 7 cookies)

1 teaspoon cornstarch

One 8-ounce package reduced-fat cream cheese, softened

One 8-ounce package nonfat cream cheese, softened

1 cup lowfat sour cream

1 teaspoon ground ginger

4 egg whites

One 14-ounce can lowfat sweetened condensed milk

1/2 teaspoon vanilla extract

1 tablespoon minced crystallized ginger

1) Preheat the oven to 300°F and place the rack in the center of the oven. Coat an 8- or 9-inch springform pan with nonstick spray. Cut a circle of parchment paper to line the bottom and a collar for the sides and place them in the pan.

2) Combine the crumbs and cornstarch and cover the bottom of the springform pan with this mixture.

3) Beat the cream cheeses, sour cream, ginger, and egg whites until smooth. Beat in the milk on low speed until all is smooth. Stir in the vanilla.

4) Pour into the prepared pan. Distribute the crystallized ginger across the top.

5) Bake for 1 hour, until almost set. Turn off the oven, leave the door open, and let the cake rest for 1 hour. This will prevent the cheesecake from cracking.

6) Remove from the oven, cool completely, and remove from the pan. Keep refrigerated. This cake stays fresh for several days.

Per Serving: Calories 218; Protein 10g; Fat 7g (Saturated 5g); Carbohydrates 28g; Fiber 0g; Sodium 272mg

Frostings

About Glazes

If a glaze is poured onto a hot cake, it will soak in and become invisible, although the flavor will be clear with every bite. Sometimes this is a nice touch. I like to pour the Orange Icing Glaze onto warm Orange Angel Food Cake. However, the same recipe will make an attractive shiny glaze when poured onto a cooled cake. Glazes harden rapidly after being made. So let the cake cool, then make your glaze and pour it over the cake immediately.

Orange Icing Glaze

Makes: enough to ice a 9-inch cake

The Grand Marnier adds a complex note to this glaze, but it can be left out if desired.

1^1/$_2$ cups confectioners' sugar
1 teaspoon minced orange zest
3 tablespoons orange juice
1 teaspoon Grand Marnier or other orange liqueur
1 teaspoon lemon juice

Sift the sugar into a bowl. Blend in the remaining ingredients until smooth. The glaze should be runny; add more orange juice if necessary. Immediately after making the glaze, pour over the top of the cake, letting some drip down the sides.

Per Serving: Calories 74; Protein 0g; Fat 0g (Saturated 0g); Carbohydrates 19g; Fiber 0g; Sodium 0mg

Lemon Icing Glaze

Makes: enough to ice a 9- or 10-inch cake

This is very nice on cupcakes, which can then be decorated with candied lemon peel.

1^1/$_4$ cups confectioners' sugar
^{1}/$_4$ to ^{1}/$_3$ cup lemon juice

Sift the sugar into a bowl. As you pour the juice into the bowl in a slow, steady stream, use a whisk to beat the icing. Stop pouring in the lemon juice when you get the consistency desired. Immediately after making the glaze, pour it over the top of the cake, letting some drip down the sides.

Per Serving: Calories 60; Protein 0g; Fat 0g (Saturated 0g); Carbohydrates 15g; Fiber 0g; Sodium 0mg

Seven-Minute Frosting

Makes: enough to frost a 9-inch cake

Named for the seven minutes that the egg whites and sugar are whipped over heat, this frosting is fluffy and shiny white.

1^1/$_4$ cups sugar
^{1}/$_4$ cup cold water
2 egg whites
^{1}/$_4$ teaspoon cream of tartar
^{1}/$_8$ teaspoon salt
1 teaspoon vanilla extract

1) Bring 2 inches of water to a boil in a pot.

2) Choose a stainless steel bowl that is the right size to rest on top of the pot. (You are making a double-boiler: a bowl is better suited for this than the straight-sided double-boiler insert.) Combine all the ingredients except the vanilla in this bowl and set it over the boiling water. Beat the icing with an electric mixer on high speed for 7 minutes. Time it—it will feel like a long time, but you don't want to stop too soon.

3) Remove the bowl from the pot, add the vanilla, and beat for 2 minutes at high speed.

4) This icing will harden quickly. It is best to ice the cake right away, but if you can't, place plastic wrap directly on the icing, making sure no air touches it.

Per Serving: Calories 101; Protein 1g; Fat 0g (Saturated 0g); Carbohydrates 25g; Fiber 0g; Sodium 38mg

Seven-Minute Almond Frosting

Makes: enough to frost a 9-inch cake

The simple Yellow Layer Cake (page 531) can be made quite elegant with this frosting.

1 recipe Seven-Minute Frosting (opposite)
1 teaspoon almond extract
2 tablespoons sliced almonds, toasted

Follow the directions for Seven-Minute Frosting, but substitue the almond extract for the vanilla. After icing the cake, distribute the almonds on top or around the sides.

Per Serving: Calories 110; Protein 1g; Fat 1g (Saturated 0g); Carbohydrates 25g; Fiber 0g; Sodium 38mg

Honey Fudge Frosting

Makes: enough for a 9 x 13-inch sheet cake

To make really rich-looking brownies, top them with this frosting.

1/3 cup honey
1/2 cup 1% lowfat milk
1/4 cup Dutch-process cocoa
1/2 teaspoon vanilla extract

1) Combine all the ingredients in a food processor fitted with a steel blade. Mix until smooth, scraping down the sides of the bowl.

2) Transfer to a nonstick saucepan and cook over medium-low heat, whisking until it starts to boil. Reduce heat to medium and cook for 10 to 15 minutes, or until slightly thickened, whisking constantly.

3) Let the glaze cool, then drizzle over the cooled cake.

Per Serving: Calories 45; Protein 1g; Fat 0g (Saturated 0g); Carbohydrates 11g; Fiber 1g; Sodium 7mg

Cream Cheese Frosting

Makes: enough to frost a 9-inch cake

I use a combination of reduced-fat and nonfat cream cheese because I don't think that frosting made with all nonfat tastes right. This version, however, satisfies me as much as a full-fat frosting.

One 8-ounce package reduced-fat cream cheese
4 ounces nonfat cream cheese
2 tablespoons lowfat sour cream
1 1/2 cups confectioners' sugar
1 teaspoon vanilla extract

Beat the cream cheeses and sour cream until soft and fluffy. Sift the sugar into the bowl and beat in. Continue to beat and add the vanilla.

Per Serving: Calories 141; Protein 4g; Fat 5g (Saturated 3g); Carbohydrates 19g; Fiber 0g; Sodium 155mg

Chocolate Cream Cheese Frosting

Makes: enough to frost a 9-inch cake

Cocoa Angel Food Cake frosted with this makes a spectacular cake.

4 ounces reduced-fat cream cheese, softened
4 ounces nonfat cream cheese, softened
2 tablespoons lowfat sour cream
1 cup confectioners' sugar
1 ounce semisweet chocolate, melted
2 tablespoons Dutch-process cocoa
1 teaspoon vanilla extract

Beat the cream cheeses and sour cream until soft and fluffy. Sift the sugar into the bowl and beat in. Continue to beat and add the chocolate, cocoa, and vanilla.

Per Serving: Calories 106; Protein 3g; Fat 4g (Saturated 2g); Carbohydrates 16g; Fiber 1g; Sodium 107mg

Marshmallow Fluff

Makes: enough to frost a 9-inch cake

This is a light, sweet, white icing that reminds me of a childhood favorite of the same name.

1 egg white
1/4 cup honey
1/16 teaspoon salt
1/2 teaspoon vanilla extract

1) Fill one-third of the bottom of a pot with water and bring to a boil.

2) Put all the ingredients into a stainless steel bowl that will sit on top of the pot. Place over the boiling water and beat for several minutes, until the egg whites expand and thicken into soft peaks. (Be careful not to overbeat to the stiff peak stage; this results in dense frosting.)

3) Remove the bowl from the double boiler and continue to beat until cool.

Per Serving: Calories 28; Protein 0g; Fat 0g (Saturated 0g); Carbohydrates 7g; Fiber 0g; Sodium 19mg

Cherry Topping

Makes: enough to top a 9-inch cake

Cherry Topping is the classic cheesecake topping, but I also put it straight onto ice cream.

One 16¹/₂-ounce can sweet cherries in syrup
3 tablespoons sugar
1¹/₂ tablespoons cornstarch
¹/₄ cup water
2 teaspoons kirsch, or other cherry brandy
   (optional)

1) Drain the cherries, saving the syrup. Measure ¹/₃ cup of the syrup and put into a small saucepan. Stir in the sugar. Bring to a boil.

2) In a small bowl, mix the cornstarch and water until a smooth paste forms. Using a wooden spoon, stir the paste into the pot. When the mixture clears and is bubbling in the center, remove from the heat. Stir in the cherries, and the kirsch, if desired.

Per Serving: Calories 58; Protein 0g; Fat 0g (Saturated 0g); Carbohydrates 15g; Fiber 0g; Sodium 2mg

Cookies

Not all cookies lend themselves to lower-fat baking. Soft, crumbly, rich butter cookies must have butter. But there are plenty of options for those times when you want a more healthful cookie. Drop cookies can be plump and moist without a lot of fat, and biscotti—those flavor-intense, twice-baked Italian cookies—don't need any oil or butter at all.

Cookies and Oven Temperature

Oven temperature is crucial to successful cookie baking. Preheat your oven a long time (mine needs a full 30 minutes). When cookies are baked in a hot oven, they set quickly and don't spread as much (desirable for drop cookies). If your oven heats unevenly, you'll need to rotate the cookie sheet once while baking. You might notice that the second or third sheet of cookies placed in the oven bakes differently than the first. That is because each time the oven door is opened, the temperature drops. So open the door as quickly as possible and close it before fussing with the cookies you've just removed.

Most cookies bake best in the center of the oven, which is why experienced bakers bake only one sheet at a time. If in a hurry, you can bake up to three shelves of cookies, moving them from shelf to shelf as they bake, but each time the oven door is opened the oven cools so that the cookies spread more and cooking time will be lengthened by several minutes.

Temperature so affects cookies that even the way a cookie sheet is constructed will change how a cookie bakes. Rimless cookie sheets are the best because they allow hot air to flow around the cookies. Insulated cookie sheets (sometimes called "air-cushioned") prevent burning, but they also keep cookies from browning, which can add a few minutes to the baking time and is not always desirable.

Overbaking is to be avoided, and a minute one way or the other can make a difference. I set the oven timer a minute earlier than the suggested baking time, then keep checking in two-minute intervals until the cookies are done. Most cookies are ready when they are lightly golden brown around the edges and their centers are set but still soft. Exceptions to this are noted in the recipes.

Chocolate Chip Biscotti

Makes: 18 biscotti

If you don't have a food processor, the batter can be mixed by hand, but the nuts must be finely ground first.

1/2 cup walnuts or pecans
1 cup unbleached, all-purpose white flour, divided
1/8 teaspoon salt
1/4 cup Dutch-process cocoa
1/2 cup sugar
2 eggs
1 teaspoon vanilla extract
1/2 cup semi-sweet chocolate chips, preferably mini-size

1) Preheat the oven to 325°F. Line a baking sheet with foil and coat with nonstick spray, or use parchment paper.

2) Finely chop the nuts and 1/2 cup of the flour in the food processor. Add the rest of the flour and the salt, cocoa, and sugar. Pulse until mixed.

3) In a bowl, whisk the eggs and vanilla. Using a fork, stir in the dry ingredients until all is moist. Using a stiff spatula or spoon, stir in the chocolate chips.

4) Put a 16-inch-long piece of plastic wrap on your work surface. Place the cookie dough on the plastic and shape it into a log about 14 inches long, 3 inches wide, and 1 inch high. Use the plastic, pulled up along the sides of the dough, to help shape the biscotti. Turn the log onto the cookie sheet, removing the plastic wrap, and place the cookie sheet in the oven.

5) Bake for 25 minutes, turning the cookie sheet once during cooking. Remove the biscotti from the oven and cool on a wire rack for 10 minutes. Reduce the oven temperature to 300°F.

6) Slice the biscotti, on the diagonal, into 1/2-inch-thick cookies. Place them with a cut side down on the cookie sheet. Bake for 20 minutes. Turn the cookies over and bake for another 25 minutes. Cool on a wire rack.

Per Cookie: Calories 95; Protein 2g; Fat 4g (Saturated 1g); Carbohydrates 14g; Fiber 1g; Sodium 23mg

Orange Biscotti

Makes: 20 biscotti

Biscotti are one of the few cookies that aren't best eaten hot right out of the oven. But these are so good, it is hard to wait.

1 cup almonds
2 1/2 cups unbleached, all-purpose white flour, divided
2/3 cup sugar
1 teaspoon baking powder
1 teaspoon baking soda
1/4 teaspoon salt
1 teaspoon vanilla extract
2 tablespoons orange juice
3 eggs
2 teaspoons minced or fine strips orange zest

1) Preheat the oven to 325°F. Coat 2 baking sheets with nonstick spray, or line them with parchment paper.

2) Finely chop the nuts and 1/2 cup of the flour in the food processor. Add the rest of the flour and the sugar, baking powder, baking soda, and salt. Pulse until mixed.

3) In a bowl, whisk together the vanilla, orange juice, eggs, and zest. Using a fork, stir in the dry ingredients until all is moist. Knead briefly in the bowl, using the heel of your hand, until a dough ball forms. Divide in half.

4) Put a foot-long piece of plastic wrap on your work surface. Place half the dough on the plastic and shape it into a log about 10 inches long, 3 inches wide, and 1/2 to 1 inch high. Use the plastic, pulled up along the sides of the dough, to help shape the biscotti. Turn the log onto a cookie sheet, removing the plastic wrap. Repeat with the other piece of dough.

5) Place in the oven and bake for 30 minutes, turning the cookie sheets once during baking so they cook evenly. Remove the biscotti from the oven and cool on a wire rack for 10 minutes. Reduce the oven temperature to 275°F.

6) Slice the biscotti, on the diagonal, into 1/2-inch-thick cookies. Place them with a cut side down on the cookie sheets. Bake for 20 minutes. Turn the cookies over and bake for another 15 minutes, until dry but slightly soft in the center. Cool completely on a wire rack before storing.

Per Cookie: Calories 130; Protein 4g; Fat 5g (Saturated 1g); Carbohydrates 19g; Fiber 1g; Sodium 124mg

Drop Cookies

Drop cookies are easy to make. No rolling. No cookie cutters. The batter is simply scooped up with one spoon, then another spoon pushes the dollop of batter onto the cookie sheet. As with many baked goods, for the best texture the batter should be handled minimally. Once baked, use a spatula to remove the cookies to a wire rack to cool. Reduced-fat cookies stale quickly. What won't be eaten in a day or two should be frozen. Defrost individually in the microwave for a warm, homebaked treat.

Oatmeal Drop Cookies

Makes: 20 cookies

Old-fashioned rolled oats provide a chewier texture than quick oats.

$1/4$ cup plain nonfat yogurt
$1/4$ cup vegetable oil
$1/2$ cup maple syrup or honey
1 cup old-fashioned rolled oats
$1/2$ cup whole wheat flour
1 teaspoon baking powder
1 tablespoon ground cinnamon
$1/2$ cup raisins
$1/2$ cup chopped walnuts (apples can be substituted)

1) Preheat the oven to 375°F. Coat cookie sheets with nonstick spray or line with parchment paper.

2) Stir together the yogurt, oil, and maple syrup, then mix in the oats.

3) Sift the flour, baking powder, and cinnamon over the wet ingredients, add the raisins and walnuts, and stir until mixed.

4) Drop large tablespoons of the batter onto the cookie sheets. Bake for about 25 minutes, until light brown.

Per Cookie: Calories 105; Protein 2g; Fat 5g (Saturated 0g); Carbohydrates 15g; Fiber 1g; Sodium 29mg

Apple and Date Cookies

Makes: 18 cookies

Dates are chewy and very sweet, making them a good choice, but any dried fruit will do. Fruit that is hard and leathery should be softened in hot water first.

$1/2$ cup plain nonfat yogurt
$1/3$ cup vegetable oil
$1/2$ cup honey
2 egg whites
1 teaspoon baking powder
1 teaspoon ground cinnamon
1 cup whole wheat flour
$2/3$ cup old-fashioned rolled oats
$1/2$ cup chopped dates
$1 1/2$ cups grated peeled and cored apple

1) Preheat the oven to 375°F. Coat 2 cookie sheets with nonstick spray.

2) Whisk together the yogurt, oil, honey, and egg whites.

3) Sift together the baking powder, cinnamon, and flour. Stir in the oats and dates. Blend until there are no dark streaks.

4) Fold the wet ingredients into the dry until everything is moist. Stir in the grated apple.

5) Drop batter by the spoonful onto cookie sheets. Bake for 20 to 25 minutes, until the centers are firm to the touch.

Per Cookie: Calories 123; Protein 2g; Fat 4g (Saturated 0g); Carbohydrates 20g; Fiber 2g; Sodium 39mg

Applesauce Cookies

Makes: 30 cookies

Use a thick applesauce, one that "plops," not pours, off a spoon.

1/2 cup vegetable oil
1 cup thick applesauce, preferably homemade (page 467)
1/2 teaspoon vanilla extract
3/4 cup whole wheat flour
1/4 teaspoon ground cloves
1/4 teaspoon ground nutmeg
1/2 teaspoon ground cinnamon
1/2 cup sugar
1/4 cup chopped nuts
2 cups old-fashioned rolled oats
1/4 cup raisins

1) Preheat the oven to 375°F. Coat cookie sheets with nonstick spray.

2) Mix together the oil, applesauce, and vanilla.

3) Sift the flour and spices into a separate bowl. Stir in the sugar, nuts, oats, and raisins.

4) Combine the wet and dry ingredients, stirring until there are no dry lumps.

5) Drop the batter by the tablespoonful onto the cookie sheets. Bake for 20 to 25 minutes, until the cookies turn light brown.

Per Cookie: Calories 92; Protein 1g; Fat 5g (Saturated 0g); Carbohydrates 12g; Fiber 1g; Sodium 1mg

Carrot Cookies

Makes: 18 cookies

These are a cookie version of carrot cake and the cream cheese frosting is good here, too.

1/2 cup plain nonfat yogurt
1/3 cup vegetable oil
1/2 cup honey
2 egg whites
1/2 teaspoon vanilla extract
1 teaspoon baking powder
1 teaspoon ground cinnamon
1 cup whole wheat flour
2/3 cup old-fashioned rolled oats
1/2 cup raisins
1 1/2 cups grated carrots

1) Preheat the oven to 375°F. Coat 2 cookie sheets with nonstick spray.

2) Whisk together the yogurt, oil, honey, egg whites, and vanilla.

3) In a separate bowl, sift together the baking powder, cinnamon, and flour. Stir in the oats, raisins, and carrots. Blend until there are no dark streaks.

4) Fold the wet ingredients into the dry until everything is moist.

5) Drop the batter by the spoonful onto the cookie sheets. Bake for about 20 to 25 minutes, until the centers are set.

Per Cookie: Calories 122; Protein 2g; Fat 4g (Saturated 0g); Carbohydrates 20g; Fiber 2g; Sodium 43mg

Banana Cookies

Makes: 24 cookies

These cookies are soft and chewy with a lot of banana flavor.

$^1/_2$ cup honey
$^1/_2$ cup packed light brown sugar
$^1/_4$ cup vegetable oil
1 egg
2 or 3 very ripe bananas, mashed (1 cup)
1 cup whole wheat flour
1 cup unbleached, all-purpose white flour
1 teaspoon baking powder
$^1/_2$ teaspoon kosher salt
1 teaspoon ground cinnamon
$^1/_4$ teaspoon ground nutmeg
$^1/_4$ teaspoon ground cloves
1 cup old-fashioned rolled oats
$^1/_2$ cup chopped pecans or walnuts (optional)

1) Preheat the oven to 375°F. Coat 2 baking sheets with nonstick spray.

2) Beat together the honey, brown sugar, oil, egg, and bananas.

3) In a separate bowl, sift together the remaining ingredients except the oats and nuts. Stir to combine. Stir in the oats and nuts. Continue to stir until no streaks of spices appear in the flour.

4) Pour the wet mixture into the dry. Stir with a rubber spatula until the batter is evenly moist but still lumpy.

5) Drop the batter by large tablespoonfuls onto the baking sheets. The cookies will spread, so don't crowd them. Bake for 20 to 25 minutes, until firm and golden.

Per Cookie: Calories 117; Protein 2g; Fat 3g (Saturated 0g); Carbohydrates 22g; Fiber 1g; Sodium 66mg

Cocoa Cookies

Makes: 24 cookies

Start to finish, these will take you under 40 minutes to make. I whip up a batch when a chocolate craving hits.

1 cup whole wheat flour
1 cup unbleached, all-purpose white flour
2 teaspoons baking powder
$^1/_4$ teaspoon kosher salt
$^1/_3$ cup Dutch-process cocoa
$^1/_2$ teaspoon sugar
$^1/_4$ cup vegetable oil
1 teaspoon vanilla extract
2 egg whites
$^1/_2$ cup honey
$^1/_2$ cup chopped pecans or walnuts (optional)

1) Preheat the oven to 350°F. Coat 2 baking sheets with nonstick spray.

2) Sift together the flours, baking powder, salt, cocoa, and sugar. Stir until no streaks of cocoa remain in the flour.

3) In a separate bowl, beat together the oil, vanilla, egg whites, and honey until frothy.

4) Pour the wet ingredients into the dry and fold together, working quickly until a pastelike batter forms. If desired, stir in the nuts.

5) Drop tablespoonfuls of the dough onto the baking sheets. The cookies will spread slightly while baking. Bake for 20 to 25 minutes, until the centers are firm to the touch.

Per Cookie: Calories 80; Protein 2g; Fat 3g (Saturated 0g); Carbohydrates 14g; Fiber 1g; Sodium 66mg

Chocolate Nut Crackle Cookies

Makes: 20 cookies

These are exceptionally good cookies, with just the right crisp yet crumbly texture.

1 tablespoon unsalted butter, softened
$^{1}/_{2}$ cup sugar
$^{1}/_{2}$ cup unbleached, all-purpose white flour
3 tablespoons Dutch-process cocoa
$^{1}/_{2}$ teaspoon baking powder
$^{1}/_{4}$ cup finely chopped walnuts
$1^{1}/_{2}$ teaspoons vegetable oil
2 egg whites, lightly beaten
2 tablespoons confectioners' sugar

1) Put the rack in the center of the oven and preheat to 400°F. Coat a cookie sheet with non-stick spray or line it with parchment paper.

2) Using an electric mixer, beat together the butter and sugar until fluffy as snow. Beat in the flour, cocoa, baking powder, and nuts. Pour in the oil and egg whites and beat on low speed until all is well blended. Press the sticky batter against the sides of the bowl until it is spread out about $^{1}/_{3}$ inch thick. Place in the freezer to firm up, about 20 to 40 minutes. Don't freeze solid.

3) Dust your hands with some of the confectioners' sugar. Roll the dough into 1-inch balls. Place on the baking sheet. When all are on the tray, dust with confectioners' sugar by putting some in a fine mesh metal sifter and shaking it over the cookies.

4) Bake for 8 to 10 minutes, until they spread slightly and are not quite firm to the touch. If desired, dust with confectioners' sugar again after the cookies have cooled on a wire rack.

Per Cookie: Calories 53; Protein 1g; Fat 2g (Saturated 1g); Carbohydrates 9g; Fiber 0g; Sodium 18mg

Gingersnaps

Makes: 60 cookies

Smell your ground ginger. It must be fresh and sharp or the flavor of these cookies won't sparkle.

1 cup whole wheat flour
1 1/2 cups unbleached, all-purpose white flour
2 teaspoons ground ginger
1/8 teaspoon ground cloves
1 teaspoon ground cinnamon
1/4 teaspoon kosher salt
1 1/2 teaspoons baking soda
1/3 cup vegetable oil
1 egg
1 egg white
1/2 cup molasses
1/2 cup honey
1/2 cup packed light brown sugar

1) Preheat the oven to 375°F. Grease cookie sheets or line with parchment paper.

2) Sift the flours, ginger, cloves, cinnamon, salt, and baking soda into a bowl. Stir until there are no spice streaks in the flour.

3) Put the remaining ingredients in another bowl. Beat with a mixer until the mixture is a little bubbly.

4) Pour the wet ingredients into the dry. Stir with a rubber spatula until the flour is completely wet and a batter forms.

5) Drop by full teaspoonfuls onto the baking sheets. The cookies will spread, so don't crowd.

6) Bake for about 6 minutes, until the cookies are firm and begin to brown. Watch them closely as they cook—they go quickly from done to scorched. Remove the cookies from the sheets and cool on racks. Store in airtight bags, where they will remain fresh for several days.

Per Cookie: Calories 52; Protein 1g; Fat 1g (Saturated 0g); Carbohydrates 10g; Fiber 0g; Sodium 43mg

Almond Loves

Makes: 30 cookies

A dollop of jam is baked into the center of each cookie, making these very pretty.

1 3/4 cups whole, blanched almonds
2 egg whites
1/3 cup honey
1 tablespoon vegetable oil
1/4 teaspoon ground nutmeg
1/4 teaspoon ground cardamom
1/4 cup fruit preserves

1) Preheat the oven to 350°F. Coat cookie sheets with nonstick spray.

2) In a food processor fitted with a steel blade, grind together all the ingredients except the preserves until a smooth paste forms.

3) Drop teaspoonfuls of the paste on the cookie sheets. With a wet spoon, make a depression in the centers of the cookies. Place a small dollop (about 1/2 teaspoon) of preserves in each depression.

4) Bake 10 to 15 minutes, until lightly golden.

Per Cookie: Calories 73; Protein 2g; Fat 5g (Saturated 0g); Carbohydrates 6g; Fiber 1g; Sodium 6mg

Chocolate Meringue Kisses

Makes: 28 kisses

Eating meringue kisses is like eating sweetened cloud puffs—but not on a humid day, when they turn tough and chewy.

1/2 cup slivered almonds
1/4 cup semi-sweet chocolate chips
1 cup sugar, divided
1 teaspoon instant espresso powder
5 tablespoons Dutch-process cocoa
1/2 teaspoon ground cinnamon
2 tablespoons cornstarch
5 egg whites
1/4 teaspoon cream of tartar
1 teaspoon vanilla extract

1) Preheat the oven to 275°F. Line 2 baking sheets with parchment paper.

2) Finely chop the almonds, chocolate chips, and 1/2 cup of the sugar in the food processor. Pulse in the espresso powder, cocoa, cinnamon, and cornstarch.

3) In a large, grease-free mixing bowl, beat the egg whites at low speed until frothy. Increase the speed and add the cream of tartar. Beat until soft peaks form. Add the remaining sugar, a tablespoon at a time, until the egg whites are firm but moist. Beat in the vanilla.

4) Using a rubber spatula, fold in half the cocoa mixture, then fold in the other half.

5) Drop tablespoonfuls of the batter onto the cookie sheets. The cookies will spread, so give them room.

6) Some people like meringue cookies a touch chewy on the inside. If you do, bake them for 40 minutes, cool them for 10, and then transfer the sheet of parchment paper to a cooling rack. When the cookies reach room temperature, they can be peeled off the paper. If you like a light, dry texture, bake for 1 hour, then leave in the turned-off oven, with the door open, for 30 minutes. Next, transfer to a cooling rack and cool completely.

Per Cookie: Calories 57; Protein 1g; Fat 2g (Saturated 0g); Carbohydrates 10g; Fiber 1g; Sodium 13mg

Brownies and Bars

Brownies and similar bar desserts are ideal for lowfat baking. Unlike cakes, they are meant to be chewy and moist, which is easier to accomplish than a cake's light crumb texture. Like most baked goods, they bake best when placed in the center of a preheated oven. Rotate the pan once during cooking to ensure even browning. Timing can vary depending on the color of the pan; a dark pan will bake the bars as much as ten minutes sooner than a light-colored pan.

Basic Brownies

Makes: 12 servings

These stale quickly. What won't be eaten in a day can be wrapped tightly and frozen, then warmed in the microwave.

2 tablespoons unsalted butter, melted
2 tablespoons vegetable oil
$1/4$ cup buttermilk
2 egg whites
1 egg
$1^1/2$ teaspoons vanilla extract
$1/2$ cup packed light brown sugar
$1/2$ cup sugar
1 cup unbleached, all-purpose white flour
$1/2$ cup Dutch-process cocoa
$1/4$ teaspoon salt

1) Put the rack in the center of the oven and preheat to 350°F. Coat an 8×8-inch pan with nonstick spray.

2) Using an electric mixer at medium speed, beat the butter, oil, buttermilk, egg whites, egg, vanilla, and sugars until the sugar is dissolved and the batter is smooth. (Medium speed will prevent air bubbles from forming.) Sift the flour, cocoa, and salt into the bowl. Using a rubber spatula, stir until all is moist and smooth. Pour into the baking pan and tap on the table to get rid of large air pockets in the batter.

3) Bake for 25 to 30 minutes, until the center of the brownies is firm to the touch.

Per Serving: Calories 157; Protein 3g; Fat 5g (Saturated 2g); Carbohydrates 27g; Fiber 1g; Sodium 69mg

Butterscotch Chip Brownies

Makes: 12 servings

Mint chocolate chips could be substituted for the butterscotch chips. Of course, both could be used (and you could throw in a few nuts, too).

$1/4$ cup vegetable oil
1 cup sugar
$1/2$ cup nonfat sour cream
3 egg whites
1 teaspoon vanilla extract
1 cup quick oats
1 cup unbleached, all-purpose white flour
$1/4$ cup Dutch-process cocoa
$1/4$ teaspoon salt
1 teaspoon baking powder
$1/2$ cup butterscotch chips

1) Preheat the oven to 350°F. Coat a 7×11-inch or 8×8-inch baking pan with nonstick spray.

2) Whisk together the oil, sugar, sour cream, egg whites, and vanilla. Add the remaining ingredients and stir until all is moist but still lumpy.

3) Spread the batter into the baking pan and bake for 20 to 25 minutes, until the center feels firm to the touch.

Per Serving: Calories 218; Protein 4g; Fat 7g (Saturated 2g); Carbohydrates 36g; Fiber 1g; Sodium 114mg

Marbled Brownies

Makes: 12 servings

The cream cheese gives these a rich, moist texture. It is tempting to eat them hot right out of the oven, but it is best to wait until they cool and the cream cheese sets.

2 tablespoons unsalted butter, melted
2 tablespoons vegetable oil
1/4 cup buttermilk
2 egg whites
1 egg
1 1/2 teaspoons vanilla extract
1/2 cup packed light brown sugar
1/2 cup white sugar
1 cup unbleached, all-purpose white flour
1/2 cup Dutch-process cocoa
1/4 teaspoon salt

Marble Ingredients
3 ounces reduced-fat cream cheese
1 tablespoon nonfat sour cream
1 tablespoon unbleached, all-purpose white flour
1 teaspoon cornstarch
1 egg white
1/4 cup sugar
1/2 teaspoon vanilla extract

1) Put the rack in the center of the oven and preheat to 350°F. Coat an 8×8-inch pan with nonstick spray.

2) Using an electric mixer at medium speed, beat the butter, oil, buttermilk, egg whites, egg, vanilla, and sugars until all the sugar is dissolved and the batter is smooth. (Medium speed will prevent air bubbles from forming.) Sift the flour, cocoa, and salt into the bowl. Stir until all is moist and smooth. Set aside.

3) With a mixer, beat together the marble ingredients until smooth.

4) Spread half the chocolate batter into the baking pan. Spoon on the cream cheese mixture and spread as best you can. This doesn't have to be perfectly even. Top with the remaining brownie batter. Spread it so that all or most of the cream cheese is hidden. Run a dinner knife through the two batters so that a white line comes to the surface. For a professional touch, draw a grid. Pulling the knife first in one direction, then back in the opposite direction for the next line will produce a chevronlike decoration.

5) Bake for 25 to 30 minutes, until the center feels firm to the touch. Let cool on a wire rack before cutting.

Per Serving: Calories 197; Protein 4g; Fat 7g (Saturated 3g); Carbohydrates 32g; Fiber 1g; Sodium 105mg

Hermits

Makes: 12 servings

These bar cookies are like a cross between ginger-bread and spice cake. If you want, throw in a few butterscotch chips.

2 eggs
1/4 cup plain nonfat yogurt
1/4 cup vegetable oil
1/3 cup apple butter
1 cup packed light brown sugar
1/2 cup molasses
1 1/2 cups unbleached, all-purpose white flour
1/2 teaspoon baking soda
1 teaspoon baking powder
1/4 teaspoon salt
1 teaspoon ground cinnamon
1/2 teaspoon ground cloves
1/4 teaspoon ground nutmeg
1 cup raisins
1/2 cup slivered almonds

1) Preheat the oven to 350°F. Coat a 9×13-inch pan with nonstick spray.

2) Using an electric mixer, beat the eggs, yogurt, oil, apple butter, brown sugar, and molasses until smooth.

3) In a separate bowl, sift together all the dry ingredients except the raisins and almonds. On slow speed, blend the wet ingredients into the dry. Stir in the raisins and almonds.

4) Pour the batter into the pan. Bake for 25 minutes, until firm to the touch.

Per Serving: Calories 301; Protein 5g; Fat 9g (Saturated 1g); Carbohydrates 54g; Fiber 2g; Sodium 167mg

Gingerbread

Makes: 10 servings

This is a dense, moist, spicy gingerbread. If desired, top each with a spoonful of Marshmallow Fluff (page 546).

1/4 cup honey, warmed until easy to pour
2/3 cup molasses
1/3 cup vegetable oil
1 1/2 cups 1% lowfat milk
1 1/2 cups whole wheat flour
2/3 cup unbleached, all-purpose white flour
1/4 teaspoon baking soda
1 1/2 teaspoons baking powder
1 tablespoon ground cinnamon
2 teaspoons ground ginger
1/4 teaspoon ground cloves
2 egg whites, beaten to a soft peak

1) Preheat the oven to 375°F. Coat a 9×9-inch pan with nonstick spray.

2) Whisk together the honey, molasses, oil, and milk.

3) Sift together the flours, baking soda, baking powder, cinnamon, ginger, and cloves.

4) Form a well in the center of the dry mixture and pour in the wet ingredients. Fold with a spatula until the batter is moist but still lumpy. Gently fold in the egg whites. This will be a thin batter.

5) Pour the batter into the pan and bake for 1 hour, until firm to the touch.

Per Serving: Calories 258; Protein 5g; Fat 8g (Saturated 1g); Carbohydrates 43g; Fiber 3g; Sodium 144mg

Chocolate Apricot Squares

Makes: 10 servings

I think apricots and chocolate are a perfect combination, but dried peaches or pears would also be good. Plump leathery dried fruit in a bowl of hot water and then pat dry before stirring it into the batter.

2 tablespoons unsalted butter, softened
$3/4$ cup sugar
2 eggs
2 egg whites
1 teaspoon vanilla extract
$1^1/2$ cups chocolate wafer cookie crumbs (from about 32 wafers)
1 cup dried apricots
$1/2$ cup unbleached, all-purpose white flour
1 teaspoon baking powder
2 tablespoons chopped walnuts

1) Preheat the oven to 350°F. Coat an 8×8-inch pan with nonstick spray.

2) Beat the butter and sugar until fluffy as snow. Beat in the eggs, egg whites, and vanilla until smooth.

3) If you need to make the cookies into crumbs, do this in the food processor first, then remove crumbs from the bowl. Next, put the apricots and the flour into the processor. Pulse until the apricots are chopped into pieces the size of raisins. Pulse in the baking powder, then the crumbs. Stir this into the batter.

4) Pour the batter into the pan. Top with the nuts. Bake for 30 minutes, until firm to the touch.

Per Serving: Calories 238; Protein 4g; Fat 7g (Saturated 3g); Carbohydrates 41g; Fiber 2g; Sodium 205mg

Apricot and Oat Bars

Makes: 10 servings

Both apple and prune butter provide body and moisture without fat, but their flavors do come through. Apple butter will give this recipe a lighter, fruitier flavor.

$1/2$ cup old-fashioned rolled oats
1 cup unbleached, all-purpose white flour
1 teaspoon baking powder
$1/2$ teaspoon salt
$1/2$ cup packed light brown sugar
$1/4$ cup vegetable oil
1 teaspoon vanilla extract
1 egg
1 egg white
$1/4$ cup apple or prune butter
One 17-ounce can apricot halves, drained and coarsely chopped

1) Preheat the oven to 350°F. Coat an 8×8-inch pan with nonstick spray.

2) Stir together the oats, flour, baking powder, salt, and brown sugar. Using your fingertips, crumble the dry ingredients until there are no lumps in the brown sugar.

3) In a separate bowl, whisk together the oil, vanilla, egg, egg white, and fruit butter. Stir in the apricots, then pour the wet ingredients into the dry. Stir until all is moist.

4) Pour the batter into the pan. Bake for 40 to 50 minutes, until firm to the touch and golden.

Per Serving: Calories 184; Protein 3g; Fat 6g (Saturated 1g); Carbohydrates 30g; Fiber 1g; Sodium 173mg

Sour Cherry Nut Bars

Makes: 10 servings

Not too sweet but not at all sour, this bar strikes just the right balance.

1 tablespoon unsalted butter
3/4 cup sugar
1 egg
1 egg white
1 teaspoon vanilla extract
1 teaspoon baking powder
1/4 teaspoon salt
1 cup unbleached, all-purpose white flour
1 cup sour cherries, pitted (if canned, drain well)
3 tablespoons sliced almonds

1) Preheat the oven to 350°F. Coat an 8×8-inch pan with nonstick spray.

2) Using an electric mixer, beat the butter and sugar until fluffy as snow. Beat in the egg, egg white, and vanilla.

3) Sift in the baking powder, then add the salt and flour. Beat at low speed until all is moist. Stir in the cherries.

4) Pour the batter into the pan. Top with the nuts. Bake for 30 minutes, until firm to the touch and golden.

Per Serving: Calories 137; Protein 3g; Fat 3g (Saturated 1g); Carbohydrates 26g; Fiber 1g; Sodium 115mg

Jam Squares

Makes: 10 servings

These gooey, delicious squares are taller than bars. They require no skill in the kitchen and are no trouble at all to make. I like them with yogurt for breakfast.

1 cup honey
3/4 cup buttermilk
1/2 cup vegetable oil
2 egg whites
13/4 cups whole wheat flour
1 teaspoon ground cinnamon
1/4 teaspoon salt
1/2 teaspoon baking soda
2 cups old-fashioned rolled oats
3/4 cup fruit preserves

1) Preheat the oven to 400°F. Coat a 9×9-inch pan with nonstick spray. If necessary, warm the honey until thin and pourable.

2) Whisk together the buttermilk, oil, and egg whites, then whisk in the honey.

3) In a separate bowl, sift together the flour, cinnamon, salt, and baking soda. Add the oats and stir to combine.

4) Stir together the wet and dry mixtures.

5) Spread half the batter into the pan. Distribute the preserves evenly on top. Pour the rest of the batter into the pan and spread evenly.

6) Bake for 50 to 60 minutes, until firm to the touch.

Per Serving: Calories 402; Protein 7g; Fat 13g (Saturated 1g); Carbohydrates 71g; Fiber 5g; Sodium 159mg

Cobblers

Cobblers are homey fruit desserts baked with a biscuit topping. Unlike elegant cakes, they can look messy and still be perfect. The fruit fillings offered here are suggestions. This is one dessert where you can improvise, so if you have a bumper crop of raspberries, adapt a recipe to make raspberry cobbler. If baking in glass, reduce the oven temperature by 25°F.

Cherry Cobbler

Makes: 9 servings

This cobbler can be made with sour or sweet cherries, canned or fresh. Adjust the sugar accordingly.

Filling
6 cups pitted cherries (if canned, drained)
2 tablespoons to $1/2$ cup sugar
2 tablespoons corn syrup
$1^1/2$ teaspoons cornstarch

Biscuit Topping
$1^1/2$ cups unbleached, all-purpose white flour
2 teaspoons baking powder
$1/2$ teaspoon baking soda
$1/2$ teaspoon salt
$1/4$ cup sugar
$1/4$ teaspoon ground nutmeg
$1/2$ teaspoon ground cinnamon
3 tablespoons vegetable oil
$1/2$ cup buttermilk
1 egg

1) Preheat the oven to 400°F.

2) Put the filling ingredients into a small saucepan. Heat to a simmer and cook until the sugar dissolves and the mixture begins to thicken, about 4 to 7 minutes. Pour the cooked mixture into an ungreased 8×8-inch baking pan or a 2-quart casserole.

3) Sift together the flour, baking powder, baking soda, salt, sugar, nutmeg, and cinnamon.

4) Whisk together the oil, buttermilk, and egg. Make a well in the dry ingredients and pour the wet ingredients into the depression. Using a fork, quickly mix together the wet and dry ingredients until the flour is moistened and lumps form. Create a ball of dough by kneading this with the palm of your hand (not your fingertips). Knead only about 5 times, until a rough ball forms.

5) Drop portions of the dough onto the fruit until the pan is covered. (A few holes are okay.)

6) Bake for 40 minutes, until the biscuit browns.

Per Serving: Calories 237; Protein 4g; Fat 6g (Saturated 1g); Carbohydrates 43g; Fiber 2g; Sodium 324mg

Blackberry-Pear Cobbler

Makes: 10 servings

Blackberries can be hard to find during their short season, but high-quality frozen blackberries are available year-round.

Filling
3 cups blackberries (if frozen, do not thaw)
4 ripe pears, peeled, cored, and sliced
1 teaspoon minced lemon zest (optional)
1 teaspoon lemon juice
1/4 cup sugar
1 tablespoon cornstarch

Biscuit Topping
1 1/2 cups unbleached, all-purpose white flour
2 teaspoons baking powder
1/2 teaspoon baking soda
1/2 teaspoon salt
1/4 cup sugar
1/4 teaspoon ground nutmeg
1/2 teaspoon ground cinnamon
3 tablespoons vegetable oil
1/2 cup buttermilk
1 egg

1) Preheat the oven to 400°F.

2) Put the filling ingredients into a saucepan. Heat to a simmer and cook until the sugar dissolves and the mixture begins to thicken, about 3 to 5 minutes. Pour the cooked mixture into an ungreased 8×8-inch baking pan or 2-quart casserole.

3) Sift together the flour, baking powder, baking soda, salt, sugar, nutmeg, and cinnamon.

4) Whisk together the oil, buttermilk, and egg. Make a well in the dry ingredients and pour the wet ingredients into the depression. Using a fork, quickly mix together the wet and dry ingredients until the flour is moistened and lumps form. Create a ball of dough by kneading this with the palm of your hand (not your fingertips). Knead only about 5 times, until a rough ball forms.

5) Drop portions of the dough onto the fruit until the pan is covered. (A few holes are okay.)

6) Bake for 30 to 40 minutes, until the biscuit browns.

Per Serving: Calories 213; Protein 3g; Fat 5g (Saturated 1g); Carbohydrates 40g; Fiber 4g; Sodium 287mg

Blueberry-Peach Cobbler

Makes: 10 servings

This is also excellent when made with canned peaches and frozen blueberries; just be sure to drain them well.

Filling
3 cups peeled and sliced fresh peaches, or two 16-ounce cans
3 cups blueberries (if frozen, thawed and drained)
1 tablespoon lemon juice
3/4 cup packed light brown sugar
2 tablespoons cornstarch

Biscuit Topping
1 cup unbleached, all-purpose white flour
1 cup whole wheat flour
2 teaspoons baking powder
1/2 teaspoon baking soda
1/2 teaspoon kosher salt
2 tablespoons sugar
1/4 cup vegetable oil
3/4 cup buttermilk

1) Preheat the oven to 400°F.

2) Stir together the filling ingredients. Put the mixture in an ungreased 8×8-inch pan.

3) Sift together the flours, baking powder, baking soda, salt, and sugar.

4) Whisk together the oil and buttermilk. Make a well in the dry ingredients and pour the wet ingredients into the depression.

5) Using a fork, quickly mix together the wet and dry ingredients until the flour is moistened and lumps form. Create a ball of dough by kneading this with the palm of your hand (not your fingertips). Knead only until a rough ball forms.

6) Drop portions of the dough onto the fruit until the pan is covered. (A few holes are okay.)

7) Bake for 40 minutes, until the biscuit browns and the fruit bubbles.

Per Serving: Calories 261; Protein 4g; Fat 6g (Saturated 1g); Carbohydrates 50g; Fiber 4g; Sodium 286mg

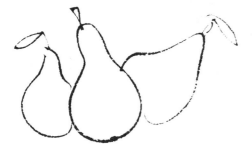

Puddings

Simple puddings, such as Vanilla (below), and desserts in the same family, such as Lemon Curd and Vanilla Cream (page 565), can stand on their own, but they can also be used as part of other desserts. Use them as a base for fruit tarts, or fill a meringue shell with them and then top with a fruit puree. Fill a parfait glass with layers of pudding, granola, and frozen yogurt. These pudding recipes can be doubled. Other puddings, like Rice Pudding and Pumpkin Custards (page 566), are meant to be served alone, or with ice cream. What unites them as a family is their creamy, homey nature.

Vanilla Pudding

Makes: 4 servings

For this pudding to set properly, it is essential to boil it for the exact amount of time. Begin timing once it is boiling, not before.

3 tablespoons cornstarch
1/2 cup sugar
1/8 teaspoon salt
2 1/2 cups 1% lowfat milk, divided
2 egg yolks
2 teaspoons vanilla extract

1) Dissolve the cornstarch, sugar, and salt with 1/2 cup of the milk in a heatproof bowl. Whisk in the egg yolks.

2) Put the remaining milk into a saucepan and heat until small bubbles appear. Slowly pour about half this into the egg yolk paste, stirring constantly, then pour it all back into the hot milk. Bring it to a boil and cook for exactly 2 minutes, stirring constantly with a hard rubber spatula.

3) Remove from the heat and stir in the vanilla. Pour into a serving dish or individual bowls and chill. Cover to prevent a skin from forming.

Per Serving: Calories 218; Protein 6g; Fat 4g (Saturated 2g); Carbohydrates 38g; Fiber 0g; Sodium 148mg

Chocolate Pudding

Makes: 4 servings

This pudding must also be boiled for the specific time; start timing once it begins boiling, not before.

1 egg yolk
1/4 cup Dutch-process cocoa
3 tablespoons cornstarch
1/3 cup sugar
1/8 teaspoon salt
2 1/2 cups 1% lowfat milk, divided
1/2 teaspoon vanilla extract

1) Put the egg yolk in a medium heatproof bowl and lightly beat it.

2) In another bowl, combine the cocoa, cornstarch, sugar, and salt. Pour in 1/2 cup of the milk and whisk until a smooth paste forms.

3) Bring the remaining milk to a boil, then immediately remove from the heat (boiling milk scorches quickly) and whisk the cocoa paste into the hot milk. Put it back on the burner, bring it to a boil, and cook for exactly 2 minutes, whisking constantly. Remove from the heat.

4) Gradually pour about 1 cup of the hot mixture into the egg yolk, whisk it smooth, and pour it back into the pot. Bring the pudding back to a simmer and cook over medium-low heat for 2 minutes. Do not boil. Stir in the vanilla. Pour into serving dishes and chill. Cover the bowls of pudding with plastic wrap to prevent a skin from forming.

Per Serving: Calories 179; Protein 7g; Fat 4g (Saturated 2g); Carbohydrates 32g; Fiber 2g; Sodium 147mg

Lemon Curd

Makes: 5 servings

Given the choice between a lemon dessert and almost anything else (even chocolate), I choose lemon, so developing this recipe was important to me. Lemon curd can be eaten alone as a pudding, or used as a base for other recipes, such as Lemon Meringue Pie (page 528) or lemon tarts.

2 egg yolks
1/2 teaspoon minced lemon zest
2/3 cup sugar
2 tablespoons cornstarch
3/4 cup water
1/4 cup lemon juice
1/2 teaspoon vanilla extract

1) Put the egg yolks in a heatproof bowl.

2) Combine the lemon zest, sugar, and cornstarch in a heavy-bottomed small saucepan. Add the water and lemon juice and stir until the sugar is dissolved. Put the pot over high heat and bring to a boil. Reduce to a simmer and cook for 1 minute. The liquid should be bubbling, but not at a rolling boil.

3) Slowly whisk about a quarter of the liquid into the egg yolks, then return it all to the pot. This prevents the egg from curdling. White strands in the curd are from egg whites not properly separated out. These can be discarded. Simmer the curd, stirring constantly, until thickened. This will take less than 3 minutes.

4) Remove from the heat and stir in the vanilla. Pour into a bowl, cover, and chill.

Per Serving: Calories 143; Protein 1g; Fat 2g (Saturated 1g); Carbohydrates 31g; Fiber 0g; Sodium 5mg

Vanilla Cream

Makes: 8 servings

This has a tinge of color from the brown sugar. For a pure white cream, use white granulated sugar.

3 tablespoons packed light brown sugar
1 tablespoon sugar
4 ounces reduced-fat cream cheese, softened
1/2 cup lowfat sour cream
1 teaspoon vanilla extract

With an electric mixer, beat the sugars and cream cheese until smooth. On low speed, beat in the sour cream and vanilla.

Per Serving: Calories 80; Protein 2g; Fat 4g (Saturated 3g); Carbohydrates 9g; Fiber 0g; Sodium 78mg

Pumpkin Custards

Makes: 10 servings

These custards will hold their flavor and texture over several days if stored in the fridge. Serve with mini-scoops of vanilla frozen yogurt.

2 tablespoons lowfat or regular graham
    cracker crumbs
2 tablespoons finely chopped pecans or walnuts
4 ounces reduced-fat cream cheese, softened
One 15-ounce can pumpkin (2 cups)
One 14-ounce can lowfat sweetened
    condensed milk
1 tablespoon brandy
$1/2$ teaspoon ground cinnamon
$1/8$ teaspoon ground cloves
$1/4$ teaspoon ground ginger
$1/8$ teaspoon ground allspice
1 tablespoon cornstarch
1 egg

1) Preheat the oven to 425°F. Coat 10 custard or muffin cups with butter-flavored nonstick spray. Combine the graham cracker crumbs and chopped nuts, then divide the crumbs among the cups.

2) Beat the cream cheese and pumpkin until creamy. Beat in the remaining ingredients until smooth. Pour into the cups.

3) Reduce the oven temperature to 350°F and bake 30 minutes, until set. Let cool for 10 minutes, then unmold from the cups.

Per Serving: Calories 196; Protein 6g; Fat 6g (Saturated 3g); Carbohydrates 29g; Fiber 1g; Sodium 107mg

Rice Pudding

Makes: 6 servings

I've mentioned elsewhere in this book how I grew up eating in New Jersey diners. Rice pudding was listed on the menu in every establishment, and when it was good, it was superb. It took me many recipe tests to come up with a rice pudding that could compare favorably with my memory.

4 cups 1% lowfat milk, divided
$1/2$ cup medium-grain white rice (not converted)
$1/2$ teaspoon minced orange zest
$1/2$ teaspoon vanilla extract
$1/4$ teaspoon ground cinnamon
$1/2$ cup sugar
1 egg
$1/2$ cup golden raisins

1) Preheat the oven to 350°F.

2) Bring 1 cup of the milk to a boil in a small saucepan. Stir in the rice and simmer until most of the milk is absorbed, about 10 to 12 minutes. Boiling milk foams up, so keep an eye on it to keep it from spilling out of the pan.

3) Meanwhile, combine the remaining milk and the orange zest, vanilla, cinnamon, sugar, egg, and raisins in a 2-quart casserole. Stir in the cooked milk and rice. Place, uncovered, in the center of the oven.

4) After baking for 30 minutes, stir. Continue to bake another 45 minutes, until a brown crust begins to form on the surface and sides. Stir again and bake for 20 minutes longer, for a total of about $1 1/2$ hours.

Per Serving: Calories 247; Protein 8g; Fat 3g (Saturated 1g); Carbohydrates 49g; Fiber 1g; Sodium 95mg

Banana Rice Pudding

Makes: 6 servings

I suppose that you could just stir sliced bananas into your serving at the table, but the bananas wouldn't take on the creamy, cooked texture, or taste quite so sweet.

4 cups 1% lowfat milk, divided
1/2 cup medium grain white rice (not converted)
1/2 teaspoon vanilla extract
1/4 teaspoon ground cinnamon
1/2 cup sugar
1 egg
1 banana, sliced

1) Preheat the oven to 350°F.

2) Bring 1 cup of the milk to a boil in a small saucepan. Stir in the rice and simmer until most of the milk is absorbed, about 10 to 12 minutes. Boiling milk foams up, so keep an eye on it to keep it from spilling out of the pan.

3) Meanwhile, combine the remaining milk and the vanilla, cinnamon, sugar, and egg in a 2-quart casserole. Stir in the cooked milk and rice. Place in the center of the oven.

4) Bake, uncovered, for 30 minutes. Stir and continue to bake another 45 minutes, then stir the browning crust and sides into the pudding, gently stir in the banana, and bake for another 20 minutes.

Per Serving: Calories 223; Protein 8g; Fat 3g (Saturated 1g); Carbohydrates 42g; Fiber 1g; Sodium 93mg

Baking in a Water Bath

Puddings are often baked in a water bath. Because water temperature can't rise above 212°F (higher than that it turns to steam), the body of the pudding sets in a constant, low temperature, and yet the top firms and browns from the direct heat of the oven. I've baked bread puddings in both water baths and directly in the oven. The texture of the custard is smoother and softer when in a bath; however, if you don't want to bother with the water bath, the pudding will taste wonderful and still set nicely, in about ten minutes less.

To make a water bath, use a pan several inches larger than the pudding baking dish. Place the pudding dish in the larger pan and pour water around it until it comes halfway up its sides. Remove the pudding dish and place the water bath in the oven to preheat. You need to start with hot water or the pudding will take much longer to bake. Once the pudding is prepared and the bath is hot, the baking dish can be carefully set in the hot water.

When the pudding is done, carefully lift the pudding dish out of the water bath. Don't try to lift the water bath out of the oven while the pudding is still inside. Not only might the water splash into the pudding, but it is likely to splash out and burn you as well. For this reason it is helpful to have the pudding in a dish with handles, or high sides that can be gripped with oven mitts.

Flan

Makes: 6 servings

Flan needs to be chilled, and can be made a day ahead of time, so it is a good choice for a dinner party. Flan doesn't need a garnish; simply sit it in a pool of its own caramel sauce on a beautiful plate. If fresh raspberries are in season, a few can be placed around each pudding.

2 tablespoons water
1/2 cup sugar
2 tablespoons maple syrup or honey
One 14-ounce can lowfat sweetened condensed
    milk
1 1/2 cups 1% lowfat milk
3 eggs
1 teaspoon vanilla extract
1/8 teaspoon ground nutmeg

1) Preheat the oven to 350°F. You will be cooking the flan in a 2-quart soufflé dish or casserole set in a water bath. Get out the soufflé dish and find a baking dish large enough to accommodate it. Put the baking dish in the oven. Bring about 4 cups of water to a boil, in a kettle or in the microwave, for the water bath.

2) Heat the 2 tablespoons water and the sugar and maple syrup in a small, heavy-bottomed pot over medium heat. Don't stir; swirl the pot. Warm through until all the sugar is dissolved. Raise the heat and simmer for 10 minutes, until the sugar is melted and the syrup is golden brown. Pour the caramel into the soufflé dish and roll the dish so the caramel coats the bottom and about an inch up the sides.

3) Whisk together the remaining ingredients. Strain the mixture through a fine mesh strainer into the soufflé dish. Place the dish in the center of the baking pan. Pour the boiling water around the pan. Take care not to splash the hot water on yourself or into the dish with the flan. Bake for 1 hour or a little longer, until the flan sets. Remove from the water bath very carefully. Chill the flan for at least 4 hours or up to 1 day before serving.

4) To serve, run a knife around the edge and invert onto a serving dish.

Per Serving: Calories 350; Protein 10g; Fat 6g (Saturated 3g); Carbohydrates 63g; Fiber 0g; Sodium 131mg

Bread Puddings

Bread puddings are homestyle desserts that do not require a pastry chef's skill to make. I've lightened recipes usually made with cream and egg yolks, yet retained the rich and silky texture and flavor. Serve them warm or at room temperature.

Apple Cinnamon Raisin Bread Pudding

Makes: 6 servings

If the bread is very sweet, leave out the 2 table-spoons of sugar.

2^1/4 cups 1% lowfat milk
1 teaspoon vanilla extract
^{1}/3 cup packed light brown sugar
2 tablespoons sugar
2 egg whites
1 whole egg
6 slices cinnamon-raisin bread, staled
1 large apple, cored, peeled, and thinly sliced

1) Preheat the oven to 350°F. Coat an 8×8-inch baking dish or a 2-quart casserole with nonstick spray. Prepare the water bath (see page 567).

2) Beat together the milk, vanilla, sugars, egg whites, and egg until foamy.

3) Tear the bread into 1- to 2-inch pieces. Stir the bread into the liquid mixture. Stir in the apples. Pour the batter into the baking dish and place into the water bath in the oven.

4) Bake 40 to 50 minutes, until pudding sets and the top is light brown and slightly crusty.

Per Serving: Calories 221; Protein 8g; Fat 3g (Saturated 1g); Carbohydrates 40g; Fiber 2g; Sodium 185mg

Peach Bread Pudding

Makes: 6 servings

I usually like to cook with fresh fruit, but this recipe is really good with canned peaches. And, because there isn't any peeling or slicing, this is one of the easiest desserts to make. Of course, if it is peach season, and you feel the inclination, fresh peaches would be wonderful.

2^1/4 cups 1% lowfat milk
1 teaspoon vanilla extract
^{1}/3 cup packed light brown sugar
2 egg whites
1 whole egg
^{1}/4 teaspoon salt
6 slices homemade-style white bread, staled
^{1}/2 cup golden raisins
One 15-ounce can sliced peaches, drained
    (1^1/2 cups)

1) Preheat the oven to 350°F. Coat an oblong 2^1/2-quart casserole or baking dish with nonstick spray. Prepare the water bath (see page 567).

2) Beat together the milk, vanilla, brown sugar, egg whites, egg, and salt until foamy.

3) Tear the bread into 1- to 2-inch pieces. Stir the bread into the liquid mixture. Stir in the raisins and peaches. Pour the batter into the baking dish and place into the water bath in the oven.

4) Bake for about 1 hour, until the pudding sets and the top is light brown and slightly crusty. Carefully remove the pudding pan from the water bath. Let rest 10 minutes before serving.

Per Serving: Calories 263; Protein 9g; Fat 3g (Saturated 1g); Carbohydrates 51g; Fiber 2g; Sodium 336mg

Cocoa Bread Pudding

Makes: 6 servings

Often, full-fat bread puddings are too heavy to be the right ending for a meal. Not this one. Cocoa Bread Pudding puffs up slightly as it bakes, its texture is soft and almost fluffy, and it tastes rich but is not too filling.

2 cups 1% lowfat milk
3 tablespoons Dutch-process cocoa
1/3 cup packed light brown sugar
1/2 teaspoon vanilla extract
1/8 teaspoon kosher salt
1/8 teaspoon ground nutmeg
3 slices homemade-style white bread, torn into pieces
1 whole egg
1 egg white

1) Preheat the oven to 350°F. Coat an 8×8-inch pan or a 2-quart casserole with nonstick spray, or use a nonstick pan. Prepare the water bath (see page 567).

2) Heat the milk until warm but not simmering. Whisk in the cocoa and brown sugar until there are no lumps of cocoa and the sugar is dissolved. Remove the pan from the heat. Stir in the vanilla, salt, nutmeg, and bread.

3) Lightly beat the egg and egg white. Stir them into the bread mixture.

4) Pour the batter into the baking dish and place into the water bath in the oven.

5) Bake for 50 minutes, until the pudding sets.

Per Serving: Calories 148; Protein 6g; Fat 3g (Saturated 1g); Carbohydrates 26g; Fiber 1g; Sodium 188mg

Lemon Bread Pudding

Makes: 6 servings

Serve this on its own, or warmed and with a scoop of vanilla ice cream.

2 cups 1% lowfat milk
1 1/2 teaspoons vanilla extract
1/3 cup packed light brown sugar
2 egg whites
1 whole egg
1/8 teaspoon kosher salt
4 slices homemade-style white bread, stale or lightly toasted
1 tablespoon lemon zest in fine strips or minced

1) Preheat the oven to 350°F. Coat an 8×8-inch baking dish or a 2-quart casserole with nonstick spray. Prepare the water bath (see page 567).

2) Beat together the milk, vanilla, brown sugar, egg whites, egg, and salt until foamy.

3) Tear the bread into 1- to 2-inch pieces. Stir the bread into the liquid mixture. Stir in the lemon zest.

4) Pour the batter into the baking dish and place into the water bath in the oven. Bake for about 1 hour, until the pudding sets and the top is light brown and slightly crusty.

Per Serving: Calories 161; Protein 7g; Fat 3g (Saturated 1g); Carbohydrates 27g; Fiber 1g; Sodium 223mg

Frozen Desserts

Although super-premium ice cream isn't part of a lowfat diet (though certainly still part of life and one of those occasional indulgences), frozen desserts are very much a part of a healthy daily diet. The recipes here are easy and fun to make and never go out of season.

Chocolate-Covered Banana Bites

Makes: 4 servings

These are messy to eat, so you may want to stick popsicle sticks in them to use as handles later.

2 ripe bananas
1/4 cup Chocolate Syrup (page 576)
1/4 cup sliced or slivered almonds, toasted

1) Peel the bananas, cut each into 6 pieces, and place on a baking sheet lined with wax paper. Insert popsicle sticks now, if desired. Freeze until solid.

2) Dip each banana into the syrup, coming up halfway on each piece. Roll the coated banana in the nuts. Freeze the bananas again on the wax paper. Do not leave in a frost-free freezer for more than a few hours without covering, since that will dehydrate the bananas.

3) Let stand at room temperature for 5 minutes before serving.

Per Serving: Calories 145; Protein 2g; Fat 4g (Saturated 1g); Carbohydrates 28g; Fiber 3g; Sodium 2mg

Purple Pops

Makes: 8 pops

Even my toddler, who doesn't like yogurt, likes these.

2 ripe bananas
One 6-ounce can frozen purple grape juice concentrate
1/4 cup water
1/4 cup plain nonfat yogurt
1 tablespoon sugar

1) Puree all the ingredients and pour into small paper cups or popsicle molds. If using cups, when halfway frozen, stand a wooden stick or plastic spoon in the popsicle to make a handle.

2) When frozen solid, unmold or peel away the paper to eat.

Per Serving: Calories 75; Protein 1g; Fat 0g (Saturated 0g); Carbohydrates 18g; Fiber 1g; Sodium 8mg

Pineapple Popsicles

Makes: 6 pops

Most popsicles are too big for toddlers to finish (or it is finished because half of it has melted on their clothes). Making popsicles at home solves this problem because they can be made as small as desired, even in ice cube trays.

One 8-ounce can crushed pineapple, drained
3/4 cup unsweetened pineapple juice
1/4 cup sugar

Puree all the ingredients, pour into popsicle molds, and freeze.

Per Serving: Calories 67; Protein 0g; Fat 0g (Saturated 0g); Carbohydrates 17g; Fiber 0g; Sodium 1mg

Strawberry Banana Popsicles

Makes: 8 pops

2 large ripe bananas, peeled
One 10-ounce package sweetened frozen
    strawberries, thawed
2/3 cup water

Puree all the ingredients, pour into popsicle
molds, and freeze.

Per Serving: Calories 54; Protein 0g; Fat 0g (Saturated 0g);
Carbohydrates 14g; Fiber 1g; Sodium 1mg

Sorbet, Sherbet, Frozen Yogurt, and Ice Cream

Frozen desserts are readily available in the supermarket in versions both delicious and healthful.
However, there are times when you might want
to make your own. Maybe you have a large
watermelon to use up, or maybe you just want
to have fun. Transforming ingredients as familiar as strawberries and yogurt into something as
smooth, cold, and delicious as Strawberry
Frozen Yogurt (page 574) can be a family event.

Some of these recipes require a frozen
dessert machine and others don't—equipment
needs are stated in each recipe. It helps to have
a freezer that is set very low (near 0°F) so that
the dessert freezes quickly and hard, which will
improve the texture. But when ready to eat, let
the container sit at room temperature for five
minutes or longer, until easy to scoop.

Lemon Sorbet

Makes: 3 servings

*Few foods are more refreshing on a hot night than
lemon sorbet.*

1 tablespoon finely grated lemon zest
1 cup sugar
1/2 cup lemon juice
1 cup water
1 tablespoon orange-flavored liqueur, such as
    Grand Marnier

Whisk together all the ingredients until the sugar melts. Proceed following the directions of your frozen dessert machine. Or, to make this without an ice cream maker, freeze the mixture in an ice cube tray. After it has set, puree in the food processor (a blender won't work). Freeze again in a container.

Per Serving: Calories 287; Protein 0g; Fat 0g (Saturated 0g); Carbohydrates 73g; Fiber 0g; Sodium 4mg

Watermelon Sorbet

Makes: 6 servings

This solves the problem of what to do with all that watermelon you brought home when you got carried away because it was on sale at the market. (This is a dilemma I face several times a summer.)

4 cups seeded watermelon
1 cup sugar
3 tablespoons lemon juice

Puree all the ingredients. Proceed following the directions of your frozen dessert machine. Or, to make this without an ice cream maker, freeze the mixture in an ice cube tray. After it has set, puree the cubes in the food processor (a blender won't work). Freeze again in a container.

Per Serving: Calories 165; Protein 1g; Fat 0g (Saturated 0g); Carbohydrates 42g; Fiber 0g; Sodium 3mg

Berry Sorbet

Makes: 4 servings

If the tiny seeds in the berries bother you (I knew someone who would not eat berries because of this), the berry puree can be pushed through a fine mesh strainer, leaving the offending seeds behind.

2 cups berries, thawed if frozen
1 cup sugar
$1/2$ cup water
2 tablespoons lemon juice
2 tablespoons orange juice

Puree all the ingredients. Proceed following the directions of your frozen dessert machine. Or, to make this without an ice cream maker, freeze the mixture in an ice cube tray. After it has set, puree in the food processor (a blender won't work). Freeze again in a container.

Per Serving: Calories 239; Protein 1g; Fat 0g (Saturated 0g); Carbohydrates 62g; Fiber 2g; Sodium 6mg

Peach Sorbet

Makes: 6 servings

Peach sorbet is lovely on its own, but don't hesitate to pair it with another dessert, like Peach Bread Pudding (page 569).

4 large or 6 medium peaches, peeled and pitted
3/4 to 1 cup sugar
1 tablespoon lemon juice

1) Puree all the ingredients. Taste and adjust the quantity of sugar, keeping in mind that once frozen it will taste less sweet.

2) Proceed following the directions of your frozen dessert machine. Or, to make this without an ice cream maker, freeze the mixture in an ice cube tray. After it has set, puree in the food processor (a blender won't work). Freeze again in a container.

Per Serving: Calories 135; Protein 1g; Fat 0g (Saturated 0g); Carbohydrates 35g; Fiber 2g; Sodium 0mg

Pineapple Sherbet

Makes: 6 servings

A sherbet differs from a sorbet in that it contains dairy along with fruit.

1 1/4 cups unsweetened pineapple juice
1/2 cup sugar
One 8-ounce can crushed unsweetened pineapple, packed in juice
2 tablespoons lemon juice
1 1/2 cups 1% lowfat milk

Whisk together all the ingredients. Proceed following the directions of your frozen dessert machine. Or freeze until mushy, blend in a food processor, then freeze again in an oblong pan until firm.

Per Serving: Calories 143; Protein 2g; Fat 1g (Saturated 0g); Carbohydrates 33g; Fiber 0g; Sodium 32mg

Strawberry Frozen Yogurt

Makes: 4 servings

If using frozen berries, they must be individually frozen, not packed in sugar.

2 cups strawberries (if frozen, thawed)
2 cups nonfat plain yogurt
1 teaspoon vanilla extract
1/2 cup sugar
2 tablespoons nonfat dry milk

1) Puree the berries, then blend with the remaining ingredients.

2) Proceed following the directions of your frozen dessert machine. Or, to make this without an ice cream maker, freeze the mixture in an ice cube tray. After it has set, puree in the food processor (a blender won't work). Freeze again in a container.

Per Serving: Calories 197; Protein 8g; Fat 1g (Saturated 0g); Carbohydrates 41g; Fiber 1g; Sodium 106mg

Banana Vanilla Frozen Yogurt

Makes: 6 servings

Use ripe—but not bruised—bananas.

2 large bananas
2 1/2 cups nonfat plain yogurt
2 teaspoons vanilla extract
1/2 to 2/3 cup sugar
2 tablespoons nonfat dry milk

1) Puree all the ingredients. Taste and adjust the sugar, taking into account that when frozen it will taste less sweet.

2) Proceed following the directions of your frozen dessert machine. Or, to make this without an ice cream maker, freeze the mixture in an ice cube tray. After it has set, puree in the food processor (a blender won't work). Freeze again in a container.

Per Serving: Calories 165; Protein 7g; Fat 0g (Saturated 0g); Carbohydrates 34g; Fiber 1g; Sodium 86mg

Honey Vanilla Frozen Ice Cream

Makes: 4 servings

This is one of the few times when the yolks are used and the whites are discarded (or, better yet, saved for another recipe).

2 1/4 cups 1% lowfat milk
2 tablespoons nonfat dry milk
1/2 teaspoon vanilla extract
3 egg yolks
3 tablespoons honey

1) Put the milk into a heatproof measuring cup. Stir in the dry milk and vanilla.

2) Heat the egg yolks and honey in a double boiler. Stir in 2 tablespoons of the milk. Pour the egg yolk mixture into the measuring cup. Return it all to the double boiler and stir constantly as it thickens. Cook for about 8 minutes, until smooth and thick (it will not be quite as dense as a true custard). Chill.

3) Proceed following the directions of your frozen dessert machine.

Per Serving: Calories 159; Protein 7g; Fat 5g (Saturated 2g); Carbohydrates 21g; Fiber 0g; Sodium 87mg

Strawberry Milk Shake

Makes: 3 servings

For extra strawberry flavor, use strawberry ice cream instead of vanilla.

2 cups strawberries
1/3 cup nonfat milk
1 tablespoon sugar
1 pint lowfat vanilla ice cream

Wash and hull the berries. Put the fruit into a blender. Puree with the milk. Add the sugar and blend. Add the ice cream and puree until smooth but still thick. Serve immediately.

Per Serving: Calories 188; Protein 6g; Fat 3g (Saturated 1g); Carbohydrates 36g; Fiber 3g; Sodium 82mg

Ice Cream Pie

Makes: 10 servings

Use a glass or ceramic dish for a pretty presentation.

20 chocolate wafer cookies
2 tablespoons melted butter
2 tablespoons vegetable oil
1 quart nonfat frozen ice cream or yogurt,
    any flavor

1) Chop the cookies in the food processor until they are fine crumbs (should make about 1 cup). Put the crumbs into a 9-inch pie pan. Drizzle on the butter and oil. Toss the crumbs and fats until lumpy. Press the crust into the pie pan until evenly thick all around.

2) Bake the crust in a preheated 375°F oven for 9 minutes. Let cool.

3) Leave the frozen ice cream out until it is slightly softened. The ice cream needs to be soft enough to spread, but not so soft that it puddles. Thaw only as much as you need, and it may help to break up the quart so that the interior thaws as fast as the outside. Spoon the softened ice cream into the crust and spread evenly. Freeze until firm. If desired, top with Marshmallow Fluff (page 546) or decorate with cookies.

Per Serving: Calories 170; Protein 3g; Fat 6g (Saturated 2g); Carbohydrates 26g; Fiber 0g; Sodium 148mg

Syrups and Sauces

Most people love gooey, sticky, sweet toppings on frozen desserts. These recipes will add calories but almost no fat, and will turn any lowfat ice cream into a luscious indulgence. For a homemade banana split, get a large bowl, slice a banana, scoop out some ice cream, and load on the toppings.

Chocolate Syrup

Makes: 8 servings

The better quality the cocoa, the better this syrup will be. We keep some on hand for making chocolate milk, too.

1 1/2 cups sugar
1 1/2 cups water
2/3 cup Dutch-process cocoa
2 teaspoons vanilla extract

In a small, heavy-bottomed saucepan, bring the sugar and water to a boil. Boil vigorously for 5 minutes. Reduce to a simmer and slowly whisk in the cocoa. Simmer for about 15 minutes, stirring occasionally, until the syrup thickens. Remove from the burner and let cool for 5 minutes before stirring in the vanilla.

Per Serving: Calories 163; Protein 1g; Fat 1g (Saturated 41g); Carbohydrates 2g; Fiber 2g; Sodium 3mg

Marshmallow Sauce for Ice Cream

Makes: 8 servings

This is a silly recipe that is a lot of fun. What better end to a meal than ice cream with marshmallow and chocolate sauces?

1/2 cup sugar
3 tablespoons water
2 cups mini-marshmallows
1/2 teaspoon vanilla extract

1) Boil the sugar and water until syrupy but not darkened, about 2 to 3 minutes. Swirl the contents of the pot; don't stir.

2) Reduce the heat to medium-low and stir in the marshmallows and vanilla. Stir gently until partially melted but still lumpy. Serve hot over ice cream.

Per Serving: Calories 99; Protein 0g; Fat 0g (Saturated 0g); Carbohydrates 25g; Fiber 0g; Sodium 15mg

Orange Grand Marnier Sauce

Makes: 4 servings

Ice cream sundaes aren't just for kids. This is an "adult" sauce.

1/2 cup orange juice
1/4 cup water
2 tablespoons sugar
2 tablespoons Grand Marnier or other
    orange liqueur
1 seedless navel orange

1) Bring the orange juice, water, sugar, and Grand Marnier to a boil. Cook until the liquids become slightly thickened. This will take about 10 minutes.

2) Meanwhile, peel the orange with a sharp paring knife, removing both the skin and the white pith beneath. Cut the segments away from the membranes. This is more trouble than just peeling and slicing, but it yields beautiful pieces of orange.

3) If you want a perfectly smooth sauce, drain the thickened sauce through a fine-meshed sieve to remove the foam.

4) Stir in the orange segments.

Per Serving: Calories 81; Protein 1g; Fat 0g (Saturated 0g); Carbohydrates 17g; Fiber 1g; Sodium 2mg

Blueberry Syrup

Makes: 12 servings

This syrup differs from blueberry sauce in that is is a smooth, thick liquid with no lumps from the berries. You can put it in a squeeze bottle (like those plastic squeeze bottles used for ketchup) and use it to squiggle decorations on a dessert.

2 cups blueberries (if frozen, thawed and drained)
1/4 cup lemon juice
1/2 cup water
1/2 cup light corn syrup
1/2 cup sugar
2 tablespoons cornstarch mixed with 1/4 cup water

1) In a medium saucepan, bring the blueberries, lemon juice, and water to a simmer and cook until the berries burst. Put through a sieve or food mill to strain out the skin and seeds.

2) Return the blueberry liquid to the pot and bring to a simmer. Stir in the corn syrup and sugar and cook until dissolved. Slowly pour in the cornstarch paste and stir until the syrup thickens and clears, about 2 minutes. Allow to cool, then store in a glass jar in the refrigerator.

Per Serving: Calories 91; Protein 0g; Fat 0g (Saturated 0g); Carbohydrates 24g; Fiber 1g; Sodium 19mg

Blueberry Sauce

Makes: 6 servings

For a Fourth of July picnic, have this and Berry Sauce (opposite) made with strawberries over low-fat vanilla ice cream.

1/2 cup water, divided
1 teaspoon cornstarch
1/3 cup sugar
1 teaspoon lemon juice
2 cups blueberries (if frozen, thawed but not drained)

1) Mix 1 tablespoon of the water with the cornstarch. Set aside.

2) In a small saucepan, bring the remaining water and the sugar and lemon juice to a boil. Add the blueberries, reduce to a simmer, and cook until a few of the berries burst.

3) Slowly stir in the cornstarch paste. Simmer and stir until the sauce thickens and clears. (Do not stir vigorously or unsightly air bubbles will form.)

Per Serving: Calories 72; Protein 0g; Fat 0g (Saturated 0g); Carbohydrates 18g; Fiber 1g; Sodium 4mg

Berry Sauce

Makes: 4 servings

This recipe can be made any time of the year with fresh or frozen berries.

2 cups berries (fresh or frozen)
1 tablespoon apple juice concentrate
1 tablespoon honey
1 tablespoon lemon juice

1) Put all the ingredients in a pot and simmer until the outsides of the berries soften. This takes only a minute or two. If using frozen berries, cook them at a low heat so that they do not turn to mush as they defrost. The apple juice concentrate can be used frozen; just scoop what you need out of the can and put the remainder back in the freezer.

2) Strain the berries and liquid through a wire mesh strainer into a bowl. You can do this by pushing it through with the back of a wooden spoon, or you can use a bowl scraper, a hard plastic semicircle made specifically for this job. Straining the berries will remove their seeds and create a smooth sauce.

3) Serve warm or chilled. The sauce stays fresh for 3 days in the refrigerator. It can be reheated in the microwave.

Per Serving: Calories 54; Protein 1g; Fat 0g (Saturated 0g); Carbohydrates 14g; Fiber 2g; Sodium 1mg

Caribbean Pineapple Topping

Makes: 8 servings

This unusal topping is really tasty.

One 20-ounce can pineapple chunks packed in juice
1/3 cup sugar
1 tablespoon fresh lime juice
1/4 teaspoon ground nutmeg

1) Finely chop the pineapple, including the juice, in a processor or blender.

2) Put the pineapple in a saucepan with the sugar, lime juice, and nutmeg. Bring to a boil, reduce to a simmer and cook, uncovered, stirring frequently, until the topping thickens to the consistency of a thick syrup. This will take about 20 minutes.

3) Store in a glass jar in the refrigerator.

Per Serving: Calories 76; Protein 0g; Fat 0g (Saturated 0g); Carbohydrates 20g; Fiber 1g; Sodium 1mg

Pineapple-Mango Sauce

Makes: 5 servings

This is very cooling after a spicy meal.

1 ripe mango
One 5¹/2- to 8-ounce can pineapple chunks
    packed in juice, drained
3 tablespoons sugar
1 tablespoon lemon juice

1) Cut the mango away from the large, oblong inner seed. Scrape or cut the flesh from the skin and put in a food processor or blender.

2) Add the pineapple, sugar, and lemon juice and puree.

3) Store in a glass jar in the refrigerator. Chill before use.

Per Serving: Calories 70; Protein 0g; Fat 0g (Saturated 0g); Carbohydrates 18g; Fiber 1g; Sodium 1mg

Maple Bananas

Makes: 4 servings

This simple technique of warming fruit in the microwave can be used for other fruits. I've made it with peeled, sliced apples and it is lovely with fresh peaches. Instead of maple syrup, you can use honey. It's versatile, too, and is good on pancakes at breakfast.

2 bananas
2 tablespoons maple syrup

1) Peel and slice the bananas. Put into a microwavable bowl.

2) Pour the maple syrup over the bananas.

3) Cover and microwave for 30 seconds. Stir and microwave for another 20 seconds, until the bananas soften but do not let them turn to mush. Time will vary depending on the microwave and size of fruit slices.

Per Serving: Calories 79; Protein 1g; Fat 0g (Saturated 0g); Carbohydrates 20g; Fiber 1g; Sodium 1mg

Sauces, Salsas, Pantry Staples, and Beverages

Tomato Sauces
583

Basic Basil Tomato Sauce

Fat-Free Tomato Sauce

Freshly Minted Tomato Sauce

Roasted Tomato Sauce

Tomato Coulis

Fat-Free Enchilada Sauce

Red Pepper Sauce

Barbeque Sauces
587

All-American Barbecue Sauce

Very Quick Barbeque Sauce

Island Barbeque Sauce

Fruity Barbeque Sauce

Teriyaki Sauce

Spicy Teriyaki Sauce

Pestos
589

Basil Pesto

Orange Pesto

Mint and Basil Pesto

Sun-Dried Tomato Pesto

Gremolata

Salsas
592

Red Salsa

Tropical Salsa

Pineapple Salsa

Orange and Pineapple Salsa

Peach Salsa

Corn Salsa

Chutneys
594

Tangy Tomato Chutney

Peach Chutney

Pineapple Chutney

Cranberry and Fruit Chutney

Rhubarb Chutney

Onion Relish

Onion and Ginger Relish

Caramelized Onions

*Fast and Fresh
Cranberry Relish*

Fish Sauces
598

Tartar Sauce

Caribbean Tartar Sauce

Cucumber Sauce for Fish

Sour Cream Lime Sauce for Fish

Other Sauces
600

Mushroom Gravy

Green Chili Sauce

Hot! Sauce

Honey Mustard Sauce

Dipping Sauces
602

Hot Mustard Dipping Sauce

Hoisin Dipping Sauce

Asian Dipping Sauce

Homemade Pantry Staples
603

Roasted Peppers

Roasted Garlic

Lemon or Orange Zest

Crystallized Ginger

Toasted Nuts

Soft Breadcrumbs

Dry Breadcrumbs

Croutons

Yogurt Cheese

Almost Sour Cream

Hard-Boiled Eggs

Garlic Oil

Rosemary Orange Oil

Herb Vinegar

Raspberry Vinegar

Garlic and Shallot Vinegar

Beverages
609

Limeade

Honey of a Lemonade

Watermelon Mint Spritzer

Ginger Beer

Microwave Hot Cocoa

Hot Mulled Cider

Tomato Sauces

The truth is that not a week goes by that I don't use a store-bought sauce. If you have a good sauce on hand, a meal can be ready in minutes. If you don't have that jar to open, the meal might not get made. However, despite the availability of excellent commercial products, I continue to make my own for many reasons. Some, like the fresh-tasting Freshly Minted Tomato Sauce (page 584), don't have store-bought equivalents. Others are tastier or more healthful because I've made them from scratch.

In any event, I keep these recipes in the freezer (tomato sauces freeze very well) and find them so useful that I often double the recipes, just so I'll have some when needed.

Basic Basil Tomato Sauce

Makes: 1 1/2 cups; serves: 3

Don't use out-of-season tomatoes; use canned whole tomatoes instead. A good brand will provide plenty of flavor. Drain and discard the juice, and chop the tomatoes before putting them in the pot.

1 1/2 teaspoons olive oil
1/2 cup minced onions
1 tablespoon white wine
4 medium tomatoes, peeled, seeded, and chopped (2 pounds)
1 cup fresh basil leaves, loosely packed, chopped
1/4 teaspoon kosher salt
1/4 teaspoon freshly ground pepper

1) Heat the oil in a saucepan over low heat. Sauté the onions in the oil for about 5 minutes. Keep the pan covered. Add the wine and cook for 5 minutes more.

2) Stir in the tomatoes, basil, salt, and pepper. Simmer, uncovered, for 15 minutes or longer.

Per Serving: Calories 72; Protein 2g; Fat 3g (Saturated 0g); Carbohydrates 11g; Fiber 3g; Sodium 176mg

Fat-Free Tomato Sauce

Makes: 5 cups; serves: 10

The onions and garlic are softened in red wine instead of being browned in oil. For the most flavor, let this rest for 1 to 3 days in the refrigerator before using.

4 cloves garlic, minced
1 cup chopped onions
1 rib celery, minced
1/3 cup red wine
One 28-ounce can tomato puree
One 14 1/2-ounce can whole tomatoes, coarsely chopped, with juice
1 tablespoon dried basil
2 teaspoons dried oregano
1/4 teaspoon dried rosemary
1 tablespoon minced fresh parsley
1 bay leaf
1 carrot
1/4 teaspoon kosher salt

1) Briefly cook the garlic, onions, and celery in a little of the wine, then add the rest of the wine, cover, and simmer for 10 minutes. If more liquid is needed, add the juice from the canned tomatoes.

2) Add the remaining ingredients and continue to simmer for at least 30 minutes and up to 1 hour.

3) Before serving, discard the bay leaf and the carrot.

Per Serving: Calories 60; Protein 2g; Fat 0g (Saturated 0g); Carbohydrates 13g; Fiber 3g; Sodium 469mg

Freshly Minted Tomato Sauce

Makes: 1 1/4 cups; serves: 3

This sauce takes only 15 minutes to cook—about the time required to bring a large pot of water to a boil.

2 cloves garlic, minced
1 teaspoon grated fresh ginger
4 medium tomatoes, peeled, seeded, and chopped (2 pounds)
1/2 cup fresh mint leaves, lightly packed, chopped
1/2 cup fresh basil leaves, lightly packed, chopped
1/8 teaspoon kosher salt
1 1/2 teaspoons olive oil

1) Combine all the ingredients except the oil. This can be done in the food processor. If using a processor, with the machine running, drop in the whole garlic cloves and a piece of ginger about the size of a teaspoon and mince. Then pulse in the tomatoes and herbs until the mixture is coarsely chopped. Add the salt.

2) Pour the mixture into a saucepan and gently simmer, uncovered, for 15 minutes.

3) Stir in the oil.

Per Serving: Calories 67; Protein 2g; Fat 3g (Saturated 0g); Carbohydrates 10g; Fiber 3g; Sodium 103mg

Roasted Tomato Sauce

Makes: 3 cups; serves: 6

This is so easy to make; all the ingredients are roasted whole, and then chopped or pureed in the food processor.

2 pounds plum tomatoes, cored
    (about 16 tomatoes)
1 teaspoon dried rosemary
4 shallots, peeled
3 cloves garlic, peeled
$1/2$ teaspoon kosher salt
$1/4$ teaspoon freshly ground pepper
2 teaspoons olive oil

1) Preheat the oven to 350°F.

2) Place all the ingredients in a baking dish. Toss to combine. Bake, uncovered, for about 40 minutes.

3) Puree or coarsely chop the roasted vegetables, making sure to include all the liquid that has oozed out of the tomatoes.

Per Serving: Calories 55; Protein 2g; Fat 2g (Saturated 0g); Carbohydrates 9g; Fiber 2g; Sodium 175mg

Tomato Coulis

Makes: $1^1/3$ cups; serves: 2

This is the one tomato sauce that should not be made ahead and frozen or it loses its lightly cooked, fresh flavor.

1 tablespoon extra-virgin olive oil
1 pound ripe tomatoes, chopped
2 tablespoons shallots, chopped
    (about 1 large shallot)
1 clove garlic, minced
$1/4$ teaspoon kosher salt, or more to taste
$1/4$ teaspoon freshly ground pepper, or more
    to taste

1) Heat a pan, then add the oil. Stir in all the ingredients, cover, and cook for 5 to 7 minutes, stirring occasionally.

2) Chop the sauce in a processor until chunky. Taste and adjust the salt and pepper.

Per Serving: Calories 117; Protein 2g; Fat 8g (Saturated 1g); Carbohydrates 13g; Fiber 3g; Sodium 262mg

Fat-Free Enchilada Sauce

Makes: 7 cups (enough for 2 batches of enchiladas); serves: 14

This recipe intentionally makes a lot. It freezes very well, with no loss of flavor, and I figured that if I was going to bother to make it from scratch, I might as well have enough for at least two meals.

$^1/_2$ cup minced onions
$^1/_2$ green bell pepper, minced
2 cloves garlic, minced
$^1/_2$ cup red wine
$^1/_4$ teaspoon kosher salt
$1^1/_2$ tablespoons ground chili powder, or more to taste
1 teaspoon ground cumin
$^1/_8$ teaspoon cayenne pepper (optional)
One 28-ounce can tomato puree
One 28-ounce can ground peeled tomatoes

1) In a medium saucepan, cook the onions, bell pepper, and garlic in the wine until the vegetables are soft. Covered, with the wine bubbling over moderate heat, this will take about 10 minutes.

2) Add the remaining ingredients, cover, and simmer for at least 30 minutes or up to 1 hour. Taste and add more chili powder if desired.

Per Serving: Calories 47; Protein 2g; Fat 0g (Saturated 0g); Carbohydrates 10g; Fiber 2g; Sodium 362mg

Red Pepper Sauce

Makes: $1^1/_4$ cups; serves: 5

This isn't a tomato-based sauce, but it can be used like one for many recipes. I've spread it on pizza, layered it in a lasagna, tossed it into pasta, and drizzled it over steamed vegetables. When red peppers, which are usually expensive, go on sale, I buy a bag and make a big batch of this sauce. It freezes well and is a welcome change from tomato sauces.

2 large red bell peppers
1 teaspoon olive oil
2 cloves garlic
$^1/_2$ teaspoon kosher salt
$^1/_4$ teaspoon freshly ground pepper
$^1/_3$ to $^1/_2$ cup reduced-sodium, defatted chicken or vegetable broth

1) Preheat the oven to 400°F.

2) Cut the peppers in half or in quarters. Remove and discard the cores and seeds. Trim off the whitish membranes.

3) In a heavy casserole dish, toss together the peppers, oil, garlic, salt, and pepper. Bake, uncovered, for about 30 minutes, until the peppers' skins begin to blister and they wilt.

4) Put the contents of the casserole (including the juice) in a blender or food mill and puree. Add at least $^1/_3$ cup broth to thin the sauce to the desired consistency. If the peppers were very large, you might need $^1/_2$ cup broth. Use immediately, or refrigerate or freeze for later use.

Per Serving: Calories 19; Protein 1g; Fat 1g (Saturated 0g); Carbohydrates 2g; Fiber 1g; Sodium 225mg

Barbeque Sauces

For the last few years I've been a judge of bottled barbeque sauces at a Barbeque Cook-Off. Every year I go home with bottles of sauces, impressed with their quality and flavor. Still, I like to make my own (my stepson likes Island Barbeque Sauce on almost everything). Barbeque sauce can turn a plain grilled turkey cutlet into a spicy meal, be stirred into strips of chicken and rolled into tortillas for a fast dinner, or be added to a stew to lend a bit of surprising flavor. Most homemade sauces stay fresh for two months in the fridge, so they never go to waste.

All-American Barbeque Sauce

Makes: 2 cups; serves: 8

This recipe takes its cue from the national brands of barbeque sauces on supermarket shelves, but it's much, much better.

2 teaspoons vegetable oil
1 cup chopped onions
3 cloves garlic, minced
1 cup ketchup
2 tablespoons apple cider vinegar
1/4 cup Worcestershire sauce
1/2 cup packed light brown sugar
1 tablespoon ground chili powder
1/2 teaspoon kosher salt
1/4 teaspoon Tabasco sauce, or more to taste
1 tablespoon Dijon mustard

1) Heat the oil in a saucepan and sauté the onions and garlic over moderate heat until golden, about 10 minutes. Keep covered between stirrings.

2) Meanwhile, combine the remaining ingredients in a bowl. When the onions are ready, stir the mixture into the pot. Simmer over low heat for 20 minutes, stirring occasionally.

Per Serving: Calories 114; Protein 1g; Fat 2g (Saturated 0g); Carbohydrates 26g; Fiber 1g; Sodium 630mg

Very Quick Barbeque Sauce

Makes: 2/3 cup; serves: 4

This mild sauce can be made in a pinch.

1/2 cup ketchup
2 tablespoons Worcestershire sauce
3 tablespoons packed light brown sugar
1/2 teaspoon kosher salt
1 teaspoon soy sauce
1/4 teaspoon Tabasco sauce, or more to taste

Whisk together all the ingredients.

Per Serving: Calories 77; Protein 1g; Fat 0g (Saturated 0g); Carbohydrates 20g; Fiber 0g; Sodium 778mg

Island Barbeque Sauce

Makes: 2 1/3 cups; serves: 9

No cooking is necessary to make this unique sauce.

1/2 cup honey
1/2 cup molasses
1/2 cup apple cider vinegar
1/4 cup ketchup
3 tablespoons soy sauce
2 tablespoons Dijon mustard
1/2 teaspoon Tabasco sauce
1/4 cup orange juice concentrate, thawed
2 tablespoons tomato paste

Combine all the ingredients until smooth (this can be done in a blender, but don't liquefy).

Per Serving: Calories 137; Protein 1g; Fat 0g (Saturated 0g); Carbohydrates 35g; Fiber 0g; Sodium 526mg

Fruity Barbeque Sauce

Makes: 2 cups; serves: 8

This deeply flavored sauce can also be used as a dipping sauce for chicken.

1 teaspoon vegetable oil
1/2 cup chopped onions
1/2 cup tomato juice
1 tablespoon Dijon mustard
One 16 1/2-ounce can plums, drained and pitted
1 tablespoon ground chili powder
1/2 teaspoon kosher salt
1/4 cup honey
2 tablespoons lemon juice
1/4 cup water

1) Heat the oil in a small saucepan and sauté the onions over moderate heat until golden, about 10 minutes. Keep the pan covered between stirrings.

2) Meanwhile, combine the remaining ingredients in a bowl. When the onions are ready, stir the mixture into the pot. Simmer for 15 minutes.

3) Let the sauce cool until it can be handled. Puree in a food processor or blender until smooth.

Per Serving: Calories 75; Protein 1g; Fat 1g (Saturated 0g); Carbohydrates 18g; Fiber 1g; Sodium 233mg

Teriyaki Sauce

Makes: 1 cup; serves: 8

Like barbeque sauce, teriyaki sauce can be used to make quick dinners out of everyday ingredients, and it can also serve as the flavoring base for a no-fuss stir-fry.

1/2 cup soy sauce
1/4 cup dry sherry
1/4 cup packed light brown sugar
1 tablespoon vegetable oil
3 cloves garlic, minced
1 tablespoon finely grated fresh ginger

Whisk together all the ingredients. Store in a glass jar in the refrigerator.

Per Serving: Calories 58; Protein 1g; Fat 2g (Saturated 0g); Carbohydrates 9g; Fiber 0g; Sodium 1032mg

Spicy Teriyaki Sauce

Makes: 1 1/4 cups; serves: 10

Red pepper flakes are widely available and thus are listed here, but if you can find it, substitute Chinese chili paste.

1/2 cup soy sauce
1/4 cup dry sherry
1/3 cup packed light brown sugar
2 teaspoons Asian sesame oil
1 clove garlic, minced
2 tablespoons finely grated fresh ginger
1/8 teaspoon crushed red pepper flakes
1/4 teaspoon freshly ground pepper
1/16 teaspoon cayenne pepper

Whisk together all the ingredients. Store in a glass jar in the refrigerator. Let rest 1 day before using.

Per Serving: Calories 49; Protein 1g; Fat 1g (Saturated 0g); Carbohydrates 9g; Fiber 0g; Sodium 827mg

Pestos

Pestos are finely minced herbs in an olive oil base. It is essential that only fresh herbs and fragrant olive oil are used. Pestos add intense flavor to any number of dishes, from soups to casseroles. They can top fish or chicken before grilling and can be spread on grilled bread. Use pesto as you would mustard in sandwiches or toss with pasta (1/2 cup livens up 1 pound of pasta). Pestos can be frozen in ice cube trays, then the cubes popped out and stored in a freezer bag.

Basil Pesto

Makes: 1 1/2 cups

Make sure your basil is very clean—there's nothing worse than gritty pesto.

2 cups fresh basil leaves
2 cloves garlic
1/2 cup pine nuts or walnuts
2 tablespoons grated Romano cheese
5 tablespoons grated Parmesan cheese
5 tablespoons extra-virgin olive oil

1) Wash the basil leaves. Dry in a salad spinner.

2) In a food processor fitted with a metal blade, puree the ingredients in the order listed, starting with the washed basil. Scrape down the sides of the processor after each ingredient is chopped. It will not become smooth until the oil is poured in. With the machine running, add the olive oil in a slow and steady stream. As soon as it is smoothly incorporated, the pesto is ready.

Per 2 Tablespoon Serving: Calories 94; Protein 3g; Fat 9g (Saturated 2g); Carbohydrates 1g; Fiber 0g; Sodium 62mg

Orange Pesto

Makes: 3/4 cup

You want a juicy orange for this pesto. When purchasing oranges, pick up one in each hand. The heaviest has the most juice.

1 orange
2 cloves garlic
2 tablespoons sliced or slivered almonds
1 cup fresh basil leaves, packed down
1 1/2 teaspoons Dijon mustard
1/4 teaspoon kosher salt
1/4 teaspoon freshly ground pepper
1 1/2 teaspoons extra-virgin olive oil

1) Grate 1 teaspoon of peel off the orange, taking care to only get the colorful outer layer and none of the bitter white pith. Then, using a knife, peel the orange, getting rid of the pith and inner membrane. Cut into quarters.

2) Mince the garlic in a food processor. Add the almonds and chop fine. Pulse in the basil. Add the orange quarters, grated orange peel, and remaining ingredients and puree.

Per 2 Tablespoon Serving: Calories 46; Protein 1g; Fat 3g (Saturated 0g); Carbohydrates 5g; Fiber 1g; Sodium 135mg

Mint and Basil Pesto

Makes: 2/3 cup; serves: 10

Once mint is planted in a garden, it tends to run amok. Some gardeners grow mint plants in pots to keep them from spreading, but not me. I'll put up with mint growing in my beans because the aroma is so wonderful. Extra mint gets used in this pesto.

2 cloves garlic
1/2 teaspoon kosher salt
1 1/2 cups fresh basil leaves, packed
1 cup fresh mint leaves, packed
1 tablespoon balsamic vinegar
3 tablespoons extra-virgin olive oil
2 tablespoons water
2 tablespoons grated Parmesan cheese

1) Mince the garlic and salt in a food processor. Pulse in the basil and mint until they are finely chopped. Scrape down the sides of the bowl several times while doing this.

2) While the machine is running, slowly add the vinegar, oil, and water until the mixture is smooth. Pulse in the Parmesan cheese.

Per 2 Tablespoon Serving: Calories 50; Protein 1g; Fat 5g (Saturated 1g); Carbohydrates 2g; Fiber 1g; Sodium 125mg

Sun-Dried Tomato Pesto

Makes: 1 cup

Sun-dried tomatoes never process into a smooth puree. Bits of skin and tomato meat will fleck this pesto.

$1/2$ cup sun-dried tomatoes (not oil-packed)
2 cloves garlic
1 shallot, peeled
$1/2$ cup fresh basil leaves, packed
3 plum tomatoes, peeled and seeded
$1/2$ teaspoon kosher salt
$1/4$ teaspoon freshly ground pepper
1 tablespoon extra-virgin olive oil

1) Bring about 1 cup of water to a boil (I do this in the microwave). Drop in the sun-dried tomatoes, cover, and let rest for about 15 minutes, until the tomatoes soften.

2) With the food processor running, add the garlic and shallot and process until minced. Add the basil and chop. Remove the sun-dried tomatoes from the soak water and drop them into the processor, along with the fresh tomatoes, salt, pepper, and oil. Pulse until it becomes a lumpy paste.

Per 2 Tablespoon Serving: Calories 34; Protein 1g; Fat 2g (Saturated 0g); Carbohydrates 4g; Fiber 1g; Sodium 123mg

Gremolata

Makes: $1/3$ cup

Gremolata is a granular-textured condiment with an intense lemon and garlic flavor. Its texture can only be achieved by mincing the ingredients with a knife, not in a machine. It is superb as a garnish on soups, tossed into pasta, or spooned onto grilled chicken.

1 tablespoon minced lemon zest
$1/2$ cup minced fresh parsley
4 cloves garlic, minced
$1/4$ teaspoon kosher salt
$1/4$ cup extra-virgin olive oil

Stir together the zest, parsley, garlic, and salt. Slowly pour in the oil while constantly stirring the gremolata until it is all well blended. This stays fresh for up to 3 days.

Per Tablespoon Serving: Calories 127; Protein 0g; Fat 14g (Saturated 2g); Carbohydrates 2g; Fiber 1g; Sodium 125mg

Salsas

Salsas are fresh vegetable relishes that can be spicy and sharp, but also sweet and mild. They are usually not cooked, but are served raw alongside other dishes. Sometimes salsa is used as an ingredient in another recipe, such as Mexican Meatloaf (page 214). The most familiar, Red Salsa, is a chunky tomato-based sauce, but many are made with other vegetables, such as corn, or with fruits. Although they often have hot chilies in them, they don't have to be mouth-burning and should not overwhelm the foods they are paired with.

Red Salsa

Makes: 2 cups; serves: 8

If you don't have a food processor, the ingredients can be minced with a knife and then combined.

1 lime
2 cloves garlic
6 scallions, quartered
2 large ripe tomatoes, cored and quartered
2 tablespoons canned sliced jalapeños
1 tablespoon fresh parsley
1/2 teaspoon kosher salt
1/4 teaspoon freshly ground pepper
2 teaspoons dried oregano
1/4 teaspoon ground cumin

1) Cut the peel and white pith away from the lime. Cut the peeled lime into quarters. Put into the food processor and pulse until coarsely chopped. With the machine running, drop in the garlic and scallions and process until minced.

2) Add the remaining ingredients and pulse until chopped.

Per Serving: Calories 18; Protein 1g; Fat 0g (Saturated 0g); Carbohydrates 4g; Fiber 1g; Sodium 157mg

Tropical Salsa

Makes: 3 cups; serves: 12

This can also be served as a side salad.

1 Granny Smith apple
2 tablespoons fresh lime juice
1 large mango
1 navel orange
1/2 medium red onion, chopped (1 cup)
2 tablespoons raspberry vinegar
1 tablespoon chopped fresh cilantro (optional)
1 teaspoon kosher salt

1) Core and chop the apple. Immediately toss with the lime juice to prevent browning.

2) Cut the pit from the mango. Peel and dice. Add the mango to the apple.

3) Cut the peel and white pith away from the orange. Cut the segments from the membranes. Squeeze the juice and pulp still clinging to the membranes into the bowl with the apple. Chop the orange and add it to the bowl.

4) Stir in the remaining ingredients. Toss gently.

Per Serving: Calories 29; Protein 0g; Fat 0g (Saturated 0g); Carbohydrates 8g; Fiber 1g; Sodium 161mg

Pineapple Salsa

Makes: 5 cups; serves: 10

When you chop salsa in a processor, you don't have to worry about handling the jalapeños. If I mince fresh hot peppers by hand I always wear rubber gloves to keep their juices off my skin and away from my eyes. (Rub your eyes once with jalapeño-touched fingers and you'll be forever cautious.)

2 tablespoons pickled jalapeño pepper, or 1 to
    2 fresh jalapeños
2 tablespoons fresh parsley
1 clove garlic, peeled
2 1/2 cups fresh pineapple, or one 20-ounce can
    unsweetened chunks, drained
1/2 green or red bell pepper, seeded
2 large ripe tomatoes, cored, seeded,
    and quartered
1 medium red onion, peeled and quartered
1/4 cup fresh lime juice
1 teaspoon kosher salt

1) Mince together all the ingredients and stir. Or use a food processor fitted with a steel blade. With the machine running, drop in the jalapeño, parsley, and garlic. Mince. Add the rest of the ingredients. Pulse to chop to the desired chunkiness. This will take only a few whirs of the processor. Don't overprocess or the salsa will become watery.

2) Store for up to 1 week in a glass jar in the refrigerator.

Per Serving: Calories 35; Protein 1g; Fat 0g (Saturated 0g); Carbohydrates 8g; Fiber 1g; Sodium 221mg

Orange and Pineapple Salsa

Makes: 1 1/2 cups; serves: 6

Chop the oranges by hand, not in a machine, to get even pieces with minimum loss of juice.

2 navel oranges
One 8-ounce can unsweetened pineapple
    tidbits, drained
1/4 cup minced red onions
1 jalapeño pepper, seeded and finely minced
1 tablespoon fresh lime juice
1/2 teaspoon kosher salt

1) Cut the peel and white pith away from the orange. Cut the segments away from the membranes and chop the segments.

2) Stir together the chopped oranges and the remaining ingredients.

Per Serving: Calories 44; Protein 1g; Fat 0g (Saturated 0g); Carbohydrates 11g; Fiber 1g; Sodium 161mg

Peach Salsa

Makes: 1 1/2 cups; serves: 6

Fresh, ripe, juicy peaches are essential.

2 cups diced peeled peaches
    (from about 2 large peaches)
2 tablespoons minced shallots
1 jalapeño pepper, seeded and finely minced
1 tablespoon lemon juice
1/2 teaspoon kosher salt
1 tablespoon chopped fresh cilantro (optional)
1 clove garlic, minced

Stir together all the ingredients.

Per Serving: Calories 31; Protein 1g; Fat 0g (Saturated 0g); Carbohydrates 8g; Fiber 1g; Sodium 161mg

Corn Salsa

Makes: 4 cups; serves: 8

This is especially good with bean burritos, or tossed into a green salad.

One 16-ounce package frozen corn, cooked and
    cooled (preferably shoepeg white)
6 scallions, sliced
1/2 red bell pepper, diced
2 cloves garlic, minced
2 tablespoons diced canned mild green chilies
2 tablespoons chopped fresh parsley
2 tablespoons chopped fresh cilantro (optional)
1 tablespoon red wine vinegar
1 tablespoon extra-virgin olive oil
2 teaspoons lemon juice
1 teaspoon kosher salt

1) Combine the corn, scallions, peppers, garlic, chilies, parsley, and cilantro in a bowl.

2) Whisk together the vinegar, oil, lemon juice, and salt. Pour over the salsa and toss to combine.

Per Serving: Calories 76; Protein 2g; Fat 2g (Saturated 0g); Carbohydrates 13g; Fiber 2g; Sodium 288mg

Chutneys

Chutneys are cooked relishes, known for their balance of sweet and sour flavors. Among their many uses they can be spread onto turkey sandwiches, used as a glaze for roasted poultry, or mixed into chicken salad. Store chutney in a glass jar in the refrigerator, where it will stay fresh for at least a month, or it can also be frozen.

Tangy Tomato Chutney

Makes: 2 cups; serves: 8

Make this during tomato season, when the tomatoes are dark red and juicy.

1/2 cup chopped onions
1 teaspoon vegetable oil
4 medium tomatoes, peeled, seeded, and chopped
    (about 1 pound)
1/4 cup packed light brown sugar
1/2 cup raisins
2 tablespoons red wine vinegar
1/2 teaspoon kosher salt
1/4 teaspoon freshly ground pepper

Sauté the onions in the oil until they brown lightly and soften. Put the cooked onions in a heavy-bottomed saucepan along with the remaining ingredients. Simmer, uncovered, for 15 to 25 minutes, until thickened.

Per 1/4 Cup Serving: Calories 80; Protein 1g; Fat 1g (Saturated 0g); Carbohydrates 19g; Fiber 1g; Sodium 130mg

Peach Chutney

Makes: 2 cups; serves: 8

Peaches can easily be peeled by scoring an X on them with a knife and then dropping them in boiling water for 1 minute. Cool in a cold water bath, drain, and the skins will slip right off.

1 cup chopped onions
1 teaspoon vegetable oil
6 peaches, peeled, pitted, and chopped
$2/3$ cup sugar
$1/4$ cup lemon juice
1 cinnamon stick
$1/8$ teaspoon ground cloves
1 bay leaf
$1/8$ teaspoon crushed red pepper flakes
$1/4$ teaspoon ground ginger

1) Sauté the onions in the oil in a small nonstick pan.

2) Put the cooked onions into a heavy-bottomed saucepan along with the remaining ingredients. Bring to a boil, reduce to a simmer, cover, and cook for 30 minutes. Remove the cinnamon stick and the bay leaf. Boil, uncovered, until the excess liquid is cooked off and the chutney thickens.

Per $1/4$ Cup Serving: Calories 107; Protein 1g; Fat 1g (Saturated 0g); Carbohydrates 26g; Fiber 2g; Sodium 1mg

Pineapple Chutney

Makes: $2^1/2$ cups; serves: 10

For the fullest flavor, serve this at room temperature, not chilled.

1 cup packed light brown sugar
$1/4$ cup fresh lime juice
3 cups pineapple chunks, drained and chopped (fresh or two 20-ounce cans)
1 teaspoon dried thyme
$1/2$ teaspoon kosher salt
$1/8$ teaspoon cayenne pepper (optional)
1 tablespoon chopped crystallized ginger

1) Put all the ingredients in a heavy-bottomed saucepan. Simmer, covered, for 30 minutes. Let rest until cool enough to handle.

2) Place in a food processor and coarsely chop. Return to the pot, and simmer, uncovered, until thickened.

Per Serving: Calories 112; Protein 0g; Fat 0g (Saturated 0g); Carbohydrates 29g; Fiber 1g; Sodium 105mg

Cranberry and Fruit Chutney

Makes: 8 cups; serves: 32

The recipe makes a large quantity because I have friends who demand a jar each autumn. Because of the quantity, it is important to use a heavy-bottomed pot—the chutney will scorch and stick in a lightweight saucepan.

1 lemon
1/2 cup apple cider vinegar
1 1/2 cups water
2 cups honey
1/4 teaspoon ground cardamom
1/2 teaspoon ground cinnamon
1/2 teaspoon curry powder
1/4 teaspoon ground ginger
1/4 teaspoon ground allspice
4 navel oranges
6 cups cranberries (fresh or frozen), sorted and rinsed, divided
1/2 cup golden seedless raisins
1/2 cup chopped dried apricots
1/2 cup chopped walnuts (optional)

1) Grate the lemon rind, avoiding the white pith under the surface. Juice the lemon and put both the juice and rind into a pot with the vinegar, water, honey, and spices.

2) Grate the rind of 1 of the oranges and put it into the pot. Peel the oranges with a sharp paring knife to remove the rind and pith. Slice the oranges and add to the pot.

3) Bring this mixture to a boil and cook for 5 minutes. Reduce the heat to a simmer and add 3 cups of the cranberries and the raisins and apricots. Simmer for 30 minutes, until the chutney starts to thicken.

4) Stir in the remaining cranberries and the walnuts and cook for another 20 minutes, stirring frequently.

Per Serving: Calories 95; Protein 0g; Fat 0g (Saturated 0g); Carbohydrates 25g; Fiber 1g; Sodium 2mg

Rhubarb Chutney

Makes: 3 cups; serves: 12

Rhubarb is not just for desserts, as this recipe proves.

2 cups chopped onions, preferably a sweet variety like Vidalia
1 1/2 teaspoons vegetable oil
1 pound rhubarb, chopped (about 4 cups)
1 apple, cored, peeled, and chopped
1/2 cup golden raisins
1 cup packed light brown sugar
1/2 cup raspberry or red wine vinegar
1 teaspoon kosher salt
1/16 teaspoon cayenne pepper
1/4 teaspoon ground ginger
1/2 teaspoon ground cinnamon

1) In a medium saucepan, sauté the onions in the oil until golden.

2) Add the remaining ingredients to the pot. Bring to a boil, then reduce to a simmer. Cook, covered, for 10 minutes. Uncover and continue to gently simmer for 20 to 25 minutes. Stir frequently because the chutney tends to stick to the bottom and burn easily.

Per Serving: Calories 123; Protein 1g; Fat 1g (Saturated 0g); Carbohydrates 30g; Fiber 2g; Sodium 170mg

Onion Relish

Makes: 4 cups; serves: 16

This relish is sweet and tangy and absolutely wonderful. Serve with Fat-Free Crispy Pita Chips (page 24) or on Crostini (page 42) as an appetizer. Serve on burgers for lunch. Serve on top of polenta as a side dish. Once you taste this relish, you'll find plenty of other uses.

2 tablespoons plus 2 teaspoons olive oil
8 cups sliced Spanish onions, or a sweet variety such as Vidalias
1/2 cup balsamic vinegar
2 teaspoons sugar
1 teaspoon kosher salt
1/2 teaspoon freshly ground pepper
2 tablespoons dry sherry

1) Put all the ingredients except the 2 additional teaspoons of extra-virgin olive oil into a heavy-bottomed nonstick saucepan. Cook, covered, over low heat for about 1 hour, until the onions are sweet and golden and almost no liquid remains. Stir occasionally during the hour.

2) After 1 hour, uncover, add the remaining olive oil, and continue to cook for about 5 minutes, until there is no liquid left in the pan but the onions are still very moist.

Per Serving: Calories 52; Protein 1g; Fat 2g (Saturated 0g); Carbohydrates 7g; Fiber 1g; Sodium 124mg

Onion and Ginger Relish

Makes: 4 cups; serves: 16

Add the ginger after the onions. This allows you to check the temperature of the skillet. If the onions sizzle, the skillet is too hot and will scorch the ginger.

1 recipe Onion Relish (opposite)
1 tablespoon finely grated fresh ginger

Follow the recipe for Onion Relish, but add the ginger in Step 1.

Per Serving: Calories 52; Protein 1g; Fat 2g (Saturated 0g); Carbohydrates 7g; Fiber 1g; Sodium 124mg

Caramelized Onions

Makes: 1 1/2 cups; serves: 6

Don't be fooled by the short list of ingredients. A long, slow cooking in a touch of oil thoroughly transforms this basic bulb from a sharp, assertive ingredient into a sweet, complex relish.

1 teaspoon vegetable oil
3 medium yellow onions, thinly sliced (3 cups)

1) Heat the oil in a 10-inch nonstick sauté pan over medium heat. Add the onions, reduce the heat to low, cover, and cook for 30 minutes. Stir occasionally. The pan must be quite hot when the onions are added so they will brown at the edges, but then lower the heat right away so a long, slow cooking brings out their sweetness. The onions are done when they shrink to one-third their raw size and are golden brown.

2) Store in the refrigerator for up to 1 week

Per Serving: Calories 29; Protein 1g; Fat 1g (Saturated 0g); Carbohydrates 5g; Fiber 1g; Sodium 2mg

Fast and Fresh Cranberry Relish

Makes: 1 1/2 cups; serves: 12

If you've always bought canned cranberry sauce because you thought that fresh was too much bother, try this.

1 orange
1 lemon
2 cups cranberries, sorted and rinsed
One 8-ounce can pineapple, packed in juice, drained
1/2 cup maple syrup or honey

1) Cut away the peel and white pith from the orange and lemon. Slice in half crosswise so the seeds can be removed easily.

2) Put the cranberries, pineapple, citrus, and maple syrup in a food processor fitted with a steel blade. Pulse until the mixture is finely chopped but not pureed.

3) Put the mixture in a saucepan and simmer gently for 5 minutes, until it just starts to thicken. Or the relish can be served raw after being left to stand at room temperature for 1 hour.

Per Serving: Calories 57; Protein 0g; Fat 0g (Saturated 0g); Carbohydrates 15g; Fiber 1g; Sodium 2mg

Fish Sauces

A piece of grilled or baked fresh fish needs little more than one of these sauces served alongside.

Tartar Sauce

Makes: 1 1/4 cups; serves: 20

Fresh tartar sauce is a far cry from jarred. I rarely eat tartar sauce at restaurants but I enjoy it when it is homemade.

1 cup lowfat mayonnaise
1 small dill pickle, minced (1/4 cup)
1 scallion, minced
1 tablespoon drained capers
1 tablespoon minced fresh parsley
1 tablespoon lemon juice
1/8 teaspoon freshly ground pepper
1/8 teaspoon Tabasco (optional)

Blend together all the ingredients.

Per Serving: Calories 21; Protein 0g; Fat 1g (Saturated 0g); Carbohydrates 3g; Fiber 0g; Sodium 170mg

Caribbean Tartar Sauce

Makes: $1^1/4$ cups; serves: 20

This tartar sauce is really different. It will stay fresh for several days in the refrigerator, although it might separate a little and need to be stirred.

1 cup reduced-fat mayonnaise
$1/4$ cup sweet pickle relish
1 shallot, minced
1 tablespoon minced fresh parsley
1 tablespoon fresh lime juice
$1/2$ teaspoon kosher salt
$1/8$ teaspoon freshly ground pepper
$1/8$ teaspoon Tabasco (optional)

Blend together all the ingredients.

Per Serving: Calories 45; Protein 0g; Fat 4g (Saturated 1g); Carbohydrates 2g; Fiber 0g; Sodium 162mg

Cucumber Sauce for Fish

Makes: $3/4$ cup; serves: 6

The cucumber lightens the dairy base of this sauce.

$1/2$ cup plain nonfat yogurt
$1/2$ cup lowfat sour cream
$1/4$ teaspoon kosher salt
$1/4$ teaspoon freshly ground pepper
1 tablespoon minced fresh dill
1 cucumber, peeled, seeded, and finely diced

Blend together all the ingredients. Chill before serving.

Per 2 Tablespoon Serving: Calories 42; Protein 2g; Fat 1g (Saturated 1g); Carbohydrates 6g; Fiber 0g; Sodium 117mg

Sour Cream Lime Sauce for Fish

Makes: $1^1/4$ cups; serves: 10

Although lemon juice is usually paired with fish, lime juice can also provide that citrus spark to seafood. Stirred in with sour cream, the sharpness is mellowed but the flavor remains.

1 teaspoon finely minced lime zest
1 tablespoon fresh lime juice
1 cup lowfat sour cream
1 tablespoon honey
$2^1/2$ tablespoons Dijon mustard

1) Grate the lime zest first, then squeeze out the juice. Save extra lime juice in a small container in the freezer.

2) Blend together all the ingredients. Chill before serving.

Per Serving: Calories 40; Protein 1g; Fat 2g (Saturated 1g); Carbohydrates 6g; Fiber 0g; Sodium 119mg

Other Sauces

The following recipes can accompany a variety of dishes.

Mushroom Gravy

Makes: 6 servings

Ladle this over meatloaf and burgers.

1 teaspoon vegetable oil
1/2 cup chopped onions
1 teaspoon sherry
1 1/2 cups sliced mushrooms, preferably the dark crimini-type mushrooms (about 6 ounces)
3/4 cup reduced-sodium, defatted chicken broth
1/4 teaspoon dried sage
1/2 teaspoon kosher salt
1/8 teaspoon freshly ground pepper
1 tablespoon unbleached, all-purpose white flour

1) Heat the oil in a small saucepan. Add the onions and cook over medium heat until they become soft and sweet, about 7 minutes.

2) Pour in the sherry, add the mushrooms, and cook until the mushrooms shrink and give off liquid.

3) Whisk together the broth, sage, salt, pepper, and flour until the flour is dissolved. Pour it slowly into the pan. Simmer, stirring frequently, about 5 minutes, until the gravy thickens.

Per Serving: Calories 23; Protein 1g; Fat 1g (Saturated 0g); Carbohydrates 3g; Fiber 1g; Sodium 221mg

Green Chili Sauce

Makes: 3 cups; serves: 12

Use this over enchiladas or serve with quesadillas.

2 cups chopped onions
4 cloves garlic, minced
1 tablespoon vegetable oil
2 tablespoons unbleached all-purpose white flour
1 1/2 cups reduced-sodium, defatted chicken broth
Two 4-ounce cans diced mild green chilies
1/2 teaspoon kosher salt
1/2 teaspoon ground coriander
3 tablespoons chopped fresh cilantro

1) In a small saucepan, sauté the onions and garlic in the oil over moderate heat until the onions turn golden. Stir in the flour and cook until it lightly toasts. Slowly pour in the broth while scraping up the flour stuck to the pan. Add the chilies, salt, and coriander.

2) Bring to a boil, reduce to a simmer, and cook 15 minutes, uncovered, over medium-low heat. Stir in the cilantro.

Per Serving: Calories 32; Protein 1g; Fat 1g (Saturated 0g); Carbohydrates 4g; Fiber 1g; Sodium 210mg

Hot! Sauce

Makes: 3^1/2 cups; serves: 14

This thick cooked sauce can be used as a condiment in addition to salsa, or as an alternative to a bottle of Tabasco on the table. Any tomato, red or green, fresh or canned, can be used.

1 teaspoon vegetable oil
^{1}/2 cup chopped onions
1 cup water
2 cloves garlic, minced
3 cups coarsely chopped tomatoes (red or green, fresh or canned)
2 tablespoons tomato paste
1 tablespoon soy sauce
^{1}/2 teaspoon ground cumin, or more to taste
1 teaspoon ground coriander
^{1}/2 teaspoon cayenne pepper, or more to taste
^{1}/4 teaspoon Tabasco sauce
2 teaspoons chili powder
2 tablespoons red wine

1) Heat the oil in a saucepan and cook the onions until softened. If necessary, add a few tablespoons of the water to keep the onions from sticking. Add the garlic and sauté for 2 more minutes.

2) Add the rest of the water, along with the remaining ingredients. Simmer, covered, for 30 minutes. Taste and adjust the seasonings as needed and cook for 15 more minutes.

Per Serving: Calories 20; Protein 1g; Fat 1g (Saturated 0g); Carbohydrates 3g; Fiber 1g; Sodium 88mg

Honey-Mustard Sauce

Makes: 8 servings (1 tablespoon each)

Any plain, steamed vegetable can be dressed with this sauce for an elegant, flavorful side dish.

^{1}/4 cup honey mustard
2 tablespoons white wine vinegar
3 tablespoons lowfat or reduced-fat mayonnaise
1 tablespoon vegetable oil

Whisk together the mustard, vinegar, and mayonnaise. While whisking, pour the oil in a steady stream into the dressing. Store in a glass jar in the refrigerator.

Per Serving: Calories 50; Protein 0g; Fat 4g (Saturated 0g); Carbohydrates 4g; Fiber 0g; Sodium 51mg

Dipping Sauces

Put these sauces in small bowls and serve with won tons, Chinese vegetable rolls, or steamed shrimp. They can also be used to spice up simple stir-fries, or can be used as dips for steamed vegetables.

Hot Mustard Dipping Sauce

Makes: 1/2 cup; serves: 12

Dry mustard provides a sharp, clear heat that you can't get with prepared mustards.

1 1/2 tablespoons dry mustard
1/2 teaspoon sugar
1/4 cup water
2 tablespoons dry sherry
1 teaspoon rice vinegar
1 tablespoon soy sauce
1 teaspoon Asian sesame oil
1 tablespoon minced scallion

Whisk the dry mustard and sugar with the water until dissolved. Stir in the remaining ingredients.

Per Serving: Calories 13; Protein 0g; Fat 1g (Saturated 0g); Carbohydrates 1g; Fiber 0g; Sodium 86mg

Hoisin Dipping Sauce

Makes: 1/2 cup; serves: 12

If you aren't familiar with hoisin sauce, this is a good recipe to start with. It is fruity, sweet, and tangy.

1/4 cup hoisin sauce
2 tablespoons water
1 tablespoon soy sauce

Whisk together all the ingredients.

Per Serving: Calories 12; Protein 0g; Fat 0g (Saturated 0g); Carbohydrates 2g; Fiber 0g; Sodium 169mg

Asian Dipping Sauce

Makes: 1/2 cup; serves: 12

Sauces don't have to be thick and creamy. This is a highly seasoned liquid that adds plenty of flavor to foods by doing little more than moistening them.

1/4 cup rice wine vinegar
1 tablespoon sugar
2 tablespoons soy sauce
1/2 teaspoon minced fresh ginger
1 tablespoon minced scallions

Whisk together the vinegar and sugar until the sugar dissolves. Stir in the remaining ingredients.

Per Serving: Calories 6; Protein 0g; Fat 0g (Saturated 0g); Carbohydrates 1g; Fiber 0g; Sodium 172mg

Homemade Pantry Staples

Some of these pantry items can be found in the market but others in this section need to be made in your own kitchen. None are difficult to prepare and they all add important elements to other recipes.

Roasted Peppers

Makes: 1/2 to 1 cup sliced peppers per pepper used

To make velvety-smooth, smoky roasted peppers, raw peppers are cooked over (or under) high heat until their skins blacken. For cooks who usually worry about burning things, this takes some getting used to. Once the skins are charred thoroughly, they slip off easily.

Any quantity bell peppers

1) Preheat the broiler or grill. Single peppers can be charred over a gas burner on the stovetop.

2) Place the peppers on a baking sheet lined with foil (to ease clean-up later) and place in the broiler, or place directly on the grill, about 4 inches away from the heat source. Cook until the skins turn black and blister, then turn the peppers (use stainless steel salad tongs) and continue to roast until they are almost entirely blackened but not burned through.

3) Place the charred peppers in a paper bag, fold over the top, and set the bag in the sink (as they steam they weep moisture and this is the tidiest place for them).

4) When the peppers are cool enough to handle, pull off the skin and trim off the seeds and veins. Slice or leave whole. Store in a glass jar in the refrigerator. To extend shelf life, cover with olive oil.

Per 1/4 Cup Serving: Calories 10; Protein 0g; Fat 0g (Saturated 0g); Carbohydrates 2g; Fiber 1g; Sodium 1mg

Roasted Garlic

Makes: 1 head garlic

Raw garlic is sharp and pungent, and it is hard to take in large amounts. But when garlic is roasted, its flavor mellows, its aroma becomes sweet, and it takes on the smooth texture of butter.

1 whole head garlic

1) Preheat the oven to 350°F. The temperature doesn't have to be exact. If you are cooking at 325 or 400°F, just adjust the cooking time accordingly.

2) Select a large head of garlic with dry, papery skin and bulbous cloves. Rub the outside layer of skin off the head. Cut off the top one-fifth of the head so that the large outer cloves are exposed.

3) Put the head in a baking dish. It is not necessary to grease or cover the pan. Bake for about 1 hour, until the cloves become soft and spreadable.

Per Clove: Calories 4; Protein 0g; Fat 0g (Saturated 0g); Carbohydrates 1g; Fiber 0g; Sodium 1mg

Lemon or Orange Zest

Makes: 1 1/2–2 tablespoons

Zest is the outer layer of the peel of citrus fruit. If the white beneath the surface is scrupulously avoided, the zest will not be at all bitter, but is the essence of citrus flavor, pure and dry. All commercially available citrus is waxed, and the wax contains fungicides that cannot be washed off. The amount is tiny and doesn't keep me from using zest; however, when I can get organic citrus, I buy it. Zest freezes well if tightly wrapped in plastic.

1 lemon or orange, well washed and dried

1) To get the most zest off a lemon or orange, use a vegetable peeler. Carefully strip the colorful outer layer off the fruit, leaving all the white pith beneath. Then mince or slice the peel according to the recipe's directions.

2) You can also use a tool called a zester. This little gadget has several sharp holes, that, when pulled along the peel, make fine strips of zest. These are beautiful and perfect as garnishes or for many recipes, especially baked goods.

3) Even if a recipe calls for only a teaspoon of zest, you should zest the entire fruit. Also, take a moment to juice the lemon or orange. Use immediately or freeze in small containers. For small amounts, freeze in ice cube trays, then pop out and store in freezer bags.

Per Teaspoon Serving: Calories 1; Protein 0g; Fat 0g (Saturated 0g); Carbohydrates 0g; Fiber 0g; Sodium 0mg

Crystallized Ginger

Makes: 1 cup

Crystallized ginger is sometimes called candied ginger. I use it a lot. I toss it in muffins, pancakes, and pies, and eat small pieces straight as a snack. It can be expensive at gourmet stores, though I've found it very fresh and reasonably priced at Asian markets. It is not difficult to make at home, but the ginger must be fresh, firm, and plump to start with.

1 cup sugar, plus more for rolling
2 cups water
1 cup peeled ginger, sliced 1/8 inch thick

1) Dissolve the sugar in the water. Heat and stir until clear. Bring to a boil and reduce to a simmer.

2) Stir in the ginger and simmer, uncovered, for 45 minutes. Place a piece of wax paper on the counter, and a wire cooling rack over that. Using a slotted spoon, transfer the ginger to the cooling rack (the wax paper catches the drips). Let drain until almost dry, which will take several hours.

3) Roll the ginger in sugar, then store in an airtight container. Crystallized ginger will last for several months.

Per Tablespoon Serving: Calories 153; Protein 0g; Fat 0g (Saturated 0g); Carbohydrates 13g; Fiber 0g; Sodium 2mg

Toasted Nuts

Nuts that are toasted have a richer, fuller, nuttier flavor than those that are uncooked. There are two ways to toast nuts. For only a few tablespoons, cook them in a dry skillet. For larger quantities, toast them in a sheet pan.

Any quantity nuts

1) *Stovetop Method*: Heat a dry, heavy skillet over a medium-hot burner. Add the nuts and cook them for 3 to 4 minutes. Toss the pan frequently so that all sides of the nuts are heated. Toast them until they begin to change color and the toasted aroma reaches you. Small seeds and nuts like sesame or pine nuts take less time. As soon as the nuts are toasted, place them on a dish and let cool. (If left in the pan, the retained heat will burn them.)

2) *Oven Method*: Preheat the oven to 325°F. Place the nuts on an ungreased rimmed metal baking sheet. (Do not use the insulated type.) Bake for 5 minutes. Shake the sheet to toss the nuts and bake for about 3 minutes longer, until the nuts begin to change color and the aroma is apparent.

Soft Breadcrumbs

Makes: 1 scant cup per slice

Sometimes called "fresh" breadcrumbs, these have to be made at home and used immediately.

Any quantity bread

1) To make a large amount of breadcrumbs, tear the bread into several large pieces and put in a food processor fitted with a steel blade. Pulse until it reaches the desired crumb size.

2) For a smaller quantity of breadcrumbs, cut the bread into tiny cubes. Do this by cutting each slice of bread into long, very thin strips, then turning it 90 degrees and cutting into strips again.

3) Use soft breadcrumbs immediately.

Per Tablespoon Serving: Calories 17; Protein 1g; Fat 0g (Saturated 0g); Carbohydrates 3g; Fiber 0g; Sodium 34mg

Dry Breadcrumbs

Makes: 2 1/4 cups

These are the finer-textured, dried crumbs. They do not have to be used right away but can be stored in an airtight container for up to 3 months or in the freezer for 6 months.

1/2 pound loaf bread

1) Cube the bread and place on a baking sheet in a single layer. Preheat the oven to 350°F, then turn off the oven. Place the baking sheet in the oven. Let it sit several hours or longer until stale and crispy through.

2) Process in a food processor until very fine.

Per Tablespoon Serving: Calories 17; Protein 1g; Fat 0g (Saturated 0g); Carbohydrates 3g; Fiber 0g; Sodium 34mg

Croutons

Makes: 4 cups; serves: 16

You can buy excellent fat-free croutons in the market. There are times, though, when I have half a loaf of homemade bread that needs to be put to use, and that is when I make croutons. It is also an opportunity to use flavored oils.

4 bread slices, $1/2$ to $3/4$ inch thick
1 tablespoon olive oil or flavored oil
   (pages 607–608)

1) Preheat the oven to 400°F. Coat a rimmed baking sheet with nonstick spray.

2) Cut the bread slices into cubes. Put in a bowl and toss with the oil. Place on the baking sheet in a single layer.

3) Bake for 12 to 15 minutes, turning the cubes over once during cooking. Croutons are done when golden brown and crispy in places.

Per Serving: Calories 30; Protein 1g; Fat 1g (Saturated 0g); Carbohydrates 4g; Fiber 0g; Sodium 41mg

Yogurt Cheese

Makes: 3 cups

This isn't exactly cheese. It is drained, thickened yogurt (known as laban in the Middle East) that tastes like cream cheese with a tang. It can be used as a spread or as an ingredient in other recipes. It is very low in fat.

1 pound plain nonfat or lowfat yogurt

1) Use yogurt with live cultures and a brand that doesn't rely on gelatin as a thickener. Put the yogurt in a fine wire mesh sieve or a colander lined with cheesecloth or a coffee filter. Set over a bowl, cover, and refrigerate for at least 12 hours and up to 24 hours. The longer it drains, the thicker and firmer it becomes.

2) Once it it the consistency you desire, put the yogurt cheese into a container and store in the refrigerator for up to 2 weeks.

Per 2 Tablespoon Serving: Calories 11; Protein 1g; Fat 0g (Saturated 0g); Carbohydrates 1g; Fiber 0g; Sodium 14mg

Almost Sour Cream

Makes: $2^{1}/4$ cups

Almost Sour Cream will stay fresh in the refrigerator for up to 4 days. (If some liquid separates out, a quick stir will make it smooth and thick again.) It can be used in salads instead of mayonnaise, baked on top of fish, tossed with vegetables, or put on baked potatoes.

2 cups 1% lowfat cottage cheese
$1/4$ cup plain nonfat yogurt

In a food processor fitted with a steel blade, blend the cottage cheese and yogurt until smooth. (To achieve a texture like sour cream, it is essential that you use a food processor fitted with a steel blade. A blender will make this recipe too thin.)

Per 2 Tablespoon Serving: Calories 20; Protein 3g; Fat 0g (Saturated 0g); Carbohydrates 1g; Fiber 0g; Sodium 105mg

Hard-Boiled Eggs

Makes: 6 eggs

Hard-boiled eggs might seem self-explanatory, but if you've ever boiled an egg only to find the yolk still runny, or tried peeling an egg only to remove half the white along with the shell, you'll want to read on.

6 eggs

1) Put the eggs in a pot and cover with water by 1 inch. Bring to a rolling boil, then reduce to a gentle boil so that the eggs don't bang around and crack. Once the water is boiling, set a timer for 10 minutes.

2) Have a bowl of cold water waiting. Using a slotted spoon, slip the eggs into the water. If the water warms up, pour it out and fill again with cold water. This quick cooling method makes shelling easy. If eggs are allowed to stay warm after boiling, the shells will pull off with the whites stuck to them. This method will also prevent the eggs from having a green tinge.

3) To peel the eggs, gently tap them all over against the counter. Peel off the shell. Rinse off any bits of shell stuck to the eggs.

Per Egg: Calories 78; Protein 6g; Fat 5g (Saturated 2g); Carbohydrates 1g; Fiber 0g; Sodium 62mg

Garlic Oil

Makes: 1 cup

Sometimes it is too much of a bother to peel and mince fresh garlic. Other times I don't want the texture of little bits of garlic in the recipe. That is when I use garlic oil. Although it is no more than oil infused with the flavor of garlic, it imparts a clear, smooth garlic flavor to foods. Once made, it lasts in the refrigerator for up to 6 months.

1 cup olive oil
2 cloves garlic, peeled

Put the olive oil and peeled cloves in an airtight glass jar. Store it in the refrigerator. As time passes, the garlic aroma and flavor will become stronger. Remove the garlic when the oil gets to the strength you desire. Then again, if you are a garlic fanatic, you can leave the garlic in until you've used all the oil. Olive oil solidifies in the refrigerator. Use a spoon to scoop out the amount you need, or bring the jar to room temperature and pour out the oil.

Per Teaspoon Serving: Calories 40; Protein 0g; Fat 5g (Saturated 1g); Carbohydrates 0g; Fiber 0g; Sodium 0mg

Rosemary Orange Oil

Makes: 3 cups

Once this flavored oil is in your refrigerator, you'll find plenty of uses for it, such as brushing fish before grilling or warming the oil in a skillet and tossing in leftover pasta.

1 orange
1 tablespoon fresh rosemary leaves and stems
3 cups olive oil

1) Preheat the oven to 275°F. Using a vegetable peeler, strip off the zest, avoiding the white pith below.

2) Put the zest, rosemary, and oil in a small ovenproof bowl or measuring cup. Heat the oil for 1 hour. Remove carefully and cool on a rack.

3) Strain into a very clean or sterilized jar. Store in the refrigerator. Bring to room temperature before using.

Per Teaspoon Serving: Calories 40; Protein 0g; Fat 5g (Saturated 1g); Carbohydrates 0g; Fiber 0g; Sodium 0mg

Herb Vinegar

Makes: 4 cups

This vinegar gets used up quickly in my house. It is especially delicious in coleslaws and cucumber salads.

1 cup fresh herbs of choice, loosely measured, with stems
8 peppercorns
1 rib celery, thinly slice lengthwise
4 cups white wine vinegar

1) Wash the herbs well and dry in a salad spinner.

2) Have ready 1 or 2 very clean jars. Divide the herbs, peppercorns, and celery between them. Pour in the vinegar. Cover tightly. Store in a cool, dark place for at least 1 week. At this point the vinegar can be strained into another clean or sterilized jar. Or the herbs, peppercorns, and celery can be left in the vinegar for a stronger taste. If so, be sure to remove them when they are no longer fully covered by the vinegar, as they can mold if exposed to air.

3) Once the jars are opened, store in the refrigerator, where the vinegar will last for several months.

Per Teaspoon Serving: Calories 00; Protein 0g; Fat 0g (Saturated 0g); Carbohydrates 0g; Fiber 0g; Sodium 0mg

Raspberry Vinegar

Makes: 3 cups

Good-quality raspberry vinegars can be purchased in any gourmet store, but this homemade version tastes fresher.

One 12-ounce package frozen raspberries, thawed
1 1/2 cups good-quality red wine vinegar
1 1/2 cups good-quality white wine vinegar

1) Drain the raspberries from their juice and place in a glass or stainless steel bowl. Pour in the vinegars, cover, and let rest 6 hours or up to 1 day in the refrigerator.

2) Put the raspberries and vinegar in a pot, bring to a boil and cook, uncovered, for 3 minutes.

3) Strain to remove the solids (a wire mesh strainer is a good tool for this) and pour into a bottle. Keep refrigerated.

Per Teaspoon Serving: Calories 00; Protein 0g; Fat 0g (Saturated 0g); Carbohydrates 0g; Fiber 0g; Sodium 0mg

Garlic and Shallot Vinegar

Makes: 4 cups

This imbues salad dressing with garlic aroma and flavor without the sharpness or texture of the raw cloves.

10 cloves garlic, peeled and lightly smashed
2 shallots, peeled and halved
4 cups white wine vinegar

1) Have ready 1 or 2 very clean jars. Divide the garlic and shallots between them. Pour in the vinegar. Cover tightly. Store in a cool, dark place for at least 1 week. At this point the vinegar can be strained into another clean or sterilized jar. Or the garlic and shallots can be left in the vinegar for a stronger taste. If so, be sure to remove them when they are no longer fully covered by the vinegar, as they can mold if exposed to air.

2) Once the jars are opened, store in the refrigerator, where the vinegar will last for several months.

Per Teaspoon Serving: Calories 00; Protein 0g; Fat 0g (Saturated 0g); Carbohydrates 0g; Fiber 0g; Sodium 0mg

Beverages

Most of the time it is too much of a bother to make a beverage. Sometimes, though, a homemade drink is the most refreshing thing to come out of a kitchen. Here are recipes for when you have the time and inclination.

Limeade

Makes: 4 servings

Fresh limeade is far, far better than store-bought frozen or bottled.

3/4 cup sugar
4 cups water
3/4 cup fresh squeezed lime juice (from about 4 large limes)
Lime twists, for garnish

Dissolve the sugar in the water. Stir in the lime juice and chill. Garnish with lime twists, if desired.

Per Serving: Calories 158; Protein 0g; Fat 0g (Saturated 0g); Carbohydrates 42g; Fiber 0g; Sodium 8mg

Honey of a Lemonade

Makes: 8 servings

On a hot summer day there are few things more welcome on a table than an icy pitcher of home-made lemonade. Sure, you can buy a bottle at the store, but it just isn't the same.

4 lemons, or 1 lemon and 3/4 cup lemon juice
3/4 cup honey
2 cups warm water
4 cups cold water
Ice cubes
Mint sprigs, for garnish

1) Wash 1 lemon well. (It is best if you can find an organic lemon.) Slice the lemon into rounds. Remove the seeds.

2) Put the lemon slices in a pitcher. Pour the honey and warm water over them. With a wooden spoon, stir the mixture until the honey dissolves in the water. Mash the lemon a few times to release the skin's flavors and some of the fruit's juice.

3) Pour in the cold water.

4) Juice the remaining 3 lemons. Each lemon should produce about 1/4 cup juice. Add the juice to the pitcher. Stir to combine.

5) Chill the lemonade and serve over ice cubes. Garnish with mint sprigs.

Per Serving: Calories 102; Protein 0g; Fat 0g (Saturated 0g); Carbohydrates 28g; Fiber 0g; Sodium 7mg

Watermelon Mint Spritzer

Makes: 2 servings

These are bubbly, pink, and fun.

1 pound watermelon
1 sprig fresh mint (about 10 leaves)
1 teaspoon lemon juice
1/4 cup seltzer or sparkling spring water

1) Cut the watermelon from the rind. Remove the seeds.

2) Liquefy the watermelon, mint leaves, and lemon juice in the blender or food processor.

3) Fill 2 tall glasses with ice cubes. Pour half the puree in each glass. Top off each glass with about 2 tablespoons of seltzer. This will make a pretty pink foam on the surface.

Per Serving: Calories 39; Protein 1g; Fat 1g (Saturated 0g); Carbohydrates 9g; Fiber 0g; Sodium 4mg

Ginger Beer

Makes: 5 servings

Some people can't get enough garlic. I can't get enough ginger. This is both sharp and sweet and goes great with spicy meals.

1/3 cup chopped fresh ginger
5 cups water
3 tablespoons sugar
2 tablespoons honey
1/4 cup lemon juice
2 1/2 cups sparkling water or seltzer

1) The ginger can be chopped in a mini-processor. Combine it with the water and sugar in a saucepan. Bring to a boil and keep at a full boil for 2 minutes. Turn off the heat and stir in the honey. Let cool completely.

2) Strain the liquid through a fine mesh sieve, pushing on the solids to extract all the flavorful juice. Stir in the lemon juice and chill the liquid.

3) Just before serving, stir in the sparkling water. The gingerade base can be kept chilled for a week and individual portions poured when desired. Mix 1/2 cup seltzer for each cup of gingerade base.

Per Serving: Calories 58; Protein 0g; Fat 0g (Saturated 0g); Carbohydrates 16g; Fiber 0g; Sodium 12mg

Microwave Hot Cocoa

Makes: 1 serving

This is as quick as opening up one of those prepackaged mixes, but is so much better. Use the best cocoa you can find—you'll be amazed at how you can taste the difference.

2 teaspoons to 1 tablespoon sugar
1 tablespoon Dutch-process cocoa
1 cup 1% lowfat milk

1) In a microwavable mug, stir together the sugar, cocoa, and 2 tablespoons of the milk until everything is well mixed. The amount of sugar needed depends on your own likes and the brand of cocoa.

2) Pour in the remaining milk and stir.

3) Microwave for about 2 minutes, or whatever works with your oven, until the milk is hot throughout but not boiling.

Per Serving: Calories 146; Protein 9g; Fat 3g (Saturated 2g); Carbohydrates 23g; Fiber 2g; Sodium 124mg

Hot Mulled Cider

Makes: 8 servings

One of my favorite ways to make guests feel at home is to have a pot of hot mulled cider greet them as arrive. The aroma wafts through the house, giving it a relaxed, cozy ambience. For large parties, when I'm mulling a few gallons of cider I take a whole orange, stud it with about a dozen cloves, and let it float in the pot.

1/2 gallon apple cider
1 cinnamon stick
6 whole cloves
1/8 teaspoon ground or freshly grated nutmeg
1 strip orange peel, about 2 inches long

Stir all the ingredients together in a large pot. Warm the mixture on the stovetop for about 15 minutes. Keeping the pot covered will reduce evaporation; however, the wonderful aromas that fill the house if the lid is left off may be worth the loss of a little cider.

Per Serving: Calories 117; Protein 0g; Fat 0g (Saturated 0g); Carbohydrates 29g; Fiber 0g; Sodium 7mg

Acorn Squash Rings, Baked, 361
Aegean Pizza, 442
African Peanut Sauce, 299
African Spinach and Peanuts, 339
Al dente, 86
Almond(s)
  Angel Food Cake, 541
  Frosting, Seven-Minute, 545
  Loves, 554
  Orange Biscotti, 549
  Sour Cherry Nut Bars, 560
Almost Sour Cream. *See*
      Sour Cream
Anadama Bread, 498
Angel Food Cakes, 539–41
Angel Hair Pasta, Lemon
      Garlic, 379
Appetizers, listing of recipes, 20–21
Apple(s), 311–13
  Baked, 515
    Brandy, with Jelly Glaze, 516
    Microwaved, for One, 516
    Spiced, with Applejack, 516
  Cake, 534
  and Carrot Coleslaw, 79
  and Celery Slaw with Honey
      Dressing, 80
  Cider Chicken Stew, 188
  Cinnamon, 312
  Cookies, Date and, 550
  Grilled, 311
  Muffins, 475
  Pie, 523
  Pie, Cranberry, 524
  Pie, More Than, 524
  Red Cabbage and, 313
  Salad, Tuna and, 430
  and Turnips, Layered, 312
  Waldorf Salad, 77
Applesauce, 467
Applesauce, Peachy, 467

Applesauce Cookies, 551
Apricot(s)
  Chicken, 173
  Couscous Pilaf, 384
  Glazed Chicken, 168
  and Oat Bars, 559
  Squares, Chocolate, 559
  Stewed Prunes and, 468
Artichoke Heart(s)
  Salad, Chicken and, 103
  Tuna Salad with Capers and, 105
Asian Beef and Noodle Salad, 91
Asian Dipping Sauce, 602
Asian Green Beans, 335
Asian sesame oil, about, 11
Asparagus, 313–17
  Frittata, 463
  in Gingerly Citrus Dressing, 314
  with Red Pepper Sauce, 314
  Risotto, 306
  Roasted, 316–17
  Sautéed, 316
  Smoked Salmon-Wrapped, 34
  Soy-Dressed, 73
  and Spaghetti, 285
  Steamed, 314
  with Warm Lemon Dressing, 315
Avocados
  Guacamole, 28
  Guacamole Caliente, 28

Baba Ganouj, 29
Baba Ganouj with Mint and
      Cumin, 29
Bacon, 11
Bacon-Stuffed Mushroom Caps, 41
Baking, defined, 8
Baking, lowfat, 530–31
Baking pans, 18, 277, 531
Baking sheets, 18
Balsamic (Vinegar)

Berries with Mint, 508
  Chicken and Broccoli, 200
  Onions, Mashed Potatoes
      and, 355
  Surprising Strawberries, 508
  Vinaigrette, 55
Banana(s)
  Bites, Chocolate-Covered, 571
  Bread, 488
  Cookies, 552
  French Toast, 458
  French Toast, -Stuffed, 460
  Frozen Yogurt, Vanilla, 575
  Maple, 580
  Meringue Pie, 528
  Muffins, Honey, 475
  Popsicles, Strawberry, 572
  Purple Pops, 571
  Rice Pudding, 567
  Sour Cream Pie, Blueberry
      and, 527
  Yogurt Smoothie, 469
Barbeque Sauces, 587–89
  Listing of recipes, 581
Barbeque(d)
  Burgers, 433
  Chicken, Orange, 171
  Chicken, Pineapple, 170
  Hot Dogs, 198
  Sandwiches, Turkey, 427
  Shrimp, 49
Barley
  with Mushrooms, 397
  Salad, Wheat Berry and, 97
  Soup, Mushroom, 130
  Soup, Vegetable, 130
  with Vegetables and Dill, 398
Bars, Dessert. *See* Brownies and Bars
Basil
  and Broccoli Ziti, 286
  Orange Pesto, 590

Pesto, 589
Pesto, Mint and, 590
and Tomato Crostini or
    Bruschetta, 43
and Tomato Salad, 70
Tomato Sauce, Basic, 583
Basmati and Lentil Pilaf, 389
Bayou Stewed Cauliflower, 329
Bayshore Meatball Subs, 428
Bean(s), Dried, 399–406. *See Also*
    Black Bean(s); Chickpea(s);
    Lentil(s); White Bean(s)
Baked, 402
Basic, 399
Chili, 302
Easy Turkey Chili, 196
Enchiladas, 273
Hopping John, 406
Layered Tortilla Casserole, 276
Mexican Mole Chili, 197
Mexican Mole Vegetarian Chili, 303
Red Rice and, 393
Roasted Vegetable Tortilla
    Lasagna, 278
Salad, Many-, 99
Split Pea(s)
    and Smoked Turkey Soup, 138
    Soup, 137
    Two-Pea Soup, 138
Stew, Belizean Vegetable and, 301
Succotash with Tomatoes and
    Basil, 373
and Tortilla Lasagna, 275
Beans, Green. *See* Green Bean(s)
Beef
    Broth, 111
    Frontier Pie with Corn Bread
        Topping, 184
    Ground
        Cooking with, 211
        Burgers, Barbeque, 433
        Burgers, Greek-Style, 433
        Burgers, Mushroom and, 432
        Chili, Mexican Mole, 197
        Meatballs, Porcupine, 215
        Meatballs, Seasoned, 216
        Meatballs, Tiny, and Spaghetti in
            Creamy Tomato Sauce, 217

Meatloaf, Mexican, 214
Meatloaf, Spinach-Stuffed, 212
Meatloaves, Muffin Tin, 212
and Noodles, 193
Sloppy Joes, Quick Confetti, 429
Stuffed Peppers, 214
Hot Dogs, Barbequed, 198
Moo Shu, 206
Roast Beef Pinwheels, Herbed, 38
Salad, Asian Noodle and, 91
Stew, Old-Fashioned, 195
Stir-Fried, and Snow Peas, 205
Stir-Fried, with Broccoli, 204
Beet Greens, Steamed, with Sesame
    Oil, 339
Beets, 317–18
    Baked, 317
    Borscht, 118
    Harvard, 318
    Pickled, 76
    Raspberry and Orange
        Glazed, 318
    Salad, Minty, 76
    Salad, Orange and, 77
Belizean Bean and Vegetable
    Stew, 301
Bell Peppers. *See* Pepper(s), Bell
Berry(ies). *See Also specific berries*
    Balsamic, with Mint, 508
    Dairy Shake, Very, 469
    -Good Muffins, 474
    Pie, 526
    Sauce, 579
    Sorbet, 573
    Swirl, Melon-, 114
Beverages
    Ginger Beer, 610
    Honey of a Lemonade, 610
    Hot Mulled Cider, 611
    Limeade, 609
    Microwave Hot Cocoa, 611
    Smoothie, Banana Yogurt, 469
    Smoothie, Dairy-Free Fruit, 470
    Smoothie, Fruit and Yogurt, 470
    Smoothie, Orange Mango, 470
    Strawberry Milk Shake, 575
    Very Berry Dairy Shake, 469
    Watermelon Mint Spritzer, 610

Biscotti, Chocolate Chip, 548
Biscotti, Orange, 549
Biscuits, 492
Black Bean(s)
    Burritos, Veggie and, 422
    Chili, 302
    Chili Egg Casserole, 465
    Dip, 31
    Dip, Layered, 32
    and Pumpkin, 404
    and Rice, 403
    Salad, All-Season, 99
    Salad, Corn and, 100
    Salad, Yellow Rice and, 100
    Soup, 136
    Soup, Brazilian Pumpkin and, 136
    Southwestern, 403
    Tostadas with Salsa and Goat
        Cheese, 38
    Whole Wheat Tostadas, 38
Blackberry and Red Currant
    Chicken, 167
Blackberry-Pear Cobbler, 562
Blanching, defined, 8
Blending, defined, 8
Blintzes, Pears as, 518
Blissful Tuna Salad, 106
Blueberry
    Bran Bread, 488
    Lemon Muffins, 474
    Pancakes, 453
    -Peach Cobbler, 563
    Sauce, 578
    Sour Cream Pie, Banana and, 527
    Syrup, 578
Boiling, defined, 8
Bok Choy, Stir-Fried, 340
Borscht, 118
Brandy Baked Apples with Jelly
    Glaze, 516
Brazilian Black Bean and Pumpkin
    Soup, 136
Bread. *See Also* Pita; Stuffing;
    Toast(s); Tortilla(s)
    Listing of recipes, 471–72
    Canapés, 34–35
    Croutons, 606
    Crumbs, 605

Bread *(cont.)*
  Garlic, American, 415
  Soup, 131
  Spreads, 448
Bread, Quick, 488–93. *See Also*
      Corn Breads; Muffins;
      Popovers; Scones
  Listing of recipes, 472
Bread, Yeast, 493–501. *See Also*
      Focaccia
  Baking tips, 493–96
  Storing and freezing, 496
  Listing of recipes, 472
Bread Pudding, 569–70
  Apple Cinnamon Raisin, 569
  Cocoa, 570
  Lemon, 570
  Peach, 569
Breakfast Polenta, 450
Breakfast Potatoes, 466
Breakfasts, listing of recipes,
      446–47
Broccoli, 319–22
  Frittata, 462
  Garlic and Lemon, 320
  Garlic Oil Pasta with, 378
  and Garlic Pasta for One, 286
  Lasagna, Carrot and, 280
  Mini-Frittatas, -Pepper, 46
  Muffins, Cheddar, 482
  Oven-Roasted, 322
  Pasta with Sun-Dried Tomato
      Pesto, 289
  and Peanuts, 320
  Pizza, Garlic and, 442
  and Roasted Peppers, 319
  Salad, Chickpea, Pasta, and, 101
  Salad, Chinese Pasta and, 90
  Salad, Wild Rice, Corn, and, 93
  Scallops, Pasta, and, 256
  Shells with Chickpeas and, 290
  Steamed, Simply, 319
  Stir-Fried
    Beef with, 204
    Garlic, 321
    Hoisin Chicken and, 202
    with Oyster Sauce, 321
    Shrimp and, 250

  Stuffed Potatoes, Ricotta and, 418
  Ziti, Basil and, 286
Broiling, defined, 8
Broths, 110–12
Brownies and Bars, 556–60
  Listing of recipes, 506
Bruschetta and Crostini, 42–45
  Listing of recipes, 21
Brussels Sprouts, 323–24
  with Chestnuts, 323
  Glazed, 324
  Oven-Roasted, and Carrots, 324
  Roasted, 323
Buckwheat, about, 396
Bulgur (Wheat)
  Salad, 96
  Salad, Feta and, 96
  Stuffed Eggplant, Feta and, 267
  Stuffed Peppers, 214
Burgers, 432–35
  Listing of recipes, 417
Burritos, 420–22
  Listing of recipes, 416
Busy Day Tortellini Soup, 128
Buttermilk, 12
  Chicken, Sesame, 171
  Creamy Herb Dressing, 59
  Pancakes, 452–53
  Two-Mustard Dressing, 60
  Waffles, 457
Butternut Squash. *See*
      Winter Squash
Butterscotch Chip Brownies, 556

C abbage
  Classic Picnic Slaw, 78
  Coleslaw with Horseradish
      Dressing, 79
  Red, and Apples, 313
Caesar Salad with Apple Dressing
      and Currants, 66
Caesar-Style Dressing, 60
Caesar-Style Salad, 65
Cajun Catfish, 223
Cakes, 530–43
  Listing of recipes, 506
  Baking tips, 530–31
Calamata olives, 12

Calories and fat, 5
Canapés, Cream Cheese and
      Caviar, 35
Canapés, Smoked Salmon, 34
Candied Sweet Potatoes, 356
Cannellini and Corkscrew
      Gratin, 405
Caper(s), 12
  Caponata, 372
  Relish, Grilled Fish with
      Currant-, 240
  Sauce, Fish Steak with
      Tomato, 238
  Sauce, Turkey Cutlets in
      Lemon-, 209
  Sauce, Turkey Cutlets with
      Rosemary-, 210
  Spaghetti alla Puttanesca, 291
  Tuna Salad with Artichoke Hearts
      and, 105
Caponata, 372
Cappuccino Mud Pie, 527
Caramelized Onions, 597
Caribbean Corn Soup, 150
Caribbean Pineapple Topping, 579
Caribbean Tartar Sauce, 599
Carrot(s), 325–27
  Baby, with a Honey-Mustard
      Glaze, 325
  Cake, 535
  Cookies, 551
  Dilled, 325
  Italian Sweet and Sour, 326
  Lasagna, Broccoli and, 280
  Lemony Squash and, 363
  and Lentils, 400
  Muffins, Ginger, 477
  Not Your Traditional
      Tzimmes, 358
  Orange Ginger, 326
  Oven-Roasted Brussels Sprouts
      and, 324
  and Peas, 346
  and Raisins, 327
  Rooted, 327
  Salad
    and Apple Coleslaw, 79
    and Mint, 80

North African, 81
Sesame Slaw, 81
and Walnut, 80
Zucchini Slaw, 82
Soup
Chilled, 118
Gingery Almond, 121
-Tomato-Orange, 120
Sticks, Marinated, 75
Casserole, Chili Egg, 465
Casserole, Mexican Zucchini, 366
Casserole, Sausage and Cheese
Egg, 464
Casserole, Tuna Noodle, 231
Casserole, Turkey Meatball and
Penne, 217
Casserole, Zucchini Cheese, 366
Casseroles
Meat and Poultry, 181–87
Listing of recipes, 153
Vegetarian, 269–76
Listing of recipes, 264
Casual Meals, listing of recipes,
416–17
Catfish, Cajun, 223
Catfish, Pecan, 223
Cauliflower, 328–30
Bayou Stewed, 329
Curried, and Peas, 329
Florets, Dressed, 328
with Garlic Breadcrumbs, 328
Roasted, with Rosemary and
Garlic, 330
Soup, 119
Celery and Apple Slaw with Honey
Dressing, 80
Cereal, 449–51
Chévre. See Goat Cheese
Cheddar
Chili-Cheese Pinwheels, 37
Macaroni and Cheese, 270
Macaroni and Cheese with
Vegetables, 270
Muffins, Broccoli, 482
Mushroom and Cheese Scalloped
Potatoes, 350
Popovers, Whole Wheat, 492
Quesadillas, Whole Wheat, 423

Sausage and Cheese Egg
Casserole, 464
Stuffed Potatoes, 418
Zucchini Cheese Casserole, 366
Cheese. See Also Cheddar; Cream
Cheese; Feta; Goat Cheese;
Parmesan; Ricotta
Lowfat and nonfat, 277
Shredded, 15
Basic Quesadilla, 423
Cottage Cheese-Dill Muffins, 480
Mini-Muffins, Jalapeño-, 39
Muffins, Turkey and, 481
Pizza, Veggies and, 439
Romano and Olive Focaccia, 503
Yogurt. See Yogurt Cheese
Cheesecake
Chocolate Marble, 542
Ginger, 543
Mousselike, 542
Cherry
and Apple Chicken, 188
Cobbler, 561
Soup, Chilled, 113
Sour, Nut Bars, 560
Topping, 547
Cherry Tomato and Watercress
Salad, 73
Cherry Tomatoes, Cheery, 368
Chestnuts, Brussels Sprouts
with, 323
Chestnuts, Roasted, 323
Chicken
Entrées, listing of, 152–54
Fat content of, 155
Baked, 166–75
Baking tips, 166
Apricot, 173
Apricot Glazed, 168
Breasts, Papaya Baked, 169
in Chili Tomato Sauce, 173
Gingered Marmalade, 167
Hoisin, 168
Lemon-Rosemary, 170
Marmalade, 172
in Orange and Tahini, 172
Orange Barbeque, 171
in Parchment, Oriental, 175

Pineapple Barbeque, 170
Red Currant and Blackberry, 167
Rolls, Lemon-Thyme, 174
Sesame Buttermilk, 171
Breaded and Baked, 155–59
Baking tips, 155–56
Chutney, 159
Crusty Horseradish, 158
in Mustard, 156
Nuggets, Honey-Mustard, 156
Nutty Honey, 157
Pecan Baked, 157
in Pesto Crust, 158
Broth, 112
Casseroles
Enchiladas, 186
Greek, 182
Mexican Corn and, 181
Pot Pie, 185
Grilled, 159–62
Grilling tips, 159
Fresh Herb Marinated, 160
Maple-Mustard Glazed, 160
Tandoori, 161
Turkish-Style Yogurt, 162
Kebabs, 162–66
Cooking tips, 162
Garlic-Oregano, 166
Honey-Hoisin, 164
Honey-Teriyaki, 164
Persian Lemon, 165
Satay, Curried Lime, 165
Tropical, 163
Yakitori, 162
Pizza, Southwest, 441
Poached, 103
Roasted, 176–80
Roasting tips, 176
Garlic, 178
Herb, 177
Lemon, 177
Orange and Lime, 178
with Red Rubbing Spices, 180
Sweet Soy, 179
Salad
Artichoke Heart and, 103
Curried, 104
Curried Fruit, Rice, and, 94

Chicken (cont.)
  and Noodle, Chinese, 91
  Poached, 103
  Raspberry, Greens, and, 66
  Tropical Pasta and, 89
  Soups, 132, 144–51
  Listing of recipes, 109
  Stir-Fried
    Cooking tips, 201
    and Broccoli, Hoisin, 202
    Honey Teriyaki, 203
    Kung Pao, 202
    Lo Mein, Hoisin, 207
  Stovetop Cooked, 188–200
    Apple and Cherry, 188
    and Apple Curry, 189
    Balsamic, and Broccoli, 200
    Burritos, 420
    Chili Pumpkin, 190
    Country, 191
    Fajitas, 199
    Fragrant, 192
    in Indonesian Sauce, 200
    and Noodles, 193
    and Rice, 190
    Roll Ups, Spicy Shredded, 427
    Stew, Apple Cider, 188
    Stew, Southern, 194
    White Chili, 197
  Stuffed Potatoes, Pesto and, 419
  Tortilla Soup with, 132
Chickpea(s)
  Curry, 303
  Dip, Garlic and Lime, 30
  Gratin, 406
  Hummus with Tahini, 30
  Minestrone, 126
  North African Vegetable Soup, 127
  Salad, Broccoli, Pasta and, 101
  Salad, Roasted Red Pepper and, 101
  Salad Bar Pesto Soup, 127
  Shells with Broccoli and, 290
  Spread, Pine Nut and, 31
  Tortilla Soup, 132
  Vegetables and, over
    Couscous, 298
Chili, Green, and Spicy Tofu
  Enchiladas, 274
Chili, Green, Sauce, 600

Chili and Lime Corn, 332
Chili Corn Bread, 487
Chili Egg Casserole, 465
Chili powder, 12
Chili Pumpkin Chicken, 190
Chili (Stews), 302
  Black Bean, 302
  Easy Turkey, 196
  Mexican Mole, 197
  Mexican Mole Vegetarian, 303
Chili-Cheese Pinwheels, 37
Chili-Orange Vinaigrette, 57
Chili-Seasoned Fish Steaks, 225
Chili-Spiced Tortilla Chips, 24
Chilled Soups, 113–18
  Listing of recipes, 108
Chinese
  Broccoli and Pasta Salad, 90
  Chicken and Noodle Salad, 91
  Chicken Noodle Soup, 146
  Cucumber Salad, 68
  Dumpling Rolls, 297
  Steamed Fish, 244
  Vinaigrette, 57
Chips
  Pita, Fat-Free Crispy, 24
  Pita, Garlic Oil, 25
  Tortilla, Baked, 24
  Tortilla, Chili-Spiced, 24
Chocolate Apricot Squares, 559
Chocolate Chip Biscotti, 548
Chocolate Cream Cheese
    Frosting, 546
Chocolate Marble Cheesecake, 542
Chocolate Meringue Kisses, 555
Chocolate Nut Crackle
    Cookies, 553
Chocolate Pudding, 564
Chocolate Syrup, 576
Chocolate-Covered Banana Bites, 571
Cholesterol, 4
Chopping, defined, 8
Chowder, Corn, 124
Chowder, Manhattan-Style Fish, 142
Chutney Chicken, 159
Chutney Cream Cheese Spread, 33
Chutney Pinwheels, 37
Chutneys, 594–96. See Also Relishes
  Listing of recipes, 581

Cider, Apple, Chicken Stew, 188
Cider, Hot Mulled, 611
Cider-Cooked Vegetables, 371
Cider-Roasted Squash and
    Shallots, 362
Cinnamon Apples, 312
Cinnamon Raisin Swirl Bread, 500
Cinnamon-Raisin Oatmeal, 449
Cioppino, 246
Citrus-Marinated Fish, 236
Clam(s)
  Risotto, Mussels and, 260
  Sauce, Linguine with Tomato
    and, 254
  Sauce, Spaghetti with, 252
  Sauce, Spaghetti with Fresh, 252
Cobbler, Blackberry-Pear, 562
Cobbler, Blueberry-Peach, 563
Cobbler, Cherry, 561
Cocoa, Dutch-Processed, 12
Cocoa, Hot, Microwave, 611
Cocoa Angel Food Cake, 540
Cocoa Bread Pudding, 570
Cocoa Cake, 532
Cocoa Cake, Zucchini, 533
Cocoa Cookies, 552
Coconut Sauce, Fish in
    Curried, 245
Coconut Soup, Indian-Style, 125
Coffee Cake, Pear and Spice, 538
Coleslaws and Slaws, 78–82
  Listing of recipes, 53
Compotes
  Dried Fruit and Ginger, 468
  Honeydew, Mango, and
    Ginger, 511
  Melon Ball, 510
  Strawberry and Melon, 511
Cookie sheets, 18
Cookies, 547–55
  Listing of recipes, 506
  Baking tips, 547–48
Cooking terms, 8–9
Corkscrew and Cannellini
    Gratin, 405
Corn, 330–33
  Casserole, Mexican Chicken
    and, 181
  Chili and Lime, 332

on the Cob
  Grilled-in-the-Husk, 331
  Microwaved, 331
  Roasted, 331
  Steamed, 331
Confetti, 332
Focaccia, 504
Fried Rice, 333
Garlicky Zucchini and, 365
Muffins, 478–79
Pear Cornbread Pudding, 414
Polenta, Double-, 409
Salad
  Black Bean and, 100
  Southwestern, 75
  and Tomato, 72
  Wild Rice, Broccoli and, 93
Salsa, 594
Soup
  Caribbean, 150
  Chicken, 149
  Chowder, 124
  Gazpacho, 116
  Leek and, 124
  Velvet, 146
Succotash with Tomatoes and
  Basil, 373
Corn Bread Stuffing, 410
Corn Breads
  Chili, 487
  Molasses, 486
  Vegetable, 486
Cornbread Pudding, Pear, 414
Cottage Cheese-Dill Muffins, 480
Coulis, Tomato, 585
Country Chicken, 191
Couscous, 384–85
  Listing of recipes, 375
Couscous, Vegetables and Chickpeas
  over, 298
Cowboy Foil-Wrapped
  Vegetables, 374
Crab, Tortilla Soup with, 132
Crabmeat Mini-Frittatas, 46
Cranberry
  Bread, Orange, 489
  Chutney, Fruit and, 596
  Muffins, Maple, 476
  Pie, Apple, 524

Relish, Fast and Fresh, 598
Stuffing, Bread and, 412
Cream Cheese
  and Caviar Canapés, 35
  and Chives Spread, 448
  -Filled Muffins, Maple, 480
  Frosting, 546
  Frosting, Chocolate, 546
  Spread, Chutney, 33
  Spread, Smoked Salmon, 448
Creole Green Beans, 336
Creole Sauce for Seafood, 231
Crostini and Bruschetta, 42–45
  Listing of recipes, 21
Croutons, 606
Crust, Pie. See Pie Crust
Crystallized Ginger, 604
Cucumber(s)
  Seeding, 68
  Salads, 68–69
  Sauce for Fish, 599
  Soup, Yogurt, 117
Cupcakes, 532
Currant Pilaf, 390
Currant Scones, 484
Curry(ied)
  Cauliflower and Peas, 329
  Chicken, Fruit, and Rice Salad, 94
  Chicken and Apple, 189
  Chicken Salad, 104
  Chickpea, 303
  Coconut Sauce, Fish in, 245
  Dressing, Mild Yogurt, 59
  Fried Rice, 390
  Lime Chicken Satay, 165
  Mashed Potatoes, 354
  Orange Dip, 26
  Pea Pilaf, 394
  Rice, 388
  Spiced Nuts, Sweet, 23
  Squash Soup, 121
  Stuffed Eggs, 36
  Sweet Potatoes and Greens, 304
  Tomato Soup, 120
Custards, Pumpkin, 566
Cutting boards, 17–18

Dairy-Free Fruit Smoothie, 470
Dal Nepal, 402

Date and Apple Cookies, 550
Deep South Boiled Shrimp
  Dinner, 251
Deep-Dish Rustica Pizza, 444
Deep-Dish Vegetable Pizza, 445
Dessert Fruit Plates, 513
Desserts, listing of recipes, 505–7
Deviled Eggs, 35
Dicing, defined, 8
Dill, Orzo with Fresh, 381
Dilled Carrots, 325
Dilled New Potatoes, 351
Dill-Poached Fish, 242
Dilly Potato Salad, 84
Dipping Sauces, 602
Dips and Spreads, 25–33
  Listing of recipes, 20
Dirty Rice, 391
Double-Corn Polenta, 409
Dough, Pizza, 437–38
Dredging, defined, 8
Dressed Cauliflower Florets, 328
Dressings, Salad, 55–60
  Listing of recipes, 52
Dried Fruit. See Fruit, Dried
Dumpling Rolls, 296–97
Dusting, defined, 9
Dutch-Processed Cocoa, 12

Eggplant
  Baba Ganouj, 29
  with Mint and Cumin, 29
  Caponata, 372
  Caviar, 30
  Lamb Moussaka, 183
  Moussaka, 182
  No-Pasta Vegetable Lasagna, 278
  Oven-Baked Ratatouille, 271
  Sauce, Spaghetti with Tomato
    and, 292
  Stuffed, Bulgur and Feta, 267
  Stuffed, Rice and Pine Nut, 266
Eggroll Wrappers
  for dumplings, 296–97
  for ravioli, 282
Egg(s). See Also Frittatas
  Casserole, Chili, 465
  Casserole, Sausage and Cheese, 464
  Deviled, 35

Egg(s) *(cont.)*
  Drop Soup, 125
  Hard-Boiled, 607
  Salad, 429
  Stuffed, Curried, 36
  Stuffed, with Smoked Salmon, 36
Enchilada Sauce, Fat-Free, 586
Enchiladas, 186, 272–74
Ethiopian Vegetables, 372
Exercise, benefits from, 5
Exotic Mushroom Sauté, 343

Fajitas
  Chicken, 199
  Vegetable, 295
Far Eastern Ginger Noodles, 382
Fast and Fresh Cranberry
    Relish, 598
Fat-Free Crispy Pita Chips, 24
Fat-Free Enchilada Sauce, 586
Fat-Free Tomato Sauce, 584
Fats, dietary
  in chicken, 155
  in food products, 5
  in stuffing recipes, 176
  types of, 3–4
Fennel, Salad with Orange and, 64
Feta
  Aegean Pizza, 442
  and Bulgur Salad, 96
  Greek Stewed Potatoes and
      Tomatoes with, 352
  Kale with Red Onion and, 341
  Mashed Potatoes with Cheese, 354
  Pasta with Vegetables and, 288
  Stuffed Eggplant, Bulgur and, 267
  and Tomato Crostini or
      Bruschetta, 43
Fiber, in healthy diet, 3
Finger Foods, 34–42
  Listing of recipes, 20
Fish. *See Also* Salmon; Shellfish; Tuna
  Cooking times for, 221
  Baked, 222–33
    in Almost Sour Cream, 224
    Catfish, Cajun, 223
    Catfish, Pecan, 223
    in Creole Sauce, 230

    en Papillote, 232
    Ginger and Lime, 226
    Golden, 229
    with Golden Raisin Sauce, 228
    Lime-Thyme, 226
    with Mint, 227
    with Mustard and Apples, 228
    Mustard and Honey, 225
    Onion and Tomato, Spicy, 230
    Orange-Herb, 227
    in a Packet, Ginger, 232
    with Pesto, 224
    Spanish, 229
    Steak Burritos, 421
    Steaks, Chili-Seasoned, 225
    Sticks, 222
    Sticks, Parmesan, 222
    Trout, Whole, in Foil, 234
    Trout, Whole, with Cornbread
        Stuffing, 233
  Burgers, 435
  Chowder, Manhattan-Style, 142
  Grilled or Broiled, 234–41
    Citrus-Marinated, 236
    with Currant-Caper Relish, 240
    Fresh Herb-Marinated, 235
    Garlic-Broiled, 236
    Maple Teriyaki, 238
    with Piri Piri Sauce, 239
    Steak in Raspberry
        Marinade, 237
    Steak with Tomato Caper
        Sauce, 238
    Swordfish and Pineapple
        Skewers, 240
  Poached, 241–44
    Chinese Steamed, 244
    Dill-, 242
    with Herbs, 242
    in Wine and Lemon Juice, 241
  Salad, Ocean and Grape, 107
  Sauces, 598–99
    Creole, for Seafood, 231
  Smoked, Spreads, 33
  Soup
    Chowder, Manhattan-Style, 142
    and Rice, Italian, 143
    and Vegetable, 142

    Stovetop Cooked, 244–49
      in Curried Coconut Sauce, 245
      Fillets, Pan-Cooked, 244
      in a Pot, 247
      Seafood Gumbo, 248
      Steak and Asparagus Stir-Fry, 249
      Stew, Moroccan, 246
      Swordfish and Broccoli
          Risotto, 261
      and Vegetables, Sweet and
          Sour, 249
Five-Spice Orange Slices, 509
Five-Spice Turkey Cutlets, 210
Flan, 568
Focaccia, 502–4
  Listing of recipes, 472
Fragrant Chicken, 192
French Bread, 501
French Dressing, 58
French Toast, 458–61
  Listing of recipes, 446
Frittatas, 462–64
  Listing of recipes, 447
  Mini-Frittatas, 45–46
Frontier Pie with Cornbread
    Topping, 184
Frostings and Glazes
  Listing of recipes, 506
Frozen Desserts, 571–76
  Listing of recipes, 507
Frozen Yogurt. *See* Yogurt
Fruit. *See Also specific fruits*
  Dessert Plates, 513
  Desserts, listing of recipes, 505
  Kebabs, 513–14
  Salad Dressing, Strawberry-
      Yogurt, 514
  Salad in a Jar, 512
  Salad with Yogurt and Mint
      Sauce, 512
  Smoothie, Dairy-Free, 470
  Smoothie, Yogurt and, 470
  Tropical Gazpacho, 116
  Tropical Salsa, 592
Fruit, Dried. *See Also* Apricot(s);
    Cranberry; Raisin(s)
  Chili Pumpkin Chicken, 190
  Chutney, Cranberry and, 596

Compote, Ginger and, 468
Currant Pilaf, 390
Currant Scones, 484
Date and Apple Cookies, 550
Granola, 450
Granola, Fruity, 451
Not Your Traditional
    Tzimmes, 358
Sunburst Salad, 97

Garbanzo Beans. See Chickpea(s)
Garlic. See Also Garlic Oil
    Peeling, 12–13
    Bread, American, 415
    and Broccoli Pizza, 442
    -Broiled Fish, 236
    Chicken, 178
    Garlicky Zucchini and
        Corn, 365
    Gremolata, 591
    and Herb Focaccia, 503
    Lovers' Potatoes, 349
    Mushrooms, Pan-Fried, 344
    Roasted, 603
        and Greens, 339
        Mashed Potatoes with, 353
        Vegetable Soup, 126
    and Shallot Vinegar, 609
    Toast, 415
Garlic Oil, 607
    Pasta, 378
    Pasta with Broccoli, 378
    Pita Chips, 25
Gazpacho, 115–16
Ginger, Crystallized, 604
Ginger, peeling and grating, 13
Ginger Beer, 610
Ginger Cheesecake, 543
Ginger Muffins, Crystallized, 477
Ginger Noodles, Far Eastern, 382
Ginger Relish, Onion and, 597
Gingerbread, 558
Gingerbread Pancakes, 456
Gingerbread Waffles, 457
Gingered Marmalade Chicken, 167
Gingersnaps, 554
Glazes. See Frostings and Glazes
Glossary of cooking terms, 8–9

Goat Cheese
    Mashed Potatoes with, 354
    Pizza, 443
    Salad, Greens, Spiced Nuts, and
        Warm, 62
    Tostadas with Salsa and, 38
Graham Cracker Pie Crust, 522
Grains, 396–98. See Also
        specific grains
Grains, Portobellos and, 396
Grand Marnier Sauce, Orange, 577
Granolas, 450–51
Grapefruit
    Broiled, Honey and Ginger, 468
    Broiled, Sugar and Rum, 469
Gratins
    Cannellini and Corkscrew, 405
    Chickpea, 406
    Potato and Vegetable, 350
    Winter Squash, 362
Gravy, Mushroom, 600
Greek
    Chicken Casserole, 182
    Cucumber Yogurt Salad, 69
    Oregano Vinaigrette, 57
    Pita Pocket Sandwiches, 426
    Salad, 65
    Stewed Potatoes and Tomatoes, 352
        with Feta Cheese, 352
    -Style Burgers, 433
    Tomato Salad, 71
Green Bean(s), 333–37
    and Almonds, 334
    Asian, 335
    and Bacon, 334
    Cooked with Salsa, 334
    Creole, 336
    Great, 336
    Gremolata, 334
    Salad, Blissful Tuna, 106
    Salad, Many-Bean, 99
    Salad, Mustard, Dill, and, 74
    Steamed, 333
    Stewed, and Potatoes, 337
Green(s), 337–42. See Also Spinach
    Preparing and cooking, 337–38
    Beet, Steamed, with Sesame Oil, 339
    Bok Choy, Stir-Fried, 340

Curried Sweet Potatoes and, 304
Dumpling Rolls, Chinese, 297
Dumpling Rolls, Ginger, 296
Housewarming Soup, 139
and Pasta, 287
and Raisins Crostini or
    Bruschetta, 44
Roasted Garlic and, 339
Salads, 61–67
    listing of recipes, 52
Gremolata, 591
Gremolata, Turkey Cutlets with, 208
Gremolata Green Beans, 334
Grilling tips, 159
Guacamoles, 28
Gumbo, Seafood, 248
Gumbo, Smoked Turkey, 198
Gumbo, Vegetable, 300

Harvard Beets, 318
Hawaiian Pizza, 441
Herb(ed)(s). See Also specific herbs
    Broiled Mushrooms, 342
    Dressing, Creamy, 59
    Focaccia, Garlic and, 503
    Fresh, Marinated Chicken, 160
    Fresh, -Marinated Fish, 235
    Poached Fish with, 242
    Ravioli, Ricotta with, 283
    Rice Salad, 92
    Roasted Chicken, 177
    Spaghetti with Fresh, 379
    Tomato Salad, Summer, 70
    Vinegar, 608
Hermits, 558
Hoisin (Sauce), 13
    Chicken, Baked, 168
    Chicken and Broccoli Stir-Fry, 202
    Chicken Lo Mein, 207
    Dipping Sauce, 602
    Kebabs, Honey-, 164
    Moo Shu Beef, 206
    Tofu Stir-Fry, 298
Honey Banana Muffins, 475
Honey Fudge Frosting, 545
Honey of a Lemonade, 610
Honey Vanilla Frozen Ice Cream, 575
Honeyed Pineapple, 514

Honey-Mustard
  Chicken Nuggets, 156
  Glaze, Baby Carrots with a, 325
  Sauce, 601
Honey-Poppy Seed Vinaigrette, 56
Hopping John, 406
Hors D'Oeuvres. *See* Small Bites
  and Finger Foods
Horseradish
  Chicken, Crusty, 158
  Cocktail Sauce, 49
  Dressing, Coleslaw with, 79
  Smoked Fish Spread with, 33
Hot Dogs, Barbequed, 198
Hot! Sauce, 601
Housewarming Soup, 139
Hummus with Tahini, 30
Hydrogenated fats, 3–4

Ice Cream
  Honey Vanilla Frozen, 575
  Marshmallow Sauce for, 577
  Pie, 576
Icings. *See* Frostings and Glazes
Indian-Style Coconut Soup, 125
Indonesian Rice Salad, 92
Indonesian Sauce, Chicken in, 200
Ingredients, in recipes, 11–16
Ingredients, measuring, 531
Irish Soda Bread, 490
Island Barbeque Sauce, 588
Italian Fish and Rice Soup, 143
Italian Meringue, 530
Italian Sweet and Sour Carrots, 326
Italian Vegetable Noodle
    Soup, 128

Jalapeño(s)
  Caribbean Corn Soup, 150
  -Cheese Mini-Muffins, 39
  Guacamole Caliente, 28
  Pineapple Salsa, 593
  Southwestern Vegetable Sauté, 370
Jam, Baked Tomato, 370
Jam Squares, 560
Jam-Filled Muffins, 479
Japanese Noodle Salad, 89
Jicama Spears, 34

Kale with Red Onion, 341
Kale with Red Onion and
    Feta, 341
Kasha, Basic, 396
Kasha and Mushrooms, 397
Kebabs. *See Also* Skewers
  Cooking tips, 162
  Chicken, 162–66
  Fruit, 513–14
Kitchen appliances, 18, 494–95
Kitchen design, 16–17
Kitchen equipment, 17–19
Kitchen pantry
  Staples, homemade, 603–9
    Listing of recipes, 582
  Stocking the, 11–16
Kneading techniques, 494–95
Knives, 17
Kosher salt, 13, 508
Kugel, Noodle, 383
Kugel, Spinach Noodle, 383
Kung Pao Chicken, 202

Lamb
  Greek-Style Burgers, 433
  Moussaka, 183
  Stew, 196
Lasagna
  Baking tips, 277
  Bean and Tortilla, 275
  Broccoli and Carrot, 280
  Mushroom, 281
  No-Pasta Vegetable, 278
  Roasted Vegetable Tortilla, 278
  Spinach, 279
  Swiss Chard, 280
  Turkey, 187
Latin Turkey Skewers, 47
Layered Black Bean Dip, 32
Layered Tortilla Casserole, 276
Leek and Corn Soup, 124
Leek Soup, Potato, 123
Lemonade, Honey of a, 610
Lemon(s)
  Bread Pudding, 570
  Chicken Kebabs, Persian, 165
  Chicken Soup, 145
  Curd, 565

Curd-Filled Meringue Torte, 529
  -Ginger Fish, 237
  Gremolata, 591
  Icing Glaze, 544
  Juice, fresh, 13–14
  Meringue Pie, 528
  Oat Drop Scones, 485
  Poppy Bundt Cake, 536
  Roasted Chicken, 177
  -Rosemary Chicken, 170
  Sorbet, 572
  -Thyme Chicken Rolls, 174
  Turkish-Style Yogurt Chicken, 162
  Zest, 604
Lemony Squash and Carrots, 363
Lentil(s)
  Brown Rice and, 401
  Carrots and, 400
  Dal Nepal, 402
  Pilaf, Basmati and, 389
  Red, Salad, 102
  Soup, 133
    Ginger, 134
    Rice and, with Sausage, 135
    Spinach and, 134
  Spinach with, 401
  Stewed, 400
Lettuce. *See* Green(s)
Lime Fish, Ginger and, 226
Lime Juice, fresh, 13–14
Limeade, 609
Lime-Thyme Fish, 226
Linguine
  with Clam and Tomato Sauce, 254
  Scallops, 255
  as udon noodle substitute, 16
  Walnut, 287
Lowfat baking, 530–31
Lowfat food products, 5

Macaroni. *See* Pasta
Mandarin Soup, 147
Mangos. *See* Melon(s)
Manhattan-Style Fish Chowder, 142
Manicotti, Spinach, 282
Maple Bananas, 580
Maple Cream Cheese-Filled
    Muffins, 480

Maple Pumpkin Mash, Spiced, 363
Maple Syrup, 14, 461
Maple-Mustard Glazed
   Chicken, 160
Maple-Stuffed French Toast, 461
Marbled Brownies, 557
Marmalade Chicken, 172
Marmalade Chicken, Gingered, 167
Marshmallow Fluff, 546
Marshmallow Sauce for Ice
   Cream, 577
Marshmallows, Sweet Potatoes
   and, 357
Matzo Ball Soup, 148
Measurement equivalents, 8
Measuring ingredients, 531
Meat. *See* Beef; Lamb; Sausage(s)
Meatball(s)
  Porcupine, 215
  Seasoned, 216
  Subs, Bayshore, 428
  Tiny, and Spaghetti in Creamy
    Tomato Sauce, 217
  Turkey, 216
  Turkey, and Penne Casserole, 217
Meatloaf
  Mexican, 214
  Muffin Tin, 212
  Spinach-Stuffed, 212
  Turkey, 213
Mediterranean Baked Beans, 405
Melon(s), 510
  Ball Compote, 510
  -Berry Swirl, 114
  Compote, Strawberry and, 511
  Honeydew, Mango, and Ginger
    Compote, 511
  Mango Salad, Mixed Greens
    and, 62
  Mango-Pineapple Sauce, 580
  Watermelon Mint Spritzer, 610
  Watermelon Sorbet, 573
  Watermelon Soup, 114
Menu planning, 9–10
  For cocktail parties, 22
  Suggested menus, 10–11
Meringue, Italian, 530
Meringue For Pie, 529

Meringue Pies, 528
Meringue Shell, 523
Meringue Tortes, 529
Mexican
  Corn and Chicken Casserole, 181
  Meatloaf, 214
  Mole Chili, 197
  Mole Vegetarian Chili, 303
  Zucchini Casserole, 366
Microwave(d)
  Baked Apple for One, 516
  Baked Potato, 348
  Corn on the Cob, 331
  Hot Cocoa, 611
  Polenta, 408
Milk Shake, Strawberry, 575
Millet Stuffed Squash, 268
Mincing, defined, 9
Minestrone, 126
Mini-Frittatas, 45–46
Mint, Fish Baked with, 227
Mint, Sugar Snap Peas with, 347
Mint and Basil Pesto, 590
Mint and Carrot Salad, 80
Mint Spritzer, Watermelon, 610
Mint Vinaigrette, Snap Peas in, 74
Minted Tomato Sauce, Freshly, 584
Minty Beet Salad, 76
Mirin, about, 14
Molasses Corn Bread, 486
Moo Shu Beef, 206
Moroccan Fish Stew, 246
Moroccan Vegetables, 301
Moussaka, 182
Moussaka, Lamb, 183
Mousselike Cheesecake, 542
Muffin Tin Meatloaves, 212
Muffins, 473–82
  Baking tips, 473
  Listing of recipes, 471
Mushroom(s), 342–45
  Barley with, 397
  Beef and, Burgers, 432
  Caps, Bacon-Stuffed, 41
  Caps, Stuffed, 42
  Gravy, 600
  Herbed Broiled, 342
  Kasha and, 397

Lasagna, 281
Mini-Frittatas, Ricotta-, 45
Pan-Fried Garlic, 344
Pearl Onions, Peas, and, 345
Portobello, Grilled, 343
Portobellos and Grains, 396
Risotto, 307
Sauté, Exotic, 343
Shiitake, Spinach, and Turkey
  Stir-Fry, 204
Shiitake Brown Rice, 392
Soup, Barley, 130
Stuffing, Sausage and, 412
Thyme, 344
and Tomato Sauce over Pasta, 290
Wild Wild Rice, 394
Mussels, 260–63
  Preparing for cooking, 262
  and Clams Risotto, 260
  in Shallot Sauce, 262
  Spanish, 263
  in Spicy Tomato Broth, 263
Mustard Dipping Sauce, Hot, 602
Mustard Dressing, Two-, 60
Mustard Sauce, Honey-, 601
Mustard Vinaigrette, 56

No-Bones Chicken Soup, 144
Nonfat food products, 5
Noodle(s). *See Also* Pasta
  Types of, 15–16
  Beef and, 193
  Buttered Egg, 377
  Casserole, Tuna, 231
  Chicken and, 193
  Ginger, Far Eastern, 382
  Kugel, 383
  Kugel, Spinach, 383
  Peanut Butter, 294
  Peking Scallops and, 257
  Salad
    Asian Beef and, 91
    Chinese Chicken and, 91
    Japanese, 89
    Sesame Soba, 90
  Soup
    Chicken, 151
    Chinese Chicken, 146

Noodle(s) *(cont.)*
   Italian Vegetable, 128
   Spanish Chicken, 145
North African Carrot Salad, 81
North African Vegetable Soup, 127
Nutrition, diet and, 3–5
Nutritional analyses, 6
Nut(s). *See Also* Almond(s);
    Peanut(s); Walnut(s)
   Nutritional value of, 4
   Chocolate Chip Biscotti, 548
   Nutty Honey Chicken, 157
   Pecan
    Baked Chicken, 157
    Catfish, 223
    Pancakes, Buttermilk, 453
   Pine Nut and
    Chickpea Spread, 31
    Rice Stuffed Eggplant, 266
   Snack Mix, 23
   Spiced, 22
   Spiced, Sweet Curried, 23
   Toasted, 605

Oatmeal, Cinnamon-Raisin, 449
Oatmeal, Rich Old-Fashioned, 449
Oatmeal, Simply, 449
Oatmeal Bread, 499
Oatmeal Drop Cookies, 550
Oatmeal Pancakes, 454
Oat(s)
   Bars, Apricot and, 559
   Drop Scones, Lemon, 485
   Fruity Granola, 451
   Granola, 450
Ocean and Grape Salad, 107
Oil, Asian sesame, about, 11
Oil, Garlic. *See* Garlic Oil
Oil, olive, about, 4
Oil, Rosemary Orange, 608
Old-Fashioned Beef Stew, 195
Olive(s)
   Calamata, about, 12
   oil, about, 4
   and Romano Focaccia, 503
   Spaghetti alla Puttanesca, 291
   Spanish Fish, 229
   Tomato Olivada Crostini or
    Bruschetta, 44

100% Whole Wheat Muffins, 473
Onion(s)
   Balsamic, Mashed Potatoes and, 355
   Caramelized, 597
   and Ginger Relish, 597
   and Herb Potatoes, 349
   Pearl, Mushrooms, and Peas, 345
   Red, and Rosemary Focaccia, 503
   Red, Kale with, 341
   Red, Kale with, and Feta, 341
   Relish, 597
Orange(s)
   Angel Food Cake, 541
   Barbeque Chicken, 171
   Biscotti, 549
   Cranberry Bread, 489
   Dairy-Free Fruit Smoothie, 470
   Grand, 509
   Grand Marnier Sauce, 577
   -Herb Fish, 227
   Icing Glaze, 544
   Mango Smoothie, 470
   Nut Pancakes, 455
   Nut Waffles, 457
   Oil, Rosemary, 608
   Pesto, 590
   Rice, 387
   Salad, Beet and, 77
   Salad, Oriental Spinach and, 64
   Salad with Fennel and, 64
   Salsa, Pineapple and, 593
   Scones, 483
   -Sesame Vinaigrette, 57
   Slices, Five-Spice, 509
   Vinaigrette, Chili-, 57
   Zest, 604
Oriental
   Chicken in Parchment, 175
   Orange and Spinach Salad, 64
   Sugar Snap Peas, 346
Orzo, 380–82
Oven temperature, 8, 166, 277, 547
Oyster Sauce, 14
   Stir-Fried Broccoli with, 321

Paella, Vegetable, 395
Pancakes, 452–56
   Cooking tips, 452
   Listing of recipes, 446

Pan-Cooked Fish Fillets, 244
Pans, 18
Pantry. *See* Kitchen pantry
Papaya Baked Chicken Breasts, 169
Parmesan
   Asparagus, Roasted, 317
   Fish Sticks, 222
   Oven-Roasted Broccoli with, 322
   Parsley Risotto, 305
   Summer Squash Packets, 367
   Toast, 414
Parsley
   Storing, 14
   Bulgur and Feta Salad, 96
   Gremolata, 591
   Orzo with Lemon and, 381
   Risotto, Parmesan, 305
Parsnips
   Cider-Cooked Vegetables, 371
   Fall Vegetable Medley, 371
   and Pineapple, 359
   Root Vegetable Soup, 123
   Rooted Carrots, 327
Pasta, 377–83. *See Also* Lasagna;
    Linguine; Noodle(s); Orzo;
    Ravioli; Spaghetti
   Cooking times, 86, 377
   Angel Hair, Lemon Garlic, 379
   Broccoli and Garlic, for One, 286
   Casserole, Baked, 269
   Corkscrew and Cannellini
    Gratin, 405
   Four Peppers and Salmon over, 254
   Garlic Oil, 378
   Garlic Oil, with Broccoli, 378
   Greens and, 287
   Hoisin Chicken Lo Mein, 207
   Hot Pepper, 380
   Macaroni and Cheese, 270
   Macaroni and Vegetable Salad, 86
   Manicotti, Spinach, 282
   Mushroom and Tomato Sauce
    over, 290
   Pasta e Fagioli, 141
   Penne
    with Mushroom, Beans, and
     Tomato Sauce, 292
    and Turkey Meatball
     Casserole, 217

with Vegetables and Ricotta
   Sauce, 293
Salads, 86–91
  Listing of recipes, 53
Scallops, Broccoli, and, 256
Shells with Broccoli and
   Chickpeas, 290
Spinach and Friends, 289
with Sun-Dried Tomato Pesto, 289
Tiny, with Almonds, 380
Tortellini Skewers, 47
Tortellini Soup, Busy Day, 128
Tortellini with Pesto and
   Sun-Dried Tomato Salad, 88
with Vegetables and Feta, 288
Vermicelli and Rice Pilaf, 378
Vermicelli Soup, Quick, 129
Pastry crust. *See* Pie Crust
Peach(es)
  Baked, with Ginger, 515
  Bread Pudding, 569
  Chutney, 595
  Cobbler, Blueberry-, 563
  Pie, 525
  Salsa, 593
  Sorbet, 574
Peachy Applesauce, 467
Peanut Butter, 14
Peanut Butter Noodles, 294
Peanut(s)
  African Spinach and, 339
  Broccoli and, 320
  -Pumpkin-Apple Soup, 122
  Sauce, African, 299
Pearl Barley. *See* Barley
Pear(s)
  Baked, Glazed, 517
  as Blintzes, 518
  Cobbler, Blackberry-, 562
  Cornbread Pudding, 414
  Poached, in Raspberry Sauce, 519
  with Red Currant Jelly Sauce, 520
  and Spice Coffee Cake, 538
Pea(s), 345–47
  Buttered, 345
  Carrots and, 346
  Couscous with Dill and, 384
  Curried Cauliflower and, 329
  Orzo with Mint and, 382

Pearl Onions, Mushrooms, and, 345
Pilaf, Curried, 394
Rice with Mint and, 388
Snow
  Shrimp and, 250
  and Shrimp Salad, 106
  Stir-Fried Beef and, 205
  and Water Chestnuts, 346
Soup, Two-, 138
Sugar Snap
  with Mint, 347
  in Mint Vinaigrette, 74
  Oriental, 346
Pecan Baked Chicken, 157
Pecan Catfish, 223
Pecan Pancakes, Buttermilk, 453
Peking Noodles and Scallops, 257
Penne. *See* Pasta
Pepper, Hot, Pasta, 380
Pepper(s), Bell
  Four, and Salmon over Pasta, 254
  Red, Roasted
   Broccoli and, 319
   and Chickpea Salad, 101
   Crostini or Bruschetta, 45
   Dip, 27
   Mini-Frittatas, Broccoli-, 46
  Red, Sauce, 586
  Red, Sautéed Garlic Asparagus
   with, 316
  Roasted, 603
  Stuffed, 214
Persian Lemon Chicken Kebabs, 165
Pesto Pasta Salad, 87
Pesto Potato Salad, 84
Pestos, 589–91
Pickled Beets, 76
Pie, Spaghetti, 294
Pie Crusts, 521–23
Pies (Dessert), 521–30
  Listing of recipes, 505
  Ice Cream, 576
Pilaf. *See* Rice
Pine Nut (Pignoli)
  Spread, Chickpea and, 31
  Stuffed Eggplant, Rice and, 266
Pineapple
  Barbeque Chicken, 170
  Chutney, 595

Fast and Fresh Cranberry
   Relish, 598
Hawaiian Pizza, 441
Honeyed, 514
-Mango Sauce, 580
Parsnips and, 359
Popsicles, 571
Salsa, 593
Salsa, Orange and, 593
Sherbert, 574
Skewers, Swordfish and, 240
Topping, Caribbean, 579
Upside-Down Bake, 536
Pinwheels, 37–38
Pita
  Chips, Fat-Free Crispy, 24
  Chips, Garlic Oil, 25
  Pocket Sandwiches, Greek, 426
  Pockets, Crispy Tofu, 425
  Salad, 98
Pizza, 436–45. *See Also* Focaccia
  Baking tips, 436
  Listing of recipes, 417
Polenta
  Basic, 407
  Breakfast, 450
  Cheese, and Vegetable Tart, 40
  Double-Corn, 408
  Microwave, 408
  Squares with Pepper Relish and
   Goat Cheese, 40
  Topped, 426
  Vegetable, 408
Pommery Potato Salad, 85
Popovers, 491–92
Popsicles, 571–72
Porcupine Meatballs, 215
Portobello Mushrooms, Grilled, 343
Portobellos and Grains, 396
Potato(es), 347–55. *See Also*
   Sweet Potatoes
  Types of, 348–49
  Baked
   Microwaved, 348
   Perfect, 348
   Sour Cream and Chives
    for a, 348
  Breakfast, 466
  Confetti, 351

Potato(es) *(cont.)*
Cups Filled with Sour Cream and
Caviar, 39
Garlic Lovers', 349
Gratin, Vegetable and, 350
Mashed, 353
and Balsamic Onions, 355
with Cheese, 354
Curried, 354
with Roasted Garlic, 353
Rutabagas and Spuds, 360
Timbales, 355
New, Dilled, 351
Onion and Herb, 349
Salads, 82–86
Listing of recipes, 53
Savory, 351
Scalloped, Mushroom and
Cheese, 350
Shredded Hash Browns, 466
Soup, Leek, 123
Stewed, and Tomatoes, Greek, 352
Stewed Green Beans and, 337
Stuffed
Cheddar, 418
Chicken and Pesto, 419
Ricotta and Broccoli, 418
Salsa and Beans, 419
Pots, 18
Poultry. *See* Chicken; Turkey
Press-in Pie Crust, 522
Protein, in healthy diet, 4–5
Prunes, Stewed Apricots and, 468
Pudding, 564–70
Listing of recipes, 507
Pear Cornbread, 414
Pumpkin
Black Beans and, 404
Bread, 490
Chicken, Chili, 190
Custards, 566
Mash, Spiced Maple, 363
Pancakes, 455
Pie, 526
Ravioli, 284
Soup, Brazilian Black Bean and, 136
Soup, Gingery, 122
Soup, Peanut-Apple-, 122

Puréed Soups, 119–25
Listing of recipes, 108
Purple Pops, 571

Quesadillas, 423–24
Listing of recipes, 416
Quick Breads. *See* Bread, Quick
Quinoa, 14–15
Pilaf, 398
Salad, Toasted, 95
Stuffed Squash, 268
Vegetable Soup, 131

Raisin(s)
Bran Cereal Muffins, 478
Carrots and, 327
Golden, Sauce, Fish Baked
with, 228
Golden, Spinach with Almonds
and, 338
and Greens Crostini or
Bruschetta, 44
More Than Apple Pie, 524
Waldorf Salad, 77
and Walnuts Pilaf, 389
Raita, Cucumber, 69
Raspberry
Chicken and Greens Salad, 66
Marinade, Fish Steak in, 237
Sauce, Poached Pears in, 519
Vinegar, 608
Ratatouille, Oven-Baked, 271
Ravioli
Filling and cooking, 282–83
Cheese, 283
Herb, Ricotta with, 283
Pumpkin, 284
Spinach and Mushroom, 284
Recipes
Menu planning with, 9–10
Nutritional analyses of, 6
Tips for following, 6–7
Red and Purple Salad, 72
Red Currant and Blackberry
Chicken, 167
Red Currant Jelly Sauce, Pears
with, 520
Red Rice, 393

Red Rice and Beans, 393
Red Rubbing Spices, Chicken
Roasted with, 180
Red Salsa, 592
Red-Cooked Turkey Skewers, 48
Reduced fat food products, 5
Relishes, 597–98
Rhubarb Bundt Cake, 537
Rhubarb Chutney, 596
Rhubarb Pie, Strawberry, 525
Rice, 386–95. *See Also* Risotto;
Wild Rice
Types of, 386
Black Beans and, 403
Brown, 386
Brown, and Lentils, 401
Brown, Shiitake, 392
Chicken and, 190
Curried, 388
Dirty, 391
Fried, Corn, 333
Fried, Curried, 390
Fried, Shrimp, 259
Fried, Vegetable, 391
Hopping John, 406
Lemon, 387
Orange, 387
with Peas and Mint, 388
Pilaf
Basmati and Lentil, 389
Currant, 390
Curried Pea, 394
Raisins and Walnuts, 389
Vermicelli and, 378
and Pine Nut Stuffed Eggplant, 266
Pudding, 566
Pudding, Banana, 567
Red, 393
Red, and Beans, 393
Saffron, 387
Salad
Curried Chicken, Fruit, and, 94
Herbed, 92
Indonesian, 92
Spanish, 95
Yellow, Black Bean and, 100
Soup, Italian Fish and, 143
Soup, Vegetable, 129

Soup with Sausage, Lentil and, 135
South of the Border, 392
Vegetable Paella, 395
Vinegar, 15
White, 386
Wild Wild, 394
Ricotta
  with Herb Ravioli, 283
  -Mushroom Mini-Frittatas, 45
  Pizza, Spinach and, 440
  Sauce, Penne with Vegetables
    and, 293
  Stuffed Potatoes, Broccoli and, 418
Risotto
  Cooking tips, 304
  Asparagus, 306
  Mushroom, 307
  Mussels and Clams, 260
  Parmesan Parsley, 305
  Spinach, 306
  Swordfish and Broccoli, 261
Romano and Olive Focaccia, 503
Root Vegetable Soup, 123
Root vegetables, 359–60
Rosemary and Red Onion
    Focaccia, 503
Rosemary Orange Oil, 608
Rubber bands, 19
Rum and Sugar Broiled
    Grapefruit, 469
Rutabagas. See also Turnips
  Fall Vegetable Medley, 371
  Mashed, and Spuds, 360
  Root Vegetable Soup, 123
  Rooted Carrots, 327
  Sugar-Glazed, 359

Saffron
  Black Bean and Yellow Rice
    Salad, 100
  Golden Fish, 229
  Italian Fish and Rice Soup, 143
  Rice, 387
  Vegetable Paella, 395
Sage Tomatoes, 368
Salad Bar Pesto Soup, 127
Salad Dressings, 55–60
  Listing of recipes, 52

Salads, listing of recipes, 52–54
Salmon
  Burgers, 434
  Lemon-Ginger Fish, 237
  over Pasta, Four Peppers and, 254
  Poached, Chilled, 243
  Poached, Chilled Whole, 243
  Salad, 107
  and Scallop Packets, 233
  Smoked Salmon
    Canapés, 34
    Cream Cheese Spread, 448
    Stuffed Eggs with, 36
    -Wrapped Asparagus, 34
  Teriyaki, 238
Salsa
  Green Beans Cooked with, 334
  Stuffed Potatoes, Beans and, 419
  Tostadas with Goat Cheese and, 38
  Whole Wheat Tostadas, 38
Salsas, 592–94
Salt, 4, 13, 508
Sandwich fillings, 429–31
  Listing of recipes, 417
Sandwiches, 425–29
  Listing of recipes, 416
Saturated fats, 3–4
Sauce(s)
  Listing of recipes, 581
  Barbeque, 587–89
  Creole, for Seafood, 231
  Dessert, 576–80
  Dipping, 602
  Fish, 598–99
  Green Chili, 600
  Hoisin, about, 13
  Honey-Mustard, 601
  Horseradish Cocktail, 49
  Hot!, 601
  Mushroom Gravy, 600
  Oyster, about, 14
  Soy, about, 15
  Tomato, 583–86
Sausage(s)
  and Cheese Egg Casserole, 464
  Lentil and Rice Soup with, 135
  and Mushroom Pizza, 440
  and Mushroom Stuffing, 412

Smoked Turkey Gumbo, 198
Surprise Muffins, 481
Sautéing, defined, 9
Scallions, 15
Scallop(s)
  Broccoli, Pasta, and, 256
  Linguine, 255
  Packets, Salmon and, 233
  Peking Noodles and, 257
  Skewers, Grilled, 241
  and Sun-Dried Tomatoes,
    Spaghetti with, 256
  Won Tons, 51
Scones, 482–85
  Currant, 484
  Lemon Oat Drop, 485
  Orange, 483
Seafood, Creole Sauce for, 231
Seafood Gumbo, 248
Serving sizes, 5–6, 436
Sesame
  Buttermilk Chicken, 171
  Carrot Slaw, 81
  Paste. See Tahini
  Soba Salad, 90
  Vinaigrette, Orange-, 57
Seven-Minute Almond Frosting, 545
Seven-Minute Frosting, 544
Shallot Sauce, Mussels in, 262
Shallot Vinegar, Garlic and, 609
Shallots, Cider-Roasted Squash
    and, 362
Shellfish. See Also Clam(s); Mussels;
    Scallop(s); Shrimp
  Cioppino, 246
  Seafood Gumbo, 248
Shells and Tuna Salad, 88
Shells with Broccoli and
    Chickpeas, 290
Sherbert, Pineapple, 574
Sherry wine, 14
Shiitake, Spinach, and Turkey
    Stir-Fry, 204
Shiitake Brown Rice, 392
Shredded Hash Browns, 466
Shrimp
  Barbequed, 49
  and Broccoli, 250

Shrimp (cont.)
 in Creole Sauce, 252
 Dinner, Deep South Boiled, 251
 Fried Rice, 259
 Salad, Snow Pea and, 106
 and Snow Peas, 250
 Steamed Marinated, 48
 and Vegetable Lo Mein, 258
Simmering, defined, 9
Skewers. See Also Kebabs
 Grilled Scallop, 241
 Latin Turkey, 47
 Red-Cooked Turkey, 48
 Swordfish and Pineapple, 240
 Tortellini, 47
Skillet Drop Bread, 493
Slaws and Coleslaws, 78–82
 Listing of recipes, 53
Sloppy Joes, 428
Sloppy Joes, Quick Confetti, 429
Small Bites and Finger Foods
 Listing of recipes, 20–21
Snack Mix, 23
Snap Peas. See Pea(s)
Snow Peas. See Pea(s)
Soba noodles, 15
Soba Salad, Sesame, 90
Sorbets, 572–74
Soups, listing of recipes, 108–9
Sour Cherry Nut Bars, 560
Sour Cream
 Almost, 606
 Almost, Fish Baked in, 224
 Almost, Tuna Salad with, 430
 and Chives for a Baked
  Potato, 348
 Lime Sauce for Fish, 599
South of the Border Rice, 392
Southern Chicken Stew, 194
Southwest Chicken Pizza, 441
Southwest Torta, 274
Southwestern Black Beans, 403
Southwestern Corn Salad, 75
Southwestern Vegetable Sauté, 370
Soy Roasted Chicken, Sweet, 179
Soy sauce, about, 15
Soybean curd. See Tofu
Soy-Dressed Asparagus, 73

Spaghetti
 alla Puttanesca, 291
 Asparagus and, 285
 Chinese Broccoli and Pasta Salad, 90
 with Clam Sauce, 252
 with Eggplant and Tomato
  Sauce, 292
 with Fresh Clam Sauce, 252
 with Fresh Herbs, 379
 Pie, 294
 with Scallops and Sun-Dried
  Tomatoes, 256
 and Tiny Meatballs in Creamy
  Tomato Sauce, 217
Spanish Chicken Noodle Soup, 145
Spanish Fish, 229
Spanish Mussels, 263
Spanish Rice Salad, 95
Spinach
 Bake, 342
 Dip, 26
 and Friends, 289
 with Golden Raisins and
  Almonds, 338
 Lasagna, 279
 with Lemon and Garlic, 338
 and Lentil Soup, 134
 with Lentils, 401
 Manicotti, 282
 and Mushroom Ravioli, 284
 and Mushroom Won Tons, 51
 Noodle Kugel, 383
 and Orzo, 381
 and Peanuts, African, 339
 Pizza, Ricotta and, 440
 Risotto, 306
 Salad
  Oriental Orange and, 64
  Strawberry-, 63
  Strawberry-, with Almonds, 63
 -Stuffed Meatloaf, 212
Split Peas. See Beans, Dried
Spreads. See Dips and Spreads;
  Sandwich fillings
Spreads, Bread, 448
Springtime Pasta Salad, 87
Squash, Summer. See Summer
  Squash; Zucchini

Squash, Winter. See Pumpkin;
  Winter Squash
Steaming, defined, 9
Stews
 Apple Cider Chicken, 188
 Lamb, 196
 Moroccan Fish, 246
 Old-Fashioned Beef, 195
 Southern Chicken, 194
 Vegetarian, 298–304
  Listing of recipes, 265
 White Bean, 404
Stir-Fries
 Cooking tips, 202
 Beef and Snow Peas, 205
 Beef with Broccoli, 204
 Bok Choy, 340
 Broccoli with Oyster Sauce, 321
 Fish Steak and Asparagus, 249
 Garlic Broccoli, 321
 Hoisin Chicken and Broccoli, 202
 Hoisin Chicken Lo Mein, 207
 Hoisin Tofu, 298
 Honey Teriyaki Chicken, 203
 Kung Pao Chicken, 202
 Moo Shu Beef, 206
 Shrimp and Broccoli, 250
 Shrimp and Snow Peas, 250
 Spinach, Shiitake, and Turkey, 204
 Sweet and Sour Tofu, 297
Strawberry(ies)
 Banana Popsicles, 572
 -Filled Meringue Torte, 529
 Frozen Yogurt, 574
 and Melon Compote, 511
 Milk Shake, 575
 Rhubarb Pie, 525
 Soup, 113
 -Spinach Salad, 63
 -Spinach Salad with Almonds, 63
 -Stuffed French Toast, 459
 Surprising, 508
 Tart, 528
 -Yogurt Fruit Salad Dressing, 514
Stuffed Eggplant, Bulgur and
  Feta, 267
Stuffed Eggplant, Rice and Pine
  Nut, 266

Stuffed Peppers, 214
Stuffed Potatoes. *See* Potato(es)
Stuffed Winter Squash, Millet, 268
Stuffed Winter Squash, Quinoa, 268
Stuffed Winter Squash, Wild
   Rice, 268
Stuffing, 409–14
  Listing of recipes, 376
Succotash with Tomatoes and
   Basil, 373
Sugar Snap Peas. *See* Pea(s)
Summer Squash, 364–67. *See*
   Also Zucchini
  Millet or Quinoa Stuffed, 268
  Packets, Parmesan, 367
  Sautéed Summer Vegetables, 364
Summertime Couscous, 385
Sunburst Salad, 97
Sun-Dried Tomatoes. *See* Tomato(es)
Surprising Strawberries, 508
Sweet and Sour Carrots, Italian, 326
Sweet and Sour Fish and
   Vegetables, 249
Sweet and Sour Tofu Stir-Fry, 297
Sweet Potato(es), 356–58
  Types of, 347–48
  Bake, 358
  Candied, 356
  and Chutney Salad, 86
  Cubes, Pan-Crisped, 356
  Curried, and Greens, 304
  and Marshmallows, 357
  Muffins, 476
  Not Your Traditional Tzimmes, 358
  Spears, 357
Swiss Chard
  Housewarming Soup, 139
  Lasagna, 280
  Sautéed, 340
Swordfish and Broccoli Risotto, 261
Swordfish and Pineapple Skewers, 240
Syrups and Sauces, 576–80
  Listing of recipes, 507

Tahini, 15
  Baba Ganouj, 29
  Chicken in Orange and, 172
  Hummus with, 30

Tandoori Chicken, 161
Tandoori Tofu, 272
Tarragon-Tomato Dressing, 58
Tart, Polenta, Cheese, and
   Vegetable, 40
Tart, Strawberry, 528
Tartar Sauces, 598, 599
Temperature, oven, 18, 166, 277, 547
Teriyaki
  Chicken Kebabs, Honey, 164
  Chicken Stir-Fry, Honey, 203
  Fish, Maple, 238
  Salmon, 238
  Sauce, 588
  Sauce, Spicy, 589
Thermometers, 18, 176
Thyme Mushrooms, 344
Toast(s). *See Also* Crostini and
   Bruschetta
  French, 458–61
  Garlic, 415
  Parmesan, 414
Tofu
  Burgers, 435
  Chinese Dumpling Rolls, 297
  Pita Pockets, Crispy, 425
  Sandwich Spread, 431
  Spicy, and Green Chili
   Enchiladas, 274
  Stir-Fry, Hoisin, 298
  Stir-Fry, Sweet and Sour, 297
  Tandoori, 272
Tomato Sauces, 583–86
  Listing of recipes, 581
Tomato(es), 368–70. *See Also*
   Tomato Sauces
  Peeling and seeding, 368
  Storing, 70
  Baked, 369
  Cherry, Cheery, 368
  Chutney, Tangy, 594
  Crostini or Bruschetta
   Basil and, 43
   Feta and, 43
   Olivada, 44
  Frittata, 464
  Greek Stewed Potatoes and, 352
   with Feta Cheese, 352

Jam, Baked, 370
Red Salsa, 592
Sage, 368
Salads, 70–73
  Listing of recipes, 52
Soup
  Bread, 131
  -Carrot-Orange, 120
  Curried, 120
  Garlic and Dill, 117
  Gazpacho, 115
  Manhattan-Style Fish
   Chowder, 142
Sun-Dried
  Aegean Pizza, 442
  Dip, 26
  Pesto, 591
  Pesto, Pasta with, 289
  Salad, Tortellini with Pesto
   and, 88
   Spaghetti with Scallops and, 256
  -Tarragon Dressing, 58
  and Zucchini, Turkish, 369
Torta, Southwest Torta, 274
Tortellini. *See* Pasta
Tortes, Meringue, 529
Tortilla(s). *See Also* Burritos;
   Enchiladas; Fajitas; Pinwheels;
   Quesadillas; Tostadas
  Heating, 420
  Casserole, Layered, 276
  Chili Egg Casserole, 465
  Chips, Baked, 24
  Chips, Chili-Spiced, 24
  Lasagna, Bean and, 275
  Lasagna, Roasted Vegetable, 278
  Moo Shu Beef, 206
  Soup, 132
  Southwest Torta, 274
  Spicy Shredded Chicken Roll
   Ups, 427
Tostadas
  with Salsa and Goat Cheese, 38
  Whole Wheat, 38
Tropical Chicken and Pasta Salad, 89
Tropical Chicken Kebabs, 163
Tropical Gazpacho, 116
Tropical Salsa, 592

Trout, Whole
  Baked in Foil, 234
  with Cornbread Stuffing, 233
Trussing chicken, 176
Tuna
  Burgers, 434
  Noodle Casserole, 231
  Salad
    with Almost Sour Cream, 430
    Apple and, 430
    Blissful, 106
    with Capers and Artichoke
      Hearts, 105
    and Shells, 88
    and Vegetable, 430
    Vinaigrette, 430
    White Bean and, 102
Turkey
  Breast, Poached, 431
  Cutlets
    Pounding, 207
    Five-Spice, 210
    with Gremolata, 208
    in Lemon-Caper Sauce, 209
    Pan-Fried, 208
    with Rosemary-Caper Sauce, 210
    Stir-Fry, Spinach, Shiitake,
      and, 204
    and Zucchini Quesadillas, 424
  Ground
    Burgers, 432
    Burgers, Barbeque, 433
    Burgers, Greek-Style, 433
    Chili, Easy, 196
    Lasagna, 187
    Meatball and Penne
      Casserole, 217
    Meatballs, 216
    Meatballs, Seasoned, 216
    Meatballs, Tiny, and Spaghetti in
      Creamy Tomato Sauce, 217
    Meatloaf, 213
    Meatloaf, Mexican, 214
    Meatloaves, Muffin Tin, 212
    Muffins, Cheese and, 481
    Picadillo, 194
    Pizza, Deep-Dish Rustica, 444
    Sloppy Joes, 428

  Sloppy Joes, Quick Confetti, 429
  Spaghetti Sauce, 215
  Salad, 104
  Salad, Walnut, Grape, and, 105
  Sandwiches, Barbeque, 427
  Skewers, Latin, 47
  Skewers, Red-Cooked, 48
  Smoked Turkey
    Gumbo, 198
    Salad, Greens, Grapefruit,
      and, 67
    Salad, Wild Rice, Grape and, 94
    Soup, Bean, and Tomato, 140
    Soup, Split Pea and, 138
Turkish Tomatoes and
    Zucchini, 369
Turkish-Style Yogurt Chicken, 162
Turnips. See Also Rutabagas
  Layered Apples and, 312
  Rooted Carrots, 327
  Sugar-Glazed, 359
Two-Pea Soup, 138
Tzimmes, Not Your Traditional, 358

Udon noodles, 15–16
Utensils, kitchen, 18, 19

Vanilla Cream, 565
Vanilla Pudding, 564
Vegetable(s). See Also specific
      vegetables
  Listing of recipes, 308–10
  Cooking methods, 311
  Nutritional benefits, 3
  Packaged, 16
  Broth, 110
  Burritos, 422
  Burritos, Black Bean and
    Veggie, 422
  Caponata, 372
  and Chickpeas over Couscous, 298
  Cider-Cooked, 371
  Corn Bread, 486
  Enchiladas, 272
  Ethiopian, 372
  Fajitas, 295
  Foil-Wrapped, Cowboy, 374
  Fried Rice, 391

  Gratin, Potato and, 350
  Gumbo, 300
  Lo Mein, Shrimp and, 258
  Macaroni and Cheese with, 270
  Medley, Fall, 371
  Moroccan, 301
  Paella, 395
  Pasta with, and Feta, 288
  Penne with, and Ricotta
      Sauce, 293
  Pizza, Deep-Dish, 445
  Pizza, Deep-Dish Rustica, 444
  Pizza, Veggies and Cheese, 439
  Platter for Dips, 27
  Polenta, 408
  Quesadillas, Thick-with-, 424
  Roasted, Tortilla Lasagna, 278
  Root, types of, 359
  Salad, Macaroni and, 86
  Salad, Mixed, 67
  Salad, Tuna and, 430
  Sauté, Southwestern, 370
  Soup
    Barley, 130
    Broth, 110
    Fish and, 142
    Indian-Style Coconut, 125
    Minestrone, 126
    Noodle, Italian, 128
    North African, 127
    Quick Vermicelli, 129
    Quinoa, 131
    Rice, 129
    Roasted Garlic, 126
    Root, 123
    Salad Bar Pesto, 127
    Tortilla, 132
  Stew, Belizean Bean and, 301
  Sweet and Sour Fish and, 249
  Tart, Polenta, Cheese, and, 40
  Won Tons, 50
  Under Wraps, 373
Vegetarian entrées, listing of recipes,
    264–65
Vegetarianism, 265–66
Velvet Corn Soup, 146
Vermicelli and Rice Pilaf, 378
Vermicelli Soup, Quick, 129

Vinaigrettes. *See* Salad Dressings
Vinegar
  Balsamic. *See* Balsamic (Vinegar)
  Garlic and Shallot, 609
  Herb, 608
  Raspberry, 608
  Rice, 15

Waffles, 456–57
Waldorf Salad, 77
Walnut(s)
  Linguine, 287
  More Than Apple Pie, 524
  and Raisins Pilaf, 389
  Salad, Carrot and, 80
  Waldorf Salad, 77
Water baths, for pudding, 567
Water Chestnuts, Snow Peas
    and, 346
Watercress and Cherry Tomato
    Salad, 73
Watermelon. *See* Melon(s)
Wheat Berry(ies)
  and Barley Salad, 97
  Sunburst Salad, 97
Wheat Germ Bread, 500
Wheat Germ Pancakes, 454
White Bean(s)
  Cannellini and Corkscrew
    Gratin, 405
  Housewarming Soup, 139
  Mediterranean Baked Beans, 405
  Pasta e Fagioli, 141
  Salad, Tuna and, 102
  Soup, Broccoli, Pasta and, 140

Stew, 404
  White Chili, 197
White Bread, 496
White Chili, 197
Whole Wheat
  Bread, 497
  Cheddar Popovers, 492
  Cheddar Quesadillas, 423
  Muffins, 100%, 473
  Pizza Dough, 438
  Tostadas, 38
Wild Rice
  Salad, Corn, Broccoli and, 93
  Salad, Smoked Turkey, Grape
    and, 94
  Stuffed Squash, 268
  Stuffing, 413
  Wild, 394
Winter Squash, 360–63. *See
    Also* Pumpkin
  Cutting and peeling, 360
  Acorn Squash Rings, Baked, 361
  Butternut Squash, Baked, 361
  Butternut Squash, Twice-Baked, 361
  and Carrots, Lemony, 363
  Cider-Roasted, and Shallots, 362
  Gratin, 362
  Soup, Curried, 121
  Stuffed, Millet or Quinoa, 268
  Stuffed, Wild Rice, 268
Won Ton wrappers, for ravioli, 282
Won Tons, 49–51

Yams, 347
Yeast, about, 493–94

Yeast Breads. *See* Bread, Yeast
Yellow Layer Cake, 531
Yellow Squash. *See* Summer Squash
Yogurt
  Cucumber Raita, 69
  Curry Dressing, Mild, 59
  Frozen, Banana Vanilla, 575
  Frozen, Strawberry, 574
  Fruit Salad Dressing,
    Strawberry-, 514
  and Mint Sauce, Fruit Salad
    with, 512
  Salad, Greek Cucumber, 69
  Salad with Dill, Cucumber, 69
  Smoothie, Banana, 469
  Smoothie, Fruit and, 470
  Smoothie, Orange Mango, 470
  Soup, Cucumber, 117
  Very Berry Dairy Shake, 469
Yogurt Cheese, 606
  Spread, Herb and Garlic, 32

Zest, Lemon or Orange, 604
Ziti, Basil and Broccoli, 286
Zucchini. *See Also* Summer Squash
  Casserole, Mexican, 366
  Cheese Casserole, 366
  Cocoa Cake, 533
  and Corn, Garlicky, 365
  Grilled, 367
  Oven Fries, 365
  Quesadillas, Turkey and, 424
  Slaw, 82
  Spears with Pesto, 364
  Turkish Tomatoes and, 369